Classics of Christian Inspiration

SEEING WITH THE EYES OF LOVE

Love is a great thing,
yea, a great and thorough good;
by itself it makes every thing that is heavy, light;
and it bears evenly all that is uneven.
For it carries a burden which is no burden,
and makes every thing that is bitter,
sweet & tasteful.

THE IMITATION OF CHRIST III.5

M000302570

Seeing with the Eyes of Love

EKNATH EASWARAN ON

THE IMITATION OF CHRIST

With an Afterword by Carol Lee Flinders

NILGIRI PRESS

I S B N : cloth, 0—915132—88—5; paper, 0—915132—87—7

Second edition, first printing September 1996

The Blue Mountain Center of Meditation, founded in

Berkeley, California, in 1961 by Eknath Easwaran,

publishes books on how to lead the spiritual life

in the home and the community.

For information please write to

Nilgiri Press, Box 256, Tomales, California 94971

Printed on recycled, permanent paper.

The paper used in this publication meets the minimum requirements of

American National Standard for Information Services —

Permanence of Paper for Printed Library Materials,

ANSI Z39.48—1984

Library of Congress Cataloging-in-Publication Data

Easwaran, Eknath.

Seeing with the eyes of love : Eknath Easwaran on the Imitation of

Christ / with an afterword by Carol Lee Flinders. — 2nd ed.

p. cm. — (Classics of Christian inspiration series)

Includes bibliographical references and index.

I S B N 0—915132—88—5 (alk. paper).

I S B N 0—915132—87—7 (pbk. : alk. paper)

1. Imitatio Christi. Liber 3. Capitulum 5 — Meditations.

2. Love — Religious aspects — Christianity — Meditations.   3. Thomas, a

Kempis, 1380—1471. 4. Meditation. I. Title. II. Series.

BV4829.E27 1996

242 — dc20   96—25350   CIP

Table of Contents

Introduction

In my state of Kerala there is a Christian tradition going back nearly two thousand years. The Apostle Thomas is believed to have come to the coast of Kerala and founded a Christian community there – a living link to Christ that would mean Christianity came to Kerala well before reaching most of Europe. In my college classes there were students from these ancient Christian families, golden-brown and dark-eyed like the rest of us and carrying similar surnames, but with given names like David, Joseph, and Peter.

However, these Christian communities are concentrated in the coastal part of Kerala, around Cochin and Travancore. My village was inland, so I don't think I had any exposure at all to the message of Christ until a Christian teacher joined the faculty of my high school. My Uncle Appa, our schoolmaster, invited him regularly to our ancestral home, and I imagine my interest in the teachings of Christ was probably first kindled by meeting this man. Not long afterwards, I left home for college – a Catholic college located some fifty miles from my village – and there I met an individual who to my mind lived out those teachings perfectly.

The headmaster of my college was Father John Palakaran, a Catholic priest from a distinguished Kerala Christian family who had taken his degrees at Edinburgh University. English, French, Latin, Greek, Sanskrit, Malayalam – in all of these he was fluent. He was a brilliant scholar, though he carried it so lightly it wasn't until years later that I realized the extent of his erudition. Father John always wore his black academic robes in the classroom. He had a deep, resonant voice, and he smoked the kind of large cigars that would become the trademark of the film star Edward G. Robinson.

The overall impression was intimidating, and as a sixteen-year-old Hindu boy fresh from the village, I was intimidated rather easily. From the very beginning, though, I sensed that this man lived for his students, and in return I gave him my utmost respect. I had a class with him just one hour a week during that first year, and I used to sit in the front row lost in admiration. I had never heard English spoken so sonorously, with such wonderful broad *a*'s. I wanted to sound just like that!

Father John was able to see that I was having a hard time when it came to speaking English. I could read it well, and write it too, but I had never spoken English before. When the instructors asked a question, I had to frame my answer in Malayalam first and then translate it into English. By the time my answer was ready, the discussion had moved on. This was thoroughly upsetting to me, because in high school I had been an excellent student.

That first year was difficult for me in another way too: I had never been away from home before. The college officials must have realized that would be the case for most of their first-year students, because they did not bring us into dormitories yet. Instead we were lodged with local families, where we could eat our meals and be treated almost as if we were at home. It was a good way to ease the transition into college life, but nonetheless I was homesick quite a lot of the time.

Father John began to understand my difficulties. His way of helping me learn to speak English was to encourage me to enter the college debate program. I wanted to do everything I could to please him, and that gave me the motivation to work extremely hard. He wasn't in the habit of paying compliments, and that didn't trouble me since my grandmother wasn't either. Instead, he supported me in quiet ways. Every now and then, for example, guessing what it would mean to me, he used to call me into his private study to talk – not in his office but in his own rooms, which were part of what we called the Bishop's Palace. He had a handsome study in the Victorian mode, and because I held him in such esteem I would look all around to see what kind of pictures were on the wall, what books he kept on the shelf – everything. His academic robes would be hanging in the corner during these visits; he would be wearing his simple white cassock.

I remember him calling me there one afternoon after he had heard me speak in class. We chatted a while and then he asked casually, "Did you have breakfast?"

"Yes, Father," I said, rather bewildered by the question. "I had a good breakfast."

"Well, then, if you had a good breakfast," he said, leaning forward full of intensity, "why did you swallow the last words of every sentence?"

It was not a question he would have to ask me twice!

It was about a year later when one of his assistants

came to me in class and said, "Father John wants you." I hurried to his rooms and found him reclining in an armchair with his feet up, puffing an after-lunch cigar.

"You have probably heard there is an intercollegiate debate coming up." I had. I knew it covered the whole region and was the most prestigious debate we could compete in – and that it was for Catholic colleges only. Since I wasn't Catholic, I hadn't even thought about participating.

"I want you to represent this college."

I was overwhelmed – I literally couldn't believe it. And what if I let him down? I must have muttered something to that effect because he cut me off with a gesture. "I'll be the judge of whether you are equal to it," he said. "I'm not consulting you."

My eyes filled with tears. When I could finally speak I started to ask, "If I fare badly . . ."

He cut me short with a cheerful shrug. "Just don't come back!"

To my great relief I found that none of the students appeared to resent Father John's decision to send a Hindu boy to represent a Catholic college. In fact, when my debate partner and I left for the event, a crowd of our schoolmates came to the train station to see us off. Still, I felt quite out of place and alone. The debate was held in a big, crowded auditorium, and besides probably all being Catholic, all the other contestants seemed to be wearing European suits.

At the end of the day, to my surprise, the panel of judges not only gave me and my partner the intercollegiate trophy; they gave me first place for individual elocution. By the time we reached our campus that night the news had preceded us, and hundreds of students met our train and followed as we carried the trophy to the Bishop's Palace.

Father John opened the door and looked at me. "So you've come back," he said.

During the four years I spent at college, without calling attention to what he was doing, Father John managed to work a great transformation in me. He helped me find confidence, but detachment as well. I was so grateful that I kept a picture of him in my room. And, inevitably, rumors got back to my village: I was said to be on the verge of becoming a Catholic. My granny only smiled. She knew that it wasn't a creed or religion I was drawn to, but the sheer nobility of the man himself.

I never considered converting, and nothing in my relationship to Father John ever made me think he expected me to. I'm sure he gave me books, for I must have been as curious about his religious background as I was about every detail of his life. He may even have given me *The Imitation of Christ.* But I was young, and my interests – encouraged by him – were wide. I had not yet reached the point where religious literature had any personal meaning for me.

In fact, it wasn't through books at all, but through the lives of individuals like Father John that the message of Christ first reached me. I have had the good fortune to know quite a number of Christian men and women like him, both Protestants and Catholics, who lived truly selfless lives. Such individuals are indeed the lamp "set high for all men to see" of which Christ spoke. Long before I took to the spiritual life myself, they helped me understand that the selfless life of which all the world's scriptures speak is also a life of beauty.

The actual writings of the world's great spiritual

teachers – from the Hindu, Christian, Buddhist, Sufi, and other traditions – did not draw me until I began to practice meditation. I was a college professor by then, so when the ground began to shift beneath my feet – when all the things I had valued and worked for were no longer enough to satisfy my deepest longings – it was natural to turn to books in search of an explanation. I looked through all the texts on psychology that I could lay hands on, but none of them shed light on what was happening to me. Only when I began to read the works of the great mystics did the ground begin to feel more solid beneath my feet.

Initially, of course, I was most at home with the mystics of Hinduism and Buddhism. But gradually I became conversant with those of the Christian tradition as well. The inspired poetry of John of the Cross enthralled me, and I found Teresa of Avila's writings on meditation vivid and practical. Reading Meister Eckhart and Jacob Boehme, I found myself wondering whether they might not somehow have dipped into the Upanishads. During this period, one figure began to intrigue me more and more – not because I knew anything about his life, but because the work he had produced, *The Imitation of Christ,* seemed to me to hold a unique place in Christian mystical literature.

It's difficult to say when I first came across the *Imitation,* but I remember the thrill of certitude that its composer was a man of deep spiritual awareness. I found it to be a practical guide to developing spiritual awareness. I could see right away why Swami Vivekananda, a direct disciple of Sri Ramakrishna and founder of the Vedanta Society, had traveled to the West with the Bhagavad Gita in one pocket and *The Imitation of Christ* in the other.

It is the special strength of a few books, and this is one of them, that down through the ages they have helped bridge the gap between cloister and household. Though the Imitation was composed in a monastic setting, its teachings are universally applicable, and they have been treasured by Protestants as well as Catholics, laypersons as well as monastics.

To explain its appeal is not simple. The autobiographical elements that make Augustine or Teresa of Avila so accessible are absent. Though the language is very apt and dignified, there are no poetic or visionary flights like those we find in John of the Cross or William Blake. For theological brilliance you would have to look elsewhere. Much of the *Imitation of Christ* is no more dazzling than a manual for woodworkers. But then, if you really want to know about carpentry, you don't want a manual that will dazzle; you want one that will tell you how to make a miter joint, how to use a skill saw, and what the best finish is for a tabletop. *The Imitation of Christ* is just that kind of book – an entirely practical manual for sincere spiritual aspirants.

The great mystics of all religions agree that in the very depths of the unconscious, in every one of us, there is a living presence that is not touched by time, place, or circumstance. Life has only one purpose, they add, and that is to discover this presence. The men and women who have done this – Francis of Assisi, for example, Mahatma Gandhi, Teresa of Avila, the Compassionate Buddha – are living proof of the words of Jesus Christ, "The kingdom of heaven is within." But they are quick to tell us – every one of them – that no one can enter that kingdom and discover the Ruler who lives there who has not brought the movements of the mind under control. And they do not pretend that our own efforts to tame the mind will suffice in themselves. Grace, they remind us, is all-important. "Increase in me thy grace," Thomas a Kempis prays, "that I may be able to fulfil thy words, and to work out mine own salvation."

The hallmark of the man or woman of God is gratitude – endless, passionate gratitude for the precious gift of spiritual awareness. Universally, from whatever tradition they come and no matter how long and hard they struggled, they agree that without divine grace no one can achieve what they have achieved. At the same time, they tell us divine grace is not something that descends at particular times and places, like lightning. Rather, it surrounds us always. Like a wind that is always blowing, said Francis de Sales; like fire, said Catherine of Genoa, that never stops burning: "In this world the rays of God's love, unbeknownst to man, encircle him all about, hungrily seeking to penetrate him."

It can be baffling, this mysterious interplay of divine grace and individual effort. The truth is, both are absolutely necessary. "Knock," Jesus assured us, "and it shall be opened unto you," and he keeps his promise. But we have to knock hard. We have to sound as if we mean business. And before we can do that, all our desires must be unified. This comes in stages, in cycles repeated over and over – the painful effort, then the breakthrough to a new level of awareness; again the effort, again the breakthrough. Sometimes it can feel like we're doing it all ourselves, but in the final stages all doubts fall away, and we realize we were in His hands from the very start. The moment we feel even the slightest attraction to the spiritual life – the moment when we first take a book on the subject off the bookstore shelf – divine grace has called, and we have answered.

In the West, the practice of meditation or interior prayer has been associated so persistently with the cloister that ordinary men and women haven't readily taken it up. "We don't have time," they say. Sometimes they add, "Besides, isn't meditation just an attempt to run away from life's challenges?"

When we look at the lives of the great mystics, however, we find ready proof that turning inward does not mean turning away from life. For the man or woman "in the world but not of it," just as well as for monks or nuns, action and prayer are the two halves of the spiritual life, as complementary as breathing in and breathing out. In prayer and meditation, we breathe in deep; in the outward action of selfless service we breathe out again, blessing the lives of those around us in meeting life's challenges head-on. This does not require a special gift. Just as each of us has been born with the capacity to breathe, we have all come into life with the capacity to draw upon the deep spiritual resources released through meditation and make a great contribution to life.

In reading *The Imitation of Christ* and commenting on it to men and women of today, I have had to come to terms with certain elements that strike the modern mind as negative. These are not unique to medieval Christianity: you can find them in other religions too.

To take one example, I have never responded favorably to descriptions of hell. To my mind, an angry mind or an envious heart is its own hell. Where traditional language might speak of sins and punishment, I speak instead, less dramatically, of mistakes and consequences.

Again, medieval writers in particular – and ascetics of all religions in general – like to use the arresting language of condemnation and subjugation. They speak, for example, of "this vile body of ours," and tell us we "must mortify the flesh." To me the body is not vile, but a useful and long-suffering friend. Here Saint Francis himself comes to my rescue when he addresses the body as "Brother Donkey." He says, in effect, "I feed him and take care of him, but I ride on him; I don't let him ride on me!" Today, instead of talking about mortifying the body and senses to bring them under control, I always speak of training them – bringing body and senses to their optimum condition, like an athlete in training.

The heart of *The Imitation of Christ,* and certainly the part that is best known, is the fifth chapter of Book III, called traditionally "The Wonderful Effect of Divine Love." It seems to me to distill the essential teachings not just of Thomas a Kempis, but of Christianity itself.

Readers who love the thirteenth chapter of First Corinthians – "Though I speak with the tongues of men and of angels" – will hear echoes of it throughout this chapter. Readers familiar with the writings of Saint Bernard and Saint Augustine will identify still other echoes and reworkings of loved passages. Was Thomas a Kempis cribbing? No, but he would be the first to tell us that the *Imitation* is not the product of anyone's imagination or poetic inspiration. He signed the book only at the very end, as a copyist would have. It was habitual among the Brothers of the Common Life, Thomas's spiritual family, to keep notebooks where the monks would jot down particularly inspiring passages from scripture or

the church fathers, or even sayings and homilies received from one another. One or more of these compi-
lations was undoubtedly the basis for the *Imitation.* Since
Thomas himself made no strong authorial claim, there
is no need for us to quibble over which parts of the text
are "really" his. In fact, Thomas summed up the question himself, neatly, early in the *Imitation* where he
wrote, "Let not the authority of the writer offend thee,
whether he be of great or small learning; but let the love
of pure truth draw thee to read. Search not who spoke
this or that, but mark what is spoken."

"The Wonderful Effect of Divine Love" is a soaring
hymn of love that stands perfectly well on its own. But
when its position in the *Imitation of Christ* is understood, it
becomes doubly interesting because it marks a sharp
turning point in the text. Books I and II have been quite
sober in tone – searching, serious, and very down to
earth. Up to this moment only one voice has been
heard, that of the seasoned spiritual teacher addressing
an audience of newly dedicated aspirants – novitiates,
perhaps. He has laid out for them the basic terms of the
spiritual life: what will be expected of them and what the
disciplines are that they are undertaking.

Book III opens in a different vein altogether. Gone is
the counselor and guide of Books I and II. We hear a
voice now that is altogether new: the clear, ringing voice
of someone who has absorbed well the lessons of the
preceding books, and now seeks nothing in life but to
become united with the Lord. Each of us, clearly, is
meant to identify ourselves with this aspirant. His first
words echo the Psalmist: "I will hearken what the Lord
God will speak in me." Ardently, again and again, he
calls out, "Speak, O Lord, for thy servant heareth. . . .

Incline my heart to the words of thy mouth: let thy speech distill as the dew." Over and over he declares his readiness to be taught—no longer by scripture, but from within. And at last, a voice replies: "My son, hear my words, words of greatest sweetness. . . . My words are spirit and life." From this moment on, *The Imitation of Christ* is a dialogue, and an indisputably mystical treatise.

Tools for Transformation

Since I will be referring to meditation through-out this book, I need to say a few words about just what I mean by the term.

When I talk about meditation I am referring to a specific interior discipline which is found in every major religion, though called by different names. (Catholic writers, for example, speak of "contemplation" or "in-terior prayer.") This interior discipline is not a relaxa-tion technique. It requires strenuous effort. It does dissolve tension, but in general, meditation is work, and if you expect to find it easy going, you'll be disappointed.

Second, meditation in this sense is not a disciplined reflection on a spiritual theme. Focused reflection can yield valuable insights; but for the vast majority of us, reflection is an activity on the surface level of the mind. To transform personality we need to go much, much deeper. We need a way to get eventually into the uncon-scious itself, where our deepest desires arise, and make changes there.

So what is meditation? It is the regular, systematic training of attention to turn inward and dwell continu-ously on a single focus within consciousness, until, after many years of daily practice, we become so absorbed in the object of our contemplation that while we are meditating, we forget ourselves completely. In that moment, when we are empty of ourselves, we are utterly full of what we are dwelling on. This is the central principle of meditation: we become what we meditate on. "Write thou my words in thy heart," says the Lord in Chapter 3 of Book III, "and meditate diligently on them."

Here is a brief summary of the form of meditation I follow, and a still briefer summary of seven other practices which support and strengthen your meditation during the day. (There is a much fuller presentation in my book *Meditation*.) Together these comprise a complete eight-point program for spiritual living, which I have followed myself for more than forty years. I warmly invite you to join me while you are reading this book.

1. Meditation

* Choose a time for meditation when you can sit for half an hour in uninterrupted quiet. Early morning is best, before the activities of the day begin. If you wish to meditate more, add half an hour in the evening, but please do not meditate for longer periods without personal guidance from a selfless, experienced teacher who is following the same method of meditation.

* Select a place that is cool, clean, and quiet. Sit with your back and head erect, on the floor or on a straight-backed chair.

* Close your eyes and begin to go slowly, in your mind, through the words of a simple, positive, inspirational passage from one of the world's great spiritual traditions. (Remember, you become

what you meditate on.) I recommend beginning with the Prayer of Saint Francis of Assisi:

Lord, make me an instrument of thy peace.
Where there is hatred, let me sow love;
Where there is injury, pardon;
Where there is doubt, faith;
Where there is despair, hope;
Where there is darkness, light;
Where there is sadness, joy.

O divine Master, grant that I may not so much seek
To be consoled as to console,
To be understood as to understand,
To be loved as to love;
For it is in giving that we receive;
It is in pardoning that we are pardoned;
It is in dying to self that we are born to eternal life.

You will find it helpful to keep adding to your repertoire so that the passages you meditate on do not grow stale. "The Wonderful Effect of Divine Love" is an excellent choice. My book *God Makes the Rivers to Flow* contains many other passages that I recommend, drawn from many traditions.

* While you are meditating, do not follow any association of ideas or allow your mind to reflect on the meaning of the words. If you are giving your full attention to each word, the meaning cannot help sinking in.

* When distractions come, do not resist them, but give more attention to the words of the passage. If your mind strays from the passage entirely, bring it back gently to the beginning and start again.

* Resolve to have your meditation every day – however full your schedule, whatever interruptions threaten, whether you are sick or well.

Meditation is never practiced in a vacuum. Certain other disciplines always accompany and support it, varying somewhat according to the needs of a particular culture or audience. Here are the remaining seven disciplines I have found to be enormously helpful in supporting the practice of meditation.

2. Repetition of the Holy Name

Meditation involves use of a memorized passage, and it requires that one sit quietly. The Holy Name, on the other hand, can be repeated under almost any circumstances, and it is so brief – a spiritual formula, really – that it will come to your mind under even the most agitating circumstances. (In fact, that is often just when you will want it!)

Repetition of the Holy Name is a practice found in every major religious tradition. Many Christians simply repeat the name of Jesus, which has been used since ancient times. So has the Jesus Prayer, still used in the Orthodox tradition: *Lord, Jesus Christ, have mercy on me.* Catholics repeat *Hail Mary* or *Ave Maria,* and many use the prayer sanctified by Saint Francis of Assisi, *My God and my all.* Choose whichever version of the Holy Name appeals to you; then, once you have chosen, stick to that and do not change. Otherwise you will be like a person digging little holes in many places; you will never go deep enough to find water.

Repeat the Holy Name whenever you get the chance: while walking, while waiting, while doing mechanical chores like washing dishes, and especially when you are falling asleep. Whenever you are angry or afraid, nervous or hurried or resentful, repeat the Holy Name until the agitation in your mind subsides.

Do not make up your own version of the Holy Name, but use one of the formulas above which have been sanctioned by centuries of devout tradition. If you repeat it sincerely and systematically, it will go deeper with every repetition. It can be with you even in the uttermost depths of your consciousness, as you will discover for yourself when you find it reverberating in a dream – or, deeper still, during dreamless sleep.

3. Slowing Down

Hurry makes for tension, insecurity, inefficiency, and superficial living. To guard against hurrying, start the day early and simplify your life so you do not try to fill your time with more than you can do. When you find yourself beginning to speed up, repeat the Holy Name to help you slow down.

It is important here not to confuse slowness with sloth. In slowing down we need to attend meticulously to details, giving our best even to the smallest undertaking.

4. One-pointedness

Doing more than one thing at a time divides attention and fragments consciousness. When you read and eat at the same time, for example, part of your mind is on what you are reading and part on what you are eating; you are not getting the most from either activity. Similarly, when talking with someone, give that person your full attention. These are not little things. Taken together they help to unify consciousness and deepen concentration. One-pointed attention is a powerful aid to meditation.

Everything you do should be worthy of your full attention. When the mind is one-pointed it will be secure, free from tension, and capable of the concentration that is the mark of genius in any field.

5. Training the Senses

In the food we eat, the books and magazines we read, the movies we see, all of us are subject to the dictatorship of rigid likes and dislikes. To free ourselves from this conditioning, we need to learn to change our likes and dislikes freely when it is in the best interests of those around us or ourselves. We can begin by saying no when our senses are urging us to indulge in something that is not good for our body or mind. The senses are the secretaries of the mind; to get the mind to listen to us, we need to bring them over to our side.

6. Putting Others First

Dwelling on ourselves builds a wall between ourselves and others. Those who keep thinking about their needs, their wants, their plans, their ideas, cannot help becoming lonely and insecure. When we learn to put other people first, beginning within the circle of our family and friends and co-workers, we deepen our own security and dramatically enrich our relationships.

It is important to remember here that putting others first does not mean making yourself a doormat, or saying yes to whatever others want. It means putting the other person's welfare before your own personal desires. That is what love is: the other person's welfare means more to you than your own. And love often requires you to say no. But when you do, it must always be said with kindness, tenderness, and respect.

7. *Spiritual Reading*

Our culture is so immersed in the mass media that we need to balance our outlook by giving half an hour or so each day to spiritual reading: something positive, practical, and inspiring, which reminds us that the spark of divinity is in all of us and can be released in our own lives by meditation, prayer, and daily practice. Just before bedtime is a good time for this kind of reading, because the thoughts we fall asleep in will be with us throughout the night.

8. *Spiritual Association*

When you are trying to change your life, you need the support of others with the same goal. If you have friends who are meditating along the lines suggested here, you can get together regularly to share a meal, meditate, and perhaps read and discuss your spiritual reading. Share your times of entertainment too; relaxation is an important part of spiritual living.

Ah, Lord God, thou holy lover of my soul, when thou comest into my heart, all that is within me shall rejoice. Thou art my glory and the exultation of my heart: thou art my hope and refuge in the day of my trouble.

CHAPTER ONE

All Shall Rejoice

Thomas a Kempis does not say "O thou Tri-partite Unity" or "Ah, Supreme Godhead and Ulti-mate Being," but "thou holy lover of my soul." His Lord is his intimate companion, his beloved sweet-heart, who can be seen and heard in the aspirant's heart of hearts. Thomas's writings, like the entire medieval period, are permeated with the beautiful understand-ing that the Lord of Love is not an abstraction at all – that, in the words of Julian of Norwich, "He is our clothing, for he is that love which wraps and enfolds us."

None of the great mystics of the period – or of any other time – will claim that this perfect intimacy can be attained swiftly or easily, any more than in an ordinary romance. Before we can become one with the Beloved there are mountains in consciousness to be climbed, fierce rivers to be forded, epic inner battles that must be fought and won. Yet, just as great worldly romances often begin with a single, telling glance, so, very often, does this one. Suddenly, for no rhyme or reason, deep within you something stirs. "When thou comest into my heart," says Thomas, "all that is within me shall rejoice." For a split second, it seems, you catch a glimpse of Someone. It may take no longer, in the words of one mystic, than an *Ave Maria*. But in that brief, glowing instant, the doubts and uncertainties of a lifetime can vanish. And suddenly the direction of your life changes.

When this experience came to the scholarly Saint Augustine, he sighed in profound relief, "No further would I read, nor needed I." And down the ages, every scholar turned aspirant has sighed with him – including Thomas a Kempis, who writes in the opening chapters of the *Imitation*: "What have we to do with genus and species, the dry notions of logicians? He to whom the Eternal Word speaketh is delivered from a world of unnecessary conceptions."

This experience is the same whether it comes to Saint Augustine in the last days of the Roman Empire, to Thomas a Kempis in medieval Europe, or to Mahatma Gandhi in British India. The truths of the spiritual life hold true for all times. Yet each period in history, each culture, imparts its own cast to the discovery of God. In our times – more than ever in history, I believe – the emphasis of civilization is on the external world. It is as if we were content to spend all our time decorating the outside of a house – the lawn, the shrubs, the trellis and the porch swing – without ever going inside, without even looking for the One who is waiting there. We never so much as knock on the door. Teresa of Avila put it very well: "It is no small pity and should cause us no little shame that through our own fault we do not understand ourselves or know who we are . . . we only know we are living in these bodies and have a vague idea . . . that we possess souls. All our interest is centered on the rough setting of the diamond, the outer wall of the castle – that is to say, on these bodies of ours."

If there is a God, we reason, he is surely outside, as is everything else that catches our attention. Vaguely, fondly even, we imagine as we go about our business that Someone is probably keeping an eye on us – like Agatha Christie's Inspector Poirot, seated bundled up in a trench coat on the Orient Express, peering out obliquely from behind the Paris edition of the *Herald Tribune*. To the murmurings from within, meanwhile – the faint stir and rustle of a presence deep inside of us, and a voice hauntingly beautiful – we turn a deaf ear. "We stuff our ears and say we cannot hear you," complained the medieval German mystic Hans Denk. "We close our eyes and say we cannot see you."

The external world, so fascinating, so glamorous, has us firmly in hand and thoroughly mesmerized. Lasting happiness is almost ours, it promises – over there, just ahead of us, right around the next corner. When we round that corner and find that happiness has eluded us, something in us says, "It's just around the next corner." Our life becomes a continual pilgrimage around corners. Yet such is human credulity that even after rounding a thousand corners, we still say, "The thousand and first, that is the one!"

As long as we believe that we are happy only when some external condition is fulfilled, so long – even when that condition is fulfilled – will there be the proviso "Now let another condition be fulfilled." It is this habit, this almost mechanical fixation of the mind, that keeps us forever chasing down blind alleyways.

But what if you get tired of looking outside? What if you decide to look within? Back you go to that house for a closer look! Now you're not so interested in the flowers in the garden or the Victorian porch swing. You are looking for a door, and you find it. And from behind it, if you press your ear against the panels, you can hear a voice, faint but vibrant: "The kingdom of heaven is within." And so is the King; so is the Queen.

Once you have made the decision to turn inward, you begin to look differently at life. Your mounting need is like a powerful searchlight, intently focused. Up to now you have trained its bright light onto material satisfactions, and finally pierced right through them. You have trained it on prestige and power with the same result. Finally, thoroughly dissatisfied, in a magnificent sweep of spiritual intuition you turn the searchlight within. And this is when it takes place: that split second of astonished certainty when you know that the Lord lives within you.

Afterwards you want nothing more in the world than to repeat the experience. You want with all your heart to gaze again into those compassionate eyes and remain longer in that healing presence. So you do just what any ordinary lover would do: you try to go back to the place where you saw your beloved last. Not a café or a library or a tennis court now, but deep within your own consciousness. It is not easy to find your way back, and nearly impossible to remain there for any length of time. But every human being has the capacity to do this; every one of us can discover the Christ within and be united with him forever. The door to deeper consciousness might seem to be locked except to saints, but we do have a key, every ordinary one of us: the practice of what Catholic mystics call interior prayer, which I call meditation.

To enter deeper levels of consciousness through meditation, we need to train our very capacity to attend. All our mind, all our desires, all our will, must be fused. In the end, this is the purpose of all the legitimate spiritual practices that have come down to us in the great religions of the world; but the most effective way I know of is to meditate sincerely and systematically on a memorized spiritual passage. If you can sit in silence, eyes closed, going through the words of the Lord's Prayer with such complete concentration that you don't even hear the lawn mower next door, your journey inward is well underway.

But of course it isn't enough to be underway; you have to know where you're going. You need a map, and this is the second reason to meditate on a deeply spiritual passage. The Lord's Prayer, the Beatitudes, the Prayer of Saint Francis, Saint Teresa's "Let nothing disturb thee" – all these are passages deeply imbued with Christ-consciousness. They are soaked with his love and dyed deep in his wisdom, and as you let each word sink into your heart in meditation, you cannot help but draw closer to the source, the Christ within. You can almost hear his voice: "Over here! You're getting warmer!"

Nothing but your own growing dissatisfaction – your sharpening hunger for meaning and permanence and abiding truth – can so challenge the hold of the world that you turn inward like this and hear for yourself the very personal invitation of Jesus Christ: "Knock, and it shall be opened; seek, and you shall find; ask, and it shall be added unto you." When Thomas a Kempis declares, "Thou art my glory, and the exultation of my heart: thou art my hope and refuge in the day of my trouble," he is celebrating precisely this discovery: that real glory and exultation, true hope and refuge, can be found nowhere but in union with the Lord, who is within.

In every time and every place where people have thought deep and hard about life, they have left some record of the feelings I've been describing, usually in symbol and myth. They describe a haunting sense of being in exile, of being a wanderer far from home. Chronic homesickness would seem to be as categorically human as the opposable thumb.

According to the Judeo-Christian tradition, it is Eden we long for – a garden home where our every need was met and we were complete. Somehow, for reasons we can't remember, we were turned out. The memory haunts us, undercutting every ordinary satisfaction, and we wander through life growing more and more hungry, feeling alienated in the world, always on the lookout.

To carry the metaphor a little further, we are all tourists in this world – looking about ourselves, trying to figure out what we ought to be feeling when we stand before this statue or that palace, and wishing at every turn that we were back home. Just eavesdrop sometime on a Grayline bus tour. I remember in India you could hear tourists murmur to each other, "Well, it's certainly not like this back home," or "George, don't you wish we could be having dinner back home tonight?" The nostalgia of world travelers is ironic, because it is usually a feeling very like nostalgia that has launched them in the first place: something about the brochures at the travel agent's, the pictures of swaying coconut palms that beckon so seductively, that makes us want to say, "There, that's where I'll find my paradise. That's what I've always yearned for." We each have our own versions. To some it's the arched ways of Oxford University, to others the gleaming white islands of the Aegean. "There – there I could be happy."

Exiles all, we know very well that we are meant to live in permanent joy and ever-increasing love, and nothing short of this will satisfy us. In the words of Mechthild of Magdeburg, "The soul is made of love, and must ever strive to return to love." There is an inward tug in everybody, a persistent voice that calls, "Come back to the source." When Thomas calls the Lord "my hope and refuge in the time of my trouble," he reminds us that we are all refugees, far, far away from our homeland.

Thou art my hope and refuge in the day of my trouble.

Even in the most intimate relationships, it is seldom that one person can remain steadfast when the other is irritated or in a depression. It takes boundless love on the part of the Lord to say, "When everything is going well with you, I understand that you might well forget me. But when things are wrong with you, when the clouds are gathering and looking dark on the horizon, why don't you come to me then?"

Who but the great lover would say this? No human being with any self-respect would allow himself to be a last resort, but Jesus is always willing. He says, "When everything has failed — when your bank has gone bankrupt and your bar has gone bar-rupt, when all friends have forsaken you and even your dog won't wag his tail for you — come to me then. I will never turn you away."

That is how dear we are to him. When we are tardy, when we delay our return to him by being selfish and self-willed, it is he who grieves. "Look at my kids! They're still stumbling down blind alleys in a far country." In a magnificent Bengali proverb, it is said that the Lord is always waiting for us with his arms open wide; and for every step we take towards him, he takes seven towards us.

Whether we like it or not, one day we are going to leave our blind alleys and begin to search for him. Nobody is ever lost; nobody ever ceases to be a child of

God. When people come to cry on my shoulder because life is not making them happy, I say, "Don't get my jacket wet. That's not going to help you. Why not let me show you how to leave this country altogether? You're ready to go home!" You may have traveled far and wide – to China, Tibet, Uzbekistan – but that is all horizontal travel, just moving about from one point on the physical plane to another. When the urge to turn inward becomes importunate, you are ready for *vertical* travel: ready to go deep within yourself in search of the divine.

Getting ready for this inward journey is a lot like preparing for a trip to India or Japan. You may start by reading about it. World travelers, you know, drop in at the travel agency and pick out a number of pamphlets from that attractive rack on the wall; then, if they get interested, they get books from the library and start reading about local customs. Here, too, you get enthralled reading the itineraries of the great travelers in the lands of the spirit: Augustine, Teresa, the Compassionate Buddha, all of whom say in much the same language, "The land of joy and love is within." And they don't talk about the places they've been the way horizontal travelers like John Gunther or Paul Theroux do. Horizontal travelers enjoy differences: different food, different customs, different ways of dress. But vertical travelers rejoice in unity. External differences are interesting for a while, but the human being's deepest need is for discovering what unites us all.

So you read, and you plan; and then slowly you

begin to get serious about making the journey. You try to balance your budget by curtailing certain expenses here and economizing there. By staying home from movies you don't need to see and keeping away from the sales, you will be able to pay your travel expenses. And just as if you were going to a third world country where health conditions are not the best, you've got to get certain shots. They are not very pleasant. But you are so eager to visit the country, you have read so much about it, that you say, "Let's go and get it over with." You even manage a wry grin.

Now you have your medical certificate, and you're ready for your passport. But here, in this very important matter of identification, there is a big difference between traveling outside and traveling inside. With horizontal travel, of course, you have to get your passport at the outset. With vertical travel, you get it at the very end of the journey. The purpose of a physical passport is to establish your identity in the limited, physical sense: Who were your parents? Where were you born? Do you have any moles? But in the deeper sense, establishing your real identity is the whole object of traveling inward.

And let's not forget the important question of luggage. You won't be allowed to take all you want – just forty pounds, no more. So you select only what is essential. You find a lot of things you can do without. Ultimately you know you may have to carry your own bags, so you try to keep them light and portable.

This is the story of getting started in the long inward

journey of meditation. Every traveler who has seen the heaven within, who has become a resident in what Augustine calls the City of God, will describe to you how difficult the journey is, how terribly challenging the conditions. But at the same time, all these voyagers will tell you how determined they were. There was nothing else in life they wanted.

The mystics don't deny the existence of the external world; it is we who deny the internal world, which they are telling us is every bit as real. There are mountains in the world within, they tell us, higher than the Himalayas. You remember that the great English climber George Leigh Mallory, when journalists asked why he wanted to climb Mount Everest, gave a very British reply: "Because it is there." Similarly, if you ask the mystics why they want to travel inwards, they will tell you, "Because God is there."

Many of you, I imagine, have ancestors who braved danger and hardship to make their home in a new land. If you could ask them what it was like, say, a hundred and fifty years ago to travel from the East coast to the West, they would tell you stories that would give you nightmares. Yet they didn't go back to Poughkeepsie or Pittsburgh; they just kept on. It is the same in meditation. "This act of will [determinación] is what he wants of us," says Saint Teresa in her autobiography. Nothing less will get us where we need to go.

But because I am as yet weak in love, and imperfect in virtue, I have need to be strengthened and comforted by thee; visit me therefore often, and instruct me with all holy discipline.

CHAPTER TWO

Weak in Love

To travel deep into consciousness through the practice of meditation you must have a huge desire, so huge it swallows up all your other desires. The onset of that desire is a sure mark of divine grace. Often it begins as a nagging, driving restlessness. To be content no longer with picking up what is floating on the surface of life, but to want only the pearls on the bottom of the sea: that is the touch of grace.

With this desire, however, comes a terrible responsibility. You know now that you must begin the long, arduous task of training the mind and senses through spiritual disciplines. Nobody has to tell you this, for the awareness wells up from deep inside. A great saint from the Russian Orthodox tradition, Theophan the Recluse, stated it unequivocally: "The principal condition for success in prayer is the purification of the heart from passion, and from every attachment to things sensual."

I had always understood there to be a connection

between spiritual awareness and certain disciplines that train the mind and senses, and for that very reason I had wanted nothing to do with the spiritual life. I imagined my body being bent with prayer and fasting, my intellect clouded with speculation, and my life deprived of health, happiness, color, and friendship.

In a sense my fears were justified, for the path to spiritual awareness is as steep and fearsome as any the human being has ever attempted. But what I could not have foreseen was how joyfully I would set out upon that path when the moment to do so actually came. That is because the desire to gain mastery over one's mind and senses does not come from some distant deity or even from a monastic rule. It comes from deep within yourself – from the Lord of Love within. Catherine of Genoa describes this experience beautifully:

> When God sees the soul pure as it was in its origins, he tugs at it with a glance, draws it and binds it to himself with a fiery love that by itself could annihilate the immortal soul. In so acting, God so transforms the soul in him that it knows nothing other than God; and he continues to draw it up into his fiery love until he restores it to that pure state from which it first issued. . . . That is why the soul seeks to cast off any and all impediments, so that it can be lifted up to God.

The thrust toward God-consciousness starts as a vague stirring – just a tug, as Catherine says – and grows little by little until in the final stages it is a relentless pull like the outgoing tide. That it makes itself known at all is an expression of grace, sheer grace; but how rapidly it grows depends entirely on how we respond. And our response, the great mystics of all traditions point out, is almost always a matter of overcoming our own self-will. This is the heart of the spiritual life for a long, long time. *Naughting* is the medieval Christian's term for what is really the aim of all spiritual disciplines: the reduction to absolute zero of everything in us that is selfish and separate.

In that sense, it's nothing extraordinary that Thomas a Kempis is asking from us here. We all have the desire for this journey; all he asks is that we feed that desire. Whenever you have a lesser desire, the practice of meditation will enable you to siphon the energy away from that desire and channel it into this tremendous wanderlust. The City of God is within. You can reach it here and now, in this very life, through the practice of meditation.

It is a demanding adventure, a difficult undertaking, but we have come into this life for nothing else. In the inspiring words of Meister Eckhart, "Man shall become a seeker of God in all things, and a finder of God at all times and everywhere, and among all people, and in every way."

Thomas has addressed the Lord in beautifully intimate words. Now he explains why he must ask his help:

*But because I am as yet weak in love, and imperfect in
virtue, I have need to be strengthened and comforted by
thee . . .*

So many people have come to me during the
last thirty years and confessed tragically, "I don't think
I have the capacity to love. I'm not strong enough to
form a lasting, loving relationship. I don't think I'm a
bad person; I just don't know how to love."

I ask them, "Have you always known how to write?"
They say no.

"Have you always known how to read?" They say
no.

"But now you are able to do both. How did you
manage that?"

"Well, I studied. I practiced a lot."

We have only to look at little children learning to
write. Just to write cat, their whole face participates in
the effort — brows knitted together, lips twisted,
tongue sticking out. Look in again twelve years later
and there they'll be on the university campus, where a
learned professor is indulging in words of thundering
sound, with lightning playing about his head. There
will be that same child, scribbling furiously and not
missing a syllable. This is what practice does, and it is
the same with love. It requires unremitting practice.
There is nothing wicked in not being able to love. You
just haven't learned to read the book of love or write in
it. You haven't mastered the skill.

So when Thomas a Kempis confides to the Lord, "I
am weak in love, and imperfect in virtue," he is saying,

"Come teach me. Come help me. I need this skill desperately; for I can see that my own capacity to love is but a drop compared with the ocean of love I have glimpsed in you." And this is just what the Lord has been waiting to hear. "God is bound to act," says Meister Eckhart, "to pour himself into thee as soon as he shall find thee ready." No one expects to learn tennis just by thinking about it, or calculus, or windsurfing. If you're serious, you'll put aside time for practice. It is the same with learning to love. It takes time.

To give yourself that time, there is one simple step that anyone can take – simple, but enormously effective. Just get up an hour earlier in the morning. Throughout the day, you will feel the difference. You have ten minutes more now to spend over breakfast with your family, ten minutes longer to get to your workplace without cursing stoplights along the way, and five minutes' leeway to chat with your co-workers when you get there.

Five minutes here, ten there, can add up to a significant change. You don't find yourself sneaking desperate looks at your watch now, and you're no longer jerked about from place to place, always just in time or a few minutes late. It's in those fresh new intervals, at the breakfast table, in the office, that you find countless little opportunities to give your attention and affection to those around you – not in one dramatic episode, but in small encounters throughout the day.

To get up earlier, you will probably want to go to bed a little earlier too. That won't come easily. For me, it meant making an honest reassessment of how I was spending my time. I sat down and wrote a list of all my obligations – my committee memberships, the concerts I liked to attend, the learned societies I had joined. Then I just started drawing lines through the ones that could be deemed inessential. I braced myself for my colleagues' reaction: "E.E.'s withdrawing! He's not pulling his weight!" But to my amazement, my presence was not missed as keenly as I'd expected. This was briefly disappointing, but soon the payoff came. Here was an hour, there was half an hour. I had more time now to really look at my students, my family, my fellow faculty members – time to really listen to them.

Of course, slowing down the day is only the first step. The hurried pace that keeps us "weak in love" originates in the mind. You might stop at someone's desk to be sociable, but that doesn't mean your thoughts have stopped. They are immaterial, after all! Most people are perceptive enough to know when this is taking place. If you're pretending to chat with them while your mind has sprinted ahead toward the conference room, you might as well take the rest of you there too.

No one can love with a mind that is going fast – or one that is divided. No one can love with a mind that is apt to swerve wildly, whether to avoid the small exigencies of daily life or to pursue something bright across the room that attracts you.

Let me suggest a small experiment. For a day or so,

think of yourself as James Joyce, or any other writer who specializes in stream of consciousness writing. With the uncritical eye of the motion picture camera, observe your thought processes when you are in different states of mind. When you are feeling irritable, take a peek. If you have occasion to be afraid or anxious, check again. If a strong desire overtakes you and you can manage to see what's going on in the mind, take note. Check your vital signs at the same time: see how rapid your pulse is, and whether your breathing is shallow and quick, or deep and slow.

If you can do this accurately – which is harder than it sounds – you will make a very interesting discovery. Fear, anger, selfish desire, envy: all these are associated with a speeded-up mind, and when the mind speeds up, it takes basic physiological processes with it. The thinking process hurtles along, thoughts stumble over one another in an incoherent rush – and, on cue, the heart begins to race and breathing becomes quicker, shallow, and ragged.

Interestingly enough, the reverse is also true. Once the mind gets conditioned to speed, not only do speeding thoughts make the body go faster, speeded-up behavior can induce negative emotions as well.

Suppose you've slept through the alarm and are in a rush to get off to work. You rip through the kitchen like a whirlwind, grabbing whatever you need as you go, trying to button your shirt while you eat your toast on your way out the door. The next time you catch yourself like this, watch and see how prone your mind

is to negative responses. Everything seems an obstruction or a threat. Your children look hostile – if you see
them at all – and even the dog seems out to ruin your
day, draping herself right across the threshold in the
hope of tripping you up. "Watch out!" the kids say
once you're gone. "It's going to be another of those
mean-mood days."

In a way, getting through the day is much like driving a car. When you're driving over sixty-five miles per
hour, you need a lot of space just to turn or stop. At
high speeds you can't see the scenery along the way; if
you try, you may get yourself killed. You might even
miss the road signs, and if a possum or squirrel is trying
to cross the road, you may not be able to avoid it. In the
same way, those who have been conditioned to race
and hurry through life often don't see people, just
blurs. When they hurt others, they are often not even
aware of it. They can injure relationships without even
knowing that damage has been done.

A speeding mind is a dangerous thing. When
thoughts are going terribly fast, they are out of control, and there is no space between them. To press the
analogy further, it's like those dangerous moments on
the freeway when cars are not only speeding but following bumper to bumper. Everyone is in danger.

A thrilling realization comes when you begin to understand this two-way relationship between speeded-
up thinking and negative emotions. If you are chronically angry, fearful, or greedy, you know well how

much damage these tendencies have done to your relationships, making you "weak in love and imperfect in virtue." And you know, too, how dauntingly hard they are to change when you approach them head-on. Their roots go deep in your past conditioning. You can talk them out, analyze them in your dreams, reason with yourself, go to anger workshops and fear seminars; still they wreak havoc, out of control.

But suppose that instead of going after chronic anger or fear directly you were to tackle the thought process itself – the mind in its Indianapolis speedway mode. When a car is going a hundred miles per hour, you can't safely slam on the brakes. But you can lift your foot off the accelerator. From one hundred miles per hour the speed drops to ninety-eight, then to ninety-five, then ninety, until finally you're cruising along at a safe and sane fifty-five. You've decelerated gradually and safely.

This is exactly what happens to the mind in meditation. You put your car into the slow lane – the inspirational passage – and you stay there, going through the words of the passage as slowly as you can. Distractions will try to crowd in, and you don't want to leave big gaps for them to rush into. For the most part, though, you just increase your concentration. In this way, little by little, you can gain complete mastery over the thinking process.

Saint Francis de Sales describes the process in more traditional language:

If the heart wanders or is distracted, bring it back to the point quite gently and replace it tenderly in its Master's presence. And even if you did nothing during the whole of your hour but bring your heart back and place it again in Our Lord's presence, though it went away every time you brought it back, your hour would be very well employed.

As you do this, your health cannot help improving, because the poor, innocent body is typically the victim of ungoverned mental activity. When I see somebody in a burst of fury, to my eyes it almost looks like a thousandth of a heart attack. When it's repeated over and over, when you get angry more and more easily, the time may come when the heart will say, "I can't take it any longer!" Of course, it might not be the heart; it might be the lungs or the digestive organs or some other physiological system or process. Whatever the result, I believe the same contributing cause is often involved: a chronically agitated mind weakening the health of the body.

People who don't easily get provoked, on the other hand, have what one researcher, Suzanne Kubasa, calls a "hardy personality." It is difficult to upset them, difficult to make their mind race out of control. As the mind slows down, I would say, you get more hardy — more patient, more secure, more healthy, more resilient under stress. Meditation is the key to achieving this end.

Visit me therefore often . . .

In the Gospel According to Saint Matthew, Jesus gives his disciples instructions in how to pray. Not in public, for everyone to see,

> But thou, when thou prayest, enter into thy closet, and when thou hast shut thy door, pray to thy Father which is in secret, and thy Father who seeth in secret shall reward thee openly.

By "into thy closet," Jesus was reminding us that real prayer takes place in the heart. As the great Russian Orthodox teacher Theophan the Recluse insists, "Outward prayer alone is not enough. God pays attention to the mind, and they are no true monks who fail to unite exterior prayer with inner prayer." To sequester oneself is only the first step. For real prayer to take place, we must shut out every external distraction and travel deep inward.

Mystics down the ages have issued a consoling assurance: when you turn to God, they say, God is turning to you. Eckhart says, in words stamped with the authority of his experience:

> You need not seek him here or there; he is no further off than the door of your heart. There he stands lingering, awaiting whoever is ready to open and let him in. You need not call to him afar; he waits much more impatiently than you for you to open to him. He longs for you a thousandfold more

urgently than you for him — one point, the opening and the entering.

The Lord is always at home deep inside each one of us, and he is always ready to greet us there. If time stretches long between visits, it's no fault of his. We are the ones who are delaying by postponing the practice of the spiritual life. "God is near us, but we are far from him," says Meister Eckhart. "God is within; we are without. God is at home; we are in the far country."

To visit the Lord, or let him visit us, we must enter the depths of consciousness through meditation. To receive the benefits of his loving instruction, we don't have to make a shopping list and keep it in our meditation room: "Lord, please give me *(a)* patience, *(b)* endurance, and *(c)* forgiveness." You don't have to ask for these virtues because in the practice of meditation, you become what you meditate on. When your attention is completely focused on the words of the passage, the words slowly begin to write themselves on your consciousness. They are no longer being heard by the ears or read by the eyes or even understood by the intellect; they are starting to be etched on your heart.

At the very instant you are praying with Saint Francis, "Lord, make me an instrument of thy peace," the Lord is doing just that. By teaching you to conduct yourself in your daily life with love and respect to everyone, whatever they say to you or do to you, you are transforming your consciousness and conduct in the image of Saint Francis.

People say to me, "Oh, but surely this is only possible

for great saints!" Much the same thing must have been said to William Law, the great Anglican devotional writer who was a contemporary of Pope and Swift, because he takes it up with deft eighteenth-century irony: "It will perhaps be thought by some people that these hours of prayer . . . ought not to be pressed upon the generality of men who have the cares of families, trades, and employments; and that they are fitting only for monasteries and nunneries."

The argument is familiar, and we've all heard it: "Meditation is a good idea for people who have time – that is, for those who have nothing better to do."

But Law counters it. Prayer is not placed before us as a duty, he says, but "recommended to all people as the best, the happiest, and the most perfect way of life. For people, therefore, of figure, or business, or dignity in the world to leave great piety and eminent devotion to any particular orders of men, or such as they think have little else to do in the world, is to leave the kingdom of God to them."

The effects of deepening meditation can be seen all through the day. Your concentration improves and your vision becomes twenty-twenty. Where you could see only blurs before, now you see forms and faces. You can read the delicately phrased messages that are written in the eyes of others. "My daughter looks worried about something. I'd better help her talk about it." Or even, "The dog! He's reminding me I didn't play with him last night." You don't hurt people now, and even if they hurt you, you are less likely to retaliate in anger.

Because you can see the whole picture, you see all the factors in the lives of those around you that are influencing their behavior.

As the rush of thinking slows down, there comes a little space between two thoughts. If someone does something to provoke you, it's not that you don't feel angry or are not aware of what the other person is doing, but now you can slowly open out an interval between two angry thoughts — half a car-length, then two, then three. Traffic thins out, so the danger of collision is lessened. You have moved out of the fast lane, where anger hurtles along, and you have dropped into the slow lane — the one where positive emotions like patience, kindness, and good will travel. The physiological benefits are many and immediate. When your thoughts slow down, your lungs breathe more deeply and your heart beats more slowly.

. . . and instruct me with all holy discipline.

But meditation alone is not enough. You can make great progress during a morning's meditation only to see it all undone at the breakfast table, when someone admits to having dented a fender slightly or overdrawn the checking account. To hold on to the precious advances you make in meditation and to extend the effects of meditation into the rest of the day, you need to practice certain supporting disciplines as well. In one form or another, though the emphasis will vary with time and circumstance, these disciplines are universal. They are undertaken wherever men and women are striving to still the mind and transcend narrow, individual consciousness.

The first of these is the use of the Holy Name, called the *mantram* in Sanskrit. Meditation is going inside to pay a formal visit to the Lord who lives in the depths of consciousness: you sit down and politely give him your undivided attention. Repeating the mantram, by contrast, is quite informal, though never casual. There are times throughout the day and night when you need to draw on the Lord for love or wisdom or strength, and you need to do it *right now,* regardless of where you are or what you are doing. Through the repetition of a simple spiritual formula like *Ave Maria,* the Jesus Prayer, or simply the name of Jesus alone, you can do just that. You're not paying a visit in person; you can't even afford the price of a phone call. Instead, you're calling the Lord collect. A wave of fear or anger is about to overtake you, or a great wave of selfish desire, and you just go out for a brisk walk repeating *Jesus, Jesus, Jesus* in your mind. The rhythm of your breathing will blend with the rhythm of your footsteps. Soon you will find that the rhythm of your mind has slowed down too, and its turbulence has subsided.

The power of this simple discipline has been laid out eloquently by the anonymous author of the *Cloud of Unknowing:*

> . . . . a naked intent directed unto God, without any other cause than himself, sufficeth wholly. And if thou desirest to have this intent lapped and folden in one word, so that thou mayest have better

hold thereupon, take thee but a little word of one syllable, for so it is better than two; for the shorter the word, the better it accordeth with the work of the spirit. . . . And fasten this word to thy heart that so it may never go thence for anything that befalleth. This word shall be thy shield and thy spear, whether thou ridest on peace or on war. With this word thou shalt beat on this cloud and this darkness above thee. With this word thou shalt smite down all manner of thought under the cloud of forgetting; insomuch that if any thought press upon thee to ask what thou wouldst have, answer with no more than this one word. . . .

When people say or do harmful things to you, you can almost see the cloud of darkness forming across your mind. It is this cloud that covers over your need to give and forgive, and it can seem as thick as a great thunderhead. But with the mantram you can just beat on that cloud until you disperse it and drive it away, and there behind it, shining like the sun, is the capacity to forgive others and draw them closer to you. It isn't always that you forget the wrongs that have been done or said, but there is no longer any emotional charge.

The use of the Holy Name is a powerful tool for deepening spiritual awareness. It is not to be confused with the practice of meditation, but when we recite the Holy Name to ourselves during the day, it allows us to draw upon the resoluteness and calm of our morning's meditation.

❧

It is time now to turn to a discussion of the aspects of the spiritual life that are more difficult to fit gracefully into our lives. We've discussed the value of meditation and the mantram in some detail. And the place and value of the disciplines of slowing down and one-pointed attention are apparent enough: learning to do just one thing at a time makes obvious sense in the context of meditation, and so does slowing down. Reading the great mystics and keeping spiritual companionship need little explanation: after all, if you're trying to become a great bowler, you seek out the company of bowlers and read books by master bowlers on how to bowl; that is all very reasonable and straightforward. But the remaining two disciplines in this eight-point program require real artistry to fit into our lives. They are skills that we learn only with trial and error after faithful effort. But to make our lives a work of art, we eventually have to master these difficult disciplines: training the senses and putting others first.

Invariably at my weekend retreats someone asks why I put so much emphasis on training the senses. It is almost always a very fresh-faced young someone who is still enjoying the wide margins that nature gives to youth — the iron digestion, the resilience to bounce right back after an all-night party or cram session, the ears that can tolerate one-hundred-twenty-decibel rock bands without flinching. Older people are a little more reticent — rather as if life itself had suggested that some degree of mastery over the senses can be helpful. I address the question in two ways.

First, I point out that training the senses is not an end in itself. Indeed, the senses have no life of their own. They are just the mind's connection with the outside world, the channels through which impressions of the world pour into the mind, keeping it endlessly busy and active. Medieval writers spoke of the senses as our "wits," for they are our means of knowing. The more varied and exciting the impressions are, the higher is the level of activity. Day and night, awake and dreaming, the mind is like the engine of a car that has been left running, consuming fuel and running down the battery.

"The eye hath not its fill of seeing, nor the ear of hearing," said the prophet of Ecclesiastes. This is where the trouble starts, for the senses are wonderful servants but poor masters. And as long as the mind is searching outward for satisfaction, the senses are likely to be in control, and the mind will follow their lead. The palate will say, "Let's eat a third piece of pie," and the mind will mutter, "Yeah, okay, sure, go ahead." You can see who's running the show. Before the mind can turn inward, to receive what is there and ready to be given, it has to become still; but the senses have to be won over first.

The mind itself is more than a match for us. But where the senses are concerned, we have a fighting chance, and in coming to grips with them, we sharpen the skills, the wit, and cunning it will take to go after the mind itself – in due time. To put it more affection-ately, I like to think of the mind as the Big Boss and the senses as five secretaries. In any bureaucracy it's diffi-cult to go directly to the boss. The mind is a real Type A, with a schedule full of places to go and people to see. You are wise to start by trying to win the good will of the secretaries. At first they are chilly and inhospitable, and for a long time the situation resembles those Hollywood movies of the 1930s where Spencer Tracy or Clark Gable breezes into an office, flings himself onto the corner of the receptionist's desk, and in-quires, ignoring her icy looks, "Hey, honey, how's the boss man today?" But gradually, just as in those highly predictable screenplays, the ice melts and the secretary becomes a staunch ally. She'll warn you, "He's there and I'll send you in, but watch your step; he's eaten three salesmen for breakfast!"

Winning over the senses, however, requires more than Hollywood charm. In collusion with the mind, they've been having the run of our life for a long time now, and they're not about to give it up.

Which brings us to the second part of my reply. Training the senses, I always emphasize, does not mean mortifying them. The senses are naturally servants of consciousness, not enemies. They are meant to serve us well; it is just that they've been badly raised. They are unschooled. "Why do you behave so terribly?" we ask in exasperation. And all they can say in response is "I can't help it!"

The senses are being stimulated all the time. Every

billboard screams that satisfaction lies outside. No one can help getting caught in that belief, and a lot of vital energy is trapped in living it out. I was no exception. But today, after many years of exacting discipline, I can count on my senses never letting me down. They might drop delicate hints about that chocolate mousse on the pastry cart, but a firm "Careful!" brings them right back to the fresh strawberries. I have their complete, joyful cooperation now – but the victory hasn't come easily.

The palate, indeed, is the ideal starting point for getting some mastery over your senses. You have five, six, a dozen opportunities every day: breakfast, lunch, dinner, and any number of between-meal snacks! No need to talk of fasting or strange diets.

You can begin simply by ceasing to choose foods that don't benefit your health and instead choosing foods that do. With this simple resolution, you'll strengthen your will and deepen your meditation – and please your physician, too.

I first became interested in changing my diet for the better under the influence of Mahatma Gandhi, when he was writing weekly articles for his paper *Young India.* One week he would write about the struggle for Indian independence from British rule, the next week about village uplift, and the third week about the value of goat's milk. Diet was an important topic for him, and he experimented all his life to discover the very best. Indians can be quite traditional about food; they always want the dishes that mother used to make. But Gandhi put tradition aside in favor of health, and his example appealed to me deeply.

I too, of course, had been brought up on Indian cuisine – first Kerala style, later Central Indian. And I had enjoyed it all thoroughly. It never occurred to me to ask what the purpose of food is. Gandhi's example prompted me to ask; and I concluded, to my great surprise, that food is meant to strengthen the body. So I started changing. I began to eat fruits and vegetables that wouldn't have appealed to me in earlier days at all. As I began to focus more on health, I found that I enjoyed salads, and that highly spiced curries no longer seemed palatable. I was prepared now to agree with Gandhi's dictum that taste lies in the mind.

On the other hand, far-reaching though these changes were, I don't think I really understood what Gandhi was getting at until much later, when I began to meditate. It was then that I made what was for me a remarkable discovery. When I needed a lot of drive to go deeper in meditation – for example, if I had a problem to solve that required more energy and creativity than usual – I found that I had only to pick a strong sensory urge and defy it. When you suddenly need cash, don't you go and shake the piggy bank? It was a little like that. I would look around intently to see what kind of cravings I had, and then I would walk up to a really big one and say, "Come on, because I am really broke." The desire would come on strong, and I would push it back and come out with both my pockets loaded.

My whole outlook on desire changed. Formerly, when a strong urge would come, I used to do what everybody does: yield to it, and not reluctantly either. Now I began to rub my hands with joy at the prospect of doing just the opposite. "Here's another desire! It's strong, so I'll gain even more by defying it." I began to understand that any strong desire, when it is defied, generates a lot of power. It's like watching the needle on your gas gauge go up! But I must confess to you that this insight did not come to me because of my own ingenuity. It came because of my teacher's blessing. I could almost feel her looking on and smiling as I recklessly flung aside one after another of these fetters and plunged ahead.

Not every desire, I should say, is to be rejected out of hand. I distinguish very carefully between harmless desires and desires that are harmful to the body or mind – or, of course, to those around you. If the desire is for food that is wholesome, you may well be able to yield with full appreciation. But if it is a desire for something sweet that you don't need, you will find you can get equal satisfaction out of refusing it. It's a deceptively simple change in perspective. Your attitude toward the body becomes very different: you see it no longer as an instrument of pleasure, but as an instrument of loving service.

From the very start, you will be able to see some benefits in training the senses. But the full reward comes only after long years of meditation in conjunction with the allied disciplines. For when the senses and the mind become still, we realize our true nature in the supreme climax of meditation. Saint Teresa of Avila describes this supreme state with an inspired simile:

> As soon as you apply yourself to prayer, you will feel your senses gather themselves together. They seem like bees which return to the hive and there shut themselves up to work at the making of honey. And this will take place without effort or care on your part. God thus rewards the violence which your soul has been doing to itself, and gives to it such a domination over the senses that when it desires to recollect itself, a sign is enough for them to obey and so gather themselves together. At the first call of the will, they come back more and more quickly. At last, after countless exercises of this kind, God disposes them to a state of utter rest and of perfect contemplation.

Our senses are groping into the external world just like bees hovering over a fragrant garden. What restaurant can I go to? What show can I see? What store is having bargain sales? At least the bees' busy search will be rewarded, but for us, as we grow more sensitive, there is only bitter disappointment; for there is no nectar in the outside world. No honey is being manufactured there; all the honey is being made inside.

Thomas a Kempis has confessed to being "weak in love and imperfect in virtue." Now he opens his heart more deeply still. In the next verse he admits to being under the sway of "evil passions" and "inordinate affections."

Set me free from evil passions, and heal my heart of all inordinate affections; that being inwardly cured and thoroughly cleansed, I may be made fit to love, courageous to suffer, steady to persevere.

CHAPTER THREE
Inordinate Affections

Most of us, I think, will hesitate here and say, "'Evil passions' might be putting it just a little too strongly. Emotional difficulties? Yes, we do have a few. A problem with anger? Yes, we can confess to that. Towering rage has gripped us on occasion. Nameless fears do torment us more often than we'd like, and jealousy is not unknown to us, we admit. But still, isn't that word *evil* a little extreme? A little . . . medieval?"

When Thomas a Kempis says "evil," however, he is not asking us to wallow in guilt. Rather he is saying, "You'd better take these characters seriously. They mean business! They're out to get you." The most ruthless hijackers can't hold us hostage more effectively than our own passions when they take over our lives. At international airports today every effort is made to be sure we don't have dangerous traveling companions, and you and I have to make the same careful inquiries where our thoughts are concerned. The fellow behind dark glasses, with the folded newspaper under his arm – look out! Interpol has a fat file on him. Don't take him with you! And that nice-looking elderly lady? That's no bag of knitting she's got draped over her arm!

Tempestuous passions like fear, anger, and greed aren't born six feet tall and armed to the teeth. They usually start as little, little fellows. You begin to dwell on an angry thought, something provoking, a genuine injustice done to you. At first it's just a little mouse gnawing at your consciousness with very small teeth. But if you keep on dwelling on it, feeding it every day by giving it more and more attention, finally it becomes the mouse that roared. In Thomas a Kempis's own description:

> For first there cometh to the mind a bare thought of evil, then a strong imagination thereof, after-wards delight, and an evil motion, and then consent. And so by little and little our wicked enemy getteth complete entrance, whilst he is not resisted in the beginning.

When we're trying to grasp a phenomenon as elusive as the mind, metaphors are exceedingly helpful. So we can think of thoughts as traveling companions – or, if we return for a moment to the language of the automobile, we can think of Thomas a Kempis's "evil passions" as cars hurtling along the freeway at top speed, too close to one another for safety. In fact it is the same thought, repeating itself over and over and over again: *IhatehimIhatehimIhatehimIhate.* . . . If we could look

more closely, we would see a break between each repetition; but as long as the mind is going so fast, we don't
see the break, so we identify ourselves with the compulsive thought. Since there is no opening in traffic for
another kind of thought – like compassion, or courage
– to come in, we are at the mercy of the one recurring
motif.

Meditation is the key to setting all this right. By
gradually slowing down our process of thinking, we
can come to see the intervals, tiny as they are, between
one angry thought and the next. Little by little, as we
bring our mind back again and again to the words of
the passage, we extend those intervals – and new possibilities arise. During the rest of the day, by repeating
the Holy Name whenever a wave of fear or anger arises,
we strengthen this process of disidentification.

In other words, through the practice of meditation,
you can gradually learn to disidentify yourself from
the powerful emotions that can turn on you and
wreck your life. That powerful emotion of *I hate him, I
hate him* is not you; it's a dangerous terrorist who has
hitched a ride on your plane. Once you can pull back
even a hair's breadth from a big wave of anger or greed
and say, "That's not really me," you've as good as
snatched the hijacker's weapon right out of his hands.

. . . and heal my heart of all inordinate affections . . .

Again, "inordinate affections" has a quaint
sound to it, like something out of an Aristotelian treatise on poetics. For a contemporary translation, you

might substitute "addictions" or "compulsive attachments." Thomas's language may be quaint, but his message is very up-to-date. He is implying that desire, which is our capacity for love, is spilling out all the time. Whether it is Belgian chocolate ice cream bars or "recreational drugs," fine wines or handcrafted jewelry, every one of these represents a hole in consciousness where love is ebbing out. Unchecked, this constant leakage will finally drain the reservoir, leaving you with an empty tank and miles from home. To find your real Self, you need every drop of the fuel that is desire. That is why it is so important to plug all those little holes one by one.

A compulsive desire is like any other thought over which you have no control. It flows continuously: *I want that, I want that, I want that,* with no space between the demands. But when you begin to deepen your meditation, two things happen. First, of course, the thought process itself slows down. Second, you develop a new kind of attitude toward desires. You get a taste of the powerful satisfaction that comes when you go against long-standing compulsions. You realize that you don't have to identify with those strong urges. Hesitantly, you begin to oppose some of them.

After a while, when a very strong, powerfully compulsive desire overtakes you and your mind just keeps chanting *I want that,* you catch sight of a tiny opening between the demands. It's only a split second in duration at first, but in time it grows long enough for another thought, another kind of thought, to make itself known. "Hmmm . . . maybe part of me does want that. Maybe part of my mind. But do I? Is it really in my long-term best interest to gratify this desire? Or my family's?"

When this happens, you are on the way to developing a supremely precious skill: when a desire comes of which you do not approve, you can draw your mind back. It is almost like reaching out, taking hold of its collar, and pulling it back gently. The desire will quietly vanish, leaving you heir to all the energy that fueled it. I began by saying, remember, that training the senses is not an end in itself; it's a preparation for training the mind. Now you can see why. You are no longer just training the senses; you are well on your way to having trained your very capacity for giving attention too. And in the process, you have begun to train the will, far beneath the conscious level.

It can be terribly painful when we see ourselves mastered by some enormous desire or compulsive attachment. We think maybe we'll never get free – think we don't have any will at all. But I always tell my friends, when they confide these feelings to me, that the will is there the whole time, only it's being carried along in the desire itself – like a baby kangaroo, riding in its mother's pouch. It's a whimsical image, but it suggests that the baby won't always stay in the pouch. One day it will heave itself out and hop away on its own strong feet.

. . . that being inwardly cured . . .

Medical scientists have achieved almost miraculous results in learning how to transplant parts of the human body. I would never deprecate their achievements, but I would point out how much more wonderful it would be to get a new mind – a mind that is always at peace, full of love and energy, always ready to work for others. This is what meditation can give us. The great Catholic teacher Hugh of St. Victor described his experience: "I am suddenly renewed: I am changed. I am plunged into an ineffable peace. My mind is full of gladness; all my past wretchedness and pain is forgot. My soul exults, my intellect is illuminated, my heart is afire: my desires have become kindly and gentle."

Indeed, this new mind brings with it enormous benefits to health. As meditation deepens and sense cravings fall away, you come to identify yourself less and less with the body. You develop a certain sense of detachment, without which it isn't possible to understand the language of the body. You can read its requests accurately now, and you'll be impressed to discover that the body has a native wisdom. Fresh, whole, natural food tastes good to the palate when the mind is not confusing it with messages planted by advertisers. Vigorous exercise feels good when the mind whispers to the body: "You were meant for motion!"

. . . and thoroughly cleansed . . .

Layer upon layer, long years of conditioning have overlaid our minds, dulling the bright glow of awareness that is our birthright. Through meditation, these layers of dust and grime are removed. Saint Catherine of Genoa has described this cleansing process with a beautiful simile:

> It is as with a covered object: it cannot respond to the rays of the sun, not because the sun ceases to shine, for it shines without intermission, but because the covering intervenes. Let the covering be removed and again the object will be exposed to the sun and will answer to the rays which beat against it in proportion as the work of removal advances.

When you meditate on a beautiful passage like the Twenty-third Psalm and take it into the depths of consciousness, it gradually washes clean the very walls of consciousness. It paints them anew with glowing pictures of the human being in the divine image. When you give your complete attention to the Prayer of Saint Francis, you are cleansing your mind. When the great stream of love from the twelfth chapter of the Bhagavad Gita pours into your consciousness, you are purifying the contents of your mind. The more inspiring the passage and the deeper it goes, the purer your mind becomes. Finally, after many years of meditation, negative thoughts will not be able to enter your mind; the atmosphere just won't sustain them.

. . . I may be made fit to love . . .

When I visit San Francisco I like to go with friends to the Marina, where we can walk for a mile or so right next to the bay. On all sides people are jogging and sprinting, while the sea gulls and pigeons scatter out of their way; and at regular intervals there are exercise stations where some are trying to strengthen their backs or calf muscles or thighs. It reminds me of my high school in Kerala, where bodybuilding was highly regarded and one of the most popular ways to show how strong you were was "making the frog leap" in your biceps.

I'm impressed by how many people are joining health clubs now, and by how much enthusiasm they have for strengthening the body. My suggestion is only this: Why not learn the exercises that will strengthen your mind as well? Where the muscles of patience are weak, as they are with most people today, one little provocation and you are ready to retaliate. You can strengthen those muscles immeasurably through meditation, so that you become, as the Bible says beautifully, "slow to wrath."

No one at the Marina, and none of the trainers at your workout club, will ever give you special exercises meant to weaken particular muscles. But spiritual teachers do this. They help you strengthen your will and patience, but they also say, "Let's see if we can't make those resentment muscles a bit flabby." Do what they say, and before you know it the muscles of resentment and hostility will just lie there. The frogs won't leap at all now, and you will be incapable of hostility.

These are secrets that aren't known in our modern civilization. But they are spelled out succinctly in the Prayer of Saint Francis of Assisi. Meditate on the prayer with the same regularity you give to your morning push-ups or jogging or swimming, and your mind will undergo so dramatic a change that you'll wish you could have "before" and "after" photographs for the newspapers.

As compulsive patterns of living fall away, all the vital energy that has sustained them will come back to you. You really are stronger now. And as compulsive attachments fall away, you become capable of slowly extending your love to more and more people. You have more and richer relationships now, and you are increasingly aware that beneath all the teeming diversity of life there is unity. Your arms are strong now. You have a long reach, and it seems like lifetimes ago that you might have described yourself as "weak in love."

The source of your newfound strength, and the keystone of the mystics' Spiritual Fitness Program, is the deceptively simple discipline that characterizes the form of meditation I teach: that is, the training of attention. I ask my students to give their complete attention to the words of the spiritual passage. I ask, too, that when their attention wanders away from the passage, as it will, they should bring it back, gently but firmly. I tell them to keep doing this over and over, thirty times in thirty minutes if need be.

I promise them that if they do this, they will develop a tremendous skill. When the mind is accustomed to wandering wherever it likes, there can be serious consequences. But see what happens when you have brought it under some control. Now when your attention begins to wander from Rosalind to Celia — as happens so often in today's world — you can bring it back to your sweetheart. Even if Rosalind has had a bad day and is taking it out on you, you can guard your love against going astray and win her undying loyalty in the process.

The wandering mind is one of the frailties of human nature. When our dear one provokes us, we say, "I wish he'd go away." We're all like that. When our beloved is self-willed and won't give us our way, we think, "Why do I have to be with her?" It is this kind of thought, repeated a thousand times, that leads finally to the tragic parting of the ways that we see all around us. And it is the capacity to break that train of thought, right at the outset, that makes us "fit to love." As Shakespeare says:

> Love is not love
> That alters when it alteration finds,
> Or bends with the remover to remove.

. . . *courageous to suffer* . . .

The modern attempt to pretend that life can be all jubilee and merrymaking is futile. We can't conceal the sorrow that throbs at the very heart of life, and it is this sorrow which provides us the means of spiritual growth.

It is a universal law of life, enshrined at the core of every great religion, that when we go after personal satisfaction it will elude us. Read the life of Saint Augustine or Saint Teresa, or of any of the other great lovers of God who have burned their fingers and made their hearts weary before they finally turned inward to find the supreme source from which all truth, joy, and beauty flow. This inward turning rarely takes place all at once; for most of us it is long and drawn out. Yet gently, over many years as our meditation deepens, we are forced to see the emptiness of what we've clung to – and indeed very often the things we've clung to break in our grasp and fall to pieces. It is a terribly painful process, and that is why Saint John of the Ladder says, "Prayer is the mother and also the daughter of tears." We grieve at what is slipping away from us, but we know there is even greater grief in holding on.

Training the senses can be very painful. So is every skirmish and every battle we undertake against self-will. At the outset, it can feel – this is no exaggeration – that something in us is dying, and dying by slow, painful degrees. Yet even as this is taking place, our experience begins to verify the beautiful and mysterious words of the fourteenth-century German mystic John Tauler. "In the truest death of all created things," he observed, "the sweetest and most natural life is hidden. In their death lies the secret of our life." This is not our world, he is saying. This world of created things is not the one we were born to inhabit. To find the world that is our own, the City of God, we must gently, gradually, but resolutely withdraw our attachment from the world of physical things.

Tauler continues: "This dying has many degrees. A person might die a thousand deaths in one day and find at once a joyful life corresponding to each of them." He is a subtle psychologist. Suppose you have a strong desire to eat something you have been conditioned to enjoy for many years. You are able to forget it for a little while, but then it comes up again. You focus more intently upon the work at hand, you repeat your mantram, and indeed the desire recedes for a while – but then, without warning, up it comes again. It's an exhilarating struggle, because even though you may not be able to erase the urge altogether, every time you manage to set it aside, you get a little more strength with which to fight, a little more vitality. You begin to taste "a joyful life" that indeed corresponds to the death of every selfish urge.

Tauler concludes magnificently by saying,

> This is as it must be. God cannot deny or refuse this death. The stronger the death, the more powerful and thorough is the corresponding life. The more intimate the death, the more inward is the life. Each life brings strength, and strengthens to a harder death . . . a death so long and strong that it seems to him hereafter more joyful, for he finds life in death and light shining in darkness.

The mind becomes still, the heart becomes full of love, and as a result the body glows and creative faculties come into play. People are drawn to you, and you become a shining lamp to all those who are around.

. . . steady to persevere.

Imposing spiritual disciplines on yourself takes tremendous courage, because it asks you to come face to face with all that is resistant and rebellious inside you. This journey into the world within is real travel, and you'll meet with quite a few unexpected adventures.

The depths of consciousness is an immense region with many levels. On every level of consciousness there is a breathtakingly different view of life, so that when you change levels you have great difficulties. It's very much like going to China: you don't know the language; you don't know the customs; you don't even know how to use chopsticks. Just so, it takes a lot of effort and experience to learn how to operate on a new level of consciousness, where the race-old sense of separateness is beginning to give way to unity. And just when you begin to feel at home in this new region, meditation deepens again, and you enter still another level of consciousness. You've just got used to China and now you're in India. You don't know how to drape a sari or put your hair in a chignon or place a little tilak on your forehead – but you learn.

Living on the surface level of consciousness, we do

not even know there is a world within – a world, what's more, with its own meteorological events. We know, of course, that here in North America we are subject to strong winds – cold ones that bring in a wintry breath from the north, or warm ones like the chinook that come across the Rockies in spring. But we know nothing about the winds that blow inside. People just don't know how to cope with the winds that blow through the mind. Where there is a hot wind, they lose their temper; when it is a cold wind, they get icy; when it's neither hot nor cold, they get bored and do ridiculous things!

With deepening meditation, you realize that when these strong winds come up, you have a choice. You don't have to bend whichever way the wind is blowing. You don't have to identify with the angry or fearful motions of the mind. Just as wind power can be harnessed, the wind of anger can be harnessed. Gandhi showed us how. The wind of greed can be harnessed, too. Francis of Assisi showed us how.

While modern civilization has made great strides in understanding the external world, it has sadly neglected exploring the internal world. Yet we live in the world within every bit as much as in the world outside. The forces of anger are great hurricanes which can destroy us and others. The forces of greed are gales that can devastate the mind. Fear is a fierce blizzard that can become a terrible burden on the human being. We need to know how these winds blow, and how they can be directed and put to work.

Whenever I see windmills on the hills around us, I am reminded that the powerful winds that sweep our region have been put to work. Similarly, "anger mills" can be set up in consciousness: we can put anger to work. When the destructive winds of anger blow, we can repeat the Holy Name, calm our mind, and turn that rising anger into compassion. Anger is raw power, power that we usually allow to dissipate in meaningless explosions. But we can learn to use anger as a motivation, as Gandhi did when he channeled his anger into nonviolent resistance. Anger, fear, and greed are all powerful forces that can help us, when transformed, to persevere on the spiritual journey. Once we have harnessed their power, they will push us forward rather than hold us back.

In the practice of meditation, what we really learn to do is to discover the world within, which is as real as the world without. I am not denying the reality of mountains, seas, rivers, or forests. But I am also at home in the world within, in which there are tremendous mountains where you can climb to the summit, look about, and exclaim with Angela of Foligno, "The world is full of God!"

Love is a great thing, yea, a great and thorough good; by itself it makes every thing that is heavy, light; and it bears evenly all that is uneven. For it carries a burden which is no burden, and makes every thing that is bitter, sweet and tasteful.

CHAPTER FOUR
A Great & Thorough Good

Unselfish love is a precious thing, and like all precious things it must be worked for. Our image of the lover may be the young man in a tuxedo dancing cheek to cheek with his sweetheart, but the reality is more like a miner digging in a deep pit for gold or for precious gems. It is hard work, and we have to dig through a lot of ordinary earth before getting anywhere near a diamond or a nugget of gold.

Many years ago, when I was a student, I was traveling with a friend by train when we passed a world-famous gold mine not too many miles from Bangalore and decided to get down and take a look. The mine was run by a British company in a place called the Kolar gold fields. Kolar is located on the vast plains of South India, so when we got out of the train I was surprised to see several huge hills. I told my friend I hadn't known there were hills like that in the area. He knew more about mines than I did, so he just laughed. All the dirt and rock that had covered the hidden gold had been removed, he explained, and there was so much of it that it had become these hills.

I remembered that dramatic terrain when the newspapers were full of the discovery in South Africa of the world's second largest diamond. Weighing in at six hundred carats, it was going to be sold for thirty million dollars. I couldn't read the accounts without trying to recall what the world's first largest diamond was. How much did it weigh? A friend who is a reference librarian helped me out: it is the Star of Africa, discovered in 1905. It weighed one and one-quarter pounds before it was cut, and it resides in the Tower of London, where it adorns the British royal scepter.

Of course, if you were to ask the great mystics of East and West, "What is the world's most precious jewel, and where is it?" they would have a very different answer from the *Guinness Book of World Records.* Jesus called it "a pearl of great price." Teresa of Avila says that the human soul "can best be compared to a mansion made of a single diamond," which the Compassionate Buddha refers to in his beautiful mantram *Om mani padme hum:* literally, "The jewel is in the lotus." Every one of us is the possessor of the most precious diamond in the world: it is hidden in the lotus of the heart, in the very depths of consciousness. To get it, we don't have to attend a sale at Christie's or Sotheby's; we have only to claim our legacy. It is always with us; it will always be with us.

The problem is, we don't know this. It is as if we had a hidden treasure in a safe-deposit box. To get the key to that box and claim the treasure, there is a certain price. Thirty million dollars is not enough. Thirty billion is not enough. Money counts for nothing in this divine marketplace, but "sweat equity" is precious. We must go deep into consciousness through the practice of meditation, and in order to do that, we must first remove tons and tons of self-will. We have to dig and dig and keep digging. If, at the end of our spiritual journey, we could see all our self-will piled up against the sky, we would be stunned.

I have always been a hardworking person, but I had no idea what unending labor meditation would exact. Almost no one can fathom this. It seems so simple at the outset that people just can't believe it's going to be difficult. "How could sitting still for thirty minutes and concentrating on the soothing words of Saint Francis be a problem?" they ask.

So they begin to sit with me in meditation, and after a month or so, when I ask how their meditation is going, they answer, "Oh, I don't find it so very difficult. Maybe I have a natural aptitude for it!"

I'm not one to throw cold water on natural aptitudes. Who knows, maybe this is one of those one-in-a-million you read about! But once a person breaks through the surface level of consciousness and begins to enter deeper levels, the story changes. Then when I say, "Your meditation must still be going very well?" there is only silence at first, and a pained look.

"Not exactly," comes the reply at last. "I don't know where I'm going any more, and when I try to meditate on the Prayer of Saint Francis, all kinds of thoughts rush in – from restaurants and swimming pools and movie theaters and dental chairs. They come and sit by my side in meditation, and I just don't know what to do."

In feigned innocence I ask, "Why don't you just tell them to go away?"

"I've tried. They just laugh at me!"

At this point, when they have all but despaired, I tell them they are actually doing much better than they think.

"Up until now," I explain, "the ego hasn't taken your efforts seriously, but now it does. Now it is beginning to feel threatened, so it is loosing all its weapons against you: distractions of every kind, and worst of all, the idea 'Oh, who am I, with all my weaknesses and wayward desires, to think I could ever follow this path to the end?' This is no time to get discouraged. Just give your attention more and more to the spiritual passage, and ransack your day for hidden opportunities to go against self-will. A little opportunity here, another there – you will see how your meditation deepens."

I add, too, that we have only to read the lives of people like Augustine and Teresa of Avila to make an enormously comforting discovery: all of these people began with imperfections, just as we do. "Look at that slag pile of self-will!" Augustine would say. "Almost touches the sky, and I had to take out every shovelful by hand! If I can commit all those mistakes and still discover this flawless diamond, don't weep over the mistakes you have committed. Turn your back upon them and start digging!"

By itself it makes every thing that is heavy light . . .

What you are removing with pick and shovel in meditation is nothing more than the will to have your own way, solidified in a thousand petty little insistences: "I must have this to drink and that to eat. I must have this kind of music to listen to and that sort of sweater to wear. I won't tolerate people who disagree with my views on contemporary art, and I will avoid the company of anyone who is richer or poorer, older or younger, darker or lighter, brighter or slower, than I am."

The cumulative weight of all these stipulations is tremendous, and much of the sorrow we experience in life has to do with our having to carry it all around. A fourteenth-century spiritual classic, the *Theologia Germanica,* says, "Nothing burns in hell but self-will." We can paraphrase aptly: "Nothing oppresses us in *life* except self-will."

The surest sign of grace, then – and it can come like a bolt out of the blue – is the desire to go against all selfish desires. Mechthild of Magdeburg describes the dawning of this desire in a soul that is just turning inward: "First, that it wills to come to God, removing all self-will, joyfully welcoming God's grace and willingly accepting all its demands against selfish desires."

To take on self-will is a joint endeavor of immense cooperation between divine grace and human effort.

It's like a matching grant: the harder we try, the more abundantly grace pours forth from within to augment our effort.

You begin, then, in little, little ways, and at first the whole business seems almost laughable. You order tortellini for dinner when you really wanted fettuccine. You ask for mineral water instead of Chianti, and fresh fruit to round everything off just as your eyes start to slide toward the dessert list. This is hardly the stuff that hair shirts are made of, but you are reducing self-will, and you do notice a certain alertness entering your life and a new mettle. Part of your mind leaps out, "But I'd so looked forward to that fettuccine." But another part now replies, "Oh, hush! Pasta's pasta." You are in the driver's seat now, in a way that can feel quite pleasurable.

Be warned, though, that progress will be uneven. You can try a more daring raid on self-will the next morning, and find you've tumbled right out of the driver's seat onto the hard pavement. But you brush yourself off and carry on, exhilarated – and keenly interested.

Most of us pay little attention to the movements of our mind over the course of a day. We don't notice how, when there are differences of opinion or when events don't work out as we'd hoped, the mind surges up and down, moves wildly to and fro, and grumbles, "I don't like this." But with our new perspective, we almost look forward to life trying to knock us off our pins.

In my own case, for instance, there is a certain very well known newspaper in this country whose editorial page contradicts almost all my views on life. Of course, I could just avoid reading it. Instead, for years I have gone out of my way to read it every day. I have actually taught myself to enjoy reading articles about the supreme importance of money. "So, it seems the measure of a nation's strength is its gross national product. Hmmm." There is no question in my mind but that I disagree. Yet my mind, as I read, is unperturbed. It makes no convulsive movements. In fact, it almost chuckles. I am able to read attentively and follow thoroughly the line of thinking.

Similarly, on evenings when I want to entertain myself with a good book, my inclination in the past would have been to turn to a volume of Robert Browning's poetry, or a play by George Bernard Shaw. Instead, I now reach for a stack of medical journals. The articles are seldom well-written; often they are even badly edited. But I read them in order to keep abreast of medical goings-on – and because of my deep interest in the connection between meditation and health, I read not in protest but with gusto. Medieval mystics mortified the flesh; I have mortified my literary sensibilities.

Once you have lost the dread of being contradicted, or even of being disappointed aesthetically, a kind of inward cheerfulness pervades your mind. You find that you think more clearly under duress, your blood pressure unaffected. You wear your opinions more loosely, carry your self-will more lightly; so you function better in life.

Tragically, when self-will is highly developed, it has

the effect of narrowing our vision of life down to a tiny peephole. When we're only thinking of what's in our immediate personal interest, we just don't see things clearly. We can't take in the larger picture. If we did, we'd see that our own welfare is neatly interlocked with everyone else's – that separateness is the illusion born of preoccupation with self. There is no more ideal place to begin breaking free from that preoccupation than in the company of our family and friends. In to-day's world where so many people, whether through necessity or through choice, plough a lonely furrow, we need to be reminded of the importance of living and working with other people – building strong, selfless, loving relationships wherever possible.

It is love that teaches us our real stature and reveals the heroism we never thought we possessed. The small renunciation that might be well-nigh impossible in a vacuum can be blessedly simple when someone we love stands to gain. This is surely part of what Thomas a Kempis means when he says that love makes everything that is heavy light. Turning down that glass of Chianti might take some doing in ordinary circum-stances, but when you're in the company of an impres-sionable teenager, you'll gladly set it aside. Or suppose you're tempted to add another antique fire screen to your collection. Hard to resist, maybe, if your aim is solely to reduce your own self-will. But if the money you save can be spent on a tent for family camping trips – something everybody can enjoy – then saying no to the temptation can be a breeze. You feel so good inside!

A knack for quiet self-sacrifice is the very life and soul of family living.

The annals of ancient monastic communities, East or West, relate how in a thousand ways members would go after self-will in acts of fierce deprivation, such as sleeping without lying down or eating only one meal a day for years on end. This approach might have had its merits; but my way is, I think, subtler, and much better suited to the world of today. Each of us can find ways to simplify our lives and reduce our needs – what we eat, what we wear, how much we drive, how we spend our leisure time. All the daily choices we make can work to reduce self-will. They can also take into account our endangered environment and all the living creatures that inhabit it. Reducing self-will needn't be a joyless exercise. It can be achieved through many little acts of love, performed over and over throughout the day.

We start, then, by recognizing that the sense of *I and mine* we've cultivated all our lives is like a coil wrapped tight around our necks, throttling us, and that the more we dwell on ourselves, the tighter it gets. Gradually, we now start extending our concern more and more to the people immediately around us, by learning to see that their needs are just as urgent as our own. As the coil loosens, we can breathe more easily. The coil is still there, but the distinction between our families' needs and our own has begun to dissolve.

This is no place to stop. It is time to enlarge the circle of attention and compassion still further. You might

forgo an evening at the theater to attend a town coun-
cil, because there needs to be a community center for
the aged and better parks for the children. Little by
little, in loving gestures, you stretch the confines of
self-will outward. You are not obliterating the old nagging *I and mine* by a frontal attack. Rather, you are extending your boundaries outward until they include
all of life. In the words of Catherine of Genoa, "Everything is mine, for all that is God's seems to be wholly
mine. I am mute and lost in God."

Not that this comes easily. I did not find it the least
bit enjoyable to forgo some of my earlier pleasures. But
when you want this more than anything else, when
you want God – not intellectually, not theoretically,
but with all your heart, all your mind, and all your
spirit – then you get the will, the wisdom, and the
courage to give up whatever stands in the way. That
"whatever" may be extremely pleasant, and you may
have been conditioned to it for a long time. But if you
want the Lord passionately enough, you will succeed
in letting go.

. . . and it bears evenly all that is uneven.

Whenever I hear someone say "I got even with
him," I want to point out, "But you didn't! You got odd
– odder and odder." When we can't let go of our anger,
when we allow it to push us about and damage our relationships, we lose something of our essential humanity. The artists of medieval Europe used to portray
anger, envy, and greed as monsters with bared fangs

and terrible horns. The contemporary teenager who describes his aggravated father as "bent out of shape" is getting at the same truth in his own wry idiom.

The ability to forgive is the hallmark of the highly evolved human being. There is no more exacting skill. And yet it is nothing more, essentially, than the seemingly prosaic capacity of withdrawing attention at will and placing it where you choose. Whatever distressing words have been spoken, whatever unkind acts have been performed, the mind that has been trained in deep meditation can turn quietly away and focus instead on the loving words, the thoughtful acts, of a happier hour.

Like any skill, this one develops with practice. Suppose you are meditating on the words of Thomas a Kempis: "Love bears evenly all that is uneven." Suddenly a much louder passage is ringing in your ears. It is as if a car with huge speakers had pulled up next to yours at a stoplight, playing a tape of something someone has said to you that day: "Charles, I think it's time both of us started seeing other people!" or "Marilou, you're just not working out as an administrator. I've decided you'd be more effective back in your old post."

The more attention you give to these dissonant voices, the louder they'll get. The only way to turn them down is to give your attention more and more to the words of the passage: "Love bears evenly all that is uneven." It is a simple skill, but it has wide applications. When you have a severe personal problem, you are naturally inclined to dwell on it, and when you do, it looms all the larger. Solutions seem more and more distant. Most problems are rather unassuming when you see them in their native costume. They only become unmanageable when you can't stop brooding on them, dressing them up as Count Dracula or Lady Macbeth.

When someone who is close to you lashes out over nothing, or lets you down in a way that really grieves you, it is natural that you should find it difficult to have loving thoughts. It is altogether understandable that you should want to move away from that person. But when you have developed the capacity to step back from the turmoil of an offended mind and look at the situation with even a small measure of objectivity, you can make a fascinating discovery. Often the person who is causing us trouble is simply making a call for help – calling in the only language he or she knows. Underneath the abrasiveness is a hidden message: "Please move closer to me. Support me. Bear with me."

We all know how much turmoil there is in living together. This is why so many follow the counsel of despair and say, "Why not live by ourselves? Why be unhappy?" But for ordinary people like you and me, the solitary life is not particularly conducive to spiritual growth. To purify our hearts of self-will, no amount of reading books can be of much help. No amount of discussion will do the job. Seminars on Self-Will Extinction are beside the point. There is only one way to undo self-will, and that is by living and working harmoniously with other people. In the sometimes painful give-and-take of life every day, you can draw upon the power released in meditation to love and support the people around you – even at the expense of your own comfort and convenience.

The mystics are unanimous: love of God makes itself seen and felt as love of our fellow creatures. Only when you have lowered all the barriers between yourself and others will there be no barrier between you and the Lord within. Deliberately, then, from the very first, you begin to chip away at those walls in consciousness. You do it in little ways, throughout the day, by trying to see the needs of others as clearly as your own and to act in harmony with them.

Another discipline that comes very naturally into the picture at this point is spiritual fellowship, spending time with others who meditate, who share your ideals and your efforts to realize them. The support you can provide one another will strengthen your meditation enormously. Don't confine yourself to fellow aspirants of your own time and place. Your stoutest spiritual allies may have lived centuries ago – Saint Teresa of Avila or the Compassionate Buddha, John Woolman or Saint Catherine of Genoa. Daily reading from the scriptures and from the lives of the great mystics is a richly rewarding side of the spiritual life.

For it carries a burden which is no burden . . .

On our village roads in Kerala, people carry all kinds of things on their heads. Whether they are bringing water jugs from the well, or carrying butter and yogurt to the marketplace, or taking baskets of laundry down to the river, everything goes on the head. This is wisdom born of experience, because it is best for the back and makes for beautiful posture.

Even so, the loads are heavy, and after a while the back begins to weary. So at intervals along our footpaths and country roads there are stone pillars called *athani*s, just the height of a man or woman. They are flat on top so that you can slide your burden off and rest for a moment. When the day is warm and you have a mile or two to travel, nothing could be more welcome than the sight of one of these pillars just ahead.

The *athani* is a humble, ordinary feature of the Kerala landscape. But it makes a glorious appearance in a tender poem written by a Kerala poet about Mary Magdalene. The poet himself was a devout Hindu, but he was so moved when he heard the story of Mary Magdalene that he retold it in Malayalam, my native tongue. He chose a particularly soft and gentle meter, to tell the Gospel story in his own Kerala way.

Mary Magdalene is described as a deeply troubled person whom the whole village looked down on for her dissolute life – someone who had despaired, in all likelihood, of ever being able to put her past behind her. When she heard that Jesus was nearby, she slipped in behind him while he was at dinner, fell to her knees, and began to weep. She washed his feet with her tears and dried them with her long, lustrous hair, because she knew that here was somebody who was incapable of sitting in judgment on her.

"Weep, lovely one, weep!" says the Lord. "Let all your suffering pour out." He knows her tears are easing a heart that has been ready to break under the weight of her grief. "You who have eyes like a doe's, your eyes are even more beautiful now when you wash away the past. Let those same tears purify your mind as well." Then he makes her a tender promise. "I will be your *athani*. Just hand over the burden of your past. My arms are strong; I can carry it all." And he adds gently, "Your sins are forgiven. Go in peace."

In the Hindu tradition, one of the names of the Lord is "the ocean of forgiveness." If we want to be united with him, we need to forgive all those around us, for in learning to forgive we move closer and closer to the Lord, who is the source of forgiveness itself.

When you begin to travel inward through meditation, you will see for yourself how many things the mind has not been able to pardon. For a while, all you can do is look at them in dismay. But if over many years you have developed compassion for others, then that same wealth of compassion will come to you when you most need it. It will equip you with a kind of spiritual eraser. Now you will be able to walk up to a memory that has spread hostility, fear, or greed in your mind for decades and just rub it out.

If anyone were to ask me about the mistakes I made in the past, I would say simply, "That was how I saw life then. Now, through the grace of the Lord, my vision has been corrected." That is why I repeat over and over again, "Don't let your mind dwell on the past." Everybody has scars from the past. Don't talk about them; don't think about them. I am the first to admit that this is a tall order. It can be done, though, through repetition of the Holy Name.

> *. . . and makes every thing that is bitter sweet and tasteful.*

Saint Bernard declared that "Jesus is honey in the mouth, music in the ear, a shout of gladness in the heart." Saint Bernard very probably repeated the name of Jesus to himself just as good Hindus do the name of Rama or Krishna. Saint Catherine of Genoa may have engaged in the same practice, for at the time of her conversion she is said to have received certain instructions directly from the Lord within. "From the *Hail Mary*," she was told, "take the word Jesus, and may it be implanted in your heart, and it will be a sweet guide and shield to you in all the necessities of life." When she was comforting the patients in the hospital she administered in Genoa, she would always urge them to "call Jesus." Biographers of Saint Francis of Assisi describe him as praying all night on occasion, repeating the same words over and over: "My God and my all, my God and my all." And in the Eastern Orthodox tradition, the practice called hesychasm consists in the repetition of the short prayer "Lord, Jesus Christ, have mercy upon me."

Repetition of the Holy Name is not a substitute for meditation. When you meditate, you need to sit down in a quiet place with your eyes closed and bring your attention to rest on the words of a memorized passage. The Holy Name, I want to emphasize, can be used under any circumstances. You can use it throughout the day to tap into the peace and security of your morning's meditation. It can be your lifeline. The more assiduously you repeat it, the stronger the rope will be, and the closer at hand in times of danger.

The most precious period of the day for repeating your mantram is at night, just as you are falling asleep. Between the last waking moment and the first sleeping moment, there is an infinitesimally narrow tunnel into the unconscious. If you can learn to fall asleep in the Holy Name, you can send it in deep where it will heal the wounds the day has inflicted; it will soothe the raw edges of daily experience. The proof that the Holy Name is doing its work is that sometimes you may hear it reverberating in your sleep.

This is the miracle Saint Paul refers to when he enjoins us to "pray without ceasing." It goes on wherever you are, whatever you are doing, protecting your mind against any negative emotion. In fact, I like to compare the Holy Name to a highway patrolman riding about on a Harley-Davidson, round and round the alleys of the mind – most of them blind. He keeps an eye on the thoughts traveling there and gives out tickets for excessive speed, for drifting back and forth across lanes, for driving too close to the car ahead. Day and night, your mantram is always on duty.

The noble love of Jesus impels one to do great things, and stirs one up to be always longing for what is more perfect.

Love desires to be aloft, and will not be kept back by any thing low and mean.

Love desires to be free, and estranged from all worldly affections, that so its inward sight may not be hindered; that it may not be entangled by any temporal prosperity, or by any adversity subdued.

CHAPTER FIVE

Great Things

These lyrical lines convey a feeling of tension between the sheer weight of ordinary life – its disappointments, its cares, its bitterness – and the longing to soar upward, free from any hindrance or entanglement. This tension hints in turn at a deeper one: between the things of this world, as Saint Teresa termed them, and the things of heaven. Clinging to the world kept her bound for nearly forty years; a deep surge of longing for higher things enabled her at last to break free.

Teresa's friend John of the Cross described this dilemma – which is the dilemma of every one of us – in a treatise on the spiritual life called *The Ascent of Mount Carmel*. The work is prefaced by a rough sketch of a mountain crisscrossed by paths. At the top of the mountain is Earthly Paradise – not heaven but heaven on earth, life as it is meant to be lived. At the bottom of the mountain you see the beginnings of two routes. One is wide and inviting; the other is small and narrow, curving about tortuously among rocky crevasses. The choice seems obvious at first glance. But as your eye travels upward, you see that the path that had seemed so attractive begins to coil back upon itself. It shrinks in size, and finally vanishes in the thick undergrowth of the lower slopes. This is the path of least resistance, of saying "Yes, of course!" to every murmur from the senses and the ego.

The other path, so hard at the outset, becomes gradually wider and easier of access as it ascends, and it carries you with increasing ease and delight all the way to the top. This is the path of spiritual discipline. The difference is this: on the one hand, a life ruled by self-will, and on the other, one that is lived for the whole.

> *The noble love of Jesus impels one to do great things, and stirs one up to be always longing for what is more perfect.*

During the Winter Olympics that were held at Calgary in 1988, everyone was impressed by a champion ski-jumper they called the Flying Finn, who was able to soar through the air for seventy meters. He looked like an eagle – head thrust forward, wings folded back. To my inexperienced eye, what he was doing looked absolutely impossible. But when I consulted friends who ski, they said, "No, it's not impossible. But it takes a tremendous lot of training." Most of the greatest ski-jumpers have practiced since childhood. Matti Nykänen, it is said, was so enraptured by skiing – the dangers so beckoned to him – that he jumped off a roof when he was only seven. It was to protect him from serious injury that his parents gave him a pair of skis and set him loose on the slopes. He was asked, "How many times do you jump on your skis?" His answer: four to five thousand times a year – which is nearly ten times a day.

Watching Matti Nykanen on television, amazed by his ability, I thought of the words of the medieval German mystic who prefaced his treatise with a warning: if you don't like challenges, he said, don't read this book. My guess is that with that warning he attracted exactly the reckless young aspirants he was after – the Matti Nykanens of the spiritual life – because the best and brightest young people want difficult things to do. They don't want us to mince words; they don't want us to coat the pill. They want tremendous challenges to pit themselves against. Meditation is the hardest path the human being can walk on; but when I tell my young friends outright how grueling the later stages of meditation can be, their faces glow at the prospect.

It's a great pity that the roiling turbulence of young men and women is so often seen as a threat to society. Rightly understood and channeled, that restlessness can be the most precious asset of any society, because it arises directly out of the need that is deepest in every human being: the need to give. It is when that need is blocked that the trouble starts, and grievously enough, the trouble often comes in the form of self-destructive behavior.

Many young people in this country have satisfied

their physical appetites over and over. Now they yearn for a higher goal. It is as if there has been an opening from inside out of which tremendous yearning, tremendous energy, comes up. It is so powerful and demanding that young people have got to find some way of putting it to work. Misunderstanding it, they do the most dangerous and meaningless things possible. The real answer is not to chastise them or be punitive, but to show them through our own example what this tremendous energy is meant for – and that the more it is utilized, the more they will get from within. It's a wonderful discovery for a young person to make: that beneath all these drives to rebel there flows this deep desire to give and to serve.

The wealth of a country does not lie in mines, factories, or shopping centers; it lies in the hearts of young people. My grandmother understood this implicitly, simple village woman though she was. Very often, living in an orthodox Hindu society, I would question some of its assumptions and try to go against them. I had all the makings of a successful rebel. But I never got an opportunity to make much of a splash because my grandmother would usually support me, even though she observed all the orthodox ways herself.

Sometimes, I have to confess, this was rather deflating. Confronted by my latest effort to challenge the time-honored ways of my village, she would only say, "The capacity to rebel is part of our human wealth. It is God-given." When the Lord is making a human being, she would explain, he takes a good measure of rebelliousness and mixes it in. He has his reasons. Rebelliousness is given to us so that in time, once we come to understand ourselves and life, we will use it to rebel against all that is selfish, base, and separate in ourselves.

Unfortunately, most of us never get that far. Not knowing what all that energy is for, we use it to rebel against parents, partner, community – whoever is around. When the time comes to rebel against ourselves, we've used up all the fuel.

When Thomas uses the phrase "the noble love of Jesus," he is describing the burning idealism that can propel a young man or woman into acts of great courage and self-sacrifice. You can see, then, how tragically we betray our young people when we hold out for them as goals a good pension plan, a rapid promotion ladder, a home in one of the best neighborhoods. Today's epidemic of suicide among children and teenagers has to do directly with this betrayal. They urgently need a sense of direction, and there is only one way to provide it: for us to transform ourselves. We need to show them, by our own example, how impatience and restlessness can be used.

It is no coincidence that whenever someone sets out to live selflessly in response to this "noble love" of God, young people gravitate to that person in large numbers. When Mother Teresa left her teaching position in Calcutta to serve the city's poor, the young women who had been her students couldn't wait to join her work. When Mahatma Gandhi set out to free India, my country's young people pressed forward from all sides.

These towering individuals had what young people are always looking for: a cause to which they can devote their lives.

Love desires to be aloft, and will not be kept back by any thing low and mean.

I have already mentioned the great teacher from the Eastern Orthodox tradition known as John of the Ladder. The name suggests a fascinating picture. You can imagine John taking his ladder everywhere, so that he can climb step by step to the highest peak of consciousness. When you are practicing meditation and following the allied disciplines, you are climbing that same ladder. You can call yourself Stuart of the Ladder, Sarah of the Ladder; and this ladder is the very best gift you can give your children. When you want to teach children how to use a stepladder, you don't lecture them; you just set it up right there in the living room. In a spiritual home, the parents set up John's ladder and show how it is to be climbed. And as the children watch, they will be climbing too; they will grow in understanding, patience, and selflessness.

In each one of us there is an upward urge – a deep inner voice that asks us to continue to evolve, growing taller day by day, until we attain our full height. But there is also another voice, loud and raucous, which keeps saying, "Remain stunted; stay selfish; stay sensuous." This is the "low and mean" side of consciousness. The spiritual life can be characterized as the long drawn-out struggle between these two voices. The voice of selfishness seems particularly loud at first, because it is so near at hand – right here at the surface level of consciousness. The other voice is very faint at the outset. But when you go deeper and deeper into consciousness in meditation, you discover gradually that your real needs are not for personal satisfaction. Go after your own satisfaction day and night, for weeks on end, and you will still feel restless and insecure. Once you start taking cues, though, from that other voice – "Be kind; think of others" – the security and peace you'd been looking for begin to fill your life and buoy your spirits. Not only that, as you listen more and more to this new voice, it becomes musical and incomparably beautiful. You don't have to force this; it comes about naturally as meditation deepens. You begin to think as urgently about the needs of others as you've been thinking about your own. All the old heaviness has gone. You feel light – "aloft," in Thomas's own words.

But at the beginning of the spiritual life, when your attention is split between these two urges, it can be very painful. I've told my Californian friends that it is like trying to climb El Capitan in Yosemite. You are burning with desire to make it to the top, only you've carefully put on handcuffs, leg irons, and a tremendous load on your back.

"Rick," the experienced mountaineer might ask, "where are you going?"

"Oh, I'm off to climb El Capitan."

"But what's all this? Leg irons, handcuffs, and a huge backpack?"

"Oh, this?" says Rick proudly. "This is my equipment, developed over a long period."

"You'll find it a lot easier," the more seasoned climber suggests, "if you can free your hands."

Rick blanches. "You mean, give up my gear? Sounds impossible to me."

But his friend persists. "Let's try it anyway."

With trepidation, Rick sets his handcuffs aside and addresses the precipitous granite face.

"Hey!" he shouts. "I can grip better! Raise myself better! I didn't know this."

Now his friend gently suggests that the leg irons could go too. Once more there is a shudder of apprehension, but clank! go the leg irons. "Hey!" Rick shouts again. "I have freedom of movement now! My hands are free! My feet are free!"

"Yeah," his friend says, "but you've still got a ridiculous load on your back. Sure, you need water and ropes. Rations for a few days, and a sleeping bag. But all this other junk has got to go." Soon there is a big pile on the ground – all the things Rick doesn't need. And if you look hard at the face of El Capitan you can see Rick moving along at a good clip, almost to the top.

In a sense, desire is the single most important word in this passage from *The Imitation of Christ*. Thomas is saying that through the choices we make in everyday life, we can strengthen the desire for spiritual awareness –

the upward drive. For example, we can read uplifting books instead of spy thrillers. We can steep ourselves in the lives and writings of the great mystics until they haunt our very sleep. And we can spend time with others who share our desire for spiritual growth.

At the same time, we can withdraw our energy and attention from those activities for which the downward impulse clamors. We can stay away from violent and sensate motion pictures. We can forgo our Saturday morning perusal of the mail-order catalogs in order to give the time freely and generously to our family. We can help staff a shelter for homeless families, or volunteer to drive meals to elderly people who are housebound.

Every deep desire is a prayer, whether you spell it out to God or not. Desire is power, and when you have a deep, strong, unified desire, the power of that desire will drive you into action. If that desire is selfless, immense creativity, initiative, and courage will pour into your hands. This great surge is the Lord answering your prayer – not from somewhere outside, but from deep within.

The Lord answers every selfless prayer, but the initial unification of desires is up to us. Many people who try meditation complain about their inability to make real progress, even though they have been meditating for some time. I always point out that the driving force that takes us upward is the power of desire, and therefore it is essential to recall desires from wasteful channels. I am not talking about right or wrong now, or moral and immoral. Even a little desire has a lot of power packed in it. We have accumulated a tremendous store of scientific and technological know-how in today's world, but very few of us suspect that it is in our desires that all our power lies. Unfortunately, most of us have no way to get at all this power. The sages tell us that if we can find a way to reach those desires in the depths of our consciousness, we will have the equivalent of a powerful booster rocket. One by one, we can recall our vital energy from sensory cravings and selfish desires and unify it through the practice of meditation into one great, shining, powerful desire that will take us right up into higher consciousness: blast off from Cape Kennedy, right there inside!

The fascinating thing about all this is you aren't always aware that you are dislodging a long-standing compulsive desire until after the fact. You are trying to go deeper in meditation, and the very intensity of your effort pulls energy in from wherever it can. You don't give up smoking; smoking gives you up. You don't give up alcohol; it gives you up. If you go deep enough, where the cravings lie, and are able to withdraw energy from those cravings, those urges cannot trouble you again.

Unfortunately, the conspiracy today is to inflate those desires. Through the talents of the advertisers we are encouraged to indulge them, intensify them. It's for our own protection, then, that we develop the skill of deflating desires. There is nothing more satisfying.

Among my own friends, I have watched with delight as addictive desires slowly deflate like so many balloons. You can almost hear the air hissing out. I have been able to anticipate this and say, "In a few weeks' time the balloon is going to be flat. Don't cry. Be glad!"

> *Love desires to be free, and estranged from all worldly affections . . .*

Thomas a Kempis is reminding us that we should not confuse love with compulsive attachment. When the great mystics speak of love, they mean the capacity to see the Lord in every living creature: not just in the immediate family, not just in a sweetheart or best friend. By love they mean the capacity to see what is in the best interest of all and act accordingly.

Love that is "estranged from all worldly affections" is not based on physical appearance. It has nothing to do with what this person can do for me or what that person can provide for me. It has only to do with loving the Self within. This kind of love grants perfect freedom. It allows us to act wisely in every situation because it widens our vision, allowing us to see the whole picture. "Love is infallible," said William Law. "It has no errors, for all errors are the want of love."

We should not be discouraged when at the outset we find this kind of love to be impossible. It is a gradual development, which grows as we release ourselves from compulsive desires and come to see that we are not the body.

That so its inward sight may not be hindered . . .

In my beautiful village there were no electric lights when I was a boy. At the end of the school day we would play soccer, and afterwards swim in the cool river. By the time we turned towards home, the shadows of evening would have fallen. Night comes swiftly in the tropics: one minute the sky is glowing with color and then suddenly it's dark. But in those days before electric light, our eyes were so accustomed to the darkness that we could skip along the paths as though it were broad daylight.

Years later, when I had gone away to the university and got used to electric lights, I came back on vacation and found I had lost this knack. I couldn't see in the dark. My friends teased me: "Hey, we thought you were getting *brighter!*"

A long time afterward, while I was living with my mother on the Blue Mountain in South India, I began taking long walks in the evenings. And one night I realized that I was seeing in the dark once again. My night vision had come back.

This experience came to mind years later when I read these striking words from Saint Augustine: "Our whole business in life is to restore to health the eye of the heart, whereby God may be seen." What Thomas a Kempis calls "inward sight" Augustine calls "the eye of the heart." We are all born with this eye, only sheer disuse keeps it closed. When it begins to open we feel as if someone has just given us an extremely high-powered flashlight. Its brilliant light allows us not only to see things but to see into them. We no longer see just the external appearance of people; we see into their hearts. This means that when we see somebody who is leading a very troubled life, we can see the circumstances that have made him that way; and we will refrain from judging him.

I have always had a special fondness for the Greek philosopher Plotinus, partly because he wanted to go to India. Like Saint Augustine, he too described an "inward sight." "You must close the eyes," he wrote, "and waken in yourself that other power of vision which is the birthright of all, but which few turn to use." When you waken this new power of vision, he would explain, you will see the One. Every philosopher has his favorite metaphors, and for Plotinus it was always "the One." There may appear to be billions people on earth, he would say, but there is really only One.

I heard a perfect illustration of Plotinus's doctrine of the One recently when a friend described taking his little boy, Abraham, to the county fair. Abe went into the hall of mirrors and found himself confronted by all kinds of versions of himself: a tall, thin Abe, another Abe who was short and round, a crooked Abe and a wavy one . . . He must have wondered, "Who are all these different people?" But then he recognized his own face in all the variations, and he concluded wisely that no matter how many Abes there appeared to be, in fact there was only one, and it was he. The illusion lay in the manipulation of mirrors.

It is very much the same story with us when we

discover our real identity. Afterwards we are never taken in by appearance. George may have a mustache, Tom a beard, and Michael both, but I am not taken in by beards or mustaches. I say, "It's all the One, *appearing* as George, *appearing* as Michael, *appearing* as Tom." This is not just a verbal statement. It is a living knowledge, which enables me to treat all of them with love, no matter what the provocation – and, when I have to oppose them, to do so with tenderness and respect.

> *That it may not be entangled by any temporal prosperity . . .*

One day, the chroniclers tell us, Saint Francis of Assisi whittled a fine cup out of wood, and when it was finished he set it before him on the altar where he carried out his private worship. He looked at it with satisfaction and said to himself, "Francis, that's a nice piece of work, if I do say so."

Then he began to pray, and soon he became deeply absorbed. But after a while, he realized that his attention had drifted back to the cup. "How perfectly the grain of the wood reflects the light! What a lustrous polish!" No sooner did he see that his thoughts had drifted from God than he got to his feet, picked up the cup, and threw it into the fire.

Stories like this are preserved carefully down through the ages because they convey priceless spiritual truths – in this case, the simple realization that attention can get caught in anything. What I would add is that when attention gets caught, our capacity for loving does too. I have known many people who say they cannot love, whose love was in fact widely distributed among a great multiplicity of objects.

We have been ruthlessly conditioned to think we can find fulfillment in possessions, to love things rather than people – so much so that when we feel an emptiness in our hearts, we go to shopping centers to fill it up. I am all for living in reasonable comfort, but when I go to shopping centers I get alarmed – not so much at the money that is being wasted as at the loss of will. No one has enough will to waste, and no one has enough energy to waste. This is the real energy crisis of our civilization: too much of our vitality and drive are being diverted into meeting the demands of personal greed.

When you go deeper into consciousness, you gradually make the discovery that your real needs are not for your own personal satisfaction and aggrandizement. Your real needs are for adding to and enriching the lives of others.

. . . or by any adversity subdued.

In the early stages of meditation, what we are doing is setting the sails of our little boats by training our attention and bringing our senses under control. As Saint Francis de Sales said, "It is not we who make the gale of inspiration blow for us . . . but we simply receive the gale, consent to its motion, and let our ship sail under it, not hindering it by our resistance." We just have to be ready – and part of that readiness is the willingness to travel light. No time now for taking on new attachments; time rather to get rid of most of the ones we already have.

When we drive across the Oakland bridge, I often see big cargo ships resting at anchor, and sometimes I notice that the bottom part of the ship is painted a different color from the upper part. A friend once explained this to me. If the boat is absolutely full, he told me, it's riding so low in the water that you can't see the second color. But when all the cargo has been removed, then it's a two-colored boat again. Most of us, when we undertake the spiritual life, are listing very low in the water, and no one can see the second color at all. This means we have a lot of unloading to do — cargo we may have been accumulating for decades. This unloading doesn't take place overnight. We can't hire a crew of longshoremen with big muscles to do the work for us. We have to unload the boat ourselves; and, worse yet, we really would rather keep most of the cargo. This is where the "adversity" Thomas speaks of comes into our lives.

My sympathies are all with you. I know the unloading doesn't come easily. You seize some heavy attachment and run to the rails with it, and then you feel such a stab of heartache that you carry it all back again.

You may try this over and over — starting to throw out, then changing your mind. And even when you do manage to get rid of some old selfish piece of luggage, there may still be pain and a twinge of regret. But toward the latter part of meditation, when you regain the "inward sight" Thomas speaks of, you begin to catch tantalizing glimpses of the other shore. There is Saint Francis of Assisi with his cowl and rope belt and sandals, and you hear him singing "My God and my all!" There is Saint Teresa, with the castanet and tambourine she played when she and her sisters danced before the Lord. When you glimpse these great spiritual figures in the depths of your meditation, and hear their song, all the longing in your heart bursts forth and you seize every selfish attachment you can lay hands on. At this point there is a danger that you will even throw out the rudder. That is where your spiritual teacher will come to your rescue – grab your arm as you're about to toss and say, "You need that rudder. And that sail! And even a few provisions. Don't get carried away!"

Nothing is sweeter than love, nothing more courageous, nothing higher, nothing wider, nothing more pleasant, nothing fuller nor better in heaven and earth; because love is born of God, and cannot rest but in God, above all created things.

CHAPTER SIX

Nothing Fuller

When Thomas says that "nothing is sweeter than love," he is speaking the language of the experienced world traveler: "I've been everywhere on this globe, friend, and I'm here to tell you there is nowhere like Bali." You could substitute "Corfu" or "the Isle of Man," but if your travels, like Thomas's, have taken place deep inside, you will speak as Julian of Norwich did: "I saw the soul, so large as it were an endless world, and also as it were a blessed kingdom . . . a worshipful city."

Until we get into the deeper stages of meditation, we cannot imagine the vast continents that spread across the immensity of consciousness. Millions of thoughts, millions of feelings, millions of urges, drives, hopes, and fears lie just below the surface level. To break through the rocky crust of the ego and enter this other world takes a powerful will and a long period of discipline. But when at last it does open and you slip through, there is a curious feeling in the pit of your stomach. You are entering a world you never thought existed at all. You see a floor that has no bottom, a roof that is endless. You see the bottomless floor of consciousness, the endless roof of consciousness, the boundless space of the room. You look out across this vast new world and you wonder, "But how am I to travel here? There is no path, and I don't know where to go!"

In the Hindu tradition, it is said that when a spiritual aspirant sets out on this epic journey, he or she needs two wings: one is discrimination, the other detachment. The words are alliterative in Sanskrit too — *viveka* and *viraga*. Both come with deepening meditation, but it is also true that if we cultivate them in our daily life, meditation will deepen.

It pleased me immensely to find that in a passage which occurs earlier in *The Imitation of Christ,* Thomas a Kempis uses the same compelling imagery: "By two wings a man is lifted up from things earthly, namely, by simplicity and purity. Simplicity ought to be in our intention, purity in our affections. Simplicity doth tend towards God; purity doth apprehend and taste him." It would be hard to define discrimination more aptly than as "simplicity in intention," hard to explain detachment more precisely than as "purity in our affections."

In the vocabulary of Madison Avenue, the man of discrimination is one who knows a fine set of luggage when he sees it. The discriminating woman is one who knows where to buy her cosmetics. Mr. and Ms. Discrimination recognize top quality in any consumer item; shoddy simulations will never take them in. In the vocabulary of mysticism, on the other hand, the measure of our discrimination is how accurately we are able to distinguish between the real and the unreal – between joy that lasts and its fleeting counterfeit, pleasure.

There is a phrase in Sanskrit that characterizes the attitude of the man or woman of discrimination: *neti, neti,* "not this, not this." They look at fame and see that it will not satisfy them. They look at power and know it will never meet their deepest needs. They pass through life very much as a discerning shopper strolls through a department store looking for just the right silk tie. "Not that one," they murmur as their eyes search the racks. "No, that won't do."

When you search tirelessly for the business suit with classic lines, the mystics tell us, it is permanence itself you are after. When you comb the shops for the most exquisite earrings, it is the allure of beauty itself that draws you. So why stay on the periphery of life? Why not go to the source of all permanence and all beauty? Only be warned that when you go on this kind of shopping spree, cost can be no object. You must be willing to stake all you have. Mechthild of Magdeburg said it boldly:

> Wouldst thou come with me to the wine cellar?
> That will cost thee much;
> Even hadst thou a thousand marks
> It were all spent in one hour!

If thou wouldst drink the unmingled wine,
Thou must ever spend more than thou hast,
And the host will never fill thy glass to the brim.

The touchstone against which we are meant to test everything in life is our driving need for joy that is permanent, for "the unmingled wine." To drink from this cup, we are not asked to close our eyes and ears to the beauties of this world — "all created things," in Thomas's words — but we are expected to see their limitations. "God has intended us for happiness," says Mechthild, "with greater love than can be imagined." The pleasures of food and drink or other sensory pursuits are genuine enough, but once we have had the tremendous experience of transforming anger into sympathy or ill will into good will, sense pleasures pale into insignificance. Only when we have tasted both kinds of experience can we assess them accurately. When Thomas says that "nothing is sweeter than love," he speaks with the conviction of one who knows that the source of all sweetness is within.

Discrimination is what lets us make wise choices. It brings with it the capacity to see where our choices lead us. It is an insightfulness that grows with use. Each time I choose what will benefit my family or my community over what will bring me a passing, personal satisfaction, I am exercising that choice-making capacity and strengthening it. My vision will become sharper. I will see more clearly, as I go along, what the results of all those choices will be. But understanding is barely half the battle where the making of wise choices is concerned. The will must be engaged too, and for that to happen we must have the second wing: detachment.

There is no more easily misunderstood term in the mystic's lexicon. Detachment is not to be confused with indifference. If you have detachment, you can be affectionate and loving, you can have rich, satisfying relationships, but you will never get caught in clinging to people or things in the hope of extracting security.

The fundamental assumption of life today is that nothing is real but the world outside us, reported to us by the senses. And the corollary of that assumption is that you and I are essentially physical beings. But as meditation deepens and you begin to bring the senses under control, you eventually make the startling discovery that you are not your body. Saint Thérèse of Lisieux, once she had made this discovery, used to describe the body as a kind of envelope, and marvel that so few of us ever try to read the message sealed inside. And her namesake, Teresa of Avila, lamented in a passage I quoted earlier: "We trouble little about carefully preserving the soul's beauty. All our interest is centered in the rough setting of the diamond, the outer wall of the castle – that is to say, in these bodies of ours."

Once you have a measure of detachment from your body, it becomes effortless and natural to act in its best interest – for example, to give it the food it needs and the exercise it requires. You establish a firm but very friendly relationship with the body. Your body will be your "buddy," and it will recognize that you are the boss.

But that's only the beginning. As meditation deepens still further, detachment allows you to realize that you are not your mind either. Up until then, all of us are subject to the whims of body and mind. If our taste buds say "Fudge brownie *now!*" it is fudge brownie now, whatever red warning lights might be flashing in our rearview mirror. And if the mind announces, "I hate that person," we have no recourse but to go along for the ride, even though we know it's going to mean a migraine.

With detachment, however, the picture changes. Slowly the physical world loses its hold on you; then, in time, an even more wonderful development comes: the clamorous world of your own emotions loses its hold too. You have come to see that you are not your body; now you realize you are not your mind either. Just as for a short period in meditation you don't hear the cars outside or the planes overhead, there will be periods now when there is no anger in your mind, no clamor of resentment, no matter what may have taken place that day in the office or classroom. It isn't that negative emotions don't arise, but now you can put the storms at a certain distance. In a big thunderstorm, everyone counts the seconds between the lightning bolt and the thunder that follows: "One, two, three – hey, that was *close!*" Similarly, when you see the lightning inside – a flicker of jealousy or anxiety – and brace yourself for the ensuing turbulence – one, two, three, four, five, six, seven, *eight* . . . you are surprised to hear only the faintest rumble. "It must be miles and miles away."

Through meditation you can learn to stand back from the heat of mental processes that are raging out of control. When you are too close, when you are too closely identified with the mind, you get badly burned. But as you move back, the heat becomes bearable. The smoke doesn't get in your eyes, so you can see more clearly. Now you find you can choose how to respond to a difficult situation.

I'm not unappreciative of the modern psychological methods of dealing with emotional problems like resentment and anxiety, but my own way is different. When I first began to meditate, I was absolutely convinced that I was my mind. But after my meditation deepened, when another person was treating me unkindly and the traditional responses – fight or flight – were right at hand, I could ask myself, "Shall I be rude in return, or shall I treat him kindly? Shall I try to understand his difficulties and support him?" The connection between stimulus and response had been severed, and I saw that I could live in freedom – I could love in freedom.

In deep meditation, after many years, you can go to the root of some of the tendencies that have been distorting your life and pluck them out clean. As best I can, I would like to describe how it felt to me the first time this took place.

It was during my summer vacation on the Blue

Mountain, treasured months when I had all the time I needed for meditation. I was becoming painfully aware about then of certain weaknesses in myself that had never been apparent to me before I took to meditation. I sat down to meditate one morning and went deep, deep inward. Not a muscle could have been moving. No distraction troubled the mind. "Like the flame of a candle kept in a windless place": that is how the Bhagavad Gita describes the mind of someone who is in deep meditation, and that's exactly how I felt at that moment. There was no movement in the mind – none to the past, none to the future; no images of any kind. All sounds had become inaudible. The senses were closed down. I was experiencing the state Teresa of Avila calls the "prayer of quiet." Consciousness itself was burning steady, motionless, and in its light I could see into the depths of my mind to where a particular weakness was located. I could see how long it had been there, how conditioned my mind had become, and how much this weakness had influenced me – not for the best – in my relationships, even in my academic work.

I had reached a deep level where attention, desire, will, and achievement all came together. Having descended to that level, I was able at last to correct that weakness, and in a sense to begin life new thereafter. It was "The End" for old, selfish ways and "Here Beginneth" for new, selfless ones. To paraphrase Meister Eckhart, I went in a pauper – well, not quite, but considerably impoverished – and I came out a prince, wealthy beyond the dreams of avarice.

This dramatic development seemed sudden, but in fact the transformation had been going on for many years. That morning was simply the climax. Saint Bernard of Clairvaux described in his own way this long, baffling, drawn-out process:

> He has quickened my sleeping soul, has aroused and softened and goaded my heart, which was in a state of torpor and hard as a stone. He has begun to pluck up and destroy, to plant and to build, to water the dry places, to illuminate the gloomy spots, to throw open those which were shut close, to inflame with warmth those which were cold, as also to straighten its crooked paths and make its rough places smooth. . . . In the reformation and renewal of the spirit of my mind, that is, of my inward man, I have perceived in some degree the loveliness of his beauty.

Meditation renews everything, because it renews the mind itself. Imagine what it would be like this very day to be handed a fresh, new mind – a mind with the dew still on it, one that won't hold resentment or carry hostility. To put it bluntly, resentments are stale food. We don't like to eat day-old bread if we can avoid it, so why should we tolerate week-old feelings and year-old grudges? This renewal of the mind is exactly what takes place each day in deep meditation. You come out of your meditation room in the morning and look around, and never have you seen a buckeye tree as beautiful as the one blooming in your backyard. And listen to that blackbird! You never knew a blackbird could sing so melodiously.

. . . nothing more courageous . . .

When we are in the grip of fear, it can feel like a profound paralysis – not at all like the furious agitation that comes with anger or resentment. But experienced meditators deal with fear exactly as they deal with the stormier mental states. They don't analyze; they don't intellectualize. They just leave the neighborhood, traveling deep in meditation to the stillness no wave of fear or anger or greed can disturb. If they find themselves too agitated or too overwhelmed to meditate, they take a fast walk repeating the mantram. The sheer momentum of the effort makes them feel as if they're leaving fear or anger in the dust, and at a deep level – below their conscious awareness – the mantram gradually breaks up the oppressive gridlock of fear or anxiety. Their breathing rhythm alters from shallow and ragged to deep and even. The mind grows steady, and by the time they get home, they are ready to act constructively.

For the illumined man or woman, fear has no meaning. No one is more courageous, and their courage has a very simple origin: once you realize you are not the body, you lose all fear of death. My grandmother was such a person. I was not a very brave boy, but Granny was the bravest person I have ever known, and it was watching her that planted the seeds of my own courage.

I was terribly afraid of death, for example, and in my ancestral home death was not hidden away as it is so often in this country today. When someone in the family died, there was a room right on the first floor of our house called "the dark room" where the body was kept until the cremation could take place. And by tradition, some member of the family had to keep watch there through the night and keep alive the flickering flame of a little oil lamp, so that the body would not be left in darkness.

Nothing could have been more terrifying to me. I couldn't even have considered spending the night in that room, and my cousins gleefully made matters worse by the stories they told of ghosts and demons. But again and again I watched Granny take on this duty without hesitation. She would just lie down on the floor by the side of the dead body, and when I asked her, "Granny, don't you get scared?" she would say, "Why? This is not your Aunt Sita; it is just her body. It's like one of her old saris. There is nothing to be afraid of." And throughout the night she would lie there in the dim light of the coconut oil lamp, repeating her mantram.

This kind of example made a deep, deep impression on me, and after a while my terrible fear of death began to ease. Today I know beyond the shadow of a doubt that I am not my body. My body is a faithful friend, but it is finite – I am not. When I do think about death, I know that when I finally shed my body it will be like a leaf or fruit dropping from the branch: a very natural conclusion to a long, loving, beneficial life.

. . . nothing higher, nothing wider, nothing more pleasant, nothing fuller nor better in heaven and earth.

Love is a dynamic process. It is meant to grow. But we have to work at it every day. Even today, after more than forty years of meditation, I work at it still. If there is somebody who gives me offense, I try to be more tender towards that person. When somebody tries to go astray, I try to move closer. It calls for unremitting endeavor.

In the early days of our youth, we all try to seek love through the body. It is a natural beginning, but millions of people get caught on that level and never progress beyond it. I never tell young people, "You haven't any idea what love means." I say, "You are on the first step of love. Let me take you up, step by step. You'll reach the stars, and from there you can love all." The body has its legitimate place, but as an instrument of love it is entirely inadequate. For one thing, to strike a note of grim realism, the body loses its strength with the passage of time; and our need is for a love that will increase without limit.

I've always enjoyed going to weddings. In India, I loved to watch the bride and groom walk together around the sacred fire. In this country, I've been deeply moved by the beautiful exchange of vows and rings. But whenever I hear the words "till death do us part," I feel tempted to stand up and shout to the bride and groom, "No, no, no! Don't accept that!" Love that is physical, death will destroy. But love that is spiritual, death can never destroy.

Love can begin as the will of two people to dissolve their separateness over the years until they are not two but one. But even that lofty state is only the beginning of love. It should go on to encompass more and more – friends, relatives, other races, other nations – until finally it embraces all of life. Then you become love itself. And life does not end in death for the person who has become love. That person is not a physical creature, but a beneficial force that can never be extinguished.

> *Because love is born of God, and cannot rest but in God, above all created things.*

It's only when a man or woman of God is well along the spiritual path that they can echo Saint Augustine as Thomas a Kempis does here. You remember Augustine's great outcry, "Thou hast created us for thyself, and our hearts cannot be quieted till they find repose in thee!" Saint Catherine of Genoa speaks the same language: "Because of its capacity for the infinite, the soul could not satisfy itself with earthly things; and the more it strained to do so, the further it moved away from the peace and joy that is God."

There is a growing sense as meditation deepens that this tremendous journey you have undertaken is not to a strange land at all, but to your first and dearest home. As you near journey's end there come moments of recognition, like those of a weary traveler returning home. Something is familiar about that stand of trees up ahead, or the low hills off to your right. The air is fragrant with flowers . . . you can almost remember their names. And your pace quickens: this is where you belong.

Eden, to me, is not a place at all. It is a state of consciousness — that state in which we transcend our physical separateness and become aware of the divine ground of existence within. That is our native state, the place where we really belong. Saint Francis is not Francis of Assisi; he is Francis of Eden. Saint Teresa is not Teresa of Avila; she is Teresa of Eden. They carry Eden around with them. That is why they are at home everywhere, and like superb hosts and hostesses, they want nothing more than for the rest of us to be at home there too.

Theologians have wrangled for nearly two thousand years over the significance of phrases like "the Garden of Eden" and "original sin." No doubt the illumined man or woman could make some astute guesses as to what might have transpired between our spiritual ancestors and a wily serpent; but the more urgent questions, they tell us, concern the here and now. Better to look at the choices we are making right now in our own daily lives and ask whether they are moving us toward Eden or away from it. The Fall is real not because it took place in prehistoric times, but because it happens every single day.

I like to imagine the serpent coming to Adam and Eve to make his pitch. "Listen," he says, "There's nothing like this! All you have to do is look out for number one. You can have your food cooked any way you like.

You can have your apartment decorated the way you want it; who cares what anybody else thinks? You can play the kind of music you like as loud as you want, enjoy yourself any way that appeals to you, make piles of money any way you can. Whatever works . . . if it feels good, do it! You don't have to care for anybody!" Remarkably similar to the message of our own mass media: happiness lies in complete and utter separateness.

Theologians speak of the Fall, while cosmologists tell us we live in the aftermath of an inconceivably vast explosion called the Big Bang. From a starting point fifteen billion years ago, the effects of the primeval explosion are still detectable by sensitive astronomical instruments: galaxies are still flying apart in all directions. This astronomical model seems a painfully accurate description of life today. Despite all our triumphs in science and technology, I think the human being has never been so distant from other human beings, never so alienated from other living creatures, from the entire environment, and, worst of all, from his or her own self. Propelled by obsessive identification with our own private needs and personalities, we hurtle away from one another at speeds that kill.

Yet in the midst of all this flying apart, this drift toward more and more intense self-will, there is a counterforce: the inward tug of love that is calling us all home.

In Hinduism we have an ancient mythic counterpart to the Fall, and it is very much in harmony with the Big Bang theory too. In the beginning, according to this myth, there was only consciousness: a vast cosmic egg full of unitive awareness. Inexplicably, in a creative burst of differentiation, this cosmic egg exploded in a thousand directions. You and I and all the rest of life are each tiny fragments of that original unity – infinitesimal bits of a vast jigsaw puzzle. Each of us carries with us a tiny bit of the cosmic yolk, a fragment of the divine. And it's that dab of yolk in all of us – the memory of unitive consciousness – which keeps us from ever being fully at home in a world of separateness.

Thomas Merton describes this infinitesimal bit of divine yolk in haunting language:

> At the center of our being is a point of nothingness which is untouched by sin and by illusion, a point of pure truth, a point or spark which belongs entirely to God, which is never at our disposal, from which God disposes of our lives, which is inaccessible to the fantasies of our mind or the brutalities of our will.

> It is this still point which enables us to work tirelessly for the welfare of all, and which draws us inward in the long return to our native state of being.

He that loveth, flyeth, runneth, and rejoiceth; he is free, and cannot be held in.

He giveth all for all, and hath all in all; because he resteth in One highest above all things, from whom all that is good flows and proceeds.

He respecteth not the gifts, but turneth himself above all goods unto the Giver.

CHAPTER SEVEN

He That Loveth, Runneth

In the early days of meditation, nothing we see in ourselves suggests that we'll ever get off the ground – no wings, no aerodynamic promise of any kind. In the language of Teresa of Avila, we stumble along like poultry, we who were meant to soar like eagles!

But once you have had even a fleeting glimpse of your real home, the tug to return is so powerful that you're like a homing pigeon, with all your attention and all your instincts trained on that shining goal. A stronger will and increased determination will make themselves felt – and you will need them, because as meditation deepens, the obstacles become correspondingly greater. My granny used to say, "The Lord will keep on raising the hurdles – not one inch less than you can jump, but not one inch more either."

In my high school days, there used to be a track meet every year on the eve of summer vacation. Typically, the students who did well in these events were not the exceptional scholars. I was a rather good student, so it was simply assumed that I wouldn't be able to run fast or jump high – or, for that matter, perhaps even walk. But even then, I had a kind of contrary streak: if I found I wasn't good at something, I just had to work at it. So I decided to enter the pole-vaulting event.

I began to practice secretly. Before anyone was up in the morning, I would go and get my pole. I did some experimenting, and soon I discovered there were tricks to pole-vaulting that no one had taught us. On the day of the school games, when the whole village was gathered, everybody looked so pained when I trotted up with my pole! I took my time, gathered my concentration, said my mantram, and took off running. I still remember the gasp of amazement – one doesn't forget these moments! – when I flew like a bird over the bar.

I was able to do this not by reading books about the pole vault, not by admiring other people vaulting, but by trying to do it myself. And that's just how it is with meditation.

He that loveth, flyeth, runneth, and rejoiceth.

Whenever I hear of any great achievement that calls for extraordinary skill and endurance, I'm fascinated by the parallels that emerge with the practice of meditation. A few years ago aviation history was made by two veteran pilots, Dick Rutan and Jeana Yeager, when they flew their specially built airplane the entire distance around the world – a voyage of more than twenty-five thousand miles – without stopping.

Millions of people must have watched the landing on television – not, I think, because it was a spectacle, but because it appeals to our desire for facing challenges and putting ourselves to the test – the same drives that propel us into the practice of meditation. When Rutan was asked why he and his friend had undertaken the trip, he said, "Just for the hell of it." I would say, "Just for the heaven of it," but we mean the same thing. There is no rhyme or reason behind all this, just that deep, driving need to fulfill oneself, to hurl oneself against the greatest imaginable challenge. "When it comes down to it," Rutan added, "this is the ultimate goal: the last plum to be picked."

Friends who were asked to describe Dick Rutan said, "Flying is his life, and his hobby too. He lives and breathes it." That's just what is required for success in meditation. You pool all your resources, fuse them until, like the *Voyager,* you can travel around the whole of life and see it as one unbroken circle. No need to stop; no need to refuel!

You can imagine how much fuel an ordinary aircraft would require to travel around the world. The designer of the *Voyager* – Burt Rutan, Dick's brother – had to make the plane as light as possible to minimize the necessary fuel supply. Just so, in the case of spiritual aspirants, one of the most severe challenges is reducing the weight of self-will to a bare minimum.

When Rutan and Yeager landed, someone asked why they had only fourteen gallons of fuel left. Had they really calculated it that closely? Rutan replied that they had carried considerably more than they would have needed under ideal circumstances. "The problem was we could virtually never fly the plane on its optimum range profile because of weather, winds, and turbulence." The pressure never let up. "Every time we'd take a minute to say 'Hey, this is really neat,' Thor would come out of the sky and run us through a thunderstorm or kill an engine."

This is exactly what happens in the deeper stages of meditation. Even if you have enormous determination and will, you can't be sure it will be enough because you have to provide for storms and turbulence — and for unintended changes of direction and retracing misdirected flight patterns as well. The way to provide this extra measure of fuel is through the conservation of energy; and that is the purpose of sense training. We don't train the senses so we can become ascetics, but simply to give us the fuel we need to make the voyage. To draw the parallel even more closely, it seems that during much of the *Voyager's* flight the fuel gauge was inaccurate. For quite a bit of the trip, they had to fly without even knowing how much fuel they had.

"I've trained all my life for this trip," Dick Rutan said. "It was a major goal of my lifetime. I spent every little bit of experience that I'd gained over a whole lifetime of flying to bring this off." If you just replace flying with meditation, you have my story.

The *Voyager,* concluded the *San Francisco Examiner,* "produced a near miracle with a mechanical package of a size that is unimposing. After nine days and 26,000 miles, in history's only nonstop circling of the globe on a single tank of fuel, Dick Rutan and Jeana Yeager eased the slim craft down to a flawless three-point landing. . . . As light as a leaf, the little craft arrived to a luminous backdrop of sun and shadow on the Mojave that fitted the occasion, and Yeager's and Rutan's modesty befitted it also. They came into victory with simple grace."

May we all match their achievement!

He is free, and cannot be held in.

Americans are often surprised to learn that in India, too, boys had the opportunity to be Boy Scouts. We had our official kerchiefs, our khaki shorts, our salute, and our own marching songs. But instead of caps, we wore turbans. And given the kind of wild animals that inhabited our forests – lions, tigers, elephants – I would suggest that our camping expeditions took considerably more courage than those of the average Scout troop in Cornwall or California.

In order to win a particular merit badge in the Boy Scouts, I had to undergo training in tying knots. I didn't know it at the time, but I could have told my Scoutmaster that all of us are already experts in tying knots. We have hard knots around our hearts – granny knots, reef knots, square knots – and we've tied them ourselves. They are the reason we cannot always be patient, secure, loving, and selfless. The training we need now is in untying knots. When we become aware of the

Lord, all the knots become untied. Everything inside becomes loose and free. Then we are able to love everybody, even those who slander us.

Whenever we brood upon ourselves and think only about our own needs, we contract consciousness so tight that it becomes a prison. But if our love and concern are given to others, if we live for the whole instead of just ourselves, no power on earth can inhibit our ability to serve and give.

There is a legend concerning Saint John of the Cross that conveys this priceless truth. John had been imprisoned by persecutors for several months, and as the days and weeks passed and he steadily weakened, he longed more and more to rejoin his spiritual companions, who had placed themselves in his loving care. And finally that selfless desire to rejoin them became so intense that it burst the constraints even of physical laws. Deep in the night, the story goes, he awoke to find his jailer asleep and the doors mysteriously unlocked. Trusting completely in the Lord's guidance, he slipped out of his cell and past more sleeping guards. Somehow he dropped down the sheer rampart and fled towards the river, only to come to a high wall. Trusting still in his guide, he approached the wall and even in his weakened condition climbed it easily. Finally, battered and weary, he arrived at the convent of Teresa and her sisters. In the morning, his jailers were too awestruck even to try to recapture him, for they sensed that he could not have made this escape unaided by God. This has been called miraculous by some; by others, simple proof that when we love very deeply we have access to unlimited strength and wisdom.

Once we've broken out of the prison house of the ego and are able to love everybody whatever they do, we are free. The real meaning of freedom is mastery over our passions and desires. We aren't born with this freedom, but we're all born with the capacity for attaining it. Nothing that anyone did to us in the past, nothing we ourselves have done, can destroy this divine capacity; it is our birthright. Yet, paradoxically, it cannot be fully realized without the cooperation of divine grace. And it takes a long, long time.

He giveth all for all, and hath all in all . . .

There is a poignant moment in the Gospels when a young man comes running up to Jesus. "Good Master," he says, "how can I win eternal life?" The Lord chastises him tenderly, "Why callest thou me good? There is none good but one, and that is God." Then he answers the young man's question by citing the commandments of Moses. "All these I have observed since my youth!" the fellow blurts out – so full of hope and eagerness.

By now Jesus has noticed that the young man is dressed in fine, expensive clothing. His heart reaches out to him, for he sees his good intentions and sees too what will be his stumbling block. There is a beautiful touch in the narrative: "Jesus, beholding him, loved him." At last he said, "One thing thou lackest; go thy way, sell whatsoever thou hast, and give to the poor, and thou shalt have treasure in heaven: and come, take up the cross and follow me." The young man hears what is being asked, and he cannot give it – at least not then. "He was sad at that saying, and went away grieved: for he had great possessions."

The story can cut us to the quick, for we all have our attachments. Each of us has some counterpart to the wealth that weighed this eager young man down. For some it may be pleasure – midwinter cruises in the Bahamas or a lifetime pass to every Giants game. The great mystics see us struggling with attachments like these, and they grow impatient on our behalf. If we could begin to imagine what immense wealth the Lord is trying to pour into our lives, they cry out, we would feel so unutterably foolish, standing here clutching doggedly at our nickel's worth of security. When the Lord offers us our divine inheritance, we reply, "Just put it down over there, and we'll take a look from here." But it is letting go first that is the real crux of the spiritual life. No one has said it more boldly than Meister Eckhart:

> Know that no man in this life ever gave up so much that he could not find else to let go. Few people, knowing what this means, can stand it long, and yet it is an honest requital, a just exchange. To the extent you eliminate self from your activities, God comes into them, but not more nor less. Begin with that, and let it cost you your uttermost. In this way, and in no other, is true peace to be found.

There is another way of understanding these simple words, "He giveth all for all, and hath all in all." It is this: illumined men and women have complete access to every bit of their vital capacities. They hold all their resources in the hollow of their hands, because they have learned to remain and act completely in the present. They give themselves completely to whatever task they are carrying out, and the astonishing result is that their resources are never depleted.

> . . . because he resteth in One highest above all things, from whom all that is good flows and proceeds.

Only the lovers of God are free everywhere and at all times, because their center is in the Lord within. In the practice of meditation we learn how to throw away all other supports. The person who is dependent upon money is not secure: just pull away his pile of bank notes and he will collapse. The person who is dependent on power is not secure: you have only to draw her crutch of power away and she will fall like ninepins. But when we put all those crutches aside and become completely dependent upon God, we are becoming completely dependent upon ourselves. Every day in meditation we renew this magnificent discovery and find, along with Saint Bernard of Clairvaux: "What a great thing is love, provided always that it returns to its origin! Flowing back again into its source it acquires fresh strength to pour itself forth again."

He respecteth not the gifts, but turneth himself above all goods unto the Giver.

Saint Augustine gave a kind of catchall definition of sin that is almost paraphrased in this line of Thomas a Kempis: "All sins are contained in this one category, that one turns away from things divine and truly enduring and turns toward those which are mutable and uncertain."

Last week, as I was passing through Ghirardelli Square in San Francisco, there was a magician performing in the central courtyard. This man had three boxes and a red ball. He opened the boxes, while all of us stood around curious to see what he was going to do. "Come closer," he said, "and watch carefully." And we did. He showed us the box, showed us the ball, then put the ball in the middle box and asked, "May I close the boxes?" "Of course!" we replied. He did so, while we all watched carefully to see if anything went up his sleeve. But nothing did.

Then he asked a young girl to come up and retrieve the red ball. She giggled and confidently opened the middle box. No ball was to be seen! Her jaw dropped and she blushed in surprise. "But I saw it go into the box!"

The magician smiled and opened the box on the left — and there, of course, was the ball.

Then he put the ball back into the same box and asked her to open it. Again there was the initial confidence, again the look of complete astonishment.

Again and again he did the trick — she still hadn't learned.

I couldn't help thinking that this is one of the cruel tricks life plays on every one of us. "I was sure happiness was there. I could almost touch it!" Over the last thirty years, so many young friends have assured me they have found the way to happiness and have gone off to pursue it. After a time they have come back broken-hearted — and then gone back and done the same thing a little later. They look just like this young girl — astonished, bewildered, full of consternation.

Being myself something of an amateur magician, I know some of the trade secrets. One is that if I can get you to watch my right hand closely, I can do what I like with the left. In the deeper stages of meditation, when Life the Magician says, "Hey, Greg, here's the red ball going into this box. Wouldn't you like to open it?" Greg can just sit back and say, "Nope."

"Why not?"

"Because I know the ball's not there."

Greg has left sorrow behind.

What the great mystics are trying to convey is the enormous contrast between the evanescent pleasures of the physical world, which can never, ever satisfy us, and the unbounded joy of loving God.

Again, no one has expressed this more powerfully than Saint Augustine:

What do I love when I love my God? Not the beauty of any bodily thing, nor the fair harmony of time, nor the brightness of the light, . . . nor sweet melodies of varied songs, nor limbs acceptable to embracements of flesh. None of these I love when I love my God; and yet I love a kind of light, and melody, and fragrance, and embracement, when I love my God.

With beautiful words and ardent passion, Augustine is saying that the love of God satisfies our hunger always. When Jesus said to the woman at the well, "I am thirsty," she gave him water. But instead of thanking her, he spoke to her as only a great spiritual teacher can: "Whosoever drinketh of this water shall thirst again, but whosoever drinketh of the water that I shall give him shall never thirst." All physical pleasures come to an end swiftly, but the joy that comes from the love of God only increases with time.

Love oftentimes knoweth no measure, but is fervent beyond all measure.

Love feels no burden, thinks nothing of trouble, attempts what is above its strength, pleads no excuse of impossibility; for it thinks all things lawful for itself and all things possible.

It is therefore able to undertake all things; and it completes many things, and warrants them to take effect, where he who does not love would faint and lie down.

CHAPTER EIGHT

Love Feels No Burden

When we can withdraw our attention from problems, they become light; but selfishness makes everything a terrible burden. Even something that is very light will become terrible, nearly impossible, when our reserves of love and compassion are running low. It is only when we give the Lord within all our love and devotion that we can say with Thomas, "Love is able to undertake all things."

I was reminded the other day of what the love of the Lord within can do for us. We were at the beach when my wife, Christine, spotted a little seal slowly looking around to see whether it had an audience. When it saw two enthusiastic spectators it performed a few numbers, including a figure eight. It came even closer and raised its bald head above the water, looking right at us with those bright eyes as if asking us to join it. Then again it began frolicking just for the sake of frolicking, diving for the pure love of diving.

At the same time I noticed two starfish lying flat on the shore, and I felt awfully sorry for them. I could imagine one saying, "How I wish I could jump and play and dive in the sea like that baby seal!" and the other replying, "You took the words right out of my mouth." While I watched, a wave came and washed them back into the sea they must have been longing for.

When we look at the life of Jesus, Thomas would say, it should bring out this longing in our hearts to be a little like Jesus. In some mysterious way, when this longing becomes deeper and deeper, all desires are withdrawn from the evanescent foam and froth of life to feed this huge desire. We lie there supine on the sand, longing and longing, and at last a great wave of grace comes and picks us up like those starfish. In other words, we need to put sustained effort into the spiritual life, but what really enables us to become aware of the Lord at last is only his infinite mercy.

> *Love oftentimes knoweth no measure, but is fervent beyond all measure.*

Love has nothing to do with ledger sheets or bottom-line accounting. Love doesn't keep records, and refuses to hire a bookkeeper. Real love has no limits, because it springs from boundless depths.

Whenever you are tempted to calculate, "If I give sixty grams of love, how much will I get in return?" love becomes a contract. For love to be a sacrament, we should be able to stand firm and steadfast each day and say, "Whether you like me or hate me, whether you light up when I enter the room or leave it at the first opportunity, I am going to love you more and more." Love doesn't insist upon reciprocity, and it never counts the cost.

> *Love feels no burden, thinks nothing of trouble, attempts what is above its strength, pleads no excuse of impossibility . . .*

I was always capable of hard, sustained work, and in the early years of my own spiritual practice I drew heavily on that capacity. I changed all my ways, reversing long-standing patterns of living, and I took great joy in doing so. As I worked my way down to the more stubborn attachments, I found it harder going, but I kept at it anyway. Finally, however, I reached a point when I felt I could go no further. What I was attempting to do appeared now to be quite literally impossible. The rest of the journey seemed completely beyond me – beyond any human being. I was plunged into grief.

Since then I have come to understand that every man or woman who has sought God-realization has undergone this anguish, that it comes at a certain stage in the spiritual journey.

For a long time, you see, you are just struggling across the foothills of the spiritual Himalayas, longing for at least a glimpse of one of those snowy peaks. A mantle of early morning frost on a good-sized hill sets your heart racing, and that night you can hardly bear to stop and camp. You forge on, and at last before you beckons a snowcapped peak – the real thing this time – and everything in you is bent on scaling it. You want with all your heart to get there, but right in front of you yawns a chasm that is miles across. "What do I do now?" you ask. "There is no road! There isn't even a track for a mountain goat. Even if I have tremendous willpower and energy, how can I travel if there is no path?" You see the peak and the chasm at just the same moment. Intense restlessness seizes you, and wild optimism alternating with despair.

People who depend on their own sheer willpower can get into trouble at this stage. But if from the earliest days of your spiritual life you have tried, like Brother Lawrence, to keep yourself in the presence of God through meditation and repetition of the Holy Name, you know what to do. With the trust and affection of a small child, you turn to the Lord of Love within and ask, "Why don't you just take me up in your arms and deposit me on the other side? I'll close my eyes and repeat your name, and leave the rest to you!"

And this is what takes place. It happened to me, and it can happen to you. Love wells up in your heart if you surrender your self-will, and devotion carries you across the chasm. You don't even feel the motion. You think you're still on the frostbitten lower slopes; then after a while you open your eyes and find yourself on the snowcapped peak. Finally it dawns on you, "I don't have to do any leaping. Whenever there is a great leap to be made, the Lord is there to take me in his arms, cradle me against his chest, and deposit me safely."

Years later, looking back on all this, I have realized that I am a very blessed creature. I am still lost in wonder at what happened to me, for I know that I could never have completed the journey under my own power. It was grace alone that enabled me to continue until the end.

This mystery has been recorded again and again in the lives of the mystics. Teresa of Avila writes in her commentary on the Song of Songs:

> An infant doesn't understand how it grows, nor does it know how it gets its milk; for without its sucking or doing anything, often the milk is put into its mouth. Likewise, here, the soul is completely ignorant. It knows neither how nor from where that great blessing came to it, nor can it understand . . . it sees that it is nourished and made better and doesn't know when it deserved this. It is instructed in great truths without seeing the Master who teaches it; fortified in virtues and favored by One who knows it well. . . . It doesn't know what to compare his grace to, unless to the great love a mother has for her child in nourishing and caressing it.

In playful language we can never forget, Sri Ramakrishna, the great Bengali saint of the nineteenth century, speaks of the same experience. He says that in the first half of our spiritual endeavors, we are like baby monkeys. The little monkey holds on to its mother while she jumps from branch to branch, and he has to hold tight because if he loosens his grip, down he'll fall.

But during the second half, Ramakrishna says, we are like kittens. The mother cat doesn't expect her kitten to hold on to her; she picks him up by the scruff of the neck. You would think she is being cruel to hold him like that; but in fact she is being very protective. The kitten just goes limp and lets the mother cat do the traveling. And when the kitten is set down on his feet again, the mother's protective love continues to surround him. He can be right on the verge of making what the feline world sees as a serious mistake, but the mother won't let him. Have you seen a mother cat reach out and slap the kitten with her paw? It hurts, and the kitten doesn't make that mistake again!

This is how faith takes root in our heart and grows. Sometimes people speak of faith as something we should cultivate on principle – no matter how the intellect balks, no matter what our own experience has taught us. My own attitude is stubbornly practical. I've never taken anything on faith that I could not test against my own experience. Today, I would say freely that I am a man of profound faith in God. But mine is a living faith. It began as the most tentative proposition: "I shall move in this direction, even when it doesn't look pleasant, and let us see what happens." As my meditation deepened, great difficulties did come my way, but over and over I have been rescued – sometimes at the eleventh hour. I could never have told you why, but my path would be cleared; courage, insight, and resourcefulness would come to me. Today, after many years of validation in my personal experience, I can claim that my faith in God has become unshakable. But that faith is the fruit of a long period of effort and clear observation — and, I would add, an open mind.

The poet Robert Browning uses a geometrical simile: all the Lord expects us to do is to draw the arc; the Lord himself will complete the circle. Have I done everything possible to train my senses, to subdue my passions, to liquidate my self-will? If I have, even if I have not been completely successful, he will augment my strivings and reward my efforts a hundredfold.

> *. . . for it thinks all things lawful for itself and all things possible.*

G. K. Chesterton was a Catholic writer who wrote the delightful Father Brown mysteries and a beautiful book on Saint Francis of Assisi. It may have been Saint Francis's life that inspired Chesterton to write:

> Loving means to love that which is unlovable,
> Or it is no virtue at all.
> Forgiving means to pardon the unpardonable,
> Faith means believing the unbelievable,
> And hoping means to hope when things
> are hopeless.

This is what the practice of meditation enables you to do.

It is therefore able to undertake all things; and it com-
pletes many things, and warrants them to take effect,
where he who does not love would faint and lie down.

When you have learned to travel far, far inside through meditation, and to place yourself at the feet of the Lord, you are able to tap into enormous reservoirs of love and wisdom. You have an ally now with deep pockets. Once you have succeeded in aligning your own will with the will of the Lord, you have made yourself invincible.

It is not that we are extraordinary people. But within us there are tremendous forces of which we are all but ignorant — forces as mighty as cosmic radiation or electromagnetism or the solar wind. We could ally ourselves with these internal forces, but we don't really believe they are there. Saint Francis de Sales, a French mystic of the seventeenth century, wrote, "Our free will can hinder the course of inspiration, and when the favorable gale of God's grace swells the sails of our soul, it is in our power to refuse consent."

In other words, propelling our boat across the sea is not our responsibility; the wind will do that. But we do have to set the sails and keep our boat yare, as sailors say. I am certain that Francis de Sales would also tell us it isn't enough just to set the sail and then go below and read *Lord Jim* for the rest of the voyage. At every stage in meditation, we need to be dedicating ourselves anew to all the disciplines. It's very much like the constant work aboard a ship at sea. The boat might be sailing along without any visible effort on anyone's part, but on deck and below there's likely to be a lot of activity. One sailor is mending sails, another is putting tar over all the cracks, still others are swabbing the decks or oiling the fittings or making sure the lines are secured. On long voyages there are periods of deadly, boring, uneventful work. For long stretches of time in meditation, too, you can't really see any progress. But when a great tropical storm bears down upon your little ship – storms of anger, fear, or greed – and not so much as a keg of molasses gets washed overboard, you feel rewarded. All that dull, dreary labor has paid off.

To re-ignite enthusiasm when it is slowly fading, the best thing you can do is to spend time with a passionately enthusiastic teacher. If you can visit him or her in person, that is ideal, but even to spend an hour reading someone like Teresa of Avila can lift you out of your doldrums. It's as if she were to stride right into your little room, look around, and say, "It's too dark in here. Let me give you a two-hundred-watt bulb!"

A spiritual teacher can help you by a kind of osmosis. But they can help you very practically, too, by giving you a thousand and one tips for tightening up the ship. It's all little, little things, but the sum total is what determines the quality of your meditation. You may have gone over the instructions in meditation over and over again and feel there is nothing more to learn, but you still need to review them regularly. The deeper significance of some of those instructions will not be clear until you have been practicing meditation over a long period of time. That is why, although I have already touched upon most of the eight disciplines I recommend for meditation, I'd like to go into some of the finer points now.

First, have your morning meditation as early as possible, and be as regular about it as you can. Most of us get hungry for breakfast at a particular time; soon you will find you get hungry for meditation at a particular time, too. As John of Kronstadt said, "Prayer is the breathing of the soul. Prayer is our spiritual food and drink." At the time when you would normally be settling down and starting a passage, the mind begins to draw inward of its own volition, no matter where you are. You'll feel a restlessness, a strong pull toward the room or corner you have set aside for meditation – and this is just how it should be.

Second, there is the recurring problem of sleep in meditation. As soon as your neuromuscular system begins to relax, there is a tendency to let go. Don't yield to those waves of drowsiness, no matter how delicious they seem. Be sure there is fresh air coming into the room and that you haven't gotten too comfortable. If you still feel you need tea or coffee, determine just how much will help keep you alert and don't drink more than that. Jumps and jitters aren't a great improvement over sleepiness.

Even when you've taken all these precautions, you may feel the passage drifting away like a kite whose string is slipping through sleepy fingers. Dimly, you see the kite zigzagging across the sky, and then it's lost. As soon as you feel this happening, move away from the back support and sit up straighter. If necessary, open your eyes for a moment and repeat the Holy Name, but do not yield to sleep. If you do, some of the later transitions in meditation will be much more difficult.

Third, keep memorizing new inspirational passages. Don't be content with just a few. Any passage can get stale with long use, but you can keep your favorites fresh for years so long as you have a repertoire of new ones on hand. This is very much like going over your ropes, like a sailor or a climber, and being sure none of them is frayed.

It's one thing to know you need new passages and it's another to carve out time in a busy life to memorize them. You may wait in vain for enough free hours to commit the entire "Wonderful Effect of Divine Love" to memory. But five minutes will open up here and there. Just keep handy an index card on which you've copied part or all of the passage you're currently working on. Don't be discouraged if at first you find it hard to memorize passages. Memory is like a muscle. You can build it up.

Fourth, there is the problem of distractions. They will be a challenge in meditation from the earliest weeks until the most advanced stages, and in warning you about yielding to them, I'll be as firm as Theophan the Recluse: "You must not allow your thoughts to wander at random, but as soon as they run away you must immediately bring them back."

Let us be absolutely clear: any thought, any idea, any association or image, anything that comes into your mind beyond the words of the passage itself is a distraction and has to be treated as a distraction. The anonymous author of the fourteenth-century mystical treatise *The Cloud of Unknowing* tells us exactly why: distractions can come with rosaries in their hands!

> It is inevitable that ideas will arise in your mind and try to distract you in a thousand ways.... Dispel them by turning to Jesus with loving desire. Don't be surprised if your thoughts seem holy.... But if you pay attention to any of these ideas, they will have gained what they wanted of you.... Soon you will be thinking about your sinful life, and perhaps in this connection you will recall some place where you have lived in the past, until suddenly before you know it your mind is completely scattered.

Distractions come in a thousand attractive shapes and colors. One of the chief sources is the innate human tendency to fantasize. It isn't only abnormal people who fantasize; everybody does. All these millions of people buying lottery tickets are thinking, "When I win the jackpot, the first thing I'll buy is . . ."

The mystics describe this impulse to fantasize as almost a zone in consciousness, a region you travel through as you move deeper in meditation. "As we pass from without to within," says Theophan the Recluse, "we first encounter the powers of imagination and fantasy." These powers are heightened in meditation, and they can paint very alluring pictures. Especially if you're artistic, it is tempting just to stay in fantasy land, build a little cottage, and never take a step further.

Anyone who has tried to meditate even a little can attest to the fantasizing power of the mind, and anyone who knows anything of life knows what havoc that power can wreak. We have a simple but profound story in India about a milkmaid who is going to the village with a pot of milk on her head. While walking she thinks, "I like dancing, and when I sell my milk I'm going to buy dancing bells. I'll fasten them to my ankles so they make music whenever I move, and when I dance —!" She starts to dance, the pot falls, and the milk she was going to sell is gone. The story applies to every one of us, for we all have our own equivalent of dancing bells and pots of milk.

Once you decide to take the problem of distractions in hand, you make some interesting discoveries. First, you find that often distractions will enter through association. A particular phrase or word in the passage might be highly charged for you, so that it is like a door that suddenly swings open and lets the mind run out. There are few thrills quite as satisfying as waiting quietly with concentration, going through the passage, and catching the mind just as it starts to steal away. Now you know to put up a sign there: "Wrong Way, No Exit."

You also gradually discover that just before a distraction comes, your concentration will begin to flicker a little. That very flicker can usher in a wave of restlessness, anger, or fear. It requires great capacity and years of experience to observe this: the mind is almost on the passage but not quite settled, and just coming up is that split second when concentration might be lost. Unless the party of distractions (they don't usually come alone; they travel with lots of relatives) sees this kind of opening, they won't try to come in. Once you have observed all this for yourself, you'll have all the motivation you need to sit up straighter and give more concentration. That's all you have to do. Don't try to fight the distractions off. Just strengthen the defense.

Even with the best of efforts, even for experienced meditators, the passage will sometimes slip away. Without knowing how you got there, you find yourself back downtown, walking along your favorite boulevard while your eyes dart pleasurably into the shop windows. When this happens, don't gnash your teeth or get depressed. Just bring the mind back – quietly, firmly – to the beginning of the passage. This is a simple but highly effective discipline. The first few times I invoked it, my mind would cry out, "No! Oh, no, not that!" It might even have had the nerve to add, "It's not fair." But once my mind saw I was unmoved, the mid-meditation excursions were over.

The purpose of all these tactics, of course, is to enable you to go through the words of the inspirational passage with complete concentration. Saint John of the Ladder states it clearly: "You must make a great effort to confine your mind within the words of the prayer." It will take years, but once you have perfected this skill no distraction will be able to enter your mind. It can come and knock on the door; you will not open it. It can ring the bell; you will just turn the volume of the passage up louder. This is what Saint Teresa did; this is what Saint Francis did. They just kept turning up the volume until it became so loud in the depths of consciousness that all distractions were drowned.

Today, when I use the words "Lord, make me an instrument of thy peace," they resonate at a deep, deep level. It is no longer a matter of words; it is now a great desire encased in words – and desire is power. When the Prayer of Saint Francis discharges its power at a deep level, you will slowly start behaving like Francis. Instead of wanting other people to console you, you will start consoling them. Instead of nursing old grievances, you will be more forgiving. You will stand up and face opposition calmly, neither flinching nor retaliating. You will become a Little Flower of South Bend, or of Minneapolis!

"It is in giving that we receive," says Saint Francis, and when these words have come to life in your heart, you keep on giving with one hand while the Lord is putting it in your other hand. You don't have to look back and ask, "Is it exhausted? Am I on the last round?"

This experience of infinite spiritual wealth is what Thomas a Kempis means when he says love is "able to undertake all things." When this great wealth pours into our hands, we cannot hold onto it for our own ends. If we've been given greater energy, we're expected by the Lord to use it to help and support others. If we didn't return these gifts in selfless work, we would be tormented by restlessness. Because we have limitless love pouring out from our hearts, endless energy driving our lives, we need to give it to everyone who comes in contact with us.

So don't look to any kind of sensation, bodily or emotional, as a sign that your meditation is deepening. The real test is, "How much am I able to love? How much am I able to give, even at my own expense, even when it is painful?" In her great work on prayer, *The Way of Perfection,* Teresa of Avila says, "Progress has nothing to do with enjoying the greatest number of consolations in prayer, or with raptures, visions, or favors. . . ." We want to ask, "Then what does spiritual progress mean?" And later Teresa gives us her answer: "For my own part, I believe that love is the measure of our ability to bear crosses."

Love is watchful, and sleeping slumbereth not.

Though weary, it is not tired; though pressed, it is not straitened; though alarmed, it is not confounded; but as a lively flame and burning torch, it forces its way upwards, and securely passes through all.

If any one love, he knoweth what is the cry of this voice. For it is a loud cry in the ears of God, the mere ardent affection of the soul, when it saith, "My God, my love, thou art all mine, and I am all thine."

CHAPTER NINE

Love Is Watchful

When we love the Lord, when we want to serve him and realize him, most of the things we call deprivations will become enrichments. Most of what we now call denials will become affirmations.

In the deepest stages of meditation, there comes the moment when it is not enough to love Christ the teacher and friend: we want to unite ourselves with Christ in his suffering, to relieve him of it, to share it. The way we do this is to relieve the suffering of those around us. The Buddha told his disciples, "Just as a mother with her own life protects her child – her only child – from harm, so let your love flow outward to the universe: a limitless love, without hatred or enmity."

Love is watchful, and sleeping slumbereth not.

Increasingly as we grow older, sleep can become problematic. Old memories come to stalk us; fears and resentments come to nibble at our security. Sleep may be a long time coming, and when it comes it is often shattered by unpleasant dreams. Small wonder that people spend five hundred million dollars each year on sleeping pills. Small wonder they come to dread going to bed at night.

But the great mystics speak very differently of both sleep and sleeplessness.

The German mystic Angelus Silesius wrote in beautiful, enigmatic language that almost echoes Thomas: "The light of splendor shines in the middle of the night. Who can see it? A heart which has eyes and watches."

Of course, the light he is describing is not physical, and the night is not only the stretch of time between sunset and sunrise. What you are doing in meditation is trying to make the unconscious conscious: to travel deep into the dark realms of the unconscious and set them ablaze with spiritual awareness. You do this in a small way each time you meditate, but you also enter the unconscious when you go to sleep at night, and one of the remarkable discoveries you will make as your meditation deepens is that you can make considerable progress during your sleep. Later on, in fact, some of the most thrilling experiences to come your way are likely to take place not during meditation and not during the day, but in the middle of the night.

This is why I place so much emphasis on a simple bedtime sequence that everyone can follow with benefit, whether their desire is for spiritual awareness or just the blessed gift of a sound night's sleep. First, put away your Agatha Christie or John le Carré. The last things you read about, or think about, or see on television, will follow you into your sleep and color your dreams.

Second, spend fifteen minutes to half an hour reading something of genuine inspirational value – ideally, works from the great mystical traditions. (Dame Agatha Christie would very likely agree with this advice: a friend told me recently that Miss Marple herself always read a few lines from Thomas a Kempis before bedtime.) When you have finished, turn off your light and begin repeating your mantram, giving it all the attention you can, and keep repeating it until you fall asleep.

To do this is much harder than it sounds. It is terribly difficult, in fact, because the period just before sleep is like listening in on a party line. Someone is talking on one line about the happenings of the day, while on another a voice keeps harping on your mistakes and shortcomings, and still a third is chattering away about tomorrow. To keep your attention on the Holy Name when all this is going on is hard, hard work. For many nights, you may not be falling asleep in your mantram at all; you'll be drifting off into your own thoughts.

If this happens, don't get discouraged; be patient and keep on trying. For just at the juncture of waking and sleeping there is a narrow entry into the unconscious, and if at that instant you are repeating the Holy Name, it will slip inside. When you have learned to fall asleep in the mantram, you may sometimes hear it in your sleep. When a nightmare is slowly tiptoeing in, the mantram will reverberate and the nightmare will vanish. All night long the name of the Lord can go on echoing, "Jesus, Jesus, Jesus," and as it does, old wounds are healed and long-standing conflicts are resolved. Diffidence gives way to confidence, and despair to faith.

In India we have a holiday called Shivaratri, "the night of Lord Shiva." On this night everybody, including the children, tells the Lord, "Every night you have to stay awake to keep an eye on us. But tonight we promise to be good so that you can sleep." We go to the temple and we spend the whole night there, repeating our mantram, singing songs of devotion, and listening to spiritual discourses so that the Lord can sleep without worrying about what we're up to.

Of course, the deeper meaning that is supposed to dawn upon us one day is, "Hey, instead of just one night, why don't we make it one week?" Then, when you have been good for one week – being selfless, putting everybody first – the Lord says "I'm beginning to feel so rested, I haven't felt this good in years. Shall we do it for one month now?" You groan, "How did I get into this?" But your spiritual life has really begun now. Finally, when you can say, "Even in my sleep I cannot feel a wave of anger or resentment against anybody," you have reached the level of spiritual awareness where every night is Shivaratri.

There is a similar episode in the life of young Thérèse of Lisieux. She was so devoted to Jesus, so close to him, that she thought of him as a child who was her joyful companion. This sweet devotion concealed an underlying strength, for even in times of adversity her love did not waver. Speaking about a painful period of aridity, she says, "Jesus was sleeping as usual in my little boat; ah, I see very well how rarely souls allow him to sleep peacefully within them. Jesus is so fatigued with always having to take the initiative and to attend to others that he hastens to take advantage of the repose I offer to him."

> *Though weary, it is not tired; though pressed, it is not straitened; though alarmed, it is not confounded.*

Here Thomas is making a mature and realistic assessment of the latter stages of the spiritual life. He warns that it's far from a bed of roses. It's not a vacation from life with all expenses paid. There will be exhaustion, he promises, anxiety, and frustration – all the mental states you might have thought you'd left behind. Only now you have some control over the mind, as well as a tremendous purpose toward which you are working. You know that these negative states will pass, that none of them can overwhelm you, because you know they exist only in the mind. This is why the famous "bookmark prayer" of Saint Teresa of Avila offers such tender consolation, and why it is such a useful passage for meditation:

> Let nothing upset you;
> Let nothing frighten you.
> Everything is changing;
> God alone is changeless.
> Patience attains the goal.

Who has God lacks nothing;
God alone fills all our needs.

Though weary, says Thomas, love is never tired. You see, as soon as you get some control over your thinking process, energy is released. Thinking consumes a lot of energy, but you never really discover this until the titanic factory of the mind closes down. When it does close down, and all the tremendous racket of the thinking process is hushed, the body benefits immediately. Vitality that isn't tied up in thinking goes to the body directly. The mind will say, "I don't need it now. You take it as a loan, but be sure you use it wisely." That is why, when you are meditating deeply and well, you can throw yourself tirelessly into selfless work. You may get weary, but the fuel tank is never drained.

Most of the time, I believe, what tires us out is not the work we do or the challenging conditions under which we do it. What really exhausts us is wanting to get something from it for ourselves. When we are entirely free from selfish desires, there is no longer a difference between rest and activity. Mahatma Gandhi described this remarkable state as follows: "Our very sleep is action, for we sleep with the thought of God in our hearts. . . . This restlessness inspired by God constitutes true rest."

Though pressed, it is not straitened . . .

Worry is probably the most energy-inefficient activity the mind is prone to. By deepening meditation, you can curtail its excessive claims on your time and vitality. You might sit down for meditation feeling burdened by terrible problems, but as you give your attention more and more to the Prayer of Saint Francis, the burden mysteriously lifts, and at the end of your meditation you find you have left all your anxieties at the feet of the Lord. The problem might still be there, but now you have the resources to begin to solve it wisely and selflessly. Gradually, when you have experienced this again and again, there comes the lively awareness that you are equal to any problem that may come to you, because you know the Lord is within, waiting to help.

Though alarmed, it is not confounded . . .

In the parts of India that are watered by the great monsoons, there are essentially two seasons – the wet season and the hot season. During the hot season, the whole earth is parched for six months, from December to June. The heat is scorching. Everywhere you see trees thirsting for water, animals panting for something to drink. By the end of May people are scanning the horizon, and when they meet at the temple or market they ask, "Did you see the monsoon cloud yesterday?" At first it's no larger than a fist, but slowly it becomes bigger and bigger, until finally it fills the whole sky, dark almost as the night. When at last the monsoon bursts, the whole sky lights up and there is a tremendous thunderclap. There is joy in this thunder, which is the rain saying, "I am coming! I am coming!"

Indian mystics who come from the monsoon

regions love to allude to these great storms to describe their own experiences in meditation—especially to the long wait before the storms. As meditation deepens, there are periods universally called "dry spells." The feeling of deprivation can be so terrible that you feel you are trudging through a real Sahara. Whatever you get, whatever comes to you, only intensifies your longing. "My soul thirsteth for thee," King David lamented. "My flesh also longeth after thee, in a barren and dry land where no water is."

These periods are painful, but they are absolutely necessary. A spiritual experience cannot take place until there has been a certain strengthening of desire. Our love has to be intense, irresistible, sustained all the time. It isn't just a question of time and regular effort, but of passion. Most people, I've observed, have a great many desires. And, because they are many, each desire in itself is rather small. These many desires are accordingly rather easy to satisfy—at least on a short-term basis. The effect of the mass media is to turn almost all of us into people with many desires. The principle behind it is simple: the more things we can be made to want, the more things we will buy. Ideally, we can be persuaded to invest in scuba diving equipment in July, a motorboat in August, and an indoor gym in September. It is the job of the mass media to multiply and proliferate our desires.

Yet I have also observed that in spite of the best efforts of Madison Avenue, there are a number of men and women who have only some desires. Because these desires are fewer, each one is bigger. These people with only some desires want satisfactions that last. They can't be manipulated as easily as those whose desires are many. They'll set their own goals.

But there is an even smaller group of people, rather rare: those who have just a few desires. My attention is always drawn to these people. If they are students, I can usually predict they will be at the top of their class. From their ranks come great scientists and brilliant artists – real benefactors of the human race.

Finally, there is that rarest type of all, the person who has only one unbounded desire which nothing on the face of the earth can satisfy. All his vitality has come into his hands; all her attention is focused like a laser. When I meet someone like this, I can predict with accuracy, "That person will not be content with anything less than realizing God. He or she will accept no substitute." From this smallest band of all, down through time, have come men and women like Teresa of Avila, Francis of Assisi, and Mahatma Gandhi.

You should not grieve if you can't honestly put yourself in this last category. Right this minute you may be riddled with many, many small desires; but gradually, through the sincere, sustained practice of difficult spiritual disciplines, you can reduce many desires into some, then some into a few, and ultimately a few into one all-consuming passion. At that point nothing finite will satisfy you: not being the head of a great country, not amassing billions of dollars, not landing in the Andromeda galaxy – nothing.

For the vast majority of ordinary people like us, it takes a long, long time to unify desires. We must be prepared for many years, even decades, of taking the energy from old desires and pouring it into this new stream. It is painful. But that's the way it is in all training, whether it is for tennis or ballet or Self-realization. Don't you say, "No pain, no gain"? It is the capacity to hold out to the very end that enables us to grow to our full stature.

As we near the goal, as our desires are becoming more and more unified, the very strength of our yearning begins to draw the Lord toward us. The Lord just cannot resist the longing of someone who is deeply devoted, and from time to time, he reveals himself in the depths of that person's consciousness. In the words of John Tauler, "When we thus clear the ground and make our soul ready, without doubt God must fill up the void."

When the monsoon cloud of grace bursts, there is no thrill like it in the world. In a second you forget all the torment of waiting, and you say, "I am never going to let you go. I am going to keep my arms around you all the time." Yet the first visits of the Beloved are fleeting. An instant and he is gone — a brief, thirst-quenching shower, and then the long drought again. It is a stunning disappointment which has fallen upon every mystic. Desolate, you throw yourself down with your heart broken into a thousand pieces, and once again there is the watching, the waiting, and the painful drawing in of all your desires.

So when grace comes, don't get excited and tell all the world, "I'm in a state of grace." You won't be for long!

There is no avoiding these long stretches of aridity, because they are part of spiritual growth. But you can safeguard yourself against feeling overwhelmed or defeated when they come your way. The key is to train the mind from the earliest days not to get elated by victories or depressed by setbacks. The mind is always on the lookout for a chance to get excited. "Did you see that, boss? I managed to stay right there on the passage for fifteen minutes straight. Let's celebrate!" An hour later, it is just as ready to wallow in despair. "I'll never be able to walk past a bakery unscathed, never! Let's find a bridge and jump off." Your job is to nip both kinds of reaction in the bud.

Finally, years later, when we are united with the Lord permanently, we ask, "How could you, who are called the Lord of Love, have been so cruel? How could you have toyed with me so?"

And the Lord will smile his beautiful, enigmatic smile and ask, "How else could I have unified your desires?"

> *But as a lively flame and burning torch, it forces its way upwards, and securely passes through all.*

When I was a boy, there were dense forests near my native village in South India. In these forests wild animals roamed at will, and out of fear of these creatures most people didn't go out at night if they could avoid it. When they did have to go out, they would carry large torches made of coconut fiber soaked in oil. These torches burned slowly, and cast so bright a glow that you could see the path quite easily. There was no fear of stepping on a cobra, and the larger animals ran the other way as soon as they saw the approaching flame.

Men and women of God are like these torches. They shed brightness wherever they go, dispelling all fears. In the Hindu and Buddhist tradition, our real Self is described as *deva,* from a Sanskrit root meaning "light" with which the English word divine is related. Our real Self is regarded as the source of all light. The deeper we go in meditation, the nearer we get to this light and the brighter its glow appears. Jacopone da Todi, a Franciscan mystic of the thirteenth century, describes it in ecstatic poetry: *Lume fuor di mesura | Resplende nel mio core,* "Light without measure shines in my heart."

Once you've caught even a glimpse of this light, you will want each day to see more of it and to bring more of it into your life. Finally you won't just see the light; you will become the light yourself. Saint Teresa of Avila, who is to me the most glamorous woman the West has produced, carried the light of spiritual awareness all over Spain, undaunted by serious ailments any one of which would send most of us to the infirmary. She said of herself that she lived in the light that knows no night.

Although many Western mystics have dropped glorious hints as to how this state can be reached, none have spelled it out more clearly than the saints of the Eastern Orthodox tradition. In nineteenth-century Russia, Theophan the Recluse wrote:

> The more [the aspirant] strives to pray, the more thoughts will quieten down, and the purer prayer will become. . . . But the atmosphere of the soul is not purified until a small spiritual flame is kindled in the soul. This flame is the work of the grace of God. This flame appears when a man or woman has attained a certain measure of purity in the general moral order of his life. Yet it is not permanent, but blazes up and then down and its burning is not of an even strength. But no matter how dimly or brightly it burns, this flame of love is always there, always ascends to the Lord and sings a song to him.

To light this flame and keep it lit, the mystics draw upon an endless source of fuel — the power that is contained in sexual desire, which is the equivalent in the human being of a tremendous oil well. It might seem perplexing to think of desire as fuel, but think of what great lengths we will go to in order to satisfy our desires. That is why I never speak negatively about sex. To me, sex is a storehouse of power. It is our wealth. Strong sexual urges are natural, but they can be trained — and they must be.

The sex drive is the "crude oil" of consciousness. Refined, it can take us all the way to the goal of life. It is so raw and powerful that it seems unfair that we should have to master it. But only a power of this magnitude will carry us to the summit of consciousness. It is said in our Hindu scriptures that when the sex faculty comes under complete control, all the vitality that has been consolidated travels through the physical system nourishing the vital organs, strengthening the immune system, and prolonging creativity into the very twilight of life.

There are a few rare individuals who seem to achieve mastery over their sexual desires with no apparent struggle, but for the vast majority it takes many years. It is a gradual development, and sex has a special significance at each stage in life. As we pass from childhood to the teen years, then to our twenties and thirties, to middle age and old age, there is a gradual evolution of the way we should look at sex and the way we should use it. It grieves me to notice how many older people retain their teenage attitudes toward sex. It keeps surprising me, because by the time we are forty all our other attitudes have changed. We don't play the games children play; we don't undertake the exploits teenagers do. We seem to have grown in most aspects, but not in our understanding of sex.

The media have a great deal to do with this immaturity where sex is concerned. If you have grown up in this country, you may simply accept the continuous propaganda that is going on. Movies and television programs, as well as advertisements for all kinds of products, inundate us with sexually charged messages and images. All of this conditioning is particularly tragic when teenagers are the target. They are so vulnerable, and in adolescence attitudes are formed that may stay with a person for life. When I first came to this country, people told me that the teenage years are the golden years. I disagree. They are the glandular years – the glands call the tune and set the tempo, too. One reason I feel so tender toward teenagers is that I know how powerful sexual drives can be and how helpless one can be to resist them.

In most parts of India, segregation of the sexes is the norm. But I come from an unusual tradition. In my family boys and girls are together even as teenagers, and this seems very healthy to me. It is good for young people to attend classes together, play together, study together. But I do not think they are ready for sexual relations. To give sex a place in a lasting, loving relationship requires enormous maturity, which even many adults do not have. It requires rare sensitivity, self-forgetfulness, and attention to the other person's needs. To expect teenagers to rise to these heights is cruelly unfair.

I have lived close to hundreds of young people and have taught thousands more, and I can attest from more than fifty years of playing Ann Landers that whenever a relationship is founded on sex, it's just a matter of time – a few months, sometimes just a few weeks – before it is disrupted. With anguish in their eyes, so many young men and women have come to me and asked, "What is the matter with us? We couldn't bear to be without each other, and now I don't even want to run into him on the street."

I tell them, "There is nothing wrong with you. But

your relationship has no foundation. Jesus put it very well when he said a house built on sand cannot last."

If they ask, "What is the lasting foundation on which you can build love?" I tell them, "Put the other person first. Learn to understand her needs, or his needs, as well as you do your own." If they have some depth, they will get very quiet and serious at this point, because putting someone else first is not easy. It's easy to give a gift or write a sonnet, but to put the other person first, you have to reduce your own self-will. When they have grasped what I'm saying, most of my young Romeos and Juliets grin ruefully, shrug their shoulders, and decide they probably aren't ready for romance yet after all. With a sigh of relief they head back to the soccer field or the ballet studio. One-to-one relationships had better wait a few years.

To learn to love takes many years, and even in the twenties it doesn't come easily. But by that time we have at least weathered the most stressful period of emotional and physiological change, and we are ready to start learning. Experience – with luck, not too bitter – has made vividly clear to us certain truths that as teenagers we could only dimly suspect. We've come to realize, probably, that like most people our deepest desire is for permanent, loving relationships. And we've watched ourselves trying in vain to build those relationships on a physical, sexual basis. The physical basis promises so much – it's such a clever salesman. But we've begun to see through the sales pitch, and we're pretty sure now that what it promises it can never deliver.

What draws us again and again into sexual involvement is that for just a moment it releases us from the deep sense of separateness that haunts every human being. In a completely loving and loyal relationship, sex can have a beautiful place, but lasting love is not based on sex. Lasting romance has two precious components: increasing respect, and tenderness that grows every day. This is what all of us want in a relationship. Once we've tasted it and the closeness it brings, we begin to move beyond the physical barrier.

Once a relationship is secure on a lasting foundation, two people who are deeply in love can enter a third stage which brings even more fulfillment: they can begin to work together for a great cause. This is the very flowering of romance. It doesn't bring just the two of them together; it draws them into a loving relationship with many, many others, who come in time to think together as with one mind, to feel together as with one heart, to work together as with a single pair of hands.

In the final stage of romantic love, you come to have a loving relationship with every creature, expressed in whatever way is perfectly suited to each. Your love for your partner has not diminished in the least; it has simply expanded to include all of life. Now you are relating to the Self, who is One in all. And indeed, this final stage is what you've wanted from the first. From there you can look back and see that sexual desire was really the yearning for unity – unity with one person to begin with, but ultimately with all of life.

All of us are given a reasonable margin in our early years to experiment with sex, but it is prudent for us to use our understanding to see what tremendous power it has and how that power can best be used. We should never allow ourselves to get despondent or discouraged. Mahatma Gandhi wanted to take a vow of celibacy, but even he confesses that he had to take it three times. The Compassionate Buddha said that if he had had one more force like sex to reckon with, he would not have made it. If spiritual giants like these found the challenge so formidable, we shouldn't despair.

For harnessing and directing the sex faculty and bringing it under our control, we are given a great instrument: the human will. A German mystic of the early Middle Ages, Gertrude the Great, describes an exchange between herself and the Lord within. "O Lord," she exclaims, "would that I might have a fire that could liquefy my soul, so that I could pour it totally out like a libation unto thee!"

And the Lord replies: "Thy will is such a fire."

> *If any one love, he knoweth what is the cry of this voice. For it is a loud cry in the ears of God, the mere ardent affection of the soul, when it saith, "My God, my love, thou art all mine, and I am all thine."*

Every time you repeat the Holy Name, it is a call for the Lord to reveal himself in your heart. When you use your mantram under great stress – of longing, of fear, even of terrible anger or anxiety – that call is truly "a loud cry" that almost pitches you into the very arms of the Lord. In the latter stages of meditation, when you have been using the mantram with all your might and the Lord doesn't seem to be responding, you'll be calling out with a keen sense of deprivation – and that will make your cry all the louder.

Teresa of Avila was so passionately in love with her Lord that he used to appear before her regularly. He had no choice! Her love was so strong that he belonged to her completely. And, of course, she belonged to him – so utterly that when she took her vows as a Carmelite nun, she ceased to be Teresa de Ahumada y Cepeda, daughter of a proud and titled aristocratic family, and chose the name "Teresa of Jesus."

Once, the story goes, a radiant figure appeared to young Teresa in a vision and asked, "Little one, what is your name?"

"Sir," she replied, "I am Teresa of Jesus" – meaning, "I don't belong to myself at all; I belong completely to my Lord." Then, taking him to be an angel and plucking up her courage, Teresa asked, "And who may you be?"

The radiant figure must have been moved by this sweet reply, for he smiled and answered, "I am Jesus of Teresa."

Enlarge thou me in love, that with the inward palate of my heart I may taste how sweet it is to love, and to be dissolved, and as it were to bathe myself in thy love.

Let me be possessed by love, mounting above myself through excessive fervor and admiration.

Let me sing the song of love; let me follow thee, my Beloved, on high; let my soul spend itself in thy praise, rejoicing through love.

CHAPTER TEN

Sing the Song of Love

When Thomas said, "My God, my love, thou art all mine, and I am all thine," the courtship period was over, for two had become one: in the beautiful phrase of John of the Cross, *"Amada en el amado transformada."* Now the lover and the Beloved are singing "the song of love" together, and their language is reckless. Let me "be dissolved" in love, "possessed by love; . . . let my soul spend itself in thy praise."

One thinks of Saint Francis preaching on his tiptoes in ecstasy or playing an imaginary fiddle to accompany a song he alone hears.

The aspirant does not ask, in this passage, that the Lord should love him, but rather that his own capacity to love be enlarged to its utmost. He asks for the supreme experience – that his soul "spend itself in thy praise, rejoicing through love."

Enlarge thou me in love, that with the inward palate of my heart I may taste how sweet it is to love, and to be dissolved, and as it were to bathe myself in thy love.

Many years ago, when I took a bungalow on the Blue Mountain and went to live there with my mother, one of my uncles came to visit us. Uncle Appa had taught me Shakespeare and opened my eyes to the classics of Western literature. He spent a few days with us and admired the magnificent views down the mountain slopes: the tea plantations, the silver eucalyptus trees, the bright blue sky. He observed the stillness of the hill country and felt how clear and cool the air was at that height. Finally he gave me a warm smile, and with a knowing look he said, "I see now why you wanted this place. You want to write poetry."

There had been a time not too long before when his guess would have been right. My passionate love of nature and my equally passionate love of poetry were really one love. They reinforced each other. And when I walked those beautiful curving roads on the Blue Mountain, whole passages from Wordsworth would come to mind:

> Five years have past; five summers, with the length
> Of five long winters! and again I hear
> These waters, rolling from their mountain-springs
> With a soft inland murmur. — Once again
> Do I behold these steep and lofty cliffs,
> That on a wild secluded scene impress
> Thoughts of more deep seclusion; and connect
> The landscape with the quiet of the sky.

But I had already reached the stage in my life when neither the love of poetry nor of nature – not even the two together – could satisfy me completely. Slowly but surely, my deep love of nature and poetry was being transmuted into an all-consuming love of the Self. A new desire was stirring within me. I wanted, in the words of Thomas a Kempis, to be "enlarged." I wanted to climb "above myself."

Up until that period, I'd have insisted that my life was full and complete. I loved writing; I loved teaching English; and I loved my vacations, too! At the end of the term, right after my last class, the horse carriage would be waiting just outside the classroom with all my luggage aboard. I would jump on it, rush to catch the Grand Trunk Express, and be reunited with my family on the Blue Mountain two days later. My colleagues were very happy to see this. "What devotion to his family!" they would exclaim.

But now that I had begun to meditate, I knew all this was not enough. Mahatma Gandhi's words went right into my heart when he said that if you don't love everybody on earth, you are not a lover of God. It was not that I was coming to love my family less, but I was beginning to love those around me equally, because now my capacity for love was growing. It was all so mysterious to me, so new. A certain creative process had begun to work in me, and I had no idea what the final result would be. All I could do was cooperate.

This can happen to every one of us, over a long, long time. We start with our own family, our partner, our child, but then gradually we extend the circle of our compassion and affection to our neighbor. Slowly, it moves on down the street. In time, our new capacity to love is so strong that it won't let us ignore the needs of homeless people on the other side of town. Then it extends to the county, then to the state. This is how it develops, and this is why it takes some years. We can say, "Oh, this is impossible!" But there is Saint Francis saying, "I have done it," and Saint Teresa saying, "I have done it." The more we love, the more we can love. This is what it means to enlarge ourselves in love.

The ordinary world of the ego and the senses is so confining! The pleasures of the palate, for instance, are so small, for all the energy we put into indulging them. That is why Thomas cries out to taste with an "inward palate . . . how sweet it is to love." It is very much the same with music, too. As a young man, Francis of Assisi had been a great lover of music. He and his friends would sing and play through the streets of Assisi late at night. Years later, however, he would describe a different kind of music – so exquisite that if it had continued even a second longer, he said, his heart would have broken in two.

My own love of poetry and nature followed much the same course. I loved poetry before – I couldn't get enough of it – but today there is a magnificent poetry woven into every moment. I loved nature before, too, but today my love is so much deeper. It goes beyond how I feel. Now I am careful to do nothing that might hurt the environment.

When this fierce desire – to throw off the old limits and become the immense Self you were meant to be – first sets in, there is a lot of anguish in it. I can testify there is both pain and rapture. Your life becomes full of contradictions. It is an unsettling state of affairs, when those old attachments by which you had defined your personality are falling away. But to compensate, when your attraction to external pleasures has weakened, inside you begin to have deep experiences in meditation. Just for a couple of seconds the mind is still. For one minute the ego falls asleep. You feel such a thrill of joy when this happens, and such fullness of love, that now you tell yourself, "Nothing has been lost."

Great mystics have conveyed this in many ways. Saint Augustine writes in the *Confessions* of just such a glimpse, and he recorded the experience in joyous language much like Thomas's: "No further would I read, nor needed I, for instantly, even with the end of this sentence, by a light as it were of confidence now darted into my heart, all the darkness of doubting vanished away."

When Augustine wrote these lines he was a seasoned veteran of the spiritual life, looking back on something that had happened long before. Decades of spiritual disciplines lay behind him, long years of labor in the service of his Lord. Those years had brought him repeated, incontrovertible experiences of God's presence within. But that first moment in a garden in Milan would remain fresh and luminous for him always, as it has for untold numbers of aspirants who have drawn courage from his story. No one has described with greater dramatic power the long, painful struggle to turn inward, and the joy of finally doing so. Even today, the *Confessions* reads like a well-paced, gripping novel – as arresting now as when it was written more than sixteen hundred years ago. I have read it many times, and I am always surprised at how contemporary the story seems, and how familiar.

Outwardly, Augustine's world bore little resemblance to ours. The pace was slower, quieter. The traffic certainly moved more slowly. There was no talk of vanishing ozone layers or acid rain. Yet hanging over everything was a brooding awareness of inconceivably great changes about to take place. The vast, all-encompassing reality, the great Roman Empire, was moribund. Sick at the center, unwell in every limb, it was dying, and dying along with it were the state religion and the elaborate civic mythologies that had shored it up. In its place, extending across the entire Mediterranean world, was a seething turmoil of competing philosophies, creeds, and cults. Augustine had left none of these unexamined. The Christian faith of his birth and upbringing had seemed too simple, too childlike, to satisfy his fierce and well-schooled intellect. Yet none of the other teachings he explored seemed to satisfy anything but his intellect.

At only thirty-two, Augustine had been appointed official imperial rhetorician for the city of Milan: he had arrived. Satisfaction, though, had not. Nothing of what he had been accustomed to enjoy — not his friendships and romantic involvements, not his formidable intellectual achievements or the quiet rewards of teaching — none of it held him any more. None of it could still the questions that haunted him day and night.

The sheer depth of his mother's religious life attracted him now as it never had before. Friends meanwhile were bringing him astonishing reports from Egypt — stories of men and, later, women who were living out the Gospel teachings with apostolic fervor. Saint Anthony was one of these. He was a giant among mystics, who issued this flawless description of deep meditation: "That prayer is perfect when you are no longer aware of who is praying or of the prayer itself."

For Anthony, the moment of truth had come when he was passing by a church where the Gospel was being read. "Go home," he had heard, "and sell all that you have, and come and follow me." The young man in the Gospels had gone away dejected, but Anthony, a successful businessman, had gone straight home to act on Jesus' words. Augustine frankly envied him, as he envied some of his friends, too, who had made what seemed effortless, almost instant transformations of life and will. For the doubts and inhibitions that held Augustine prisoner now were not intellectual but personal. He had tried so many times to reform himself, only to fall back with renewed ardor into his old untrammeled ways. "Lord, give me chastity, but do not give it yet." Augustine can be looked upon as the patron saint of everyone who has ever vacillated on the path to God-consciousness!

At last, tormented after weeks and months of struggle, he hurled himself out of doors one afternoon only half conscious of where he was, and stumbled into the garden of the friend's house where he was staying. Suddenly, from nowhere visible, he heard a child's voice say, "Pick up and read, pick up and read." He rushed to his copy of Saint Paul's Epistles. Could he hope to be as fortunate as Anthony? Would the book speak to him? Opening it, he read the first lines his hand fell upon: "Not in rioting and drunkenness, not in chambering and wantonness, not in strife and envying; but put ye on the Lord Jesus Christ, and make not provision for the flesh, to fulfill the lusts thereof." Not a text that would speak to every one of us, but to Augustine, very much the man-about-town, the wrangling intellectual and ambitious academician, it struck hammer blows. Surely this was the Lord speaking directly to him.

Years later, looking back on that first revelation, Augustine laments in the language of a very personal love, "Too late came I to love thee, O thou Beauty both so ancient and so fresh; yea, too late came I to love thee. And behold, thou wert within me, and I out of myself, where I made search for thee. You were inside, Lord, all the while, and I was looking in all the wrong places."

Down through time, across one generation after another, the *Confessions* has provided a universally recognized pattern for what happens to a human being when he or she turns inward. I, too, felt a shock of recognition when I read Augustine's story. I was just a few years older than Augustine when my own universe began to tilt wildly on its axis. I had established myself as a successful writer and professor of literature. No one had declared me an imperial rhetorician, to be sure, but I was head of the campus speech and debate society. I had strong interests in music and drama; I was deeply fond of my students and my work. Yet I, too, had discovered, just beneath the surface satisfaction of it all, a profound sense of insufficiency.

Like Augustine, I had a mother who was deeply established in my ancestral faith. Like him, I had remained outside – skeptical, unconvinced, for all my growing hunger. Meanwhile, the world around me was undergoing unprecedented changes. The vast British Empire that had ruled India for nearly two hundred years was crumbling as surely as Rome's had crumbled, and with it was crumbling the implicit faith I had placed in everything Western. And if Saint Anthony and Saint Ambrose were bright sources of light for Augustine, just so was Mahatma Gandhi for me. His ashram near Nagpur seized my imagination as irresistibly as Saint Anthony's desert enclaves had seized Augustine's.

Saint Augustine wrote vividly about the way old desires crowded about him and tugged at his sleeves; and when I read those lines, I thought he could have been describing my own experience. And I had come up just as hard as he against the utter instability of my mind and will, those sometime friends: "The mind gives an order to the body," he used to say in frustration, "and is at once obeyed. But when it gives an order to itself, it is resisted." Throughout his long and painful struggle, Augustine drew gratefully on his friends for support. But his staunchest spiritual ally, his best friend of all, was without question his mother, Monica. For me it was my grandmother and my mother. It was through their grace, at long last, that I could sing in chorus with Augustine, "Too late came I to love thee, O thou Beauty both so ancient and so fresh . . . "

When people ask me, "Haven't you lost the normal satisfactions of life?" I say, "No! All I have lost is insecurity and inadequacy." I've lost the feeling I was just a plaything of life, without any sense of direction. I feel at home in the world now and comfortable in the universe. I have relationships with all life, and I feel sure this is a romance that will go on life after life. I know that when Saint Francis speaks of Brother Sun and Sister Moon, he is not just being poetic — he is speaking out of a very practical knowledge that beholds the entire world as the manifestation of God's love.

> *. . . that with the inward palate of my heart I may taste how sweet it is to love . . .*

There is a passage in the *Confessions* where Augustine recalls a point early in his own spiritual development when, he says, "I heard thy voice from on high crying unto me: 'I am the food of the full-grown.'" He is referring to one of the first discoveries you will make on the spiritual path. Just as you begin to change your food habits when you start meditation, soon you see that you must change the way you feed your mind as well. Personal pleasure and profit are junk food for the mind. They don't nourish; they don't even satisfy. You still feel hungry afterward. Just as we select food that nourishes the body – fresh, whole foods, foods brimming with nutrients – we learn to do the same for the mind. Kind thoughts, compassionate thoughts, thoughts directed to the welfare of everyone around will be the mainstay of our diet.

When Augustine hears God speaking, he replies in effect, "All right, I won't go on eating in those Carthaginian hot spots – but what do I eat?" Then comes the answer, very dramatic, when the Lord says, "And then thou shalt feed on me." Stop eating mind-food that is bad for you, he says, and soon you'll be ravenous. The inspirational passages will look so good!

Augustine wonders, "What'll happen then?" Again the answer comes straight: "Nor shalt thou change me to thy substance. Thou shalt be changed into mine." This is exactly what takes place. The human being becomes a divine force.

After many decades now, meditation is for me a great banquet. In the early hours of the morning, at the holy hour that in India we call *brahmamuhurta,* I get a call from inside saying, "Sit up and meditate! A great banquet is spread for you." Meditation is the nourishing feast that fills my hunger. It is the current that recharges my batteries. It rejuvenates me and heals my wounds.

. . . and to be dissolved . . .

Chemists will tell you there are compounds which resist almost any solvent. I would say that self-will falls into this class. If you put self-will in acids, it'll come right through. Put it in alkalis; it will still be there. Bury it, for that matter, and it will grow. There is no simple, fast way to get rid of self-will. But if you can learn over years of effort to put the needs of others first, you will find your self-will beginning to dissolve. When you think more and more about others, it's like applying a super-solvent from within. As you move closer to others, you will move closer to the Lord within, who is your real Self. After many years you actually begin to lose yourself in the Lord of Love, and in so doing, you truly find yourself. This transformation is not just spiritual, either; it invades the body and the mind as well. There is a radiance about your appearance, a splendor about your personality, that evokes the deepest response in everybody who is sensitive.

There is no way God can be known to us other than by our becoming part of him. To try to understand the supreme reality we call God through the intellect is like trying to study the sun with a candle. To become lost in him is the highest mode of knowing. Saint Bernard of Clairvaux stated it magnificently:

> Just as a drop of water mixed with wine seems
> entirely to lose its own identity while it takes on the

state of wine and its color; just as iron, heated and glowing, looks very much like fire, having divested itself of the original and characteristic appearance of iron; and just as air, flooded with the light of the sun, is transformed so that it appears not so much lighted up as to be light itself, so it will inevitably happen that in illumination, every human affection will then, in some ineffable manner, melt away from self and be wholly transformed into the love of God.

When I go deep in meditation, I lose myself in the Lord within and become one in spirit with him. I'm like the little drop of water Bernard describes, and my Boss is a great sea of wine.

. . . and as it were to bathe myself in thy love.

In India on a warm, tropical afternoon, there is nothing equal to jumping into a cold river. You are not just in a little tub of water; you become part of the river. Just so, when you see the divine current that flows in the depths of every human being and can keep your eyes on it always, you will be bathing in a river of love.

When I gave classes on the Berkeley campus back in the sixties, there was a loose-limbed Irish setter named Ludwig who used to spend most of his time in the waters of the fountain in front of the Student Union. In fact, Ludwig was something of a mascot, and the fountain was unofficially known as Ludwig's Fountain. We all used to enjoy watching him splash about and throw great plumes of water up to sparkle in the sunlight.

Every one of us, I told my students, has a fountain playing like that in the depths of our consciousness, and we
can all take instruction from Ludwig — go there and
play and swim and refresh ourselves. The waters of life
are not outside; they are right within.

Let me be possessed by love . . .

Don't ever be possessed by things. I appreciate
everything about modern civilization that makes life
comfortable, but if you look carefully, you can see that
we are beginning to be possessed by our possessions.
The proof is that we feel if we cannot have a particular
thing — a particular car, certain clothes, a home computer — we ourselves are incomplete. It is this haunting
sense of inadequacy that the media are exploiting, particularly in that interesting phenomenon called "impulse buying." You go to a supermarket to buy a can of
cocoa and you come back with a big brown bag full of
things. Why? Oh, they were on sale, and they were
stacked up right next to the cash register. When things
can reach out and compel you to buy them, they have
stolen a bit of your capacity to love. That is why the
simple life is a very loving life, in which all our precious
capacity to love is preserved.

*. . . mounting above myself, through excessive fervor
and admiration.*

Once all your desires are unified, there comes
a point in meditation when prayer ceases to have
words. The words of the inspirational passage fall

away, and your consciousness becomes a field of unified desire which draws you beyond the world of words and thoughts. This is a mysterious state, and it can be frightening to find yourself plunged into its depths. Theophan the Recluse describes it and allays our fears, making it clear that this is a stage all seekers pass through:

> Further on in this state, another kind of prayer may be given which comes to a man instead of being performed by him.... The spirit of man comes upon man and drives him into the depths of the heart as if he were taken by the hand and forcibly led from one room to another. The soul is here taken captive by an invading force and is kept willingly within as long as this overwhelming power of prayer still holds sway over it.

This is a perfect description of what happened to me during the deeper stages of meditation. I used to say, "This is enough! I have gone deep enough; I don't want to go any farther." But something kept dragging me down into a deeper place, out into a brighter room.

You, too, may come to a stage where you feel there is a power driving you from behind, drawing you from in front. At that time, because of the depths you have reached in meditation, it is very important to throw yourself into selfless and concentrated work in harmony with others. This is for your own safety. It's important also to eat nourishing food in moderate quantities. Regular, vigorous exercise is important at this time, and so is wholesome entertainment. The body and the nervous system both have to be strengthened to withstand the impact of these tremendous developments.

Gradually, at this stage, meditation will cease to be a discipline. It will become a source of such ravishing joy that there is the danger of wanting to bask in it. This is where you safeguard your progress by making a rich contribution in your outward life. You have inhaled; now you must exhale. You find yourself in possession of joy that never deserts you, for if others are in distress, you have the great joy of being able to relieve their pain. If they are happy, you have the great joy of sharing their happiness. You live in a world of joy. You don't have to go anywhere in search of joy; joy comes in search of you. Saint Anselm of Canterbury describes his own experience: "I have found a joy that is full and more than full. For when heart and mind and soul, and all the man are full of that joy, joy beyond measure will still remain."

Let me sing the song of love . . .

"When your life becomes a song," said a Bengali mystic, "the Lord listens."

Years ago I visited the home of a friend and we were seated on the terrace together. The wind was blowing, and I heard the dulcet tinkling of bells. Looking around, I saw there were wind chimes which were making sweet music out of the wind. I could well imagine a storm coming and the music becoming even sweeter – a hurricane, and the music becoming a kind of symphony. The lover of God lives very much like the wind chime. When joy comes, he sings a sweet refrain; but when sorrow comes, oh! the song becomes sweeter; and when great trials come, tremendous hymns burst forth from his consciousness.

The Greek philosopher Plotinus loved to talk about human consciousness using this same language of music. "We are like a chorus," he said, "who stand around the conductor but do not always sing in tune because our attention is diverted by looking at external things."

Imagine the London Philharmonic Orchestra in one of those outside theaters, performing under the direction of a great conductor. What would you think if the members of the wind section kept gazing out into the audience while the violinists followed the planes overhead and the percussionists kept falling asleep? You'd want your money back. "There is no music here," you'd tell the gentleman at the ticket office. "There is no orchestra here! Everybody is doing his own thing." Plotinus says we are all living like that, unaware of the divine conductor within.

"But when we do behold him," Plotinus adds, "we attain the end of our existence and our rest. Then we no longer sing out of tune, but form a truly divine chorus about him. In that chorus the soul beholds the fountain of life, the fountain of creativity, the principle of being, the cause of good, and the root of the soul." I cannot express to you in words what this divine harmony is like. There is not a discordant note anywhere, not even in the unconscious. The symphony goes on playing even in sleep.

Let me follow thee, my Beloved, on high . . .

Just as on a high mountain there is a timberline beyond which no trees can grow, so there is a point in consciousness beyond which no thoughts can grow, no selfish desires can take root. We may think, "Who wants to live at an elevation where there is no thought? No cravings to brighten our lives?" But those who climb to that point and come down for our benefit say, "Oh, but the air is like champagne there. You have no idea how it goes to your head! The view will take your breath away. Absolute truth can be seen, and absolute beauty too."

Mountain climbers train to climb the Himalayas for many, many years. Meditators, similarly, train for decades to climb the Himalayas of the soul. When they stand at the peak and look around, they say: "The world is full of God! I see now that in everyone there is the divine. There is a continuing relationship between mountain and sea, forest and river, and all living things."

Don't be content to climb only the Sierras or the Alps. As Saint Augustine said, that is not enough: "People travel afar to marvel at the heights of mountains, the mighty waves of the sea, the long courses of great rivers, the vastness of the ocean, the movements of the stars, yet they leave themselves unnoticed!"

Let my soul spend itself in thy praise, rejoicing through love.

Before I took to meditation, I had no idea what wealth I had locked up in my heart. I was like someone spending out of a checking account, watching anxiously each month as "Checks Written" overtook "Cash in Balance," completely unaware that in the depths of my consciousness there was a great savings account that I could draw on, a vast trust fund in my name. After many years I was finally able to go deep in meditation and unlock this treasury. Then I discovered how rich I was, and with that discovery came the immediate, passionate desire to lay hold of that vast wealth of love, wisdom, and resourcefulness and pour it out at the feet of the Lord.

Let me love thee more than myself, nor love myself but for thee: and in thee all that truly love thee, as the law of love commandeth, shining out from thyself.

CHAPTER ELEVEN

The Law of Love

Just as the law of relativity can be verified in England or in Japan by English or Japanese physicists, the law of love that Thomas expresses in these verses can be verified by lovers of God both East and West. Reading selections from Meister Eckhart, for example, is almost like reading selections from the South Indian mystic Shankara Acharya. In fact, since meister and acharya signify the same thing, we can as well say "Meister Shankara" and "Eckhart Acharya," so deep do the similarities go. Similarly, there are two marvelous women mystics, one from India and one from Europe, who sing of the love of God and dance in ecstasy to express their love of God; and when translated into the language of the heart, there is no difference between Mechthild of Magdeburg and Meera of Rajasthan.

About three hundred years separate them. Meera was born around 1498; Mechthild, between 1207 and 1210. Meera shed her body before she was fifty;

Mechthild lived to be eighty or more. Both of them adopted the rich devices of courtly love poetry to compose their songs for the Lord within, and the similarities between the two are remarkable.

Meera was born a royal princess of the Rajput people. Her menfolk were brave warriors who fought the Mogul emperor in Delhi. She herself grew up cherished and protected, in an atmosphere of music and dance; but as her spiritual life deepened, she displayed the courage of the Rajputs more brilliantly than her most formidable uncles and brothers.

When Meera was just a little girl, she received an image of Lord Krishna from a wandering teacher who saw great spiritual promise in the girl, and from that day onwards she felt she was betrothed to Krishna. In accordance with the customs of her people, she was married at about eighteen to a prince from a nearby state. For years she struggled to fulfill her new family's expectations of her and still remain the passionate devotee of Krishna that she couldn't help but be. At last, after she had survived three attempts on her life and innumerable assaults to her spiritual life, she answered the call of her first and only love. Carrying nothing with her but her vina, the stringed instrument with which she accompanied her songs, she walked out of her royal palace and never came back. For the rest of her days she wandered through northwest India composing love songs to Lord Krishna — songs which are sung throughout India even today. Legend has it that as Meera was singing in a Krishna temple one day, her longing for him reached such a height that before her companions' eyes she simply vanished into the figure of her divine Beloved.

About Mechthild's childhood we know very little, but her poems suggest that she too was brought up in a courtly setting. When she was about twelve she had her first spiritual experience, a "greeting" from Christ that was so powerful that afterward the worldly life never exerted any real pull. At twenty-three she left her family and moved to the town of Magdeburg, bent on severing any attachment that might hinder her pursuit of the Lord within. Mechthild's native state of Thuringia was in a period of spiritual awakening then, and Magdeburg was a place where women seekers in particular were coming together in loosely-bound spiritual communities within a lay movement known as the Beguines. Mechthild lived in Magdeburg as a Beguine until she was an elderly woman. In 1270 she went to live in the famous convent of Helfta, where she died in 1297.

Mechthild drew upon the richness of chivalric poetry to express her love of God. Mostly she just scribbled her songs on pieces of paper that were not collected until much later. By 1300, however, Mechthild's songs were being circulated around Europe, and tradition has it that when Dante wrote his *Divine Comedy,* it was she the great poet was describing when he wrote of "a solitary woman moving, singing, and gathering up flower on flower – the flowers that colored all her pathway." It is a beautiful image, and one very much in the spirit of Meera too, for it suggests that the lives of those who dedicate themselves to the service of God are not austere at all. They are lives strewn with flowers, full of joy, full of love.

> *Let me love thee more than myself, nor love myself but for thee . . .*

Meera writes, in vivid images drawn from everyday life:

> None can break the bond between you and me,
> none but you, O Lord of the world.
> You are the tree, Krishna,
> and I the bird that sits on the branches singing.
> You are the river, Krishna,
> and I the fish that swims in joy from bank
> to bank.
> You are the green hill, Krishna,
> and I the peacock dancing,
> with flashing plumes spread.
> Accept Meera's devotion, Lord of the world!

Mechthild's intimate tone echoes Meera's:

> Thou shinest in my soul
> As the sun on gold.
> When I rest in thee, O Lord,
> My bliss is manifold.
> Thou clothest thyself with my soul
> Who thyself art its mantle.

Both these great mystics appeal to their Lord in irresistibly sweet language. Meera teases, "Some people say

I flirted with you, others that I cheated you, but I got
you, Krishna!" And Mechthild sings just as playfully:

> I seek thee with all my might.
> Had I the power of a giant thou wouldst
>   quickly be lost
> If I came upon thy footprints.
> Ah, my love, run not so far ahead,
> But rest a little lovingly
> That I may catch up with thee!

And both of them rise to the very heights of poetry
when they describe their longing for permanent union
with the Beloved. From Mechthild:

> Even should all creatures lament for me,
>   none could fully tell them
>   what inhuman need I suffer.
> Human death were far gentler to me
>   than to be without you.
> I seek thee in my thoughts
>   like a bride seeking a groom.

And from Meera:

> In life and death you are my friend,
> My only friend.
> Without your presence
> I am lost in the maze of life.
> Ask my heart and it will tell you
> Whose face it is seeking always.
> This world is but a shadow play
> Where family and friends flit by.
> I pray to you with folded hands
> And beg you to heed my prayer.

Mechthild and Meera are adamant: if you want to be united with the Lord, there can't be anything else you want more. There comes a point in every great mystic's life when he or she is put to the test: nothing can be held back. Mechthild reveals on one occasion that God actually said to her, "To have all that mine is, you must let go of all that thine is." And in one of the most precious of all Hindu scriptures, the Bhagavatam, there is a verse that has inspired people like me down the ages all over India. It is very much in keeping with these lines from Thomas a Kempis, because it contains the supreme secret of devotion. "If you want to be united with me," the Lord says, "you must lay hold on whatever it is in life that gives you most delight – whatever it is you think you cannot live without – and give it to me. Infinite are the blessings that will follow."

To make this gift – to look about you and find what gives you most satisfaction in life and say, "Here, Lord, it's yours!" – is next to impossible. For my own part, I can attest that I was in love with my work and in love with life as I was living it then. My students were dear to me, and I to them. That was my whole world. All my attention had been flowing into it, and I would never have been able to imagine that I could live without it.

But as your need for the Lord within – call him Christ or Krishna, call her the Divine Mother – as that need becomes more and more imperious, circumstances start to change. If you were to ask me how I was able to give up a career and way of life I loved so much,

I would have to say that it wasn't through my own effort at all. It was through my grandmother's grace that everything changed in such a way that if I hadn't voluntarily let go, it would probably have been taken from me anyway. That kind of divine banditry is considered to be one of the highest forms of grace.

Mechthild describes in magnificent poetry her own response when from deep within she heard the divine voice say, "Hand it over!" God says:

> "Thou huntest so for thy love.
>   What bringest thou me, my queen?"

> "Lord, I bring thee my treasure.
>   It is greater than the mountains,
>   wider than the world,
>   deeper than the sea,
>   higher than the clouds,
>   more glorious than the sun,
>   more manifold than the stars.
>   It outweighs the whole earth."

The Lord lets her know he's interested, and asks:

> "What is the name of thy treasure"

And the soul replies:

> "Lord, it is called my heart's desire.
>   I have withdrawn it from the world,
>   denied it to myself and all creatures.
>   Now I can bear its weight no longer.
>   Where, O Lord, shall I lay it?"

The Lord is so pleased that he opens his arms to her and bids her come:

> "Nowhere shalt thou lay it
> But in my own divine heart
> and on my human breast.
> There alone wilt thou find comfort
> And be embraced by my holy spirit."

Mechthild has set aside everything in her life that could have separated her from her Beloved, and now she is lost in union with him. This is what mystics of every spiritual tradition call the Divine Marriage, and in their passionate descriptions of this state they call forth the romantic in each of us. Henry Suso, who lived just a hundred years later than Mechthild, writes ingenuously: "I will set down here a short description how it is when the Bride thus embraces the Bridegroom, for the consideration of the reader, who perhaps has not yet been in this wedding chamber. It may be he will be desirous to follow."

And that is just how it is. Each of us, Suso suggests, approaches the spiritual life at our own pace. Few rush right into this marriage. Instead, first, we get an invitation. It seems innocent enough: "Please come and help us celebrate." We go and sit at the back and look around. Maybe we even attend the reception, and have a couple of glasses of champagne and a piece of cake. That is how we begin. The next time we come as a friend of the bride's. We get a good seat in the third row, and as the bride and bridegroom come down the aisle they look at us and we manage to give them a warm glance in return. Then, as chance would have it, at the next wedding we find ourselves standing right up there next to the altar as a bridesmaid or a best man. It doesn't seem like a bad idea at all! And finally, the great day comes when we are there as the bride or bridegroom. The ceremony passes, we exchange rings, and at last, in a symbolic gesture with universal meaning, we lift the veil and gaze into the eyes of our Beloved.

In the words of Meister Eckhart, "As long as the soul has not thrown off all her veils, however thin, she is unable to see God. Any medium, even a hair's breadth, between the body and the soul stops the actual union." In Sufism, the mystical tradition of Islam, it is said that with every stage in deepening meditation, you remove one veil. The lover, the spiritual aspirant, is yearning to see his divine Beloved, who is heavily veiled. One veil falls away – the physical – and you can see the Self a little more clearly. The mental veil falls away and you see more clearly still. Finally, when the ego falls – the veil of self-will – there is the Beloved, revealed in all the beauty and all the love we have been longing for.

One Sufi poet used to ask, "Do you know why God is veiled from you? Would you like to know what the veil is?" We all say, "Of course!" And he replies, "You yourself are the veil. If you remove yourself, you will be able to love all." Our modern civilization says just the opposite: "Thicken the veil! Make it opaque! Wear many layers piled on top of one another!" As a result, not only can no one see us, we cannot see either. Love is not blind, you know; love sees. "Love hath no errors." Only when you love can you see everybody's needs.

It's a wonderful paradox: it is when you have seen God in your own heart, in the depths of meditation, that you see him everywhere, even with your eyes wide open. In the great climax of meditation, when self-will is extinguished and the mind becomes still, you see the whole universe as the manifestation of God's love. You love everybody now because you see the Self in them, and not only human beings but animals too – elephants, sea lions, sparrows, every living thing. Wherever you go, you'll see only unity. You will find the universe friendly. For me it is one world, in which not only are all human beings part of my family, so are the seas, the mountains, the rivers, the trees. After all, it isn't governments and corporations that supply me with oxygen; it is plants and plankton. They are my dear friends, my kith and kin. This is the ultimate reach of the supreme marriage that takes place deep in meditation: I am joined in marriage to all of life.

At weddings in North India, it is customary to apply distilled rose water to the wrist of each guest. It is so fragrant and lasts so long that wherever you go afterward, people will smile and say, "Hey, you must have come from a wedding!" Just so, the Buddha says, when you meet a lover of God, you take a little of that fragrance home in your heart. You will be more patient, more understanding, more secure, more selfless. That is why people loved to be around saints like Francis of Assisi and Teresa of Avila. We instinctively seek the company of men and women like this, and when we find them, we feel so comfortable – not even talking, just being nearby. Once you have begun to meditate, you will find this taking place in your own home. A kind of quietly healing influence can be felt wherever there is even one person whose mind is at peace and whose heart is full of love.

. . . and in thee, all that truly love thee . . .

In the eleventh century, Saint Anselm composed a beautiful prayer in which he asks the Lord, "Teach me to seek thee, and reveal thyself to me when I seek thee; for I cannot seek thee except thou teachest me, nor find thee except thou revealest thyself."

Often God reveals himself through the men and women who love him with all their heart. If you ask any illumined teacher from the Hindu tradition what is the best way to deepen your love for God, he or she will reply, "Through the company of those who have realized God." This is the unspoken, powerful attraction that men like Francis of Assisi and Meister Eckhart exerted on those around them in medieval Europe, and this is why people sought out Julian of Norwich and Catherine of Genoa for spiritual counsel.

There is no equivalent to the highly personal and intimate communication that goes on between an earnest seeker and a realized man or woman. In my own life, without knowing why, I began early to seek out such people. I didn't try to talk with them; it was enough just to·look at them.

It began when I was a graduate student at the University of Nagpur, when every weekend I used to love to visit the railway station. Nagpur is located at a crossroads between north and south, east and west, and the great trains from all parts of India came through. I would wait on the platform, and sooner or later most of the important political figures would pass by. And one of them, like Gandhi, was much, much more than just a political figure. Badshah Khan was a great man of God, and although he came from a Muslim race that is one of the fiercest on earth — the Pathans, of the mountainous regions around the Khyber Pass — he had become so ardent a devotee of nonviolence that we called him the Frontier Gandhi. He was so tall that he had to stoop to come out of the train. His laughter and speech were like sweet music — so gentle coming from such a huge mountain of a man! It was from those encounters on the railway platform that I received from him the inspiration to write his life's story, *A Man to Match His Mountains*, many years later.

There were more of these precious encounters with spiritual figures, and each of them came without any effort on my part. Through one of my campus colleagues I was privileged to meet Meher Baba. Much later another friend took me and Christine to the ashram of Swami Ramdas, where we sat and watched him looking like the most ordinary fellow in the world as he shaved himself and fiddled with the dial on his radio to get the morning news.

Soon afterwards, when Christine and I were visiting Vrindavan, the place where the historic Krishna lived, I learned by happenstance that a beautiful woman saint named Anandamayi Ma was there in her ashram that day and accepting visitors. I ran back to get Christine, and we arrived just in time. There was quite a large crowd. I remember several Indian visitors trying to touch Anandamayi Ma's feet, which is our way of paying deep respect. She prohibited them gently, directing each of them to her mother as if to say, "It is her feet you should touch, not mine; for it was she who brought me into this life." As we were leaving, this gracious and saintly woman took a garland from her own neck and put it around Christine's.

From all of these encounters, I have drawn a precious and rare kind of sustenance. I call them my "teachers at large," for each of them transmitted to me a glimmering of my own deepest Self. But most powerful of all, and most telling for the whole course of my life, was my meeting with Gandhi.

Those were critical years in India's struggle for independence from British rule, when terrible problems confronted the country. I yearned to have a part in solving them, but I was very young, and it was impossible for me not to feel overwhelmed. In search of guidance, I made a kind of pilgrimage one day to Gandhi's ashram, outside a town called Wardha. I walked the six or seven miles from the railroad station, and when I arrived I found that a crowd had gathered around the little cottage where Gandhi had been meeting with his co-workers for several hours. I felt sure he would be fatigued when he appeared, that his step would be dragging and the last thing he would want to see was a crowd of people. But when the door opened and Gandhi stepped out, he looked as bright and vital as someone who'd slept eight hours. "Come on," he gestured at us, and he set out walking at a clip that soon had most of us panting. For a moment — just an instant — our eyes met. That is all I was conscious of at the time, just a look. But many years later I began to understand that in a deep, mysterious way, that look continued to give me strength. I realized that a wordless communication must have taken place, though I didn't know how to decode it at the time and had to keep it "pending" until much later.

> *. . . as the law of love commandeth, shining out from thyself.*

One of the first and most eloquent opponents of slavery in this country was the Quaker, John Woolman, who deeply loved the *Imitation of Christ*. Here is his own testimony to the "law of love":

There is a principle which is pure, placed in the human mind, which in different places and ages hath had different names. It is, however, pure and proceeds from God. It is deep, and inward, confined to no forms of religion, nor excluded from any, where the heart stands in perfect sincerity. In whomsoever this takes root and grows, of what nation soever, they become brethren in the best sense of the expression.

God has given us several laws. The law of gravity is a divine gift, and so is the law of unity. We have discovered the one, but not the other. The law of gravity governs the external world; the law of unity governs the internal world. Just as all the planets and all the galaxies are held together in an immense unity by gravitational forces, human beings also, the mystics say, are held together by the law of unity – beginning with the members of the family and extending to all other families, beginning with one nation and extending to all other nations.

These are not pious platitudes; they are living laws. It is because we have broken them that there is war, there is famine, there is hostility between man and woman, child and parent, friend and friend. But whenever we see a person who has patience, we are seeing that law of love shining through. The love of the Lord, the glory of the Lord, shines out through every human being to the extent that he is able to bless them that curse him, that she does good to those who harm her. It starts with each one of us.

Love is active, sincere, affectionate, pleasant and amiable; courageous, patient, faithful, prudent, long-suffering, manly, and never seeking itself.

For in whatever instance one seeketh oneself, there he falleth from love.

Love is circumspect, humble, and upright: not yielding to softness or to levity, nor attending to vain things; it is sober, chaste, steady, quiet, and guarded in all the senses.

Love is subject, and obedient to its superiors, to itself mean and despised, unto God devout and thankful, trusting and hoping always in Him, even then when God imparteth no relish of sweetness unto it: for without sorrow, none liveth in love.

He that is not prepared to suffer all things, and to stand to the will of his Beloved, is not worthy to be called a lover of God.

A lover ought to embrace willingly all that is hard and distasteful for the sake of his Beloved, and not to turn away from him for any contrary accidents.

CHAPTER TWELVE

Love Is Subject

The fruit of the spirit, said Saint Paul, "is love, joy, peace, long-suffering, gentleness, goodness, faith, meekness, temperance; against such there is no law." In other words, these are the real qualities of the Self. For the great majority of us they are hidden and weighed down by masses of self-will, but at the first opportunity they will rise from below the surface level of consciousness.

This is one of the thrilling developments in deepening meditation. Your mind has not yet become completely still, but it is certainly quieter, and as the turbulence dies down, you begin to see wonderful qualities rising from deep within. Gradually – gracefully – they will come into play in your daily life. It is really very much like watching a plum tree or a peach tree bursting into blossom. When somebody is angry at you, the desire to help that person will thrust aside your own angry replies, because you will feel the pain of the other person's anger and want to relieve it.

When somebody is being rather obnoxious and your normal desire would be to move away, you will find yourself trying to move closer instead.

In the Indian tradition, the symbol for this wonderful development is the lotus. One of its Sanskrit epithets is *pankaja,* from the word *panka,* "mud," and *ja,* "born." The lotus is born in the mud at the bottom of a lake and finds its way up through the waters until it reaches the surface, where it extends its rosy petals like a chalice of light in the rays of the morning sun. Similarly, even though our capacity to love is born in selfishness and a few strong personal attachments to people near us, it can slowly begin to rise, through the practice of spiritual disciplines, moving upward through the waters of life. You begin by loving A, B, or C, but you end by becoming love itself.

Mystics who use the language of spiritual courtship to describe their experience will often refer to the later stages of meditation as a kind of "holy fecundity." It is the mystics' capacity to bring goodness into the world, whatever their context. In Jesus' own words, "By their fruits ye shall know them."

Teresa of Avila, for example, who felt herself to be a bride of Christ, makes a careful distinction between the honeymoon and the marriage itself. For some time after she first attained spiritual awareness, she was subject to sudden raptures *(arrobamientos)* which would sweep her without warning into the embrace of the Lord within, and altogether out of everyday existence. Over time, however, people close to her observed that she was no longer subject to these spells, and they asked her whether she missed them. Teresa smiled and said no: "I've found a better way to pray." She had moved out of the honeymoon stage, and now all the fire and passion of those earlier experiences had come under her conscious control. She could pour her love uninhibitedly into the Lord's work.

Sometimes we are disconcerted to learn that mystics don't live happily ever after. They don't seek to. They ask only to be united with God, even in suffering, and to be instruments of his love.

Let us now touch upon each of the precious qualities Thomas attributes to the man or woman of God:

Love is active . . .

My granny was active all her life. If there was a great feast, she didn't just call the young girls and say, "You do the work." She said, "Help me," and seated together they would slice great piles of okra, eggplant, and green beans – enough for our whole joint family, which numbered about a hundred people. Slowly, one by one, the girls would say, "Granny, I'm falling asleep!" And she would smile and say, "Go to bed then." Toward the end she might be seated there alone, chopping and slicing until daybreak. When my mother would come and ask, "Wouldn't you like to sleep now?" Granny would reply, "Isn't it time to go to the temple?" And that would be the beginning of another day.

In a village society that expected an aristocratic family like mine to rely on servants, my granny really stood out. "She milks her own cows!" people would say. And she could have had the cowherd do it. More than that, when necessary she would clean the cowshed with her own hands. When I asked her, "Granny, why don't you let Appu do it?" She told me, "The cows give us milk. They help take care of us; shouldn't I help take care of them?" She also enjoyed a pithy Kerala saying: "Your own gums are better than somebody else's teeth." She was always independent, and she liked hard work.

Sometimes there is a misconception about the spiritual person: an image of someone who is nice enough, but who doesn't get much done. This couldn't be farther from the truth. When you meditate deeply, you get into danger if you just stop acting. You need meaningful, engaging work, work that adds to the benefit of all. When you have gone a little way in meditation, instead of rushing about doing a myriad different things, you learn to act efficiently in ways that are harmonious with your goal; you don't waste time and energy on meaningless activity. You become very active, but in a controlled, focused way. This compatibility of action and contemplation is one of the little known secrets of the meditative life.

. . . sincere, affectionate, pleasant . . .

Bernard Shaw said that if you want to judge a person's character, watch him or her in a quarrel. It's a penetrating remark. Do unkind words shoot out of his mouth? Do unkind things fly from her hand? Similarly, when I want to know how someone is doing in meditation, I just observe that person when he or she is provoked. For just as a ship is tested in a storm, so your spiritual awareness is really tested when anger builds up around you, just daring you to function freely in the emotional turmoil. If you are able to use courteous, kind, considerate language in the midst of towering waves of resentment, your meditation gets A-plus.

Being sincere, affectionate, and pleasant takes a lot of inner toughness. We don't usually associate affection with strength, but there is a very close connection. When it comes to tender, loving relationships, candlelight dinners are fine; but if you want to see whether two people are truly in love, watch them when one is angry. If they're in love, the other should be able to calm that person down; that is one of the "wonderful effects of divine love." Furious words may be flying about your ears, but you just stand there foursquare to all the winds that blow. Such a person is firm, like a mountain or a rock. You remember that Jesus said of Peter, whose name means "rock" in Greek, "Thou art Peter, and upon this rock I shall build my church." For building homes, too, this kind of rock makes the best foundation. When even one member of a household has the security that comes of deep meditation, the house can stand firm. When the storms are blowing, instead of moving away, the lovers will move closer. When danger threatens there won't be two; there will be just one.

For lovers who would reach this state, the precious secret is to cultivate what I call a slow mind. When you learn to meditate, you are slowly shifting the mind from overdrive down to high, then to second, and finally into neutral. Then you have unlimited patience. When someone is angry with you, you can listen to his point of view with such detachment and attention that sometimes you'll say, "Hey, he's right – I'm wrong. I can learn from him."

When I first came to this country, I picked up an apt simile from the laundromat. These machines were so new to me that I watched them with fascination. When you first put your clothes into a dryer, I observed, they whirl around so fast that you can't make out anything; you can't tell your shirt from your socks from your pajamas. But as the machine is about to stop, it slows down. Then you can even read the writing on your T-shirt: "Only Elephants Should Wear Ivory." Similarly, I told my new American friends, when thoughts slow down, we can see them clearly and set them right.

Our best defense against the fast thinking that plunges us into anger is the Holy Name – particularly when it is combined with a really fast walk. In India, some of these essential strategies of the spiritual life are handed out with a delightfully light touch in a little story. One such story concerns a wandering sage who was asked by a villager what to do about anger. "That's simple," the sage said. "Whenever you get angry, just get outside and walk as fast as you can, repeating to yourself the Holy Name: *Rama, Rama, Rama.*" Time passed, and it was months before the sage's wanderings led him to that village again. His villager disciple ran to greet him, but the sage could hardly recognize him. He looked calm and secure but exceptionally fit as well, strong and bronzed by the sun. "I'm glad to see you looking so well!" the sage exclaimed. "What is the secret of your good health?" "Oh," the man answered with an embarrassed smile, "I've been living mostly in the open."

. . . and amiable . . .

One of the finest exercises in making your life a work of art is not to regard anybody as an enemy. This can be exceedingly hard. Most people are basically good, but there are some rare individuals, perhaps because of their past, who just can't help returning unkindness for kindness. If you have to deal with them every day – they may even be part of your family! – it can be almost more than you can bear.

The miracle of meditation is that in the long run, even if somebody is unkind to you, you can still return kindness. Even if somebody tries to pull you down, you can pull him up by returning good for evil: blessing those that curse you, in Jesus' words, and doing good to those who hate you. In India, the symbol for this precious capacity is the sandalwood tree. The great mystic Shankara explained why in a haunting poem:

> I have visited many countries,
> Seen many sights,
> But never have I seen anything
> Like the sandalwood tree.
> The more you cut it,
> The more you burn it,
> The more you grind it,
> The more fragrance its hoarded sap will yield.

This is a perfect description of Mahatma Gandhi or Teresa of Avila. The more they were attacked and libeled, the more radiant they became with love. In order to love, we have to learn to suffer. To me, this is the message of Jesus. In our own century, it is Mahatma Gandhi who showed us that love is the sure remedy for even the greatest of evils, war. "Nonviolence," he claimed, "in its dynamic condition, means conscious suffering. It does not mean submission to the will of the tyrant, but it means the pitting of one's whole soul against the will of the tyrant. Working under this law of our being, this 'soul-force,' it is possible for a single individual to defy the whole might of an unjust empire."

. . . courageous . . .

"Perfect love," said Saint John, "casteth out fear." Courage is a quality that follows deepening meditation. It implies complete faith in God, whom you know to be present in the depths of your consciousness.

Saint Francis of Assisi lived for some time among the people of his region who had contracted leprosy. He bathed them, nursed their wounds, and did everything in his power to relieve their suffering. But to his nearest followers he confided how much resistance in himself he had had to overcome before he could do this. For as a young man, before he was drawn to God, he had been unwilling to go even within miles of the leper houses, and even then he would cover his nostrils in repugnance. But one day – when, in one chronicler's words, "he was beginning to think of holy and useful things" – a leper approached him and stretched out his disfigured hand for alms. Francis tossed him some coins and turned away, revolted to the point of nausea. But then he seems to have seen suddenly that it was Jesus who asked, Jesus in a leper's flesh; and "made stronger than himself," in one of the great understatements of hagiography, he ran back to the man and kissed him in great joy. In that moment of recognition, that sure instinct that the Lord dwells in all, Francis overcame his fear and his repugnance forever.

Courage isn't just something that happens in the lives of the saints and martyrs. The vicissitudes of everyday relationships can call forth enormous courage in every one of us, once we determine to act in the deepest interest of everyone around. For example, putting others first does not mean saying yes to everyone. Love often expresses itself in saying no. When you allow people to exploit you, you aren't just hurting yourself; you are helping the exploiter to hurt himself as well. It requires enormous judgment, and bravery too, to oppose nonviolently people we love – to fight the sin but not the sinner. In time, we can lovingly wear them down with our patience, and when we see signs of regret and reconciliation, we make friends again and completely forget the barrier that stood between us.

To give an example, when I was coming to this country from India, I traveled by ship with many other Fulbright scholars – including some from Pakistan, whose relations with India were strained to the brink of war. At the dining table, these fellows would try to take it out on me as if I were the prime minister. "Why does your country do this?" they would ask in angry tones. I said, "I'm a plain professor; what do I have to do with setting foreign policy?" But they kept making unpleasant cracks, meal after meal, until the other Indian scholars finally just went to another table.

Now, before I had taken to meditation, I confess I would have done the same. I have never cared for controversy, and there seemed to be nothing gained by staying and arguing. But now I was secure. It was not that I didn't understand their cracks or that their open animosity wasn't painful, but I refused to give them the satisfaction of driving me out. I was convinced that differences in our political opinions need not stand between us as human beings. They kept on baiting me, but I never replied – and I never lost my courtesy, either. This went on almost until we reached Marseilles. There we parted company: they were going on to Gibraltar; I disembarked to take the train for Paris. And the interesting thing was that just as I was leaving, they gave me a party. It was a deeply human response. They were really embarrassed, and with simple courtesy they asked, "Please forgive us for what we have said."

The lovers of God don't play Pollyanna. They don't bury their heads in the sand and say, "Oh, everybody is good; everybody is loving" – not at all. They know the world is a harsh place, and the times we live in are difficult and dangerous. But they have enough security, endurance, and love to remember that all these upsets are on the surface. Beneath the anger and agitation, through every human being a river of love still runs.

. . . patient . . .

The spiritual life calls upon us to be both patient and impatient. Without a certain measure of impatience, you're not likely to cut through all the million and one fetters that tie you to limited, self-willed living. I was as impatient as any of you in the first half of my spiritual life, almost reckless in throwing aside whatever looked like an impediment to becoming aware of God. But in the second half I came to realize that the results of my efforts weren't in my hands at all. Even to have come as far as I had was due entirely to the grace of God. You could say that I became more patient at that point, in that I was more willing just to give full effort and let things take their course. Even so, there was a lot of impatience in the second half, and a lot of suffering too. As Gandhi says, the nearer you are to the goal, the further away it appears to be.

After a retreat some years ago, when the participants were taking leave of me, one man lingered until the very last minute and then came to me, gave me a hug, and said, "You have stolen my heart; why can't you steal my mind?" It was a beautiful question, because it expressed so tenderly the mix of patience and impatience that everybody comes to feel on the spiritual path.

. . . *faithful* . . .

To our modern world, the word faith is highly suspect. It seems to imply a lack of intellect, almost a naive gullibility. But every one of us acts on faith every day of our lives. When we get into a car, we put our faith in everybody else on the freeway not to drive into us; we put our faith in the company that built our car, the mechanic who has repaired it, even the engineers who designed the highway. This isn't to say that our faith is unquestioning: we try to be alert when we're behind the wheel, and we choose our mechanic carefully. But once we have done our part, we are willing to trust the car and the roads to get us where we are going in one piece.

This is all the faith I have ever asked anyone to place in God: the same faith you put in your car. You should feel free to place in the Lord who has created the world at least as much faith as you put in the state highway department.

The Hindu scriptures make a bold statement about faith: "You are what your faith is." If you believe money will make you happy, you will go after money. If you are convinced fame will make you secure, you will court fame. Why? Because in the words of the Bible, "As a person thinketh in his heart, so is he." Not "as a person thinketh in his head," for these beliefs come from a much deeper level than the intellect. In the Orthodox tradition, they say whatever spiritual knowledge you have in the head doesn't become real until you bring it down into the heart through spiritual disciplines. Because of the tremendous distance, this takes many, many years.

. . . prudent . . .

There may come moments in meditation when extraordinary experiences take place, and you will be tempted to let your mind soar and bask in the wonder of it all. But every good spiritual teacher will tell you to pay no attention to these occurrences. They have nothing to do with indicating the quality of your meditation, and if you start pursuing them, you can get lost in a kind of Alice's Wonderland of the mind – which, of course, is just what the mind wants you to do!

The real test of deepening meditation is not in the visions we see or voices we hear, but in our capacity to really see the faces of those around us and really hear their voices. Were you able to look through a teenage mask of stony indifference this morning and see the deep yearning for respect and affection it concealed? Did you reach out in love? If so, your meditation is coming along splendidly, no matter how uneventful it might seem.

If by chance you do experience something out of the ordinary – if Saint Teresa should whisper a loving word or two in Spanish as you are falling asleep, or Saint Francis and his sparrows should turn up in a dream – do not dwell upon the experience or become elated. You will only lose the benefit.

. . . long-suffering . . .

A better contemporary translation for this word "long-suffering" would be "enduring." Those who are spiritually aware have an almost endless capacity to endure hardship, mostly because all their attention is given over to the hardships of others. They scarcely notice their own pain and suffering because they are doing everything they can to relieve the suffering of others.

My grandmother demonstrated this marvelous capacity throughout her life. There was one occasion when a painful growth had developed on her back – a carbuncle, I think – and my mother called in a surgeon to remove it. The physician wanted to give Granny an anesthetic, but she insisted it wasn't necessary. She lay down and he performed the surgery, but he was terribly distressed to see that tears were running down her cheeks. "I told you it would hurt!" he said. "Why didn't you take the anesthetic?" Granny just shook her head. "I'm not crying because of the pain," she said in a low voice. "I'm crying because my daughter is crying." My aunts still tell this story because it captures Granny's stature and her sweetness, as well as the tender bond between her and my mother.

. . . *manly* . . .

I would add, of course, "womanly." I come from a matriarchal society, one of the rarest societies in the world, where men and women are called upon not to compete with each other but to complete each other. Most of the men in my family really look upon our women as better guides to life than we men are. My spiritual teacher was my grandmother, and my mother was her teaching aide. I used to consult with girl cousins who were no older than I, because I respected the quiet wisdom they could bring to any question I might have.

The Hindu tradition has passed down a magnificent figure for worship which conveys the cherished ideal of completion between man and woman. God is represented in this figure as half masculine and half feminine – on one side the soft curves and draped sari of a woman, on the other the supple strength and chiseled features of a man. This is to remind us that in every man or woman who has discovered the divinity within, the best of what is feminine and the best of what is masculine come together. Great figures like Francis of

Assisi, Mahatma Gandhi, and Teresa of Avila appeal deeply to men and women alike.

> . . . *never seeking itself. For in whatever instance one seeketh oneself, there he falleth from love.*

Nobody who is trying to get purely personal satisfaction out of a relationship is in love. Thomas a Kempis puts it even more strongly by saying that that person "falleth from love": he gets hurt, and he hurts others too. In a sense, this is the central paradox of life: the more we seek our own pleasure, our own way, the more unhappy we become. Again, Meister Eckhart said it magnificently: "Where creature stops, there God begins. All God wants of you is for you to go out of yourself in respect of your creatureliness and let God be God in you."

To borrow the language of contemporary science, the man or woman who has no self-will is a kind of superconductor. It's a powerful metaphor, because in superconductivity electricity encounters virtually no resistance. Scientists and technologists tell us that superconductivity can allow for unheard-of techno-logical progress — for example, levitating trains — achieved with small machines, little pollution, and noninvasive technology. Similarly, when a person has no self-will, he or she is always aware of the unity of life. Whomever he meets he will meet at a deep level. No barrier can come in her way. That's why such a person is able to console others — comfort them, nourish them, and strengthen their relationships.

Love is circumspect, humble . . .

In an interview with Mother Teresa of Calcutta, a reporter said to her, "Humble as you are, it must still be an extraordinary thing to be a vehicle of God's grace in the world." She answered, "But it is his work. I think God wants to show his greatness by using our nothingness. I am like a little pencil in his hand. That is all." Mahatma Gandhi always claimed to be no more than an ordinary man – and he was ordinary, until he followed the call coming from within. Then he became, after many years of transformation, a powerful force for good in the world.

In my own life, grace came through both my mother and my grandmother. My grandmother was like a tree of which my mother was the flower, and to the extent my own life has borne fruit, all the credit goes to them. In a sense, I have done nothing but live out what began with them.

As your meditation deepens, you will come to see in how many beautiful ways others have shaped your life and set your feet on the path. It's the mark of the self-realized man or woman that like Mother Teresa, they will refuse to be congratulated on anything they have accomplished.

. . . and upright, not yielding to softness . . .

Saint Francis was described as almost fragile in appearance, delicate as a reed. Gandhi weighed only a hundred pounds at the time of his death. And my grandmother was probably smaller than either of them. Yet when they took a stand, no one on earth could move them. The combination of tenderness and toughness made them irresistible. To be tender without toughness is sentimentality. To be tough but not tender is cruelty. But in a great spiritual figure, the two qualities are perfectly balanced. To be gentle you first have to be secure.

. . . or to levity, nor attending to vain things.

It's always remarkable to me to observe in restaurants the gravity with which people study the menu: the thoughtful frown on the forehead as the choices are made, the close consultation with a friend who has eaten there before. And often, if there is a slight discrepancy between the dream as it is offered and the reality on the plate, the waiter is told to go back and restore our faith.

It is the same in the department store: the utter absorption with which people exercise their sacred right to choose – between stripes and plaids, synthetic fibers and natural ones, double-breasted and classic . . .

These are all "vain things," in the vocabulary of Thomas a Kempis, not worthy of our serious attention; and in giving ourselves over to them, we weaken our capacity to love. That is why Jesus says, "Lay not up for yourselves treasures upon earth, where moth and rust doth corrupt and where thieves break through and steal." Don't chase after things that come and go; settle only for what abides. Why store things that get rusty almost overnight? Why try to possess things which might be stolen tomorrow? Instead, why not have things that increase with the passage of time? "Lay up for yourselves treasures in heaven."

We're all susceptible to those advertisements that enjoin, "Watch your money grow." But the mystics remind us that while money may grow, the satisfaction we get from it shrinks. Mother Teresa of Calcutta said in an interview that from her observations of life, the more money people have, the poorer and more insecure they become. That is because our real wealth is not money but desire. Once we come to realize this, we understand the importance of investing our desire-capital well. One of my responsibilities as a spiritual teacher is to play the part of a wise stockbroker. When I see someone investing heavily in short-term pleasures, I say, "Sell out now!" Don't hold on to worthless certificates in the hope that they'll go up in value. Build yourself a solid portfolio, full of high-yielding investments. Buy all the shares you can in selfless living.

It is sober, chaste, steady, quiet . . .

So much of what passes for joy in today's world is really only excitement – and once you have begun to experience even for a moment what it is to have a still mind, you will understand that excitement is a form of pain. That is why the exultant grin of the lottery winner can so easily be taken for a grimace.

The wellsprings of joy and fulfillment are within, and they can only be discovered by the man or woman who has gone beyond pleasure as well as pain. It takes many years to achieve this, because the entire nervous system must be reconditioned. It has to be strengthened to withstand the tremendous impact of the flood of love and joy that will one day surge up from within.

There is no contradiction between a sober, quiet exterior and an interior that is full of light and love. It is a terrible misunderstanding to think mystics are killjoys or wet blankets. Mystics are *give*joys; they are *warm* blankets. When life is cold, they will wrap you in warmth. When you feel desolate or abandoned, they will remind you that you are the beloved child of God.

. . . and guarded in all the senses.

You can train your senses through meditation so effectively that when the tavern or the casino is pulling them in, you can just say "Withdraw!" and they will obey you.

Analogies from the automotive world come so naturally in modern life that I have hit upon one to explain the value of this precious skill. When you leave your car somewhere, you turn off the engine, lock it, and take the key with you. Otherwise, anybody can climb in and drive your new Volvo away. Similarly, when the desire for a double martini comes and tries to get in the driver's seat, you say, "The key is in my pocket. And that's where it's going to stay!" It's absurd to think that by acquiring this control over our senses, we are losing the joy of life. Rather, we are gaining security and joy.

Love is subject . . .

None of us is unemployed. All of us are born to be servants of God. We are all born on earth to make life a little better than we found it. And until we understand this and begin to carry out our job, a feeling of frustration will always haunt us. In whatever capacity – teacher, carpenter, doctor, engineer, gardener, computer programmer – we become fulfilled when we use our talent, our training, our time and energy, for the benefit of all, without questioning what we'll get in return.

. . . and obedient to its superiors . . .

Thomas a Kempis was writing in a monastic context to people who had taken the threefold vow of poverty, chastity, and obedience. Most of us are not members of monastic communities, but we are engaged in essentially the same effort to eradicate self-will as Thomas's fellow monks. For this reason I would like to offer a set not of vows but of watchwords for twentieth-century aspirants.

First, where poverty is concerned, I like to recall a verse in Sanskrit composed by Bhartrihari, a poet who, according to tradition, was a king who renounced his kingdom to take up the spiritual life. He said, "You are rich, and your clothes are of silk; I live in a cottage and wear simple clothes. Yet I am content with what I have; these disparities are deceiving. Poverty is when one's desire for things is never satisfied. When the mind is at peace, who is the poor man and who the rich?"

Spiritual poverty, in other words, is a state of mind rather than the state of your bank balance. That is why instead of telling my friends to embrace lives of poverty, I suggest simplicity. There is a beautiful art to consciously reducing your needs in accordance with the limitations of our small planet. "Live simply," says the trenchant slogan I see on some bumpers now, "so that others may simply live."

Second, chastity. In all the monastic traditions of the world, the vow of chastity is a time-honored approach to mastering sexual drives. For those who choose to live in a lasting, loving relationship, I suggest an alternative that can be much more challenging and much more fulfilling: to live in unswerving loyalty to your partner. The conditioning of life today makes this exceedingly difficult, but the rewards are enormous.

The third traditional monastic vow, which Thomas a Kempis refers to here, is obedience – and here I like to set forth the ideal of unity, putting the needs of the whole before our own personal satisfaction. When it comes to our own needs we must always be ready to bend: to compromise at the periphery while standing firm at the center.

The self-willed person is rigid, like someone with only one bone. Give him a push and he falls and breaks into a dozen pieces. The Lord has given us all these bones for a reason: we can bend in every direction, and

that is our glory. It is our capacity to bend when necessary to accommodate others, knowing we will not
break, that gives us security.

During the rainy season in northern India, the
Ganges River rises from the Himalayas and pours
down the mountains in torrents, uprooting huge trees
as if they were matchsticks. Our scriptures say that one
day a sage saw this terrific sight and asked, "Mother
Ganga, how is it that you uproot these mighty trees but
leave the rushes and grasses to flourish?" She replied,
"Big trees cannot bend, so I have to uproot them. The
rushes and grasses bend and let me pass."

Those who are strong enough to bend their will
gracefully to benefit others, to lower themselves effortlessly to serve others, have little to fear from the
fierce currents and turmoil of life. They will be tested,
true, but they will survive and flourish.

. . . to itself mean and despised . . .

We needn't let Thomas's medieval language
alarm us here. He is saying only what Gandhi said: "I
am the most ambitious man in the world: I want to
make myself zero."

*. . . unto God devout and thankful: trusting and hoping
always in him, even then when God imparteth no relish
of sweetness unto it.*

Every one of us at times cries out, "Oh, the
Lord hasn't come! I've been at this five months, ten

months, three years, and he still isn't here! What's the matter?"

At times like this every great mystic will counsel patience. And if we are sincere, we do try to be patient – at least with a kind of impatient patience.

I think it is for our safety that the Lord doesn't come in a helicopter. He comes in a bullock cart, trundling along the back roads, because he knows that to a certain extent we have to suffer and reflect and learn.

Once you've learned to take a long view of spiritual development, you begin to see certain patterns and trust them. Progress in meditation doesn't follow a straight line. It comes in fits and starts, and typically a leap forward is preceded by a period of doubt – not so much of the path itself as of your own capacity to stick it out. This kind of uncertainty can bring enormous suffering, because you know now that nothing else on earth can satisfy you.

For without sorrow none liveth in love.

God is love, but God can also be a tyrant – for our good. When we go after things that can only bring insecurity and ugliness, it is out of his great love that the Lord may hit us hard. On occasion he is forced to take up what G. K. Chesterton called the "holy hammer." It goes against his nature for the Lord to hurt us, but often there is no other way he can draw our attention. If he tries to tap us on the shoulder, we pay no heed. If he says from within, "Hey, you!" we plug our

ears in a frenzy of activity. But one good, hard blow —
and we listen!

For the good student, a gentle rap on the knuckles
can be enough. But most of us just go on taking the
blows until someone close to us has to whisper, "I say,
you aren't doing so well. You're always hostile and agitated, and your knuckles are all scraped and swollen!"
We might try to say, "Oh, I was born like this. I can take
it." But inside, we know the pain is mounting. In traditional language, the Lord within is trying to tell us that
we've been making wrong choices. But it is just as accurate to use more modern language: wrong choices
bring painful consequences. "If you think or act with a
selfish thought," the Buddha says, "suffering will follow you, as the wheel of a bullock cart follows the foot
of the bullock."

Training the mind to avoid repeating wrong choices
is rather like giving the body a vaccine. The reason you
don't get chicken pox more than once, scientists tell
us, is that the body has a kind of biochemical memory.
After one attack of a virus, the immune system becomes educated: the next time it sees that enemy cell, it
releases its own killer cells to swallow it up. It is because
of this precious capacity of the body that vaccines are
effective. One small lesson – a very light case of the disease – and no second lesson is needed; the immune
system is ready. In the same way, we should be able to
learn from a light run-in with jealousy or resentment
not to contract the disease again.

Viruses, of course, are particularly cunning crea-tures. They can put on all kinds of fancy clothes. We get flu over and over because the immune system doesn't recognize the many viruses to be the same old flu: a false nose, a wig, a changed walk, and the immune system is deceived. Similarly, many of the mistakes we make are subtle; they overtake us before we see them coming, and every time they come they look a little different. But here, too, we are given some margin for learning. In time we should be able to see through all the disguises and recognize self-will and selfishness for what they really are. Then we remember the harm they do us. In this sense, meditation is like a long pro-cess of immunization. You close your eyes, make a fist, find the vein in your mind, and in goes the vaccine: "Where there is hatred, let me sow love; where there is injury, pardon . . ."

To put it very simply, the purpose of the pain we undergo in life is to help us go beyond pain.

> *He that is not prepared to suffer all things, and to stand to the will of his Beloved, is not worthy to be called a lover of God.*

More than twenty-five years ago I was invited to the Spiritual Life Institute in Sedona, Arizona, to give a series of talks, and while Christine and I were there we were taken to a beautiful chapel on a hillside. Cactus flowers were in bloom all around, and the deep red of the rocks and sand stood out magnificently against the strong blue of the desert sky. We walked in the front door and found ourselves standing before a life-sized crucifix carved by a sculptor who had wanted us to receive the agony of the Passion in full measure. I wasn't prepared for it, so the suffering went straight in. When I saw the elongated body with outstretched arms, the hollow eyes and the lips parted in pain, it was as if Christ himself were pleading to us, "Why don't you take me off the cross?"

Wherever we see anyone suffering, Christ is telling us, "That is me you see – your Beloved." Jesus on the cross says, "Help me!" when he sees how much suffering we have caused all over the world, by striking out against one another and conniving at exploitation.

Many of the great Christian mystics heard this cry from their Lord and found themselves rushing to his aid. Catherine of Genoa felt herself almost thrown headlong out of her privileged existence as a Genoese aristocrat into the slums of the city, where she nursed the victims of plague, syphilis, and poverty for nearly thirty years. Catherine of Siena spent most of her much shorter life struggling to heal the wounds of an entire country that was torn by war, corruption, and schism. And today, Mother Teresa of Calcutta lives out her love for Christ in tender service to suffering humanity all over the world. The same interview I mentioned earlier included this exchange:

"What did you do this morning?"

"We prayed."

"When?"

"At half past four."

"And after prayer?"

"We continue to pray through our work by doing it with Jesus, for Jesus, and to Jesus. That helps us put our whole heart and soul into doing it. Serving Jesus in the dying, the crippled, the mentally ill, the unwanted, the unloved – they are Jesus in disguise."

When love reaches its highest pitch, it is eager to embrace any amount of suffering for the sake of the beloved, and it feels that suffering as joy. In the furthest reaches of prayer, the human being enters a mysterious world where by a strange kind of alchemy, two distinctions are dissolved. One is the distinction between joy and sorrow; the other is the distinction between oneself and the rest of life. This is the supreme mystery enshrined by all the world's religions. It is the mystery Saint John of the Cross was trying to convey when he spoke of "the wound that burns to heal." Meister Eckhart says it most plainly: "He who suffers for love does not suffer, for all suffering is forgot."

> *A lover ought to embrace willingly all that is hard and distasteful for the sake of his Beloved, and not to turn away from him for any contrary accidents.*

No one has etched this great truth into human consciousness more indelibly than Francis of Assisi. The chroniclers describe how one day, late in his life, Francis went to visit a mountain – his mountain, in fact, because a devoted follower had actually deeded it to Francis for his Order to use. The mountain was called La Verna, and legend claimed that the deep crevasses running down its sides had opened up in a great earthquake on the day Christ was crucified. Francis knew he was near his death and wanted to draw as close as he could to the Master he had served so passionately. So that he could be completely alone, he established himself on a rocky ledge of the mountain which could be reached only by crossing a single log. He gave his companion, Brother Leo, permission to bring him water and recite matins once a day, but otherwise he remained alone. More than a month passed while he prayed and waited. At last he entered a state of deep contemplation and asked the Lord for two graces before he should die. The first was that he feel in his body and soul the suffering Christ had undergone at Golgotha. The second was that he feel in his heart the exceeding love for all that had brought Christ there to be crucified.

Francis remained a long time in prayer. Then, the chroniclers say, "Through love and through compassion he was wholly changed into Jesus." At one and the same instant, he felt exceeding great joy and unspeakable grief. The suffering he felt was so great that it invaded his body, and blood began to flow out of his palms and feet and side as it had from the wounds of Jesus in the Passion. Francis concealed these wounds as best he could, but his followers observed them – saw that he could no longer place the soles of his feet on the ground, and that his garments were perpetually bloodstained. He carried with him, too, the marks of Jesus in his heart: "a burning flame of divine love."

To love, Saint Francis teaches, is to feel pain. When you have attained full awareness of God, you have the joy of being able to relieve pain, but the pain itself you cannot escape. That is why Jesus is called the Man of Sorrows. Gandhi, too, was a man of sorrow, and that is why he was a man of joy. He was a man in pain; that is why he was a man in love. To be a lover is to be a martyr. If you are a lover of all life, you feel a dagger in your heart wherever people are treated cruelly, wherever any living creature is in pain. You suffer the pain, but your suffering releases endless energy that flows forth in creative action. Saint Francis's love still floods the world, and Gandhi's love still pours into it like the Ganges itself.

Martin Luther King Jr., said, "If you have not found the cause for which you are willing to lay down your life, you have not yet begun to live." Words like these strike us with terror, because we believe if we do find such a cause, then the Lord could well say tomorrow morning, "Okay, put your head on the block." But in fact, it is often when we are prepared to give up our life for the sake of the Lord that he wants us to live long, because then we are able to serve him.

When spiritual teachers talk about meditation, they often speak of putting an end to sorrow. It is easy to misunderstand this. "Don't you feel any grief, then?" I am sometimes asked. And of course I do. It is not that I do not feel pain; but the pain that is in my heart today comes of seeing the pain of others. All my capacity for sorrow, which I used to waste on myself, has been turned into compassion. And the joy that comes of being able to relieve pain never goes away. In the deepest stages of meditation, when I became aware that everybody's suffering is mine and that I had developed a capacity to help, I began to find an unlimited joy.

As a child I had always been sensitive to suffering, but whenever I asked myself what I could do to relieve suffering around me, the answer had always been, "Nothing. You're too small." But my capacity to feel suffering grew with deepening meditation, little by little. And my desire to relieve suffering kept deepening with my capacity to feel it. Today I know that once a person becomes one with the Lord, he or she feels the suffering of all. Yet there is a simultaneity of suffering and joy, far beyond the duality of pleasure and pain. Now I am prepared to face any amount of pain, because the Lord has granted me the immense desire to relieve the suffering of others.

When we change our way of seeing – when, after years of spiritual striving, we begin to see with the eyes of love – we will live in a different world. If we give others deep respect and trust, and bear all suffering with patience and internal toughness, we will find ourselves in a compassionate universe. The eyes of love see the core of goodness in the hearts of others, and that is how I see the world today. It is not that I fail to see suffering and sorrow. But I understand the laws of life and see its unity everywhere. All I ask is that I may ever see this vision, and ever serve the Lord of Love in every living creature.

THOMAS A KEMPIS

The Wonderful Effect of Divine Love

1

Ah, Lord God, thou holy lover of my soul, when thou comest into my heart, all that is within me shall rejoice.

Thou art my glory and the exultation of my heart: thou art my hope and refuge in the day of my trouble.

2

But because I am as yet weak in love, and imperfect in virtue, I have need to be strengthened and comforted by thee; visit me therefore often, and instruct me with all holy discipline.

Set me free from evil passions, and heal my heart of all inordinate affections; that being inwardly cured and thoroughly cleansed, I may be made fit to love, courageous to suffer, steady to persevere.

3

Love is a great thing, yea, a great and thorough good; by itself it makes every thing that is heavy, light; and it bears evenly all that is uneven.

For it carries a burden which is no burden, and makes every thing that is bitter, sweet and tasteful.

The noble love of Jesus impels one to do great things, and stirs one up to be always longing for what is more perfect.

Love desires to be aloft, and will not be kept back by any thing low and mean.

Love desires to be free, and estranged from all worldly affections, that so its inward sight may not be hindered; that it may not be entangled by any temporal prosperity, or by any adversity subdued.

Nothing is sweeter than love, nothing more courageous, nothing higher, nothing wider, nothing more pleasant, nothing fuller nor better in heaven and earth; because love is born of God, and cannot rest but in God, above all created things.

4

He that loveth, flyeth, runneth, and rejoiceth; he is free, and cannot be held in.

He giveth all for all, and hath all in all; because he resteth in One highest above all things, from whom all that is good flows and proceeds.

He respecteth not the gifts, but turneth himself above all goods unto the Giver.

Love oftentimes knoweth no measure, but is fervent beyond all measure.

Love feels no burden, thinks nothing of trouble, attempts what is above its strength, pleads no excuse of impossibility; for it thinks all things lawful for itself and all things possible.

It is therefore able to undertake all things, and it completes many things, and warrants them to take effect,
where he who does not love, would faint and lie down.

5

Love is watchful, and sleeping slumbereth not.

Though weary, it is not tired; though pressed, it is not
straitened; though alarmed, it is not confounded; but as
a lively flame and burning torch, it forces its way
upwards, and securely passes through all.

If any one love, he knoweth what is the cry of this voice.

For it is a loud cry in the ears of God, the mere ardent
affection of the soul, when it saith, "My God, my love,
thou art all mine, and I am all thine."

6

Enlarge thou me in love, that with the inward palate of
my heart I may taste how sweet it is to love, and to be
dissolved, and as it were to bathe myself in thy love.

Let me be possessed by love, mounting above myself, through excessive fervor and admiration.

Let me sing the song of love, let me follow thee, my Beloved, on high; let my soul spend itself in thy praise, rejoicing through love.

Let me love thee more than myself, nor love myself but for thee: and in thee all that truly love thee, as the law of love commandeth, shining out from thyself.

7

Love is active, sincere, affectionate, pleasant and amiable; courageous, patient, faithful, prudent, long-suffering, manly, and never seeking itself.

For in whatever instance one seeketh oneself, there he falleth from love.

Love is circumspect, humble, and upright; not yielding to softness, or to levity, nor attending to vain things; it is sober, chaste, steady, quiet, and guarded in all the senses.

Love is subject, and obedient to its superiors, to itself mean and despised, unto God devout and thankful, trusting and hoping always in him, even then when God imparteth no relish of sweetness unto it: for without sorrow, none liveth in love.

8

He that is not prepared to suffer all things, and to stand to the will of his Beloved, is not worthy to be called a lover of God.

A lover ought to embrace willingly all that is hard and distasteful, for the sake of his Beloved; and not to turn away from him for any contrary accidents.

Afterword by Carol Lee Flinders

Like a vast river with a wide and fertile flood plain, *The Imitation of Christ* has touched and nourished more lives, but for the Bible itself, than any book in the Western world. Written in the context of Catholic monasticism, its depth and power are nonetheless felt universally. Saint Thérèse of Lisieux memorized it in its entirety, and Saint Ignatius of Loyola commended it for daily study. The New England Quaker and reformer John Woolman seems to have read it with deep appreciation. "In reading his writings I have believed him to be a man of true Christian spirit." (That may sound like faint praise, but for a Quaker of Woolman's time to praise a Roman Catholic in any fashion took some doing!) *The Imitation of Christ* was the book Dag Hammarsköld carried with him on the flight that ended in his death. Dame Edith Cavell read it nightly, and it was cherished by the martyred Protestant minister Dietrich Bonhoeffer. In the Coptic monasteries of Egypt today, it is a treasured spiritual manual. The book has found its way into fiction, too: Dame Agatha Christie's Miss Marple reads a chapter each night, and at the critical moment when George Eliot's heroine Maggie Tulliver has nowhere left to turn, it is the *Imitation of Christ* that bears her up.

So beguiling are the bends and twists of this great river, and the charm of the towns it passes through, that we forget to look for the tiny wellspring in the high country where it starts. Indeed, the location of that wellspring is a vexed issue. Some remarkably vitriolic essays have been written on the probable authorship of this spiritual classic! Part of the difficulty is that the book is more a distillation than an original production. On every page one finds quotations or paraphrases from scripture, from the church fathers, and from writings of the first members of the Brothers of the Common Life. We have no manuscript copy, moreover, on which anybody has actually claimed authorship.

There is little to go on, and as Easwaran reminds us in his introduction, Thomas himself asked that we "search not who spoke this or that, but mark what is spoken." Still, for many of us authorship is a compelling matter. When we love a book, we want to know about the life behind it. Is it of a piece with the book? Besides, it isn't just the cumulative wisdom of all those citations that makes the *Imitation* a perennial favorite; it is that voice—so warm and compassionate, despite the gravity of the teachings; so tender and yet, here and there, just a little wry.

Fortunately for those of us who care, the scholarly world has reached accord on the question of authorship. Names like Jean Gerson and Saint Bernard of Clairvaux are no longer proposed with any seriousness. Thomas a Kempis is the recognized author, so long as we understand that the whole notion of authorship didn't mean in his time what it does today—particularly where spiritual writings were concerned. When a man or woman was able to inspire others, by spoken as well as by written word, it wasn't thought to be through any special gift of their own. The Holy Spirit was working through them. The interesting question is, then, what is it about such a human being that allows the Holy Spirit to work through him or her?

Typically, to find the answer to this question, we do best to stay clear of the more tumultuous population centers of times past, looking instead to quieter places: backwater towns, lively with the warmth of longstanding relationships, slow paced and simple: places like Ruysbroeck, the village where Jan of Ruysbroeck was born; Norwich, the English cathedral town where Julian lived and wrote; and Deventer, another cathedral town, this one set in the Yssel Valley of what is now the Netherlands . . .

✑

Thomas Hamerken was thirteen, maybe only twelve years old – for the chronicles don't jibe – when he traveled a hundred miles or so from a tiny village outside Cologne to the prosperous, busy town of Deventer. The year was 1392. His father's name meant "he with a little hammer"; he was probably a carpenter. Kempen was the name of the village from which he came, and it was the village, not the father, who would be remembered for having given Thomas to the world.

Handsome brick buildings lined the busy streets of Deventer, streets that were laid out around the stone cathedral of Saint Lebwen, built six hundred years before to honor the Anglo-Saxon missionary who had first brought the word of Christ to this part of Europe. Deventer was considerably quieter than nearby Rotterdam, but culturally it was much more active: the recorded demand for books during the fifteenth century is astonishing. Everything Thomas saw when he arrived there was new to him, but not unknown, because his older brother John had told him all about it – had told him, too, about the cathedral school he would be attending, and, most glowingly of all, about the Brothers of the Common Life, who were doing so much to smooth the way for young scholars. John had been through the Deventer schools himself, drawn like other boys from throughout the Rhineland by the school's excellent reputation. In time he had been drawn still more irresistibly by the sanctity and fellowship of the Brotherhood itself. From the dormitories maintained by the Brothers for boys like himself, it had been an easy step into the Augustinian monastery at nearby Windesheim, established just eight years before by the founder of the Brothers of the Common Life, Geert Groote.

Both the Hamerken sons had taken their earliest lessons from their mother, who ran a small school in her home. But village schools equipped a child only to read and write. The "chapter schools," also called "Latin schools," were located in larger towns. There boys between nine and fifteen would learn Latin and dialectics in preparation for the Trivium and the Quadrivium of one of the great universities. Even if he were only twelve, then, Thomas was far from being the youngest scholar to be making his own way in the world.

The schools were generally run by the town governments, but there was no general system for boarding the students. A popular sentiment did prevail – "A bed, a beer, and a stew for the love of God" – and most of the pious people of Deventer complied; but boys need more than one meal a day, so many ended up begging. Their scholarly performance under those circumstances couldn't have been first rate.

All this has to be put in perspective, of course. Historian Barbara Tuchman points out that most little boys of the period were packed off in one direction or another by their seventh year: the nobleman's son to a friend's castle, to learn the fine arts of thrashing and bashing; the peasant's son to someone else's shop or farm to be apprenticed. "If children survived till age seven," she explains, "their recognized life began, more or less as miniature adults."

Still, no matter how impassively the world may have regarded all those children, children they still were. "When I was a child," Saint Paul reminds us, "I spake as a child, I understood as a child," and it seems fair to impute to that young boy in a strange town feelings of confusion and apprehension – particularly when we find out he hadn't a penny to his name.

Thomas a Kempis was one of life's lucky ones, though, and he never stopped being grateful for it. For on his way into Deventer, he had dropped in at the monastery at Windesheim to see his older brother, and John had told him to go see the vicar, Florent Radewijns, as soon as he got into town.

Foremost among the Brothers now that Groote himself was gone – in fact, Groote's chosen successor and the only one of his associates whom he had asked to take holy orders – Radewijns was a man of great spiritual stature. Unhesitatingly, he took the boy into his vicarage and lodged him there until he found suitable quarters with "a devout matron." Seeing that the boy had no money, he provided books and paid his tuition.

Increasingly, the Brothers had made the protection

and nurturing of these young boys their special apostolate: finding homes with good families, making sure
they could afford books, and finally even setting up
well-supervised dormitories where the boys got not just
a beer, a bed, and a stew, but help with their homework
and spiritual guidance as well. Did they need income?
The Brothers instructed them in the valued art of
manuscript copying, and found them work, too. Florent Radewijns appears to have been the moving force
behind this concern and the work it fueled.

Years later, Thomas a Kempis would write a biography of Radewijns to inspire his own novices to greater
spiritual efforts, and his deeply felt gratitude infuses the
work. "Master John Boheme," he tells us,

> who was Retor of the scholars, was a friend to
> Florentius [Radewijns]. And when the time to pay
> the fees was come, each scholar brought what was
> justly due, and I also put my fee into his hand. . . . He,
> having some knowledge of me and aware that I was
> under the care of Florentius, said, "Who gave thee
> this money?" And I answered, "My lord Florentius."
> "Then go," said he, "take back his money, since for
> love of him I will take nothing from thee." So I took
> back the money again . . . and said, "The Master hath
> given back my fee for love of thee." And Florentius
> said, "I thank him and will repay him, after another
> fashion with gifts more excellent than money."

In the years to come, Thomas would have considerable contact with Radewijns. He carried messages for
the revered man and often attended to his simple needs
at mealtimes. He describes his mentor in choir:

He did not gaze about with wandering eyes, but stood very quietly turning towards the altar with all restraint and reverence. . . . And as often as I saw my Master Florentius standing there, I was careful not to chatter. . . . Once on a time it happened when I was standing near him in the choir that he turned to share our book for the chanting, and he, standing behind me, put his hands upon my shoulder – but I stood still, hardly daring to move, bewildered with gratification at so great an honor."

What a sweet-natured, entirely devout soul Thomas a Kempis appears to have been: "simple" in the most exalted sense of the word; seamless, absolutely undivided. His life is virtually without event. From the dormitories of the Brothers, just like his brother John, he would move into the monastery at Mount Saint Agnes, and there live for virtually all his ninety-one years (ninety-one in those days!). He was an exceptional copyist and the composer of a great many spiritual works besides the *Imitation of Christ*. He held the office of subprior, which made him master of the novices, for years on end. A brief stint as provisioner proved, apparently, calamitous, and it's amusing how much satisfaction his biographers have taken from that. A fellow monastic leaves us this description: "As he meditated, the tips of his toes alone touched the floor, the rest of his body . . . lifted heavenwards, whither his soul tended with all its desires."

One yearns for a more telling, more personal glimpse of Thomas a Kempis, but his official biography is disappointingly vague. The only real insights we have into his personality emerge out of reading the biographies he wrote of other members of his spiritual circle. These portraits were gathered into a volume called *The Founders of the New Devotion.* Insofar as he'll ever be, the "real" Thomas is here. Not that you get any direct information about his own life — he was a monk, after all, and in a sense monks have no personal life. Still, he is a writer, and it's often the small things a writer or a photographer or painter focuses upon that tell you who he or she really is. So beautifully do these other lives shine through that you come away feeling that Thomas's greatest gift is to be a perfect medium, clear and pure.

Thomas offers many proofs, for instance, of Florent Radewijns' sanctity. None, though, is sweeter than this:

> So too, in the month of May, the season when the wild herbs that are used as medicaments have their highest virtue, the good Father did not forget his poor; knowing that many were weak, ulcerous, and full of sores, he made them to come to his house upon an appointed day and hour to receive certain medicines, and to have their bodies bathed in warm water infused with aromatic herbs. And when they had been thoroughly bathed and washed he made ready for each a most cleanly bed for sudorific treatment. And after receiving a cup of wine, and some words of comfort, they went away with great joy to their own homes. . . .

A delight in the natural world that is almost Franciscan pervades his accounts. He plays with etymologies for Radewijns' name. Florentius, he speculates, could mean *flores colligens,* "the gatherer of flowers," for he had gathered so many clerks and Brothers "in the flower of their age" to serve and love the Lord. He takes an episode from Radewijns' youth, so very slight that you wonder how he even chanced to hear it:

N I L G I R I P R E S S

Post Office Box 256

Tomales, California 94971

Stamp

Nilgiri Press publishes books by Eknath Easwaran on how to lead the spiritual life in the home and the community. Ask your bookstore about them – or fill out this card and return it to us. We will send you a catalog of our books and audio tapes along with a free copy of our newsletter containing a schedule of retreats and workshops. *Thank You.*

_____

Name (Please print or type)

_____

Street

_____

City   State   Zip + 4

_____

Title of the book in which you found this card.

_____

How did you hear about this book?

_____

*Book store where you bought this book.
(Please include city and state.)*

It happened upon a time that he was invited with many others to a marriage, and when they were upon the way together, being most eager to pleasure his friends and to make merry with them, he did as follows for their gratification: cutting down green branches from the trees, he took them and empowered those who sat in the carriage in such wise as greatly to win their favor.

Thomas goes on to allegorize — this was the high Middle Ages, after all — but what we retain is the image itself, of the young man so eager to please his friends, slashing away at the hedgerows, clambering over the carriage to pile up the greenery, teasing the laughing couple as they disappear inside a leafy canopy . . . doing exactly what the moment called for, for such is always the genius of deeply spiritual individuals.

&

Of the author of *The Imitation of Christ,* then, we still have only the faintest sketch. But as I've suggested, the *Imitation* is not so much the work of a single man as it is of an entire spiritual movement, and of that movement we can pull together quite a clear picture.

As you turn the pages of *Founders,* you get a feeling not only for the individuals themselves but also for the extraordinary atmosphere Thomas Hamerken had walked into there in Deventer. "Pear seeds grow into pear trees," said Meister Eckhart, "and God-seeds into God-trees." Thomas a Kempis was a God-seed, without question. But for his life to have unfolded as perfectly and fragrantly as it did, the soil had to be perfectly prepared, too.

～

Historian Barbara Tuchman has asked us to see in fourteenth-century Europe a mirror of our own times. Her best-selling book *A Distant Mirror* is subtitled *The Calamitous Fourteenth Century*. The catalog of woes is stunning: war, plague, schism, oppressive taxation, bad government, insurrection, brigandage. Even the weather seemed to be pitted against humankind, for climatic shifts that began in the early part of the century made for lower temperatures, heavy rains, and a shortened growing season. In the wake of all this, famine spread, weakening the population so that it would be all the more susceptible to the plague.

One can set forth the essentials of Thomas a Kempis's life with almost no reference to any of these events. As a cloistered monk, his daily life was spent entirely with individuals who, like himself, had turned away from the world and put all their attention to their own reconstruction. By temperament he was reclusive, never so happy as when, in his own words, he had "a little book in a little nook." What he wrote and did could have been written and done in almost any century.

But just one generation earlier, the founder of Thomas's spiritual community was living a radically different kind of life, one much more in the roiling, passionate, and anguished tradition of Saint Augustine. Geert Groote, founder of the Brothers and Sisters of the Common Life, was an enormously appealing, highly idiosyncratic figure of tremendous energy and talent—a man who did nothing, ever, by half measures. Geert Groote was a man absolutely of his own times. In contrast to Thomas's life, Groote's was shaped by events and forces that were quite without precedent.

First, and most spectacular, was the Black Death, which swept through Europe in wave after terrible wave throughout the second half of the fourteenth century, reducing the population by a third within the first three years, and ultimately by half. Groote's own parents died in the first assault, and he himself would succumb to one of the later epidemics. The terrible swiftness of the disease (typically one died within three to five days of contracting it), its ugliness, and the inconceivable suffering it brought — the horror of lifeless bodies that amassed too rapidly to be buried, the decimation of entire towns and the emptying of whole monasteries — seems to have benumbed the minds of those who witnessed it. Barbara Tuchman points out that chroniclers say astonishingly little about the plague, and speculates that it simply overwhelmed them. Some things, perhaps, just cannot be assimilated.

Second, the church itself was in a state of profound disarray. The Great Schism did not officially begin until 1378 (ending in 1417), but it had been a long time developing. The years of the dual papacy, and the preceding period as well, were profoundly demoralizing to the entire Christian world. The division cut across countries and cities, then villages, and ultimately families.

Overlaid across all of this, and continuing through five generations, there was the Hundred Years' War, begun in 1339. Fought, technically, between France and Britain, it drained and savaged most of northern Europe before it ended in 1453.

Geert Groote was born in the year 1340. He was just seven the year ships from the Black Sea port of Caffa docked in Messina, Sicily, carrying a deadly cargo from the East. By the next year, 1348, the bubonic plague was advancing northward across Europe, and the town of Deventer was bracing itself in the few small ways it could. The hospital was enlarged, the public cleansing department was set to work, and some simple disinfectants, like white vinegar, were stored in the city hall.

Not that anyone put much store by these measures. This was the Black Death, an implacable and terrible judgment against humanity. Better to ready your soul than the hospital. The plague struck Deventer in 1350, and by the end of summer both Geert's parents were gone. Under relatives' guardianship, Geert resumed his schooling when the town returned to relative normalcy. He studied at the same chapter school Thomas a Kempis would attend forty years later. At fifteen he went off to Paris for further studies. He would have been accompanied, one can be sure, by a trusty manservant, for Geert lived most certainly at the privileged end of the social scale. His inheritance was ample, and he spent freely — entertaining his friends and wearing the showiest, most elegant clothing to be had.

Groote was an unusually able student. Normally the Master of Arts degree would have required seven years of residence and the age of twenty. Groote took his at just eighteen, with only three years in residence. This degree equipped him to teach everywhere, and allowed him to continue his own formal education in medicine, law, or theology. Indeed, he continued in all three! For the next ten years he was truly a professional student, not only in Paris but in Cologne and Prague as well, teaching part-time while he studied, so avid for learning that no one line of study would content him.

His degrees had endowed him with mastery in the liberal arts. Eventually he would feel most at home in the practice of law, but immediately after receiving his degree he applied himself to the natural sciences, and that entailed some travel through murky waters. The study of the natural world and the study of magic — black and white — were utterly entangled at that time. The physical world was known to be infused and animated by the spirit world: you couldn't imagine trying to manipulate the one, or even understand it, without somehow propitiating the other. Astronomy and astrology were indistinguishable, and so were chemistry and alchemy.

By 1362, Groote was back in Paris, studying law and theology. The ecclesiastical infrastructure was in those days a rough equivalent to today's corporate world: a vast and complex system having as little to do with genuinely spiritual issues as the upper managerial echelons of General Motors do with building automobiles, but offering splendidly remunerative opportunities to adroit young men. Well schooled in canon law and theology, Groote could look forward to entering the service of a cardinal or officiating at one or another great cathedral, and in any case he could and did begin to apply now for "prebends," incomes attached to several different positions.

By his own reckoning and his biographers', the young Groote could be faulted on at least two counts: an urgent desire to be great in the eyes of the world and the arrogance that is almost inevitable in young people who move as swiftly and easily across the hurdles of academia as he did. He had, on the other hand, a gift for friendship. All his biographers remark his personal attractiveness. The friends he made during his student years would stand by him later, and would go to great lengths, when the time came, to assist in his conversion — to claim, in fact, chief responsibility for it.

If Groote sounds like something of a butterfly, the impression is probably wrong. He was just twenty-five years old when his townspeople called a meeting, at his house, to discuss an exceedingly delicate, persistent dispute with the city of Utrecht — a taxation question that needed to be resolved once and for all. Would Groote represent Deventer at the Papal Court in Avignon? They offered him a large sum of money to cover the expenses, but he refused the money and went on his own hook. In two years he succeeded in winning the case. Back to Paris then, surer than ever of a brilliant future as a scholar and clergyman. Two canonries fell into his hands.

Everything was in place now, by the laws that govern a particular kind of life, for a dramatic change in direction. Groote had done what he'd set out to do, seen what he'd wanted to see; and he was increasingly unhappy. Friends issued warnings: "You're frivolous, Geert — look at your clothes!" "This dabbling in sorcery — it's playing the devil's game." Perfect strangers issued oblique warnings. Finally, as in the lives of Saint Francis and Saint Teresa of Avila, a severe illness struck him and brought him close to death.

Groote's recovery coincided with his decision to reverse the direction of his life. There was an enormous amount of undoing to do, and piece by deliberate piece he fell to undoing it. Had he indeed spent a fortune on high fashion? He adopted a simple clerical habit and later would wear only the oldest, most tattered and nondescript clothing. Had he too eagerly sought wealth and office? He would resign all his prebends and finally give away even the use of his own home. Had he drawn others into the practice of astrology? He would actively speak against the dubious arts from now on. Had he – well, never mind, but he would avoid the company of women altogether for the remainder of his life. It was to "unmarried women devoted to God" that he signed over his house, reserving only a few small rooms at the back for himself, sealed off from the rest of the house.

Groote needed time in seclusion to consolidate all these changes, and to think out what the remainder of his life would be. He entered a Carthusian monastery and stayed – as a guest, not a novice – for three years. While there he completed a remarkable document, his *Conclusions and Propositions*. This would be a kind of blueprint for the rest of his life. It would be cherished by the Brothers, and much of it would find its way into the *Imitation.*

From the very first resolution flows all the rest: the service of God and the salvation of his soul were his principal tasks in this world. No temporal good whatsoever would impede him. Groote was not going to live out his years in a monastery. His *Propositions* were designed to allow him to live in the world while not of it. He would attend Mass every day – attentively and reverently. His only line of study now would be spiritual books, and he lists the ones he deems suitable. In food and drink and sleep, he would be abstinent: no meat, and very little wine.

In the fine points he can seem a bit fussy: "Seventh, take but one cooked pear after thy meal, and that not of inordinate size, or three of the very smallest." But the drift is clear: he would make each moment of the day count as he strove to remake himself in Christ's image. The overall tenor is buoyant, large-minded, and very carefully tailored to his own failings: "Likewise after the example of Bernard, utter no word by which thou mayest seem to be very religious, or endowed with knowledge." Practicality pervades: "It is better to do one action well with great deliberation than through lack thereof to be thrown out of one's course. . . . The same habit of deliberation should prevail in writing and speaking and in action also, because it is impossible to seek therein the glory of God if a man so impetuously rush into a matter that his whole strength is occupied in it. Learn then to be slow and restrained in action."

Seeking to establish himself in continual prayer, he would utter short, ejaculatory prayers, as the Desert Fathers had, throughout the day. From "Geert the Great," Thomas à Kempis writes, he had become "Geert the Humble." It's worth emphasizing this, because the very hallmark of the Brothers and Sisters of the Common Life was their utter humility, warmed and balanced by a heartfelt appreciation of one another.

For Groote, the *Propositions* constituted a highly personal "statement of intent," a promise to himself. Though their end result was a life virtually indistinguishable from that of the Carthusian monastery he'd been living in, they were not formal vows, and the distinction was all-important to him. He wasn't opposed to monastic orders on principle, but he was sure that a truly God-centered life could be lived anywhere. He wanted to find and live out the essentials of such a life, quite apart from institutional settings that may or may not facilitate it.

Groote's avowed intention was to lead others to God in two ways: the example of a holy life, and the active work of preaching and writing. The former he would begin immediately, closeted in relative seclusion in the back rooms of his house at Deventer, immersed in prayer and study. Living only barely "in the world," he attended Mass daily, prayed and meditated each morning, and sang the canonical hours, hard at his books the rest of the day. He lived on pea soup most of the time – it could simmer at the back of the stove untended. If he invited friends to supper, he made up for the scanty fare by reading to them from a shelf of spiritual books kept next to the table!

To expand his library, Groote borrowed books and had them copied. He would invite young clerks to his house in the evening, instruct them in the art of copying, and pay them for their work. Soon the evenings were given over more and more to spiritual discourse; out of these meetings would evolve, in time, the Brothers of the Common Life. The basis of that life, as of Groote's own, would be abandonment of earthly goods, adoption of a "common life," chastity of thought and word as well as deed, and annihilation of their own will. "Obedience" was not construed so much as obedience to a superior as rather an openness to one another – a willingness to be corrected and chastised by one another, and inspired. Groote felt these principles should be the basis of life for any follower of Christ, monastic or otherwise. And it was on this, the content of the spiritual life, that he placed all his attention. Of himself and his followers he exacted no vows, insisting instead upon a daily, individual renewal of intention which no merely external routine would supplant.

External conditions would in time force more formal definition of the Brothers and Sisters — their legal defense even — and those same conditions would help compel the formation of monasteries and convents. But Groote moved slowly and reluctantly in that direction. Never did he reject monasticism outright, but seemed rather to be trying to open out another avenue, to bring the spiritual life into the reach of more people than those called to holy orders: it troubled him that the word "religious" generally meant monastics. He sought the irreducible core.

In many ways, one is struck by similarities between Groote and Mahatma Gandhi. Groote's patched grey outer garment, his moth-eaten cap, were as much legend as Gandhi's spotless white loincloth would be. Scolded once by a friend, he tried to explain, "I do this, not because I have nothing better, but in order to conquer myself." His wheelbarrow full of books, jostled over the rough dirt roads of the Yssel Valley, were as much a trademark as the watch that Gandhi pinned to his one garment. Like Gandhi, too, he saw in manual labor a precious aid to spiritual growth. "Labor is a wonderful necessary to mankind in restoring the mind to purity." What spinning was for Gandhi's satyagraha movement, book copying was for the Brothers.

In the larger sense, too, the resemblance holds. The political crisis of Groote's time and place was the Great Schism. But he refused to address it directly, for he saw the schism itself as merely a symptom of much deeper ills — just as Gandhi saw British domination of India to be symptomatic of more far-reaching problems. Both men were trained lawyers, and both had a deep interest in medicine. Medical metaphors came naturally. The disturbance in the highest office of the church, said Groote, was like a severe headache, which indicated that a disease had been going on for a long time and had finally brought the body to the verge of collapse.

"But all of us are acting like inexperienced physicians," he said, "and try to remove the symptoms without taking care of the causes of the illness." For Groote, the causes were in the moral and spiritual inadequacies of the church members and clergy, and the only cure was reform at the level of individual lives: "trickle-up," very much in the Gandhian mode. To this end he would use all his training and rhetorical skills. Nor would he stay in the cities. Like Gandhi, he traveled tirelessly into the smallest villages, and like Gandhi, he was enormously well received. Like Gandhi, too, he grasped the importance of the local and the vernacular – his village preaching was in the local dialect.

His reception was phenomenally enthusiastic, in a time and place when preaching was not generally well received. Often he would speak all morning, then send his congregation home for a meal, meditate while they were gone, and address them again in the afternoon. Central to all his sermons was the theme of the imitation of Christ: in selfless love for one another, and consequent willingness to suffer ourselves to relieve the suffering of others, we conform to our Lord and become one with him. The special target of his entire preaching effort was clerical abuse, a preoccupation which grew directly out of an enormous respect for the office itself. Stung by his criticism, certain of the clergy turned on him and had him silenced, so that after only three years of active preaching he was forbidden to continue. Initially, he was devastated; he wrote of a "schism of his heart," and feelings of terrible uncertainty and indecision. Yearning to address the spiritual needs of his people, he appealed through a friend to Pope Urban VI to be reinstated.

Waiting for his appeal to be considered, he retired to a quiet estate outside of town, where he could spend long, uninterrupted hours in prayer and meditation. Almost immediately he was able to place himself again in the hands of God. Exultant, he poured his renewed trust and faith into a letter, "On Patience": to imitate Christ means to follow him in his passion, suffering if need be all the difficulties and pains inflicted on one by worldly-minded people. Many Christians are willing, he points out, to take up a cross they've made themselves, like penitential exercises, prayers and fasting; but the cross which God has made for them, the one that is really theirs, they throw down in horror.

Serene, then, he waited and busied himself in several ways. He translated parts of the Breviary into Dutch, and devoted himself for the first time to the formation of his disciples. He heard out a request on the part of some of these who wanted a more remote setting better suited for meditation. He gave his assent and selected a site near the town of Zwolle, where in two years the monastery of Mount St. Agnes would open. This would be the home of Thomas à Kempis. Groote's biographers agree that he had several motives for approving the foundation. One was that antagonism from several monastic and mendicant orders was very high. The fact that the Brothers took no vows and lived out in the world was taken as an unspoken rebuke. Establishing a community of a recognized order, the Augustinian canons regular, should allay hostility; but in case it did not, the Brothers would have a place where they could come and be safe.

Groote seemed now to be acting out of a long view of things to come — as though, some of his biographers think, he knew his remaining time was short. He turned over his library and house at Zwolle for the use of the Brothers. Then in August 1384, a friend contracted the plague. Groote went to care for him without hesitation, and fell ill himself. Knowing he was near death, he appointed Florent Radewijns to lead his followers. "Behold, " he said with characteristic flair, "I am being called by the Lord. Augustine and Bernard are already knocking at the door." After giving his final instructions regarding the foundation at Mount St. Agnes, he died — having fallen far short, for all he could see, of what he'd intended. Soon after his death, there came from Rome the Pope's reply to his appeal. It was favorable — had he lived he would have been licensed to preach once again.

This one man, then, whose essential act was simply to turn himself around, who gave himself so unrestrainedly and unabashedly — humbly and headlong — managed, in the words of Thomas, "to undertake all things, and bring many of them to pass, and warrant them to take effect." He was not a saint, except in the local and vernacular sense — sufficient entirely to the time and place he occupied. He'd begun by grooming himself for a role in the church hierarchy, but he ended instead, like Saint Francis, seeking to rebuild the church from the ground up — each brick being men and women whose very lives were Christlike.

The stones he set in place stood firm, and great things rose upon them. Mount St. Agnes was built, and the Windesheim foundation too. Under their protection, the Brothers were able to continue their apostolate with the students of Deventer. By 1460 there were some fifty congregations of Brothers and Sisters. Convents were founded also that bore the same relationship to the Sisters of the Common Life. Within a hundred years, the Windesheim chapter numbered ninety-two houses, and from this chapter there spread a far-reaching, powerful reform of convents and monasteries all over northern Europe. And finally, from that first community, Mount St. Agnes, whose site Groote himself selected, there would issue the incalculably precious and influential book *The Imitation of Christ*.

Index

emotions
external world, 28–30

Faith, 152–153, 232–233
Fall, the, 128–129
fear: spiritual responses to,
124–125; and use of Holy
Name, 53–54, 125
forgiveness, 88–90, 93
Founders of the New Devotion, 259,
Francis de Sales, 14, 47–48,
112–113, 154
Francis of Assisi: and attachments, 110; and greed, 76;
and Holy Name, 94; as illumined teacher, 215; and
life's purpose, 13; and music, 188; and suffering of
Jesus, 248–250; using his
Prayer in meditation, 20,
50, 161; view of body, 16
freedom: vs. dependence, 141;
from selfish desire, 138–139

Gandhi, Mahatma: and an-
ger, 76–77; Easwaran's
meeting with, 217–218; and
humility, 237; as inspirational resource, 193; and
life's purpose, 13; and love,
187; resemblance to Geert
Groote, 269–270; and sexual desire, 182; and sorrow,
250; and suffering, 228; and
training of senses, 58–59;
view of inward journey, 28;
and young people, 101–102
Garden of Eden, *see* Eden
Gerson, Jean, 254

Gertrude the Great: and sexual desire, 182
grace, 14, 15; and desire, 148;
and desire for inward
journey, 39–41; and Easwaran's mother and grand-
mother, 237; expressions of,
41; and human effort, 83–
84; mystery of, 151–153; and
unifying of desires, 174–175
gratitude, 14
Great Schism, 263, 269–270
Groote, Geert, 256, 262, 263–
272

Hamerken, Thomas, *see*
Thomas a Kempis
Hammarskjold, Dag, 253
happiness, *see* joy
hardship, *see* suffering
health: and benefit of meditation, 52, 68; and speeded up
mind, 48
hell, 16
Hinduism: counterpart to the
Fall, 129–130
Holy Name: as call for Lord,
182–183; as tool for transformation, 21–22, 55; uses
of, 21–22, 52–53, 54, 94–95,
124, 125, 226–227; using at
bedtime, 167–168
home, as metaphor, 32–34
Hugh of St. Victor, 68
human body: detachment
from, 119–120; as
instrument of service, 60;
mortification of, 16;
see also health

humility, 237
Hundred Years' War, 263
hurry, *see* mind, quieting

Ignatius of Loyola, 253
illumined teachers, 11–12,
    215–218
Imitation of Christ: appeal of, 13,
    15–18, 253; authorship
    question, 254–255, 261;
    Easwaran response to, 11,
    12–13; in literature, 253–
    254; medieval quality of, 16,
    27, 63–64, 65; power of fifth
    chapter of Book III, 16–18;
    as practical manual, 14–15;
    see also Thomas a Kempis
immune system analogy, 245–
    246
impatient patience, 231–232,
    244
inordinate affection, *see* selfish
    desire
inspirational passages: impor-
    tance of, 31–32; in medita-
    tion, 20–21, 69; Prayer of
    Saint Francis of Assisi, 20,
    50, 161; variety of, 157
inward journey: experience of
    Augustine, 28, 35, 37, 127,
    189–194; experience of mys-
    tics, 27–31, 127; and grace,
    39–41, 83–84, 148; prepar-
    ing for, 34–37; *see also* medi-
    tation
inward sight, 108–110

Jacapone da Todi, 176
Jesus Christ: and attachments,
139–140; instructs disciples
    in prayer: 48-49; and life's
    purpose, 14; and Mary
    Magdalene, 92–93; and suf-
    fering, 165, 246–248; view of
    selfless love, 80–81
John of Kronstadt, 156
John of the Cross, 12, 97, 138,
    185, 248
John of the Ladder, 73, 160
journeys, *see* inward journey;
    travel analogy
joy: in depth of meditation,
    200; vs. pleasure, 117, 118,
    143–144; real vs. sensory,
    239–240; vs. sorrow, 248,
    250
Julian of Norwich, 27, 115, 215

Khan, Badshah, 216
kindness, 225–228; *see also* love
King, Martin Luther, Jr., 250
knots, untying, 137–138
Kubasa, Suzanne, 48

Law, William, 50–51, 107
law of unity, 219
light, spiritual awareness as,
    176–177
likes and dislikes: freedom
    from, 23; *see also* senses
Lord: calling with Holy Name,
    182–183; as living within,
    30–34; union with, 196–
    197, 212–215; *see also* Self, real
lotus, 80, 222
love: and absence of self-will,
    236–237; and action, 223–
    224; vs. attachment, 107;

becoming, 222; and courage, 228–231; and endurance, 234–235; enlarging capacity, 185, 187–189; and faith, 232–233; and humility, 237; as job, 241; and kindness, 225–228; masculine vs. feminine, 235–236; need for practice, 42–43; and obedience, 241–243; and patience, 231–232, 244; physical vs. spiritual, 126–127; vs. possessions, 110–111; and prudence, 233–234; vs. self-will, 86–88; vs. sexual desire, 179–181

LOVE NEVER FAILETH

Love vaunteth not itself,
is not puffed up;
doth not behave itself unseemly;
seeketh not her own,
is not easily provoked,
thinketh no evil . . .
Love never faileth.

I CORINTHIANS 13

Love Never Faileth

❧

EKNATH EASWARAN

ON SAINT FRANCIS,

SAINT PAUL,

SAINT AUGUSTINE &

MOTHER TERESA

❧

With Introductions by Carol Lee Flinders

❧

NILGIRI PRESS

Second edition, first printing August 1996

The Blue Mountain Center of Meditation, founded in
Berkeley, California, in 1961 by Eknath Easwaran,
publishes books on how to lead the spiritual life
in the home and the community.
For information please write to
Nilgiri Press, Box 256, Tomales, California 94971

Printed on recycled, permanent paper.
The paper used in this publication meets the minimum requirements of American
National Standard for Information Services - Permanence of Paper for Printed
Library Materials, A NSI Z39.48—1984

Library of Congress Cataloging in Publication Data:
Easwaran, Eknath.
Love Never Faileth / Eknath Easwaran on Saint Francis, Saint Paul, Saint
Augustine & Mother Teresa with introductions by Carol Lee Flinders. — 2 nd ed.
p. cm. — (Classics of Christian inspiration series)
Includes bibliographical references and index.
ISBN 0—915132—90—7 (alk. paper). —
ISBN 0—915132—89—3 (pbk. : alk. paper)
1. Spiritual life. 2. Spiritual life — Christianity. I. Title.
BL624.E165 1996
282'.092'2 — dc20 [B] 96—25217 CIP

Table of Contents

Introduction by Carol Lee Flinders

It happened to Augustine, and it happened to Francis of Assisi – in a garden, to the one; to the other, in a dilapidated chapel. To Paul it happened while he was Saul the tentmaker, on the road to Damascus, engulfing him in a light so bright he saw nothing for three days afterward. And to Teresa, a Sister of Loreto, it happened as she sat on a train headed for Darjeeling – happened so simply and quietly there's almost nothing to tell.

"God spoke to me," they say, and their lives compel our belief. Struck down by love, charged then to live it, they are no longer Augustine or Francis or Teresa but "Saint" or "Blessed" or, to millions of God's homeless and hungry children, just "Mother." No longer a finite human being but a force, barely contained in flesh and bone. "Not I, not I, but Christ liveth in me."

The pattern is never exactly the same twice. With Paul, for instance, there seems to have been a complete and radical reversal: Saul of Tarsus gone in a flash; Paul, "the new man," there in his stead, and no one more surprised than he. With Mother Teresa, on the other hand, there is no sudden transformation, but a simple, gradual unfolding – one long, pure, unflinching acquiescence. (Asked for "legends" about Mother Teresa as a young nun, one of her earliest associates protests, "But there are no legends about her. Mother Teresa is completely normal.") These are extremes. Set down all similar "cases" and they fall somewhere between, but always there seems to be that "still, small voice," coming just when it's needed most.

One envies them so, these great souls who know themselves "called," know without a doubt that what they are doing has divine sanction and even complicity. It is hard not to think of them as almost superhuman. Setting them apart as "Saint Thus and Such" only makes matters worse.

In fact, Easwaran's purpose in looking at the lives and words of these individuals is not to set them apart from the rest of us, but to connect us to them, directly and vitally, in the manner of a physician readying a patient for a transfusion. Individuals like Bernard of Clairvaux, Catherine of Siena, George Fox, John Woolman, Saint Vincent de Paul, and Teresa of Avila have elevated the period of history in which they lived, and they continue to inspire even now. Yet there is nothing any of them did, Easwaran would insist, that isn't within the reach of every human being.

Years ago, when Easwaran was giving the nightly classes in meditation with which he began his work in this country, he used to enjoy describing his first and only trip to Yosemite National Park. It gave him a chance to tease without mercy the friend who'd taken him there – this had been his first exposure to the American passion for the Right Equipment, the Perfect Campsite, the Well-Built Fire. But he had a point to make too.

As day faded into night, he recalled, the din on the valley floor was intolerable. Transistor radios, car engines, parents and children calling out to one another – you might as well have stayed in downtown Berkeley. By ten o'clock, though, the last radio was turned off and the last exuberant child bedded down. Silence fell across the campground. And in the silence, audible at last, he heard the faint, murmuring music of a stream that passed just ten feet from his tent. He hadn't even known it was there.

Just so, he tells us, the "still, small voice" of God murmurs within every one of us all the time — advising us, consoling and strengthening us — an endless wellspring of wisdom and inspiration. The only reason we don't hear it as clearly as Francis or Augustine did is that we've allowed too many other noises to drown it out: the raucous voice of self-will, the clamor of selfish desire, the shrill tones of anxiety and fear. Silence them one by one, through meditation and the allied disciplines, and Francis's experience at San Damiano or Augustine's in his garden will no longer seem like a fairy tale at all.

Hearing the stream is one thing: following it to the source, the clear, pure spring itself, is another. Looking at the lives of the great men and women of God, one gathers that there is a reciprocity between prayer, or meditation, and action — a powerful mandate to live out what is heard in the depths of consciousness, and a deepening of the inner life each time you do. Small tasks lead outward into larger ones, the ante rising with each willing response, as the individual becomes a more and more perfect instrument of the divine will.

It is in the final stages of this process, says Easwaran, that you make an endlessly astonishing discovery. When the senses have been brought under control, when the mind is stilled and self-will extinguished and the voice you've heard just barely, just for seconds, is finally distinct — loud and clear at long last — you realize that it is your own. Your innermost self is inseparable from the Lord.

Each ordinary one of us, then, conceals an immense power for good. That power, the capacity for "love in action," is who we really are, and we conceal it at terrible cost to the world and ourselves. Among the darkest fears of our time is that of repression. Don't repress your anger, we're taught, and above all don't repress your sex drive . . . Yet our most powerful drive, our very identity, is closeted away — hotly denied.

From this point of view, individuals like Saint Paul, Saint Augustine, Saint Francis, and Mother Teresa are spectacularly uninhibited and supremely themselves. And never has the world been in greater need of the love and strength that flows through such people. What better reason, then, to look at each in turn . . .

SAINT FRANCIS

Introduction by Carol Lee Flinders

The loves and writings of the great spiritual figures are so wonderfully diverse that for almost all of us one or another speaks with special force. Saint Augustine, for instance, has long been a special favorite of people with an intellectual bent – those who have pressed the rational mind to its limits and said finally, "No, no, there has to be more than this." To those with no intellectual pretensions whatsoever, figures like Rose of Lima or Joseph of Cupertino are particularly dear.

Francis of Assisi, though, belongs to everyone. He is the saint with whom just about everybody believes they have a special, private understanding.

It's not immediately clear why. If you really look at what he was doing and how he lived – the ashes he would scatter across a dinner that looked a little too good, the single rough garment he wore, tied at the waist with a rope, the crude thrown-together huts where he and his Brothers spent long, prayerful, icy-cold winter nights – if you look at it squarely, nothing could be more off-putting. Not that it was peculiar – Francis only did what people have always done when they yearn to loose spirit from flesh. But it doesn't typically endear them to others.

Nor does he seem to have possessed other qualities that

usually inspire a following. Crude as his assessment was, considering that he himself was a Friar, Brother Masseo can probably be forgiven for blurting out one day, "Why after you? Why after you?" – adding in explanation, "You are not beautiful to look upon; you are not a man of great knowledge; you are not of noble birth. Why, then, does all the world follow you?"

Francis sought, in the words of his own Rule, "to follow the teaching and the footsteps of our Lord Jesus Christ," which for him meant a life of intense and prayerful austerity. He was not the first man or woman to do so. What sets him apart, though, what keeps his memory warm and alive all over the world today and makes him perhaps the most beloved of saints, is that he made it look like fun.

Compared to the thousand-odd manuscripts that remained in Augustine's library at Hippo, we have almost nothing written by Francis. A last testament, a couple of poems, a few letters – no scriptural commentary, no theological treatise. Francis was mortally suspicious of the world of letters. He chose instead to teach by and through his own actions. So it is most appropriate that the real memorial to the Little Man of Assisi is his life – a life chronicled as lovingly and attentively as almost none has been before the modern period: by Thomas of Celano, by Saint Bonaventura, by his own Brother Leo, and by many, many others. At least once in a generation, someone is inspired to retell his story: writers as diverse as Nikos Kazantzakis and G. K. Chesterton, filmmakers as dissimilar as Roberto Rossellini and Franco Zefferelli. And always, shining through even the most poignant or downright harrowing episodes, there is that joy – exceeding joy – just barely subdued.

"Why after you?" There was no questioning "why"

when Francis was the leader of Assisi's young men about town. He was charming, witty, generous, and musical — a troubadour who composed love songs, the life, soul, and pocketbook of every party. A serious illness cut across all this when he was twenty-two, plunging him during his recovery into a newly introspective mood. After the second of two failed attempts to take up a life of soldiering, he entered a period of even deeper soul-searching.

He would spend his days now in the ruined church of San Damiano outside Assisi, and it was on one of those days that he heard a voice, coming, he thought, from the crucifix: "Go hence, now, Francis, and build up my church, for it is nearly falling down." His response was literal and immediate — and pivotal. Within a few months, he had left forever the home he grew up in and had given himself over entirely to his new calling.

Over the next two years, Francis rebuilt three churches that had fallen into bad disrepair. But this was only the beginning. For he soon realized that his real mission was to infuse vitality and strength into the Church itself — and this he did, in every way conceivable.

Francis's work began with the founding of the Friars Minor, the "Little Brothers" of Christ, who would go out into the world preaching and extending spiritual friendship everywhere. Not long after came the order founded by — and named after — his first woman disciple, Clare. To the Poor Clares there still clings the fragrance of a romance so pure and perfect as to have made the entire Courtly Love tradition look vulgar in comparison. No less important, though, was the Third Order, which adapted the Franciscan pattern for men and women, married or single, whose calling was not monastic. They were to care for the sick and give to the poor, detaching themselves from whatever wealth they might possess and using it as

God's stewards. Pledged to make peace with their enemies, to restore ill-gotten gains, never to bear arms, and never to accept public honors, members of the Order were a strong force for peace in the violent and unstable social structure of the thirteenth century.

Francis's real contribution, though, goes far beyond the institutional. So profound was his devotion that it awakened a great depth of feeling in others: he quite literally taught the people of his region, and generations to come, how to worship.

There was Christmas, three years before Francis would pass away, when he arranged that in the little town of Greccio a replica of the stable at Bethlehem should be constructed, complete with donkey, ox, and manger. Bearing candles and torches, all the men and women of the region came together. "The night was lighted up like the day, and it delighted men and beasts. . . . The woods rang with the voices of the crowd and the rocks made answer to their jubilation." The mystery of the Incarnation came to life anew for everyone there. "The saint of God stood before the manger, uttering sighs, overcome with love. . . ." The mass was celebrated, Francis sang the Gospel, and then he preached "charming words concerning the nativity of the poor King and the little town of Bethlehem." To one man in particular there came a wonderful vision. "He saw a child lying in the manger lifeless, and he saw Francis go and rouse the child, as from a deep sleep. . . ." The symbolic meaning was lost on no one.

Francis sought to identify himself so completely with Christ that His love would reenter the world through His servant. That could only mean one thing to him, which was to seek nothing for himself and offer everything to God. To the suffering he had always imposed upon himself — the privation of every creature comfort — there came to be added the enormous sorrow of seeing his own Order torn apart by dissension and finding himself unable to restore it to unity. Finally, in seclusion on the mountain La Verna, whose great cracks and fissures were believed to have opened up at the moment when Christ was crucified, he lifted his heart to God in perfect abandonment of self — and he was answered. From that time forth, Francis would bear on his hands and feet, and in his side, the unremittingly painful marks of Christ's own anguish.

❧

I have said "he made it look like fun," and that must seem flippant by now. But in fact this was the enormous paradox of Francis's life. He wedded himself joyously to poverty, called her his bride, his Lady, and played the exuberant bridegroom to the hilt. He was always the troubadour, the *"jongleur de Dieu,"* who taught that good cheer is not just a kindness to all around, but one of the three ways to obtain peace (obedience and prayer being the other two). "Rejoice always," he would say, because it's when the soul is dark and troubled, sullen and lonely, that it turns to the world to seek comfort. "Spiritual joy arises from purity of heart and perseverance in prayer." Ebullience, therefore, and a marvelous sense of good theater are the hallmarks of Francis's life and his way of teaching.

The lives of saints are shot through, for instance, with accounts of Lust Overcome. To call it merely "lust" doesn't really say it, of course — doesn't imply the quieter yet often more tenacious yearnings for home, children, and partner that help make the monastic calling so arduous. The lone monk or nun keeps grim vigil night after night in a narrow cell while the demons of the mind itself

dance around them, and eventually — archetypally, anyway — those demons are banished. Nowhere, though, do
we read that any of them except Francis burst right out of
that cell — a hut in his case — into the snow outside, rolled
in it bared to the waist, and then piled it up into *seven*
(that's right, seven) snow people.

"Here they are, Francis," he exulted. "Here is your family. The big one over there is your wife. Those are your
children, and there are your two servants."

"But Francis," he chided himself. "They're cold. Have
you nothing to put on them? If you do not, then aren't
you glad you have only your God to serve?"

In fact, Francis never abandoned his desire for a family.
He simply expanded the normal idea of what a family is
until it embraced all women, all children, and all men —
all animals and birds and even insects. The sun and moon
he took as siblings and finally even the very elements: "Sister Water, which is very useful and humble and precious
and chaste"; "Brother Fire . . . beautiful, jocund, robust,
and strong."

It's as if, when he ran out of that hut, he brought the
whole Western spiritual tradition with him and showed
us once and for all that nothing is excluded from the spiritual life: that all forms of love are perfectly realized by the
man or woman who leaves selfish desire behind.

The longer you study his life, the more obvious are the
parallels with other saints. And yet there's no one like
him, and that's the beauty of it. G. K. Chesterton, one of
his most hopelessly smitten biographers, pointed out that
you could never anticipate what Francis would do or say
in a given situation. But once he had done it or said it, all
you could say was "Ah, how like him!"

Did Brother Masseo's challenge go unanswered, then?
Did Francis just smile enigmatically and go on his way?

No, the chroniclers tell us. Beaming with delight (months at a time would probably pass without his getting such an opportunity to forbear) he raised his eyes to heaven and remained for a time absorbed in God. Then he knelt down and gave thanks, and when he turned at last to his Brother, said:

"Would you know why they follow after me? Because the eyes of the Most High God have not seen anywhere among the sinners anyone more vile, or more imperfect, or a greater sinner than I. . . . He has elected me to confound the nobility, the majesty, the right, the beauty, and the wisdom of the world, in order to make it known that every virtue and every good thing comes from Him and not from the creature."

❦

From the very beginnings of Easwaran's work in this country, Saint Francis has been a cherished presence. Do we balk at the idea of bringing the body and senses under some measure of control? There is Francis, characterizing his own body as "Brother Ass." "He needs you to feed him," Easwaran elaborates, "and to feed him only so much as he needs – to shelter him, and give him rest when he's tired, and be kind to him in every way, a true friend. But make no mistake – you are the rider, not he!"

Do the finer points of "putting others first" keep eluding us? Lessons in *caritas* leap out from every page of Francis's life, like the night when a Brother cried out in his sleep, "Brothers! I die of hunger!" Swift was Francis's response — but exquisitely tactful. All the Brothers were awakened; all were called to the low table, and all were commanded to break bread together, while Francis spoke tenderly of the danger of excessive mortifications. The friar who had cried out was never named.

There may be no more perfect distillation of all that Francis lived for than the simple prayer Easwaran invariably suggests for use in meditation, which begins, "Lord, make me an instrument of thy peace. . . ."

Lord, make me an instrument of thy peace.
Where there is hatred, let me sow love;
Where there is injury, pardon;
Where there is doubt, faith;
Where there is despair, hope;
Where there is darkness, light;
Where there is sadness, joy.

O divine Master, grant that I may not so much seek
To be consoled as to console,
To be understood as to understand,
To be loved as to love:
For it is in giving that we receive,
It is in pardoning that we are pardoned,
It is in dying to self that we are born to eternal life.

Make Me an Instrument

[I]

When I first came to this country, in 1959, I looked hard for a suitable meditation passage for the West. In this Prayer of Saint Francis I found the perfect answer. During all these years I have been recommending it to everyone because, as you can see, it is a very rare thing: an attempt to reverse almost all the ordinary tendencies we find in human nature. It gives us a blueprint for making our life a blessing for everyone.

In this profoundest of prayers, Saint Francis confides in us how the son of Pietro di Bernardone was transformed into a son of God. We too can aspire to such a transformation by making his Prayer an integral part of our consciousness. This cannot be done through reading or discussion, which take place only on the surface level of consciousness. It can only be done by regular, systematic meditation. If we meditate on Saint Francis's words diligently and with enthusiasm every morning, the marvelous transformation that Francis worked in himself will gradually be effected in us too.

This word "meditation" means many different things to different people. It has been applied to dancing and to listening to music and even to letting the mind wander, which is just the opposite of meditation. I want to explain right from the outset that when I talk about meditation, I mean only one thing: systematically training the mind to focus completely on a lofty ideal until that ideal absorbs our every faculty and passion. In the West this focusing of the mind is often called "interior prayer" or "contemplation," the word "meditation" being used for a kind of disciplined reflection on a single religious theme (such as the Passion) and its significance. But whatever term is used, the practice I am referring to is universal. It has been described in every major spiritual tradition. If you look at the writings of early figures of Christianity like the Desert Fathers, I think you will agree that they would immediately recognize the method I myself follow and teach.

For those who are not familiar with this method, a brief summary will clarify the references to meditation I make throughout the rest of this book.

Instructions in Meditation

Begin by devoting half an hour every morning as early as convenient to the practice of meditation. If you want to meditate more, have half an hour in the evening also, but do not meditate longer than half an hour at a time.

If you do not have a meditation room in your home, a special corner set aside for that purpose will do. Whichever you choose, your meditation place should be quiet. Keep it simple and attractive with a few religious pictures if they appeal to you.

Sit in a straight-backed chair – one with arms – or cross-legged on the floor, with spinal column erect and eyes gently closed. As your concentration deepens, you may begin to relax and fall asleep. If so, draw yourself up and move away from your back support so that you can keep spine, neck, and head in a straight line.

To meditate on the Prayer of Saint Francis, you will need to know the words by heart. (Until you learn them, you can begin with a passage from Scripture that you already know, such as the Lord's Prayer or the Twenty-third Psalm.) Go through the words in your mind as slowly as you can, letting each word drop singly into your consciousness like a jewel. Do not follow any association of ideas, but keep to the words of the Prayer. If you are giving them your full attention, you do not have to turn them over in your mind; the meaning cannot help sinking in.

Similarly, when distractions come, do not resist them; that way they will seize your attention. Instead, simply try to give more and more attention to the words of the Prayer.

It is said that once Saint Francis carved a small cup and was so pleased with his handiwork that his eyes kept wandering back to it even during prayer. When suddenly he realized that the cup was taking his thoughts away from God, he picked it up and flung it into the fire. We don't need to be that severe with ourselves, but if you find that your mind has wandered completely away from the Prayer, just go back to the first word of that stanza and begin again. Adding to your repertoire of inspirational passages from the scriptures or great mystics will help to keep the words of the passage from growing stale.

After long and strenuous endeavor, the day will come when the windows of your senses close down completely and you are able to meditate with one-pointed absorption on the Prayer. Saint Teresa of Avila described this stage vividly:

> You will at once feel your senses gather themselves together; they seem like bees which return to the hive and then shut themselves up to work at the making of honey; and this will take place without effort or care on your part. God thus rewards the violence which your soul has been doing to itself, and gives to it such a domination over the senses that a sign is enough, when it desires to recollect itself, for them to obey and so gather themselves together. At the first call of the will they come back more and more quickly. At last, after many and many exercises of this kind, God disposes them to a state of absolute repose and of perfect contemplation.

In this book I give a practical commentary on passages for meditation from four great Christian exponents of what I call "love in action." My hope is to make these passages more meaningful for those who want to meditate on them and then translate their ideals into action. But although I often comment line for line, let me repeat that what I am recommending you do in meditation is very different. When you go through these words in meditation, your mind will want to follow all kinds of associations. This is not getting absorbed in the Prayer; it is wandering away from it. As you meditate on these precious words, give them all your attention. Gradually they will become part of you, reflected in everything you say and do.

The central principle of meditation is that we become what we meditate on. Over time, the transformation taking place in our character and consciousness is bound to show itself in our daily relations. Part of this transformation is accomplished in meditation, but the rest is done during the day. Meditation generates power that needs to be put to constructive use, particularly in healing our relationships. Francis once said that we pray to partake of the peace of the Lord, but that the hours of the day are meant for spreading this peace in the places where people dwell. When things go wrong at home, for instance, we need to try to remain patient and sympathetic. When someone at work is curt to us, we need to harness the strength found in meditation to move closer and show that person some special kindness.

The Holy Name

To do this, it is a great help to learn to use the Holy Name — a powerful spiritual formula which, when repeated silently in the mind, has the power to transform consciousness. There is nothing magical about this power; it is simply a matter of practice, as you can verify for yourself.

Repetition of the Holy Name is a practice found in every major religious tradition. Many Christians simply repeat *Jesus, Jesus, Jesus.* The Desert Fathers repeated the Prayer of Jesus, which Eastern Orthodox Christians use even today: *Lord, Jesus Christ, have mercy upon me.* Catholics may also use *Hail Mary* or *Ave Maria.* Choose whichever version of the Holy Name appeals to you; then, once you have chosen, stick to that and do not change. Otherwise you will be like a person digging little holes in many places; you will never go deep enough to find water.

Repeat the Holy Name whenever you get the chance: while walking, while waiting, while doing mechanical chores like washing dishes, and especially when you are falling asleep, anytime you are not doing something that requires your attention. Whenever you are angry or afraid, nervous or hurried or resentful, repeat the Holy Name until the agitation in your mind subsides. All these states of mind are power running against you, which the Holy Name can harness and put to work.

I might mention that not just any phrase has this

power. By and large, it is good not to make up your own version of the Holy Name but to use a formula that has been sanctioned by centuries of devout tradition. Most words and phrases denote something to us only at relatively superficial levels of awareness; below that, in the unconscious, they mean nothing. If you repeat the Holy Name sincerely and systematically, however, you can verify for yourself that it goes deeper with every repetition. It can be with you even in the uttermost depths of your consciousness, as you will discover for yourself when you find it reverberating in a dream – or, deeper still, during dreamless sleep. When you awake, the thrill of this great experience will remain with you, reminding and inspiring and enabling you to be a little calmer and kinder throughout that day.

In the case of Saint Francis, we find this practice arising spontaneously from the depths of his ardent love. The *Fioretti* or *Little Flowers of Saint Francis,* the earliest collection we have of stories about Francis and the early Order, relates that the nobleman Bernard of Quintavalle, before he enlisted himself as a disciple, wanted to find out for himself whether young Francis of Assisi was a sincere lover of God; so he invited him to his wealthy home.

"Saint Francis accepted the invitation," the chronicle continues,

> and took supper with him, and stayed the night also; and then Bernard resolved to make trial of his

sanctity. He got a bed prepared for him in his own room, in which a lamp was always burning all night. Saint Francis, in order to conceal his sanctity, entered the room and immediately threw himself on the bed and feigned to sleep. Bernard also resolved to lie down, and began to snore loudly, as if in a very deep slumber.

Thereupon Saint Francis, believing that Bernard was really asleep, immediately rose from the bed and betook himself to prayer, and raising his eyes and his hands to heaven with the greatest devotion he said, "My God and my all!" So saying, and shedding many tears, he remained until morning, constantly repeating "My God and my all!" and nothing more.

Meditation and the repetition of the Holy Name go hand in hand: meditation is for the quiet hours of morning and evening; the Holy Name can be used at any other time of day or night. Together these two help us to change negative habits at a depth our ordinary will cannot reach. Francis once said that our knowledge is as deep as our action. Many people are victims of habits, such as smoking or drinking, which they know to be harmful, but still they are unable to give them up. If this knowledge is driven deeper into their consciousness through meditation and the Holy Name, it can free them from the tyranny of undesirable habits to follow wiser patterns of behavior. One of Francis's contemporaries, an historian who had been a student at Bologna and heard Francis speak on the Feast of the Assumption, described him in this way:

His habit was dirty, his appearance insignificant, his face not handsome. But God gave his words such power that many noble families, between whom there had been much old-time enmity and spilled blood, allowed themselves to be induced to make peace. And all felt great devotion and reverence for him. . . . He was not silent about wrongs that he saw, but gave everything its right name. And it seemed to each who listened that the poor little man from Assisi talked to him alone, as if all the words he heard were directed to him, and one after another, like well-aimed arrows sent by a master hand, thrust their points into his heart.

This is precisely what we experience in meditation as the holy words of Saint Francis's Prayer penetrate our hearts.

Let me now try to bring out some of the practical profundity of these words, drawing on my own experience.

[2]

Without spending a single moment beating about the bush, Francis comes straight to the point of the spiritual life: *Lord, make me an instrument of thy peace.* Our first priority is to reform ourselves; without that, how can we expect to help other people reform themselves? It is the living example of a man or woman giving every moment to making love a reality that moves our hearts to follow. We do not have to call ourselves religious to serve as examples of love and unity. We do not need a bumper sticker that says, "You are following an instrument of the Lord." Our everyday actions speak for themselves.

Just as the example of Jesus inspired Francis a millennium later, Francis inspired thousands of people even during his own lifetime. Near the end of his life, while he was making a mountain journey, Francis's health failed. His companions went into a farmyard to borrow a donkey for him to ride. On hearing for whom it was intended, the peasant came out and asked, "Are you the Brother Francis there is so much said about?" Receiving a nod from one of Francis's companions, he added, "Then take care that you are as good in reality as they say, for there are many who have confidence in you." Deeply stirred, Francis kissed the peasant in gratitude for this reminder of just how much such an example could mean even to people he had never met.

How can we go about making ourselves such an example? To begin with, as long as we are full of ourselves, our own small desires and self-centered thoughts, we leave no room whatever for the Lord to work in our lives. Jesus says simply, "Thy will be done." The implication is clear: to live in harmony with the divine will, our petty, selfish, personal will – self-will – has to go. When we ask to be made instruments of peace, what we are really asking for is the boundless determination to empty ourselves of every ugly state of mind that disrupts relationships – anger, resentment, jealousy, greed, self-will in any form.

Transforming these negative states of mind into their positive counterparts is not at all an easy task. Selfish desires and resentments masquerade as part of us, part of our personality. In reality they are only a mask, which can be removed to reveal our real personality. Mystics call this mask self-will. I often call it the ego. Either name means the self-centered drive to get what I want, have my own way, whatever the cost to others. This is the source of all selfish and destructive behavior.

In English fiction there is a fascinating character known as the Scarlet Pimpernel. He shows up here, then there, then here again, breaking the law for what he considers worthy causes, but the authorities can never lay eyes on him. That is how the ego behaves. It simply is not possible to challenge him to a duel. He will not reply to your invitation; he will never pick up your gauntlet; if you shout at him, your echo will shout back at you. But there are a million little ways in which you can slowly track the ego to its lair.

If someone were to pull over to the side of the road in San Francisco and ask me how to get to Los Angeles, I wouldn't say, "Go north." Everyone knows you have to go the other direction. Similarly, spiritual figures like Saint Francis tell us, "Don't follow your selfish desires and angry impulses; that is the way to emotional bankruptcy." But we reply, "Oh, no! I know what I'm doing. It's obvious which way is better." Francis would insist, "Please believe me. If you go that way, you will become more insecure. People will slowly lose their respect for you, and you will lose respect for yourself. Eventually you will not feel at home anywhere on earth. Instead, let me show you a secret trail that will take you slowly round so you can surprise the ego in his sleep. He'll never know what hit him."

Like most people I have met in this country, I too was conditioned at an early age by talk about not "repressing" the ego. I believed that if you defy a strong selfish impulse, sooner or later your frustrations will explode. The lives of men and women like Saint Francis, however, show us just the opposite: reducing the ego for the sake of fulfilling a higher goal, a loftier desire than self-interest, is not repression but transformation. The signs are sure. Repression bottles up our energy, so that it can make itself felt only in destructive ways. When this energy is transformed, however, it is released every day in creative ways that we can see: patience, resilience under stress, skill in building bridges between others and ourselves.

When a selfish urge is crying out for satisfaction, then, that is an ideal opportunity to summon up your will and go against that urge. Because so much of our vital energy is caught up in pampering these selfish impulses, they offer us a long, long trail right into the depths of consciousness. When we defy the impulse and use its energy for some selfless purpose, we are following a trail that will eventually allow us to get around the ego.

These are the dynamics of spiritual transformation. The route is always there and it is always open; that is its promise. We must be prepared for many, many years of arduous hiking over rough terrain. Very likely we are going to have lapses; some very attractive detours may distract us temporarily. All that we are asking the Lord for is the determination to do our best to stay on the right trail and go forward.

As a practical first step toward becoming an instrument of peace, we can try our best not to harbor grudges. One suggestion is that when you have a falling-out with someone, instead of deciding on the spot that you are not going to come within ten feet of that person, try going out for a really fast walk, repeating the Holy Name in your mind until the immediate wave of anger rolls over you. (If a fast walk is not feasible, sit down quietly to repeat the Name.) Then you can make a simple effort to recall some of the good things that person has done for you. He may have let it go by when you said something particularly unkind to him one time; or perhaps when you got sick she took care of you. Anger makes us utterly forget all these incidents, so that for a while we see only the dark side. When we remind ourselves that even though at present we may be nursing a very real injury, the past has brought us kindness and aid from this person, our anger will find it difficult to burn for very long.

On another front, I have come to feel that one of the cornerstones of peaceful relations everywhere is the capacity to avoid becoming wedded to one's own opinions. Francis repeatedly warned his brothers about trying to "embrace poverty while keeping the purse of your own opinion." When we do not have this capacity, arrogance often makes its ugly appearance. At the mere hint of disagreement we get agitated, and our views are liable to come out clothed in harsh tones and intemperate language. The message to the other party is clear: we have scant respect for him or her as a person. Nothing wounds more deeply or muddies the original issue more thoroughly. It is then that war breaks out. We need not think of war only in terms of the War of the Roses or the landing on the beaches of Normandy. Skirmishes are fought in the dining room all the time; guerrilla warfare is often waged in the kitchen.

Where there is hatred, let me sow love.

To the south of my ancestral home in Kerala, South India, beautiful rice fields stretch almost to the horizon. When I was a little boy, every morning during the planting season I would be awakened just after dawn by the sounds of the villagers plowing the land with their bullocks, talking and singing as they worked. First the tiny seedlings must be planted.

Somebody goes along with a big basket, planting them one by one in a row, so carefully that when you look at rice growing, it looks like a gigantic green carpet. Later each seedling must be transplanted. All in all, it is difficult to believe that these minute seedlings are going to bear such a rich harvest.

You and I can go in for a similar kind of hand labor. When you plant just one kind word with somebody who has been unkind to you, though it is only a tiny seedling, it is going to bear a rich harvest. A lot of people get the benefit – secondhand, thirdhand, fourthhand – from our little kindnesses. Every time you focus on what brings people together instead of what drives them apart, you are planting a long row of these seedlings. Every day – in the office, at school, in the kitchen, at the store – everyone has opportunities for this kind of hand labor. We may think our opportunities are hardly worth the trouble, but little things like kindness catch on and spread.

In Kerala we have a giant, fierce-looking plant called elephant nettle. It seems to flourish in every nook and cranny, and you have only to walk by for it to stretch out to touch you. One little touch and you feel as if you have been stung. By the time you get home, you have a blister that won't let you think about anything else until it goes away.

My grandmother, my spiritual teacher, was expert at driving home great truths with homely illustrations. She used to say, "A self-willed person is like an elephant nettle." That is why the moment we see somebody who is given to saying unkind things, we make a detour. We pretend we have just remembered something that takes us in another direction, but the fact is that we just don't want to be stung. "I promise not to go near the elephant nettles," I always assured my granny. But when it came to a classmate I did not like, she would say, "Here, you have to learn to grow. Go near him. Let yourself slowly get comfortable around him; then give him your sympathy and help take the sting out of his nettleness."

I am not one of those philosophical people who say, "No matter what you do to me, it is all right." Certainly not! When someone is being unkind, whether to me or to somebody else, I feel a loving obligation to remonstrate with him, kindly but firmly. When a person senses that we have his best interests at heart, when he knows we will not move away from him whatever distress he is causing, we can remonstrate and at the same time support him in his efforts to overcome his problem.

Where there is injury, pardon.

When children cry, my mother used to remind me, they are really trying to speak to us. They have some problem and do not know how to explain what is bothering them, so they use the only language they have: lifting the roof off. Grown-ups usually go in for a more subtle style. When they get really annoyed, they let loose with some choice epithets, stalk out of the house (often tripping over the threshold), and growl something rude to the first person they see. We understand this more easily than an infant's tantrum, but it is just as childish. When a baby raises the roof, most people do not respond by taking it personally and getting hostile; they try to find out what the problem is and solve it. Saint Francis is reminding us that there is no more reason to take grown-ups' annoyance personally than we do children's.

No one would claim for a second that this kind of response comes easily. Dealing with acrimonious situations and self-willed people with a calm patience requires toughness, the inner toughness that real love demands. In matters like these, one of Francis's earliest disciples, Brother Juniper, won a reputation for his naive ingenuity. Once, when a superior reprimanded him with great severity, Brother Juniper was so disturbed by the grief he had caused that in the middle of the night he jumped out of bed, prepared some porridge with a big lump of butter on top, and took it to his superior's room. "Father," he said, standing at the door with the bowl of porridge in one hand and a lighted candle in the other, "today when you reprimanded me I noticed that you were hoarse from excitement. Now I have prepared this porridge for you and beg you to eat it; it is good for the throat and chest."

The superior impatiently told Brother Juniper to go away and let him sleep.

"Well," said Brother Juniper simply, "the porridge is cooked and has to be eaten, so please be so kind as to hold the light while I do the eating." His superior must have laughed in spite of himself, and we are told that he was sporting enough to sit down with Brother Juniper so they could eat the porridge together.

Most of us will never be so ingenuous as Brother Juniper, but we can still learn to head off resentment in every way possible. The more resentment is allowed to grow, the more damage it is going to do. Resentment is like swallowing a seed from the elephant nettle: soon our whole insides will ache from top to bottom from its stinging, and we won't have the vaguest idea how to get rid of it. Just think about the comparison a little. Not only will that resentment wreak havoc with our emotional well-being, it will gradually break down the functioning of our physical system as well.

Resentment will defend itself with a foolish argument: "Well, it's my own business." Not at all. In the first place, unless the person against whom you nurse the grudge is extremely secure, you are making that person into an agitated missile who is going to injure a lot of others. This is no exaggeration. Resentment is contagious, much more so than a virus. In a home where it is allowed to fester, everybody gets infected: the children, the children's playmates, even the dog. But kindness is even more contagious. Whenever people see somebody facing harsh treatment with quiet security, with a kind of infectious good humor, they get infected too. "How I wish I could do that!" they marvel. We can use kindness to inoculate those around us against the dread disease of resentment.

Where there is doubt, faith; where there is despair, hope.

I keep up with a variety of magazines and newspapers, and I find a lot of people throwing up their hands. Many tell us civilization is doomed, perhaps even the planet itself. I am not one of those who claim all is well no matter what is happening. On many fronts, the horizon *is* dark. But who is responsible for all these crises? Not the three Greek sisters of fate, not the Power which created us. It is we ourselves who are totally responsible; therefore it is we who can set these wrong situations right.

The shining examples of spiritual figures like Saint Francis stand as monuments of hope. They had to face adversities of every description, opposition from every imaginable kind of entrenched self-interest. Often they were able to make use of such problems to spur themselves on. When we take a good look at the state of the world, we are sometimes inclined to say, "There is nothing to be done." If we would only turn to the example of Saint Francis we would have to admit, "It's not impossible, really. Look what he was able to accomplish. Why can't we manage some of the same?"

When I was in India, I came across a number of American expressions that baffled me. One was "pulling yourself up by your own bootstraps." I resolved that when I came to this country, I would look for some person performing this acrobatic feat! This is the marvel of meditation – a marvel I have never been able to get over. Nobody pulls you up; you pull yourself up. It should appeal enormously to the justly lauded spirit of American ingenuity. Francis himself said, "More than all grace and all the gifts of the Holy Spirit . . . is the conquering of yourself." You go to work on your own mind and change whatever needs changing, making yourself into the kind of person most suited to meeting the challenges of the day. There is cause for enormous hope here.

None of us need be ashamed or embarrassed if ghosts out of our past come and whisper, "Remember what you did in high school? All the escapades you took part in? How unkind you were, how you wasted so many opportunities?" To me, this sort of guilt is a trick the ego plays to make us doubt ourselves. It is most unfair. Here we are looking back at our behavior of ten or twenty or thirty years ago and judging it by our standards of today. Who has not made mistakes at some tumultuous period in life? If you ask me personally, "Did you?" I will say, "Plenty." And if you ask, "Well, don't you too feel guilty about what you did?" I will say, "I'm not proud of it, but that is how I saw life then."

If you want to judge yourself, the only fair way is to judge yourself with today's eyes as you are today. Look at yourself straight on and ask, "Have I been selfish today in any way?" If you have a competitive streak, this is where you can make good use of it. Just say, "Today in such and such ways I have been somewhat selfish, but tomorrow I'll do better."

Where there is darkness, light.

On a dark night when you are stumbling along the road trying to pick your way home, what would you say if somebody came up and offered to help with a flashlight that has no battery? People who are quick to anger or who nurse grudges have no battery in their flashlight; we would do well to tell them, "Please don't bring your flashdark here." Isn't there a battery called Eveready? Well, resentful people have a battery that can be called Neveready. By refusing to let their compassion shine, they darken the path of everyone around them. On the other hand, people who are patient and who can love you more than they love themselves have a flashlight that shines in all directions at the same time.

There are many different sizes of flashlights. I have one by my bedside which is the size of a fountain pen. I can hardly see anything with it, but it is better than the dark; at least it shows you where the walls are so that you avoid walking into them and banging your head. That is the first stage of our transformation: we appear as little fountain pens of light. A group at a party is saying, "I can't see any good in Ebenezer at all," and we chime in, "Oh, he has helped me out a few times."

As we are able to work more comfortably and

harmoniously with people, we will find that instead of a penlight we hold a normal, hand-sized flashlight. People begin to look to us for advice and solace. They like to be around us because we somehow make them feel more secure. Finally, when we see the spark of divinity burning in the people around us, we are like a big beacon. People are drawn to us, because they find that by our light their paths become clear and well marked.

Where there is sadness, joy.

This line touches me deeply. Saint Francis is quietly bringing home to us a tremendous responsibility. Our influence, whether for sadness or for joy, reaches everywhere. We cannot ever say, "I live alone in an attic off Fourth Street. This line does not apply to me." Don't you ride on a bus where thirty people see how solemn and sad you look? Everywhere we go we affect people.

Once a student of mine in India thought he had found an answer to this. I met him on campus and said to him casually, "I've been noticing how downcast you look these days. It grieves me. Is there anything I can do?"

"There is no need for you to be concerned about the way I look," he replied politely enough. "It's my face." "Yes," I agreed, "it is your face. But it is we who have to look at it."

Francis himself was far from being a solemn-faced ascetic. Often he went about singing softly, and on the road he liked to regale his companions with songs of God's glories which he composed himself – in French, the language of the troubadours. "We Friars Minor," he exclaimed once, "what are we except God's singers and players, who seek to draw hearts upwards and to fill them with spiritual joy?" Their joy was so great that "when they returned from their work at evening time or when in the course of the day met on the road, love and joy shone out of their eyes, and they greeted each other with chaste embraces, holy kisses, cheerful words, modest smiles. . . ."

[3]

Francis's second stanza begins beautifully: *O divine Master. . . .* We can all think of ourselves as the Lord's footmen and handmaids; he is the Master, the one and only boss. It is a superstition to believe that we are unemployed at any time. We are all born with our appointment orders: "You, Morton E. Hazelby, are hereby instructed to contribute to life on earth and continue contributing until the last breath of the life I have given you is spent." Those of us who take the terms of this order to heart become secure and respected wherever we go.

The ideal of living as the Lord's servant was embodied with consummate grace by Francis's dear disciple Clare. Though she held the office of abbess and all the Sisters at tiny San Damiano convent looked up to her as their spiritual leader, it was Clare who most often served them at table, pouring water over their hands and waiting upon them. She took personal care of any Brothers and Sisters who happened to be sick, and did not hesitate to take on any chore, however lowly, that needed doing. When Sisters came home from working outside the convent, Clare washed their feet with her holy hands. And at night she often got up to put the covers back on a Sister who had uncovered herself in her sleep, for fear she might become chilled.

> *Grant that I may not so much seek to be consoled as to console.*

Beggars, lepers, all who suffered were sacred in Saint Francis's eyes. Whatever he had he would willingly give to someone more in need. Often he gave away his hood, a part of his habit, or even his trousers to beggars, so that his companions had their work cut out for them just keeping clothes on their beloved Francis's back. But there was a deeper object in his giving too. One day in Perugia he met a man he had formerly known who was now reduced to utter poverty. The man complained with great bitterness at having been treated so unjustly by his master. "I will willingly give you my hood," begged Francis, "if you will forgive your master his injustice." The man's heart was moved. He forgot his hatred, it is said, and was filled with the sweetness of forgiveness.

As a boy, when I was feeling sorry for myself because of difficulties in school or with someone in the village, my grandmother used to tell me gently, "This is not sorrow; this is self-pity. Self-pity weakens, but sorrow for others strengthens and ennobles human nature." This is a distinction worth remembering, particularly in times of distress. Whenever we feel life has been hard on us, instead of going off to our bed-room and locking the door, that is the ideal time for turning our grief outward and putting it to work as compassion for the sorrows of others. After all, every-one faces misfortunes in life – now and again, severe ones. If, in the midst of our own troubles, we can go to a grieving neighbor or to someone sick and offer help, we will find that while we are lifting their spirits, we are lifting our own as well. This is a perfect recipe both for nipping depression in the bud and for spreading consolation.

To be understood as to understand.

When I first took to meditation, my attitude toward my students underwent a substantial change. You know, when you have been talking in class for five days running about Wordsworth's view of nature and on Friday you ask one or two simple questions and can get no satisfactory answer, it is natural to feel a bit exasperated. "Why can't they follow?" I used to ask myself. "Or, if they can't follow, why can't they at least read through the text at home so they can answer simple questions?"

Gradually, however, I began to develop a more compassionate attitude. It struck me forcefully that words like Saint Francis's were meant not only to be repeated in meditation but to be applied, even in mundane situations on a university campus. I began to understand, for example, that it was unreasonable to expect a good performance from a student who had an irresistible tendency to daydream and procrastinate. With that insight, my exasperation evaporated. I saw such problems now from my students' perspective, and instead of wishing they were different, my attention went to getting to know those students and helping them learn better habits. Teaching became a matter of not merely conveying knowledge, but of showing how to live.

Understanding is the first thing to jump out the window when two emotionally involved people get into a quarrel. "He just doesn't understand me!" is a grumble that frequently reaches my ears. Saint Francis, I suspect, would reply, "What does it matter? The real question is, do you understand him? Have you tried to understand his point of view?" The honest answer would usually be no. Strong emotions plug up our ears like those foam earplugs which expand into the opening of your ear to prevent even a single wave of sound from getting through.

I have yet to hear of anyone who did not understand his or her own side of a quarrel in minute detail. "See, my hay fever is acting up now because my prescription ran out, and I had this terrific headache from our youngest son yelling at me. So when my husband came into the kitchen and slammed the door for no reason, I just let him have it." Our private prosecuting attorney in the mind has built up an open-and-shut case. That is the problem: we shut the case too soon. As any experienced judge knows, every case has two sides. Fairness demands that we give equal time to the defense, who is inside us too. The other side deserves the same hearing and the same benefit of the doubt that we give ourselves as a matter of course. This is detachment. If we can practice it, quarrels can be settled amicably before they ever come before a jury.

To be loved as to love.

Now we get down to the nitty-gritty of romance. Millions of people today voice the heartfelt complaint that they feel lonely and unloved. It is a serious condition. Here Saint Francis is saying, "I know the cause of the malady and I know the secret of its complete cure." No matter what the relationship may be, when you look on another person as someone who can give you love, you are really *faking* love. That is the simplest word for it. If you are interested in making love, in making it grow without end, try looking on that person as someone you can give your love to – someone to whom you can go on giving always.

Learning to love is like swimming against the current of a powerful river; most of our conditioning is in the other direction. When the river by my village used to flood with the advent of the monsoon rains, we boys liked to try to swim across without being swept downstream by the current. To tell you the truth, I never succeeded. The only time I came close was the time someone told me there was a crocodile after me. But a few of my cousins were such powerful swimmers that they could fight the current and reach the other side exactly opposite from where they had set out. It is simply a question of developing your muscles: the more you use them, the stronger they get. Similarly, when you put the other person's welfare foremost every day, no matter how strong the opposing tide inside, you discover after a while that you can love a little more today than you did yesterday. Tomorrow you will be able to love a little more.

There is no end to love. It does not confine itself to just one person or one family. Most of us seem to feel that if Romeo, say, begins to care deeply for Juliet's nurse, his love for Juliet will somehow be diminished; Juliet should feel jealous. If he learns to extend his love to her brothers, the nurse should feel neglected too. There is no conflict. Romeo still loves Juliet and still cares for her nurse; it is just that he is coming to love everybody. He can be completely loyal to his sweetheart, Juliet, and completely loyal in all his other relationships as well. The beauty of this kind of love is that it never divides; it will bring Juliet, her nurse, and her brothers closer together than they ever were before.

For it is in giving that we receive.

This is one of the most incredible paradoxes in life. We think, naturally enough, that if we go after what we want, we will probably get it; then we will be happy and secure. The mass media intone this line of thinking like a litany: grab, grab, grab! Yet sooner or later the whole smorgasbord of things to get causes every sensitive person to ask, "If I go on grabbing and grabbing, at what point is it that I become secure and feel no more need to grab?" This question can lead to some far-reaching answers. Our needs are much too big to be satisfied with things, no matter how many we can manage to acquire. Often, it seems, the more we try to get, the more acutely we feel those needs.

We are used today to thinking in terms of presents – Father's Day presents, Mother's Day presents, birthday presents, Christmas presents. The great excitement at Christmas is looking in our stocking and opening gifts. Francis might ask, "Don't you want to find your stocking filled with good things every morning?" We *can,* every morning after meditation. But we cannot expect to find our stocking filled if we leave it hanging there full of stuff. There will be no room for the Lord to put anything in unless we empty ourselves every day by giving all we can in the way of kindness and loving help. Then every morning we will find ourselves full again – of love, of understanding, of forgiveness, of energy with which to carry these gifts to others. Saint Francis has been telling us in every line of this Prayer that this is the Lord's way of giving: the more we share what we have, the more he wants to give us from within.

Every day we can receive these gifts and every day we can share them, whether people are friendly to us or not. The more we share, the more we will win the love and respect of others – and the more we win their love and respect, the less our turmoil and troubles. Personal burdens will lie lightly on us. Our deepest need is for the joy that comes with loving and being loved, with knowing we are of genuine use to others. For everybody who has problems or who wants to go forward steadily on the spiritual path, my recipe would be to do more for others and think less about yourself. Hang up an empty stocking and every day you will find your life filling more and more with joy.

It is in pardoning that we are pardoned.

Late in his life Francis found himself compelled to give over his place as head of the order to Brother Elias, who thereafter became very keen on improving the conduct of his Brothers. When Elias came to him with complaints and plans to penalize some of them, Francis gave him strong advice: "See to it that no Brother in the whole world, however he may have sinned, is permitted to go from you without forgiveness if he asks for it. And if he does not ask for forgiveness, then ask him if he does not want it. And even if he comes before your eyes a thousand times with sin, love him more than you do me, that you may draw him to the Lord; . . . for the healthy need no physician, but only those who suffer illness."

The forgiveness Francis is prescribing here is not a matter merely of saying "I forgive you; let bygones be bygones." No amount of talking can prevent the seed of resentment from taking hold in our heart. True forgiveness requires that we not only not take personally any harsh thing said or done to us, but that we make an all-out effort to understand the other person's situation. Then, even if we get angry for a few minutes and think, "That Mortimer!" we know it will soon turn to "Well, he comes from a discordant home, and nobody showed him how to object nicely." When this happens, we know that resentment doesn't stand a chance. But Francis is zealous in his recommendation that we follow up this forgiving with genuine acts of kindness, which can actually cure the impulse of the other person to say or do something harsh again.

It is in dying to self that we are born to eternal life.

We all have deep within us an overwhelming desire to lose ourselves in love. In practical terms, this is what loving the Lord means. Saint Francis is reminding us again that the way to live in the presence of the Lord is to find that love which flows all the time, regardless of people's ups and downs, which brings together not only our own dear ones but all others as well. Finding this love requires a lot of labor and anguish, but it is this labor, which we accomplish by meditating and incorporating the other spiritual disciplines into our daily life, that opens the floodgates of love.

Loving the Lord has the miraculous power to change us. We all know how, when a young man feels drawn to a young lady, his personal appearance improves overnight, his language becomes more refined, his taste in reading and entertainment takes on a softer, more romantic bent. In the same way, as we begin to understand better what pleases the Lord, our personality begins to change. We make more of an effort to be patient with people, and even if anger does come up, it has less sting. We start to sympathize with the difficulties others are facing. This is an inescapable transformation.

If you ask lovers of God how they can find joy in effacing themselves, they will tell you, "Otherwise, I don't stand a chance; my Lord won't even look at me. He will say, 'Who wants this angry grouch around?' This gives us all the determination we need to empty ourselves. When we succeed, even a little, we feel ourselves moving that much closer to him." They do not deny that this can be distressing, but they assure us that the joy we find in this growing love will give us motivation to face distress with equanimity.

In time, we begin to enrich our life with concern for everybody, with giving our time and our energy to helping others. By directing our attention to others' welfare, we make our own life fuller and more beautiful. This is the source of the incredibly selfless, undemanding love we see in someone like Saint Francis, which seems to us so uncanny. It is what Saint Bernard was hinting at when he explained, "I love because I love; I love in order that I may love." *When I do not love,* he is trying to tell us, *I am parted from my Lord; and that I cannot bear.*

MOTHER TERESA

Introduction by Carol Lee Flinders

Threading her way carefully along the run-
down sidewalks of San Francisco's Mission District,
between the stumbling derelicts and the weary bag ladies,
the dull-eyed, bewildered adolescents and the children –
silent, thin, and much too wary – there passes a young
woman dressed so distinctively that even here, in this
motleyest of neighborhoods, one notices her. She is a
nun. Her head is veiled, a crucifix hangs at her left shoulder, and she wears the blue-bordered white sari of the Missionaries of Charity, known better, though not officially,
as the Sisters of Mother Teresa of Calcutta.

In all the United States, there is no city more expensive
to live in than San Francisco. To be poor in San Francisco
is therefore particularly arduous. That is one reason why
the Missionaries of Charity have come here, to the city
named (the irony was never intended, and by most it's still
not sensed) after Saint Francis. It was among some of the
most desperately impoverished people on earth that
Mother Teresa began her work of love, and now that
members of her order have been invited into cities around
the world, they still work, for the most part, among the
poorest and hungriest.

The physical privations of San Francisco's less-than-lucky account only in part, though, for the presence of the Missionaries of Charity. One could cite places that have not been so blessed where the apparent need is greater. But the poverty of the West, Mother Teresa believes, falls with a special weight, and cuts with its own keen edge:

> When I pick up a person from the street, hungry, I give him a plate of rice, a piece of bread, and I have removed that hunger. But a person that is shut out, that feels unwanted, unloved, terrified, the person that has been thrown out from society — that poverty is so hurtable and so much, and I find that very difficult. Our Sisters are working amongst that kind of people in the West.

Just as Saint Francis did in creating the Third Order, Mother Teresa has opened the way for people of all situations in life to participate in her work. Some are formally organized as Co-Workers, who meet regularly to pray together and who assist in the work materially by collecting clothing, making bandages, and fitting out the dispensaries. But in the widest sense, we all have a role to play.

To the work carried out by the Missionaries of Charity among the most destitute people in India and elsewhere, not everyone is called. But where that other kind of poverty is concerned, "The poverty of the spirit, of loneliness and being unwanted," whose consequences are ultimately just as serious, there, she insists, we all have a vocation. "This is the hunger you and I must find," Mother Teresa reminds us, "and it may be in our own home."

Her counsel is simple and direct. Begin where you are, she tells us — extend your love to the people right around you. Fill your homes with love and let that love radiate outward. "We must make our homes centers of compassion," she says, "and forgive endlessly." And she makes what some might think a very tall claim:

> I think the world today is upside-down, and is suffering so much, because there is so very little love in the homes and in family life. We have no time for our children, we have no time for each other; there is no time to enjoy each other. If we could only bring back into our lives the life that Jesus, Mary and Joseph lived in Nazareth, if we could make our homes another Nazareth, I think that peace and joy would reign in the world.

When the Nobel Prize for Peace was given to Mother Teresa in 1979, the award announcement commended her "for work undertaken in the struggle to overcome poverty and distress in the world, which also constitute a threat to peace." To give public recognition to the role that hunger and homelessness have in causing war was a very good thing for the Committee to have done. It is interesting, though, that Mother Teresa herself did not speak in quite those terms — said nothing about how if people have enough to eat, and clothing to wear, they're not as likely to enter into war.

Instead, in a characteristically broken but impassioned rush of eloquence, she appealed to every one of us: "And I think that we in our family — we don't need bombs and guns to destroy. To bring peace, just get together, love one another, bring that peace, that joy, that strength of presence of each other in the home. And we will be able to overcome all the evil that is in the world."

Which is to say, Mother Teresa believes in miracles, or at least in what might seem miraculous today. She believes, for she has experienced it and watched it in others, that within each of us is an enormous, indomitable power for good. Her version of peace goes far beyond the absence of war — and that is why she is such a powerful force for peace.

Reflecting on the subtle change that took place in Calcutta as awareness of Mother Teresa's work spread, one observer has remarked that it was as though for the first time, in that city of bottomless need, there was a safety net. In Mother Teresa's own words, "Ordinary people are beginning to get concerned. Before, they used to pass by a person dying on the streets, but now, when they see something like that, they immediately do something. If they can't get an ambulance, they bring the person to us by rickshaw, or taxi, or take them to Kalighat, or they phone us. The big thing is that they do something; it's wonderful, eh?"

The image of a safety net applies to the Missionaries of Charity in an even deeper sense, though, well beyond the good they do directly and consciously. That is because, in the quietest, most unassuming way possible, without saying a word, they challenge the view of human nature on which contemporary civilization rests — and with it, all the cynicism and despair that flow from that view. They "bear witness" to a very different picture.

Not everyone grasps what these sisters mean when they say "We do it for Jesus," or when they paraphrase his words: "In the poor it is the hungry Christ that we are feeding, it is the naked Christ that we are clothing, it is to the homeless Christ that we are giving shelter." Words are only words, after all. Yet the meaning comes through. Describing a visit to one of Mother Teresa's Homes in Calcutta, one writer recalls "a young American who was plainly radiating God's love. . . . He was administering to the particularly wretched cases with a tenderness other men his age use to express their first breathless outpourings of love. He was from New York, a Jew; he had traveled all over but, man, he had never seen anything like this. So beautiful, so beautiful."

At every opportunity, Mother Teresa reiterates the endlessly astonishing fact about the work — the fact this young man from New York had unwittingly stumbled upon and that Saint Francis put so simply: "It is in giving that we receive." Going forth in love, reaching out with love, they have found, in men and women who have every reason to behave otherwise, courage, gratitude, and enormous sweetness. And out of this experience comes a rock-solid faith — infectious, highly communicable, shining out from the eyes of everyone who possesses it — in the essential goodness of us all.

Mother Teresa describes a man brought to them, near death, who said, "I have lived like an animal in the street, but I am going to die like an angel, loved and cared for."

"And it was so wonderful," she adds, "to see the greatness of that man who could speak like that, who could die like that without blaming anybody, without cursing anybody . . . this is the greatness of our people. And that is why we believe what Jesus has said: 'I was hungry — I was naked — I was homeless . . .'"

Strip away the highly-colored facade of life today, slow down its heated pace so you can get a good look, and it's easy enough to see the assumptions that underlie it — assumptions that add up to a definite view of human nature: that we are finite, limited, and essentially powerless creatures, defined by our needs and desires, compelled in a world of scarcity to fight for them, and successful to the extent we gratify them.

It's a dismal verdict, reinforced by books, films, advertisements, and it has eroded every tender and sturdy bond that ever linked us one to another. Can a phrase like "the family of man" have any resonance at all, any power to move us, if the word "family" has none? Mother Teresa doubts it.

So much of what goes on under the name of peace work is in fact simply anti-war work. But what Mother Teresa suggests, implicitly as well as in words, is that the greatest, most effective and powerful way to oppose war is to wage peace – to wage love – to pour out your energy and concern from a source that is, in fact, endless.

Easwaran's essay on Mother Teresa addresses that basic challenge she sets before us: love. He is a seasoned teacher, and he knows very well that in the heart of his hearer one question is reverberating: "But how? How can I take this very limited and ineffectual self and make it into a powerful force for good?"

"Thou shalt love the Lord thy God with thy whole heart, with thy whole soul, and with thy whole mind." This is the commandment of the great God, and he cannot command the impossible.

Love is a fruit in season at all times, and within reach of every hand. Anyone may gather it and no limit is set. Everyone can reach this love through meditation, spirit of prayer, and sacrifice, by an intense inner life.

Hunger for Love

There is hunger for ordinary bread, and there is hunger for love, for kindness, for thoughtfulness; and this is the great poverty that makes people suffer so much.

Our modern civilization is so physically oriented that when we hear the word hunger, we immediately think in terms of vitamins and minerals and amino acids. It seldom occurs to us that just as the body develops problems when it does not get adequate food, the person who is deprived of love – or worse, who finds it difficult to love – becomes subject to problems every bit as serious. I am not referring merely to emotional problems, though these of course are included. More and more evidence indicates that lack of love not only leads to loneliness, despair, and resentment, but eventually may even lead to deterioration of the vital organs. Researchers have made a good case for connecting cardiovascular accidents like heart attack with selfishness, isolation, alienation, and bereavement, all of which can be traced to lack of love. And a brilliant San Francisco cardiologist, Meyer Friedman, traces many cardiovascular problems to a syndrome of thought and behavior called "Type A personality," exhibited by men or women who are "aggressively involved in a chronic, incessant struggle to achieve more and more in less and less time, and if required to do so, against the opposing efforts of other things or other persons."

In fact, I would say, if they are allowed to continue, such ways of thinking and acting place us at risk for more than just cardiovascular problems. When we are continually driven by a strong desire to get something for ourselves – success, pleasure, reputation, power – we live in stress all day long, day in and day out, seven days a week. We grow increasingly anxious about getting what we want, and get angry more and more often when we can't get our way – all of which only makes the demands of our desires more fierce. The body adjusts to this state of stress by keeping adaptive mechanisms like elevated blood pressure switched on almost all the time. And after a while, not surprisingly, part of the system breaks down. The medical community would be precise: "Cause of death: myocardial infarction." That is a cause, but not the first cause. We could say with equal accuracy, "He died of greed and from always putting himself first. He died from never having learned to love."

In other words, when spiritual figures like Mother Teresa talk about our need to love and to be loved, the need is not metaphorical. Mother Teresa is not talking about spirituality alone; she is talking about good nutrition. Resentment, hostility, alienation, and self-ishness are deficiency diseases. You can have all the essential amino acids, vitamins, and minerals known and unknown but if you cannot love, you are not likely to remain in good health.

We can think of Mother Teresa as a perfect physician. She has her protocols, set forth in the Sermon on the Mount and Saint Paul's "epistle on love," and the signs and symptoms of deficiency are all too easy to recognize. She puts a thermometer to modern industrial civilization, checks its blood pressure, and gives her diagnosis without hesitation: "Acute spiritual malnutrition. The patient is trying to meet all his needs with selfishness; love is crowded out." But malnutrition is reversible. Just as negative emotions like anger, fear, and greed have great power to harm, Mother Teresa knows what to prescribe to heal: good will, patience, overriding love for all.

We scarcely know today what this word *love* means. Most often it is used for physical relationships which have very little to do with love. Such relationships are based on physical satisfaction, which means that when the satisfaction goes – as all physical satisfactions must – the relationship falls apart. Love is not based on sensations; it is a lasting state of mind. At its highest – love pure and perfected, love that is completely selfless – it never asks what it can get but only what it can give. Physical sensation leads only to spiritual starvation; pure love nourishes and heals.

Usually a good physician will not write a prescription without some accompanying instructions: plenty of rest, lots of fluids, and so on. Certain conditions have to be fulfilled for the prescription to be most effective. Similarly, if love is prescribed as the remedy for our condition, to perfect pure love we need five things. The first is time. Second is control over our attention. Third comes energy, vitality. Fourth, we need discrimination. And fifth, we must have awareness of the unity of life.

Let me elaborate on these one by one.

Time

An obsession with time has been so worked into our social system that we scarcely notice we have left no time to love. Everywhere the slogan is Hurry, Hurry, Hurry. Yet to be aware of the needs of others, to spend time with others, to speak and act with patience and consideration, we must have time – a lot more time than most of us have at present.

On the one hand, this is a matter of simplifying our lives, dropping less important activities in order to allow more time for what matters most. But it is also essential to slow down our pace of living, so that we can free ourselves from the time-driven thinking and behavior characteristic of modern life.

One of the most effective steps to take here is simple: get up early. If you wake up late, rush through breakfast, run for the bus, and reach your office ten minutes after everyone else has settled down, that is the pace you are going to maintain throughout the day. It is not only inimical to health; it is also inimical to happiness, for it crowds out love. When we rush, we cannot even see people; they are just phantoms. We are too much in a hurry to catch the little signs in a person's eyes or around the corners of the mouth which say, "You're stepping on my feelings. You're letting me down." All the mind can think of is *Me, me, me* –"What *I* have to do, and how little time I have to do it."

When people ask how they can learn to love more, therefore, I sometimes say enigmatically, "Get up earlier." Allow plenty of time for meditation, and then come to breakfast not only with an appetite but with time – time enough to eat leisurely, to talk with others at the table, and to get to work five or ten minutes early so that you can chat a little with your co-workers. All too often, we do not see the people we work with as individuals. They are not just mannequins in an office; they are people very much like us. They have homes, raise houseplants, play with their dogs, worry about finances, go to the beach, enjoy musicals. When we see people as just like us, we usually find them likable.

Eating leisurely is especially important where children are concerned. They are not only assimilating their oatmeal, they are absorbing everything they see and hear. It is a great disservice to try to hurry them through a meal. We need to give them time to ask questions that cannot be answered, to tell stories punctuated by long pauses while they search for a particular word, even to upset a glass of milk, and still get off to school on time; all this is part of a loving breakfast. In these terms, I suspect that there are few people today who have a truly loving breakfast. All too often the term is reserved for a doughnut or some precooked flakes of cellulose heated up in a microwave oven, which is neither loving nor a breakfast.

"You can afford to say 'Go slow,' Uncle," my little niece Geetha used to complain with exasperation. "You don't have to go to school." I have to confess that I took my time at meals even when I *did* have to go to school; it is something I probably absorbed from my grandmother, who never felt pressured. So even if it is your first day at high school, even if you have a big day at the office and a hundred things to accomplish before noon, let your breakfast be unhurried. There is never any need for an unkind word, a numb tongue, or a cold shoulder. If you do not have much to say, you can always listen with attention. And please do not read the newspaper at the table. Millions of people, I think, use the morning paper not so much for the news as for a shield. They are shielding themselves from love.

Mother Teresa, I was interested to see, draws the same unexpected connection between time and love. "Everybody today seems to be in such a terrible rush," she observes, "anxious for greater developments and greater riches and so on, so that children have very little time for their parents. Parents have very little time for each other, and in the home begins the disruption of the peace of the world."

Attention

Slowing down is closely connected with one-pointed attention: doing one thing at a time, and doing it with complete attention. In the case of rushing, for example, the problem is not only one of speed. Our attention is riveted on ourselves – *our* needs, *our* deadlines, *our* desires – so there is no attention to give to those around us, who have needs and desires and perhaps even deadlines very much like our own. Especially for children, we need to slow down so that we can give them our attention, which they require as much as food and sleep.

Meditation is essentially a matter of learning to direct and maintain a steady flow of attention. Then, during the day, we continue to train the mind by keeping it one-pointed on the job at hand.

Interestingly enough, a many-pointed mind seems to be characteristic of the Type A personality. Dr. Friedman called it by an exotic name, "polyphasic thinking," but it is extremely common, and not just among high-powered executives. Many people, for example, find it difficult to stay interested in anything except themselves. While they are listening to you and saying, "Yes, how true," their attention wanders away, and they start planning the evening's menu or doing a few stock market calculations in their head. When they are driving, instead of concentrating on the road, they turn on the radio and start going over some old memory or rehearsing an argument with the boss. In such cases, there is no focus of attention. The mind is jumping about like a grasshopper, and there is no control over it.

Through practicing meditation and giving full concentration to one thing at a time, we can learn to direct attention where we choose. This is an almost miraculous skill, with applications to the practice of love that are as simple as they are essential. When we can give complete attention to the person we are with, even if she is contradicting our opinions on tax reform or explaining the peculiarities of Roman law, boredom disappears from our relationships. People are not boring; we get bored because our attention wanders. Giving someone our full attention says clearly, "You matter to me. You have my respect."

Attention is very much like a dog. Some years ago my friend Steve acquired a large, affectionate, and utterly blithe-spirited retriever pup whom his son named Ganesha. Ganesha had a lot of energy, and he had never been trained; he was accustomed to doing whatever he liked. If you put him in the yard, he would dig under the fence. Leave him in the bedroom and he would chew up your slippers. Take him for a walk and in a minute he would be halfway across a field chasing a deer. So Steve started to train him. For a while, I thought it was the other way around: Ganesha would bark and then Steve would run after him. But now, after a lot of patient practice, Ganesha has learned to heel and to expend his energy on a fast run at the beach instead of on bedroom slippers.

Attention can be trained in a very similar way. At first it wanders restlessly all over, looking into everything and everybody. But if we put it on a short leash and recall it many, many times, the great day will come when it will heel and obey. Then it becomes an alert, invaluable companion – very much like a well-trained sheep dog, which I have seen follow all kinds of complicated instructions. Over the years, I have come to the conclusion that there is no limit to the degree to which attention can be trained. That is how responsive it is.

Almost every disruption in human relationships – between parent and child, man and woman, friend and friend, worker and co-worker – can be prevented by learning control over attention; for with attention comes loyalty, interest, desire, trust. I can illustrate with the most fascinating of relationships: the romantic. Suppose *Romeo and Juliet* had turned out differently, and the two lovers had married and settled down to a normal domestic life. After a few years, as sometimes happens, Romeo's attention gets restless, and Juliet loses her attraction. Once the very sight of her made him think of flowers and bubbling brooks and the "light, sweet airs of spring"; now she just reminds him of the laundry and his morning espresso. Once he used to hang on her every word; now he answers everything with "Fine" and "Have a nice day." After a while his attention falls on Rosaline, his old flame.

Now *she* reminds him of flowers and brooks; his attention grabs onto her and will not let go.

If he could read what most of us read today, the advice he would get is, "Follow your desires. That is where happiness will be." That is just where unhappiness will be. If Romeo's attention cannot stay with Juliet, how is it going to stay with Rosaline? After all, Juliet is the same Juliet, no less attractive than before. But Romeo is also the same Romeo. If he cannot get control over his attention, happiness can only get farther and farther away.

The moment you hear the brook babbling and start thinking about spring, withdraw your attention completely from Rosaline and focus it on Juliet. With practice, we can focus our attention by choice just as intensely as it is focused by first love. Then Romeo will find that every day with Juliet is as sweet as the first. Every morning he will be able to exclaim with fresh wonder, "It is the east, and Juliet is the sun!" And the love between them will grow deeper and richer every day. As Teresa of Avila says, *"Amor saca amor"*: love draws out love.

Energy

To love, we have to be able to do things for others, even if it is inconvenient. We have to be able to do things we do not like even when we seem to have no willpower or energy. When we know we should help Johnny with his homework but have only enough energy to drop into a beanbag chair with a martini, one way of looking at the problem is that we are out of gas. Why? We eat good food, get enough sleep; we have plenty of energy for doing things we like. How can we get more energy, so that we can give more love?

When people ask me this, I usually point out, "You already have a lot of energy." As far as human beings are concerned, there is no real energy crisis. All of us have vast amounts of vitality. But we fritter it away, letting it flow out wastefully through one hundred and one channels.

Here again, there is a close connection with attention. Energy drains out when we let the mind go on working, repeating the same thought over and over. I have seen learned names for this phenomenon too, but I would compare it simply with a broken record. When a phonograph record becomes scratched, you know, the needle jumps the groove and keeps repeating the same few words or notes. The mind jumps its grooves too. It begins playing one of its little tunes – "Roses are red, violets are blue, Tchaikovsky is great and so are you" – and all of a sudden it is "Tchaikovsky, Tchaikovsky, Tchaikovsky . . ." That is all that most guilt complexes amount to, most compulsive memories, most resentments, most obsessions: sitting there like the little dog listening obediently to "His Master's Voice" while the same old thought goes round and round and round. There is no serious mental malady here, only a minor mechanical problem.

When we know how to meditate well, if the mind slips into a negative groove, we can lift it up gently and set it down on something positive.

This is not turning away from problems or playing Pollyanna. It is simply good energy conservation. Whatever problems we might have, dwelling on them is only going to magnify them, and waste a lot of time and energy in the process.

To put it another way, negative thoughts such as anger, resentment, greed, and worry are like holes in a tank, through which vitality drains. A few weeks ago, as we were driving to San Francisco, a car passed us leaving a trail of gasoline. About half an hour later we saw the same car parked on the shoulder of the road, out of gas. That is just what most of us do with the mind. It is full of energy, yet we go through life trying to punch as many holes in it as possible, multiplying our desires, our possessions, our anxieties, our frustrations until by the end of the day we have scarcely any energy left at all. The biggest of these holes is selfish desire. Thérèse of Lisieux was once asked by her older sister why she, Celine, was not making faster progress on the spiritual path. Thérèse took Celine's thumb and wrote on it playfully, "Too many desires." Vitality leaks out through every selfish desire. The more we want for ourselves, the less energy we shall have, and therefore the less capacity for love.

When we find it difficult to love other people or to put them first, we can think of it as a personal energy crisis. I read a lot today about the crisis with fossil fuels.

Many people still talk as if the only solution is to find some other source of power, but that is not enough; it is equally necessary to reduce consumption. The same is true when we are talking about our personal energy, our vitality. Here we have no atoms to split or fuse, no windmills to make, no sun to draw on for an alternative source of energy; we have to conserve what we have and make it last.

If we lived in a house with only one big battery's worth of electricity, we would be turning off lights right and left. If we had just one tank of fuel oil or gas, we would always be ready to turn down the heat. Similarly, when we are not using the mind, we can learn to turn it off. When some fierce desire is prompting us into action, we can learn to turn off the heat. The power is not lost. Instead of being wasted, it is consolidated as tremendous reserves of vitality, security, and self-mastery.

In today's consumer world, a lot of power is wasted in producing items which are neither necessary nor beneficial. But buying less and owning less conserves personal energy as well. Shopping for things we do not need, for example, wastes a lot of vitality, even if it is only window shopping; energy flows out with every little desire. It is a surprising connection, but an extravagant shopper will find it difficult to love. When such a person goes shopping, he or she scatters love like largesse all over the department store basement. We can become bankrupt in love this way, just as we can in money. So if you want a good, stiff test of your

capacity to love, go into your favorite store some day –
preferably when there is a sale – and see if you can
walk straight through, looking neither left nor right,
and come out unscathed. It may sound impossible,
but it *can* be done.

Discrimination

This brings us to the fourth essential of love:
the capacity to discriminate between right and wrong
desires. The criteria are simple. Right desires benefit
everyone – including, of course, ourselves. Wrong
desires may be very pleasing, but they benefit no one –
again, not even ourselves. The problem that arises is
that wrong desires can be very skillful impersonators.
They put on a three-piece suit and a false mustache
and present themselves suavely as Mr. Right, the
benefactor of all; if they happen to be just what we
like, that is only a happy coincidence. To love, we need
to be able to recognize right desires and yield to them,
which is a pleasant but rare state of affairs. But much
more importantly, we need to be able to recognize
wrong desires and resist them, which is very, very difficult.

Again, I can give a small example from my own life.
This morning my friend Laurel prepared especially for
me some waffles made with finely ground almonds.
They were not only a delicious, loving gift; they were
also nutritious. So when she came to the door I wel-
comed the whole combination with open arms – her,
the waffles, and my mind's desire to eat them. On the

other hand, if I had come to the kitchen and found a package of frozen waffles lying on the table with a note saying, "I have to go to my golf lesson. Just pop these in the toaster according to the directions on the package" – well, if I *had* had a desire for waffles I would have told that desire, "Please stay out. I don't want to eat these; I don't want to see them; I don't even want to hear about them."

Most wrong desires, I admit, are not so easily resisted. We have to draw on every militant instinct we have to take on the desire person to person. We don't even know we have this choice. When a big desire comes, we think we have to yield. There is some pleasure in yielding; but if I may say so, there is much more lasting satisfaction in resisting, even if at first we do not win. The very attitude of resisting wrong desires is the beginning of good health, vitality, and love.

Not only that, resisting wrong desires actually generates energy. Whenever we can defy a powerful, selfish desire, immense power is released into our hands. I do not think this is even suspected outside the major religions of the world, yet it is the secret of all spiritual work and transformation.

Our desires are not our business alone; they are everybody's business. Whenever we resist a selfish desire, even if we do so for no one in particular, that is an act of love – just as every time we yield to a selfish desire, it shows want of love. The reason is simple: everything we do affects others, whether directly, through the environment, or by the force of our example. To me, for instance, smoking shows lack of love. First, the capacity for love is actually caught in that compulsion. But more than that, the smoke is harmful for everyone, and the example tells even casual passers-by, "Don't worry about the surgeon general. Don't worry about consequences; don't even think about the future. If it feels good, do it!"

Pelé, the great Brazilian soccer player, has long been in a position to command a king's ransom for endorsing commercial products. He has never given his endorsement to any brand of cigarettes, and I was very pleased to hear him give the reason in simple English: "I love kids." That is a perfect choice of words. He *does* love kids. He knows that in most of the world they will buy anything with his name on it. Therefore, though he came from a very poor family, no amount of money can tempt him to do something that will mislead young people or injure their health. To love is to be responsible like this in everything: the work we do, the things we buy, the food we eat, the people we look up to, the movies we see, the words we use, every choice we make from morning till night. That is the real measure of love; it is a wonderfully demanding responsibility.

Awareness of Unity

Discrimination, then, leads us naturally to the last quality for love: the awareness that life is one indivisible whole. This is the very basis of love. Any violation of the unity of life, whether it is between individuals, between nations, between us and the environment, or between us and our fellow creatures, is a failure of love. Everything that separates diminishes love; everything that unifies increases it. Lack of love divides; wealth of love heals.

To take just one aspect of this, you may recall Mother Teresa's brilliant truism: "It is always people you meet everywhere." Beneath the thinnest shell of differences, every one of us is very much the same, whether we live in Asia, Africa, Antarctica, or America. In times of nationalism or of international tension we forget this; if we remembered, no nation would ever go to war.

Once we realize the unity of life, we see the whole planet as a single family, whose welfare is indivisible. Most of us would not dream of tearing up our front yard, filling our garage with garbage, burning the porches for fuel, spraying noxious chemicals around the house, and then telling our children, "We're moving out. You can have whatever is left." That is exactly how we should feel about the earth. When we love all life as our family, it will be impossible for us to waste anything. We will want to share whatever we have — air, water, oil, food – not only with those who are alive today but with the children of the future, all of whom are our own.

Learning to love is not a luxury. It is a vital necessity – especially perhaps today, when the whole world, threatened with violence on every side, is starving for love and unity. "In the home," Mother Teresa says, "begins the disruption of the peace of the world." Similarly, it is in the home that the peace of the world is preserved. In nourishing our family, our community, and finally our world with love, turning our backs on ourselves when necessary to give what the world so desperately needs, we become, in the words of Saint Francis, instruments of peace.

SAINT PAUL

Introduction by Carol Lee Flinders

All we know of Saint Paul is what we are told in the Acts of the Apostles, and what he tells us himself in his letters to the small communities of new Christians he had founded in cities like Corinth, Thessalonica, and Rome. Put every scrap of information together and you still have a very incomplete picture. It is incomplete by modern standards – we have no physical description, for example – but telling, all the same.

The turning point in Paul's life – the part of the story everyone has heard – is that on his way to Damascus, armed with letters from the high priest in Jerusalem which authorized the arrest of any Christians he could locate, he was struck down by a blinding light (it was or was not perceived by his companions, depending on which account you read) and heard a voice that said, "Saul, Saul, why dost thou persecute me? . . . I am Jesus whom thou persecutest." Saul asks what the Lord would have him do. "Arise," he is told, "and go into the city, and it shall be told thee what thou must do."

So began the heroic ministry of the Apostle Paul and the dissemination of the Gospel throughout the Gentile world.

If this were all we knew of Paul's conversion, the whole

train of events would seem disturbingly arbitrary. "The Lord works in mysterious ways," of course. But was there nothing in Saul's character that would help us make sense of such a radical change?

In fact, we do know more.

We know, to begin with, that Saul was a brilliant young man. He must have been, for he had had the privilege of studying with the greatest rabbi of the time, Gamaliel. We know that his family had attained Roman citizenship, which wasn't easy for Jews at that time.

We know, moreover, that he was passionately religious. By his lights, his foremost duty to the God of Israel was to root out the pernicious new faith by whatever means were at hand. He was fully prepared to live by those lights. "As for Saul, he made havoc of the church, entering into every house, and haling men and women committed them to prison." He was a man obsessed, his consciousness unified around a single purpose.

I have mentioned that one of the basic disciplines that Easwaran prescribes as a sure way to deepen one's meditation is the art of one-pointedness. By way of explaining its function, he has always insisted that the capacity to throw oneself heart and soul into something — tennis, ballet, politics, woodcarving — is in itself a sign of aptitude for the spiritual life, no matter how unlikely the individual might appear or how worldly the activity of choice.

Concentration, Easwaran believes, is the key to genius in any field, because when we can withdraw all our attention from everything except the one object or question or challenge at hand, we get access to inner resources that are normally locked away out of reach. In this sense, even a powerful emotion like anger or desire, when it unifies our attention completely, can open a door into deeper consciousness. The account of Saul's embarking for

Damascus — "breathing out threatenings and slaughter against the disciples of the Lord" — suggests that he was in just such a state.

What had stirred him to such a depth?

Just a few days before, Saul had been witness to an event of enormous significance in the history of early Christianity: the stoning to death of Stephen, its first martyr. Stephen had been preaching the Gospel to powerful effect — so powerful that his antagonists charged him with blasphemy and brought him before the high priest. Instead of refuting the charge, Stephen recounted the history of the Jews since the time of Abraham, and in the telling, he identified himself with the prophets who foretold the coming of the Messiah and his persecutors with those who had resisted the Holy Ghost. Frenzied, the crowd "gnashed on him with their teeth." Stephen was unaffected. "Being full of the Holy Ghost, they looked up steadfastly into heaven, and saw the glory of God, and Jesus standing on the right hand of God." He said as much, and his hearers "stopped their ears, and ran upon him with one accord; and cast him out of the city, and stoned him."

There is an expression to describe someone who does not join in an assault, but who stands by and tacitly supports it: "He held his coat." This is almost literally what Saul did in Stephen's case. "The witnesses laid down their clothes at a young man's feet, whose name was Saul. And they stoned Stephen. . . . And Saul was consenting unto his death." Whether Saul was present when Stephen addressed the crowd in the synagogue, whether he too "saw his face as it had been an angel," we don't know. But there can be no doubt that he saw him at the moment of his death and heard him "calling upon God, and saying, 'Lord Jesus, receive my spirit,'" and finally, "'Lord, lay not this sin to their charge.'" Stephen falls dead at the feet of Saul. Like a young lion who has tasted blood, Saul hurls himself into the pursuit of Stephen's fellow Christians. But it is no good. Something has happened to him, and within days he is brought down himself. "Trembling and astonished," he receives his orders: "Arise and go into the city, and it shall be told thee what thou must do."

Quite without Saul's awareness, something was transmitted at the moment of Stephen's death: a seed, or — more appropriately, to borrow the metaphor Easwaran uses in such instances – a depth charge, equipped with a delaying device so that the explosion in consciousness takes place days or weeks later.

What happened to Paul was dramatic – of cataclysmic proportion. But it bears on the lives of every one of us insofar as it is the prototype of something that, in a much less astonishing way, happens all the time — and not just to saints or martyrs.

Any man or woman who hopes to leave the world a more habitable place for their having passed through has reason to reflect at some point upon the enormous disparity between the ranged Powers That Be and the apparent powerlessness of the single, well-meaning individual.

History refutes this disparity, teaching us again and again, through the lives of great reformers like Mahatma Gandhi and Martin Luther King Jr., like Teresa of Avila and Catherine of Siena and John Woolman and many, many others, that the dedicated individual is in fact immensely powerful. Study their lives, see how many minor miracles had to take place to bring their work to fruition, and you begin to see that latent in human affairs, ambient in the very atmosphere – slumbering in every one of us — there is tremendous power for good: the moral equivalent of atomic power, and just as ubiquitous.

Gandhi never tired of bearing witness to that power. In 1946, when an American journalist asked, "How can we prevent the next war?" Gandhi replied: "By doing the right thing irrespective of what the world will do. Each individual must act according to his ability without waiting for others, if he wants to move them to act. There comes a time when an individual becomes irresistible and his action becomes all-pervasive in its effect. This comes when he reduces himself to zero."

Easwaran has a phrase to describe the strange magic by which the bottomless wellsprings of love, courage, and resourcefulness in all of us can be tapped. He speaks of a "stirring of the unconscious." Look deep into the eyes of a man or woman who knows what he or she is about and something in you stirs – rises up out of long sleep to answer them, just as it did in young Saul. When the Bible speaks of "bearing witness," then, words are not at issue. The real aim is the kindling by one individual in another of their divine potential: "deep calling unto deep."

Another way of putting this is to say that our real nature, yours and mine and everyone's, is love. Whatever other gifts we may have, we are at our most effective when we let ourselves act out of love. No one has conveyed this with more conviction and eloquence than Saint Paul himself, in the passage that follows – a perfect one for use in meditation.

Though I speak with the tongues of men and of angels, and have not love, I am become as sounding brass, or a tinkling cymbal. And though I have the gift of prophecy, and understand all mysteries, and all knowledge; and though I have all faith, so that I could remove mountains, and have not love, I am nothing. And though I bestow all my goods to feed the poor, and though I give my body to be burned, and have not love, it profiteth me nothing.

Love suffereth long, and is kind; love envieth not; love vaunteth not itself, is not puffed up; doth not behave itself unseemly; seeketh not her own, is not easily provoked, thinketh no evil; rejoiceth not in iniquity, but rejoiceth in the truth; beareth all things, believeth all things, hopeth all things, endureth all things.

Love never faileth: but whether there be prophesies, they shall fail; whether there be tongues, they shall cease; whether there be knowledge, it shall vanish away. For we know in part, and we prophesy in part. But when that which is perfect is come, then that which is in part shall be done away.

When I was a child, I spake as a child, I understood as a child: but when I became a man, I put away childish things. For now we see through a glass, darkly; but then face to face: now I know in part; but then shall I know even as also I am known.

And now abideth faith, hope, love, these three; but the greatest of these is love.

I CORINTHIANS 13

Epistle on Love

[1]

Saint Paul's "epistle on love" (I Corinthians 13) is an eloquent, practical little manual for loving, so pregnant with meaning that I recommend it to everyone for use in meditation. Some will prefer the King James Version, with its elevated beauty of language. Others will find that the words of a contemporary translation speak to them more directly. It does not matter; this is a personal choice. What is important is to translate Saint Paul's words into our thought and action, and for that purpose I want to comment on this masterpiece of Christian mysticism almost line by line to show its application to daily living.

"Earnestly desire the higher gifts" of the spirit, Paul begins, "and I will show you a more excellent way." The way of love is perfectly suited to our times. Instead of telling friends you are leading the spiritual life, which sometimes makes people raise their eyebrows, you can say, "I'm learning to love." It is the same. "He who loves not knows not God," Saint John says; "for God is love."

Learning to love in this way is the most difficult, the most demanding, the most delightful, and the most daring of disciplines. It does not mean loving only two or three members of your family; that can often be a kind of ego-annex. It does not mean loving only those who share your views, read the same newspapers, or play the same sports. Love, as Jesus puts it, means blessing those that curse you, doing good to those that hate you; that is the real measure of love. Of course, words like these describe great lovers of God. But little people like us can learn to love like this too. The first condition is simple: we must want to love. Desire is the basis of all learning.

In the style of his Master, Paul is asking, "Do you want to love – not just those who like you but even those who dislike you, the very sight of whom sends you hurrying in another direction?" All of us, I think, would like to answer yes. All of us really want to love. Nobody wants to be hostile, angry, or afraid, and all these states arise from lack of love. But we do not know how to love; and perhaps we do not even know that love can be learned.

Here Mother Teresa has given us a practical clue. Universal love, she points out, is first learned in the home. The family is our primary school for love, for it is within the circle of the family that we see ourselves most easily as part of a larger whole. When sociologists say that the days of the family are numbered, this is like saying that the days of our love are numbered. To love is to live, and not to love is to have nothing to live for.

Once we earnestly desire to learn this, we start to school in love. Most of us do not begin by blessing those that curse us. That is graduate school. We start with first grade – being kind to people in our family when they get resentful. Eventually comes high school, where we learn to move closer to those who are trying to shut themselves off from us. College means returning good will for ill will. Then we are no longer simply mastering words and behavior; we are actually changing the way we think. And finally we enter graduate school: "Return love for hatred." There we learn to give our love to all – to people of different races, different countries, different religions, different outlooks, different strata of society, without any sense of distinction or difference.

Paul, I must say, can really strike hard. His words are utterly contemporary. "I may have all the knowledge in the world," he says. "I may be able to speak fourteen languages, including one or two that are spoken only by angels. I may have crossed the Atlantic in a canoe with only a cat for company. What does it matter? If I haven't learned to love, I am nothing."

Here we have an authentic standard for the worth of our lives, the value of our times. Paul is asking, "How much are you worth?" If we reply airily, "Oh, about five hundred thousand dollars," he won't bat an eyelid. "I'm not asking about your bank account," he'll say. "I'm asking what you are worth."

"Well," we tell ourselves, "after all, this Paul comes from Asia Minor. Probably he doesn't understand English idioms, or maybe this is some kind of Greek pun." But Paul is being literal. We are conditioned to think of value in terms of money; it scarcely occurs to us that "what are you worth?" has nothing to do with money at all.

When we measure people and situations in terms of money, values become secondary. To give just one example, take a man who manufactures and sells weapons – or, for that matter, one who manufactures or advertises cigarettes, ignoring all the evidence about what smoking does to health. He may rent a Santa Claus suit at Christmas and fill stockings with gifts to express his affection, but Paul would still say, "He doesn't know how to love." When he learns, he will not be able to make money through activities that bring suffering to other people or other creatures.

The more we measure life in money, the less room there is for love. To show how far this can go, every day we read in the papers or hear from a neighbor that somebody's house has been broken into or somebody's wallet "lifted." The root cause of this kind of crime is our obsession with money and material possessions, which we ourselves have fostered – in our entertainment, our advertisements, our whole way of living. If we really desire to reverse this trend, we have to stop measuring people in money and start measuring them in love. If a woman has a million dollars in the bank, there is no connection with the kind of person she is. Instead of asking how much she has, we should ask, "How much does she give?" How much of her time does she give to others? How much of her work goes to benefit others? Only then do we begin to measure her real worth.

Again, take the business of moonlighting. I never learned this word in India, you know. When I first heard it in this country, I naturally assumed it was something romantic. But moonlighting is the opposite of romantic when its purpose is just to provide more "discretionary income." Instead of bringing people together, it can actually divide them. You want a second car so you don't have to share the first; then your partner wants another TV so you can each watch the program of your choice. Finally you are down to dual toasters, his and hers. When this happens, you are actually moving apart. Of course, there are extreme situations when a person has to hold two jobs. But the vast majority of us show our love much better if we give our time and energy to our families instead of taking a second job to buy them more things.

Somebody who loves easily, who can turn his back when necessary on personal profit or pleasure, is rich in love, a real tycoon in tenderness. Conversely, somebody who thinks only about himself – who can't think about the fellow next door or the family from the other side of the tracks, who can't identify with people from another race or country or color — that person is a skinflint. He won't give a tender thought to anybody.

At the University of California, Berkeley, there is a hill overlooking a beautiful outdoor theater. When I was there in the sixties, if Howlin' Wolf came to the Greek Theatre, graduate students whose stipends had run out or freshmen who had blown their remittance at the pizza parlor would creep up to watch from Tightwad Hill, where without a ticket they could make out Mr. Wolf's silhouette and occasionally hear him howl. This is a compassionate way to look at people who cannot think about others — they watch life from Tightwad Hill. But at the same time, it shows that by their own token they are not worth much. After all — at least in the days when I was there — it took only five dollars to go to the Greek Theatre. To go instead to Tightwad Hill, you have to be either the flintiest of skinflints or utterly down-and-out.

Here, I think, it is good to give people a wide margin of understanding, especially when they are young. In India, where families often make severe sacrifices to send a son or daughter to college, everyone is patient with a student who is out of cash. If you are waiting in line for tickets with two or three friends, for example, and your turn comes at the box office window, everyone understands if you suddenly discover that your shoelace has come loose. You bend down to tie it, giving your friends a chance to buy your ticket, and everybody knows there is no question of generosity or stinginess; you simply do not have the capacity to pay. Similarly, when someone suddenly gets angry, you can think to yourself, "Well, his shoelace has just come untied." Whatever he was doing before, he has to bend down and look at his feet; he hasn't got attention to give to anything else. When a person can't think about anything except himself, all he has time for in life is tying shoelaces; after two or three steps they are undone again.

The truly wealthy person, on the other hand, is one who has a genius for not thinking about himself. He or she simply forgets to ask questions like "How does this affect my feelings?" When I was in Berkeley, it was impossible to pass a pizza parlor or coffeehouse without finding two people intimately discussing each other's subconscious. A great lover has a genius for not thinking about his subconscious. All his sensitiveness is opened out to those around him.

Such people have a genius for happiness as well. They don't get offended because they are not brooding on themselves. Similarly, they don't get upset. If you are unkind to them, they can oppose you kindly – not because they feel hurt, but because they understand the damage your ill will does to you. If you insult them, they will feel sorry for you; you are exposing yourself as a miser.

If we could only realize it, all of us are billionaires in love. Our inner resources are infinite. By keeping the doors to this interior treasury closed, we have learned to live like paupers, sometimes even bankrupting our lives and the lives of those around us. Most of the conditions of modern life which we decry and suffer from today, particularly the sharp rise in violence and crime, have not been imported from some other planet. We ourselves have made our society what it is; we have made our world what it is. But there is a very positive side to this: if we have done all these things, we can undo them also. By drawing on our vast capacity for love, every one of us can make a lasting contribution to world peace.

In this sense, Saint Paul's Epistle is a detailed, practical guide for "profiting from a financial crisis," which will tell us not how to get more from life but how to give more – how to make ourselves rich in love.

[2]

Love suffereth long, and is kind; love envieth not; love vaunteth not itself, is not puffed up; doth not behave itself unseemly.

My grandmother was fond of a Sanskrit saying: "Patience is the ornament of the brave." Patience, not retaliation, is the real badge of courage. I would add, patience is equally the mark of love.

To be a good teacher, you need patience. To excel in anything you have to have patience. But if you want to love – which means, in my language, if you want to live – patience is an absolute necessity. You may be dashing, glamorous, fascinating, and alluring; you may be tall, dark, and handsome, lissome, lovely, and blonde, or whatever the current fancy may be. Without patience, you cannot be called a great lover; it would be a contradiction in terms.

"Well," most of us say, "I guess that leaves me out. Patience has never been my strong suit." Very, very few of us are born patient, especially today. Our age has been called the age of anxiety, the age of anger; I would say simply, it is the age of impatience. Almost everybody is impatient. You see it in supermarket lines, on the highway, on the tennis court, in the schoolyard, in the political arena, on the bus. With all this we have begun to believe that impatience is our natural state. Fortunately, love is our natural state, and patience is something that everybody can learn.

Some years ago, reading about Saint Teresa of Avila, I fell so in love with her that I borrowed a cassette course in Spanish from the library and tried to learn a few words, mostly to find out how Teresa's little poems must have sounded. Unfortunately, the people who produced the course did not have this purpose in mind, because the dialogue was "Would you be so kind as to introduce me to your cousin?" and "I have no cigars or cigarettes." (I wanted to say, "Good!") But my love for Saint Teresa was so great that despite these obstacles, I managed to learn enough to follow her when she comes out with one of those wonderfully simple lines of hers. One sentence I remember always: "*La paciencia todo lo alcanza.*" Patience achieves everything; patience attains the goal.

I have to confess that I did not have time for

conversing with a tape recorder about cigarettes and cigars, so I returned the cassette to the library. But if I had persisted all the way to Lesson 52, I am sure I would be reading the *Interior Castle* in Spanish and reciting lines from John of the Cross in a good Castilian accent. That is the purpose of such courses: you do Lesson 1, then Lesson 2, and fifty-two lessons later you speak Spanish. Of course, these methods are not flawless. I remember a cartoon showing a man and his wife in a European restaurant staring at a big platter on the table in front of them, on which there is a sewing machine covered with spaghetti. The wife is saying, "I *told* you not to try to order in Italian!" Self-help has its hazards, but by and large, if you do your lessons diligently and keep on plodding, you will reach your goal.

It is exactly the same with patience. If you find somebody irritating, don't avoid that person; you would be missing a precious educational opportunity. Being with people is an essential part of the course. Most of us, when we see someone exasperating coming up our front steps, want to get into the closet, pull an overcoat in front of us, and call out, "There's no one home!" If you really want to learn patience, however, you will say, "Great! This is Lesson 10 in the course," and open the door with a smile.

On the Blue Mountain, my wife and I had a good friend who had come to India from England as a missionary and later joined Mahatma Gandhi. One of this lady's frequent visitors was an acquaintance with such difficult ways that the very sight of her was enough to elevate our friend's blood pressure. One day she asked me, "What should I do? Should I hide when I see her coming and refuse to answer the door?"

"No, no," I said. "Just repeat the Holy Name – *Jesus, Jesus, Jesus.*"

After a week or so she came to me again. "It's no use," she said. "Once I hear that particular knock, my mind gets agitated before I even think of Jesus."

I got a good idea. "Make it a race," I suggested. "The moment you see her turn in at the gate, start the name of Jesus going. See if it can get into your consciousness before she reaches the door."

Our friend kept at it with British bulldog persistence. I never asked how the race was going, but one day I was pleased to hear her announce, "Oh, by the way, do you remember my friend so-and-so? I don't get agitated around her any more. When I see her coming up the walk, the Holy Name dashes along next to her and beats her to the door."

This is one of the simplest ways of learning to be patient. When irritation calls and demands an immediate answer, the Holy Name puts it on hold, giving the mind a few precious minutes to prepare itself so that it can push the harsh words back. In other words, the Holy Name gives us a chance to respond to events the way we choose.

There is a close connection between speed and impatience. Impatience is simply the mind being in a hurry; that is why one of the steps in my eight-point program is slowing down. Our culture has become so speeded-up today that we scarcely have an opportunity to learn to be patient; everyone is in too much of a hurry. People in a hurry cannot be patient. People in a hurry cannot love. To love you need to be sensitive to those around you, which is impossible if you are always racing through life engrossed in all the things you need to do before sunset. In fact, I would go to the extent of saying that a latecomer will find it difficult to love; he will be in too much of a hurry. A late riser will find it difficult to love; she will be going through the day trying to catch up.

Of course, it is easy to be patient when people agree with you. It becomes difficult when others criticize you or contradict you or do not do what you want. This kind of contrariness is part of life. If all five and a half billion of us thought and spoke and acted alike, the world would be about as interesting as a condominium with every room the same. Fortunately, we come from different homes, went to different schools, hold different jobs, have been exposed to different influences. Naturally, when we get together in close relationships, we differ in all kinds of ways, some of them not very pleasant. If we are going to love, we have to accept difficult relationships; that is life. But this is not a matter for resignation. When you love, you live among difficulties not with resignation but with rejoicing.

The secret of this is profoundly simple: these differences amount to no more than one percent of who we are. Ninety-nine percent is what we have in common.

When all you see is the one percent of difference, life can be terribly difficult. But when you cease thinking only about yourself, you see the much larger whole in which all of us are the same, with the same fears, the same desires, the same hopes, the same human foibles. Instead of separating us, the one percent of superficial differences that remains makes up the drama of life.

When I came to the University of California on my first visit to this country, I remember going to a little store on Telegraph Avenue and asking for some half-and-half. In India we learned British English, of course, so l pronounced the words as the English do, with broad *a*'s as in *father*: "ha'f and ha'f." The man just stared. "What?" I repeated myself: "I would like some half-and-half." He couldn't understand. Finally he went and got his wife, who fortunately was a little more patient. She brought me a little carton and explained, "You'll have to excuse my husband. You see, we say it 'haffen haff.'"

That is all the difference between us. Isn't there a song, "You say *tomayto* and I say *tomahto*; let's call the whole thing off"? That is all most quarrels amount to. If you can keep your eyes on what we have in common, you will find that most quarrels disappear. You can anticipate other people's behavior and help them change it too, if you only remember that the other person has feelings which are just as easily hurt as yours. He too appreciates it when other people are kind. She too appreciates it when you are patient, even if she herself is irritating: in fact, she is ninety-nine percent you. Being with people who are different is not only unavoidable; it is a precious, vital necessity. Without the company of those who differ from us, we grow rigid and narrow-minded. Those who associate only with people their own age, for example, lose a great deal: the young have much to learn from the old, and older people from the young. Similarly, if you are a blue-collar worker, it is good to know an intellectual with a Ph.D. or two; it will cure you of any awe you might have of experts. If you are a university graduate, there is no reason to stop speaking to your high school friends who went straight into work. Even the difference between an egghead and a hardhat is only one percent. Their feelings, their responses to life's perennial problems, are very much the same.

Most disagreements, in other words, do not really go very deep. They are not settled by arguing. They are not solved through analysis and synthesis. They are resolved, or dissolved, through patience. Without patience you start retaliating, and the other person gets more upset and retaliates too. Soon you have two people out of control. Instead, listen to what the other person is saying. How can you even answer if you do not listen? Repeat the Holy Name, refrain from answering immediately, and when you can, try a smile or a kind word; it can do so much to relax the atmosphere. Little by little you can try a kind phrase, then a kind sentence. When you become really expert in love, you can throw in a kind subordinate clause.

This actually quiets the other person. Kind language is a sedative. When you answer harsh words or disrespect with kind words, you are writing a prescription and passing it to the other person: "Take this. It will keep your blood pressure down and calm your mind."

This is a vital skill, for whatever our role in life – student, teacher, doctor, parent, carpenter – we can't depend on people doing what we say in just the way we like. If you are a doctor, for example, you cannot expect to get patients who are well-behaved, courteous, and prepared to carry out instructions cheerfully. You are going to get many whiny children and irritable adults. You will see people who are short-tempered, ask embarrassing questions, demand to see your diploma, and wouldn't dream of following instructions they do not like. This is part of being a doctor. But every patient like that is a lesson in love. When the nurse comes in and says, "You've got a real pill this time, doctor," you can say, "Terrific! I'm getting a lot of lessons today; I'm going to learn patience fast." Maybe the patient hasn't slept. He has been in pain for forty-eight hours, hasn't been able to eat his breakfast; do you expect him to be an angel? If you can be patient with him, it may help as much as any medication. It is not only drugs or surgical procedures that help your patient. At least as important is the faith that you are not just doing a job for pay or for some personal research interest; you are concerned about his welfare.

"Love suffereth long and is kind," Saint Paul says.

There is a close connection; sometimes patience is the greatest part of being kind. This word "kind" is so simple that we seem to have forgotten what it means; it opens a great avenue of love. One medieval Western mystic asks, "Do you want to be a saint? Be kind, be kind, be kind." I would say, "If you want to be a great lover, be kind, kind everywhere, kind to all."

This is the rub. Most of us can be kind under certain circumstances – at the right time, with the right people, in a certain place. Otherwise we simply stay away. We avoid someone, change jobs, leave home; if we have to, we move to southern California. But as Jesus says, being kind when it is easy to be kind is not worthy of much applause. If we want to be kind always, we have to move closer to difficult people instead of moving away.

Thérèse of Lisieux, a charming saint of nineteenth-century France who died in her early twenties, was a great artist at this. In her convent there was a senior nun whose manner Thérèse found offensive in every way. Like many of her sister nuns, I imagine, all that she wanted was to avoid this unfortunate woman. But Thérèse had daring. Where everyone else would slip away, she began to go out of her way to see this woman who made her skin crawl. She would speak kindly to her, sometimes bring her flowers, give her her best smile, and in general "do everything for her that I would do for someone I most love." Because of this love, the woman began to get secure and to respond.

One day, in one of the most memorable scenes in Thérèse's autobiography, this other nun goes to Thérèse and asks, "Tell me, Sister, what is it about me that you find so appealing? You have such love in your smile when you see me, and your eyes shine with happiness." Her very image of herself has changed; for the first time in her life, perhaps, she has begun to think, "I must be a lovable woman!" That is the healing power of kindness, which we should never forget even though we are so seldom able to observe it. "Oh!" Thérèse writes. "How could I tell her that it was Jesus I loved in her – Jesus who makes sweet that which is most bitter."

In every disagreement, I would say – not only in the home but even at the international level – it is really not ideological differences that divide people. It is lack of respect, which I would call lack of love. Most disagreements do not even require dialogue; all that is necessary is a set of flash cards. If Romeo wants to make a point with Juliet, he may have elaborate intellectual arguments for buttressing his case, but while his mouth is talking away, his hand just brings out a big card and shows it to Juliet's face: "I'm right." Then Juliet flashes one of hers: "You're wrong!" You can use the same cards for all occasions, because that is all most quarrels amount to.

What provokes people in a quarrel is not so much facts or opinions, but the arrogance of these flash cards. Kindness here means the generous admission – not only with the tongue but with the heart – that there is something in what you say, just as there is something in what I say. If I can listen to you with respect, it is usually only a short time before you listen with respect to me. Once this attitude is established, most differences can be made up. It may require a lot of hard work, but the problem is no longer insoluble.

When two people quarrel, they take for granted that they are adversaries. That very attitude is the problem between them, not the difference of opinion. We think that a quarrel has to have a right side and a wrong, a winner and a loser. With this attitude, both sides are losers. The problem is not solved; at best it is simply terminated. The difficulty is in the way the lines are drawn: "This is you against me." It is not; it is you and me against the problem. To resolve our differences, I have to push the problem over to the other side and pull you over to my side; then we can plan together to solve the problem. After all, we have a common goal: how to resolve that problem to the satisfaction of both sides.

"Love envieth not; love vaunteth not itself, is not puffed up." There is a common element here. Our usual idea is that when love is intense, jealousy has to creep in. Saint Paul is reminding us that when love is present, jealousy *cannot* creep in. Similarly, when jealousy is present, there is no room for love; we are thinking of ourselves. And everything is distorted. You see some little thing – a remark, a look, a handkerchief in someone else's possession – and you brood on it, make up all kinds of fanciful explanations, put two and two together and get twenty-two. Jealous people do not see what is there; they see what jealousy puts there. And then, tragically, they start thinking and acting as if all this were true.

In village festivals in India, we have a version of the "old shell game" that is played with three coconut shells. The showman says, "Put your rupee down, friends! I'm going to show you just where I put this ball. Place your rupee near that shell. If the ball is still there when I lift the shell up, I'll give you ten rupees back!" He shows everyone the ball, then lifts one of the coconut shells, puts the ball into it, and returns it to its place. "You saw me do it," he says. "If you believe your own eyes, why not put your money down?"

Somehow there is always a surprising number of villagers to say, "How simple! Instead of working all day, why not accept this foolish fellow's invitation? After all, I have sharp eyes. I saw where he put the ball." One by one, they put their money down. Some hold back; but as their neighbors step forward they say, "Well, if Raman is going to go home nine rupees richer, why shouldn't I?"

The man allows some time for all this; he even lets people arrange to borrow. Then he raises the coconut shell – and there is no ball.

I could have wept every time this happened, especially when I saw the look on those villagers' faces. Most of them didn't have a rupee to lose. And they just couldn't believe their eyes. "We *saw* it there!" They were all so sure.

Anyone who knows even a little about magic knows that the ball was never placed under the shell. It goes back into the man's palm. That is just what happens in jealousy. "I saw this. I saw him. I saw her. I saw them." What did you see? Jealousy is a great magician; insecurity is a house of mirrors. Saint Paul reminds us, "Love trusts all things." Where there is jealousy, we *cannot* see clearly. Even if it develops that there is some reason to be jealous, I would still say trust people. Trust those you love. Most people will respond.

There is another side of jealousy, and that is competition. Competition, as the British economist E. F. Schumacher says, is usually no more than jealousy and greed. You want something that somebody else has, or something you think somebody else has. Whether you need it is irrelevant. If Jack or Martha has it, you feel inferior unless you can have it too. Without comparing yourself with Jack or Martha, of course, this cannot happen. When I hear talk about "keeping up with the Joneses," I ask, "Who are these Joneses?" Keep up with your Self – with the spark of divinity within you. Let the Joneses keep up with their Self.

Jealousy can be so meaningless! Whatever assets you may have, if you are jealous, you will not be able to see those assets or give them their real worth. All you will see is something you do not have, compared with which your assets amount to nothing.

Fortunately, freedom from jealousy can be obtained by everybody. All that is required is to stop comparing yourself with others, which is one of the marvelous applications of training attention. Jealousy comes from insecurity. The answer to jealousy, therefore, is not to acquire other things or to prove yourself superior to other people, but to move closer to people around you and make yourself more secure. The more secure you are, the less jealous you will be. On the other hand, the more you move away from others and compare yourself with them, the more jealous you have to be.

"Love is not boastful," insists Saint Paul. "It is not arrogant or rude." This too is a matter of attitude. The same lack of security that makes us feel inferior to some people can make us feel superior and behave with arrogance to others. We may not go around blowing our own trumpet, but we can be boastful in a much subtler, more insidious way. When we are angry, we are being boastful. When we deprecate someone, we are being boastful. Insecure people often get a dubious satisfaction in finding fault with others like this. Instead, Paul would say, why not support them and try to help them correct their faults? Whenever you find someone who is not as skillful as you are, or as efficient, or as secure, instead of criticizing or comparing, the best service you can render is to help and support. If it is necessary to oppose or correct that person, you can always do so with sympathy, kindness, and respect.

As you practice these skills of love – patience, kindness, not being arrogant, not being rude – your capacity for them will grow. In whatever field of service you have chosen, your influence will expand. "Blessed are the peacemakers," Jesus said, "for they shall be called children of God." We can all be peacemakers. We may start in a very small place – the home, the office – but gradually we may find ourselves in situations where we can make a lasting contribution to the safety of our neighborhood or the welfare of the world.

This is not an exaggeration. Every one of us is concerned about the threat of war today, when armed conflict even between small nations on the other side of the globe can plunge us all into nuclear disaster. I still remember vividly the words of President Kennedy: "If we do not put an end to war, war is going to put an end to us."

When we are angry in our home, we are conducting a little war. In European history, you may remember, there is the Thirty Years War. In the home it is only a Thirty Minutes War, but these conflicts have their consequences too, which extend beyond the walls; we take them with us wherever we go. We may have guerrilla warfare in the kitchen. I have seen Cold War on the same block. Personal resentments, personal hostility, lack of courtesy, lack of respect for others: the sum of all this, the mystics tell us, is what erupts into international war. War, we should all remember, does not come about through forces of nature. It is made, declared, waged, and continued by men and women like you and me.

Conflict and disharmony, in other words, are not only problems of personal relationships. National decisions too are made by individuals. It is not uncommon to see the government of one country behave with arrogance towards other countries, even other races; and the problems that result are very much the same, only vastly more dangerous. Similarly, the frightful arms races in which so many countries are caught today – fueled, I am sorry to say, by sales from the United States – is defended throughout the world as a matter of national security. I would not hesitate to say this is national insecurity, the most dangerous kind I can imagine. And this business of retaliation – "You did this to me, so I am going to do that to you" – has brought us frequently to the brink of world war.

Love has an essential, practical place in all human affairs, even among nations. It shows itself not in exploitation but in cooperation, in a readiness to look upon all countries as members of the same human family on the same very limited planet. With the threat and danger of global war growing precipitously, we cannot afford any longer to emphasize the one percent of differences among nations. We need to do everything possible to apply the way of love even at an international level: to approach other countries with respect, pursue mutual understanding with tireless patience, keep our eyes resolutely on what we have in common with other nations rather than on our differences, and above all remember that no country on earth faces a more disastrous problem than the problems we face together – violence, poverty, inhumanity, and the despoliation of our globe. It is not my nation against yours, but all nations together against these menacing problems which make this, without exaggeration, "one world or none."

[3]

Love seeketh not her own . . .

Saint Paul gives us a sure, simple test of a loving relationship: love does not insist on its own way. If you want to apply it, see how much you can turn your back on self-will, on having your own way, for the sake of the one you love. When I first came to this country, I heard a song that I've never forgotten:

> Oh, what a beautiful mornin',
> Oh, what a beautiful day.
> I got a beautiful feelin'
> Everything's going my way.

According to Messrs. Rodgers and Hammerstein, that is a song of love. Paul would disagree wholeheartedly. The real lover sings, "What a beautiful morning! What a beautiful day! Everything is going your way." That is the challenge of love.

You can test yourself with this every day. How about breakfast? Do you insist on your own way? Suppose you get up with your heart set on blueberry pancakes: all you can think about in meditation is butter and maple syrup. You come to the breakfast table rubbing your hands in anticipation. "Where are those pancakes? I'm famished!" And your partner says, "Guess what? I've made Belgian waffles this morning, just for you."

If you have strong likes and dislikes, your jaw drops; you sit down like a martyr. "Why couldn't you have made Belgian *pancakes?*" This kind of question can really hurt.

"That's not what Belgium is famous for," your partner says. "It's waffles. Belgian waffles."

That is the time to start changing. The great lover looks up bravely, rubs his hands together with gusto, and says, "Bring them on!" You pour on a lot of maple syrup to drown every trace of Belgian waffle, and then you really go through the pile. "These are good!" you can say. "If I'd known they'd be like this, I wouldn't even have mentioned blueberry pancakes."

It is the same at work. Most of us have our little quirks about how we approach a job, and about how we do it too. Josephine, say, likes to put her file folders in the cabinet sideways. That is how she has always done it, so she finds her system very easy to use. If you want to increase friction, you can insist on your own way. But if you want to love, listen to your co-workers patiently; respect their ways. When you have to correct someone, you can always do so kindly and respectfully.

This is not at all easy; it can even be grueling. But like an athlete in training, you are training for love.

Love, like any skill, is learned through incessant practice. As Saint Francis de Sales says, we learn to speak by speaking; we learn to run by running. And we learn to love by loving; there is no other way.

After training all day you are exhausted, and so is your partner. When you come home in the evening, all you want is to be left alone. "After all," you say, "haven't I earned it?" Unfortunately, this is like a marathon runner coming home from her workout and saying, "Wow, I really ran hard today! I deserve a three-scoop sundae." Just like her, you're still in training.

The tennis finals are on tonight. You have your own TV in your bedroom, and every cell in your body is crying out, "Why not? Lock yourself in, set yourself down with a can of something that made Milwaukee famous, and just let your mind go with the match." But there is a knocking at the front door – your little boy's friend from across the street. "Hi!" he says. "Billy said you could help us tonight with our square roots."

Square roots! You thought you had heard the last of them twenty-five years ago. Haven't you paid your dues? "I'm sorry," you want to say. "I've been adding up figures for eight hours today and I've had it. The U.S. Open is on tonight and I intend to watch it." But then you catch the look in Billy's eyes, and you make yourself smile. "Okay," you say. "Tell me again what a square root is, and I will help you find some."

To me this shows great love. You may think you are only relearning mathematics that night, but in fact you are doing something much more important: you are learning to love, and by your example you are teaching those children how to love too.

"Love does not insist on its own way." This does not mean never doing something we enjoy. But Saint Paul asks, "Why not widen the circle of what you enjoy?" Instead of enjoying only the things we like, we can teach ourselves to enjoy things that other people like as well – our partner, our children, our friends.

This is a marvelous capacity. The Plaza, say, has been building up to a Beatles festival all month long. For one night only, you can sit through hours of the Beatles and recall the good old days. Naturally, you have been keeping that evening open ever since you saw the billing. But since you're not sure what your family will think about it, you haven't mentioned your plans.

The great night arrives; tunes have been running through your mind all day. At the dinner table, you clear your throat. "Ahem! What would you all think of a movie tonight?"

"Oh, dad! How did you know?" Little Jeanie has the movie page of the paper right by the chair. She has been taking ballet lessons this year, and tonight – how wonderful! – the Bijou has Baryshnikov in a film version of *Swan Lake*.

Your heart drops into your shoes. You can't make head or tail of ballet; you can't even say Baryshnikov's name. And you've been looking forward for so long to Paul McCartney and his friends! But you can see how much it means to Jeanie, so you force yourself to get up and smile. And you go and sit cheerfully through the whole thing. You don't just close your eyes and sleep, either. You don't pretend to watch while drifting off into a world of fantasy, recalling *Yellow Submarine*. You watch Baryshnikov through Jeanie's eyes, giving the performance your best attention and trying to understand what it is that captures her imagination. In that very exercise you are showing love.

Afterwards Jeanie's ballet teacher comes up with her eyes glowing. "I've never seen anyone watch ballet with more attention! You must be a great lover of the arts." She peers at you more closely. "Perhaps you have even studied at the Bolshoi in your younger years."

"Actually," you reply apologetically, "it's Jeanie who loves it. But I love Jeanie, so I am going to learn to love it too."

Of course, you have to use your discrimination. If Jeanie wants to see *Friday the 13th Part XXXIII*, you don't say, "Well, I love you, so I'll learn to enjoy watching mayhem and mutilation right along with you." You say, "I love you, so I'll take you to *The Black Stallion* instead." There is room for a good deal of artistry in this. You know the great harm that violence in the media does, especially to young people. But on the other hand, you don't just say, "I forbid you to go!" Instead, you harness Jeanie's moviegoing desire to a better alternative: a good film, a really entertaining play, a special outing, something she will enjoy but which stimulates sensitivity, sympathy, or understanding.

For people who have difficulties in loving, this is one of the surest ways to train. It applies not only to a family; you can do it with your friends also. Those who are really daring can even take out an enemy or two. It's a splendid opportunity. Pick out someone you really dislike and say, "I've got two tickets for *Best of Enemies* tonight; why don't you come along?" If you think it is hard to concentrate on Baryshnikov with your little girl at your side, just see what happens when Mr. Grump is there instead! Your attention will wander continuously, flickering from the screen to your animosity. Your mind will beg, "Let me be anywhere else!" By facing obstacles like this, love grows by leaps and bounds. Just keep repeating the Holy Name and concentrate on the screen; you will see how much power the Name can generate.

Many years ago, when my mother was still living with us here in California, a friend of ours decided to amuse her by bringing a tiny frog. She placed it on the table, and I was startled to see it hop once or twice in a lethargic sort of way. Since she was a pediatrician, I thought perhaps she had brought in a frog with anemia. Then I noticed that she had a little switch in her hand; when she pressed the switch, the toy would leap.

My mother was not particularly impressed.

Coming from a small Indian village, she thought it strange that a full-fledged physician should be playing with an electric frog. But I exclaimed, "That's just what the Holy Name can do!" It is a kind of mental power switch. Every time you use it, you get a little jump. If you keep on repeating it, you can jump right over an obstacle in the way of love.

Actually, the Holy Name has a much closer connection with medical practice than that frog. Violated self-will can cause a lot of physical problems. Most people are aware that stress can be terribly harmful on the body, but few realize how much emotional stress comes from inflated self-will. We insist on our own way, and when we do not get it, we blow up – in anger, frustration or insidious chronic resentment, all of which in the long run damage the vital organs severely. Love is essential not only for emotional health but for physical well-being too; kindness and patience are excellent preventive medicine.

People who have very little self-will don't much mind being contradicted. They have enough patience to say, "Well, if it releases some of your tension to blow up at me, go ahead." This is a particularly daring kind of love. The interesting thing is that when people find they cannot provoke you, they often do not keep trying. Usually they become quite decent when they are with you; they reserve their irascibility for someone they can provoke instead.

"Love," says Paul, "is not easily provoked, thinketh no evil." Being irritable and being resentful both come from self-will. If you have pronounced likes and dislikes, which is the manifold expression of self-will, irritation and resentment will be your constant companions. There will be things or people to irritate you throughout the day.

This can be seen even among great artists, where likes and dislikes are often virulent. There is a famous hotel in London, the Savoy, which used to attract some of the best-known actors, actresses, and literary figures around. One English actor was so particular about his room at the Savoy that when he arrived, everything in the room had to be exactly the way it was when he left, even if he had last been there a year ago and was only going to stay for a few days. To him it was his room, and if so much as a cup was on a different corner of the table, he would get insecure and raise a fuss. The management, of course, found tactful ways of dealing with such difficulties. When this great artist left, the hotel staff photographed his room meticulously; then they went ahead and rented it to someone else. When they heard that he was returning, they would take out the photographs and rearrange everything to match.

Many of us behave this way. We may not be so transparent about it, but we too have to have everything in the "right" place – that is, the way we like it. This goes not only for things but for other people. Our friend George is expected to talk this way; if he does not, we get irritated. Suzy is not expected to act that way; if she does, we feel resentful. Instead of trying to get people to keep changing with our moods, which is not likely to be successful, Saint Paul suggests, "Why not make yourself secure?" Let people change their attitude if they like; let the management change the furniture. Why should that affect our security or undermine our love?

A vague sense of irritation is so common today that many of us scarcely notice it. Virtually no one is exempt. We may not be able to pin it on any cause or refer it to any particular person, but some days there is a general sense of dissatisfaction which is just waiting to break into anger. When you sit down to breakfast or walk into the office, it is as if your mind is looking around like a hawk and saying, "What's going to irritate me today?" That is the time to be especially vigilant. Usually we feel it is the other person's job to be vigilant. "Watch out! I'm in a bad mood today. I got up on the wrong side of the bed; so I am forced to say something rude to the first person I see, and you are it." In all fairness, it is we who should watch out. What happens in our minds is our business to control.

For this kind of vague, subclinical irritation – what Dr. Friedman calls "free-floating hostility" – the Holy Name can be very effective. When a baby is crying and the mother needs to finish her work, she sometimes puts a pacifier between the baby's lips and it satisfies him for a while. The Holy Name is a pacifier for grown-ups. When you feel irritable, just put it between your lips and keep it there – *Jesus, Jesus, Jesus,* or whatever it may be. When the irritation is gone, you can take the Holy Name out.

Resentment and irritation come easily when the mind wanders, which it always will until it is trained. Resentment, for example, is a common burden on those who like to live in the past. It is essentially because we are not completely here in the present that a part of our attention gets caught in the library of the past. Like a graduate student at the university, attention has a cramped carrel in this library, piled with musty memories. If the print is small, the mind studies it with a magnifying glass until one minor incident fills the field of vision. And of course there are tapes to listen to; if the memory is faint, the mind has a dial that can take the little remark Suzanne made last summer and amplify and replay it to our heart's content. The mind gets caught; it has wandered in and now it cannot leave.

When I went to the shoe store with some children the other day, they all came out with balloons, most of which exploded in the car. But one survived; its owner held it very carefully between his hands and kept gazing at it admiringly. When we reached home, where the other children had only bedraggled-looking pieces of rubber, this boy's balloon even seemed to have swelled in size.

That is what we do with resentment: we take a memory, dwell on it, and inflate it with our attention. In the end it becomes like one of the huge traveling balloons we used to see in the skies above Sonoma County, in which for a handsome sum you could have a champagne breakfast on the prevailing air currents and perhaps enjoy the thrill of landing in a haystack or drifting out to sea. Resentment, however, offers no champagne. All we are served is a big breakfast of negative feelings.

Here, too, the answer is the Holy Name. If you keep on using it, the big balloon of resentment that can sweep you so far from reality begins to shrink until it is too small to lift even your pet poodle. Finally it bursts, just as those of our children did in the car. When this happened, of course, the children cried. But we adults can laugh when a resentment bursts; so much of a burden falls away!

"Love rejoiceth not in iniquity, but rejoiceth in the truth." When we are thinking about ourselves, it can be very difficult to see clearly what is right and what is wrong. One of the simplest ways is to ask whether what we are planning is for the good of the whole – our family, our neighborhood, our globe – or only for our own benefit or interest. Love, says Paul, cannot be private; it cannot be exclusive. It enjoys what is good for all, in which the good of each individual is included.

"When I was a child, I spake as a child, I understood as a child, I thought as a child; but when I became a man, I put away childish things." I was watching children in nursery school the other day. When they do not get their way, it is their prerogative to cry; it is their privilege. But a loving parent will have enough detachment to see that letting children have their way all the time will make life terribly difficult for them later on. Wherever you find adults having difficulty in listening to constructive criticism, the seeds of that difficulty were planted in early childhood. By not saying no, we can cripple a child for life.

This is a toddler's way of expressing disapproval – kicking his legs, upsetting his milk, and then lifting the roof. When we get older we say instead, "I'm not going to speak to him. When I see him coming, I'm going to look away." "I'm not going to work with her any more; I'm going to sit in my room and read *Gone with the Wind.*" When we do this, we are still children. To grow up, as Saint Paul says, we have to reduce self-will. That is the very essence of love. If you have to have your way, if you cannot go against your likes and dislikes for another person's sake, how can you love? At best you can have a kind of affection that comes and goes. Love does not ebb or fall; it is a continuing state of consciousness. When you love a person, you love that person always. Then the nexus of likes and dislikes is cut. You can want to see the Beatles all day long and when the choice with Baryshnikov comes up, there is no conflict; you can drop your preference effortlessly and find joy in your daughter's enjoyment.

This joy can be multiplied over and over. If there is such joy in loving one person, how much more is there in loving all! The more people we love, the greater our joy. When self-will vanishes and all barriers to love fall, we actually are in love with everyone; we have five and a half billion reasons for living.

[4]

For we know in part, and we prophesy in part. But when that which is perfect is come, then that which is in part shall be done away.

In his infinite love, the Lord has drawn a curtain between us and what may come. When my friends Laurel and Ed were designing a calendar, they worried for a while about what holidays to print in the boxes. They had to include Christmas and Hanukkah and Yom Kippur, of course, but how about Ramadan and Krishna Jayanti? How about Secretaries' Day and Gandhi's birthday? To put things in perspective, I suggested, "Suppose you could make a calendar showing everything that would happen in the coming year." We would be afraid to get out of bed, you know.

My grandmother's attitude toward the future was very practical. "Why do you want to know?" she would ask. "If you learn to love, you can face the future under any circumstances." Today, after years of arduous practice, I have no anxiety whatever about the future, though with the work of our meditation center I share many heavy burdens. I understand now that if we live wisely and selflessly today, only good can come of it, whatever else the future may bring.

Time past and time future, to paraphrase T. S. Eliot,

N I L G I R I   P R E S S

Post Office Box 256

Tomales, California 94971

Stamp

Nilgiri Press publishes books by Eknath Easwaran on how to lead the spiritual life in the home and the community. Ask your bookstore about them — or fill out this card and return it to us. We will send you a catalog of our books and audio tapes along with a free copy of our newsletter containing a schedule of retreats and workshops. *Thank You.*

_____

Name (Please print or type)

_____

Street

_____

City   *State*   *Zip + 4*

_____

Title of the book in which you found this card.

_____

How did you hear about this book?

_____

Book store where you bought this book.
(Please include city and state.)

are both contained in time present. Just as our situation today is the result of what we have thought, said, and done in the past, what we think, say, and do today is shaping our tomorrow. The future is not fixed; it is in our hands. Instead of getting extrasensory glimpses of something that may or may not happen, Paul says, isn't it much more important to live wisely here in the present? The future will take care of itself.

Similarly for this business of tongues. It is, I agree, useful and interesting to learn languages. Our University of California offers courses in more languages alive and dead than most mortals have ever heard of. But even if it offered "Tongues of the Angels 101," how would that help us to love? Whether or not we can talk with Saint Peter in the vernacular of heaven, he is still going to ask, "Have you learned to love? Do you insist on your own way? Can you be patient and kind?"

In Indian bazaars and marketplaces, street performers of all kinds try to attract attention with a fascinating patter. They know one or two sentences in each of about ten Indian languages, and before they start juggling or bring out their trained monkeys, they run through all these variations for the benefit of passersby from different parts of India. I used to enjoy listening to them very much. But after the patter was over I would walk away, because usually that was the best part of the performance.

Similarly, Paul says, you may know the word for love "in the language of men and of angels"; it will not help you to love. No kind of knowledge can serve much purpose in bringing about the transformation of character, conduct, and consciousness which love entails.

All of us who have been associated with colleges or universities know how many people travel around the world learning new languages or looking into old ones. The mystics tell us unanimously, "There is a first-priority task awaiting you at home." As Socrates puts it, "Know thyself." Jesus says, "Forget yourself." It is the same: to know our real Self, we have to forget our small, personal self, the ego. Until we do this, everything else can wait. It is not that it is unimportant to learn Ugaritic or translate Panini's grammar into Turkish. But first let us discover who we are and learn to love.

For there is not much time. Every Saturday evening I think to myself, "Another Saturday has come. Another week has gone." Do not ask for whom Saturday comes; it comes for thee. Every day when the sun rises and sets it should be a reminder to us: our lives too have risen; our lives too are going to set. There is an extraordinarily sensitive kind of human being for whom this realization goes like an arrow into the depths of consciousness. For such a person all other priorities gradually dwindle; the most urgent priority in life becomes the realization of God.

How much of our time is preoccupied with the future! To keep abreast of the fascinating tendencies of our times I look at a number of papers regularly, beginning in the morning with the *San Francisco Chroni-*

cle and the *New York Times.* Usually I concentrate on the news, but if Christine says, "This column is especially good today," I read that too. In the evening I get the *San Francisco Examiner,* and from the university campus I get the student perspective in the *Daily Californian.* And on weekends I make my way through the Sunday edition of the *New York Times,* which is mammoth, probably the biggest paper in the world. Quite a lot of the mammoth is ads.

What interests me is that most of this vast amount of paper is unnecessary. A few months ago, for example, you could have put thirty days worth of newspapers into one sentence: "Will so-and-so run again or not?" That was all anybody had to say. Instead of cutting down all those trees and running the presses overtime to bring out "tomorrow's news today," why not just send out a postcard? All this to look into the future! If you try to apply Paul's advice here, you will find there is very little to read. We have a pungent phrase in my mother tongue: *charvita-charvanam,* "chewing what has already been chewed." Once you have chewed it, why go on chewing over and over for thirty days?

"For our knowledge is imperfect," Saint Paul says, "and our prophecy is imperfect." This holds true for all human knowledge; it applies to a world that is constantly changing. Economics, for example, has absorbed human interest for thousands of years; yet as someone remarked recently, it is still in the Stone Age. My college economics professor, a good teacher, was candid with us from the very first day. "This is not a course in poetry or art," he warned. "Economics is called 'the dismal science.'" The more I studied it, the better I understood why. Nothing in it is certain. I think it is Truman who remarked that what the country needs is a one-handed economist: everything is always "On the one hand . . . but then, on the other . . ."

There is a story (probably apocryphal) about a maharaja in British India who went to the London School of Economics to study under Harold Laski. Laski was an institution; as Galbraith would say, he was "present at the Creation." For many influential people, what Laski said was law. This maharaja felt he had benefited so much from Laski's instruction that when his son came of age, he sent him to Laski too.

Naturally when the boy returned to India after his first year, his father was eager to hear what his former professor had learned in the twenty years since he had been his student. He asked his son, "What subjects did you have to write on for your exam?" The boy told him, and his father shook his head in disbelief. "The university must have become fossilized," he said sadly. "The great man has grown senile. Those are the very same questions he gave us when I was there." And he added, "When you go back, please give my regards to your professor and ask why he is still asking the same old questions."

The boy did as he was told. When he returned to his father again, it was with a terse reply from Laski:

"True, the questions are the same. But the answers have all changed."

It is the same in the not-so-dismal sciences. If you want to see the mutability of knowledge, open a textbook of medicine from just fifty years ago. You will find how many certainties have become ambiguities, how many cure-alls have become either cure-nothings or cause-alls. This does not reflect a flaw in medicine; change is the nature of knowledge. Similarly, I remember one of our own Berkeley astronomers making a public statement that took me by surprise. "We astronomers seem to have erred," he said, "in what we have been saying about this particular phenomenon."

"Really?" asked the reporters. "In what way?"

"It seems the truth is exactly the opposite of what we thought."

In contrast, no spiritual teacher has ever recommended impatience as the answer to insecurity. No scripture has ever said, "Get angry and be healthy" or "Be greedy and be loved." It is always the same old story, the same old timeless truths. When someone objects to me, "There is nothing new in what you are saying," I reply, "Of course not. That is why these truths are so valuable." What would Saint Paul's advice on love be worth if twenty years later he had to say, "Recent advances in the theory and practice of love have made it necessary to issue this revised edition"?

Similarly, love does not change. As Shakespeare says, "it is an ever-fixèd mark." By this criterion, love that comes and goes with fortune is not love. Shakespeare gives a memorable illustration of this in the character of Sir John Falstaff, a huge, boastful, outrageous, endearing old soldier. Young "Prince Hal," before he became King Henry V, did his share of painting the seamier side of London red, and he and Falstaff were close cronies. Despite his coarse nature Falstaff was a loving man with a loving heart, very fond of his friend Hal. When the prince is about to be crowned king of England, Falstaff is overjoyed. He goes about telling all his disreputable friends, "Whatever you want, just ask me. Do you want a position at the palace? Want to get into Parliament? Declare war against Finland? Just ask me; my Hal is going to be king." At the coronation, he rushes up with his unlikely crew to embrace his friend in front of all the courtiers and nobility. And King Henry, in one of the great scenes in Shakespeare, looks down at him and asks his court, "Who is this man? I know him not." When we next hear of Falstaff he is a broken man, who dies of a broken heart.

We are so physically oriented that we think this is dramatic metaphor. Dying in an automobile accident we can understand, but "dying of a broken heart"? It is not metaphor. Death from bereavement does not take place immediately, but loss of love takes away the will to live. Correspondingly, love brings life; love heals and makes whole. The more you love, the more reason you have to live. The more you love, the more precious your life will be to everyone around.

[5]

For now we see through a glass, darkly; but then face to face: now I know in part; but then shall I know even as also I am known.

I saw an advertisement the other day which said, "I like my real me. And my clothes show my real me." I wanted to object, "If that is your real you, it will be going to the cleaners once a week." We forget that clothes are just the covering; they are not the contents. Similarly, the body is just a covering. The face you see in the mirror is not your real face. Until you realize the Lord, Saint Paul would say, you have not seen your real face; you have not even seen the faces of those around you.

When we are angry, we are hiding our real face. When we are greedy or resentful or afraid, we are wearing a mask. Love means taking off all these masks. When we do this, we see the Lord in everyone – as Nicholas of Cusa says, "the Face behind all faces."

Our personality, in other words, is just a kind of makeup. Getting angry is like taking out a jar of red choleric face powder and smearing it around our eyes and mouth. Many people, I am told, put creams on their faces and then go to sleep in the hope of improving their complexion. One of the most remarkable recommendations I have heard of is avocado paste. It shows how easily we human beings can be taken in. Any sensible person would object, "Avocado paste is for making guacamole." It's not for the face; it's for eating with corn chips. Who knows? Someday we may be told that rubbing bing cherries around the eyes will give a permanent reddish tint that the covers of fashion magazines will extol. I don't know how much it helps to sleep with your eyes covered by guacamole or bing cherries, but if you fall asleep with anger makeup on, you are likely to wake up with crows-feet under the eyes. Even for physical beauty, we need to take off the makeup of anger.

Stage makeup can be so elaborate that it takes hours to put on. It also takes hours to get it off. Anger makeup is taken off by not getting angry. It may take years to remove it completely, but every bit that is taken off reveals a little more of our natural beauty. Once it is all off, we do not need to add any makeup for beauty. It is already there; our real face shines with love.

I wish you could look through my eyes at someone who is angry; you would never want to be angry again. I used to say this to the freshmen in my English classes, and it really went home. For some reason, if you tell people that anger is a thousandth of a heart attack, it may not have much of an effect. But if you say, "It makes your face look like a prune," everybody responds. You can see so many face-marring influences at work in anger; each little capillary announces, "I am not pretty." When we stop dwelling on ourselves, on the other hand, our skin and eyes and smile begin to shine with beauty.

When we see the Lord within us face to face, as Saint Paul puts it, we see simultaneously that the Lord shines from every face around us. In terms of physical knowledge – names, nationalities, hair colors, Social Security numbers – to know everyone would require many lives. But to understand others as they really are, all we have to do is know ourselves.

"But when that which is perfect is come, then that which is in part shall be done away." That is the key sentence. Jesus says, "Be ye perfect, even as your Father in heaven is perfect." It *is* possible to become perfect in love. In the fullness of love, all imperfections pass away. "Love is infallible," says William Law. "It has no errors, for all errors are the want of love."

This kind of love can never be broken, not even by time or death. It is a force which is not at all dependent on the physical body. If you love a particular person more than yourself, this force cannot be disrupted when the body dies. Every act and thought is a force in consciousness, and consciousness is not dissolved at death. Just as waves go on spreading long after a pebble is dropped into a lake, the force of love continues to operate.

Love becomes perfect when the mind is stilled and self-will ceases. Then we live in love always. Physically, of course, we still inhabit a body in San Francisco or

Saskatoon. But inwardly we live in a very different world, the Land of Love: as Teresa of Avila says, in the light that has no night.

I have to admit that I still enjoy travel literature. Most of the papers I read have weekly articles offering all sorts of enticements. You can travel by camel or kayak, paddle around with penguins on a raft in the Antarctic, even take courses while you go from place to place. This is horizontal travel, where you stay on the surface of life. But what I find much more fascinating is vertical travel. This is meditation, the whole purpose of which is to take us to the Land of Love in the utmost depths of consciousness.

For a long, long time we may not get very far on this journey. We may even spend a few years sitting in the foyer of the travel agency, falling asleep over the brochures. But a few insist on traveling deep. Then meditation ceases to be a dull, dreary discipline; it becomes a daring, even dangerous adventure. And once you look around beneath the surface, wanderlust gets whetted as on your first world cruise. It is like seeing Hawaii for the first time; everything seems absorbing: the leis, the coconut palms, the mangoes and papayas at every meal. "This is really interesting!" you say. "So different from Peoria!" Then you go to Australia, which is different still; each kangaroo and koala is captivating. As you go further the language changes; things become more difficult to understand. I remember passing through France on my first trip to this country from India. I might as well have been deaf. *Qu'est-ce que c'est?* was just sounds to me; I didn't even know it was a question. All this is very much like what happens in the depths of meditation as we move from one level of consciousness to another.

By and large, this development takes place in two ways. It may come on so quietly that you are scarcely aware of anything happening. But if you are meditating earnestly along the lines I recommend, it is more likely that very gradually, over a long period of time, you will become absorbed in the words of the passage. Concentration deepens, so that the words come more and more slowly. Then, perhaps for only a minute or two, the words dissolve in silence. But although they have disappeared, their meaning remains, very much as the fragrance remains after a vase of roses is taken from a room. When you return to the passage, you are in a different realm of consciousness. You don't understand the language. The words may just seem noises. But little by little, the way your eyes grow accustomed to the darkness when you enter a theater, you begin to understand where you are. In time you will learn to walk about in this new realm, to understand the sounds and sights and feel at home.

Over the years you pass through level after level like this, just the way one travels from one country to another, until finally you reach the very seabed of consciousness. This is the Land of Love. The whole personality is flooded with love, from the surface to the center. You not only love completely, you become love itself: a permanent, unifying, universal force. All you ask of life is to go on loving and giving.

SAINT AUGUSTINE

Introduction by Carol Lee Flinders

"Is not happiness precisely what all seek, so that there is not one who does not desire it?"

Most of us would answer this question, which Augustine asked himself in his *Confessions,* rather brusquely. "Everybody knows that. It's no more than a truism."

To take the truism one step further, wouldn't nearly every one of us accept readily that no matter which specific thing we may be pursuing at a given moment, it is joy, lasting joy, we are hoping against hope to turn it into? Yet for Augustine, even as a young man, this very question opened the door to further questions:

> But where did they know [happiness], that they should desire it so? Where have they seen it, that they should love it? Obviously we have it in some way, but I do not know how. Unless we knew the thing with certain knowledge, we could not will it with so certain a will. . . . May it be that one gets joy from this, one from that? One man may get it one way, another another, yet all alike are striving to attain this one thing, namely, that they may be joyful.

So began a line of inquiry, a search — for the thing "we have in some way, but I do not know how" — that was to last a lifetime. Not only that, this search was destined to engage, eventually, the leaders of the Christian Church at a most critical point in history.

Though Augustine's mother, Monica, sought to bring him up as a pious boy, his own passionate temperament took him down many of the byways familiar to every ordinary adolescent. Growing up in fourth-century Roman North Africa, he saw many traditions mingle — and clash. The backdrop was formed of the folkways of his native North Africa, which were usually termed "pagan." Against these loomed the orthodox traditions emanating from the Roman seat of empire, including a Christianity which young Augustine scrupulously avoided. Then from the Near East were spreading Manichean ideas, which found a place in the imagination especially of the young. Augustine's description of college life in Carthage strikes startlingly familiar chords in anyone who has spent time on a cosmopolitan campus. Fraternities of Eversores, which translates roughly as "upsetters," delighted in terrorizing students and teachers alike; to be one of them, Augustine notes, was "a notable way of being in fashion."

As part of his college syllabus Augustine read a book by Cicero, and the entire direction of his life was changed:

Suddenly all empty hope for my career lost its appeal, and I was left with an unbelievable fire in my heart, desiring the deathless qualities of Wisdom. I should not chase after this or that philosophical sect, but should love Wisdom, of whatever kind it should be.

Even more critical, perhaps, was his encounter in Milan with the bishop of that city, Ambrose. Augustine was a teacher of rhetoric, and it was Ambrose's brilliance in the pulpit that drew him to his services. But it was the content of those sermons that kept him there. For the first time, Augustine realized one could be an intellectual and a man of God at the same time.

One day someone told him the story of Anthony and the Desert Fathers, who had begun their own kind of experiment in Egypt not long before. Inside Augustine something cataclysmic burst; he turned to his companion and cried, "What is the matter with us? These men have none of our education, yet they stand up and storm the gates of heaven."

He took refuge in the garden. After a long bout of tumultuous conflict, he ended by demanding of himself, "How long shall I go on saying 'Tomorrow, tomorrow'? Why not make an end of my ugly sins at this moment?"

Weeping, reiterating his bitterly heartfelt questions, Augustine flung himself down under a fig tree. All at once he heard the voice of a child, singing what sounded like the refrain of a game: "Take it and read, take it and read." Take what? Read what? He was sure he knew. Seizing the book he had just been reading, the Epistles of Paul, he opened it and read: ". . . not in reveling and drunkenness, not in lust and wantonness, not in quarrels and rivalries. Rather arm yourselves with the Lord Jesus Christ, and spend no more thought on nature and nature's appetites."

The crisis was past; his path was clear. Augustine sought from Ambrose himself instruction in the mysteries of the catechism, was baptized, and soon set sail for North Africa again with two lifelong friends, to devote, as a monk, all his energies to his interior search.

Most Christians of that period held that the sincere desire to receive the grace of God, manifested in the act of baptism, ensured freedom from sin. Yet Augustine, given to unremitting self-examination, came to see very quickly that the simple desire to be free from sin was not nearly enough. "What temptations I can resist, and what I cannot, I know not," he confessed. He found himself far from being able to rest content with being "saved" in the abstract. He wanted a personal faith that could save him in reality, and a method by which he could painstakingly strive to perfect his human personality. It was in meditating profoundly on the words of Jesus and of Paul that he began to see his own shortcomings in stark relief. Then, methodically, in the style of a contemporary man in a desperate situation, he undertook the lifelong endeavor of confronting his own weaknesses face to face.

He ran directly into the obstacles all of us face. He calls these obstacles "chains of habit," the habits of mind, like self-centeredness and greed, that we all cultivate in our ignorance, which bind us to sinning as surely as iron shackles bind a prisoner. It is because of these mental habits that our intentions to do good, no matter how sincere, often have very little impact on our actions. He then set himself a series of critical questions: "How then can sin be overcome? Is there no free will in us, to do as we think best? How are we to approach a Good that has no substance?" In his *Confessions* he attempted to detail for us, much in the fashion of autobiographical self-revelation so popular today, his struggle to answer these doubts.

The *Confessions* is the first spiritual autobiography in the Western world. Augustine was a true pioneer in the depths of the human soul. He wrote as a guide, appealing to his own experience to illustrate the numberless twists and turns of the mind along the route towards the universal spark of divinity within. In analyzing himself, Augustine was analyzing all mankind. God's will, he concluded, cannot even be guessed at, let alone followed, till a man breaks away from the bonds of his own twisted will.

The ultimate value of his route is attested by the fact that he did indeed find, at its end, a goal, serene, lovable, fulfilling:

> ... And this is happiness, to be joyful in thee and for thee and because of thee, this and no other. Those who think happiness is any other, pursue a joy that is apart from thee and is no true joy.... Yet the reason may be that what they cannot do, they do not want to do with sufficient intensity to make them able to do it. Why are they not happy? Because they are much more concerned over things which are more powerful to make them unhappy than truth is to make them happy, in that they remember truth so slightly. There is but a dim light of memory in men; let them walk, let them walk, lest darkness overtake them.

Augustine did not have the benefit of a well-developed mystical tradition. For antecedents he had to reach back to Jesus the Christ in the New Testament and to the apostle Paul, and of their inner lives there were only vague hints as to specifics. It was up to Augustine to find a vocabulary in which to express that experience. His was a seminal mind. From the several major cultural traditions with which he was familiar, he pulled out luminous threads of truth and wove them together in the light of his own experiences of the divine, weaving the shining fabric out of which the Christian faith as we know it has grown. Into this fabric he admitted the whole of human experience, rejecting nothing from the full range of emotions, motives, and their effects. That is what makes it a truly universal scheme. The keynote of Augustine's faith is a passion for God, which breaks out in moving passages throughout the *Confessions*:

And I marveled to find that at last I loved you and not some phantom instead of you; and I did not hesitate to enjoy my God, but was ravished to you by your beauty. Yet soon was I torn away from you again by my own weight, and fell again with torment to lower things. Still, the memory of you remained with me and I knew without doubt that it was you to whom I should cleave; though I was not yet such as could cleave to you.

This passion is often termed "the communion of love." It has become, as Evelyn Underhill puts it, "the heart of the Catholic faith," and in Augustine it fueled a life of heroic action on many fronts. His sermons and pamphlets and books, founded as they are on solid sensibility, are the groundwork upon which great spiritual figures in later centuries — Saint Bernard of Clairvaux, Richard of St. Victor, Saint Thomas Aquinas, and others — built painstakingly, describing and classifying the Christian mystical tradition into stages and substages of contemplation until a marvelous edifice took shape. Their writings in turn guided people as diverse as the Italian reformer Catherine of Genoa, the mystic poet Dante, the Spanish crusader of the spirit Teresa of Avila, and even Martin Luther. All these and myriad others, each with his or her unique blend of rapture, literary expression, and heroic social action, nurtured what is most enduring in Western civilization, and in each we can hear distinct echoes of Augustine.

Yet Augustine had pressing work in his own lifetime. Christianity, despite its official sanction, was not popular in many areas of the Roman Empire. Moreover, there were currents within the church, the Donatists in particular, which threatened to tear it into bickering factions.

Finally, the Western world in Augustine's time was poised on the brink of chaos. Whole races of barbarians had settled within the Empire; Augustine knew it was only a matter of time before they overran it completely. There was no time for bickering if the Church was to survive with its spiritual heart intact. Augustine dared to envision the "followers after perfection" as shining beacons for a world growing dark, and did not want to see the unique and particular quality of Christian revelation compromised. He took upon himself the awesome task of defining, as precisely as possible, the nature of that revelation for future generations.

The example of his group of monastic friends at the cathedral in Hippo, a spiritual enclave in the very heart of society from which pastors and bishops went out to serve the people, proved vital. After the fall of Rome, monastics gradually established communities on the fringes of civilization. They cleared and planted tracts in the wilderness, creating stable centers around which settlers gathered. Their influence spread all over Europe. When other educational institutions had vanished, they played a critical role in keeping the best in the classical tradition alive. Over the following tumultuous six hundred years, these communities remained precious repositories of the Christian revelation. Augustine's writings, along with the New Testament, were their principal sources.

Augustine went a long way toward defining what it means to adhere to a life of impassioned faith while at the same time acting in this world with consummate balance, formed of sensibility and compassion. Just as his words were a raft for people throughout the Middle Ages, when whole cultures were succumbing to the tides of change, they can be a lifesaver for people like us too, who live near the culmination of a long Age of Reason — and are still searching for a joy that lasts. Here, in the beautiful passage from the *Confessions* (Book IX, Chapter 10) which follows, Augustine has handed us a road map to that longed-for land. Yet, inevitably, it is up to us to do our own walking: "Let them walk, let them walk, lest darkness overtake them."

Imagine if all the tumult of the body were to quiet down, along with all our busy thoughts about earth, sea, and air;

if this very world should stop, and the mind cease thinking about itself, go beyond itself, and be quite still;

if all the fantasies that appear in dreams and imagination should cease, and there should be no speech, no sign:

Imagine if all things that are perishable grew still – for if we listen they are saying, "We did not make ourselves; he made us who abides forever" – imagine, then, that they should say this and fall silent, listening to the voice of him who made them and not to that of his creation;

so that we should hear not his word through the tongues of men, nor the voice of angels, nor the clouds' thunder, nor any symbol, but the very Self which in these things we love, and strain beyond ourselves to attain a flash of that eternal wisdom which abides above all things:

And imagine if that moment were to go on and on, leaving behind all other sights and sounds but this one vision which ravishes and absorbs and fixes the beholder in joy; so that the rest of eternal life were like that moment of illumination which leaves us breathless:

Would this not be what is bidden in scripture, "Enter thou into the joy of thy lord"?

AUGUSTINE, CONFESSIONS IX:10

Entering into Joy

[1]

*Imagine if all the tumult of the body were to quiet
down, along with all our busy thoughts about earth,
sea, and air. . . .*

This is a vivid way of describing the throng of
traffic in body and mind, between which there is a
vital, intimate connection.

With its intricate networks of transport and com-
munications, we can compare the body to a state. It
has its major arteries or freeways, its vessels like state
highways, its capillaries or county roads. Altogether
every human body contains five thousand miles of
roads in its cardiovascular system, and they are busy
every minute. Goods are trucked in to local tissue
communities in a steady stream, while waste products
are carried back out in empty vans.

Our nervous system, our communication network, is even more elaborate. I should make it clear
that when I talk about the nervous system, I mean

more than the tissues enumerated in *Gray's Anatomy*. The nervous system is essentially a process. The brain and the rest of the anatomical nervous system are the physical components that enable this process to function in the body – in computer language, the hardware. But the software, the processes which determine how the physical hardware is used, is the mind. These are not two distinct systems, but two aspects of one: how our nervous system responds to the world reflects the processes of our mind.

In this sense, we can think of the nervous system as a great highway like U.S. 101, which travels the length of the West Coast. Highway 101 is a busy artery; in places it has several lanes for traffic in both directions, divided by a median strip with elaborate plantings. Instead of speeding cars, however, imagine flashing thoughts and emotional impulses. In fact, our internal freeway is much more crowded than Highway 101. In the nervous system it is always five o'clock on a Friday afternoon; every moment carries peak traffic.

Whenever I ride along 101 and gaze up at the exclusive homes on the hills above the maelstrom of speed and noise, I wonder, "Who would ever want to live *there?*" Who would want to lie in bed at midnight listening to the roar of trucks, the din of cars? Yet we scarcely seem to notice when the mind is like this, though the result is stress throughout the day and often into the night as well.

When driving at freeway speeds, we are expected to keep several car-lengths between us and the bumper of the vehicle in front. In the nervous system no such rules of thumb are taken seriously. Thought-traffic is frenzied, almost by definition. Yet if each thought could just keep its distance from the next, we would find our mental traffic much easier to control. That is what quieting the mind means. When you look down from your hillside home overlooking the freeway of the mind, the traffic looks like one long, continuous blur. A burst of anger, for example, appears to be a smooth, rational flow of thought. This is the effect that speed of thought has on our perception of the mind. But if we can get traffic to slow down, we can examine each thought individually and even make out the bumper stickers: "If You're Looking for Fun, Follow Me" or "I Maintain My Right to Blow My Stack." I see stickers like these on cars; the stickers on thoughts are no more rational.

Unlike the freeway, however, traffic in the nervous system usually moves in only one direction: toward what we like and away from what we dislike. Over millions of years of evolution, the nervous system has been conditioned to be attracted by what is pleasant and repelled by what is unpleasant. Here the human mind makes an evolutionary contribution of its own: it begins to label as "pleasant" or "unpleasant" not merely physical sensations, but everything in its experience. In every situation, in other words, our characteristic response is "I like this" or "I don't like that." We can rationalize our decisions any way we want; ultimately they come down to this: "I am going to do this because I like it"; "I'm not going to do that because I can't stand it." We may know all about inductive and deductive logic, yet the simple ventriloquism of likes and dislikes escapes us: we say we make decisions, and nobody is more deceived than we ourselves. Similarly, when I witness a quarrel, it doesn't usually strike me as two people trying to convince each other of the logic of their positions; it strikes me as two people trying to deceive each other. "This is what I like, so you ought to like it too." Where is the logic in that?

The more I understand of human personality, the more impressed I am by how deep likes and dislikes can go. The process starts from our earliest days. Listen to the protests of a child when you try to get him to do something he doesn't want to do, or when you try to deprive her of something on which she has set her heart! In a child this kind of behavior can be easily forgiven, but later on it becomes a terrible handicap. People who allow their likes and dislikes to grow rigid become paralyzed when things don't work out the way they want. Relationships become a source of constant turmoil. In every circumstance, having strong likes and dislikes means trouble; a lower level of likes and dislikes means less tension and better performance. I would go to the extent of predicting that when you have quieted your likes and dislikes, your performance will be better in every area of life.

᳇

In particular, having fewer likes and dislikes provides immense protection from stress. This is a popular subject today. Courses in stress reduction and management are increasingly attractive, as more and more people learn what damage a stressful life can do. But there is a good deal of confusion, even disagreement among experts, as to what the word *stress* should mean; so it is important here to be clear. According to Dr. Hans Selye, the "father of stress research," stress is the body's nonspecific response to a real or perceived threat. "Nonspecific" means that defense mechanisms (such as the fight-or-flight reaction) are triggered all over the body – unlike, say, the response to a bee sting, which is usually specific to the area that has been stung. You can imagine the damage these mechanisms can do to the body's major organs when stress becomes chronic.

What provokes the stress response? Broadly, there are two kinds of stressors. One kind is environmental, physiological, physical; the other is psychological. Dr. Selye says:

> Mental tensions, frustrations, insecurity, and aimlessness are among the most damaging stressors, and psychosomatic studies have shown how often they cause migraine headache, peptic ulcers, heart attacks, hypertension, mental disease, suicide, or just hopeless unhappiness.

It is important to realize that unlike physical agents and situations, these and similar stressors are not external. They are produced by our state of mind. Frustration is not caused by Aunt Susie, but by our response to Aunt Susie: after all, her friends at work might respond to the same Susie quite differently. Mental depression, a terrible stressor, is not caused by a situation like being out of work, but by our response to being out of work. No one enjoys not being able to find a job, but what destroys a person's spirit, saps vitality, and sometimes even undermines the will to survive is not the fact of unemployment but the mind that is thrown into depression.

This is a subtle but very important distinction. Wherever possible, it is good to avoid external sources of stress like pollution-laden air or living in the flight path of a busy airport. But we should realize that many other things in our lives which we perceive as stressful – such as our job, where challenges and change may confront us daily – may not actually be stressful in themselves. Often the stress comes from our response. It is a great mistake, therefore, to think of "managing" stress by changing jobs or avoiding any of life's legitimate challenges. Dr. Selye, in fact, emphasizes that we live in a world full of stressful situations, and to run away from stress is to run from life. But by changing our mental responses, we can learn to manage stress: not merely to survive it, but to flourish in it.

Mahatma Gandhi is a perfect example of this.

When I first went to see him in his ashram in Central India, I was in my twenties and just out of college. People came from all over the world to see Gandhi then, because India's independence movement was in full swing and making international news. But most of them had come to see Gandhi the political figure, the man who was freeing a nation without firing a shot. I wanted to see Gandhi the man.

When I arrived at the ashram, I was told Gandhi had been in high-level negotiations with Indian and British political leaders throughout the day. Tensions ran high on both sides in those years. Great Britain, in the throes of the Great Depression at home, was losing control of India, the jewel of its empire and its major source of revenue; and on the Indian side leaders were pulling in different directions on fundamental issues, each trying to pull Gandhi with him. He was in his sixties then; imprisonment and a fearful "fast unto death" had taken a serious toll on his health. I knew that his daily schedule called for him to get up before dawn, keep busy all day, and often not get to bed until midnight or later. Recalling all this in front of the door of his cottage, I expected to see him come out exhausted, with the cares of a nation blearing his eyes and bowing down his shoulders.

Instead the door opened suddenly and out came Gandhi with his famous toothless smile, his eyes sparkling and full of love, as relaxed as if he had been doing nothing more challenging than playing cards. He must have just cracked a joke, because the men and

women who came out with him, these austere statesmen and politicians, were laughing like children;
somehow their burdens had been lifted too. The stress
of that day hadn't touched him in the slightest. He
strode off for his evening walk with the light, swift step
of a teenager, beckoning to us visitors to follow, and I
remember I almost had to run to keep up with him.
Many years later, friends who had worked closely with
Gandhi told me that in his sixties he had three times
the energy that most of us have in our prime. Yet he
worked without tension, even in the midst of trials
and sorrow.

Today people look at Gandhi's example and marvel, "What an extraordinary man!" Gandhi himself
would say just the opposite: "Oh, no. Very ordinary."
To me that is his greatness, his real stature. If he had
been born a spiritual prodigy, able to cope with stress
as effortlessly as those children I used to see on television who could work huge square roots in their heads,
what hope could he offer little people like us? It is precisely because he began life as such an ordinary figure
that his example holds unlimited promise. "I have not
the shadow of a doubt," he assures us, "that every man
and woman can achieve what I have, if he or she
would make the same effort and cultivate the same
hope and faith."

Today, to explain his secret, I often come back to a
phrase he used: "an undivided singleness of mind."
That is a revealing clue. A one-pointed mind is slow

and sound, which gives it immense resilience under stress. With a mind like this, we always have a choice in how we respond to life around us.

Virtually all psychological stress, I would say, comes from the rush and hurry of a frantic mind, which jumps recklessly to unwarranted conclusions, rushes to judgments, and often is going too fast to see events and people as they truly are. Such a mind keeps the body under continual tension. It is constantly on the move, desiring, worrying, hoping, fearing, planning, defending, rehearsing, criticizing; it cannot stop or rest except in deep sleep, when the whole body, particularly the nervous system, heaves a sigh of great relief and tries to repair the damage of the day. Simply by slowing down the mind – the first purpose of meditation – much of this tension can be removed. Then we are free to respond to life's difficulties not as sources of stress but as challenges, which will draw out of us deeper resources than we ever suspected we had.

↩

"Anxiety" is a useful term psychologists have for a particularly elusive kind of stress-related problem. Anxiety is as nonspecific in the mind as stress is in the body: faced by one threatening event, such as the loss of a job or the death of someone we love, the mind responds with fear and self-doubt in every area of life, in every relationship. Increasingly too clinicians refer to "free-floating anxiety," which is not triggered by any particular kind of external event but persists from situation to situation, characteristically when the ego feels threatened.

Primary care physicians admit that much of their work these days is an attempt to help people deal with anxiety, even though many of them would agree that anxiety is not a medical problem – in other words, that it has no medical solution. They prescribe tranquilizers or refer to a growing array of therapies, but by and large they are quick to confess that they are at a loss and are treating symptoms because they cannot reach the cause.

In the language of mysticism, as long as there is a division in consciousness between "I like this" and "I don't like that," that division itself will breed stress. It will be a breeding ground for anxiety. Just as malarial mosquitoes flourish in stagnant, marshy pools, anxiety flourishes in divided minds. Augustine delineated this split in consciousness in unforgettable terms:

> Who would choose trouble and difficulty? In adversity I desire prosperity; in prosperity I fear adversity. Yet what middle place is there between the two, where one's life may be other than trial? There is sorrow and sorrow again in the prosperity of this world: sorrow from the fear of adversity, sorrow from the corruption of joy. There is sorrow in the adversity of this world, and a second sorrow and a third from the longing for prosperity, and because adversity itself is hard, and for fear that

endurance may break. Is not life on earth trial without intermission?

The key to anxiety, as to psychological stress in general, is this: it is not so much an event or circumstance that brings on an attack of anxiety; it is the significance we ascribe to that event, the way we interpret it in our own mind.

I remember a classic illustration of how the mind works in this regard, where a woman spending the weekend in a prominent hotel in New York was kept awake throughout the night by someone banging away on a piano in the suite next door. The next morning, tired and irritated beyond belief, she stormed into the manager's office and demanded, "How can you allow such a thing to happen? I'm holding you personally responsible!"

"But madam," the manager responded smoothly, "that suite is occupied by the great Paderewski. He must have been practicing for his concert tomorrow in Carnegie Hall. People will be paying a small fortune to hear him play for a couple of hours, and here you have been able to listen to him all night long."

"Paderewski! In that case, please let me keep the room after all." And the same woman who had spent a whole night fussing and fuming, tossing and turning in frustration, sat up the next night with her ear glued to the wall, listening in devoted delight.

The same event that triggers anxiety in one person may be shrugged off by a second and even prompt a deep, resourceful response in a third. Again I can offer Gandhi as an illustration. When Gandhi arrived in South Africa at the age of twenty-three, he was an utter failure: in fact, his only reason for being in South Africa was that he had been unable to make a go of it in India. He had left home with his spirit apparently crushed. And as soon as he arrives in South Africa, he is bullied and thrown off a train for wearing a colored skin in a first-class railway car. Thousands of Indians must have suffered this kind of humiliation. Most, I imagine, responded with anger, fear, and then resignation, carrying away a deep injury to their sense of worth. But Gandhi's response plunged him into the depths of his being, where he made a decision that took decades to bear full fruit: never to submit to injustice and never to use unjust means to win a cause. It could have been one of the most stressful experiences in his life. Instead, as he later told the American missionary John Mott, it was the "most creative."

When we feel threatened by someone, often the cause of our anxiety is not that person at all; the cause is our perception of that person. We are put under stress by our dislike. But we can slowly learn to change our perception of others, no matter how they act, and thereby free ourselves from this kind of stress. This is the longest, most drawn-out fight we will ever find in life. Yet in the long run, no one can escape this fight. Every one of us must someday wage this battle within ourselves, against our own selfish, violent judgments of other people. Anxiety is only the warning system, warning us that something destructive is at work within and that we ourselves are its victims.

⊹

Through meditation and the enthusiastic observance of its allied disciplines, such as slowing down and keeping the mind one-pointed through the day, we can learn to do something that sounds impossible: when thoughts are tailgating each other, we can slip into the flow of mental traffic, separate thoughts that have locked bumpers, and slowly squeeze ourselves in between. It sounds terribly daring – the kind of stunt for which professionals in the movies are paid fortunes. Yet most of us critically underestimate our strength. We can learn to step right in front of onrushing emotional impulses such as fury and little by little, inch by hard-won inch, start pushing them apart. This takes a lot of solid muscle, in the form of willpower; but just as with muscles, we can build up willpower with good, old-fashioned practice.

As you learn to do this, you will find to your immense surprise that there is not the slightest connection between another person's provocation and your response. There seemed to be a connection because of the rush of the mind: your perceptions were crowding and pushing on angry thoughts of response. Now that those thoughts have been separated, your perception of the other person's behavior has lost its compulsive force.

We all believe there is a causal connection between perception and response; that is why virtually everyone reacts to the provocation of others. But from my own hard-won experience, I can tell you that it is possible, by strengthening the muscles of the will, to push thoughts and impulses so far apart that if someone gets annoyed with you, you can be even more considerate than before; if someone speaks rudely, you can answer with kindness.

This is what living in freedom means, and it is essentially a matter of getting over rigid likes and dislikes. When this freedom is won, a good deal of the mind's rush-hour traffic subsides. There will be an occasional car on your internal freeways, running a useful errand. Now and then there may even be a well-tuned Harley-Davidson. But by and large, the freeways of body and mind will be amazingly quiet.

Before we can experience this kind of peace of mind, however, a lot of hard work needs to be done. We must find a "middle place," as Augustine puts it, between likes and dislikes: in practical language, a new vital track within the nervous system on which our energy can travel.

At present, as I said earlier, our internal freeway is set up only for one-way traffic, one-way responses, conditioned by our likes and dislikes. When we have to go against our dislikes or do something unpleasant for the sake of others, it is like driving the wrong way into a one-way street. All the traffic of the nervous system is against us, honking, dodging, and complaining bitterly. Very much the same thing occurs when we have to deny ourselves something we want: it is like stalling our car across two lanes of rush-hour traffic, a highly unpopular maneuver. In general, I would say that many psychosomatic ailments like allergy and asthma may be the result of going against a dense, one-way stream of traffic of likes and dislikes: the nervous system cannot brook it, and the body complains. But we can learn to open up traffic in both directions; and when we do, we can move in either direction freely. This gives us the freedom to choose our responses even in tense, difficult situations.

But this is not just a matter of removing a road-block or two. For practical purposes, half the mind's freeway has never been constructed; we have to lay down a whole new road. Many years of sustained, often frustrating effort must go into building this road, but you will be more than satisfied when you see where it can take you. At first the endeavor may not seem so difficult. The terrain is flat, so to speak, and if you encounter an obstacle, you can build a detour without much extra work or cost. At this stage of getting over likes and dislikes, you probably are not sacrificing anything you care about deeply. But as you proceed, you run into places where likes and dislikes have hardened into habit. These are sedimentary formations of self-will, which can stop spiritual enthusiasm cold. Most of us never attempt to climb over these petrified habits of mind or to go around them. They hem us in, limit our vision, and prescribe our action.

That is why Augustine speaks of habit as the main obstacle in the life of every human being. The enemy is our selfish conditioning: some of it imposed from the outside, by circumstances, by friends, by the media; some of it imposed by our own choices and behavior. In the long run this selfish conditioning saps our will, until we finally forget that we have the choice of fighting it. Augustine describes this process in a vivid passage in his *Confessions*:

> The enemy had control of my will, and from that had made a chain to bind me fast. From a twisted will, desire had grown; and when desire is given satisfaction, habit is forged. When habit passes unresisted, a compulsive urge sets in. By these close-set links I was held. . . .

Popular psychology and the mass media insist that we indulge our whims and desires – often, in the case of the media, for somebody else's financial gain. This is not a moral issue to me; it is a thoroughly practical one, and Augustine states the reasons concisely. Every time we give in to a whim, especially a whim that benefits nobody, our will is weakened a little. Gradually, giving in becomes a habit; habit becomes conditioning; and conditioning binds our responses hand and foot.

Giving in to a whim comes down to likes and dislikes again – "I like this, so I'll do it"; "I don't like that, so I'll avoid it." To me this is a rather unchallenging pastime. Enjoying meaningless little pleasures and avoiding unpleasant chores is all a matter of coasting downhill; no effort or will is required. Working through a monolithic habit of likes and dislikes, by contrast, is a tremendous challenge that draws out all kinds of hidden resources. When you try it, you feel very much as if you were tunneling through a mountain of solid rock.

In the hills of Sausalito just north of the Golden Gate Bridge is a tunnel, called the Rainbow Tunnel ever since someone painted a rainbow over the arched entrance, through which Highway 101 snakes on its way north. To get a highway for two-way traffic, we have to cut tunnels like this through our likes and dislikes. Each tunnel can take months of hard labor; sometimes we have to endure long periods of frustration. You keep on trying to tunnel through the mass of habit, defying old desires, and for a long time you find no evidence that anything is happening. Here an experienced guide can be of enormous support. "Just keep on tunneling," he or she assures you again and again. "If you don't give up, you're sure to break through eventually." And after months – sometimes, for a really big compulsion, even years – you finally see a ray of light coming through from the other side.

Most of us have grown so used to giving in to little desires that we forget the role of the will. When we neglect the will, as Augustine says, and allow a desire to get stronger and stronger, we may find that opportunities for satisfying that desire come our way with increasing frequency. If we look closely, however, we generally find that we have been going out of our way to find opportunities. If we could interview a strong desire, it would have a fascinating story to tell: "He's been chasing *me!* I don't have to do a thing." We may not think we have made a conscious decision to pursue a particular object of desire, but on the unconscious level, a desire is a decision. One very effective way to strengthen the will, therefore, is to be extremely vigilant about not letting ourselves be put into situations where we are likely to be swept away by our desire. "Lead us not into temptation" means precisely this: don't put yourself into situations where your will is in over its head.

As a young man, Augustine had all the desires any normal person has. That is why he can understand and sympathize with our difficulties and conflicts. His advice is practical. "I do not blame you, I do not criticize you," he once told his congregation, "if worldly life is what you love. You can love this life all you want, as long as you know what to choose." And, I would add, as long as you have the will with which to choose it. We need both: the discrimination to see what is best in the long run, and the will to make wise decisions when the pleasures of the moment present a more attractive alternative. When we have both these capabilities, all the innocent pleasures of life can be ours to enjoy. In other words, this is neither license nor a plea for asceticism; it is a plea for building up our will.

Strengthening the will by defying strong selfish desires requires a long, grueling fight. But for those who are daring, there comes a turning point: you discover that there is more satisfaction in defying a desire than in yielding to it. After I tasted this fierce satisfaction of self-mastery, my perspective on life changed dramatically. From then on, I understood that building up the will could work wonders; and I started in defying desires joyously.

The psychology of this is fascinating. You are taking the joy right out of the hands of the desire and holding it up as booty: "Now I have the joy without you!" Desire comes as a bully pointing a pistol at you and demanding your life's savings, and like Humphrey Bogart you just take the gun out of his hands. When you can do this, your entire frame of reference changes. Most of the pleasures of the world pale into insignificance. It is not that they are no longer pleasant, but your capacity for joy is no longer limited to a few pennies of sensory pleasure; it is immense beyond belief, beyond all bounds. We can throw all our capacity for rebellion into this kind of heroism, defying our conditioned dependence on trivial likes and dislikes. In doing this, we break out of a narrow world into a new realm of freedom.

Repeating the name of the Lord can be of enormous help in this. When the Holy Name is repeated it becomes like a jackhammer, rattling away at the wall of solid rock that is conditioning. The amount of rock you dislodge per hour is not of primary importance; what is important is the number of times you remember to use the Holy Name and the enthusiasm with which you repeat it. Put as much enthusiasm into it as you can muster. When you can recall the Holy Name in times of stress, you will be making much more progress than you realize.

With the Holy Name, of course, goes meditation. Daily meditation enables you to bore deep into the rock of a compulsive like or dislike and set charges of dynamite at strategic points. Once meditation reaches a certain depth, the words of an inspirational passage like the Prayer of Saint Francis – "Where there is hatred, let me sow love" – can be truly explosive. Gradually deep cracks in the structure of self-will appear. Then the name of the Lord can serve as the kind of loader I saw the other day repairing a county road: it comes and clears the rubble from those explosive charges, so that the work of laying your new road-bed can proceed.

ও

Imagine if the very world should stop, and the mind cease thinking about itself, go beyond itself, and be quite still: if all the fantasies that appear in dreams and imagination should cease, and there be no speech, no sign. . . .

This idea of a still mind is unfamiliar to almost all of us, even threatening. We have conditioned the mind to go up and down: when we get our way, the mind gets excited; when we cannot have our way, the mind sinks into depression. Nobody wants depression, but excitement is another matter; without it, we feel, life is not worth living. So we go after excitement, and after every wave of stimulation comes a trough of depression. If we could gain enough detachment to watch the mind at work, it would look like a seesaw on the playground.

This phenomenon is closely related to something that is fast becoming a way of life today: distraction. At bottom, the habit of distraction stems from a desire to keep the mind in turmoil all the time. During World War II there was a Berlin-Rome axis; this false belief about the mind is the propaganda of what we might call the mind-body axis. To be really alive, we feel, the mind has to be stimulated constantly.

I have teacher friends who complain that most children today have difficulty in concentrating; their attention span is very short. This is often a direct result of distractibility. In fairness, this is not usually the children's fault. Modern civilization sets a premium on distraction, and the mass media are in front of children's eyes and in their ears to tell them constantly, "Keep your mind jumping! If you don't, you'll get bored."

Meditation is particularly effective in undoing this habit the mind has developed, for what distracts it again is its likes and dislikes. We should be able to put the mind on any subject and keep it focused there without any effort or protest, whether it likes the subject or not. This is what I call expert driving: you start the mind out on your mental highway, glide smoothly up to fifty-five, and cruise along in the same lane without any weaving in and out. When you can do this, you make a most rewarding discovery: everything you do with attention becomes interesting. This one skill can banish boredom forever.

Likes and dislikes tend to be most pronounced in our attitudes towards other people. If we want to be free to respond in kindness, free to love, free to contribute to others' welfare, we have to work constantly to keep our mind from heaving up and down. Otherwise we cannot even know what people around us are like. All that we know, if I may paraphrase a distinguished neuroscientist, is our own nervous system. When we say "I don't like that person," what we really mean is, "This is what my nervous system is recording: If I try to work with him I get migraine; if I talk to him, I break out in a rash; if I have to spend a few hours in his company, I can't sleep at night." We are not saying anything at all about that person; we are talking about our own signs and symptoms.

Similarly, when someone insults us, it is helpful to remember that that person has not really seen us at all. He is busy reading an EEG in his own head, and the report he is getting is highly negative. Instead of erupting at him, we should be able to say to ourselves, "Poor fellow! His nervous system is showing a highly destructive pattern." When you can do this, you can remain comfortable and secure in the face of wilting criticism. All your sympathy will go out to the person who is being unkind. This is a direct result of a still mind, and it is the very basis of compassion. It means you will be able to return sympathy for ill will, love for hatred, as Jesus recommended.

Every time your nervous system is making EEG recordings under the prompting of dislikes, it is putting you under stress. When Jesus says "Bless them that curse you; do good to them that hate you," it is your own health and peace of mind he is trying to safeguard. Being consistently kind is the best way to make your nervous system strong, healthy, and resilient. The best health insurance in the world, fittingly enough, is love. The surest immunity against the bacilli of suspicion and hatred comes with compassion.

Our goal is the capacity never even to think ill of others. But this does not mean we should fail to oppose other people lovingly when necessary. When someone is making a mistake or acting unkindly, putting up tender opposition is often a demonstration of just how much we care. But it is essential to oppose kindly, without withdrawing personal support, and not for the purpose of getting something we want or having our own way. And we must be prepared for the other person's aggravation. Yet after his initial displeasure at having been opposed, every sensitive person will realize that it is because we care for him so much that we have planted ourselves squarely in his path. In the long run, this will add respect and depth to our relationship.

With someone you are allergic to, my granny had a direct, daring way of tunneling into dislikes: try sitting down next to that person and starting up a pleasant conversation. You do not need to stay long; five casual minutes will do. It is the effort that counts. It may be painful at the time, but miraculously, over time, you are likely to find your allergy subsiding – not only with regard to that particular person, but toward anybody who happens to be discourteous to you or who contradicts you. This is an answer to many emotional problems that are rampant today, which we normally recognize only when they show up in statistics like the divorce rate. This simple skill will improve your health, your vitality, and ultimately even your physical appearance; for the mind in turmoil takes away from the beauty of our face, the beauty of our movements, the beauty of our voice, the beauty of our life.

On the other hand, always making yourself the frame of reference – which is precisely what having strong likes and dislikes means – is like spending the day being thrown like a Frisbee between conflicts. By evening you will be more tense than before, and so exhausted that you cannot face the problems you have created for yourself. Instead of allowing the mind to spin its numberless wheels, it is in our own best interest to extend ourselves by working hard and giving as much time and energy as we can to other people. If you want a good friend, don't think about yourself. Be a good friend to all, think about the needs of everybody else, and you will be your own best friend.

Look at how a powerful negative emotion like jealousy can manipulate the significance we assign to events and words and gestures. Jealous people see things that are not there, and they act on what they see by the light of their own insecurity. The answer to jealousy lies in working to make ourselves more secure by not allowing the mind to dwell on its petty grievances, annoyances, and fears, and by keeping our hands and mind reasonably occupied with selfless work. Selfless work is magnificent for security as well as for personal growth.

Here again the name of the Lord can be of enormous help. In my early years in this country, I was once in a cavernous indoor shopping mall and was startled to see something flashing down a wall. I had no idea what was going on until someone explained to me that this was a pneumatic mail chute. At the bottom was a huge mail bin from which a busy clerk gathered up hundreds of postcards and packages and got them ready for the post office. This is what happens when you go on dropping the name of the Lord into your mind. Especially when you are upset, keep on dropping it over and over like so many special delivery letters. We never see what happens to them, but deep within is a divine Clerk eager to collect all our hand-addressed appeals even when we have forgotten the stamp.

One of the miracles of the Holy Name is that it can help prevent thoughts and actions from becoming compulsive, simply by keeping the mind gainfully employed. Anger is always compulsive. Nobody really wants to get angry or to be resentful; that is the nobility of the human being. We get resentful because we think we cannot help getting resentful, and that is where the repetition of the name of the Lord comes in.

The farther you progress, the more clearly you will see the effect that bouts of excitement and anger have on the mind. One tantrum because you didn't get your way can cause giant mudslides in your hard-won tunnels. Instead of spending every day digging deeper into the rock, you find yourself having to spend days, weeks, sometimes months clearing out the debris.

In one particularly wet winter in northern California, we had such torrential rains that the roadway on the north side of the Golden Gate Bridge was in danger of washing down the cliffs into picturesque San Francisco Bay. It would have taken months and a good deal of the state highway budget to construct a new highway through the solid rock. Instead, the state engineers decided to shore up the existing road. They drilled deep holes into the underlying bedrock, inserted steel beams, and filled the holes back up with cement. Now this part of the highway is actually a bridge over the unstable earth. The name of the Lord is like those steel beams, and we can insert it whenever our self-control starts to slip. The Lord is there supporting us; all we have to do is maintain contact with him. He can help us avoid the pitfalls of daily living, saving us time and energy which we can use for making further progress. And with him shoring us up, we can be sure there is no chance of suffering the acute embarrassment of landing in the Bay.

There are serious long-term consequences from repeated lapses too. We begin to think that perhaps we are not going to make it to the other side of the mountain after all, that we can never learn to deal with the particular problems we face. I believe it was Sir Richard Steele who, when asked how he spent his days, replied candidly, "In sinning and repenting." You do a lot of strenuous digging, then yield to some tantrum or temptation, and there you are, digging out the same old ground again. So whenever you feel your mind is beginning to slip, indicating an impending mudslide of self-will, that is the time to be immediately on the alert. Then it is that the name of the Lord can help shore up your will.

I understand from the newspapers that some of the oldest highways in this country, the throughways in and around the big Eastern metropolitan areas, are in critical need of repair, and no one knows where to find the necessary funds. This is bad news for commerce, but in the conditioned highways of the mind it is a happy state of affairs. When your like-and-dislike throughways are splitting open and grass is sprouting up in the cracks, don't give them any attention with which to repair themselves. Just let them crumble quietly.

Augustine is trying in these lines to help us understand why we need to train our senses and learn to harness negative emotions. On the basis of the evidence provided by some of the greatest of mystics, this arduous effort is an unavoidable part of spiritual growth. Teresa of Avila, by her own candid account, spent nearly twenty years in this kind of tunneling. None of us therefore need be surprised if our road too is uphill for a long, long time. Many years of hammering away at the massed inertia of sense-conditioning and mind-conditioning is our lot.

Yet all in all, it is not very helpful to look on difficult situations and difficult people as impediments. We can look on them as opportunities, our great helpers. Everybody has difficulties in life; nobody can manage to get around this valuable training period. It is largely when we are not able to view difficulties as opportunities for growth that they become insufferable. We can learn to see frustrating circumstances or annoying acquaintances as opportunities to contribute more, opportunities to grow and to help other people grow. Without serious obstacles, I am afraid, very few of us would ever grow up. This is the purpose of obstacles: to give us the skill and confidence to face even bigger, more formidable obstacles.

Whenever people live together or work together, it is only natural that there be a certain amount of friction. There is nothing surprising about this. But every time you find yourself in a situation where you are getting hot under the collar, you can use the Holy Name to push angry words apart and stick in their place the desire to stand firm, stay patient, and help the other person calm down. Look at the drama of it: your blood pressure is hitting the ceiling, your eyes are getting bloodshot, all your juices are flowing in the wrong direction. To be able to remain patient and come out with kind words at such a time is making a U-turn right on the anger freeway. I'm told this used to be called "doing a brodie," after someone who presumably lived to tell the tale. On a highway, doing a brodie is a death-defying act, but on the highways of the mind it is life-affirming. When your mind is racing along some emotional freeway at top speed, headed straight for disaster, I don't think anything in life can equal the thrill of learning to do a brodie on the spot and drive back calmly in the opposite direction. Everyone will stop to stare and say in admiration, "Right on the freeway!" And after a while, everyone who sees you will want to learn how to do this too.

Often what prevents us from going against likes and dislikes in daily living is the enormous amount of mental furniture we keep. People can be very particular, you know, about how their household furniture is arranged. "My velveteen armchair goes here, a foot and a half to the left of the brass floor lamp. And my abstract acrylic sculpture has to sit on the far right-hand corner of the inlaid mahogany coffee table." We get used to a particular arrangement, and anything that disturbs it disturbs us as well. This is how we arrange the likes and dislikes in our mind too, and it limits us severely in our capacity to communicate with others and draw closer to them. The person whose mind is not crammed with likes and dislikes, whose taste in mental furniture is more in the "minimalist" mode, can go into any circle of people from any walk of life and communicate beautifully. He or she can rearrange the furniture of the mind effortlessly, as the situation demands; yet the resulting configuration will always be practical and beautiful. Teresa of Avila puts it plainly: "To have courage for whatever comes in life – everything lies in that."

Once we correct our perception of life around us, freeing it from the context of "I like" and "I don't like," all events are just events. They are neither pro nor con; they do not work for us or against us. The only thing we lose in this change of perception is our mental turmoil; for when you see everything as it is, you find there is no cause for personal sorrow. You gain compassion, you gain precious insight into others, and you gain the capacity to help them see more clearly, provided they want to see.

This does not take away from the joy of life; it brings added joy. When I take my friends out, I don't think anybody enjoys it more than I do. I enjoy it even if everything goes wrong. One bright afternoon several months ago I set out with four friends for an evening in Berkeley, where we had season tickets for the performances of the Berkeley Repertory Theatre. Sultana had prepared us a sumptuous picnic dinner with quiche, fresh bread and fruit, and two elaborate salads, which she packed carefully in the trunk. Halfway to Berkeley it started to rain.

We arrived at the university campus, hoping to find a warm, dry spot where we could eat, and discovered that the trunk of the car had suddenly decided that it was not going to open. We tried calling some locksmiths, but it seemed that was a busy night for locksmiths. So we tried several restaurants suitable for vegetarians, all of which were unfortunately closed. We made it to the theater just in time to see the curtain rise.

All the time this was happening, I was watching my mind. How would it react? I found it hadn't bothered me a bit that everything had gone wrong. We enjoyed ourselves anyway, simply being out together, and I felt as relaxed as if everything had gone precisely as planned. When your mind is still, you are free to enjoy whatever comes. This is a precious skill. My grandmother used to remind me often that ups and downs are the very texture of life. "But," she would add, "you don't have to go up and down with them."

Of course, I have to add that I have no objection to everything going smoothly. I don't look forward to fiascoes or complain, "Everything went just right. What a ghastly day!" I enjoy good news, a pleasant evening, a successful turn of events. Yet if you take my blood pressure on such occasions, you will find it completely normal: no excitement, just a quiet sense of joy. I have found that excitement, far from adding to enjoyment, actually takes away the capacity to enjoy.

After years of hammering away at them, I have been able to reduce my likes and dislikes to a negligible level. In most matters, I really do not have any personal preferences, which means that my mind almost never gets upset over any personal affront or inconvenience. All my vital energy is free to deal with the things in life that really matter: the welfare of others, the spiritual growth of those who look to me for guidance, problems like violence and stress-related disorders where the work of our meditation center can play a vital role.

It takes many years to realize the velocity of the thinking process, or the immense power behind its speed. The mind is a twelve-lane freeway, and mind-traffic obeys no known speed limits or driving laws. The whole purpose of meditation is to slow down the pace of this tumultuous traffic, and the struggle to do so can go on for years and years. Yet if you can bring the full power of your mind under control, you will have a turbocharged engine at your disposal. This is the only effective way to deal with stress and anxiety, and the only way to have true peace of mind. Then, instead of sticking to the old roads of conditioned living, you can have a real adventure: strike out cross-country into unexplored territory, where all your responses are free. You will be laying down a totally new road deep into consciousness, in search of a new land of love and joy.

[2]

Imagine if all things that are perishable grew still
— for if we listen they are saying, "We did not
make ourselves; he made us who abides forever" —
imagine, then, that they should say this and fall
silent, listening to the very voice of him who made
them and not to that of his creation. . . .

In commenting on Augustine's second stanza, I want to try to bring to light some of the volcanic forces that work far, far below the surface strata of consciousness, forming the individual human personality as we see it – manifested in all the seemingly incomprehensible quirks of daily behavior. They are incomprehensible precisely because we are rarely able to see below the surface to what lies deep within: the currents which give rise to explosive emotional upheavals. All these wonders of the interior world we can see for ourselves when we take up the amazing journey into consciousness on the submarine that is meditation. This is a journey that takes us into the murky origins of our personal emotional responses to events around us. But we can travel deeper still: we can discover the place where the tremendous forces that ignite these responses can be resolved.

This is not at all a fantastical voyage. These descriptions do not proceed from the imagination of visionaries. When I point out landmarks along the way, they are landmarks which mystical pioneers like Francis and Augustine have discovered for themselves in the depths of their own consciousness. These landmarks exist; they are real. That is the reason why the journeys of the great mystics, as they themselves insist, are applicable to little people like you and me. In describing for us their routes in glowing words, they have furnished us with actual charts into deepest consciousness. By meditating profoundly, as they did, and following the same kind of challenging disciplines, you and I can discover these hidden territories for ourselves.

If we are to claim our rights to the enormous terrains within, with their untold wealth and precious human resources, there is no other way I know on earth than following for ourselves these same dynamic disciplines. Foremost among these, and indispensable, to my way of thinking, is the regular, systematic, and enthusiastic practice of meditation.

❧

Let me begin by delving into the long development of the individual human personality. We can actually begin deep in the past, at a time when the earth itself was still being formed. We usually think of the earth as inert, inanimate. Let us for a moment think of it as Mother Earth, a living, loving woman. Bumper stickers remind us, "Every mother is a working mother." The earth too is a working mother, and she has to work hard indeed to support the array of plants and creatures — ourselves included — which make up her enormous brood. Just as remembering to love and respect our human mother for all she has done for us is a duty we should all hold dear, we should show the same kind of respect, consideration, and love for our mother the earth. This loving remembrance is the spiritual basis of ecology.

Corroboration for this animated view of the earth comes from a veteran science writer, Guy Murchie. "In a very real sense," Mr. Murchie writes, "the earth is alive like an animal. Like an animal it stirs in its sleep, it breathes air, it grows." In fact, the strange early picture of the earth that geophysicists have arrived at is reminiscent of the body of an adolescent, its muscles aching to exert themselves in the processes of expansion. "Its wounds heal; its juices circulate. Its skin metabolizes. Its nerves crackle quietly with vital messages." The story of the development of the human body, Murchie points out, is inextricably intertwined with that of the development of the earth. "My body was shaped in the rivers where vertebrates developed and lungs were born. And my apprenticeship was in the trees, where I grew my hands. . . . After the uplifting of the continents produced the grassy fields, I learned to stand up and look far, and outthink the lion."

In *Evolution and Ethics*, the eminent nineteenth-century biologist Thomas Huxley suggested another dimension to this picture of human evolution:

Every day experience familiarizes us with the facts which are grouped under the name of heredity. Every one of us bears upon him obvious marks of his parentage, perhaps of remoter relationships. More particularly, the sum of tendencies to act in a certain way, which we shall call "character," is often to be traced through a long series of progenitors and collaterals. So one may justly say that this "character" – this moral and intellectual essence of a man – does veritably pass out from one fleshly tabernacle to another, and does really transmigrate from generation to generation. In the newborn infant, the character lies latent, and is little more than a bundle of potentialities. But very early, these become actualities; they manifest themselves in dullness or brightness, weakness or strength, viciousness or uprightness; and with each feature modified by confluence with another's character, if by nothing else, the character passes on to its incarnation in new bodies. The Indian philosophers called character, as thus defined, "karma."

In five billion years the amoeba has become me. This is not a blind, arbitrary growth; each of us has played the major role in his or her own development. In every short lifetime, we are the result of what we have thought and done; at the end of each life, we shall be the sum total of all we have thought and done before.

Thinking, in this sense, can be construed as a rehearsal for action. This life of ours is full of the mind, actually made out of the mind: in Huxley's sense, a mind that can trace its continuity back over many previous generations. When Augustine began to see the extent of this process we call the mind, he was amazed:

> Great is this power of memory, exceedingly great, O my God, a spreading limitless room within me. Who can reach its uttermost depth? Here are men going afar to marvel at the heights of mountains, the mighty waves of the sea, the long courses of great rivers, the vastness of the ocean, the movements of the stars, yet they leave themselves unnoticed!
>
> In the innumerable fields and dens and caverns of my memory, innumerably full of innumerable kinds of things present either by their images or in themselves or by certain notions or moods . . . in and through all these does my mind range, and I move swiftly from one to another and penetrate them as deeply as I can, but find no end. So great is the force of memory, so great the force of life!

Some people, when faced with the force of our evolutionary past, throw up their hands and say, "I am powerless! My fate is already determined, and there is nothing I can do about it." They are ignoring the bright side to this mind of ours. There is no need to refer to any supernatural power, nor even to any external power, for escape; we shape our own destiny. My destiny has been placed entirely in my own hands. It is the continuous improvement I am able to make in the quality of my thinking that decides my rate of spiritual growth, decides the quality of my life today and of my life tomorrow. In a large measure, the quality of my thinking decides even my physical health – a fact that has some surprising implications.

As I said earlier, there is a quiet correspondence between the kind of body I have and the kind of mind I have. Each of us, by the thoughts we think and the actions we take, has influenced the physical body we inhabit and the physical environment in which that body moves. One Christian mystic exclaims, "My sin is stamped upon the universe!" Fortunately, the opposite is also true: each of us can say, "My goodness is stamped upon the universe." The fragment of divinity which is in me, which is in all creatures and all people of all races, has been revealed more and more, bit by bit, through this billion-year process of growth we call evolution, and it is continually being revealed anew. I can see this divine spark shining even through the eyes of our dogs. This awareness that they are not merely kith and kin, but living manifestations of the same spark of divinity, fills my heart with love for them. When this awareness dawns, it becomes a joyful responsibility to protect the lives of all creatures.

This divine spark travels through time from stage to stage of evolution. Our dog Ganesha reveals a little more of this spark than does, say, a tiger in the forest. Our main advance in evolution over the friendly animals is that we have the capacity to "look far," as Guy Murchie says, into the consequences of our actions.

Human beings who are violent of mind, in this view, still have one foot in the animal world. When we get angry, for instance, we do not think of the consequences of our words and actions, either for the victim of our anger or for ourselves. In this sense, no matter how much we may hail our times as the age of technological miracles, we are far from seeing the end of evolution.

In the history of the world there has been a certain blessed number of humans who have determined to go beyond their personal conditioning of mind and body so as to identify with the needs of all life. Such people, like Augustine or Teresa of Avila, may look like the rest of the human race to a casual observer, yet they no longer live in the limited, physical world. They live in the state we call God-consciousness, from which there is no fall. These pioneers in consciousness are able to show us a goal to which we should make every effort to direct our own individual evolution. By ourselves we would have a great deal of difficulty discerning this goal, for the increments by which we evolve toward it without intense personal effort are indeed small.

Looked at from a contemporary perspective – say, that of Einstein's "world line," the continuous thread that traces life through space and time – a fascinating picture emerges: of consciousness evolving through time, through the long travail of evolution, picking up conditioned responses in every individual creature's life and accumulating them in the collective heritage of humankind. To make the image even more picturesque, we can liken consciousness, traveling through time, to a wind: starting up as a tiny breeze, then picking up momentum as it adds responses, getting stronger and stronger as it blows through the phenomenal world to its end. Just as a wind blowing through a garden picks up a slight fragrance from the lilacs and roses and carries their fragrance on, though the lilac blossom and rose themselves may last only a couple of weeks, so the immaterial legacy of every life is carried by the wind of consciousness through evolution, and every creature is touched by it. Further – particularly in the human context – the conditioning and the responses of various creatures mingle and act on one another, so that this evolutionary heritage becomes richer and more complicated through time.

Of course, all this makes an extremely elaborate picture. In a sense, we can look on one person's anger as a million years old! That is why retaliation makes absolutely no sense: patience, given the whole history of human personality, is much the most sensible policy. Besides anger, fortunately, we have some redeeming qualities mixed in too: a bit of tenderness, an underlying willingness to forgive. As Augustine observed:

> Who can map out the various forces at play in one soul? Man is a great depth, O Lord. The hairs of his head are easier by far to count than his feelings, the movements of his heart.

Of all these negative forces and feelings, I would call anger the single emotion most characteristic of our times, so much so that this could be called the Age of Rage. Angry, violent personalities are offered in contemporary entertainment and taken as models of behavior. Even the news media, for some reason, seem to consider it a duty to bring violent heroes and heroines before our eyes – if possible, every day. All this adds immeasurably to the burden of violent conditioning which each of us carries through this lifetime.

This seemingly imaginative history has very practical contributions to make to our understanding of personal problems. When a person comes into this life with certain pronounced proclivities, such as a tendency to erupt in rage, he is going to find himself again and again in frustrating situations where the pent-up hostilities inside him ferment until they find violent outlets. In this view, such people are as much the cause of these situations as they are victims of circumstance. They cannot avoid responsibility for getting into frustrating situations, any more than they can avoid responsibility for their anger.

As a result, if this proclivity goes unchecked, they may well develop serious health problems. Some researchers, for example, have drawn a connection between an anger-prone personality and heart disease. I find this quite reasonable, for anger places the heart and the rest of the circulatory system under tremendous stress. Digestive problems may well be another long-term correlate: a person prone to anger may develop an ulcer in the digestive tract because the stomach will be in turmoil much of the time. Of course, I am not denying that external factors play a part in bringing on ill health. Yet the mystics go far deeper: they point out that we actually bring with us into this life the tendencies that lead us into the activities, occupations, relationships, and behavior which bring these external factors onto the scene. When they say that we are responsible even for our health, they are not being occult; they are talking good, sound sense.

Yet, as I said, there is a very hopeful side of this comprehensive picture of evolution. No matter what our tendencies, each one of us has a choice. Even if we come from an angry home, went to school with angry teachers and classmates, and have an angry partner, spiritual disciplines can help us to use the same context and relationships to improve the quality of our life. This is the glory of the human being: we always have that choice. So when you are living with angry people, put up with them cheerfully and don't withdraw your support from them. It will help them a good deal, but even more, it will help you. It will not only undo some of the angry conditioning which you brought with you into this life, but also add greatly to your stock of patience, good will, and compassion. All this is the best health insurance I know.

This is going to be tough. Yet if I may be a bit morbid in the interests of highlighting choices, isn't surgery tough? Surgery is a frightful procedure, as any sensitive physician will admit. I can appreciate a man like Norman Cousins saying that to go into the intensive care unit of a hospital will upset any normal human being. Surely, artificial valves and the like are helpful. Yet these and similar remedies are meant only to deal with symptoms; the real cause of our physical problems – for instance, anger – usually goes untouched. How can the symptoms not reappear in time?

Former Secretary of State Dean Rusk once remarked that partial disarmament is like building a bridge halfway across a river. From the spiritual view of health, surgery and pharmacology are the same: they are partial solutions, a bridge halfway across the chasm of ill health. I do understand that there are special circumstances which call for surgery. But even then, to achieve real, lasting health we have to change our way of thinking: not merely our lifestyle but our thought-style. This is where meditation comes in.

Some of the most magnificent figures in the history of mysticism have begun with severe emotional problems, even serious physical handicaps. So there is no need for any of us to feel downcast about our situation or the particular difficulties we face, provided we do everything we can to purify our mind. Meditation is essentially a discipline for slowing down the furious activity of the mind; and if you can gradually bring your mind to a state so still that no movement, no thought, can arise except those you yourself approve, your mind will have become pure. We have no need to teach pure motives to the mind. All that is necessary to make the mind pure is to undo the negative conditioning to which it has been subjected; then we will be left with pure, unconditioned awareness. "Be still," the Bible says, "and know that I am God."

We can call this long process character rebuilding. Our first character in this life has been inherited: prefabricated, if you like, for the most part by negative conditioning. In this, I am grieved to admit, most of us have precious little say. Now it is our job to rebuild our character, almost from the foundation up. The priceless advice of the mystics is that inside, at the core of our being, we already have a Resident Architect, and that our first task – in which they are more than willing to help us – is to come up with an appropriate set of blueprints.

When we meditate on passages which bear the imprint of these pure minds' experiences of God, we find that their words are like the working drawings a contractor follows. "Let the scriptures be the countenance of God," Augustine advises. "Look into the scriptures, the eyes of your heart on its heart." This is exactly what we are doing in meditation when we give all our concentration to the words of an inspirational passage like this one from Augustine: we sink gradually into the heart of the author's experience until we see through his or her eyes. At the end of this book I give a list of such passages from scripture and the mystical giants of the Christian tradition. They make perfect blueprints for this job of character rebuilding.

⟿

I touched earlier on the subject of anxiety. With crippling emotional ailments so common today, this is a terribly important subject. Here I would like to venture a few suggestions about the nature of anxiety, which will make clear how closely it ties in with the picture of personality development I have just described.

Wisps of anxiety float into the lives of even very successful people. They can afflict even those who are blessed with abundant health. There is no easy way to account for these wisps, and most of us can find no safe bastion against them. Yet isn't it telling that in a civilization where dependence on external satisfactions is most marked, anxiety is epidemic?

Imagine if the ball-and-socket joint in your hip were dislocated. Your leg would be out of joint, and you would not be able to do much of anything without being aware of the discomfort twenty-four hours a day. You could not sit anywhere without thinking about it. The slightest movement would make you wince, and walking would become an excruciating chore. The mind can get out of joint like this too, so that we go through life with everything a little off, a little wrong. Many people today report a strange sense of not being at home anywhere, of not fitting in; often they use words like "loneliness" or "alienation." Whatever they try to do, part of them seems to wish they were doing something else instead. Frustration at not being able to curb these symptoms can lead to severe depression. Often the perpetrator of this kind of trouble is anxiety, and it needs to be interpreted from a depth which secular psychology cannot reach.

Anxiety can be particularly acute when we find ourselves confronted by death. This gives another valuable clue to its origin. Most of us find the death of another person or creature deeply unsettling, yet after a time we usually manage to submerge our feelings and carry on. For someone deeply sensitive to the transitory nature of life, however, an encounter with death can leave scars that last a lifetime. As a teenager Augustine witnessed the untimely death of a bosom friend, and suddenly a trapdoor opened into deeper awareness. He was devastated. "I thought death suddenly capable of devouring all men, because he had taken this loved one."

In the very depths of our consciousness, which we can call the collective unconscious, is written the story of our evolution in its entirety. Millions of times during the course of our evolution we have suffered the loss of our parents, our partners, our children, our friends. Millions of times we ourselves have gone through the agonies of death. In the unconscious is a complete record of all this – not so much of the details, but certainly of the main events. Just as each of

us bears the physical marks of millions of years of evolution, mentally too we have a complete library of
subtle impressions gleaned from the last five billion
years: instincts, primal emotions, the deeply conditioned responses of fight and flight, and much, much
more.

The main reason why none of us are consciously
aware of these deep, traumatic records is that life
would then be impossible for us. Who would be able to
sleep in peace tonight if he remembered all the times
that parents and children, partner and partner, friend
and friend have been parted? I am not speaking here
about a mere intellectual awareness that all of us are
born to die. If you knew in your heart that everybody
is bound to be parted by death, you would find it terribly difficult to carry on the routine of everyday life.
For this crucial reason the mind has drawn a merciful
veil over the contents of the unconscious, allowing
human beings to go on living "in the valley of the
shadow of death."

The word "anxiety" is an exceptionally weak term
for expressing the depths of feeling from which arises
this vague uneasiness, this unsettled sense of being out
of place and running out of time. Generally we can
only ascribe it to external events, if we succeed in linking it to anything at all. But what is actually happening is that a wisp of memory is rising, whispering to us
from deep within that nothing external in life is
secure, nothing physical ever lasts. The body wears
out; the senses grow dull and the intellect feeble; no

relationship between two physical creatures, no matter how loving, outlasts the passage of time. These are the sorry facts of life. The astonishing thing is that even though we study biology and see old age and death coming to people on every side, in our heart of hearts none of us believe that this is going to happen to us too. Even so, through all the discreet veils that are cast over the immense canyons of the unconscious, faint wisps like mist rising out of mountain valleys escape through tiny crevices in the mind and come floating up into daily life. Such are the deep springs of anxiety.

No matter how hard we may try, in the long run none of us can escape the devastating fact of death. Yet an encounter with death, as in the case of Augustine, can leave us changed decidedly for the better. It can prompt us forward on the long search for something secure in life, something that death cannot reach.

Many people, of course, do not particularly desire to be prompted forward like this. "I don't like to think about such things," they may say. "I'm happier carrying on as if nothing is going to happen." For such people, the mystics have a penetrating question: If you are truly happy inside, why do you feel the need to go looking for happiness outside? This is spiritual logic at its deadliest. It is because we need some temporary relief from these nagging, floating wisps that we go around shopping for pleasures. Though we may not admit it willingly, those who have experimented to a reasonable extent with the smorgasbord of physical pleasures understand that the pursuit of pleasure, at bottom, is not a search for joy but an attempt to escape for a time from pain. What we may not realize is that this pain is written into the very archives of consciousness.

For these reasons, I would say, anxiety can be a good augury. It is much better to be a little aware of what is written within us than to walk blithely along the boardwalk of life saying, "There is nothing at all inside, so I might as well take it easy." It is much more useful to know that something within will not allow us to be at home with inherently insecure, inherently precarious circumstances. This is a very constructive way of looking at anxiety: it shows the positive side, and it offers something we can do about it too.

Suffering, of course, has always had a bad press. Nobody likes it and people will go to enormous lengths to avoid it. Yet suffering too can have a positive side; it is not the total villain we make it out to be. It can act as a potent motivator, pushing us into more sensitive ways of relating to people, more healthy ways of thinking and behaving. We know that in tragic cases where the body loses its capacity to feel pain, it has effectively lost its alarm system. Heat, for example, doesn't hurt such people, so nothing prompts them to pull their fingers away until they are badly burned. Sensitivity to emotional pain can play the same educational role for the mind.

This term "sensitivity," which we use so glibly these days, has come to mean being sensitive to one's own feelings. "I get hurt very easily," we say, "so please be extra nice to me." It is really an implied threat. Isn't there a shrub called "sensitive plant," which you have only to touch lightly for all the leaves to droop and hide? This is what most of us mean by being sensitive: ignore us for a little while or chance to say the wrong thing, and emotionally we fold right up. I would not call this sensitivity; it is simply preoccupation with oneself. The only kind of sensitivity worth cultivating is sensitivity to the needs of others, and to cultivate that, preoccupation with ourselves has to be reduced.

Most people cannot be very compassionate towards others for the simple reason that they are not sensitive to anyone except themselves. The less you dwell on yourself, the more your sensitivity will open out to the needs and feelings of others. Every time you hurt someone and then grieve inside because of it, you are attending a valuable seminar on sensitivity. It is a seminar on the deepest and most personal level, the experiential, and it is infinitely more effective than anything we can attend for college credit. The credit comes to us directly, when we change our behavior and don't hurt people again. "Everybody's feelings can be hurt," we realize, "just like my own. I have to take others' feelings into consideration in everything I do."

In learning how to make good use of pain, we can gain helpful clues from men who know pain well: boxers. When you have a strong desire to strike out at someone – probably it is someone with whom you are emotionally involved – part of your mind is convinced that yielding to this urge will bring you satisfaction. That is the basic problem. If you have some measure of detachment at the crucial moment, you can actually watch the urge get hold of your right hand and drag you into the ring to take a swing. At that time, if you can be sensitive to the pain you will cause the other person, you can free your hand from the urge's grip.

Gradually, after a great struggle, you can build up the strength of will to deliver a left hook to the bullying urge itself. The person who is going to feel the force of the blow, of course, is you: the part of you that is entangled in wanting to strike out. That is the painful part of it all. But in the long run, it is also you who will be free.

I have seen snapshots in the newspaper of chaps after a rugged bout: battered beyond belief. Yet their desire to win was so great that they were hardly aware of the pain. They were so concentrated on the glory and the adulation and the cash that goes with winning that a lot of the capacity to feel pain was flowing into that. Similarly, we can actually come to feel a fierce sense of joy in battling these entrenched urges that have dominated our lives, and in seeing them hit the canvas – finally, for good.

These are all clues to the mind's real capacities for self-help. That is why I say that the way to deal with mental anguish is to dig deeper and discover a more profound source of motivation. Your energy will flow into that, just as water flows to a lower level. That is exactly how desire flows to deeper sources of satisfaction than the ones which promise purely personal gain.

Look back on some of the moments in your life when you were longing for something very much. Weren't you able to endure pain cheerfully at such times for the sake of the greater joy to come? Similarly, all of us find joy in suffering a personal loss for the sake of someone we love. We can learn to feel such love for more and more people; it is at bottom a matter of extending our sensitivity. This can go to such an extent that if somebody is pointedly unkind to us, our immediate response will be to feel sorry for that person. No urge to strike back will be able to get a grip on our mind. Even when we have to oppose a person we can work this miracle, which is what is meant by "fighting the sin but winning over the sinner." Then the mystics ask a marvelous question: when you find joy in suffering so that others can benefit, how can sorrow come to you?

The best way of dealing with anxiety and distress, therefore, is not to run away from them but to see them as tugging at our sleeves, trying to be helpful. "Go ahead," they are trying to tell us, "take a look inside!" That is precisely what meditation is: a conscious, controlled look inside. When anxiety is so deep-rooted, after all, it is not to be dispelled. It has something to teach us. Once, in the middle of an impassioned sermon, Augustine stopped, looked at his parishioners a few moments, and said musingly:

"You are thinking that I am saying what I always say; and you go on doing what you always do." Then a fiery sobriety came into his voice: "Change, change, I beseech you! The end of life is always unpredictable. Each man walks with a chance of falling." In order to effect real changes in our life, changes that can leave us vastly better able to deal with the exigencies of human existence, it is essential to learn to control in some measure this unpredictable thinking process of ours.

The first way in which meditating regularly can be of immediate help is in teaching us to increase our powers of concentration. In every possible arena of life, learning to improve concentration is as important as striving to lessen likes and dislikes, which I have already discussed at length. By now I need only a couple of minutes' observation to gauge a person's powers of concentration and to guess with fair accuracy at the problems he or she may be having in daily living. Poor concentration brings problems everywhere.

Most of us have much better concentration than we imagine. When you are doing something you enjoy immensely, don't you find you can give it your attention easily? That is the marvel of concentration, and joy flows from it naturally. All of us possess this capacity in some measure. To deepen it and bring it under our beck and call, we need to work on extending it to illumine activities and people which at present we do not particularly enjoy. This too, you can see, comes down to overcoming likes and dislikes, which are a constant source of trouble in daily life.

The gains will be notable on many fronts. For one, thoughts from the past cannot break in on the person who has developed his concentration. He has built a kind of citadel around his mind, a great fortress in the tradition of the most memorable ever to be constructed on medieval European mountaintops. Images and impressions from the past, fears and dreams of the future, cannot enter that fortress unbidden. Attention is a drawbridge that he can lower whenever he chooses.

On the other hand, those of us who have not developed our powers of concentration in this way are as vulnerable as cities with low walls. Any anxiety, any fear, any petty desire can jump over the walls and disrupt the mind whenever it likes. This is one reason I find it so easy to sympathize with the plight of our young people today: they have precious little opportunity to develop their concentration. Their attention span seems to be broken up into smaller and smaller fragments of time: in school, in their recreation, and particularly by the media. It frightens me to see some of the difficulties they are headed for in life.

To bring all this down to a mundane level, I could easily write a book on the spiritual side of shopping. Here you are, wanting to pick up a new umbrella, and you step into a department store. There are a lot of things to see in such a store, all cunningly arranged so that in order to get at anything, you have to look at everything else first. An hour or two later you emerge with bagfuls of articles, none of which you needed when you went in. I have seen this happen hundreds of times. In such cases, the mind is not content with waiting for distractions to jump over its walls and get in; it is so eager to be distracted that it jumps over its own walls and runs about the store like a willful child.

In shopping, I would say, make up your mind in advance exactly what you want to buy; then go in, pick up what is on your list without looking left or right, and rush straight for the exit, preferably stopping at the cashier's on your way. Only upon reaching the safety of the sidewalk should you pause to catch your breath. These days this is largely a question of self-defense. Surviving a shopping trip calls for concentration and detachment, a valuable commodity which most retailers assume their customers lack completely.

Another benefit, less prosaic, is this: when you have trained your mind to concentrate, it cannot get trapped in an old memory. To get trapped, the mind has to leave the freeway of attention at an off-ramp. Usually what happens is that instead of heading directly for San Francisco, say, you look around suddenly, see the Bay directly in front, and realize with a jolt that you have taken the wrong exit and are heading for the Richmond Bridge. "Well, I've come this far," you sigh. "I might as well just go to Berkeley instead." This is the way most of us go through a normal day, never quite sure where we are going to end up. Then, at the end of each distracting thought, we are faced with the problem of how to get back on the road where we last turned off. If we can learn to keep our attention in one lane most of the time, which is what sustained concentration amounts to, we will actually find it difficult to get trapped in memories of any kind. We will be amazed at how much anxiety, much of which is triggered by ancient memories, will then disappear from our life.

The applications of improved concentration go much deeper than we may think. Even in the most intimate of personal relationships, most of us still live inside our own private mental worlds. The walls between us and the realms of the past are so low that our attention is often occupied in the past instead of the present, leaving us very little attention to give to those we want to love. Despite our best intentions to draw closer, all kinds of distracting thoughts – likes and dislikes, attachments and aversions, private moods, dreams and desires – come in anytime they like, keeping other people at a distance. We yearn for closeness and find, more often, disappointment.

Here Augustine echoes the experiences that almost all of us go through, starting often in our adolescence. "What I needed most was to love and to be loved. I rushed headlong into love, eager to be caught. Happily I wrapped those painful bonds around me; and sure enough, I would be lashed with the red-hot pokers of jealousy, by suspicions and fear, by bursts of

anger and quarrels." The journey into deeper consciousness is one we must take up if ever we are to find
the love, the closeness, and the fulfillment we all so
earnestly desire.

[3]

*. . . so that we should hear not his word through
the tongues of men, nor the voice of angels, nor the
clouds' thunder, nor any symbol, but the very Self
which in these things we love, and strain beyond
ourselves to attain a flash of that eternal wisdom
which abides above all things. . . .*

In talking about deeper levels of consciousness, I realize I am asking for a leap of the imagination.
Let me try to make these levels more real by giving
you a concrete metaphor.

Imagine swimming around in a very deep lake: the
lake of the mind. We know how to swim effortlessly
on the surface; modern life is quite good at teaching us
all kinds of ingenious strokes for this. It supplies us
with Styrofoam lounge chairs to keep us floating pleasurably on the surface of life forever. Yet the sensitive
person, whatever his or her station, cannot help
becoming aware over time how much distress is
involved in the struggle merely to stay afloat. For
some reason, peace of mind simply doesn't seem
attainable; the mind seems to be capable of stirring up
a never-ending succession of waves.

Life on the shimmering surface of consciousness,

we are someday forced to admit, isn't everything it's supposed to be. We come to the uncomfortable realization that there is simply no guarantee of security anywhere in life on the surface, no thing or situation to hold on to. At some point, sooner or later, every sensitive person reaches a certain level of frustration where he or she is ready to dive, if only to find out what lies below.

Yet this doesn't mean that doubts don't remain. Turning inwards can be a frightening prospect. Most people feel nervous when they don't have anything to look at; their attention is used to homesteading in their eyes. They have to have some noise to listen to, or they become uneasy; their ears cannot deal with the void. That is human conditioning. Sooner or later, most of us encounter the haunting fear that if we turn our senses inwards, which is what diving into the murky waters of consciousness means, we may lose everything enjoyable in life. This fear is one of the most formidable obstacles between us and the capacity to dive deeper.

Most of us accept this barrier. "Oh, that's how my desires are," we say. "They flow in every direction, and there's nothing I can do about it." I say, "You can do a great deal about it." We can learn to deepen some desire-channels and fill up others. When our desire flows compulsively toward overeating, for example, that is a simple matter of never having tried hard enough to curtail the flow of desire when it was smaller. Every kind of addiction begins like this. Then, once the channel has been cut, attention flows into it without even asking our permission; that is what conditioning means. It is for this reason that I speak so often about the need to train our senses: vigilance keeps habits and addictions from taking undue advantage of us, from turning us into victims. Yet even if we have allowed ourselves to be victimized, any conditioned habit can be changed through the practice of meditation; even the strongest addiction can be undone.

The practical element in training the senses is willpower. I used to have many friends who counted themselves beatniks, and their frankness could be quite disarming; when I talked about the importance of willpower, they would sigh and say, "We don't have any!" Even if you find yourself in this embarrassing situation, you can build up a strong will with two simple exercises. One is to train your senses vigilantly; the other, which I will take up in a minute, is to work on letting go of selfish attachments. Both can be painful, but both are extremely rewarding as well.

Meditation is the king of interior engineering projects. Through it we can divert the flow of our attention from channels of desire we do not approve and direct it into new channels of thinking, feeling, and responding. "If a man will work an inward work," Meister Eckhart says beautifully of this kind of engineering, "he must pour all his powers into himself as into a corner of the soul, and must hide himself from all images and forms. Then he can work." That describes meditation very well. What it can do is truly amazing, as you can discover for yourself. I have seen long-standing addictions simply fall away from people who are meditating sincerely. Meditation cut a new channel for the vital energy which flowed toward that particular desire; as that energy began to flow elsewhere, the addiction lost its power to command attention and withered away, much like a plant that ceases to receive water. Instead of watering a compulsive habit like overeating, vital energy began to flow toward goals that are much more deeply fulfilling.

When you can sink to deeper and deeper levels of consciousness in meditation, you will find that attention flows naturally back to its source like creeks of vital energy – from the eyes, from the ears, from all the senses. On the surface, if it seems to you that you don't have much energy or willpower, the reason may be that a good deal of energy is flowing into these sense-creeks without your even being aware of it. In meditation, instead of flowing outward, this vitality begins to be consolidated as a huge reservoir of energy within.

ɤ

The second great obstacle to diving into deeper consciousness is the fear of giving up strong personal attachments. For most of us, our strongest attachments are to people. But I am not saying we should give up close, loving relationships. The precious secret we can learn here is that when we give up our selfish attachments to people, we can draw closer to them than ever before.

Most of us assume that by wrapping our attachments tighter and tighter around us, like a life jacket, we can manage to stay afloat in the storms of life. This belief is one of the basic currents in our conditioning, dating perhaps from a very early age of evolution when survival was the day-to-day challenge of existence. But fierce personal attachment has long since outlived its place in the human scheme of things. Augustine describes our predicament vividly:

> I was held back by mere trifles, the most paltry inanities, all my old attachments. They plucked at my garments of flesh and whispered: "Are you going to dismiss us? From this moment we shall never be with you again, for ever and ever. From this moment you will never again be allowed to do this thing, or that, for evermore"— things so sordid that I beg you in your mercy to keep the soul of your servant free from them.

In reality, selfish attachments only keep us from seeing beneath the separate surface of life, where constant change and turmoil are the law. Instead of a life jacket, they turn out to be a straitjacket.

Personal entanglements are like the lotus plants with rose and white petals that used to flourish in the ponds around the village where I grew up. After a strenuous game of soccer under the hot tropical sun, we boys loved to go swimming in those ponds, and one of the games we liked best was a kind of underwater tag. If you know about lotuses, you know that hundreds of tentacle-like vines rise up through the water from the mud deep below to support the delicate flowers you see floating so calmly on the surface. Just when you are trying to dive quickly to avoid being tagged by your pursuer, those vines can wrap themselves around you. The more you flail and try to pry yourself loose, the more you get entangled. Many times I have seen a friend have to be rescued from their clutches before he ran out of breath and drowned in their embrace.

Where I see passionate entanglements played up mercilessly today is in the exploitation of "sex appeal." Everybody, for every apparent purpose from art to advertising, seems to be trying to get in on the act. To take one ridiculous instance, why I should be lured to buy a particular model of car because it has sex appeal has always been a mystery to me. There is no earthly connection. This unceasing emphasis on the physical element of life is doing untold damage to relations between man and woman. In any relationship based on physical attraction, heartbreak has to follow. In a play I saw recently one character observes trenchantly that the average lifetime of such a relationship is ten days!

Each of us has been through relationships like this. The question is not so much whether physical attraction is an appropriate basis for a relationship; I would say it is no basis whatsoever. Physical attraction is never constant. It sets in motion a cycle of expectation and disillusionment that can go on and on and on. Often we have to learn to live with a high level of anxiety in such relationships, which over time destroys our emotional security, disturbs our peace of mind, and can even wreck our health. Some relationships never recover from the effects.

In something so basic, so strongly conditioned, as physical attraction, any amount of advice has practical limitations. We may have to go through such a relationship more than once to see for ourselves how most of the rewards we fantasize about go to pieces. The person who lives in a world of fantasy will often blame the other for letting him down. Perhaps, for example, Juliet expects Romeo to come to her balcony every morning and launch into "It is the east, and you are the sun . . ." Three days after the honeymoon, she feels crushed when she is greeted at breakfast with nothing more romantic than "Where's the coffee?" Many torrid relationships sputter because of just such inflated expectations, which demand of life something that it simply cannot give.

Yet I am not trying to imply that close relationships are impossible. Through experience, most of us come to realize that in love nothing comes as easily as we expected. Everything beautiful has to be worked for. We need to begin by accepting each other as we are, but we also need to help each other to grow. Both partners should support each other tenderly while working to overcome their drawbacks, trying always to put each other first so that they enlarge the area where the circles of their lives overlap. Finally the great day will come when those circles are not two but one. Then every day will be full of joy.

The desire to draw closer to others is our inherent wealth in life; to try to deny it is dangerous in the extreme. Instead of being driven by it or trying to suppress it, we can learn to harness this tremendous drive so that its enormous power and wealth of feeling flow into our daily life. Then our love will reach out to everybody, and all who come within our orbit will feel its healing effects. This is capitalizing on the propensity that every one of us has to get attached, instead of letting it lead us around by the nose.

The surest way to do this is easy to understand. All of us have a deep desire to love and to be loved; we can learn to expand that desire to wanting everybody around us to be loved. Instead of considering only our own needs, we can begin by thinking more about the needs of our immediate family. Wherever we go, wherever we are, we can remind ourselves to remember the needs of those around us and ask if we are helping to meet those needs. The result will be a tremendous consolidation of vitality; for there will be that much less time and attention for worry, anxiety, diffidence, or depression.

When we are kind and helpful to people around us – when we are tender to our neighbors' children, for instance, just as if they were our own – we are really harnessing this great drive for affection. Ultimately it can reach the size of a well-managed river, bringing love to everybody. That is the power of attachment, and that is the wider purpose for which it was certainly created. Everybody has this power in abundance, and everybody has trouble harnessing it too. Don't despair, therefore, if it takes a lot of work to remove the selfish element from your relationships. The more people you can love, the freer you will be in every situation, and the less you will be troubled by the urge to get emotionally entangled with one or two. Even your most intimate relationships will flourish as a result.

Here again meditation comes in. The words of the inspirational passage can open an arrow's entry into deeper consciousness, especially in times of tribulation. Through that tiny opening you can peer straight down into the recesses of the mind, thousands of fathoms deep, where our desires are unified, everybody's best interests are the same, and the qualities of compassion and forgiveness reign. If you can keep your attention focused on that shaft of light, help can come to you from the very depths of consciousness, from your own deepest resources of divinity. Augustine describes such an experience:

> That was all, just not to desire what I wanted and to want what you wished. But where was my free will in that grueling time? From what deep recess was it called up at that turning point, in which I bent my neck to your light yoke?

The darker side of selfish attachments is a grueling lesson to learn. Gradually, however, with experience, our faith grows that deep within us the Lord is willing and able to take responsibility for our ultimate welfare. Slowly we can surrender our personal will to his immeasurably more profound purpose. Bit by bit, we can work ourselves loose from the grip of compulsive emotional entanglements in the faith that our capacity to love and be loved will thereby be magnified a millionfold.

⊸

Just as every country has its own geographic and cultural milieu, every region of the mind, every level of consciousness, has certain salient characteristics. Traveling to these inner continents is very much like visiting foreign lands. As we move into these subconscious realms, one of the first startling landmarks comes when the senses suddenly take their bags and say, "This is where we get off." They grab their guitars and tennis racquets, pick up their bulging suitcases, and wave: "See you when you get back!" From that point on, we will find that our concentration improves dramatically.

When I first descended into these fascinating depths in the early days of my meditation, I observed that as long as I did not attempt to follow any association of thoughts, my concentration was generally very good. But as soon as I followed even a legitimate line of thinking, such as reasoning about the meaning of the words, my mind would slip surreptitiously off the freeway of concentration and onto a detour. For someone whose concentration had always been an asset, this was a revealing surprise. Since then I have come to the sad conclusion that half the trouble the mind gets us into is the result not so much of thinking but of thinking about thinking. There is literally no end to it. To avoid this kind of exhausting mental meandering, we need to learn how to dive to a level of consciousness so deep that thoughts themselves are suspended, where the thinking process is stilled.

If we work at spiritual disciplines diligently, there comes a time when we find ourselves standing in a land where thought has no visa, not even as a tourist. The customs officer on the dock points his finger ceremoniously and says, "Sorry, but you thoughts won't be needed here." On their way back up the gangway to the ship, thoughts meet words coming down with all their baggage. "We were sent back," they say. "How can you guys expect to be allowed in?" It is this land, where the mind is utterly still, that Augustine is trying to give us a glimpse of in this passage I have called "Entering into Joy."

In the beginning, it is a rather disorienting place. We are used to navigating with the mind and senses; when they are temporarily left behind, we need time to get our bearings and learn to walk. Augustine describes this as "a lamentable darkness in which my latent possibilities are hidden from myself, so that my mind, questioning itself upon its own powers, feels that it cannot rightly trust its own report." This kind of experience marks the beginning of true detachment from the mind.

I can illustrate with a more familiar situation. When I go into a movie theater for a bargain matinee, for a few moments I can't see a thing. My eyes, used to the dazzling California sunlight outside, are temporarily rendered useless, and I have no idea of where to find a seat. This is somewhat the way it feels to plunge below the level of discursive thought in meditation: you don't see anything that looks like life as we know it, and you feel blind and confused. You are entering the unconscious, trying to become conscious, and everything is unfamiliar.

In this sense, teachers like Augustine function somewhat like movie ushers who come up to us in the darkness and say, "Do you see that corner there? Fourth row to the left; there's a seat right by the aisle." We stand still for a few minutes, and soon we can make out a few heads directly in front. Finally we can see the seats and reach them without stumbling. The same thing happens in meditation; it is simply a matter of training our inward eyes.

Don't children attending their first swimming lessons have a healthy fear of putting their faces under water? They are afraid they are going to drown. This is the feeling we can get when we begin to break loose from some of our long-cherished emotional attachments. When I was first meditating, I had the same fears all of you must have. All kinds of struggles were going on inside me, and it took time and effort to overcome them. But once the waters closed over my head and I began to get my bearings in these new realms, I knew this was what I had been looking for and longing for, and all my energy went into diving deeper.

Experience has taught me that when we put our heads under and dive deep, leaving selfish attachments on the surface, we find a joy that is a million times what any surface sensation can give, and a love that at its fullest expression embraces all of life. Every mystic gives us this same assurance: you feel like a fish swimming in the sea of light, of love, of joy that is the Lord. When you face the fear of losing these sensory satisfactions, try to remember that what is waiting for you far below the surface is infinite joy, infinite love, infinite life.

Remember this too when you find yourself getting wrapped up in the events of the day. Whatever you are enmeshed in personally during the day, part of your attention in meditation will be on that. It will act like an inflatable inner tube around your middle, preventing you from diving below the surface. No attachment is worth the price you will be paying: you can take my word for it, and the word of the world's great saints and mystics too. I assure you that in letting go of personal attachments, you are not losing anything except your frustration; you are not letting go of anything but your old insecurities.

While you are meditating, don't be thinking about

anything whatsoever. Concentrate completely on the inspirational passage. When your concentration is complete, you will not have any impediments on the surface; you will sink naturally deeper and deeper. Then no distraction will have any compelling force behind it. It will not bother you; it will not oppress you; it will have no power to deflect you from your purpose. Eventually you will reach a level where self-ish desires won't even come to you any more; only the desires you desire will come to you. In no way do you lose your capacity to desire. What you gain is freedom.

❧

Augustine's expression "strain beyond our-selves," in my practical interpretation, implies that we must push the frontiers of our awareness deeper and deeper.

When we are able to travel into the deepest recesses of consciousness, we discover that we need no longer be hemmed in by circumstances or personality traits or even by the conditioning of our past. In a sense, each of us is a child of our past. Our childhood upbringing, our neighborhood environment and the cultural milieu in which we grew up, the schools we attended, the movies we have seen, the books and magazines and newspapers we have read, the com-pany we have kept – all these have molded our present character and conduct. Yet when we travel deeper into consciousness and approach the forbidding threshold between the conscious and unconscious realms, we realize that the emotional residue from all these factors can gradually be erased from our lives. As this is done, we uncover latent positive qualities: strong, selfless, loving characteristics that have been there all along.

If you do not know how to travel into these depths, if you make no effort to practice meditation and to incorporate spiritual disciplines into your life, you do not have a tool for remaking yourself. In that case, I would agree with modern psychologists who insist that we are bound by past conditioning to act in certain ways. Yet spiritual disciplines, particularly meditation, hold out hope for millions of people whose past conditioning oppresses them – people who may come from unhappy homes, for instance, who may not have received the love that is their divine birthright. Whatever our past, none of us need resign ourselves to being lifelong victims of circumstances beyond our control. I can readily understand a young person, for example, feeling resentful at having been neglected or abused, and we need to work hard to change the attitude of neglect with which many children today seem to be raised. Yet I wish from the bottom of my heart that these disciplines could be presented persuasively to our young people, for they offer a real alternative to the bitterness and the destructive habits to which this sense of being a victim often gives rise. Here is a method, I would like to tell them, with which they can take the energy they spend in expressing their frustration and put that energy to use undoing the damage that has been done.

As we travel deeper into consciousness, we find we can push many of our limitations further and further. We can give ourselves room to move about in, room to expand. We need no longer live with the vague feeling of being crimped, cabined, and confined.

The vast majority of people, to take just one illustration, keep very little distance between the way their minds work and the way they themselves act. This is a very restrictive habit. When I was on the faculty of my university in India, we used to see Hollywood films in which a ventriloquist named Edgar Bergen appeared with a puppet called Charlie McCarthy. Mr. Bergen would place Charlie on his knee and ask solicitously, "What do you want?" Charlie would say, "A good, stiff drink." Most of our urges, I think, have learned over time to be ventriloquists much more accomplished than Edgar Bergen. We come home from the office tired and tense and our body announces, "I need a good, stiff drink!" We don't stop to realize that this is merely the mind doing its routine. Mental urges, in fact, are past masters of this devious art. Like everyone else, I too used to be under the mistaken impression that my mind and I were one and the same; when my mind urged me in a polished, well-inflected voice to do something, I actually used to go out and act on it. Today, after years of training myself not to identify with the mind, I sometimes get amused remembering this. "Here you are, a reasonably bright fellow, able to lecture at length on English literature and the mechanics of language. How could you possibly have fallen for this ego ventriloquist?" As my meditation deepened, I learned how to keep more distance from these promptings. If my mind began to complain about someone, I wouldn't allow it to influence my words or actions. I was free to choose my own responses: kind words, patience, and respect.

Most emotional problems, I have since found, can be solved with this one master strategy: put some distance between yourself and your mind. It calls for a lot of daring, I admit. But in this country you have been brought up in a society that sets a premium on daring; why not put it to the best use possible? You will not only be getting over your resentment of a particular person; you will also be getting over the tendency to waste time and precious energy resenting. When you gain this kind of detachment from the mind, life loses most of its sorrow and frustration. You can listen to opposition with complete respect, without ever compromising your own views.

I have attended a great many committee meetings in my lifetime; on a large university campus like the one where I taught, difficult issues have to be discussed frequently, and on each issue different people can hold very different points of view. But the biggest obstacle to easy communication and the resolution of important issues, I found, was not differences of opinion; it was lack of respect for other people. In my experience, the person who doesn't respect other opinions is the person who is inclined to believe that he knows everything and nobody else knows anything. Others are not likely to support him in this position, so he generally finds himself in a distinct minority. Working to respect the opinions of others is an effective way to encourage detachment in ourselves, and it brings a good deal of peace of mind as well.

Whatever your mind is saying, try to listen to it with detachment. If it insists, "This is what you want," you should furrow your brow and counter, "How do you know?" This can save you so many health problems, so many emotional crises, so much frustration and unnecessary heartbreak. It will be a struggle, but you have my assurance, and the assurance of great mystics like Augustine, that it is a struggle you cannot lose. This doesn't mean that your life will be free from quarrels or that you will never again find yourself in tense situations; these are the texture of life. But if you can gain this kind of detachment, the agitation in your mind will be kept to a minimum, the wear and tear on your nervous system will be much less, and you will be free from that sinking feeling that you haven't done very well in your relationships.

↪

More than on any other quality, I believe, winning lasting freedom depends on the cultivation of plain, simple patience. It is impatient people who are liable to get suddenly anxious or discourteous. Patience acts as a shield against inner turmoil of every kind. It keeps the mind steady even in the midst of turbulent situations, which is one of the secrets of maintaining robust health. Patience is true preventive medicine on every front.

We can develop patience quite simply by pushing in the direction of patience: greater and greater patience, more and more often, in the everyday vicissitudes of life's normal situations and relationships. When you try to be more patient with someone difficult, you are extending the limits of your patience. When you refuse to act on anger or frustration even when provoked, you are deepening your own security. Every day you can go to bed knowing that your limitations have been pushed back a little more, that a little more negative conditioning has been erased.

Gradually we are working our way toward a critical realization: we can actually go beyond the mechanisms of the mind entirely. Thinking, however useful it may be at times, is not the highest human faculty; it is only a stage in development. If, for example, in the throes of evolution we had stopped with instinct, saying, "This is the highest possible mode of knowing," our human future would have been stunted: I would not be seated here writing these words, nor would you be reading them. Like instinct, reason is only a way station. When friends and I go to Berkeley to see a play, we sometimes stop halfway along to stretch our legs. But we don't get so involved in stretching legs that we forget to go on to the theater. Thought, in the same vein, is a useful but temporary stopping station; it should not be considered a permanent solution to the problems of living. Just as we were able to rise above instinct and to develop reason, if not always common sense, the mystics say we should learn to pass at will beyond discursive thinking and enter into a higher mode of knowing.

The way people sometimes praise the achievements of this century, you would think they have concluded that this is journey's end; we have made it. I think we are entitled to question whether we have even arrived at an age of reason, much less of higher awareness. When the age of reason is established, the nations of the world will not spend a million dollars a minute on destroying each other. Nobody will feel compelled to advertise harmful habits in prestigious magazines. We will make only things that are useful and beneficial, and we will do everything in our power to see to it that our children grow up healthy, secure, and loved. Until then, I think we can look on the age of reason as a stage toward which humanity in the twentieth century is at best slowly moving.

In this passage from the *Confessions,* as a pioneer in the evolution of consciousness, Augustine is implying that each of us is still evolving, and that we shouldn't get bogged down too long in the thinking process. This is a revolutionary concept. Isn't it Einstein who says that the highest mode of knowing is the mystical? Great geniuses in many fields have had some access to the mystical mode of knowing; that is why they were able to leap over accepted conceptual thinking and make tremendous discoveries. With the practice of spiritual disciplines, such moments of insight can become permanent states of awareness. The source of abiding wisdom is within each one of us, waiting to be discovered so it can inform our lives. But we need to keep evolving toward that wisdom, which requires tireless effort.

With spiritual wisdom comes a tremendous realization: there is no joy in anything that is only for oneself. Private satisfaction ends almost as soon as it begins. This is what we discover when we dive into the deepest realms of consciousness, where joy resides. In virtually every field of human activity we can see people chasing some temporary pleasure, admitting that it is not what they expected, and then going on to chase the same will-o'-the-wisp in some other form while life ebbs away. Clinging like this to what is limited and temporary, the mystics tell us, is the cause of all our sorrow.

We can extend this diagnosis to the level of nations. Any country that tries to find security without contributing to the security of the whole globe is bound to find itself riddled with insecurity, one characteristic sign of which is the insane arms race we see so many nations trapped in today. All we have to do is read the newspaper to see this law being borne out in every area of the globe.

Wherever we have a tendency to quarrel, to turn

resentful, to demand equal opportunities for pleasure and profit, the door to the deeper realms of joy is shut. I would even go to the extent of saying that the door to lasting health is shut. We need to remind ourselves of this every day, and one simple way to do so is by repeating the Holy Name. We can use the innumerable bits and pieces of time during the course of even a very busy day to keep fresh this remembrance that the joy of all is my supreme joy; private pleasure at the expense of others is my supreme pain. Living in a civilization where this concept is seldom put forward, we need to keep this reminder before us as often as possible.

Teresa of Avila has given us a simple secret for putting this recipe for joy into action: *Amor saca amor,* "Love begets love." When you live or work with a person who is always loving, even when opposing you, slowly you start changing for the better. To become like this, you have to learn to step aside and get yourself out of the way. That is the secret of perfect relations, of perfect love. *God is love* is an aphorism that expresses the highest of spiritual truths. If we want this divine state to be ours right here on earth, during this very lifetime, we have to work assiduously to remove from our consciousness everything that is private, separate, and self-centered.

Without a sincere effort to get ourselves out of the way, we can't understand the needs of the people closest to us; we can't even see them clearly. Often, for example, even good parents have goals for their children that their children do not share, goals that may not be in anyone's best interests. Here I have to pay a tribute to my grandmother, who never heard of educational psychology – or, for that matter, of any other kind of psychology. The summer I finished high school, living as I did as part of a rather large clan, I was barraged by opinions – from uncles, aunts, brothers-in-law, sisters-in-law, everybody – about what I ought to do with the rest of my life. The only person who didn't try to put pressure on me was my grandmother; she kept her counsel to herself. But at the very end of summer vacation, as I was taking leave of my family to go off to college, she called me over to her and whispered in my ear, "Follow your own star."

To love completely, it is not enough if we care deeply; we must also be detached from ourselves. To know what is best for someone, I have to be able to step aside from my own prejudices and preconceptions, slip into that person's shoes, and become one with him temporarily, looking at life through his eyes rather than my own. When I step back again, I will have seen his needs from the inside; only then can I see clearly how to serve those needs with detachment and compassion. This does not mean conniving at weaknesses he may have; it means that through constant love and support, I can help him to correct those weaknesses. This is the path, the strait and narrow path, that leads to real love.

✧

Why do we find it so desperately difficult to get ourselves out of the way?

Augustine began by asking us, "Imagine if all the tumult of the body were to quiet down, along with all our busy thoughts. . . ." Every private urge we have can be expressed in terms of noise. A craving for french fries whispers to us urgently in, say, five decibels; a thirst for a cocktail, in ten decibels. Resentment's rasping voice reaches some fifty decibels, and the demands of the ego himself drown out all other sounds. We have innumerable urges like this speaking up continually, and the more often we give in, the louder they cry. It adds up to a tremendous lot of noise.

In fact, I think the mind must be more noisy than the runway of an international airport. Cumbersome urges are landing on our sense-ways at all hours, screeching to a halt at our mind-gates. Desires are taking off continually on flights of hoped-for satisfaction. Huge jet cravings zoom through the skies, breaking the sound barrier. I remember a British advertisement for the Concorde flight from New York to London: "You'll reach your destination before you take off." That kind of promise might have been penned by the ego.

In talking about stillness of mind, Augustine is trying to let us in on one of the most closely guarded secrets of human existence: if all these thought-planes, incoming and outgoing, could be grounded even for a few moments, we would hear the marvelous music that is going on inside always.

One summer many years ago a friend took me on an excursion to Yosemite National Forest, which must be one of the most spectacular in this country. But by the time evening fell there were so many radios going, in campers and out around campfires, that I wondered to myself, "Why did we have to come so far just to hear the same old noise?" Only when the radio-listeners fell asleep and the radios were silenced did I hear the music of a tiny stream, babbling along only a few yards from our campsite. It had been running on all that time, but in the midst of the hubbub I hadn't even known it existed. Its song was so glorious at that moment that it seemed to me almost as if the stream were singing, "I may come and I may go, but the Lord goes on forever."

On the strength of my own experience in meditation, I can assure you that a divine stream of wisdom is flowing in your heart always. When the mind is quietened, you can hear it running blissfully through the very depths of consciousness. As you listen to this song carefully, with complete concentration, from somewhere comes a soft whisper of unshakable certitude: "You are not a finite creature, a separate fragment that one day will pass away. You are infinite and whole, and you will never die." I don't think any greater assurance can come to a human being.

Augustine describes marvelously his own step-by-step descent to this seabed of consciousness:

Thus by stages I passed from bodies to the soul which uses the body for its perceiving, and from this to the soul's inner power, to which the body's senses present external things; and from there I passed on to the reasoning power, to which is referred for judgment what is received from the body's senses. This too realized that it was mutable in me, and rose to its own understanding. It withdrew my thought from its habitual way, abstracting from the confused crowds of phantasms that it might find what light suffused it, when with utter certainty it cried aloud that the immutable was to be preferred to the mutable, and how it had come to know the immutable itself. Thus in the thrust of a trembling glance my mind arrived at That Which is. Then indeed I saw clearly thy "invisible things which are understood by the things that are made."

At this level of awareness the external world is far, far away. You have traveled to an enormous depth, and you know with certainty that this world to which you have descended is much more real, and what you understand at this depth much more valid, than what you see on the surface. On the surface, for example, we feel that it is natural for people to quarrel, for nations to go to war. "It's only human," we say. Now we realize in the depths of our soul that quarreling and fighting are not natural at all. What is natural is loving everybody, seeing everybody as one.

After this experience, even if another person is

offensive or uncooperative, we will easily be able to hear the music of the Lord above the discordant notes of the ego. This is one very practical way in which this supreme discovery can help us in our day-to-day work and relationships. Awareness of this unnamed voice gives you faith in people, and that faith enables them to see themselves in a much more positive light: as a spark of divinity, with undiscovered resources of love, wisdom, and security.

The joy that accompanies this realization of unity is so tremendous that if it were to come upon us suddenly, the nervous system would not be able to bear it. Fortunately it takes many, many years for ordinary people like you and me to reach this state. Even some of the greatest of mystical figures have been physically immobilized for days and nights by the impact of this joy. John of the Cross gives us a taste of its intensity by likening it to the rapture of a tryst between two lovers. Here are the concluding stanzas of his poem "In a Dark Night," which distills in lyric language the course of meditation:

> In a dark night,
> Inflamed with love's impatient longing
> – Oh what good fortune! –
> I went out unseen,
> My house being now all silent;
> . . .
> I lost and forgot myself,
> My face resting on my Beloved;

> All things ceased, and I surrendered myself,
> Leaving my cares
> Forgotten among the lilies.

It takes many years for us to build up our nervous system, our emotional endurance, so that we can receive the impact of these waves of pure joy and still carry on our daily responsibilities. For the world can ill afford to be deprived of the precious contribution such a person can make. This is the underlying purpose of the various disciplines I have been describing to you: first to make this divine experience possible, and then to allow us to function beautifully in everyday life once this experience has been attained. This stream of joy is flowing forever in your consciousness and mine. If anybody asks, "Then why don't I hear it myself?" Augustine gives the answer: the noise of our physical urges and the agitation of the mind is drowning it out. "Be still," the Bible says, "and know that I am God." Augustine, when he finally discovered this joy lying hidden within him, exclaimed,

> Late have I loved thee, O Beauty so ancient and so new; late have I loved thee! For behold, thou wert within me and I outside; and I sought thee outside and in my unloveliness fell upon these lovely things that thou hast made. Thou wert with me and I was not with thee. I was kept from thee by those things, yet had they not been in thee, they would not have been at all. Thou didst call and cry to me and break open my deafness; and thou didst send forth thy

beams and shine upon me and chase away my
blindness; thou didst breathe fragrance upon me,
and I drew in my breath and do now pant for thee.
I tasted thee, and now hunger and thirst for thee;
thou didst touch me, and now I burn for thy peace.

Augustine is expressing one of the most joyful real-
izations we can make on the spiritual journey: it is the
Lord alone who all along has been subtly drawing our
attention ever deeper within. Sometimes he uses the
magnetic pull of love, which is naturally the way we
prefer to be drawn toward perfection. But sometimes,
when we do not respond, he must resort to the cor-
rective pressure of pain and sorrow.

In the end, however we are led, none of us will be
able to resist the overwhelming power of the Lord: his
wisdom, his love, his joy, his peace. But through meditation and its allied disciplines, by "straining beyond
ourselves," each of us can make this epic journey
infinitely shorter and sweeter.

[4]

*And imagine if that moment were to go on and on,
leaving behind all other sights and sounds but this
one vision which ravishes and absorbs and fixes the
beholder in joy, so that the rest of eternal life were
like that moment of illumination which leaves us
breathless. . . .*

Now we are going to hear, from the mouths
of mystics who have experienced it for themselves,
just what effects the realization of God wrought on
their daily lives. Buried in their accounts somewhere
must be hidden the key to the mysterious transformation of their lives – the key that enabled them, according to their own times and temperaments, to bring
the joy, the wisdom, and the absorbing peace of that
eternal inner realm to bear in this fragmented world.
These precious accounts must hold many clues that
we, in our round of mundane activities, can apply in
our efforts to make our lives a gift to those around us.

Augustine emphasizes that the cacophony of physical and mental urges has to be quieted before we can
hear the eternal stream within us. Saint Teresa of
Avila, who wrote openly and in detail of her interior
experiences, calls this the Prayer of Quiet. "This true
Prayer of Quiet has in it an element of the supernatural." Those who experience it, she means, are no
longer ordinary. In some sense they have become
extraordinary, in that they have connected their

body, their mind, and – most important – their will to the divine will within. She goes on:

> We cannot, in spite of all our efforts, procure it for ourselves. It is a sort of peace in which the soul establishes herself, or rather in which God establishes the soul. All her powers are at rest. She understands, but otherwise than by the senses, that she is already near her God, and if she draws a little nearer, she will become by union one with him. One feels a great bodily comfort, a great satisfaction of the soul. Such is the happiness of the soul in seeing herself close to the spring, that even without drinking of the waters she finds herself refreshed.

Here we encounter a subtle attitude that seems to set the mystics apart. "We cannot, in spite of all our efforts, procure this for ourselves; it is a sort of peace ... in which God establishes the soul." Augustine voices the same attitude: "Far be it from me, O Lord, to think that I am happy for any or every joy that I may have. For there is a joy which is not given to the ungodly but only to those who love thee for thy own sake, whose joy is thyself." This joy is a gift – and there is no other way to come by it.

Teresa concludes her description with these ecstatic lines:

> It seems to [the soul] that she wants nothing more. Indeed, to those who are in this state it seems that at the least movement [of the mind], they will lose this sweet peace. They are in the palace close to their

King, and they see that he is beginning to give them his kingdom. It seems to them that they are no longer in this world.

They find themselves in the realm of love, they say wonderingly: the realm of reality. Their bodies continue to function in this phenomenal world of ours, but their center no longer lies in a world subject to change and decay, to sorrow and suffering. It is, as Augustine so graphically puts it, fixed in permanent joy.

&

Yet a great dilemma still presents itself: how are we to cultivate this attitude of theirs until God himself is pleased to grant us the experience they describe?

"It seems that at the least movement" of the mind, Teresa says, "they will lose this sweet peace." This is a formidable clue. When you dive into the deeper realms of consciousness you realize what a noisy factory the mind is, churning out thoughts day in and day out. Most of us are unaware how abrasive this activity is; we have never tasted the healing silence of the world within. Like those who live in the flight paths of a big international airport, we say, "What noise?" We simply don't hear. When I read about people who enjoy scenes of cruelty in movies, for instance, what I hear them saying is that nothing registers of the turmoil in the mind. They have turned their sensitivity to OFF.

Go to a wilderness area, where the sounds of civilization do not reach, and you will understand how great is the contrast between the surface level of awareness and these deeper realms. The silence seems magnified by comparison – and, by the same token, much more eloquent. I suspect this is one of the strongest reasons why city-dwellers take every opportunity to "get away from it all." They relish the chance to escape the noise around them, and to quiet a little the din inside.

Ultimately, however, there is only one place where you and I can find rest: in the depths of our consciousness. Everywhere else we wander is not our true home. I can tell you truthfully that within reason, I have tasted every legitimate satisfaction life has to offer. That is why I would have no hesitation in standing on any platform in the world and saying, "There is no comparison between the joy I find in the depths of my heart and everything I knew before."

Teresa describes in unforgettable words the consolation this experience brings:

Rapture is a great help to recognize our true home and to see that we are pilgrims in this life. It is a great thing to see what is going on in our home, and to know where we are someday going to live. For if a person has to go and settle in another country, it is a great help to him in undergoing the fatigues of his journey that he has discovered it to be a country where he may live still, in the most perfect peace.

Augustine addresses his Lord in strikingly similar terms:

 Nor in all these things that my mind traverses in search of you, do I find any sure place for my mind save in you: in whom all that is scattered in me is brought into one, so that nothing of me may depart from you. And sometimes you admit me to a state of mind that I am not ordinarily in, a kind of delight which could it ever be made permanent in me, would be hard to distinguish from the life to come.

Yet the hard fact is that this is but a flash of delight, as he says, a brief moment of wisdom and utter peace. It cannot be sustained for long. It fades. "So I returned to my old habits," Augustine says, "bearing nothing with me but a memory of delight and a desire, as if for something of which I had caught the fragrance but which I had not yet the strength to eat."

Even after you have this ineffable experience, it seems, years of arduous endeavor still lie ahead before your glimpse of the divine can be made permanent. In the depths of meditation you may experience the Prayer of Quiet for a few moments – the space of an *Ave Maria,* as Teresa puts it. But the state to be aimed at, in which that moment of joy goes "on and on," is having this supreme stillness in your heart with your eyes wide open and your senses alert, in the midst of the hurly-burly of daily existence.

Meister Eckhart has a picturesque yet comprehensive way of describing how this miracle of miracles was worked in him: "I was made all of one piece by you, my most sweet God." Wherever you cut the God-conscious person, he says, you will find him the same. Working or playing, with people or alone, awake or asleep, he will be aware of the unity underlying life. This is the real meaning of that elusive phrase "carrying out the will of God." It means, in effect, that you live in joy always.

Peace of mind, in other words, is not an end in itself. It is a means, a phase in one's spiritual growth, and there is much more growth yet to come. The Prayer of Quiet is a great bridge leading from an uncoordinated life of self-centered activity to a new, unified life of selfless action. With it we leave behind our old world, our old habits of mind, in order to go on to greater, wider worlds of loving work.

࿐

The secret to be gleaned from these accounts is delineated by Augustine himself in a marvelously practical prayer:

Thou dost command faithfulness. And when I knew, as it is said, that no one could be faithful unless God gave it, even this was a point of wisdom: to know whose gift it was. For by faithfulness we are collected and bound up into unity within ourself, whereas we had been scattered abroad in multiplicity. Too little does any man love thee, who loves some other thing together with thee; loving it not on account of thee, O thou Love, who art ever burning and never extinguished! O Charity, my God, enkindle me! Thou dost command faithfulness: grant what thou dost command and then command what thou wilt.

This last is the famous sentence which so startled the ecclesiastics of Augustine's time. What he is saying is revolutionary: that true faithfulness to the will of God can only arise out of some personal experience – in the form of a gift – of its unrivalled power, which can come only when we have reduced our self-will almost to zero.

This kind of assertion is common from mystics. It sets them apart. Yet understandably enough, it gives rise to grave misgivings among those who would like to arrive at this faith but have not had the personal experience that validates it. "Can we not have true faith," they wonder, "unless it is given to us? What then is the point of all this effort and self-sacrifice which is put before us as the way to reach God?"

My answer would be simple: every ounce of effort makes it that much easier for the experience to be given to us. Everything we do matters. Meditating matters very much; so does remembering to repeat the Holy Name. Working hard and selflessly, eating nutritious food in moderate quantities, getting enough exercise, staying calm and kind through the problems of the day: all these matter a good deal. They are, in fact, our real job in life; our other activities are secondary.

On questionnaires we are often asked who our employer is. Each of us is really Self-employed: employed by our innermost Self, the Lord. When we waste time in idle pursuits, when we quarrel, the Lord tries to remind us that we are doing all this on company time: time that belongs to everybody. Isn't your pay docked when you do personal things on company time? The same thing happens in life, though we do not usually make the connection. When we do selfish things, we lose some of our vigor, some of our peace of mind. That is the Lord, trying to alert us that we are wasting precious time.

Those most fortunate few who have had direct experience of the unity underlying seemingly separate phenomena immediately make the connection between their thoughts, their actions, and their peace of mind. When Teresa had to justify her course of action to her Church superiors, she didn't say that a careful survey of previous and analogous situations had produced such and such a recommendation, or that UPS delivered a twenty-page computer printout specifying what she was to do. She would say in complete faith, "His Majesty came himself and told me what to do." This is what becoming established in God means: the welfare of the whole speaks to you, direct and urgent. And the tone of the message is not, "The boss phoned a half hour ago; kindly call him back at your leisure." The Lord says, "Teresa, I am talking to *you*. Give me your complete attention." There is a certitude about that voice, a certitude which can baffle a person who is not used to hearing it. Augustine describes this clearly and dramatically:

> And thou didst cry to me from afar: "I am who am." And I heard thee, as one hears in the heart. And there was from that moment no ground of doubt in me: I would more easily have doubted my own life than have doubted that truth is.

What the Lord tells you is simple. To Francis of Assisi it was "Rebuild my church"; to Augustine, a line from Paul. The actual words are not particularly important; the message is clear and universal: "Live for all. Their joy is your joy." After such an experience it does not matter who tells you, "You didn't hear any such thing. This is not true!" As Pascal says, this truth carries its own validity. It is self-evident.

There is no way of describing the effect of these experiences except by referring to one's own life. I do not ascribe much importance to visions and voices; I look at how a person actually lives. If your experience of unity is genuine, you cannot possibly live for yourself alone, because that is the sum and substance of this call: "Live for all. Work for all." And if you say, "What about a vacation once in a while?" the Lord will be blunt: "I'm giving you a lifelong vacation! That ego of yours, which has always been telling you to stand up for your pleasures and fight for your rights, has been put out of his misery. Now, at long last, you can have a real vacation."

When most of your mental hullabaloo has been quietened, you respond easily and immediately to the sanctity of life. Wherever you see it violated, from a very deep level something in you springs into action. The other morning, after a brisk walk on the beach, I had returned to the car and was scraping the sand off my shoes when out of the corner of my eye I saw a cat leap off a sandbank onto a tiny bird. My response was so fast that I nearly succeeded in grabbing that bird out of the cat's mouth before it realized I was there. I didn't blame the cat; that is its nature. Yet I had to try to save that bird: that, after all, is my nature.

Once you have personal experience of the unity of life, your joy will lie in relieving distress wherever you find it. This requires detachment and enormous faith in human goodness. Only the person who has practiced spiritual disciplines regularly can face sorrow over and over with unflagging faith in the divine core of human nature. Yet when attention is unified, you can see straight into the heart of a person; whatever he does, whatever she suffers, you know that core of divinity remains intact.

Some years ago I read that physicists had designed a microscope that can resolve objects as minute as one billionth of an inch. Who can imagine such a thing? Who can even honestly believe that anything so small as an angstrom exists? Yet here are physicists stating confidently that they can observe the atomic structure of almost any solid material. When attention is unified, it has much the same penetrating capabilities. You can observe minute connections linking thoughts and events in the very depths of the unconscious.

Augustine describes for us what he saw when he looked through the microscope of unified attention: ". . . the glory of that ever-fixed eternity in which nothing passes, but the whole is present." And he asks searchingly: "Who shall hold the heart of man, that it may stand still and see how eternity, ever still standing, neither past nor future, utters the times past and to come?"

All of us have this inherent capacity to glimpse eternity; we have it in abundance. But for the most part we direct it towards very limited goals, frittering away its power on things that have scant capacity to satisfy our enormous appetite for joy, unity, and meaning. This misapplication is the root of our frustrations in life. "Why are men not happy?" Augustine asked himself. "Because they are much more concerned over things which are more powerful to make them unhappy than truth is to make them happy, in that they remember truth so slightly."

There is an enormous charge in memory; that is why so many of these mystics frame their statements in terms of time. When you remember an offensive remark that someone dear said ten years ago, you get offended all over again. Imagine how many unpleasant memories of this sort we must have, each with a certain negative charge, lying around in the lower stacks of the library of consciousness. In these archives there are no harmless reports; these memories are more like time bombs ticking away, waiting for a suitable occasion to explode.

Now imagine, if you will, a state of mind in which you have defused the pain and pleasure charges of every memory in your consciousness. This is one of the operating principles of meditation: if you can bring your mind back to the present every time it wanders away, you will eventually not have to deal with old anxieties at all. Your memories will still be there in the lower stacks, but they will have no hold over you.

I can remember the kind things people have said to me over the years; I remember some of the unkind things too. I remember events that have been good to me and those which have not been so good. But because I keep my attention focused on the present, these memories have no more charge. That is the real answer to problems of anxiety about the past, with its selfish attachments and ridiculous mistakes. It is equally the remedy for those otherwise inevitable fears for the future. When the mind becomes one-pointed, focused like a laser, its immense power is not diffused by anxiety or fear. You can use it effectively for lifting the burden of past and future, and for helping others to lift these burdens too.

This is not repression. When you repress a potent

memory, you make it stronger. You have forced it below the conscious level of awareness, but although it is out of sight there, it commands more attention than ever. What I am talking about is the skill of withdrawing attention from any moment but the present. When you can do that, the emotional charge of a memory is not suppressed and hidden; it simply evaporates. What gives memories and fears power over us is their capacity to soak up our attention; when that capacity goes, their burden falls away.

Even one glimpse of deepest awareness has enormous practical repercussions. In these moments of peace your vital organs and nervous system rest, and even though it may last only a short while, the quality of that rest is of the highest. You come back into the phenomenal world refreshed, recharged, invigorated, ready to face any challenge. This makes every day precious, every single hour precious, so that you become almost constitutionally incapable of wasting time now. In a sense you come back a new woman, a new man, with the mandate to use your newly harnessed energy in work that promotes the health, happiness, and harmony of all.

I wish I could find some way to convey the wonder of this. In meditation you can go into a vast treasurehouse inside. You have a kind of latchkey: you can go in anytime and draw out as much as you like. The manager, the Lord, sits there behind his big desk and says, "Go in and help yourself. Stuff your pockets. Only make sure you go back and use it all for others."

That is the agreement, which he has got in writing, so to say, sealed with your very life. Thus meditation works miracles: it recharges your enthusiasm and restores a robust optimism for life. It is the supreme education.

Living on the surface of life as we do, we don't suspect what a treasure trove of love and wisdom we have within. If I knew of a simple, painless way of unlocking this treasure, I would be the first to give it. But as far as I know, there is no way to enter and make use of these untold riches except by practicing meditation and integrating its allied disciplines into our daily life. There is no shortcut around the travail of this journey into consciousness, and those who have traversed it testify that it is the ultimate test of human endurance. Yet this is the very challenge that appeals to people. It banishes boredom and brings the dew of freshness to every day. There can be no failure in this effort: for as you go deeper and deeper into your consciousness, you discover that you have vast resources of which you never dreamed: resources with which to help yourself, to help your family and community, to contribute to your society, to change the very world for the better. The unending miracle of these resources is that they are there within every one of us. We have only to dive deep to discover them.

So it is this we can all aim for: not having mystical experiences, but making our life a gift to the members of our family and our society, just as it has been given as a gift to us. If spiritual experiences do come our way, they will serve to inspire us and further fuel our efforts. Here I am realistic enough to recognize that most of us have drawbacks and failings that stand between us and this loftiest of goals. That is why I appreciate it when people say, "Don't talk philosophy to me. Don't talk about sweetness and light. Tell me precisely what meditation can do to help me: one, two, three, four, five."

I respond very favorably to this businesslike approach. I reply, "I too am a man who means business. My business is the same as everybody else's business: learning to live in love and act in wisdom, at home and at work, with people we like and with people we don't like too." Money plays no part in this kind of business. Material possessions, prestige, power over others, have no role whatever. You can observe people at the highest levels of success; in the home life of the most respected politicians, the most eminent scientists, the most inspired artists, and the most effective businessmen you will find the same human problems: conflicts, anger, frustration, disappointment, depression. Their lives do have a bright side, but they make it clear that neither money nor prestige nor power can enable us to make our life a gift worth giving.

What meditation can do, gradually, is nothing less than re-educate our very habits of mind, so that we can respond to difficult times and difficult people with patience, resourcefulness, and compassion. It can teach us to respect opposition when we meet with it, evaluate it with detachment, and hold true to our convictions with kindness and persuasion if they stand the test. These are great arts in the field of living, which every one of us can learn through meditation.

For me, the selfish person is simply uneducated. The stubborn, self-centered person is ignorant of the most elementary skill in life – the skill of living in harmony with others. Just as people can be taught to read and write so well that they can someday compose poetry or dash off persuasive, cogent reports, we can teach our mind to respond the way we want it to respond. That is the long and the short of meditation. Impatient people can learn to become patient. Those with a history of crippling insecurities can learn to be secure. Those who are lethargic can make themselves energetic in their efforts to serve a worthy cause. Those who are self-centered can learn to widen their sphere of concern to include more individuals than themselves. There is no greater curriculum than these skills, no finer art, no more useful science.

For a reading list in this curriculum, we have the accounts of the mystics of every major religious tradition, whose experience of the eternal, when everything is said and done, is the same. Reading these accounts is an important step in spiritual education, for there is much to unlearn in the conditioning of the mass media. But no amount of reading can enable us to change ourselves; contrary habits of mind are much too deeply engrained. What we try to do in meditation is drive the most inspiring testimonies of these beacon spiritual figures deeper and deeper, until they actually get below our habits of mind and begin to change them.

The surface strata of consciousness are so hard, so densely packed with impressions, that we have to drill for years just to make a dent. It is really rough going! But once you break through to a deeper level, if you listen carefully, you will be able to hear the words of Saint Francis or Saint Augustine falling like jewels into the living waters of deepest awareness. One proof that this is taking place is that you may hear these words being recited in your sleep – a sure sign that they have penetrated so deep that they cannot help influencing your daily action.

But it is not enough, as I said earlier, simply to meditate on inspiring words; we have to try every day to translate them into our behavior. When Augustine speaks of making the peace of meditation "go on and on," this is what he means: we must learn to extend our awareness of unity to everyone around us through the course of every day. Augustine under-scores the necessity of this daily labor when he prays: "I hope that God, in his mercy, will make me remain steadfast on all the truths which I regard as certain."

This requires a lot of practice, I can assure you. Right after morning meditation you walk into your first classroom: the breakfast table. When your twelve-year-old tries out some highly contemporary sarcasm on you, he is administering a midterm; when your partner seems bent on provoking a full-scale verbal war over the scrambled eggs, that is a final exam. Finals are tough; you can't expect them to be a cinch. If everybody got an A, the lesson wouldn't be worth learning. But if you pass, you don't dare pat yourself on the back; bigger tests are sure to be around the corner. Whatever your domestic scene, you can look on it as a tough prep school for learning how to practice the words you meditate on every morning and evening.

One essential part of this lesson is time. I have to repeat this because in the breakneck pace of our age it is so easily forgotten. I am always surprised at how little time people spend together in many homes today. Rushing out to beat the competition to a few extra dollars seems to enjoy higher priority than does learning the basic skills of living. In the long run, by getting our values turned around, we pay an awful price. Nothing in the world is worth the expense of forgetting how to live. What use is a fortune – even if you win it, which is scarcely assured – once you have forgotten how to live?

I used to counsel people, "Why don't you get up a little earlier – even if it means going to bed a little earlier! – so you can spend a little more time with your family or friends in the morning and get the day off to a happy start?" In an atmosphere of frenzied friction, even the finest meal will turn to ashes. The person who starts the day with a peaceful, happy breakfast is likely to be a better stenographer, a better doctor, a better librarian, a better scientist, a better friend.

When you arrive at work, that too is a good time to remember the words of your meditation: "Make me an instrument of thy peace." It takes all kinds to make up an office or shop or classroom. What the miracle of meditation promises is simple: of course it takes all sorts, but you can learn to work in harmony with every sort imaginable – especially since what prevents us from working in harmony is usually no more than lack of patience.

When a person has difficulty working with others, you have only to scrutinize his behavior to hear his mind saying, "These people don't know anything! Why don't they pay attention to me?" Patience decrees that we be ready and willing to learn from anyone. An open attitude disarms everybody; that is its charm – and its magic. "Here is someone who is willing to listen," we say to ourselves. "Maybe I can pick up a few things from him too." It is as simple as that. After all, our life can't begin to be a gift until others are willing to receive it.

Sometimes I hear people complain, "Oh, in my job I've got to go on filing from morning till night. I never get to do anything challenging." What is as important as the job we do is how we do it, how well we can work in harmony with those around us – which, for most of us, is challenge enough. This is especially true of work done in service to others. The way violence is escalating today, both in our streets and around the globe, I don't think there is any limit to the value of work done in the spirit of harmony and peace. We may not be great figures on the world stage, we may not hold a job that shows spectacular results, but the world cannot afford to lose the contribution of anyone who is working for forgiveness, harmony, and tolerance, even if only on a small scale. Any such work is a precious gift.

When we look with sensitivity at the life of Jesus, bringing comfort and consolation to millions of people, I think most of us say to ourselves at some level, "How I would like to be like that in some small measure!" In his early days as Francesco Bernardone, the cloth merchant's son, Saint Francis was not a particularly spiritual figure. Neither was young Augustine in the days when he was painting Carthage red. What overwhelmed them, as it has overwhelmed hundreds of other seekers who went on to become towering spiritual figures, was this immense desire to remake themselves in the image of Jesus.

Even ordinary people like you and me can dedicate ourselves to this loftiest of endeavors; and when we do so earnestly, our body begins to glow with health, our mind becomes gradually more and more secure, our intellect grows more lucid, our will becomes unbreakable, and our life becomes a gift to everybody who looks on it with an open heart. These are the benefits of taking up the spiritual search in earnest: one, two, three, four, and five.

[5]

. . . leaving behind all other sights and sounds but this one vision, which ravishes and absorbs and fixes the beholder in joy . . .

I am now going to take up the most valuable — and probably the most misunderstood — of treasures that we have: desire. Desire is the fuel we have been given for this long, arduous journey into the depths of consciousness. What often makes the journey longer and more arduous than it need be, if I may say so, is our tendency to fritter desire away, in an endless round of pursuits which lead us nowhere.

Spinoza once pointed out succinctly that desires are not decisions. We have very little choice in them. Yet desire is raw power, of a magnitude at least as immense as that of nuclear energy. It is absolutely incumbent upon all of us to work to harness this power within us, so that what we do, we decide in freedom.

Once we see desire for what it really is, interestingly enough, doing something out of purely personal motives will no longer be pleasant. Doing things with the desire to help others, on the other hand, will give us enormous pleasure. With this understanding, the whole alignment of our desires undergoes a transformation.

Do you remember Augustine declaring, "By faithfulness we are collected and bound up into unity within ourself, whereas we had been scattered abroad in multiplicity"? It is this basic change of attitude with respect to desire, more than anything else, that opens up the vast treasury within. By a natural process, our capacity to desire actually grows with our capacity to make our actions a gift to others. Sensory desires, for example, are only nickel-and-dime satisfactions. It is only when we don't have a wider frame of reference than ourselves that we believe they hold out the promise of great pleasure. When we widen our horizons to encompass a greater breadth of life, we can evaluate these pleasures more shrewdly. Some of the greatest of mystics experimented with their senses rather freely in their earlier days. When they reach a state of unlimited compassion and concern for others, they admit, "Those were mere pennies. Now I am in possession of wealth beyond my wildest dreams!"

✧

"What happens to sense pleasures, then?" people naturally want to know. "Should we aim to become bleak ascetics?"

"Why is it that I don't see you playing in the sandbox any more?" I ask, by way of answer.

"The sandbox?" they wonder, taken aback. "The sandbox is for kids."

Picture grown-up men and women getting into the sandbox and playing happily for hours together with toy shovels and buckets! That is something like the picture these mystics must get when they see you and me throwing our energy into pursuits as limited as sense pleasures, which run through our fingers like sand. With their vastly wider perspective, they are able to look far down the road and see that the only possible outcome of this kind of play is increasing frustration.

Every human being has been granted a huge reservoir of desire; we all have it in abundance. Measured against this immense reservoir, the senses have a ridiculously limited capacity to satisfy our enormous appetite to know and to love. You remember Augustine's question: "Why are men not happy? Because they are much more concerned over things which are more powerful to make them unhappy than truth is to make them happy, in that they remember truth so slightly." It is the existence of this truth that we need to be reminded of as often as possible.

When I hear adults, who should know better, going around complaining, "I want all the pleasures of the senses that I enjoyed in my teens," I would like to put before them the example of my young friend Jessica. It wasn't very long ago that I saw her playing with dolls. I understand there are dolls now which, if you press a button, actually get a fever. Perfect for playing hospital! But Jess has graduated from dolls to people. She has worked hard to become an accomplished nurse, and now she is helping and comforting real patients. In the same way, now that we are grown up, our joy should consist in helping others. Once we so much as taste this joy, we will feel no need to play at being children again.

When I use the word love in this connection, I do so advisedly; the popular sense of the word tends to be superficial. I use it in the deeply spiritual sense, where to love is to know; to love is to act. If you really love, from the depths of your consciousness, that love will give you a native wisdom. "When what is known, if even so little, is loved," Augustine writes beautifully, "this very capacity for love makes it better and more fully known." With this capacity you perceive the needs of others intuitively and clearly, with detachment from any personal desires; and you know how to act creatively to meet those needs, dexterously surmounting any obstacle that comes in the way. Such is the immense, driving power of love.

Great mystics like Augustine and Teresa take this one relentless step further. If you really love, they ask, how can you act selfishly? They find it impossible to waste a day, even an hour, that could be used for helping others. For spiritual giants like these, in other words, to love is to act.

Mystics resort to the language of love often. They know that the Lord is the true fulfillment of our deepest need to love. This is a certitude stamped with their personal experience, and it sometimes strikes me that they are dying to share with us this crucial secret. Augustine speaks to his Lord with direct passion in the *Confessions,* calling on him as "God of my heart," "God, my sweetness," and "O my late joy!" God has become the focus to which he directs all his love, thus magnifying its intensity immeasurably. "This is happiness," he tells us: "to be joyful in thee and because of thee: this and no other."

Then he gives a devastating diagnosis of our failures in love:

> ...Yet the reason may be that what they cannot do they do not want to do with sufficient intensity to make them able to do it.

Each of us wants abiding joy. We want it more than anything. Yet we can find abiding joy, Augustine is telling us, only in loving with all our heart, with all our will. All our time and all our energy must be caught up in this all-consuming effort to love. A person like Augustine ultimately fills himself to bursting with this one uplifting desire, so that he floats free from the need to try constantly to satisfy a hundred and one smaller desires. Every cell of his being fills with this love, "which ravishes and absorbs and fixes the beholder in joy."

"Love desires to be aloft," Thomas a Kempis exclaims exuberantly in his *Imitation of Christ,* "and will not be kept back by any thing low and mean. . . . He that loveth, flyeth, runneth, and rejoiceth; he is free, and cannot be held in." Augustine tries to give us some way of grasping this great joy, if only vaguely, by comparing it to more self-centered pleasures:

> But what is it that I love when I love You? Not the beauty of any bodily thing, nor the order of seasons, not the brightness of light that rejoices the eye, nor the sweet melodies of all songs, nor the sweet

fragrance of flowers and ointments and spices, not manna or honey, not the limbs that carnal love embraces. None of these things do I love in loving my God.

Yet in a sense I do love light and melody and fragrance and food and embrace when I love my God: the light and the voice and the fragrance and the food and embrace in the soul, when that light shines upon my soul which no place can contain, that voice sounds which no time can take from me, I breathe that fragrance which no wind scatters, I eat the food which is not lessened by eating, and I lie in the embrace which satiety never comes to sunder. This it is that I love when I love my God.

It is exercise that helps this great love grow inside us. It is giving in to anger and jealousy and resentment that stunts it and holds us, with their heavy weight of turmoil and conflict, down on the ground. Most of the advice the mystics give us aims to promote one thing: the exercise of our love. If we do not understand this purpose, their advice can sound platitudinous – or worse still, quite mad.

If there ever was a spiritual madcap, it was Jesus the Christ. "Bless them that curse you. Do good to them that hate you and despitefully use you." People must have rushed back to Jerusalem shouting, "There's a madman loose on some mountaintop, telling us to love our enemies!" It is in Saint Francis of Assisi that we can see the attitude Jesus wants us to take up: "Lord, keep me floating in the empyrean of love for you, so that I cannot even remember to bump against others with my self-will. When I begin to sink back down under my own weight, have the mercy to give me an enemy or two on whom I can practice my love!" This is the kind of daring on which love thrives.

In this sense, the lovers of God never allow themselves to sober up. With ceaseless practice, they keep themselves drunk with the spirit of love day and night. When we have the privilege of hearing about their exploits or reading their intoxicating words, we say to ourselves: "I want to get into this tavern too! I want to sit on that high stool and say to the Divine Bartender, 'The usual, please. A double shot of sympathy, on the rocks.'" We look dazedly and see, perched on stools all around, the men and women of God. There is Teresa, holding tight to the bar to keep from floating away. There is Francis, hardly able to utter his favorite prayer, "My God and my all." There is Augustine, murmuring something about "God, my sweetness." This mysterious joy that knows no limits is our true heritage, the fulfillment that the travail of human evolution is urging.

When we practice meditation with all the enthusiasm we are capable of, when we repeat the name of the Lord, and most of all when we work harmoniously with difficult people and remain kind and respectful in the midst of provocation, we are drinking deep of the Lord's healing mercy. I sometimes see stickers on cars, proclaiming, "God loves you." God is love. He can be nothing else. When we work to live up to this supreme ideal of charity, we become conduits for his love, instruments of his peace. This is what is meant by God's forgiveness: when we embody his love, we will not be capable of doing anything that causes sorrow to another creature.

In the depths of our heart the Lord is pleading: "Come close and look at me, come deeper and deeper and become one with me, and you will be blessed wherever you go." We may think our heart is hungry for success, hungry for pleasure, but the mystics assure us, "Oh, no! What your heart is hungering for, what everyone's heart is hungering for, is the revelation that our real personality is divine."

☙

The great doubt that comes to everybody is: "I don't know how to do this. I don't really think I can love that way." Here the miracle of love comes in.

If you look at popular novels, at gossip magazines, at syrupy soap operas and movies, you come away with the impression that falling in love is something that just happens. Here you are, sauntering down Fourth Street minding your own business, when suddenly you spy a certain someone coming out of a shop and you fall in love as if into a manhole. True love is much harder to come by than that.

The mystics are the world's authorities on love. When Saint Teresa says *"Amor saca amor,"* she is giving us the basic principle: "Love begets love." One of the most beautiful things about love is that even today it cannot be purchased. It cannot be stolen, it cannot be ransomed, it cannot be cajoled, it cannot be seduced. *Amor saca amor:* only genuine love begets love.

All of us have been conditioned, even though we may not put it in such crass terms, to believe that if you love me six units, I should love you at most six units in return. I can feel secure in loving you six units because you have already committed yourself that far. But if you get annoyed with me and stomp out, slamming the door, I should get annoyed in return – and pull back, at least temporarily, my six units of love. This is the type of bargain that more and more so-called lovers strike today. Saint Teresa would say uncompromisingly, "Don't pretend that this is love. It falls more accurately under the heading of commerce." Shakespeare put the matter in perfect perspective: "Call it not love that changeth."

The whole thrust of what Teresa is confiding to us is simple: With practice, everyone can learn to love like this; everyone can live in endless love. After all, even if you don't learn Esperanto, your life is not necessarily going to be dull and drab. Even if you are not intimately acquainted with ancient Sumerian sculpture, you can make it through life without suffering serious depression. But – and this has to be drilled into the ears of the modern world – if you do not learn how to love, everywhere you go you are going to suffer.

Even in the wealthiest home, discord can leave the

members bankrupt. Ask people who "have it all": several luxury cars in the circular drive, large-screen satellite TV setups in every bedroom and den, heated pools and saunas and exercise machines, priceless originals scattered casually throughout the house. If they live in disharmony, they will be the first to admit, "Life is miserable. I wake up in the morning dreading to go to the breakfast table. I come back in the evening with a sinking feeling in my heart." These are the simple facts of life.

One trend I see which only focuses domestic disharmony is competition. "How much money does he bring in? How much does she bring in?" We should divide up our chattels and responsibilities fair and square, legal-minded advisors warn us, even to the "ownership" of our children. Millions of people have absorbed this criterion. The real question to keep asking ourselves is, "How much am I making my life worthy of being a gift?" Saint Francis says perfectly, "It is in giving that we receive." Right on, as my young friends would say. What matters is not who brings in more or invests more or inveigles more; it is who gives more. That person is the real provider, the true light of the home.

Children, likewise, can exercise their love. When they find their parents slowly moving apart, they can help bring them together with their love. Where grandparents are squabbling, parents can work to reestablish peace. Everybody can learn to play this great mediating role. I know of no greater gift.

❧

Still, practicing this kind of love is not easy. After I give a talk people sometimes come up to me distraught and tell me: "But you don't know the atmosphere in my home! You haven't met my office mates!"

I hasten to assure them, "You don't have to give me the details. I wasn't raised in a cave." I grew up in a large joint family, where we couldn't escape rubbing shoulders with one another at every turn. Later I worked on campuses with thousands of students, and must have attended hundreds of meetings where faculty members from all departments often differed with each other with passionate conviction. I am perfectly well aware that in every context there can be people who are difficult – every bit as difficult as we ourselves can be at times. Wherever we turn in life, we are liable to run into challenging predicaments.

When I was teaching on university campuses, however, I was also practicing meditation and trying to translate the teachings of the mystics into my daily life. Gradually I learned to cease looking upon challenges as difficulties, and began to see tense situations as opportunities to put my growing love to use. We can do this everywhere; the family context is perfect.

In every family, for example, there is likely to be somebody with a bit of Jonathan Swift. Swift, you know, had a sardonic tongue and a rather black sense of humor; he is said to have worn mourning on his birthday. This sort of thing has an inhibiting effect on everyone, and naturally enough, when the Jonathan of our own family enters the room, others may try to make themselves scarce. Not the person who is trying to take love seriously. She learns to come up with a genuine smile and says, "Come in, Jonathan! I've been looking forward to seeing you." To herself she can add in a whisper, "I need the opportunity to deepen my patience."

As we become more aware that the same spark of divinity is in all of us, we will find opportunities everywhere to make that divinity more evident. We won't see anybody as an enemy; we will see everybody as a friend. Every event, however difficult or potentially threatening, can be used to help carry out what the mystics call "the will of the Lord": to love, to forgive, to be kind.

In other words, these are daily exercises, very much like aerobics. You don't stop when your heart rate gets up to 85. You say, "My target rate is 120," and you keep at it until you get there. When your heart is accustomed to 120, you can start aiming for 130, then for 140. Where physical conditioning is concerned, everybody accepts this process.

It is exactly the same process for increasing patience. The resting rate for patience is zero: you say, "I don't have any patience at all. I blow my stack at the slightest provocation!" I commiserate with such people by patting them on the back and reminding them, "That is where everybody starts." But as you learn to meditate, you get more and more capacity to draw on. After a while, when Jonathan goes out of his way to provoke you, you find you can bear it cheerfully for half an hour. With continuing practice, you reach the point where you can get through an entire Saturday morning without losing control. From seven-thirty until noon, you are so patient that you begin to relish your show of self-mastery. After lunch – wisely, I would say – you make yourself scarce again, because your patience has run dry. But if you keep at it with the same diligence in every arena of personal affairs, the great day arrives when you can be patient around poor Jonathan throughout the weekend. He does his level best to provoke you, but you say to yourself, "Oh, no, you don't! Those days are over. Nowadays I can be patience itself."

There is a remarkable statement in mysticism which I am now going to translate into the language of learning to love. Through sheer exercise, over a long, long period, we do not just love Jonathan or Josephine; we become love itself. Our love radiates to anyone who comes within our orbit; we simply lose the knack of doing otherwise. It does not matter whether the person seated beside us has been unpleasant to us for years, perhaps has even opposed us; that is immaterial. What matters is that our very nature now is love. At all times, in every situation, we are at our best with everybody. This is the answer to our most profound prayers.

We need to stretch the frontiers of this miracle as

far as we can. To me, any person who even thinks about waging war – economics and politics completely aside – needs desperately to learn how to love. Saint Teresa's principle "Love begets love" does not apply only to personal relationships; it works on the level of nations just as well. Here again, Saint Francis is a marvelous teacher. How do we make ourselves into instruments of world peace? How can we forge our nation into an instrument of world peace? Francis replies, "Where there is hatred, let me sow love; where there is injury, pardon." He does not mean it as an incantation for special state occasions; it is given to us as a dynamic exercise.

I have enjoyed the opportunity of wandering through a good number of countries. Everywhere I made the same discovery: what divides one people from another is just one percent of superficial differences; in the other ninety-nine percent, we are all the same.

On my way to this country from India, I spent a week in Paris with other Fulbright scholars. My friends were intent on catching glimpses of the Louvre, the Eiffel Tower, the Left Bank, and (I suspect, though they spared me the details) the Folies-Bergère. I spent my days in the lovely city parks, watching French children happily at play. "Just exactly like Indian children," I used to say to myself. "Where is the difference?" On my return to India I was invited to speak before many groups, and always I was asked searching questions about the United States. I could see that they looked on this continent as another world, and Americans as a different kind of people. Imagine their surprise when I responded, "They're the same as you and me. People there like to be treated kindly, just like people here."

Today doubts about the future of mankind are part of the emotional atmosphere. I feel dispirited when I hear that young people, confronted with hard choices in their lives, are saying more and more often: "What does it matter? By the time I'm grown up, they'll probably have blown the earth sky-high!" Too often these doubts are justified by the actions they see so-called responsible leaders taking. Worldwide, the governments of nations are spending six hundred billion dollars every year on developing and manufacturing weapons of destruction; half a million educated, intelligent scientists are working hard at this task. What is desperately needed are personal examples of another attitude, another way of living.

If we could only remember the simple truth that people everywhere are ninety-nine percent the same and only one percent different, we would be saved a lot of headaches, and we would still have that intriguing one percent to make living a delight. Sometimes I wish a few politicians would take to meditation; then they would find it difficult to overlook the fact that all of us have the same basic needs. We all cherish health, happiness, and love; and we all desire, most important, to live in peace and harmony.

In today's shaky world, believe me, everybody takes hope from you when you have some awareness of the unity of life. Remember Francis's line: "Where there is despair, let me sow hope." Even those who sometimes belittle your efforts cannot help thinking after a while, "This just might show us the way out of our troubles." None of us can afford any longer to think in terms of living just for ourselves, or even of living just for our own family. When you can return good will for ill will, love for hatred, you are restoring the faith of everyone around you in these timeless values. As you begin to take this responsibility seriously, your life slowly takes on the greater meaning that all of us dearly desire.

Giving people grounds for hope is exactly what we are doing when we strive every day to make love the basis of our lives. I read a deeply moving article about a group of peasants in Central America who managed to flee the terror rampant in their homeland by swimming a river into the neighboring country. Sympathetic people from this country are going down to live with them in shifts in an effort to discourage military units from harassing them. The one thing these peasants talk about most is their former archbishop, who, in the face of a brutal civil war, spent his time pleading with his people to lay down their weapons. Though he was assassinated for these efforts, his people will never forget his example. As they say over and over again, in the simplest words imaginable: "He who falls for the people will live in the people."

᭡

In this we have an enormous responsibility: to keep in good health, not so much for our own sake but so that we can go on giving this gift as long as possible. Doctors, nurses, and medical technicians can be valuable allies in this sacred task, but the primary responsibility is ours alone. Health is something we have to educate ourselves to maintain, beginning with a nutritious diet, appropriate exercise, work which benefits others, loving relationships, and the enthusiastic observance of spiritual disciplines.

Here I continue a step beyond conventional medicine. In order even to contract illness, I would say, bacteria and viruses and environmental stress are not enough; we must have a certain susceptibility to illness. The immune system is not simply a physiological network, and it is clear that there are wide differences in how different individuals resist disease. Some people exposed to a particular virus get sick; others, though exposed to the same conditions, do not. Similarly, we know that spontaneous remissions – often termed "miraculous" – do occur. All this is because there are many, many factors involved in resistance, and number one, in my opinion, is the mind. The highest, most effective kind of resistance – to illness of any kind whatsoever, even to the ravages of time – is a deep, deep desire to live for others. This is a tremendous force, which I can testify to from my own life.

I am talking now about the deepest roots of the human being. Psychologists know the vital necessity of the will to live; yet when you live only for yourself, how deep can the will go? My will to live springs from the love that floods my heart when I realize that the Lord himself finds it possible to inhabit your heart and mine; and this love expresses itself in the myriad choices I make in my daily life. Most of us have experienced firsthand the benefits we reap from loving two or three people. Imagine what love for five or six billion people can do!

All of us can be much healthier than we are, much more secure. Most of us can live much longer than we expect to, and work more actively right into the evening of our life. Even in our nineties we can be productive, creative, cherished, and respected, because our life has become a shining gift. The time to cultivate the habits of living that make all this possible is now.

↩

> *. . . so that the rest of eternal life were like that moment of illumination which leaves us breathless. Would this not be what is hidden in Scripture, "Enter thou into the joy of thy lord"?*

For a few rare people, it is not enough to have access to the treasury within. They fall so deeply in love with the President of the bank that they long to know him personally, to live with him forever. Augustine makes this desire understandable for us in a startling story:

> Suppose, brethren, a man should make a ring for his betrothed, and she should love the ring more wholeheartedly than the betrothed who made it for her.... Certainly, let her love his gift: but if she should say, "The ring is enough; I do not want to see his face again," what would we say of her?... The pledge is given her by the betrothed so that, in his pledge, he himself may be loved. God, then, has given you all these things. Love him who made them.

Even for those fortunate souls who have been given ready access to the treasury within, and who go in at will and stuff their pockets with love, wisdom, energy, and the creative capacity to inspire others to improve their lives, there may still be a massive door deep inside with a gold-plated sign: "Do Not Enter." This intrigues them. They linger outside the door, listening to get some idea of who might be lodged within. Distantly they may hear someone singing *Ave Maria* in a lovely baritone; and more than anything, they long to see the singer with their own eyes.

Once we hear this voice in our heart of hearts, all our desires come together. We take to standing at this door within for hours on end, hoping against hope that one day it will open. We keep on knocking softly, longing for the moment when the voice inside responds, "Come in."

This is the point at which the mystics advise us, "You may have to bring your sleeping bag and camp outside that door for years. You never know when it will open, or even whether it will open at all." Yet if people can camp on the sidewalk for tickets to the World Series, surely we can do as much for the Lord! This is the period when all our loyalty and endurance are tested. For we have it on good authority that the Lord has a one-way window, and although we have not yet glimpsed him face to face, as Paul says, he is watching us continuously to check on the deepest desires of our heart. We have to keep ourselves at our very best each moment; and we have to give our very best, standing ready to love and respect even those who offend us or try to do us wrong. The exercise of love never becomes more daring.

Yet throughout this trying period, we know in our heart of hearts that true and lasting joy is not long off. "She understands," Teresa says of the soul at this stage, "that she is already near her God, and that if she draws a little nearer, she will become by union one with him." We actually find ourselves looking for opportunities to "do good to them who hate us," the more swiftly to enlarge our love.

Finally the huge oaken door opens a crack, hesitates, creaks, then opens a little wider. . . . We stand there holding our breath. For what we see within, in all its breathtaking loveliness, is the Lord himself, our deepest Self, our true divinity. There and then we go beyond time, beyond place, beyond circumstance, beyond change, decay, and death.

> I entered into my own depths, with you as guide;
> and I was able to do it because you were my helper. I
> entered, and with the eye of my soul, such as it was,
> I saw your unchangeable light shining over that
> same eye of my soul, over my mind. . . . He who
> knows the truth knows that light, and he that
> knows the light knows eternity. Love knows it.
> O eternal truth, true love, beloved eternity!

That is Augustine's on-the-spot, eyewitness account. Later, when he has a chance to put his insights together, he gives us an unforgettable description of his vision:

> What art thou then, my God? O thou, the greatest
> and the best, mightiest, almighty, most merciful and
> most just, utterly hidden and utterly present, most
> beautiful and most strong, abiding yet mysterious,
> suffering no change and changing all things: never
> new, never old, making all things new; ever in
> action, ever at rest, gathering all things to thee
> and needing none; sustaining and fulfilling and
> protecting, creating and nourishing and making
> perfect; ever seeking though lacking nothing.
> Thou lovest without subjection to passion,
> thou art jealous but not with fear; thou canst
> know repentance but not sorrow, be angry yet

unperturbed by anger. Thou canst change the works thou hast made, but thy mind stands changeless. Thou dost find and receive back what thou didst never lose; art never in need but dost rejoice in thy gains, art not greedy but dost exact interest manifold. Thou owest nothing yet dost pay as if in debt to thy creature, forgivest what is owed to thee yet dost not lose thereby. And with all this, what have I said, my God and my life and my sacred delight? What can anyone say when he speaks of thee?

The illumined man or woman sees divinity in everyone: the same Lord disguised as billions of human beings. If you ask me how many people there are in this country, my truthful answer would have to be "One." At the customs gate on the entrance to San Francisco International Airport, I would put up a subtle sign: "United States of America, Population One." There are over two hundred fifty million bodies in this country — two hundred fifty million costumes, if you like; two hundred fifty million vehicles. Yet there is only one driver, one wearer, one Self. This universal vision Augustine posed poetically as the loftiest of harmonies:

God is the unchanging conductor as well as the unchanged Creator of all things that change. When he adds, abolishes, curtails, increases or diminishes the rites of any age, he is ordering all events according to his providence, until the beauty

of the completed course of time, whose parts are the
dispensations suitable to each different period,
shall have played itself out, like the great melody
of some ineffable composer.

☙

This vision is within the reach of every
human being. To live in abiding joy and unfailing
love, to serve everyone to the best of our abilities, to
call the whole world our family: this is the magnificent destiny for which the human being is meant.
When the mystic is asked, just as I have been asked
many times, "What is the way by which we can reach
this destiny, claim this legacy, grow to have our head
crowned with the stars?" the reply is simple: "Unify
your desires."

The reward, I can assure you, is worth everything
we can give, every sacrifice we can possibly make.
Catching even a glimpse of this glory will make every
hardship seem slight by comparison. We must strive
to unify all the petty, personal streams of desire that
motivate us until desire for everlasting love surges in
us like a mighty river whose only outlet, whose only
fulfillment, is the sea of love we call the Lord.

In the *Imitation of Christ,* Thomas a Kempis expresses
this longing in a passionate prayer:

> Enlarge thou me in love, that with the inward palate
> of my heart I may taste how sweet it is to love, and to
> be dissolved, and as it were to bathe myself in thy
> love.

Let me be possessed by love, mounting above myself through excessive fervor and admiration.

Let me sing the song of love, let me follow thee, my Beloved, on high; let my soul spend itself in thy praise, rejoicing through love.

Let me love thee more than myself, nor love myself but for thee: and in thee all that truly love thee, as the law of love commandeth, shining out from thyself.

There is a picturesque way of portraying this strange predicament in which we humans find ourselves. Imagine for a moment the Lord standing in the deep vault of the heart, just waiting for us, with all the joy, all the fulfillment we could ever want, calling over and over again, "Come and take it all!" In our congenital deafness, we think the call must be coming from outside. We hear echoes resounding everywhere. Searching them out, one by one, we are more and more confounded not to find the source of the voice. Still it calls to us – in the form of unfulfilled longings.

In the most practical of terms, the fact that the Lord is indeed our deepest, our inmost Self means that we should never give up on ourselves, never give up on anybody on earth. Nobody is lost. The Lord is not going to leave us – indeed, without him there is no life. Even if we have to be dragged home, so to speak, every soul's calling is to be united with him one day. This final, joy-filled homecoming, this reunion, we bring closer every day that we strive to make our life the kind of gift that is worthy of Him whose gift our very life is.

An Eight-Point Program

Here, as I promised, is a brief summary of the eight-point program for spiritual living which I have been referring to throughout this book. This is the program I myself have followed for almost half a century. Much fuller instructions will be found in my book *Meditation* and in a set of cassettes by the same title.

1. *Meditation.* The heart of this program is meditation: half an hour every morning, as early as is convenient. Instructions will be found on pages 21 – 25; some passages for meditation are listed on page 279.

2. *Repetition of the Holy Name.* This is so simple a practice that it is easy to underestimate its importance. By and large, though it is one of the oldest and most powerful of Christian disciplines, it has survived only in certain monastic traditions. Once you try it, however, I think you will agree that it is also perfectly

adapted to the needs of lay people caught up in the demands of a busy life in the twentieth century. Suggestions for how to use the Holy Name will be found on pages 26 – 29; I have given many more illustrations and applications in my book *The Unstruck Bell*.

3. *Slowing Down.* Hurry makes for tension, insecurity, inefficiency, and superficial living. To guard against hurrying through the day, start the day early and simplify your life so that you do not try to fill your time with more than you can do. When you find yourself beginning to speed up, repeat the Holy Name to help you slow down.

It is important here not to confuse slowness with sloth, which breeds carelessness, procrastination, and general inefficiency. In slowing down we should attend meticulously to details, giving our very best even to the smallest undertaking.

4. *One-pointedness.* Doing more than one thing at a time divides attention and fragments consciousness. When you read and eat at the same time, for example, part of your mind is on what you are reading and part on what you are eating; you are not getting the most from either activity. Similarly, when talking with someone, give that person your full attention. These are little things, but taken together they help to unify consciousness and deepen concentration.

Everything you do should be worthy of your full attention. When the mind is one-pointed it will be secure, free from tension, and capable of the concentration that is the mark of genius in any field.

5. *Training the Senses.* In the food we eat, the books and magazines we read, the movies we see, all of us are subject to the dictatorship of rigid likes and dislikes. To free ourselves from this conditioning, we need to learn to change our likes and dislikes freely when it is in the best interests of those around us or ourselves. We should choose what we eat by what our body needs, for example, rather than by what the taste buds demand.

Similarly, the mind can be said to eat too – through the senses. We need to be very discriminating in what we read and what we go to see for entertainment, for we become in part what our senses take in.

6. *Putting Others First.* Dwelling on ourselves builds a wall between ourselves and others. Those who keep thinking about their needs, their wants, their plans, their ideas cannot help becoming lonely and insecure. The simple but effective technique I recommend is to learn to put other people first – beginning within the circle of your family and friends, where there is already a basis of love on which to build. When husband and wife try to put each other first, for example, they are not only moving closer to each other, they are also removing the barriers of their ego-prison, which deepens their relationships with everyone else as well.

7. *Spiritual Reading.* Our culture is so immersed in what the mass media offer that it is very helpful to balance our outlook by giving half an hour or so each day to spiritual reading – something positive, practical, and inspiring, which reminds us that the spark of divinity is in all of us and can be released in our own lives by meditation, prayer, and daily practice. Just before bedtime is a particularly good time for this kind of reading, because the thoughts you fall asleep in will be with you throughout the night.

8. *Spiritual Association.* When we are trying to change our life, we need the support of others with the same goal. If you have friends who are meditating along the lines suggested here, you can get together regularly to share a meal, meditate, and perhaps read and discuss your spiritual reading. Share your times of entertainment too; relaxation is an important part of spiritual living.

By practicing this eightfold program sincerely and systematically, it is possible for anyone to realize the supreme goal of life. Even a little such practice begins to transform personality, leading to profoundly beneficial changes in ourselves and in the world around us.

Additional Passages for Meditation

To be suitable for meditation, an inspirational passage should come from the scriptures or great mystics and be positive, practical, and personal in its appeal. Here are some of the passages I frequently recommend in addition to those used in this book:

Psalms 22, 23, and 100

The Sermon on the Mount Matthew 5–6 (especially the Beatitudes, Matt. 5:3–16, and the Lord's Prayer, Matt. 6:9–13)

The Wonderful Effect of Divine Love Thomas a Kempis, *Imitation of Christ* I I I . 5

Four Things That Bring Much Inward Peace Thomas a Kempis, *Imitation of Christ* I I I . 23

Lord That Giveth Strength Thomas a Kempis, *Imitation of Christ* I I I . 30

Index

viewing of, 244–245

disease, *see* health

divinity: awareness of, 260–261; evolutionary aspect of, 182–183; seeing in others, 227, 270–271; as universal spark, 139, 260–261; *see also* unity of life

Earth: and human evolution, 178–179; and unity of life, 77; *see also* nations; unity of life

Eckhart, Meister, 203–204, 234

eight-point program, 275–278

energy: conserving, 73–74; and love, 70–74; and negative thoughts, 71–72; rechanneling flow of, 204

eternal life, 267–269

evolution: and anger, 184–186; and anxiety, 189–192; and conditioning, 183–184; and consciousness, 183–184; and divine spark, 182–183; and human mind, 181–182; impact on human personality, 177–189

Faith: validation of, 236–240

forgiveness, 50–51

Fox, George, 8

Francis de Sales, 112

Francis of Assisi: memorials to, 13; overview, 12–19; Prayer of, 19, 20, 21–22, 23, 29–52; seeing attitude of Jesus in, 255; universality of

appeal, 12, 13, 15, 29; validation of faith, 237; writings of, 13, 19, 20; as young man, 14

free-floating thoughts, 118, 153–154

Friars Minor, 14

Friedman, Dr. Meyer, 62, 67, 118

future, 122–123, 135

Gamaliel (rabbi), 81

Gandhi, Mahatma: and power for good, 83, 84; in South Africa, 156; and stress, 150–152, 156

giving, 48–50; *see also* kindness

God, *see* Lord

governments, *see* nations

Habits of mind: Augustine's view of, 139, 160; getting over, 159–164; retraining through meditation, 164, 244–246; tyranny of, 28; *see also* conditioning; desire; likes and dislikes

happiness: Augustine's search for, 136, 140; *see also* joy

health: and anger, 62–63, 185–186, 187; and living habits, 265–267; and need for love, 61–63

heredity, 180; *see also* evolution

Holy Name: basic instruction, 26–28; choice of, 26; and concentration, 115; and consciousness, 27; defined,

129; defined, 63; desire to
learn, 87–89; and energy,
70–74; and health, 61–63; as
intended destiny, 271–273;
learning to give, 47–48;
living life as gift to others,
243–249; losing of self, 51–
52; as measure of wealth,
89–94; and one-pointed
attention, 67–70; and
physical relationships, 63;
practicing through meditation, 259–262; qualities
needed for perfecting, 64–
78; as state of mind, 63; and
time, 64–67; as very nature,
262; *see also* kindness
Luther, Martin, 141

Mantram, *see* Holy Name
meditation: basic instruction,
22–25; benefits of, 197–201,
242–243; concentration
in, 210–211, 214; and consciousness, 132–134, 177–
178; defined, 22, 275; and
distractibility, 165–166; and
Holy Name, 28; impact on
behavior, 246–248; inspirational passages for, 23, 24,
25, 188–189, 209, 279;
morning aftermath,
246–248; and one-pointed
attention, 67–68; as
opportunity for growth,
39–40; for overcoming
conditioning, 164, 187–189;
and personal entangle-

ments, 209–210; and
Prayer of Francis of
Assisi, 21–22, 23; for retraining habits of mind, 244–
246; and transformation,
25; translating into action,
9, 25; use by Augustine, 139
memory, 181, 240–241; and
one-pointed attention,
119–120, 199–200; and
resentment, 119–120
mind: and Augustine's
Confessions, 145–177;
evolutionary aspect of, 181–
182; gaining distance from,
216–218; habits of, 28, 139,
159–164, 244–246; improv-
ing concentration, 197–
199; and likes and dislikes,
147–148; need to slow
down, 173–177; and
nervous system, 145–147;
obstacles to stillness,
164–171; overcoming
jealousy, 169; quieting of,
145–177, 187–189, 224–225;
singleness of, 152–153;
suspending thought
processes in meditation,
211–212; traffic analogy, 145,
146–147, 157;
see also consciousness
Missionaries of Charity, 54,
55, 57
Mother Teresa, 7–8; and
hunger for love, 61–64;
overview, 54–59; and unity
of life, 77; view of time, 66

getting out of the way, 222–224; vs. having likes and dislikes, 166–171; joy in, 221–223; as opportunity for growth, 172–173; opposing kindly, 167–168

Repression, 10, 241
resentment: and energy, 71–72; and forgiveness, 50–51; heading off, 38; and Holy Name, 118–119, 120, 170–171, 173; and memory, 119–120; and self-will, 117–120
Richard of St. Victor, 141
right desire, *see* selflessness
Rusk, Dean, 187

Sacred passages, *see* inspirational passages
Saul of Tarsus: and one-pointed attention, 81–82; and stoning of Stephen, 82–83; transformation of, 80, 83; *see also* Paul
Schumacher, E.F., 106
scriptures: use in meditation, 23, 24, 25, 188–189, 209, 279
security: and selfless work, 169
Self, real, 124, 269, 273
selfish desire: as drain on vital energy, 72; getting over, 159–164; giving up selfish attachments, 205–210; power of defying, 75–76; vs. right desire, 74–76

selflessness: effect on security, 169; and right desire, 74–76
self-pity: vs. sorrow, 44–45
self-will: extinguishing, 9; getting over, 159–164; and Holy Name, 116; as noise, 9; and Paul's "epistle on love," 110–122; and resentment, 117–120; ridding self of, 30–32
Selye, Dr. Hans, 149, 150
sense pleasures, 251
senses: controlling, 9
sensitivity: to needs of others, 193–197; to pain, 193–194, 195
Sermon on the Mount, 63, 279
Shakespeare, William, 128
shopping: need for one-pointed attention, 198–199; as waste of energy, 73–74
Sisters of Mother Teresa of Calcutta, 54, 55, 57; *see also* Mother Teresa
slowing down, importance of, 276; *see also* mind, quieting
sorrow: vs. self-pity, 44–45
spiritual association, 278
spiritual reading, 278
Steele, Sir Richard, 171
Stephen (Christian martyr), 82–83
stress: and Gandhi, 150–152, 156; and health, 62–63; and likes and dislikes, 149, 167;

Classics of Christian Inspiration

⌘

ORIGINAL GOODNESS

Blessed are the poor in heart,
for they shall see God.

MATTHEW 3:8

Original Goodness

EKNATH EASWARAN

ON THE BEATITUDES

OF THE SERMON

ON THE MOUNT

NILGIRI PRESS

I S B N : cloth, 0—915132—92—3; paper, 0—915132—91—5

Second edition, first printing August 1996

The Blue Mountain Center of Meditation, founded in
Berkeley, California, in 1961 by Eknath Easwaran,
publishes books on how to lead the spiritual life
in the home and the community.
For information please write to
Nilgiri Press, Box 256, Tomales, California 94971

Printed on recycled, permanent paper.
The paper used in this publication meets the minimum requirements of American
National Standard for Information Services - Permanence of Paper for Printed
Library Materials, A NSI Z39.48—1984

Library of Congress Cataloging in Publication Data:
Easwaran, Eknath.
Original goodness : on the beatitudes of the Sermon on the Mount /
Eknath Easwaran. — 2nd ed.
p. cm. — (Classics of Christian inspiration series)
Includes bibliographical references and index.
ISBN 0—915132—92—3 (alk. paper).
ISBN 0—915132—91—5 (pbk. : alk. paper)
1. Spiritual life. 2. Meditation. 3. Beatitudes. I. Title. II. Series.
BL624.E175   1996   291.4′4 — dc20   96-25371   CIP

Table of Contents

CHAPTER I
Original Goodness

I have spoken at times of a light in the soul, a light that is uncreated and uncreatable . . . to the extent that we can deny ourselves and turn away from created things, we shall find our unity and blessing in that little spark in the soul, which neither space nor time touches.
— *Meister Eckhart*

These words, addressed to ordinary people in a quiet German-speaking town almost seven hundred years ago, testify to a discovery about the nature of the human spirit as revolutionary as Einstein's theories about the nature of the universe. If truly understood, that discovery would transform the world we live in at least as radically as Einstein's theories changed the world of science. "We have grasped the mystery of the atom," General Omar Bradley once said, "and rejected the Sermon on the Mount. . . . Ours is a world of nuclear giants and ethical infants." If we could grasp the mystery of Eckhart's "uncreated light in the soul" — surely no more abstruse than nuclear physics! — the transformation in our thinking would set our world right side up.

Meister or "Master" Eckhart – the title attests to his scholarship, but seems even better suited to his spiritual authority – lived almost exactly at the same time and for the same span as Dante, and both seem born to those lofty regions of the spirit that do not belong to any particular culture, religion, or age but are universal. Yet, also like Dante, Eckhart expressed perfectly something essential about his times. The end of the thirteenth century was a period of intense turmoil in Europe, and the Rhine valley, where Eckhart was born, was the breeding ground of various popular religious societies which alarmed conventional Christians. Yet a God who could be known personally and a path by which to reach him were what an increasing number of people yearned for, and Eckhart's passionate sermons, straining to convey the Absolute in the words of the street and marketplace, became immensely popular.

And what did he teach? Essentially, four principles that Leibnitz would later call the Perennial Philosophy, because they have been taught from age to age in culture after culture:

*First, there is a "light in the soul that is uncreated and uncreatable": unconditioned, universal, deathless; in religious language, a divine core of personality which cannot be separated from God. Eckhart is precise: this is not what the English language calls the "soul," but some essence in the soul that lies at the very center of consciousness. As Saint Catherine of Genoa put it, "My me is God: nor do I know my selfhood except in God." In Indian mysticism this divine core is called simply *atman,* "the Self."

⋆Second, this divine essence can be *realized.* It is not an abstraction, and it need not – Eckhart would say *must* not – remain hidden under the covering of our everyday personality. It can and should be discovered, so that its presence becomes a reality in daily life.

⋆Third, this discovery is life's real and highest goal. Our supreme purpose in life is not to make a fortune, nor to pursue pleasure, nor to write our name on history, but to discover this spark of the divine that is in our hearts.

⋆Last, when we realize this goal, we discover simultaneously that the divinity within ourselves is one and the same in all – all individuals, all creatures, all of life.

Words can certainly be ambiguous with ideas such as these, and "mysticism" is no exception. In this book, a mystic is one who not only espouses these principles of the Perennial Philosophy but lives them, whose every action reflects the wisdom and selfless love that are the hallmark of one who has made this supreme discovery. Such a person has made the divine a reality in every moment of life, and that reality shines through whatever he or she may do or say – and that is the real test. It is not occult fancies or visions or esoteric discourses that mark the mystic, but an unbroken awareness of the presence of God in all creatures. The signs are clear: unfailing compassion, fearlessness, equanimity, and the unshakable knowledge, based on direct, personal experience, that all the treasures and pleasures of this world together are worth nothing if one has not found the uncreated light at the center of the soul.

These are demanding criteria, and few people in the history of the world can be said to have met them. I shall often refer to these men and women collectively as "the great mystics," not to obscure their differences, but to emphasize this tremendous undercurrent of the spirit that keeps resurfacing from age to age to remind us of our real legacy as human beings.

On this legacy the mystics are unanimous. We are made, the scriptures of all religions assure us, in the image of God. Nothing can change that original goodness. Whatever mistakes we have made in the past, whatever problems we may have in the present, in every one of us this "uncreated spark in the soul" remains untouched, ever pure, ever perfect. Even if we try with all our might to douse or hide it, it is always ready to set our personality ablaze with light.

When I was growing up in South India, just half an hour's walk from my home was a lotus pond so thickly overlaid with glossy leaves and gleaming rose and white blossoms that you could scarcely see the water. One of the Sanskrit names for this most exquisite of flowers is *pankaja,* "born from the mud." In the murky depths of the pond a seed takes root. Then a long, wavering strand reaches upward, groping through the water toward the glimmer of light above. From the water a bud emerges. Warmed by the sun's rays, it slowly opens out and forms a perfect chalice to catch and hold the dazzling light of the sun.

The lotus makes a beautiful symbol for the core of goodness in every human being. Though we are born of human clay, it reminds us, each of us has the latent capacity to reach and grow toward heaven until we shine with the reflected glory of our Maker.

Early in the third century, a Greek Father of the Church, Origen, referred to this core of goodness as both a spark and a divine seed – a seed that is sown deep in consciousness by the very fact of our being human, made in the image of our Creator. "Even though it is covered up," Origen explains,

> because it is God that has sowed this seed in us, pressed it in, begotten it, it cannot be extirpated or die out; it glows and sparkles, burning and giving light, and always it moves upward toward God.

Eckhart seized the metaphor and dared take it to the full limits it implies:

> The seed of God is in us. Given an intelligent and hard-working farmer, it will thrive and grow up to God, whose seed it is, and accordingly its fruits will be God-nature. Pear seeds grow into pear trees, nut seeds into nut trees, and God-seed into God.

"Its fruit will be God-nature"! What promise could be more revolutionary? Yet Eckhart, like other great mystics of the Church before and after him, does no more than assure us of his personal experience. The seed is there, and the ground is fertile. Nothing is required but diligent gardening to bring into existence the God-tree: a life that proclaims the original goodness in all creation.

The implications of this statement are far-reaching. Rightly understood, they can lift the most oppressive burden of guilt, restore any loss of self-esteem. For if goodness is our real core, goodness that can be hidden but never taken away, then goodness is not something we have to get. We do not have to figure out how to make ourselves good; all we need do is remove what covers the goodness that is already there.

To be sure, removing these coverings is far from easy. Having a core of goodness does not prevent the rest of personality from occasionally being a monumental nuisance. But the very concept of original goodness can transform our lives. It does not deny what traditional religion calls sin; it simply reminds us that before original sin was original innocence. That is our real nature. Everything else – all our habits, our conditioning, our past mistakes – is a mask. A mask can hide a face completely; like that frightful iron contraption in Dumas's novel, it can be excruciating to wear and nearly impossible to remove. But the very nature of a mask is that it can be removed. This is the promise and the purpose of all spiritual disciplines: to take off the mask that hides our real face.

↶

It is said that the English astronomer Sir Arthur Eddington, when he announced to a bewildered world the first experiments vindicating Einstein's theories, was asked by journalists, "Is it true that only three people in the world understand the theory of relativity?" Eddington took his time, then replied in carefully puzzled tones, "Who is the third?"

That is roughly where we stand today with this discovery of original goodness. I began by saying that if Eckhart's words were truly understood, they could turn our world right side up. Yet the same has rightly been said of the Sermon on the Mount, which has never been in danger of enjoying sweeping acceptance. Mystics speak boldly and call us all to follow; but the price is high, and few want to listen.

But from time to time mysticism does flourish, often in response to some deep need in a troubled age. The late Middle Ages must have been such a period in Western Christendom, for it fostered one of the most remarkable flowerings of the Perennial Philosophy the world has known. The amazing popularity of Eckhart's sermons, delivered with the ardor and humanity of a Saint Francis but about as accessible to the average person as a talk on quantum mechanics, is just one piece of the evidence. From roughly 1200 to *1400,* from Saint Francis himself to Thomas a Kempis, there arose not only some two dozen of Christianity's greatest mystics but also a wave of popular response among the common people.

What has this to do with us at the end of the twentieth century? A great deal, I think. The fourteenth century was a time of turbulence not unlike that of our own age – "a distant mirror," to use the historian Barbara Tuchman's phrase. The popular appeal of a man like Eckhart, a quiet friar who did no more to rouse a following than preach in church about things the intellect can scarcely grasp, is evidence that however abstract the concept of original goodness may seem, ordinary people do need and respond to the idea of a spark of the divine in their own soul. The reason is simple: nothing else can fill the hunger in the human heart. Even today, with abundance within reach for more people than ever, we need something more than the physical world can offer.

Last Christmastime I sat in a café inside a fashionable department store, watching the shoppers come and go. Most of them, I thought, had not come to buy things they already wanted. It was as if they had come looking for something to want – something that might fill a nameless need, even if only for a moment. Above the glittering displays a poster bearing the name of the mall promised proudly, "The Fantasy Is Real."

To me, it is a comment on the nobility of human nature that even in the midst of such a smorgasbord of things and activities and sensations, we still feel a need for something real. For although modern civilization has made remarkable progress in many fields, it has neglected others that are vital for well-being. "Progress is a good thing," said Ogden Nash, "but it has been going on too long." Material progress does improve well-being up to a point; but beyond that point, instead of lifting us upward, it only leads us around in circles. Making things, buying and selling them, piling them up, repairing them, then trying to figure out how to dispose of them: for sensitive people, boredom with this carnival cycle began some time ago. A consumer culture is not the goal of life.

None of us need feel guilty if we have been caught in the games of profit and pleasure that industrial civilization holds up for us as life's goal. These are stages that a society goes through, just as a child plays and then discards what he or she outgrows. What matters is not that we may have made mistakes in the pursuit of physical satisfactions; what is important is to learn from these mistakes as quickly as we can that wealth, possessions, power, and pleasure have never brought lasting satisfaction to any human being. Our needs go too deep to be satisfied by anything that comes and goes. Nothing but spiritual fulfillment can fill the void in our hearts.

Today, I think, millions of people find themselves at a crossroads, forced to ask penetrating questions that in simpler times were the province only of philosophers: *What is life for? Why am I here? Is there more to me than this body? Is happiness a foolish dream; can it actually be found without closing my eyes to what I see?* New Age philosophies, and new sciences too, search for answers. But do we really need new answers to enter a new age? The questions are frankly old, and human nature has not changed. Are the answers of religion out of date? Have we forgotten the daring pioneers of the spirit who discovered and tapped a reservoir of joy, wisdom, and healing within – and who insist that we can tap it too?

We have forgotten, is the delicate answer, and it is not entirely our fault. The reason why we do not learn of these discoveries is that they are so rarely understood – cannot be understood, in fact, except by those who try to live them; and if understanding Einstein was difficult when relativity was new, shall we expect to learn in school about things "uncreated and uncreatable"? Among the disturbing trends of our age is the tendency to identify the human being as nothing more than a biochemical entity and then argue, "There is no such thing as spirit. How can the center of personality be something that 'time and space cannot touch'?"

Yet even this skepticism is not new; in a sense, it is nothing more than the modern echo of an age-old doubt. As Hans Denk, a German mystic of the sixteenth century, exclaimed to God, "Men flee from thee and say they cannot find thee. They turn their backs and say they cannot see thee. They stop their ears and say they cannot hear thee."

Centuries before, Eckhart had urged:

> You need not seek God here or there: he is no farther off than the door of the heart. There he stands and waits and waits until he finds you ready to open and let him in. You need not call him from a distance; to wait until you open for him is harder for him than for you. He needs you a thousand times more than you can need him. Your opening and his entering are but one moment.

One of my deepest desires is to convey this simple truth to the millions of people today who seem at a loss for what to live for, and especially to the young. I have seen estimates that at least half a million of our teenagers attempt suicide each year. In a free and affluent society such as ours, why would so many of our children come to the conclusion that their lives are not worth pursuing? It is tempting to point a finger at specific causes like drugs, but the president of the Youth Suicide National Center in Washington looks deeper. Our young people are profoundly troubled, she says, because "their sense of future is gone."

Environmental disaster, and domestic violence, and th4e spread of war are enough to undermine anyone's sense of future. Yet even more damaging, in my opinion, is the lack of a sustaining purpose. With a higher goal, human beings can face any challenge. But without a goal, the spirit withers, and when the natural idealism of the young is blocked, their energy eventually breaks through into uncontrolled and often self-destructive channels. Most young people I know do not really want an easy life. They long for challenge: real challenges, all the bigger because their capacities are so huge. All they ask is something to live for. But we have become a culture without large goals, with nothing but material abundance to offer the hunger in their hearts.

In almost every country and every age, there are a few men and women who see through the game of personal satisfaction and ask themselves, "Is this all? I want something much bigger to live for, something much loftier to desire." Nothing transient can appease this hunger. It touches something very deep in us, caught as we are in our predicament as human beings: partly physical, partly spiritual, trying to feel at home in the world into which we have been born. What is the reason for this gnawing dissatisfaction? The world's great spiritual traditions all give the same answer: we are not wholly at home in this world of change and death. The body may belong, but the spirit is in exile here, a wanderer, a stranger in a strange land. And we long for home.

In Western symbols it is Eden that stands for "the soul's true home" from which we have somehow been banished. In this sense, Eden is not so much a place as a state of consciousness. We may conceive of the Creation in time and space, but it is essentially our separation from our native state of original goodness which marks our advent into the world as seemingly separate individuals – in traditional language, the Fall.

Yet although we feel exiled from this state, our exile is only apparent. Like the rabbi in the Hasidic tale who walks back and forth over buried treasure every day without ever guessing what is beneath his feet, every moment we pass unaware over the core of goodness in our hearts.

The scientific account of the creation of the universe suggests a modern metaphor for Eden and the Fall. Before the Big Bang, physicists tell us, all the matter in the universe must have been compressed in an incomprehensible point, before time and outside space. Matter and energy were one in that primal state. Even in the first few seconds of creation, the universe was mostly light. Ordinary matter, in the infinite variety we experience today, devolved from pure energy flung into space and time by the explosion of creation.

In the same way we might speak of Eden as a state of

pure, unitary consciousness, logically prior to the differentiation between matter and mind. Just as there was a point before time when all matter and energy in the universe was one, there is a state of awareness in which all creation is one. The Fall is then the Big Bang: the process of individuation, which seems to scatter this unitary consciousness into fragments, leaving each of us with a shard of Eden in our hearts.

Physicists tell us that the elements created in the Big Bang are present throughout the universe, from the soil in our gardens to the gas clouds of the farthest galaxy. Many years ago, when people were lining up in San Francisco to see a rock our astronauts had brought from the moon, I picked up a rock from the road and thought to myself, "This too is a moon rock. There's no difference." Fragments from the Big Bang lie all around us, just as in distant stars. In the same way, the mystics say, a trace of our original divinity is present in every creature. In some, like Saint Francis of Assisi, it is highly revealed; in others it is more heavily veiled; but that divinity is present throughout creation.

Jewish mysticism puts this idea into haunting imagery. Shekinah, the Presence of God, is dispersed throughout creation in every creature, like sparks scattered from the pure flame of spirit that is the Lord. And each spark, seemingly alone in the darkness of blind matter, wanders this world in exile, seeking to return to its divine source.

Yet the Fall is not just an event that took place in 4004 B.C. It is still going on. Just as radio telescopes can pick up faint echoes of the Big Bang, we hear echoes of our fall into separateness every day. Superjets may have brought New York and Paris closer than ever, but I doubt that individuals have ever been more distant. And like island universes, we seem to be rushing apart at an accelerating speed. We are increasingly alienated from others and from ourselves.

In this interpretation, when Adam and Eve ate the fruit of the tree of knowledge, what they tasted is what the Sanskrit language calls *ahamkara:* literally, "I-maker," the sense of being "an island unto oneself" – something separate from the rest of life, with unique needs and peremptory claims.

This is a highly tempting fruit. If I were a playwright, I could write an entertaining play in which the serpent comes and sells the apple of separateness to Adam and Eve. "Hey, try this! Nothing could be more natural: just be yourself and take care of number one. You can have your food just the way you like it. You can decorate your apartment any old way you choose. You can play only the music you like, at any hour of the day or night. You can wear any kind of clothes you like. You can make any amount of money, by any means, and spend it on anything under the sun. Avoid people you don't like; you can even keep them off your block. Go to sleep when you want, get up when you want . . . you don't have to care for anybody!" That is the serpent's message, and among other things it makes us ideal, insatiable consumers. My sympathies are all with Adam and Eve when they fell for this. Don't we twentieth-century men and women, sophisticated as they come, go on falling all too easily for the same old apple?

To me, the serpent is not a villainous figure. He is simply an effective salesman. The serpent was only doing his job; he had to sell. "Don't blame me," he might well protest. "They didn't have to buy. I was able to tempt them because they were temptable." Talk about smooth! The word serpent comes from a Sanskrit word which means to slither about, to be smooth in one's movements: so smooth that nobody suspected there was a price to pay for what he offered, and exorbitant finance charges too.

For what seems such tempting fruit at the beginning slowly begins to cause stomachache. Separateness becomes a habit and finally a compulsive state of mind. This is a tragic development, for a person who can think only of himself, someone who explodes when things do not go her way, is a fragile, alienated, and very lonely individual. And the tragedy does not stop there; that is why I said that the Fall is still continuing. In the end, it is this driving sense of separateness – *I, I, I; my* needs, *my* wants, apart from all the rest of life – that is responsible for all the wars in history, all the violence, all the exploitation of other human beings, and even the exploitation of the planet that threatens our future today.

Yet what we seek when we fall for the serpent's pitch is very natural. What *do* we want from life, judging not by our words but by our actions? Very simple, basic things, common to all. We want to love and to be loved. We want happiness and fulfillment, though we may have differing ideas of what that means. We want a place in life, a way of belonging, a sense of purpose, the achievement of worthy goals — whatever it takes; otherwise life is an empty show. And, of course, we want never to die.

These are natural desires, and no amount of experience can erase them from our hearts. Why? Because these are the demands of Eckhart's "little spark" of the spirit, and that spark is real and inalienable: "nearer to us than our very body," as the Sufis say, "dearer than our very life."

These yearnings are not wrong, then. What happens is that we interpret them wrongly. They are messages from the spirit which have somehow got scrambled by the world of matter, and we lack the decoder by which to understand. That scrambling is what Hindu mysticism means by the much-misunderstood word *maya:* the wishful, willful illusion that the thirst in our hearts is physical and can somehow be slaked by physical experience. We wander searching for the right things in the wrong places, seeking Eden in the world of the senses, and life itself seems to delight in frustrating us.

"The soul is a pilgrim," said John Ruysbroeck, one of the great Rhineland mystics who succeeded Eckhart, "for it sees its country." But until we glimpse our "soul's true home," we are not so much pilgrims as tourists. Being a traveler is one thing, but no one really likes to be a tourist. Nothing is ever quite right: the food, the beds, the chairs, the customs. We shake our heads and mutter under our breath the universal tourist's complaint: "Back home . . ."

Deep below the level of conscious awareness, the world's mystical traditions tell us, that refrain goes on constantly in every heart. *Back home . . .* And a brilliant contemporary of Eckhart's, Mechthild of Magdeburg, gives us the reason. "The soul is made of love," she exclaims — made of love, just as the body is made of flesh — "and must ever strive to return to love. Therefore, it can never find rest nor happiness in other things. It must lose itself in love. By its very nature it must seek God, who is love."

In everyone there is this inward tug, this call to return. But because we are turned outward, our hearing gets confused. The call seems to be coming from outside. What we seek is always just around the corner . . . and when we reach the corner, it has ducked out of sight down the block. Yet human nature is so strong that even after turning corners a thousand times, we still say, "The thousand and first — that's going to be the one!" Life becomes a pilgrimage around corners.

But there comes a time when corners no longer beckon. We know from bitter experience that they only hide blind alleys. This juncture is critical; for once one reaches it, nothing on earth can satisfy for long. Those with drive may plunge into restless activity. The more frustrated they feel, the more things they try – globetrotting, solo climbing, cars, clothes, casinos, commodities futures. But the desire to wrest meaning from life only grows more urgent as frustration mounts.

Later, looking back, this utter restlessness may prove to be the first touch of what traditional religion calls grace. It means that a person has grown too big to be satisfied with petty satisfactions that come and go. But the crisis is real. If we do not understand the message, frustration can turn desperate or self-destructive – not only for an individual, but for a whole society. Each age has its own kind of suffering, the natural consequences of mistaken values it pursues, and the suffering of our industrial age is loneliness, alienation, and despair. Alienation can cause terrible harm; for it is when we feel isolated and alone that we lose sensitivity to others, and obsession with private desires and fears fills up our world. Walk the streets of any inner city today and you will see the fruits of separateness all around you, the anguish of a society in which even children and the aged are cut adrift and left on their own.

There comes a time in the growth of civilizations, as with individuals, when the life-and-death questions of material existence have been answered, yet the soul still thirsts and physical challenges cease to satisfy. Then we stand at a crossroads: for without meaningful aspiration, the human being turns destructive. Spiritual fulfillment is an evolutionary imperative. Like a snake that must shed its skin to grow, our industrial civilization must shed its material outlook or strangle in outgrown ideals whose constructive potential has been spent.

In the end, then, life itself turns us inward – "away from created things," as Eckhart says, to "find our unity and blessing in that little spark in the soul." The end of the Fall is the Return. Alienation is the heartache of feeling out of place in a senseless universe. Its purpose is to turn us homeward, and all experience ultimately conspires to that end. "Whether you like it or not, whether you know it or not," Eckhart assures us, "secretly Nature seeks and hunts and tries to ferret out the track in which God may be found."

This is a most compassionate view of human nature. Even when we are busy accumulating possessions with which to feather our little nest, planning a hilltop castle with garage space for half a dozen new cars, Eckhart would say we are really looking for God. We think, "If I can fix up my place just right, with a little bar and sauna in my room and my own entertainment center at my fingertips, then I'll feel at home!" But we will never be at home except in Eden.

"The man of God never rejoices," Eckhart declares. We think, "Just what I suspected! Every saint is really a sourpuss." But then he explains himself: "The man of God never rejoices, because he is joy itself."

When all hostility, all resentment, all greed and fear and insecurity are erased from your mind, the state that remains is pure joy. When we become established in that state, we live in joy always.

That state of joy, hidden at the very center of consciousness, is the Eden to which the long journey of spiritual seeking leads. There, the mystics of all religions agree, we uncover our original goodness. We don't have to buy it; we don't have to create it; we don't have to pour it in; we don't even have to be worthy of it. This native goodness is the essential core of human nature.

The purpose of all valid spiritual disciplines, whatever the religion from which they spring, is to enable us to return to this native state of being – not after death but here and now, in unbroken awareness of the divinity within us and throughout creation. Theologians may quarrel, but the mystics of the world speak the same language, and the practices they follow lead to the same goal.

It is in this light that this book presents the Beatitudes – the series of eight verses from the Sermon on the Mount which begins, in Matthew's version, "Blessed are the poor in spirit, for theirs is the kingdom of heaven." Each chapter takes one of the Beatitudes as a spiritual law which has the power to uncover the "uncreated light" in the depths of personality when we allow it to shape our thoughts and actions.

I want to make it clear, however, that this is not an attempt at Biblical commentary. I am content to leave explication and exegesis to scholars. In these chapters I simply comment on some of what the Beatitudes mean to me after decades of effort in trying to translate them into my life. I have chosen Matthew over Luke not for any theological reason, but because these are the words written on my memory half a century ago by a man I revered: the principal of a small Catholic college in Kerala, South India, who taught me through his personal example what Christ's teachings mean in daily living.

Meditation

Whatever our religious beliefs – or even if formalized religion is anathema – it is possible for every one of us to uncover the core of goodness of which Eckhart speaks. It has nothing to do with theology and everything to do with practice. In other words, what we say we believe in is not so important; what matters is what we actually do – and, even more, what we actually are. "As we think in our hearts, so we are." Goodness is in us; our job is simply to get deep into our consciousness and begin removing what stands in the way.

Doing this, however, is no small task. I would go to the extent of saying that there is no way to accomplish this today except through the systematic practice of meditation.

How can I make such a sweeping statement? Because I mean something very particular and practical by the word "meditation." Although it is a spiritual discipline, meditation stands above the differences that define the world's great religions. Meditation is not dogma or doctrine or metaphysics; it is a powerful tool. Everyone can use a shovel, regardless of his views on the dignity of hand labor. Similarly, everyone can use meditation to dig into consciousness and change it to conform with her highest ideals.

On the one hand, then, when I talk about meditation, I am referring to a specific interior discipline which is found in every major religion, though called by different names. (Catholic writers, for example, use terms like "contemplation" or "interior prayer," reserving the word "meditation" for another very specific spiritual practice.) So when I say that meditation is necessary for uncovering the God-seed in your heart, you can see that I am not closing a door on anyone at all. On the other hand, a great many activities called meditation are quite different from what I mean, so it is important to be clear.

When I first came to this country from India on the Fulbright exchange in 1959, practically no one talked about meditation. I could use the word without much concern that my audience might misunderstand. Today the scene is very different. If you want to learn about meditation, you can go to a library and find more than a hundred books in print on the subject, not counting the articles in popular magazines. And if you look in the Yellow Pages, you can find institutions from karate schools to hospitals offering to teach you how to meditate – each in a different way. With so much activity on the stage, I have found it necessary to say precisely what I mean or court confusion.

First, meditation as I teach and practice it is not a relaxation technique. I respect teachers and health professionals who use the word in this way, but we have the testimony of great mystics from every culture and every age that meditation requires strenuous effort. If you expect to find it easy going, you are going to be disappointed.

True, meditation does relieve the tensions of the day. But so does a ten-mile run, which is a lot of work at the time. And meditation does go on relieving tension at a deeper and deeper level, as knots and conflicts in personality are undone. But in general, especially at the beginning, meditation is work; the rewards come during the rest of the day.

Second, although there are highly respectable schools of meditation which rightly emphasize that their goal is not relaxation but awareness, their methods often involve heightening awareness of some physiological activity like breathing. I respect these methods in the hands of an experienced teacher, but to me meditation is essentially an interior discipline. The mind needs to turn inward, and to do this we have to forget the body during the period of meditation. (Interestingly enough, it is just when we forget about the body that it functions at its best.)

Third, meditation as I teach it is not visualization, nor is it drifting in a reverie and imagining pleasant things. It is not letting the mind wander, "guided" or unguided, nor observing thoughts flow by in quiet detachment. If we could really watch our thoughts in that manner, our emotions would have no power to seize hold of us – which means we would never lose our temper, never think a hostile thought, never feel afraid.

Finally, it is important to distinguish meditation from disciplined reflection on a particular theme. I stress this because many eminent spiritual figures have used the word in this way. Reflection on a spiritual topic can yield valuable insights; but for the vast majority of us, reflection is an activity on the surface level of the mind. To transform personality we need to go much, much deeper. We need a way to get eventually into the unconscious itself, where our contrary thoughts and deepest desires arise, and make changes *there*. That is the purpose of meditation.

So what *is* meditation? It is the regular, systematic training of attention to turn inward and dwell continuously on a single focus within consciousness, until, after many years, we become so absorbed in the object of our contemplation that while we are meditating, we forget ourselves completely. In that moment, when we may be said to be empty of ourselves, we are utterly full of what we are dwelling on. This is the central principle of meditation: we become what we meditate on.

Meditation, then, means training the mind: teaching our thoughts to go where we tell them and to obey themselves while they are there, much as we train a puppy. We begin by learning how to train our attention – both in meditation and during the rest of the day – until eventually we make our mind calm, clear, and concentrated as a laser, which we can direct and focus at will. This is a tremendous skill, as you can appreciate if you have ever tried to take your mind off some nagging personal problem and concentrate completely on the job at hand. In any particular subject, this capacity for one-pointed attention is the essence of genius; anyone who has it is bound to make a mark in his or her field. But when you have this kind of mastery over your attention in everything you do, you have a genius for life itself: unshakable security, clear judgment, deep personal relationships, compassion that no adversity can break down.

Yet this is only the beginning of where meditation can lead. In its deeper stages, meditation means reconditioning the unconscious itself: taming the most powerful forces we can encounter, our own desires. Below the surface of personality, all of us are torn by conflicting urges; that is the human condition. In training the mind to dwell on a lofty ideal, we gradually drive that ideal deep into consciousness and release the will to translate it into action. Conflicts in personality are resolved, so that what we believe in, what we do, and what we think become one. Training attention brings mastery of most personal problems, but this reconditioning of the unconscious brings a complete transformation of personality.

When I say these things before a new audience, I always expect some intellectual questions and objections. But every now and then, someone will come to me afterward and say, "Great! But what do I actually do?" I want to throw my arms around such people and exclaim, "Oh, thank you for asking!" That is just the kind of question a teacher longs to hear. Here, then, in brief, is the method of meditation I teach. (There are full instructions in my book *Meditation,* along with descriptions of the rest of my eight-point program.)

  * The very best time for meditation is early morning – as early as you can make it. Set aside a time when you can sit for half an hour in uninterrupted quiet. If you wish to meditate more, add half an hour in the evening, but please do not meditate for longer periods without personal guidance from an experienced teacher who is following this same method.

  * Select a place that is cool, clean, and quiet. Sit with your back and head erect, on the floor or on a straight-backed chair.

  * Close your eyes and begin to go slowly, in your mind, through the words of a simple, positive, inspirational passage from one of the world's great spiritual

traditions. (Remember, you become what you meditate on.) I recommend beginning with the Prayer of
Saint Francis of Assisi:

> Lord, make me an instrument of thy peace.
> Where there is hatred, let me sow love;
> Where there is injury, pardon;
> Where there is doubt, faith;
> Where there is despair, hope;
> Where there is darkness, light;
> Where there is sadness, joy.
>
> O divine Master, grant that I may not so much seek
> To be consoled as to console,
> To be understood as to understand,
> To be loved as to love;
> For it is in giving that we receive;
> It is in pardoning that we are pardoned;
> It is in dying [to self] that we are born to eternal life.

You will find it helpful to keep adding to your repertoire so that the passages you meditate on do not grow
stale. My book *God Makes the Rivers to Flow* contains other
passages that I recommend, drawn from many traditions. But whatever your background, I suggest you begin by giving Saint Francis a try. You will find that his
words are both personal and universal and that they
have great power to heal old wounds deep in the mind.
If words like "Lord" bother you, remind yourself that
you are addressing the divine spark within your own
heart: not some imposing figure seated on a throne in
the far reaches of the heavens, but the very core of your
own self.

* While you are meditating, do not follow any association of ideas or allow your mind to reflect on the meaning of the words. If you are giving your full attention to each word, the meaning cannot help sinking in.

* When distractions come, do not resist them, but give more attention to the words of the passage. If your mind strays from the passage entirely, bring it back gently to the beginning and start again.

* Resolve to have your meditation every day – however full your schedule, whatever interruptions threaten, whether you are sick or well. If you miss one day, goes an old Hindu saying, you will need seven days to make it up.

Meditation is simple, but it is far from easy. One friend asked me recently why I call the Beatitudes "strategies." Isn't the word borrowed from war? It is. But the spiritual life too is a battle. Mystics call it the war within: the conflict between what is spiritual in us and what is selfish, between the force of goodness and the powers of destruction that clash incessantly in every human heart.

"There is no greater valor nor no sterner fight," attests Eckhart. As always, Eckhart is terse and to the point: because "he who would be what he ought to be must stop being what he is." That is the challenge of the spiritual life – and that challenge is part of its appeal. It is precisely because the quest to realize God is so difficult that those who are really daring – and there are many in this country – should be eager to take it up. In fact, the mystics say, all the daring and aggressiveness in human nature is given to us for one supreme evolutionary purpose: to remove what covers our original goodness so that we can reveal more and more of God in our own lives.

To that end, we can take up the Beatitudes one by one as strategies for winning the war within.

CHAPTER 2
Purity of Heart

Blessed are the pure in heart, for they shall see God.

When I was a boy, growing up in a village in South India, just an hour's walk from my home was a dense jungle where wild animals roamed at will. Often I used to thrill to the trumpeting of an elephant, and rumors abounded among the children that tigers strayed from the jungle at night and prowled the village paths. You can imagine some of the nightmares I had as a child, dreaming that a tiger had crept into my room and was padding noiselessly toward my bed . . .

Suppose, now, that at just such a moment of terror you could somehow have entered my dream – just as you are, wide awake. "Wake up, Easwaran! There's no tiger. You're just dreaming, safe in your own bed."

Still asleep, I would think you were part of my dream. "What do you mean, there's no tiger? I can see it with my own eyes. I can smell it and feel its hot breath on my face. If you don't believe me, see how my pulse is racing. Feel my forehead; it's wet with the dew of fear.

My whole body is flooded with adrenaline for fight or flight – preferably flight! All the evidence of my senses tells me that tiger is real, and if you're not going to do anything to help me, you might as well not have come."

At that point, you might grab me by the shoulders and shake me awake. Only then would I look around and say sheepishly, "Oh, yes, it *was* a dream. My heart is still pounding, but I can see there never was a tiger at all."

We are used to calling dreams unreal, but that is not entirely accurate. How do we decide that the world of our senses is real? Dream experience can be full of sensory detail, and as far as the nervous system is concerned, those sensations are the same as those of waking life. We can see, feel, taste, smell, or hear things in a dream so vividly that the body actually responds with the chemistry of desire, anger, or fear. Even after we wake up, the illusion of reality may remain. And when nothing is left but the memory, how much difference is there between a waking experience and a dream?

"Dreams are real as long as they last," the psychologist Havelock Ellis once observed. "Can we say more of life?" It is a provocative question, and one which the mystics ask as well, but from a different perspective. When we wake up from a dream, they say, we do not pass from unreality to reality; we pass from a lower level of reality to a higher level. And, they add, there is a higher level still, compared with which this waking life of ours is as insubstantial as a dream.

To put it more bluntly, we are living in our sleep, dreaming that things like money and pleasure can make us happy. When they do not, it's a nightmare. When you read the Beatitudes, think of Jesus entering our dream world and showing us how we can wake up, just as from a dream, into a higher reality: the kingdom of heaven here on earth.

Yet until we do wake up, nothing sounds more absurd than the assertion that we are dreaming – and nothing seems more solid than this world of the senses. Why should this be so? If original goodness is our real nature, why are we unable to see it?

The mystics' answer is simple: because we see life not as it is but as we are. We see "through a glass darkly," through the distorting lenses of the mind – all the layers of feeling, habit, instinct, and memory that cover the pure core of goodness deep within.

To explain this, Christian mystics have drawn a comparison with a glass lantern clouded with oil and soot. To see the light, we have to clean the panes. In modern terms, the panes are the mind: the layers of consciousness that make up our personality.

As we might expect, Eckhart uses even more vigorous language. There are many of these layers, he says, each doing its part to hide from us who we really are:

A human being has so many skins inside, covering the depths of the heart. We know so many things, but we don't know ourselves! Why, thirty or forty skins or hides, as thick and hard as an ox's or a bear's, cover the soul. Go into your own ground and learn to know yourself there.

One of the easiest ways to understand how the mind itself distorts the way we see is to take a closer look at sensory perception. We like to think of sight, sound, touch, smell, and taste as direct encounters with the real world, but that is not really accurate. What we actually encounter are the images we form from the electrochemical data the senses supply to the brain. In other words, we see not so much with the eyes as with the mind, for it is the mind that arranges and interprets the information of the senses according to its own conditioning. "Hard" and "round," "red" and "green" are not qualities in the world outside; they are concepts. Even a kitchen table is a table only in the mind.

Today the "new physics" is a popular topic. Almost everyone is prepared to consider the proposal that physical objects are not necessarily what they seem. For example, the desk at which I am writing is not really solid; it appears solid because of the limitations of my instruments of observation. If human beings were sentient clouds of X-rays, we would not call a desk solid; we would be able to walk right through it. Lead would be solid, but wood would be part of the atmosphere. And if our eyes registered radio waves instead of what we call visible light, we would not see a desk at all. My study might look like a kind of beach, awash with the flotsam of rock music broadcasts and the evening news.

Similarly, there is no red carpet here beneath my feet, although I would attest confidently that there is – and so would you if you were here. There is an object which we agree to call "carpet," yet there is no redness in it; the redness is in my mind. To our black cat, Luther, who regards my study as his, everything would be what we humans call gray; or, more precisely, things would have no color at all. In Luther's feline world there might be no object "floor" as distinct from "carpet," only "warm space" and "unpleasantly cold." Color, and all the other qualities that make a thing what it is, depend on the particular modes of perception given us by our five senses.

Nothing in the external world, then, really is what we see. (We might press the point and say that we never really encounter the external world at all.) This is a sobering realization, so we can be glad that no one takes it too seriously. For matters of convenience, we all accept what we know to be a faulty position: that what we see is what is there, and that each of us sees the same world.

I want to make it clear that when the mystics talk about layers of consciousness, they are not talking theory. They are describing regions of experience so nearly palpable that each one has an almost optical effect on the way we see life. The world within has vast domains which, though we never consciously visit them, shape our perception, understanding, and behavior.

This is not a merely mystical notion. "Our normal, waking consciousness," says the brilliant American psychologist William James,

> rational consciousness as we call it, is but one special
> type of consciousness; whilst all about it, parted
> from it by the filmiest of screens, there lie potential
> forms of consciousness entirely different.

This is no mystic speaking; this is a hardheaded scientist, virtually the father of the pragmatic school of psychology, speaking from his own experience. While you are sitting there in your chair reading, he says, vast regions of personality lie open in the world within: the force fields of the unconscious, which shape our thought and action. "We may go through life without suspecting their existence," James continues,

> but apply the requisite stimulus, and at a touch they are there in all their completeness, definite types of mentality which probably somewhere have their field of application and adaptation. No account of the universe in its totality can be final which leaves these other forms of consciousness quite disregarded. How to regard them is the question, – for they are so discontinuous with ordinary consciousness. Yet they may determine attitudes although they cannot furnish formulas, and open a region though they fail to give a map. At any rate, they forbid a premature closing of our accounts with reality.

"How to regard them is the question": that is, how to see them, how to study and know and master them. That is the purpose of meditation. "Looking back on my own experiences" of these deeper states, James continues, "they all converge towards a kind of insight. . . . The keynote of it is invariably a reconciliation. It is as if the opposites of the world, whose contradictoriness and conflict make all our difficulties and troubles, were melted into unity."

Contemporary physicists sometimes say that instead

of the observable universe of classical physics, they have to deal with a "participatory universe" in which, at least on a subatomic level, the act of observation participates in the result. The mystics say something similar but even farther reaching: each of us lives in a truly participatory universe of his or her own making.

This is difficult to grasp. We can accept that the senses, although useful, do not report life as it really is; but to be told that the mind, too, while useful, is a distorting medium – that is more than most of us will buy. At least where the senses are concerned, we are generally in agreement: this desk is solid, whatever physicists may say. But where the mind is concerned, consensus is out. All of us have our own individual perceptions.

To begin with, it is our mental apparatus – our feelings, memories, and desires – that selects what we even perceive. Out of the vast confusion of data that our senses present, it is the mind that decides what registers. Anything that fails to fit our interests or understanding is not introduced to our attention. What we see – and therefore the world we live in, our world as opposed to others' – is a function of our own thinking.

Have you ever had the experience of hearing one acquaintance described by another and wondering to yourself, "Is that really the same man?" Or perhaps you and a friend stray for the first time onto sensitive ground, some question of politics or race or religion, and you think, "I've never really seen that person before!" And in matters of the heart, everyone knows how infatuation can fool us, though at the time that is how we actually see. While the flames of desire are high, ask a Romeo to describe his Juliet. "So gentle, so thoughtful, always ready with something nice to say." Ask him again when the relationship is over; you may think he is talking about a different person.

More accurately, he is a different person. That is why his perceptions have changed. "I just didn't see clearly then," he would say. "Now I know what she's really like." But that is neither true nor fair. Before, Romeo saw Juliet with the eyes of desire; now, that desire is gone and he sees different things. Both perceptions have truth in them and falsehood, and neither view is whole. What we see is a function of what we desire.

It is in the mind that we experience life, and the mind is never really clear. You know that when your mind is angry, its findings are not reliable; you see things differently when it quiets down. When your mind is afraid, its view is faulty; you find things to be afraid of everywhere. And when your mind is surging with a strong desire, you see everything in terms of satisfying that desire – which raises a big question mark over anything the mind tells you to do.

And below these relatively superficial levels, beneath the emotions we are ordinarily aware of, lie layer on layer of the unconscious mind. These are the depths an unknown fourteenth-century mystic called vividly the "cloud of unknowing," where primordial instincts, fears, and urges cover our understanding so that we see nothing except ourselves.

The deepest flaw in the mind is what Einstein called

the "kind of optical delusion of consciousness" that makes us see ourselves as separate from the rest of life. In my interpretation of the metaphor of Eden in the previous chapter, this fundamental fracture in consciousness is the I-sense, the Big Bang that triggers our Fall into separateness. Like a crack in glasses that we must wear every moment of our lives, this division is built into the mind. "I" versus "not-I" runs through everything we see.

Imagine if some genius invented a set of binoculars with conflicting lenses, so that each eye saw things differently from the other. It would confuse you completely. You would go after something or someone and trip over things you did not even see, then get up wondering why you fell. "Why is life so unfair?" Isn't that how it is? In the same way, the mystics say, we are looking at the world – all of us – through two conflicting lenses at the same time, one of which sees only "I, I, I" and the other "Not me! Not mine!" In practical terms, it means we see life divided in every way: my needs as opposed to yours, my family as opposed to yours; my country and not yours, my race, my religion . . . "I am right, so you must be wrong"; "What I like is good, so what I don't like must be bad": the refrain goes on and on.

To see life as it is, all these refracting influences have to be removed so that consciousness is pure and clear. "If the doors of perception were cleansed," as Blake said in famous lines, "everything would be seen as it is, infinite."

Blessed are the pure in heart, for they shall see God. Jesus is not being rhetorical. He is describing in simple language what the realization of God means. When the distorting instrument of the mind is made clear, we see life not as a collection of fragments but as a seamless whole. We see the divine spark at the center of our very being; and we see simultaneously that in the heart of every other human being – in every country, of every race – though hidden perhaps by clouds of ignorance and conditioning, that same spark is present, one and the same in all. The Flemish mystic Ruysbroeck explains:

> The image of God is found *essentially* and *personally* in all. Each of us possesses it whole, entire and undivided, and all of us together [do] not [possess it] more than one person does alone. In this way we are all one, intimately united in our eternal image, which is the image of God.

Blake's words about the "doors of perception," of course, are familiar to us today largely because of Huxley's experiments with mescaline, which encouraged so many young people to play with hallucinogens in the sixties. Today, almost a generation later, I think most thoughtful people understand that drugs never "cleanse" the senses; they only cloud the mind, adding one level of unreality over another. It is the mind that must be made pure, and that means that everything that distorts it must be quieted or removed.

In mysticism the mind is often compared to a lake, whose waters become clouded with mud when the lake is agitated. Only when the murk of our thoughts, desires, and passions settles does the mind become calm and clear. When the mind is completely still, the mystics say, unstirred even in its depths, we see straight through to the ground of our being, which is divine. On this, the mystics of all religions are in agreement. "Be still," says the Lord, "and know that I am God." And the Upanishads, the purest source of the Perennial Philosophy in the world, add:

> When the five senses are stilled, when the mind is stilled, when the intellect is stilled, that is called the highest state by the wise. They say yoga is this complete stillness in which one enters the unitive state, never to become separate again.

When we finally wake up from this long, lurid dream of separate existence, the mystics tell us, we will just rub our eyes; we will not believe how we used to see. The illusion of separateness will be gone, and we will see life as one indivisible whole: men, women, and children, "the beasts of the field and the birds of the air," all the created universe. This is not just intellectual knowledge or poetic vision. The vision of unity transforms our lives from the inside out. In that moment of transcendental insight, says Ruysbroeck,

> we are wrought and transformed . . . and as the air is penetrated by the sun, thus we receive in quietude of spirit the Incomprehensible Light, enfolding us and penetrating us. And this Light is nothing else but an infinite gazing and seeing. We behold that which we

are, and we are that which we behold; because our thought, life and being are uplifted in simplicity and made one with the Truth which is God.

"We behold that which we are, and we are that which we behold." Perfect words. "As a man is, so he sees," Blake once wrote to a critic:

I see everything I paint in this world, but everybody does not see alike. To the eye of a miser a guinea is far more beautiful than the sun, and a bag worn with the use of money has more beautiful proportions than a vine filled with grapes. The tree which moves some to tears of joy is in the eyes of others only a green thing which stands in the way. . . . But to the eyes of the man of imagination, Nature is Imagination itself.

Similarly, to the eyes of the man or woman of God, nature is God himself. So Angela of Foligno, a Franciscan just one generation after Francis and a contemporary of Eckhart's, exclaims in one of the most quoted passages in Christian mysticism:

The eyes of my soul were opened, and I beheld the plenitude of God, wherein I did comprehend the whole world, both here and beyond the sea, and the abyss and ocean and all things. In all these things I beheld naught save the divine power, in a manner assuredly indescribable; so that through excess of marveling the soul cried with a loud voice, saying "This whole world is full of God!"

Sometimes this revelation comes in one swift, wordless opening into eternity, as happened to Julian of Norwich:

> . . . he showed me a little thing, the quality of an
> hazel-nut in the palm of my hand; and it was round
> as a ball. I looked thereupon with the eye of my
> understanding, and thought: What may this be? And
> it was answered generally thus: It is all that
> is made. And I marveled how it might last, for
> methought it might suddenly have fallen to naught
> for littleness. And I was answered in my understand-
> ing: It lasteth and ever shall last, for that God loveth
> it. And so All-Thing hath Being by the love of God.

Or it may come less dramatically, though with equal authority, in a quiet moment of insight that transforms one's life completely – as happened at the age of eighteen to Brother Lawrence, a simple lay brother of the Carmelite order in seventeenth-century France. An anonymous chronicler describes Brother Lawrence's experience:

> In the winter, seeing a tree stripped of its leaves, and
> considering that within a little time the leaves would
> be renewed, and after that the flowers and fruit
> appear, he received a high view of the providence
> and power of God which has never since been effaced
> from his soul. . . . This view had set him perfectly
> loose from the world and kindled in him such a love
> for God that he could not tell whether it had
> increased in the more than forty years that he had
> lived since.

Can we expect, then, to spend Friday afternoons in the park gazing at hydrangeas and one day walk home full of wisdom? Probably not. Insights of this order do not really come as a bolt out of the blue. The unitive visions of Angela, Julian, and Brother Lawrence must have been prepared for deep within their hearts, surging to the surface when the time was ripe for the veil to be torn away. In traditional language, they had already made themselves pure in heart. How many young men had passed that same stripped tree and seen nothing but bare branches? But within the one particular teenager who would become Brother Lawrence, a realization was stirring to life; the tree was merely a catalyst.

"If your heart were sincere and upright," says Thomas a Kempis, "every creature would be unto you a looking-glass of life and a book of holy doctrine." The pure in spirit, who see God, see him here and now: in his handiwork, his hidden purpose, the wry humor of his creation. "Heaven lies about us in our infancy," wrote Wordsworth, and in that sense the mystic is always a child.

The Lord has left us love notes, wondrous *billets-doux*, scattered extravagantly across creation. Hidden in the eye of the tiger, the wet muzzle of a calf, the delicacy of the violet, and the perfect curve of the elephant's tusk is a very personal, priceless message: "God is love, and he who abides in love abides in God, and God in him."

Watch the lamb in awkward play, butting against its mother's side. See the spider putting the final shimmering touches on an architectural wonder. And absorb a truth that is wordless. The grace of a deer, the soaring freedom of a sparrow hawk in flight, the utter self-possession of an elephant crashing through the woods – in every one of these there is something of ourselves. From the great whales to the tiniest of tree frogs in the Amazon basin, unity embraces us all. Lose sight of this unity, allow these creatures to be exploited or destroyed, and we are diminished too.

꘠

Friends often tell me, "But I can't make myself pure! I have very negative thoughts. A person like you wouldn't understand just how negative!" I assure them that indeed I do understand. How many are born pure in heart? Yet in all the major religions, superb teachers have given clear instructions in how to make our minds pure so that divinity can shine forth: how to transform our personality from self-centered to selfless, from unconcerned to caring, eventually even from human to divine.

Intellectual study cannot be of much help in this transformation. Only meditation, the systematic turning inward of attention, can take us deep into consciousness where the obstacles to a pure heart hide.

From this point of view, meditation can be described as nothing more or less than the purification of consciousness, by removing everything that obstructs our vision of the divine core in others and in ourselves. This process is described in a remarkable mystical document of thirteenth-century Europe called *Cleaving to*

God, attributed to a great predecessor of Eckhart's known as Albertus Magnus:

> We must cast out of our minds the impressions and images and forms of all things which are not God so that we may look upon God within our own soul; for the soul is more intimately and more closely present to each thing than each thing is to itself. When we enter deeply into ourselves, the eye of inner vision is opened and a ladder is prepared by which the soul may ascend to the contemplation of God.

For myself, however, I prefer a more positive way to explain how meditation works: not as trying to "empty the mind," which is misleading, but as trying to *still* the mind, by bringing all its turbulent activity to acute focus on a single point.

In meditation, when you go through an inspirational passage such as the Prayer of Saint Francis with complete attention, each significant word or phrase drops like a jewel into the depths of consciousness. With each sentence you are absorbing the loftiest image of human nature. When your absorption in the passage is complete, nothing else will remain in your consciousness. Saint Francis's ideals will gradually displace all negative thoughts, so that little by little, divinity begins to shine through. Your mind is empty of yourself, true; but that is also to say it is full of God.

This may sound simple, but it is far from easy. Ask the mystics themselves: they will tell you how hard it is to get deep beneath the surface of the mind and remove everything that is not in harmony with the core of divinity within. The miracle is that it can be done at all. In spite of how the horizons of knowledge keep expanding, the one thing almost no one even suspects today is that it is actually possible, with a good deal of effort, to penetrate the depths of the unconscious mind and bring about the kind of unifying changes which will make a new person of us. This is the best-kept secret of the ages: that any one of us can become the kind of person he or she dreams of becoming.

Meister Eckhart calls this process "the pauper becoming the prince." Of which kingdom? The most important in the world: the realm of our own thoughts, over which very, very few of us can claim to have authority. This sovereignty confers real power, much more significant than the might of kings; for everything of value comes from the way we think. That is the power that meditation can put into our hands.

"I have not the slightest doubt," Mahatma Gandhi said, "that prayer is an unfailing means of cleansing the heart of passions." The same is true of meditation. Gandhi was a lawyer, you know, and very finicky about his words. He never put anything into print that was not true in his own experience. "But," he adds, "it must combine with the utmost humility. Prayer is an impossibility without a living faith in the presence of God within" – that is, without faith in the core of goodness in others and in ourselves. We have to be patient with ourselves, Gandhi is reminding us, and not demand miracles overnight. Always keep in mind that this center of purity is there, however unlikely that may seem, and keep on trying to uncover it. Whether the results are seen by us or not, every bit of effort helps.

I want to repeat: even some of the greatest of spiritual figures had a lot of work to do to make their consciousness pure enough for divinity to shine through. When someone treats you unfairly or unkindly, it is only natural for your mind to be flooded with resentment; everybody's mind works that way. But the day can come when you scarcely remember what resentment means. It is not that you will be blind to others' behavior, but that negative responses will not even arise in your mind; and when negative thoughts do not arise, you respond to every situation with love. This is what it means to be "pure in heart." No one should expect total freedom from negative emotions, but this innocence of heart is something we can aim at every day.

Besides meditation, there is another powerful tool for purifying consciousness that can be used at almost any time during the day. Meditation is a demanding discipline, but even children can learn to use what in Sanskrit is called the *mantram.*

The mantram, or Holy Name, is a short, potent spiritual formula for the highest that we can conceive, and it is found in the annals of every major religion. According to tradition, the earliest Christian communities used some form of the Prayer of Jesus – simply the name of Jesus, or a variation like *Lord, Jesus Christ, Son of God, have mercy* – in precisely the same way as Mahatma

Gandhi repeated *Rama, Rama,* or as Jewish mystics have repeated the Shema or *Ribono shel olam,* "Lord of the universe."

You will find full instructions for using the mantram in my little book *The Unstruck Bell,* but briefly, the mantram can be repeated silently in your mind whenever your mind is running off at the mouth – which for all of us is likely to be much more often than we suspect. Instead of worrying, fussing, fretting, fuming, steaming, simmering, daydreaming, or woolgathering, repeat the mantram. Nothing will be lost, and you will find that every repetition helps to steady your mind and sharpen your appreciation of life around you.

I wish I could share with every person in this country what repeating the name of the Lord can do. It "restoreth the soul," in David's beautiful phrase, as you will see for yourself if you give it a try. It brings energy, security, and self-confidence, and, especially in the turmoil of the teen years, there is probably no skill of greater value.

The Lord's Prayer begins, "hallowed be thy name." How do we hallow the name of the Lord? By driving it deep into the mind until it becomes a kind of channel into deepest consciousness, through which we can draw increasing reserves of patience, love, insight, and understanding.

This does require determination, I admit. I used to hunt through my days for opportunities to repeat the Holy Name, scavenging leisure moments like those curious characters who dowse for buried treasures at the beach, scanning every inch of sand with a metal detector at the end of a long wand. It calls for a great deal of patience, but the effort pays off. Today, because of all that effort, I no longer have to make myself repeat the Holy Name. It repeats itself, warding off every negative state of mind.

From the *Cloud of Unknowing,* written by an anonymous English mystic in the second half of the fourteenth century, comes one of the most stirring pieces of instruction I have seen on the protective power of the Holy Name:

> And if thou desirest to have this intent lapped and folden in one word, so that thou mayest have better hold thereupon, take thee but a little word. . . . The word shall be thy shield and thy spear, whether thou ridest on peace or on war. With this word thou shalt beat on this cloud and this darkness above thee. With this word thou shalt smite down all manner of thought under the cloud of forgetting. Insomuch that, if any thought press upon thee to ask what thou wouldst have, answer with no more words than with this one word. . . . And if thou wilt hold fast to this purpose, be sure that that thought will no while bide.

Translate that into contemporary terms and you will understand why the mantram is so effective in dealing with addictive habits and compulsive behavior. Whenever the mind starts to clamor for something you do not approve, this unknown mystic says, repeat the mantram. When your attention gets hold of the mantram, it is off the compulsion; then you are free again to think and act as you choose.

Again, in modern terms, this "cloud of unknowing" is the unconscious. When the Holy Name is established in these depths, it brings choice and the will into areas ordinarily beyond human reach. Eventually the mantram will be constantly on alert. It will hide behind the bushes of your mind like a highway patrol cruiser, waiting to nab any speeding thoughts and intoxicated desires that start weaving out onto the road. Even at night, in your dreams, the mantram will block unsavory thoughts that are trying to sneak in unnoticed. This vigilance is what Brother Lawrence called "practicing the presence of God." Those who are established in this presence, Eckhart said, carry God with them wherever they go.

Like meditation, repetition of the Holy Name can be thought of as a way of communicating with the Lord within. But it is much less formal. Meditation is something you do at a certain time and place every day, always following the instructions carefully. But you can repeat the mantram at almost any time, whenever your mind is agitated or idle.

༄

It must be admitted that the active life and the contemplative life do appear at times to exclude one another. But on the other hand, we have the assurance and the example of deeply committed men and women of God that the two actually require each other. Meister Eckhart says explicitly, "What a man takes in by contemplation, that he pours out in love."

Saint Teresa of Avila and Saint John of the Cross, two of the greatest figures in world mysticism, carried on a kind of lover's quarrel on this point for many years. Teresa, a master of interior prayer and a brilliantly practical teacher, was also one of the world's greatest activists, constantly harassed by difficulties in founding and strengthening the convents of her Sisters of Carmel. And John was a born contemplative whose deeply interior life scarcely touched the earth except when he paused to set down some of the most lyrical poems in Spanish literature. As Teresa's confessor, he kept urging her to conserve her strength and indulge her genius for meditation, leaving to others the business of household accounts and quarrels within her convents. Yet how could she not stir herself when there was work to do, and when she felt the call was coming from her Lord himself? So the tender wrangling went on, up until her last days.

After Teresa slipped from this world, it astonished those close to her to see John, devoted until then to a life of seclusion and prayer, throwing himself heart and soul into the work she had had to leave. Yet there were some who saw no contradiction; as Ruysbroeck had pointed out two centuries before, "love would ever be active: for its nature is eternal working with God." The love released in the unitive vision fuses contemplation and action, meditation and selfless service:

[God] demands of us both action and fruition, in such a way that the action never hinders the fruition, nor the fruition the action, but they strengthen one another. . . . [Thus such a person] dwells in God; and yet he goes out towards all creatures, in a spirit of love towards all things, in virtue and in works of righteousness. And this is the supreme summit of the inner life.

↬

If we were "inwardly good and pure," says Thomas a Kempis, we would be able to "see and understand all things well without impediment." When the heart is pure, nothing stands between ourselves and God within.

When I began teaching English, at a college in Central India, I had many Muslim students in my class. The young men sat on one side of the room, and the girls, hidden behind veils, sat on the other. The boys I could see, of course – their high foreheads, aquiline noses, and determined chins, characteristic of the old Muslim families of that area. But the girls' faces I could not see at all. How was I to tell whether my learned orations on Othello and Hamlet made any sense behind those veils? For an enthusiastic new teacher, it was a frustrating situation.

I went to my Muslim colleagues on the staff. "What do you do?" I asked. "I can't see the girls' faces, so I can't tell if I'm getting through to them."

My friends smiled. "We're used to it," one of them said, "so we've learned to sharpen our eyes. To us, the veil is not nearly so concealing as it seems. Focus your attention and you'll find you can see much more than you think."

He gave me some pointers, and with practice I found that I could catch the rustle of silk that hid a smile, tell from which young lady a particular giggle was coming. Before long I felt completely at home.

Against this kind of background, the mystics of Islam describe God as hidden by seven veils, each a particular layer of consciousness. As meditation deepens, we begin to see through these veils more and more clearly. The dazzling diversity at the surface of life gradually loses its power to distract and confuse us. Finally, in the tremendous climax of meditation which Indian mysticism calls *samadhi,* we actually pierce the veil of multiplicity and change. Then we see, at the very heart of existence, a reality that abides: "uncreated and uncreatable . . . which neither space nor time touches."

This kind of intense concentration is always required to see order and meaning in the world around us. Scientists find laws in the apparent confusion of sense experience in very much the same way. From the outset they operate on the firm faith that a meaningful pattern does exist, and that faith focuses their attention and their training. With unified vision they seize upon patterns that hold true against all tests.

The mystics too are certain that life makes sense. They too set out, as the British biologist Sir Peter

Medawar puts it, fired with the "rage to know." Nothing will do until they have penetrated the unity they know must lie at the heart of life. And when they begin to understand what the Sufis say — "You yourself are the veil that stands between you and God" — there arises a burning desire to get everything petty and selfish in that small self out of the way. But we start out, as a scientist does, with that first provisional faith that meaning is there to be found. "This is the reason," Augustine says, "that we trust what we are to believe before we see it: that by believing we may purify the heart, whereby we may be able to see."

But what actually focuses our vision? In a word, desire: the ardent passion to see and understand. What we are asked to do is just what Jesus and Moses emphasized in ringing words: "Thou shalt love thy God with all thy heart and with all thy soul." Then we shall see him: not with our eyes, Eckhart says, "as one sees a cow," but as a living presence in every creature.

No one begins like this. We start out with a lot of desires for many things, and when we hear Jesus' injunction, the reply that our lives give is, "Of course, Lord! There are some attachments to other things — my sauna, my van, my new sound system and Nautilus machine. But whatever love is left after that, I'll gladly give to you." And the Lord says patiently, "Why don't you keep that too? I'm prepared to wait."

Blessed are the pure in heart. We are used to thinking of purity in terms of cleansing, but in practice this unification of desires is the key. "Purity of heart," says Kierkegaard, "is to will one thing." As meditation deepens, the desire to go even deeper slowly absorbs all kinds of lesser desires. Activities that are less important to us begin to fall away. But those desires do not really disappear. Their power is simply drawn up into a deeper current, the longing of the soul for fulfillment.

Hidden inside, all of us carry a purifying fire. It may be banked with ashes that seem cold to the touch, but a spark of the divine is there nonetheless, ready to leap into life. This "hidden fire," as William Law called it, is nothing less than love of God. It is latent in every one of us, even the most jaded, the most disillusioned, the most embittered, because that spark is the one part of us that we can never lose. It wants surprisingly little encouragement to flare into vibrant life and shed light and warmth all around.

The rest of the Beatitudes tell us how this is to be done.

CHAPTER 3
Humility

Blessed are the poor in spirit, for theirs is the kingdom of heaven.

When I first came to this country, I was invited to give a series of talks on meditation and mysticism in San Francisco. I was interested to find several confirmed beatniks in my audience. They didn't think much of traditional religious language, and they didn't like mincing words; when they disagreed with me, they said so straight. One evening, without intending to, I shocked them by quoting a passage referring to heaven and hell.

"You're such an educated, cultured person," a friend objected afterward in dismay. "How can you believe in these medieval ideas?"

"To tell the truth," I answered, "I don't really think they're medieval. I have seen quite a few people actually living in hell – and one or two in heaven." Whenever we get swept away by a selfish urge or a wave of anger, we are in hell; we can almost feel the sulfurous fumes of insecurity and fear. If we get so angry that we can't sleep, we are overnight guests in hell's hotel.

"Well, that's different," my friend replied in relief. "Now you're just being metaphorical. I thought you really believed it."

"Hell is no metaphor," I said, "and neither is heaven. Hell and heaven are states of consciousness. Doesn't Jesus say the kingdom of heaven is within? And mental states are real — in fact, in some ways they are even more 'thingy' than things. If I were to throw this pen at you, you might get a little bruise. But if I said something unkind and you couldn't stop thinking about it, your resentment might burn for years. It might even aggravate your ulcer."

"I thought you were talking about sin," he said a little grumpily. "I just don't hold with those old ideas about sin and punishment."

"I don't usually talk about sin," I admitted: "not because it's not real, but because when you go on saying 'I'm a sinner, I'm a sinner,' you're actually thinking of yourself as a sinner. You expect yourself to do wrong things, so you're that much more likely to go on doing them. I like to emphasize original goodness: 'I'm a saint, I'm a saint – potentially.'

"But," I added, "my real objection to those 'old ideas' is that they make it sound as if punishment is heaped on our heads by some wrathful God outside us. Heaven and hell are inside. We don't have to have somebody punish us for doing wrong; we punish ourselves. Sin is its own punishment."

This approach appeals to me deeply, and since those

early days I have found that it makes good sense to a modern audience too. It is not really a new idea – Christian writers since the Desert Fathers have spoken clearly of these things, and no one is more precise on the subject than the Buddha. But today it appeals to our scientific temper. We do not have to be punished for getting angry, for example; anger is its own punishment. The next time someone flies into a rage before you, watch objectively and you will see what it does to the body, pumping up blood pressure, flooding vital organs and tissues with adrenaline, and subjecting the body to all kinds of physiologic stress. When I see someone getting angry, I think to myself, "That's a thousandth of a heart attack!" These things add up, and people have actually died of a cardiovascular accident brought on by the thousandth burst of rage.

More subtly, dwelling on yourself is its own punishment. All of us find ourselves a fascinating, satisfying subject to contemplate . . . until the results begin to accumulate. The effects are easier to see with someone else: the person who thinks about himself all the time, who can scarcely think about anything except in connection with his own needs, becomes the most wretched creature on earth. Nothing really goes the way he wants, and that preoccupation with himself that seemed so pleasant and natural becomes a wall that keeps everyone else outside. It's a lonely, tormented life. Perhaps the most painful irony is that this wretchedness too is just dwelling on oneself. Once the habit is formed, the mind cannot stop, even when it makes us miserable.

Here spiritual psychology cuts to the heart of the matter in one incisive stroke. All these habits of mind that can make life hell, the mystics say, can be traced to one central flaw of attention. To call it self-preoccupation comes close: the habit of dwelling on my needs, my desires, my plans, my fears. The more deeply ingrained this pattern of thinking is, the mystics say, the more we make ourselves a little island isolated from the rest of life, with all the unhappiness that has to follow. This is not a moral judgment; it is simply the way happiness works. Asking life to make a selfish person happy, my grandmother used to say, is like asking a banana tree to give you mangoes.

But there is a better word for this habit of mind: self-will, the insistent drive to have our own way, to get what we want, whatever it may cost. Self-will has a million forms, but every one of them is a kind of torment. Whenever we feel life is being unfair to us, whenever we hurt because people are not treating us right or paying us attention or giving us our due respect, nine times out of ten what is hurting is our self-will. An anonymous mystical document known as the *Theologica Germanica* says succinctly, "Nothing burns in hell except self-will." No God has to punish us for being self-willed; self-will is its own punishment, its own hell.

"Blessed are the poor in spirit, for theirs is the kingdom of heaven." The meaning of the Biblical phrase here is not "poor-spirited." It is just the opposite of being full of ourselves — that is, just the opposite of being full of self-will. When we are in the grips of self-will, life cannot help stepping on our toes, and we cannot help being thrown into turmoil when things do not go our way. On the other hand, in those moments when we forget ourselves – not thinking "Am I happy? Am I having fun yet?" but completely oblivious to our little ego – we spend a brief but beautiful holiday in heaven.

The mystics tell us that the joy we experience in these moments of self-forgetting is our true nature, our native state. To regain it, we have simply to empty ourselves of what hides this joy: that is, to stop dwelling on ourselves. To the extent that we are not full of ourselves, God can fill us – in fact, the mystics say daringly, he has to. "When we thus clear the ground and make our soul ready," says John Tauler, a pupil of Eckhart's and a brilliant mystic in his own right,

> without doubt God must fill up the void.... If you go out of yourself, without doubt he shall go in, and there will be much or little of his entering in according to how much or little you go out.

And Eckhart adds, in his wonderfully pungent way: "God expects but one thing of you, and that is that you should come out of yourself in so far as you are a created being and let God be God in you."

How far modern civilization has gone to the other extreme! Self-will has always been human nature, but today it is almost worshipped in some circles. Unselfishness is considered old-fashioned and unnatural, and to be happy, some professional psychologists say, we have to learn to assert ourselves, attend to our personal needs first, "look out for number one."

To be sure, there are reasons for these extreme positions. People think that being unselfish is boring, that a selfless person cannot possibly enjoy life because he is constantly making himself a doormat, that to have a high sense of worth you have to have a big ego. These are just misunderstandings, but the observation remains true: our age sets a premium on self-will in aggressiveness, competitiveness, and self-aggrandizement; that, we are told, is the route to joy.

Yet to live as a separate creature, cut off from the rest of life, is just the opposite of joy. The Persian mystic Jalaluddin Rumi summed up the spiritual quest in one quiet sentence: "Pilgrimage to the place of the wise is to find escape from the flame of separateness." Ultimately, self-will becomes a solid wall that keeps others out and ourselves walled in. Imagine trying to walk around the Great Wall of China, fourteen hundred miles of meandering masonry clinging to every hill and valley as far as the eye can see. That is what trying to get around self-will is like. When we feel intense anguish in a personal relationship, more often than not what pains us is not differences of politics or taste; it is just self-will in another of its disguises, hurting because it cannot have its way.

I like to think of self-will as love turned around. Love is energy, and self-will is that energy focused on oneself. We can learn to free that energy, and when we do, our lives will fill with love – which is what living in heaven means.

In today's competitive climate, often those who are aggressive about imposing their will on others are labeled "successful." But the accomplishments of such people are often sadly short-lived, while the damage they do themselves and others can be far-reaching. When self-will is excessive, we end up offending others, feeling offended, and lashing back, and that undoes everything worthwhile we might achieve.

People with little self-will, on the other hand, seldom get upset when life goes against them. They do not try to impose their way on others, or get agitated or depressed or defensive when people hold different views. Being intolerant of other views, Mahatma Gandhi used to say, is a sign that we don't have enough faith in our own. To get agitated and angry when opposed shows a certain insecurity. If we really believe what we believe, we will not be shaken when someone challenges it.

Gandhi was an excellent example of this. It is said that he was at his best when he was criticized; it made him even more respectful and compassionate, and made him reach deeper into himself to find new ways of answering. I try to practice that in all kinds of little ways. Every day, for example, I look at a very influential newspaper whose editorial viewpoint contradicts everything I stand for. And I enjoy it: the writing is often excellent, and the differences in perspective help me to understand opinions I would otherwise never hear. I can give full attention to opposite opinions, and learn from them, because my faith in spiritual values is un-shakable.

The reason for this, of course, is that these are not just my values. They are timeless, and my faith in them comes from many centuries of experience. If somebody challenges what I say about heaven being within, I don't get upset. It is Jesus who said it, and he is quite capable of defending his words himself.

Many years ago, I had a friend from Chicago who came to hear my talks in Berkeley every week. When he was about to return to Chicago he came up to say good-bye. "I've really enjoyed your talks," he told me. "And I like your sense of humor. But you know, I still don't believe a word of what you say."

I laughed and wished him well. Nobody likes to hear about self-will.

About twelve years later that fellow showed up again, looking much more than twelve years older. There were tears in his eyes when he came up to me and said, "Every word you say is true."

I comforted him by saying, "They are not really my words. They are the words of the great spiritual teachers in all religions, who have verified them over and over in their own lives. It takes most of us a certain amount of suffering to learn that they are true."

Even those who profess no religion can come to these same conclusions. Here is an outburst from one of my favorites in my college days, George Bernard Shaw:

This is the true joy in life, the being used for a pur-pose recognized by yourself as a mighty one; the being thoroughly worn out before you are thrown on the scrap heap; the being a force of nature instead of a feverish selfish little clod of ailments and grievances complaining that the world will not devote itself to making you happy.

But security means much, much more than confidence in one's views. It pays richly in personal relationships. People with little self-will are so tremendously secure that they do not rely on other people to satisfy their needs. They will never try to manipulate you, and they are free to be loyal always. They will stand by you through thick and thin; you know you can count on them, no matter what the situation.

This kind of confidence is the very basis of love. Without this foundation, every relationship is apt to wane. You may honestly believe that this particular friendship is forever; this is what you have always been looking for. But whatever you want to believe, the nature of the mind is to change, and the more self-willed your mind is, the more likely it is to change its tune when things do not work out just right. Somebody once came to my talk on meditation and told me afterward, "This is what I have been looking for all my life!" She must have gone home and thought about it, because I am still looking for her.

↩

All of us have tasted the freedom and happiness that self-forgetfulness brings, although we may not have known it at the time. In watching a good game of tennis or becoming engrossed in a novel, for example, the satisfaction comes not so much from what we are watching or reading as from the act of absorption itself. For that brief span, our burden of personal thoughts, worries, and conflicts is forgotten; and then we find relief, for what lies beneath that burden is the still, clear state of awareness we call joy. The scientist doing concentrated research, the artist absorbed in creative work, is happy because she has forgotten herself in what she is doing. Einstein had this genius for absorption in surprising measure.

But nowhere will you find personalities so joyous, so unabashedly lighthearted, as with those who have lost themselves in love for all. That is the universal appeal of Saint Francis of Assisi, the perfect image of his Master. In our own time, many millions have glimpsed this kind of joy in the film footage of Mother Teresa. To look into the eyes of men and women like these is to see what joy means.

After centuries of civilization, you would think we would have discovered that there is only one way to be completely happy, and that is to forget ourselves in working for others. It's a perplexing paradox: so long as we try to make ourselves happy, life places obstacles in our path. But the moment we turn away from ourselves to make others happy, our troubles melt away. Then we don't have to go looking for joy; joy comes looking for us.

In any age you will find a few men and women who have this marvelous gift of self-forgetfulness. In our own century there is the luminous figure of Gandhi, whom I met and walked with as a college student when I visited his ashram at Sevagram. The experience had a tremendous impact on my life. Gandhi had spent the day in meetings with political leaders who came to him for guidance in matters that affected the lives of four hundred million people; I expected to see him emerge in the evening tired and burdened. I could scarcely believe my eyes when the door swung open and Gandhi burst through, radiant and vital, joking as if he had been relaxing all day. When the time came for his evening walk, most of us had to run to keep up with this diminutive, frail-looking giant who carried the burdens of a continent with effortless grace.

It was in the evening prayer meeting that I began to understand his secret. Gandhi was seated in his usual place beneath a tree, and as the tropical sun disappeared, men and women around him took turns reciting prayers or singing hymns from different religious faiths. The atmosphere was charged. Although Gandhi neither spoke nor moved, I could not take my eyes off him as his secretary, Mahadev Desai, began to recite his favorite verses from the Bhagavad Gita, which begin:

> He lives in wisdom
> Who sees himself in all and all in him,
> Whose love for the Lord of Love has consumed
> Every selfish desire and sense craving
> Tormenting the heart. . . .

Gandhi's eyes closed in meditation, and he slipped into such deep absorption that he scarcely seemed to breathe. Suddenly I understood what I was seeing: he had forgotten himself completely in those words, which embodied the ideals of his life, and in that absorption all the burdens a person might carry in such work were lifted from his shoulders as if by the Lord himself. It was a complete renewal.

Gandhi did not try to conceal his secret. "I am trying to reduce myself to zero," he said again and again; and in making himself zero, his love expanded to embrace the world. "My life is an indivisible whole, and all my activities run into one another; and they all have their rise in my insatiable love of mankind."

Remember Tauler's words: when we get ourselves out of the way, "God must fill up the void" – and the less there is of ourselves, the more he can pour in. For most of us, the idea of making ourselves zero sounds unattractive until we actually see someone like Gandhi. Then it is abundantly clear that this is not lack of personality but its fulfillment in joy.

These are secrets which the practice of meditation can slowly reveal to us. As we penetrate the layers of self-willed conditioning in our own consciousness and begin to see the divinity within, we see beneath these layers in everybody else as well. Then we realize that our own deepest needs – for love, harmony, meaning, peace of mind – are their needs too. The welfare of family and community and planet becomes more important to us than our own, for in it our own welfare is included. All this leaves very little time to think about ourselves, and that is the secret of happiness.

It is from this kind of giving that joy comes: not

from having a lot of desires that must be satisfied, but from reducing personal desires to free time and energy for helping those around us. If I may illustrate with my own small example, I have enjoyed all the satisfactions that a person in India could have. I come from an ancient and very loving family and benefited from a good education, which gave me the best in both Indian and Western culture. As a university professor, sharing with young people my love of literature, and as a writer and public speaker, I achieved success in the fields I loved most. By Indian standards, I had everything one could desire. So I speak with an authentic voice when I say that today, when my personal desires are zero, the joy and love that I enjoy are, to quote the Upanishads, a million times what they were then. Every day my life is a million times richer.

All of us, when we hear talk like this, whisper in a quiet corner of our hearts, "Give up all personal desires? Can't I keep one or two of my favorites and settle for just five hundred times more joy?" This is a reasonable question. It takes many years of meditation to see that no matter how pleasant it may seem to indulge ourselves, every selfish craving is a thirst that cannot be quenched, a hunger that gnaws relentlessly at our peace of mind.

Once we grasp this deep in consciousness, there surges in our heart an even more powerful force: the desire to go against all selfish desires, to be free from cravings once and for all. Every step we take toward this goal brings such a sense of relief that today, one of my few personal prayers is to ask my Lord, "Never let me fall into the snare of selfish desires again!" I want every one of my desires to be for the welfare of all; that is what gives my life joy and meaning and fills my heart with love.

In the end, the goal of all spiritual seeking is to live in this state of self-forgetfulness permanently. This continuous awareness of God is to be achieved not after death, but here and now; that is what brings heaven on earth.

The Buddha uses the much-misunderstood word *nirvana* to describe this simple miracle. *Nir* means "out"; *vana,* "to blow": attaining nirvana means blowing out the burning flame of self-will, making ourselves poor in selfhood so as to be rich in God. But this is not just an idea from the mysterious East. Here is Saint Teresa of Avila on that state:

> While the mind is separated from itself, and while it is borne away into the secret place of the divine mystery and is surrounded on all sides by the fire of divine love, it is inwardly penetrated and inflamed by this fire, and utterly puts off itself and puts on a divine love. Thus conformed to the beauty it has beheld, it passes utterly into that other glory.

And here is Louis de Blois, a Benedictine monk who lived in sixteenth-century France:

> When through love the soul goes beyond all working of the intellect and all images in the mind, and is rapt above itself, utterly leaving itself, it flows into God: then is God its peace and fullness. It loses itself

in the infinite solitude and darkness of the Godhead; but so to lose itself is rather to find itself. The soul is, as it were, all God-colored, because its essence is bathed in the essence of God.

The Lord's Prayer says plainly, "Thy will be done." But before his will can be done, our will – self-will – has to go. William Law put it precisely: "To sum up all in a word: nothing hath separated us from God but our own will, or rather our own will is our separation from God."

Here, again, we must remember that words like Lord and God do not refer to some higher being in another galaxy. We are talking about a barrier that separates us from our own deepest self, the very source and ground of what makes us human and gives meaning to our lives. Therefore, Eckhart says, "the soul is blessed perfectly when it follows the revelation of God back to the source from whence it came, their common origin, letting go of its own things and cleaving to his, so that the soul is blessed by God's things and not its own."

The more self-will we have, the more difficult it must be to trace consciousness back to its source. What would you think of trying to climb Mount Everest with a trunk full of memorabilia strapped to your back? Self-will weighs us down not a bit less, and the "ascent of Mount Carmel," as John of the Cross called it, begins with lightening the load.

None of us need feel disheartened when we begin to see that our self-will is grossly inflated. That is the human condition, and it is no reason to give up and accommodate ourselves to living at the spiritual equivalent of sea level. All of us can learn to reduce this excess baggage and climb.

Self-will, in other words, is not something we have to learn to live with. It can be reduced to a bare minimum, even eliminated entirely, and every step of this reduction allows the radiance of personality to shine a little brighter.

Let me suggest three effective ways in which this can be done.

1. Meditation

The purpose of meditating on an inspirational passage such as the Beatitudes or the Prayer of Saint Francis is to empty the mind gradually of all thoughts other than the words of the passage. As Gandhi said, we are emptying the mind little by little, like a man emptying the sea with a cup. Thomas Merton quotes Dom Gueranger's beautiful description of this purpose:

> The words of God, of the saints, as we repeat them over and over again and enter more and more deeply into their meaning, have a supreme grace to deliver the soul sweetly from preoccupation with itself in order to charm it and introduce it into the very mystery of God and of his Christ.

This process takes years, perhaps a lifetime. But benefits accrue from the very beginning. As preoccupation with ourselves diminishes, security builds. We find we have greater patience — and not just with others, but with ourselves as well. Things that used to cause stress and agitation no longer ruffle us, and people we used to find difficult start to show a brighter side. For all these reasons, and others too, our personal relationships blossom; and that, for many of us, is the richest dividend of all.

Gradually the day will come when you sit down for meditation and find your attention growing completely absorbed in the words of the inspirational passage. You will not hear the cars on the road nearby, or the planes flying overhead; you will not be aware of the chair you are sitting on. You will not even be aware of your body – and when you forget your body, you no longer live in the physical world.

When concentration is complete like this, not only space but time ceases to exist. You cannot think about the past or the future; every ray of attention is focused on the present moment. When there is no past, then no ghosts from the past – in particular, no anger or resentment – can come to make your life miserable. And when there is no future, there can be no anxiety or fear. In the mystics' language, you are delivered from the burden of time into the eternal Now.

It is not that you forget what happened yesterday when you lose the bond with the past; you just don't think about yesterday. And once your mind has learned not to think about yesterday, most internal conflicts evaporate. It is as simple as that, because thinking about them is what makes them so real and oppressive. When meditation becomes so profound that the past falls away, old conflicts and the residue of emotional entanglements will fall away too. This "unburdening of memory," as John of the Cross calls it, brings an immense relief from the burden of past mistakes.

Similarly, it is heaven to be free of worry about tomorrow. I have many responsibilities, but I don't worry about them. I plan, I work hard, but I don't get anxious about results. When you develop this marvelous capacity to hold attention steady on the present, like the flame of a candle in a windless place, most anxieties evaporate. There is no reason to worry about what tomorrow may bring. If you live today completely in love – hating no one, hurting no one, serving all – then tomorrow *has* to be good, whatever comes.

2. Slowing Down

Living completely in the present, of course, is possible only with a quiet mind. The reason it is important to go through the words of a meditation passage *slowly* is to put a brake on the restless rush of the mind.

The faster thoughts go, the less control we have over them; that is what leaves decisions in the hands of dubious drivers like self-will. All negative thoughts are fast. Fear, resentment, greed, and jealousy rush through the mind at a hundred miles an hour. At such speeds we cannot turn, cannot stop, cannot keep from crashing into people. In fact, at speeds like this we are not really driving at all. We are hostages, trussed up in the trunk, and self-will is at the wheel.

If only I could show you what I see going on in the mind when someone gets angry! It is like watching thoughts whirling around in one of those clothes dryers at the laundromat, tumbling faster and faster. When the mind gets going like this, we have no more self-control or sensitivity to others than Conan the Barbarian.

Fast thinking has implications for the body too. People whose thoughts spin faster and faster become victims of the speed habit of their minds. Eventually any little thing can upset them – trifles and pinpricks that they should laugh about, if they notice them at all. This kind of turmoil takes a heavy toll on health, and evidence suggests that emotional instability may leave the body more vulnerable to illness and reduce its capacity for healing. Uncontrollable anger, for example, seems to be associated with hypertension and heart disease and is a component in severe breathing problems. Mind and body are not separate; they are aspects of one organism, and problems in the mind, when they become chronic, cannot help but affect the body too.

Even good health, then, calls for slowing down – and not just in meditation. We have to learn to keep the mind from racing during the day, and that means slowing down the whole frantic pace of modern life. There is an intimate connection between a hectic life-style and a hectic mind. Get up early, have your meditation without hurrying, talk to your children at breakfast, be kind to those around you. Even if the coffee isn't quite perked, what does it matter? Harmony is more important. And get to work early enough to chat with your colleagues; take a little time to get to know them better. You will find all this extremely useful in reducing self-will. When you are always in a rush, you cannot handle self-will because you cannot even see others' needs. You don't have time to be thoughtful or kind.

When meditation deepens, thoughts begin to slow down naturally. Then the temperature of self-will begins to drop. I wish I had a thermometer that could measure this. If genetic engineers can make biochemical markers in tobacco plants glow in the dark, why can't we have a gauge to show when self-will is heating up? As a matter of fact, with a little detached observation, it is not hard to see this happening in someone else. There are all kinds of signs, though some vary from person to person, and one sure pattern is that all the machinery of body and mind speeds up, from heart rate to speech. The trick is to be detached enough to see this happening in ourselves – and then be able to take steps promptly to correct it.

Here the mantram offers immediate, effective first aid. When you find self-will rising – when you find yourself getting angry or afraid, or some strong desire is about to get out of control, or you feel you have to get your way or you will explode – start repeating your mantram, or Holy Name, in your mind and, if possible, head for the door for a good, fast walk around the block. (Walking is one thing it's good to do fast, particularly a mantram walk at emergency time.)

Hold on to your mantram as if your life depended on it – in some respects it really might. You will find that there is a close connection between the rhythm of the mantram, the rhythm of your footsteps, the rhythm of your breathing, and the rhythm of your mind. Walk briskly, and keep going for at least a good two or three turns around the block. Quickly you will find these rhythms blending, steadying your breathing rate and slowing down the furious pace of your thoughts. By the time you get back your mind will be clearer, and a good deal of your agitation will have quieted down – simply by slowing down the mind.

I have seen people do this in the midst of an impossible situation and come back calmer in just fifteen minutes – forgiving instead of angry, kind and creative instead of frustrated and hostile. That is the power of the mantram, and the effect on other people involved has to be seen to be believed.

3. *Putting Others First*

A third way to dissolve the strata of self-centered conditioning is by learning to think of other people's needs before our own. This is perhaps the most important, the most difficult, and the most rewarding challenge on the spiritual path. Tender, truly loving relationships are the essence of serving the Lord in all.

The longer you go on meditating, the more you will see that whenever there is a problem in personal relationships, the cause is not really differences of opinion or life-style; it is self-will. A large ego – mammoth self-will – is like one of those mobile homes you sometimes see under tow on the freeway, with red flags sticking out on both sides. I try to move into the lane farthest away from them, even before I get close enough to see the sign that warns, "Wide Load." They can suddenly invade your space, drifting into your lane. Unfortunately, some people are like that too. With so much emphasis on being aggressive and competitive, on "doing your own thing" and "looking out for number one," millions of people have developed such rampant self-will that they too ought to carry little red flags in their belts, so that others can give them plenty of room to maneuver.

On the other hand, there are a few rare people who will give you their lane if necessary and say, "We'll pull over; you go ahead." Jesus says that these are the people who live in heaven. They don't just drive off onto the shoulder and give up the road; they have a destination too, and it is important for them to get there. But they know how to yield gracefully, how to look far ahead and undo a dangerous situation when they see an accident coming. Such people not only are safe drivers, they make the road safer for the rest of us as well.

If just one person in the family does this, a home becomes heaven. Even an office can become heaven! Putting others first is an infectious example that affects everybody around. In Berkeley in the sixties, an institution sprang up called the Free University. All of us maintain a free university of our own, where we teach by what we are. Especially where children are concerned, the home is a seven-day-a-week school of education for living.

But putting others first does not mean telling them yes all the time. Love often shows itself in the inward toughness that is required to say no to an attitude or desire that we think will bring harm. Parents have to do this often, for children who grow up without hearing no from their parents will be terribly brittle when they have to take no from life itself – and, worse, they will have a hard time saying no to themselves.

But loving opposition, whether to children or to adults you live or work with, has to be done tenderly and without any anger or condescension. Otherwise you are likely only to be adding more self-will to the flames. This is a difficult art. Go slowly, and remember that it is always better not to act in the heat of the moment. Whenever time allows, instead of responding immediately to an unwise demand, take a mantram walk first, meditate, and then speak when you can do so with kindness and patience. Remember, too, that the very best way to change someone is to begin with your own example.

These are skills that everyone needs in order to love, and most of us have not learned them. Relationships break down easily today not because people are bad but because they are illiterate in love. Knowing how to read and write and manage a computer does not educate us for lasting relationships. To be literate in love, we have to learn to reduce self-will.

Today, after many, many years of experience, I can look at a romantic relationship and make a fairly accurate guess as to whether it will last. I don't even have to observe the couple during a crisis; their behavior in little everyday incidents tells me a great deal. All I have to do is ask myself, "Is each person ready to put the other first?" If the answer is yes, that relationship is likely to grow deeper and more rewarding with the passage of time, whatever problems may come. But if the answer is no, that relationship may not be able to withstand even a little of the testing that life is bound to bring. Though I may not be able to predict the specific incident, sooner or later, self-will may rebel when things don't go its way.

I have heard the most cultured people, in the most affectionate of relationships, saying hurtful things, simply because they have not learned to train the mind never to indulge in any kind of harm. That is the purpose of meditation. "When a man's ways please the Lord," the Bible says, "He maketh even his enemies to be at peace with him." That is a beautiful insight into the trained mind. Today everything I do is to please the Lord, so my life is very simple. It is not that I don't face complicated problems; every day life brings increasing challenges, but I have learned to face them without inner turmoil. All I do is ask what would please my Lord. I am no longer interested in pleasing myself or in pleasing anybody else in particular; I want only to please God.

Putting others first is an area in which the mind can often play tricks on us. Interestingly enough, often when we think we are thinking of others, putting their needs first, we are really just trying to please – which means we are really thinking about ourselves. You can see how slippery self-will can be.

"Nothing burns in hell but self-will." What penetrating words! An outburst of self-will may seem justified at the time, but for those who are sensitive, a stab of remorse follows all too soon. This is a good sign. It is much better to be sensitive, suffer from our mistakes, and learn not to repeat them than to go through life leaving a trail of broken relationships and wondering why we hurt inside.

This way of learning is terribly painful, but almost all of us should expect it. I, for one, did not manage to avoid it. My mother must have been born kind; in seventy years I don't remember her uttering a hurtful word to anyone. But I was like everyone else. As children do, I sometimes said hurtful things that I was ashamed of afterward, and when I did it would torment me. I would toss and turn throughout the night, and the next morning I would go straight to my cousin or whoever it was and say, "I hope what I said yesterday didn't hurt you." To make it worse, he would look at me blankly and ask, "What was it?"

I used to complain to my grandmother, "This isn't fair! He is the one who should feel hurt, and he doesn't even remember it. Why should I be the one who can't sleep?"

"That is the makings of what is in store for you," she would say mysteriously. "That is the way you learn." I didn't understand, and I could never get her to explain.

But she was right: my motivation grew. If somebody said something rude to me, I learned to hold back a rude response and think, "Oh, no. I don't want to lie awake at night!" That is how it began. Today that reversal of conditioning has gone so far that if someone says or does something unkind to me, I feel sorry for that person, not for myself.

Self-will, the mystics say, will always cause us pain.

The least we can do is learn from it. When you make a mistake and cannot sleep at night because of it, use the power of your pain to drive your mantram deep into your consciousness, where it can heal the wound and help bring the desire not to act on self-will again. The purpose of suffering is for us to learn one of life's most important lessons: as Jesus patiently points out again and again, it is much better to suffer and learn than to cause suffering to those around us. That is why you will never hear a good spiritual teacher asking anybody, "Are you having fun?" The real question is, are you growing? If you are, well and good, even if it hurts. If we could grow up by having fun, I would be all for it. Unfortunately, however, a diet of fun often stunts human growth.

Lessons like these are learned partly at night, when the past may not let us rest, and that is where the mantram is invaluable. Scientists are doing significant research in the realm of sleep, but I don't think the modern world yet knows as much about sleep as these lovers of God. Saint Francis said that particularly at night, he felt the pain of Christ in his own body – the suffering of him who bore in himself the sorrows of all the world. That is how far sensitivity can go. Few of us aspire to those rare heights, but all of us suffer in our sleep more than we know, when hurtful things we have done and said follow us into deeper consciousness. Recently I came across a haunting passage from the Greek tragedian Aeschylus:

And even in our sleep pain that cannot forget falls

drop by drop upon the heart, and in our own
despair, against our will, comes wisdom to us by the
awful grace of God.

This happens much more often than we are aware
of, particularly when we become more sensitive to our
own self-will as meditation deepens. Sleep then becomes an important part of spiritual growth.

Here a little preparation can go a long, long way.
When you are ready for bed, there are a few simple
things you can do to make your night better.

First, have your meditation again in the evening for
half an hour. As Gandhi said, we should make prayer
the key of our morning and the bolt of our evening.

Then do a little spiritual reading, even if only for fifteen minutes. Choose something that is completely
positive and inspiring, either a passage from the scriptures or the direct words of a great mystic who has realized God. There is great poetry in the mystics,
delicious humor, profound insight, words with life and
power of their own to seal your day with a lofty image
of what the human being can become.

Then, after you put your book aside and tuck yourself in, close your eyes and start repeating your mantram until you fall asleep in it.

This is not as easy as it may sound. Other thoughts
will try to push the mantram away. But through sheer
persistence you can achieve a minor miracle. Between
the last waking moment and the first sleeping moment, there is an arrow's entry into deepest conscious-

ness. If you can send your mantram in through that narrow gate, it will go on repeating itself throughout the night, healing old wounds and restoring your soul for the next day. Those who have learned to do this, in Brother Lawrence's phrase, go forward even in their sleep.

Today, after many years of practice, my mantram stands at the entrance to my mind throughout the night. If negative thoughts come, it just says, "Sorry, you need a pass." Don't bouncers work as long as the bar is open? The mantram too is quite happy to work all night, and when you fall asleep in it, the name of the Lord will run through your mind until you wake up, healing body and mind with its quiet harmony.

This is a harsh world we live in. People have grown used to using rough, unkind language and to doing harmful things. If you can remember not to retaliate in words and actions, eventually you will find it impossible even to think hurtful thoughts. Then your self-will is nearly zero, and instead of causing others pain, your very presence will help and heal. This is the extraordinary light that mysticism throws on the human mind: as self-will is reduced, what shines forth is love. You don't have to borrow it from the saints and stuff it into your consciousness. It is there in all of us, if only we are willing to get ourselves out of the way.

CHAPTER 4
Simplicity

Blessed are the meek, for they shall inherit the earth.

On January 2, 1989, *Time* magazine skipped its customary cover feature on the Man or Woman of the Year. Instead, the cover illustration showed the Planet of the Year: an "Endangered Earth" trussed up in string, the subject of stories on threats to its life and welfare that had dominated the news in the previous twelve months.

This break in tradition was not prompted by any one particular event: not the nuclear accident at Chernobyl, which may take its toll for generations, or even the ongoing loss of our tropical forests, an ecological folly which might wipe out half of the species of life on earth and turn present croplands to deserts. What prompted *Time*'s choice was not so much catastrophes like these as the innumerable accidents and incidents which keep coming to remind us that the "acceptable risks" of modern civilization may add up to an uninhabitable world.

One such accident, still vivid in my memory, was the industrial fire in Switzerland in 1986 which spilled some thirty tons of deadly chemicals into the Rhine. This beautiful river, famed in song and legend, was polluted with poisons whose cumulative effects are unknown. Millions of fish were killed, and decades will pass before we know what damage has been done to the microorganisms which form the basis of the river's ecosystem. In West Germany alone, more than forty thousand villages lost their supply of drinking water.

I have seen the effects of some of these disasters with my own eyes. Not long ago, for example, some of the most beautiful beaches of northern California were engulfed in a huge oil slick, washed northward from an exploded tanker that sank outside the Golden Gate. On the islands and coastlands, some of which are wildlife refuges, one could see seabirds trapped in oozing slime. Hundreds of volunteers turned out to rescue these graceful creatures – seagulls, godwits, sandpipers, and the like – carefully wiping the brownish-gray scum off their bodies; for if its wings are seriously encumbered, a seabird dies.

Aside from the ecological tragedy, the confusion visible in these birds haunted me for a long time. How close their plight is to that of the human being! As Thomas a Kempis reminds us, the soul requires two wings to soar above the pull of worldly things. One is purity, which enables us to keep our eyes on the divinity in every human being. The other is simplicity: and not merely in our lifestyle, John of the Cross would say, but simplicity in our desires; for having many desires, often at cross purposes, is what creates complication and confusion in our lives.

Neither of these qualities, Thomas implies, is enough in itself to lift us up. If either is weak, we will flounder on the beach like one of those poor tarred birds. But together, when they are strong, purity and simplicity enable the soul to soar aloft.

In the name of simplification today we are asked to take the most remarkable steps: to buy food processors and microwave ovens, open charge accounts, install a telephone in every room, pay a travel agent to plan our next vacation down to the last waiter's tip. It is exhilarating to be reminded here that the real meaning of simplicity is singling out what is worth living for, and then shaping our lives around what matters and letting go of everything else.

Thoreau tells us in clear, haunting words, "I went to the woods because I wished to live deliberately, to front only the essential facts of life, and see if I could not learn what it had to teach, and not, when I came to die, discover that I had not lived." What are the essentials of life? What must we learn if we really mean to live?

"The earth is the Lord's," says the psalmist, "and the fullness thereof; the world, and they that dwell therein." Familiar words – perhaps too familiar. Do we hear them question the basis of our lives? Seas, mountains, forests, air, other people and other creatures: all these belong not to us, but to the Lord. You and I are just tenants here, with rights of tenancy, no doubt, but with responsibilities too. Our divine landlord expects us to look after our home, this green earth. And we are not doing a very good job.

One of the most impressive things about the Rhine pharmaceutical plant accident was its impact. The story attracted press attention around the world, but by the next week, except in the countries immediately affected, it was all but forgotten. Only a few concerned voices were heard to plead that these are not just noteworthy incidents, but clues to a larger pattern. Industrial technology is like a drug. Drugs cause a cluster of actions in the body, some of them intended and others incidental to the purpose, but it is only in the mind that the "side effects" can be separated from the effects that we desire. Ecological effects too are as much a part of industrial production as the plastics and chemical creations that justify it in our eyes. The more we depend on those products, the greater the impact on the environment has to be – and soon, the litany of the news reminds us, we had better assess the total cost.

"Well," we ask, "if we don't like the cost, what are we supposed to learn from ruined rivers and air that's not fit to breathe? What is the planet trying to tell us?" The answer is, "Simplify your lives." Industrial technology has a welcome place in helping to make life safer and more comfortable, but when we let it get out of control it becomes the world's greatest enemy. Technology is not an end in itself. It is a means to an end, and that end is human health, happiness, and welfare. When it begins to produce the opposite results, it is time to decide how much we really need. Technology should be not our master but our servant.

A simple life does not mean a life of poverty. There is plenty of room for material comfort and personal satisfaction while living lightly on the planet, making a contribution to life instead of threatening it. Simple living, to me, is the art of using minimum means to attain maximum results – just the opposite of what happens when we get caught up in the obsessions of a consumer society. Later in this chapter I will suggest some ways to simplify while living life at its richest.

To live simply is to live gently, keeping in mind always the needs of the planet, other creatures, and the generations to come. In doing this we lose nothing, because the interests of the whole naturally include our own.

"Blessed are the meek, for they shall inherit the earth." The danger facing our planet lends new meaning to Jesus' words. Most of us are properly suspicious when someone tells us to be "meek" or "humble"; it sounds unctuous and just the opposite of strong. Charles Dickens has a curious character called Uriah Heep who is always proclaiming how "'umble" he is. His job is 'umble, his home is 'umble, his character is 'umble. All he really is, unfortunately, is 'ypocritical. No one wants to be like Uriah Heep.

Yet the meekness that Jesus suggests is a most attractive quality. Like "poor in spirit," it means the absence of self-will, the opposite of the kind of personality that asserts its dominance over everything and everyone around. It is not the arrogant that shall inherit the earth, but those who are gentle with its resources and its creatures. In claiming nothing for themselves, they have everything, for everything is theirs to enjoy as part of the whole.

Saint John of the Cross tells us in Zen-like terms:

> In order to enjoy everything,
> Desire to get joy from nothing.
> In order to arrive at possessing everything,
> Desire to possess nothing.
> In order to arrive at being everything,
> Desire to be nothing.

"To enjoy everything, desire to get joy from nothing." If it sounds unattractive, that is only because we don't understand. The key is our desires: are they self-directed, or are they for all? Don't ask life to please you, John is telling us; ask how you can give. Then you are free to enjoy in good times and bad, in ups and downs, whatever life brings. Desire nothing just for yourself; then the whole world is yours. It multiplies joy a millionfold, and no one has proclaimed the joy of it more gloriously than the English mystic Thomas Traherne:

> You never enjoy the world aright, till you see how a
> sand exhibiteth the power and wisdom of God . . . till
> every morning you awake in Heaven; see yourself in
> your Father's Palace; and look upon the skies, the
> earth, and the air as Celestial Joys. . . . You never
> enjoy the world aright, till the Sea itself floweth in
> your veins, till you are clothed with the heavens,
> and crowned with the stars: and perceive yourself to

be the sole heir of the whole world, and more than so, because men are in it who are every one sole heirs as well as you. . . . Till your spirit filleth the whole world, and the stars are your jewels; . . . till you love men so as to desire their happiness, with a thirst equal to the zeal of your own; till you delight in God for being good to all: you never enjoy the world.

Traherne and John of the Cross give us a glimpse of the towering strength and self-control that gentleness and humility require. The stamp of the mystic, if I may put it paradoxically, is a proud humility. Francis of Assisi erased every trace of ego from his personality; yet no one was ever more personal, and Francis carried himself through life with the proud assurance that, in the words of Saint Paul, "not I, but Christ liveth in me."

Mahatma Gandhi had the same combination of humility and unshakable self-assurance. When he was asked if he were free from ambition, he replied, "Oh, no! I am the most ambitious man in the world. I want to make myself zero." I used to remind myself of this in the early days of my meditation, when many relatives and friends said, "You have such promise; why do you want to throw all this away? Don't you have any ambition?" I wanted to tell them that my ambition was only beginning. Previously I had wanted only to be a good teacher and a great writer, perhaps win the Nobel Prize in literature; now I wanted to make myself zero like Gandhi.

The source of this "proud humility" is the awareness of the divine spark within our heart. With that at our center, what can we not do? George Bernard Shaw wrote: "You see things; and you say 'Why?' But I dream things that never were; and I say 'Why not?'" That is the spirit of this meekness that Jesus extols. In this country of ambitious people, I may be the most ambitious of all, for I believe that you and I, in our own lifetime, can make our streets safe and bring harmony to our homes, simplicity to our lives, and depth to our personal relationships. We can clean up the environment for our children and grandchildren. And I won't be content with simply banishing nuclear weapons; I want to banish war itself. So if people tell you that meditation stifles motivation, you can tell them that this is what motivating forces like ambition are really for: to stir us to action on behalf of all.

It is when these instincts are harnessed for the welfare of the whole that we get the fullest reward life can give. Ambition for oneself only makes a person narrower. It is when our desires reach out to embrace all of life that life fulfills them – and much more generously than we could ever anticipate. "God is ready to give great things," says Eckhart, "when we are ready, for righteousness' sake, to give up everything."

This message is repeated again and again in the teachings of the great religions: it is when we live to serve the Lord in all that we inherit our full legacy of joy. When Gandhi was challenged to sum up the secret of his life in three words, he replied with a quote from an Indian scripture, the Isha Upanishad: "Renounce and enjoy!" These lines, he said, contain all the wisdom we need to steer a safe course through the crises of our industrial age:

The Lord is enshrined in the hearts of all.
The Lord is the supreme reality.
Rejoice in him through renunciation.
Covet nothing. All belongs to the Lord.
Thus working may you live a hundred years.
Thus alone will you work in real freedom.

۞

"The earth is the Lord's, and the fullness thereof." If we take these words as more than mere poetry, they mean that you and I are trustees. The resources of our planet have been entrusted to every one of us together, and like any good bank trustee, we are expected not to squander them but to invest them wisely for our beneficiaries: the rest of life, especially the generations to come.

This view has far-reaching consequences. The trust includes not simply the lives and resources of the planet, but inner resources too. The fact that nothing on earth belongs to us personally has some very practical implications, all of which come down to a simpler life: simpler in its externals, and so gentler on the earth; but simpler too in our inner lives, where desires are fewer but immeasurably richer and more productive.

To begin with, when you regard your life as a trust, you realize that the first resource you have to take care of is your own body.

This can be startling. Even your body is not really your own. It belongs to life, and it is your responsibility to take care of it. You cannot afford to do anything that injures your body, because the body is the instrument you need for selfless action. That is the fine print of the trust agreement: when we smoke, when we overeat, when we don't get enough exercise, we are violating the terms of the trust. If you want to live life at its fullest, you will want to do everything possible to keep your body in vibrant health in order to give back to life a little of what it has given you.

This approach has helped thousands of people I know to give up harmful habits such as smoking and drinking, without my ever preaching at them or belittling them. I keep my eye on that core of goodness. Life is crying for the contribution of every one of us, and it stirs people to learn that most of us have no idea of the capacities we have hidden inside, or what tremendous energy can be released when we free ourselves from habits that drain our energy and tie our hands. When we begin to simplify our lives, ways of giving back to life appear without our ever having to ask.

In everything, simplicity is the key to trusteeship. A simple life conserves not just our personal resources but the earth's.

A good place to begin simplifying is with this "frenzy of consumerism," to use Pope John Paul II's apt phrase – this endless cycle of buying and producing beyond any reasonable need. Everywhere I see shopping malls cropping up like alien mushrooms. I can appreciate the convenience of a pleasant, sheltered place with a few good shops selling useful things, but how many do we really need? When I go to a mall I don't often see people come to get the thing they need and then go home.

Many come just to pass the time, looking for something to spend money on.

It is not only money that is thrown away in "recreational shopping"; this aimless activity is such a tragic waste of time and attention. When shoppers go home, they leave part of their capacity to love behind in the shopping mall. Even if they don't spend money, they spend their energy. Only when this fever of buying and accumulating things quiets down can we begin to give that energy and attention to family and community, where they are desperately needed. If each of us can simplify in little ways, far-reaching changes are within our power.

Take gift-giving, for example. Is it really necessary to celebrate every birthday, anniversary, promotion, and "holiday" established by a greeting card manufacturer with a gift that is often neither useful nor desired? Why not give a gift of ourselves – of our time, attention, thoughtfulness, affection? "The most sublime act," wrote William Blake, "is to set another before you." If you have grown estranged from someone, you can move a little closer; you can begin paying attention to those you have ignored. And beyond the circle of those we live and work with, there are a great many people who desperately need love and attention and no end of deserving causes that need help.

This is one of the hidden problems of consumerism: it wastes the time and drains the energy we need for personal relationships. I don't think most people realize how much vitality can trickle away in a visit to the shopping mall. It's not only buying; just gauge how you feel at the end of a day of window-shopping. In terms of the impact on your personal energy reserves, you have written a big energy check and handed it over just for the time spent, even if you never wrote a check for a purchase and took things home.

A good deal of vitality escapes through the eyes, especially when desire comes into play. One simple tactic of defensive shopping, then, is to keep close watch over what your eyes are doing. Don't waste time and energy letting your eyes wander and then find that your mind and your desires have ambled along after. Don't let yourself be taken in by advertising tactics designed to make you pick up carefully placed "impulse" items. Keep your mantram going, keep your attention on what you are there for, get it, pay for it, and leave. When you get home, not only your checking account but your energy level will be relatively intact, leaving you more to spend where it really counts.

But the worst threat from a consumer society is the toll it takes on the environment: in the burning of fossil fuels, in the release of toxic industrial wastes, and finally in the problems of how to get rid of the trash. I am not against buying things that are needed; my objection is that so many of the items produced for us to buy are neither necessary nor beneficial, and in environmental terms, all of us pay through the nose just to have them in the stores, whether we buy or not.

Now, none of these things is in the stores because manufacturers hate clean air. None of them is produced just to fill up chain store shelves. They are there because people buy them, and manufacturers will go on making more so long as we go on buying. To escape from this sad-go-round of pollution and waste is simple: we must each begin to weigh our desire for an item against what it costs the environment to produce it – and then start saying, "No, it's not worth it."

In other words – just as John of the Cross would have told us! – even cleaning up the environment leads to managing our desires. Simplifying life implies throwing out things and activities we do not need, but what goes furthest is cleaning out the mind. The mind is an immense garage stuffed with desires, and every one we manage to throw away means a pile of plastic that need never be produced because we have no compulsion to buy.

For many of my friends, the most persuasive side of this appeal is the benefit to the next generation. Each time you are about to make a purchase, ask yourself, "What will this cost our children in clean air and pure water?"

Years ago I read an excellent article by Carl Sagan and Ann Druyan which took this tack. On behalf of their young daughter and all the world's children, they appealed to the newly elected president of the United States: "Give Us Hope for the Future." "It is no longer enough to love, feed, shelter, clothe and educate a child – not when the future itself is in danger," they observed. "Being a conscientious parent today also means working to preserve and to protect the nation and the planet – now, before it's too late." They urged the president to recognize pollution as a crime against the future:

We have been treating the environment as if there were no tomorrow — as if there will be no new generations to be sustained by the bounties of the Earth. But they, and we, must drink the water and breathe the air. . . .

I agree wholeheartedly with these concerns, but I do not expect government or industry to take the initiative in solving problems for us. My appeal is to the people. If we take these matters into our own hands, they can be dealt with without legislation or costly government intervention, which without our support might even make the situation worse. Problems like pollution do not appear out of nowhere. They develop through thousands of little, individual acts, and that is just how we can reverse them. In countless ways, each of us can begin to assume our trusteeship duties and take responsibility for the earth, air, and water.

Most of us, for example, do not give much thought to where our household trash goes after the truck pulls away. Yet what to do with the discards of industrial civilization already poses questions we cannot answer, and the problem is getting worse.

In 1988, *Time* magazine reported that the amount of trash generated in this country had increased by eighty percent in the previous thirty years. The United States produces more trash per person than any other country — roughly twice as much as Japan and Western Europe — and we are running out of places to put it. About half the landfills in this country have already closed, and the Environmental Protection Agency predicts that one third of those remaining will be filled to capacity in five to ten years.

Now, I have always been proud of living in California, which produces such a rich variety of vegetables, fruits, nuts, and grains. When Indian friends ask me if I have become an American, I like to reply, "No, I have become a Californian." On this question, however, I have not. California evidently holds the world's record in the production of personal waste: about twenty-five pounds of trash per week from every man, woman, and child.

Some of this, apparently, could easily be recycled or composted: glass, paper and cardboard, newspapers, grass clippings from lawns. But recycling is only a partial solution. Much of the material we throw away is not recyclable or even biodegradable. It has to go somewhere, and as landfills close down, the temptation becomes stronger to ship it out on barges and dump it into the ocean. "Out of sight, out of mind." Perhaps, but not out of our lives. Trash dumped at sea is finding its way home. I have seen once-beautiful beaches looking like trash heaps – covered with junk, from "disposable" fast-food containers to dangerous medical waste – and beautiful marine animals such as seals and sea gulls choking on plastic bags and dying of chemical burns. I still remember a dying seal looking at me in mute appeal as if to say, "You people are supposed to protect us. You are the trustees of our world. Why aren't you doing your job?"

Some states and cities are passing strict antipollution laws, with stiff fines for offenders. Instead, why not generate less trash? If each of us produces twenty-five pounds of trash a week, why not begin by cutting it down to twenty? If you're meditating, you might aim at fifteen – or even ten. The connection with simplifying is plain: the less we bring home, the less we have to throw away; the less we buy, the less will be produced. Everybody can do this, and the spirit is contagious.

Similarly, there are lots of ways in which we can each help restore the purity of our air.

First of all, we can dramatically reduce both fossil fuel use and air pollution simply by cutting back on unnecessary driving. I have nothing against automobiles; it is our overuse of automobiles that is getting us into trouble, making the air more and more laden with smog, the freeways more and more congested. Cities counter by building more and wider roads, but this only adds to the problem by encouraging more cars. Southern California, which has grown on the promise of a lavish network of freeways, is a perfect example. Traffic there is so thick that cars move at an average of thirty-three miles per hour – and by the year 2000 this rate is expected to drop to fifteen!

The San Francisco Bay Area is moving rapidly toward this kind of congestion, and planners talk of adding lanes to the highway. Meanwhile, every time I travel to the city I am struck by the spectacle of car after car after car with just one person inside. Common sense suggests a simple and elegant solution: why not travel two to a car? If everybody did it, we would have cut the traffic by half – and cut by half the tragic toll of traffic accidents, which, according to one commentator, can be compared to fighting the Vietnam War on our freeways every fourteen months.

If traveling two to a car can cut the problem in half, you can see how each member of a carpool counts. When I go to San Francisco, I usually take three or four friends along; I fill up the car. Carpooling is not only efficient and easy on the environment, it's good companionship. The extra fifteen minutes needed to drive a few miles to pick up a passenger, to wait a few moments if necessary, are not time wasted. I understand that each year the average American car pumps its own weight of carbon into the atmosphere. In those fifteen minutes you have kept one car off the road for one day; what could you have done in a quarter of an hour to make an impact like that? And if you use the time for repeating the mantram, you have added to your own spiritual growth as well.

Another alternative to cars – a favorite of mine – is trains. They can be made fast, efficient, safe, and clean, as we can see from what Japan has done. The railway system is beginning to expand here too, as more and more people discover how pleasant train travel can be. When I first came to this country, I traveled from New York to Kansas by train, then from Kansas to Minnesota and from there to California, and I enjoyed every hour. You can take your work along if you like; you can read, meditate, or play with your children.

Finally, I would like to put in a word for the simplest, safest, and surest mode of transportation ever: walking. Nothing beats walking for simplicity. You don't need any special equipment, only a good, comfortable pair of shoes; and you don't have to train for it or learn any special skills. The only novel suggestion I have about walking is to take the mantram along. After meditation, my wife and I start our day with a walk on the beach repeating our mantram. We have kept up this routine for the past twenty-five years, even in the sort of weather that makes one want to stay in bed. The earth is a joy in the quiet hours of early morning, and the mantram renews the mind; we come back renewed for a long day of hard, selfless work.

In the 1960s, even in California, we were looked upon as a trifle eccentric for doing this. Today, I am happy to report, brisk walking is recognized as one of the best forms of aerobic exercise you can get. Add the mantram and you get a near-perfect tonic for body, mind, and spirit at once. You can walk to your bus or carpool stop and use some of your commute time for getting in shape, so that you arrive at work refreshed and calm, even glowing. Little everyday errands can be opportunities for boosting your well-being while you help the environment. How often do we automatically hop into the car and drive a few blocks to mail a letter or pick up some groceries? In many cases, walking takes about the same amount of time.

In today's world we are getting hemmed in on all sides, and ironically, a lot of the hemming in comes from the automobile. I have read that the average person can now expect to spend about six months of his or her life just sitting behind the wheel waiting for red lights to change! Why not break free and walk or bicycle to the corner store? Your body will be strength-ened and your nerves soothed, your senses will be sharpened and refreshed, and your heart will become more attuned to the rhythm of the seasons and the beauty of the Lord's creation.

A second way to restore the purity of the air is to protect trees, from your local juniper to the tropical rain forests that sustain life as we know it. These forests may be on the other side of the globe from most of us, but they affect our lives here and now – and our every-day behavior affects them too.

Rain forests are disappearing at the rate of twenty-seven million acres per year – or, to bring the figures closer to home, we are losing an area of rain forest the size of a football field every second. Much of this destruction takes place just to raise cattle for beef. Already two thirds of the rain forests in Central Amer-ica have been lost to cattle pasture.

This kind of rampant deforestation is especially dev-astating because of what it does to the greenhouse ef-fect – the overall warming of the globe, heightened by industrial pollution, which threatens to shift climate as drastically as the Ice Age. Slash-and-burn clearing methods release huge amounts of carbon into the air, increasing the global warming effect just the way a smokestack does. And, of course, such methods leave far fewer trees to take up the carbon dioxide and give back oxygen. In countries where deforestation has been allowed to continue, the results have been desertifica-tion, erosion, floods, and starvation.

Scientists are only beginning to discover the rich

biological diversity hidden in these primordial forests; it is said they contain more than half of the known species of flora and fauna. Each year thousands of these species are destroyed forever, and we cannot even begin to guess at what effect these losses will have on the delicate balance of our ecosystem.

The picture is grim, but there is a bright side: everyone can help directly, simply by switching to a vegetarian diet. Vegetarianism is scarcely a deprivation today. With major health organizations like the American Cancer Society recommending that we eat less meat and more fresh fruits and vegetables, there are all kinds of good vegetarian cookbooks to show how delicious vegetarian cuisine can be.

Here is where the power of gentle persuasion can come into play. You can share your enthusiasm with your friends, and when you go out to eat, you can ask for vegetarian food. As more and more people do this, that is what restaurants will slowly begin to provide. When I first came to the Bay Area, people thought I had some ailment when I asked for vegetarian food. Today, with so many people asking, there are excellent vegetarian restaurants; some, in Berkeley and San Francisco, have a national reputation for excellence. That is what the demand of little people can do.

For me, the real joy of vegetarianism is knowing that my meals are not at the expense of any living creature. "All creatures love life," the Buddha says. "All creatures fear death. Therefore do not kill, or cause another to kill." Animals have as much joy in living as we have; if we have lost this perspective, it is simply because of our conditioning. Animals are not just animals to me: our scriptures call them "four-footed people." When I hear about the misery veal calves undergo, I feel almost as if they are crying out to me, "Please tell people that we love life too."

Besides not eating meat, everybody can help to reverse the greenhouse effect by simply planting a few trees. Experts say that urban tree planting can greatly reduce atmospheric carbon dioxide while helping keep the earth's surface cool. In urban areas, where there are few trees to offset the heating effect of cars and factories, temperatures are often as much as ten degrees higher than in the surrounding countryside. Planting trees can cut home energy bills as well. It has been shown, for example, that air-conditioning costs can be lowered by as much as half by planting a few shade trees on the southern and western sides of a house.

The American Forestry Association estimates that there are a hundred million spaces around American homes and communities where additional trees can be planted. We can each take part in this, and the children can join in too. Children love working side by side with adults in activities they know are meaningful. I learned this from my grandmother, who was the wisest child psychologist I have ever known; I enjoyed doing things with her much more than I ever liked playing with toys.

So please get together with your children and start planting trees. It is very inexpensive – just a few cents for a seedling – and the benefits are beyond calculation. Your children will enjoy the time you spend together, and fifteen years later they will remember the trees you planted together, which give them shade, save them energy, and fill their air with oxygen.

And why stop with trees? Gardening is another activity that anyone can share with family and friends. Growing your own food, as far as possible, and supporting growers who use organic methods, are simple and effective ways to reduce the problem of pesticide-tainted produce as well as the pollution of our water with runoff from agricultural chemicals. A small kitchen garden needn't take a great deal of space; even apartment dwellers can usually find room for a few containers. And in many areas, community gardens are springing up – a wonderful blend of good nutrition, recreation, and community spirit.

↬

Simplifying your life, then, does not mean cutting back on anything of value. It means learning the delicate artistry of making your every action count, taking notice of the needs of the whole. You can think of it as a skill – and, as with any other skill, the more you practice it, the more opportunities you will find to put it to use, bringing your creativity and ingenuity into play.

This is one of the joys that come when you see your life as a trust. When your desires are focused on the welfare of the whole, all your faculties are magnified. Nothing is lost; on the contrary, your vitality and creativity increase, and so does the joy you feel at knowing you are leaving the world a little better, a little more hopeful, for those to come.

In this view, not even our time, talent, and resources are our personal property. They are precious resources that the Lord has given us in trust – meant to be spent freely, but for the benefit of all.

This throws fresh light on every aspect of life – our work, our relationships, and even the way we spend our leisure time. For example, I find it curious that people associate the idea of vacation with going somewhere else. For me, the very best vacation is to forget myself in working hard for a meaningful, selfless cause with people I know and love.

This is the kind of vacation I would like everybody to have: working to bring joy into the lives of others; working to remove the problems that face our children. Work like this, without wanting anything in return, is serving the Lord in all.

The mystics tell us that we are born for one purpose: to expand our awareness until we see everyone on the face of the earth as our very own, our kith and kin. Distant as it may sound, the joy of this all-embracing love is within the reach of us all, and we don't have to wait until the afterlife to taste it. Every step along the way brings greater happiness, love, and richness to life.

More than three thousand years ago, sages who belong not just to India but to the whole world gave us one of the earliest spiritual treasures known to history, the Rig Veda. Listen to a prayer addressed to all of us:

Meet together, talk together.

> May your minds comprehend alike.
> Common be your action and achievement,
> Common be your thoughts and intentions,
> Common be the wishes of your heart,
> So there may be thorough union among you.

Unity is strength; unity is the purpose of love. In relationships it may begin with physical expression, but holding hands and dancing cheek to cheek is just the surface of love. Two hearts becoming one, two lives becoming one: that is the meaning of love. We just don't know the signals. We don't know the code.

But Francis broke the code; Teresa of Avila deciphered its signs. Teresa said, *"Amor saca amor."* Love begets love. When we give love, we draw love to us from everyone around us, and in that love is the highest heaven a human being can know. When you give yourself to all, the mystics say, you no longer love just one person here and another there; you become love itself.

This is a heavenly insight into the depths of the human heart. We begin by loving just one or two people, but the day will come when we catch the entire world in our love. Imagine the joy of loving all creatures, all people, the whole of nature! As the Upanishads say, everywhere such a person goes, he or she is at home in a compassionate universe:

> Those who see all creatures in themselves
> And themselves in all creatures know no fear.
> Those who see all creatures in themselves
> And themselves in all creatures know no grief.
> How can the multiplicity of life
> Delude the one who sees its unity?

CHAPTER 5
Patience

Blessed are they that mourn, for they shall be comforted.

Years ago my wife and I went for a walk in a particularly lovely part of Berkeley, high in the hills on the fringes of Tilden Park. Now and then through the lush greenery we glimpsed a breathtaking panorama of San Francisco Bay. The homes there in the Berkeley hills, built over shady ravines filled with manzanita and bay laurel trees and alive with the song of birds, are handsome and costly. Many of them probably represent the lifetime efforts of their owners, who have managed to surround themselves with beauty and an enviable measure of privacy.

But as we looked out across the bay toward San Francisco and the Golden Gate, we saw a curious brown layer of air. Even at this height, auto and industrial fumes had spoiled the atmosphere so much that my eyes were smarting. And on every lot I saw a sign prominently displayed: "Property Protected by Burglar Alarm System." Fortunate as these homeowners are, they have not managed to escape the problems of pollution and crime that we have created for ourselves as a society.

Moreover, the security these homes afford is limited at best. Visible a little higher up the hill were charred tree stumps and a lone chimney, grim reminders of a grass fire that had swept the hills a few years earlier, sparing these particular houses at the instance of a chance shift in the wind. Like an ironic comment on the whole scene, someone's burglar alarm whined on in the distance, triggered perhaps by a wandering cat.

I wonder if there is anyone who has not dreamed at some time of devising a perfect world, a never-never land where no sorrow can intrude. We may not realize it, but most of us cling to this dream in our heart of hearts. Even while we are working and saving for that storybook home in the perfect neighborhood, I suspect, what lingers stubbornly at the back of our mind is the story of Shangri-La, the hidden city of perfection untouched by tears and time.

Not only the pursuit of wealth and possessions, but many of our other activities as well stem ultimately from the desire to isolate ourselves from sorrow. Even immersing ourselves in hobbies, intellectual pursuits, or relationships can be attempts to create a little world where beauty and harmony are permanent, where disorder and distress cannot enter. We can spend the better part of our lives attempting to construct the perfect personal environment, a kind of bubble that will insulate us against everything that is unpleasant. But sorrow is woven into the very texture of life. Pain, disappointment, depression, illness, bereavement, a sense of inadequacy in our work or our relationships... the list could go on and on. "Dispose all things according to your will and judgment," says Thomas a Kempis; "you will always find that of necessity you must suffer somewhat, either willingly or against your will; and so you shall always find the Cross."

Is there meaning in this pattern, in the inescapable mingling of sorrow and joy? The mystics say there is. If tears are a fact of life, they have several lessons to teach us, and the first is to learn to keep on an even keel through life's inevitable storms. When we master this skill, a good deal of personal sorrow falls away. "Life will always be full of ups and downs," my grandmother used to say. "But you don't have to go up and down with them. You can teach your mind to be calm and kind whatever comes."

Meister Eckhart, when asked by his close friends to leave them a message that would sum up all he had ever said, replied:

Some people want to recognize God only in some pleasant enlightenment, and then they get pleasure and enlightenment but not God. Somewhere it is written that God shines in the darkness where every now and then we get a glimpse of him. More often, God is where his light is least apparent. Therefore we ought to expect God in all manners and all things evenly.... Someone may now say: I should be glad to look for God evenly in all shapes and things, but my mind does not always work that way.... To which I reply: That is too bad! ... Whatever the way that

leads you most frequently to awareness of God, follow that way.... But it would be nobler and better to
achieve rest and security through evenness, by
which one might take God and enjoy him in any
manner, in any thing, and not have to delay and
hunt around for your special way. That has been my
joy ...

Imagine the immense security of what Eckhart describes: to "take God and enjoy him in any manner, in
any thing"! Evenness of mind in any situation; the ability to enjoy life thoroughly when everything about
you is going wrong, and to remain steady, loving, and
creative even when tragedy strikes. Meditation is a tool
that can enable us to do just that – to keep the mind on
an even keel under all circumstances. The benefits flow
both ways: the steadier you can keep your mind during
the day, the deeper your meditation will be.

꘎

Training the mind to stay steady brings
another precious benefit: it protects us from the physiological impact of negative emotions and stress.

There is plenty of evidence today to suggest that destructive mental states like anger, depression, anxiety,
and resentment have a serious impact on physical
health. The medical sciences have made tremendous
strides in the past century, yet I have no doubt that
meditation will prove as important as medicine in
keeping the body well. The function of meditation is

twofold: it calms and slows the mind, and by driving the words of an inspirational passage deep into consciousness, it gradually transforms corrosive negative emotions into positive states of mind which release vitality and spread a protective shield against the stress of life.

Some of the most interesting insights in medicine concern what appears to be almost an epidemic of stress-related disorders. We like to reassure ourselves that the infectious diseases that plagued past centuries have been brought under control, some even wiped off the face of the globe; yet if medical experts from another age were to observe us today, they might comment, "The job is not yet done. So far, your industrial progress has traded one kind of epidemic for another." I have read estimates that two thirds of the people who seek help from family physicians suffer from conditions arising out of stress. There is evidence that stress is a major risk factor in six of the worst killers in modern industrial societies: cardiovascular disease, cancer, pulmonary disease, cirrhosis of the liver, accidents, and suicide.

Dr. Herbert Benson, professor of medicine at the Harvard Medical School, is one of the most respected of the thousands of physicians who maintain that traditional efforts are no longer adequate to deal with the stress of modern life. Dr. Benson recommends meditation as "a natural antidote to tension." He and dedicated associates like Joan Borysenko have done important work in exploring how what he calls "the relaxation response" — essentially, repetition of a mantram in the mind for a short period once or twice a day — can be used as therapy for relieving stress. This kind of work may go a long way toward preventing some of the major health problems of our times.

But as stress researchers realize, full health is more than just the absence of disease. It means a dynamic harmony of body and mind which allows us to live at our full physical, emotional, and spiritual potential. In this state of "full wellness," stress is not merely something to cope with. To Dr. Hans Selye, stress really *is* "the spice of life." Trying to avoid stressful events, Dr. Selye says, will not help us to improve our emotional health. Instead of trying simply to survive stress, we should aim at flourishing under it, making use of anything life brings. Translated into spiritual terms, that is precisely the ideal Meister Eckhart gave us: "evenness, by which one might take God and enjoy him in any manner, in any thing."

To attain this state, we need a way to get deep into consciousness where the emotions and perceptions that make life stressful arise. When meditation penetrates below the surface of consciousness, as in sustained concentration on an inspirational passage, it becomes more rejuvenation than relaxation. By transforming negative states of mind, it actually guards us against destructive thinking habits, which makes it invaluable simply as health insurance. My own belief, based on decades of observation, is that this kind of meditation not only confers a measure of resistance against some serious ailments, but also releases the inner resources to function vigorously and effectively right into the evening of life.

On one point, medical science and mysticism concur without question: we have no way to rid life of unfortunate events; a minimum of stress is part of the human condition. This is the stress that we can learn to thrive on.

Beyond that minimum, however, there are kinds of stress that we impose on ourselves by our own ways of thinking, both individually and as a society. These sources of stress may be difficult to get rid of, but they are not ordained by fate or God. They are consequences of human choices, and when they impose a severe toll on health and happiness, there is no virtue at all in learning to live with them. In fact, learning to live with them may sometimes mean learning to die with them.

In this class fall some of the most deeply rooted consequences of our industrial civilization and its values: stressors like polluted air, food, and water and the ever-present threat urban violence. Other causes come from personal ways of thinking, which shape our behavior and decisions: the kind of work we do, where and how we do it, where we live, how we spend our leisure time. All of these show an intimate connection between the way we think and the sources of sorrow in our lives.

To give just one instance, a recent survey disclosed that people who live close to the Los Angeles International Airport have a much higher rate of hypertension and heart disease than those who live in a quieter environment. For many people, as one of the directors of a major stress institute points out, the principal source of stress in their lives is their lifestyle itself.

This kind of stress is avoidable, even if the cost is a less lucrative job or a lot of time and effort spent on making changes in City Hall. But it is important to understand that even if we do everything we can think of to remove outside sources of stress from our lives — even if, like Ronald Colman in the movie *Lost Horizon,* we can somehow find our way to Shangri-La — stress will still pose a threat because its principal source is the mind. A person whose mind is well trained can manage in the midst of a stressful environment. Noise and pollution will take their toll on the body, but vitality and resistance will remain high. By contrast, a person whose mind is out of control can suffer from stress while lying on a quiet beach in Saint-Tropez.

On the whole, Americans are exceptionally concerned about their health. Yet most of us give ninety-nine percent of our attention to caring for the body and almost nothing to preventive care for the mind. Some of the most widely prescribed drugs in our country today are Inderal for hypertension, Valium for anxiety, and Prozac for depression. This is the only treatment most of us know.

I am not saying that these drugs are not useful under the guidance of a skilled physician, but I do not believe that drugs can ever get at the emotional components of such conditions. All they can do, which is helpful but not healing, is control symptoms. For healing, what is required is much more sweeping: not only changes in lifestyle but changes in thought-style. You can eat a perfectly balanced diet, sleep at night on the lullaby of a waterbed, and homestead in the most remote of woods, but if your thoughts do not obey you, you will still be subject to stress.

As long as we are resentful, for example, stress has to dog our footsteps. It is the same with jealousy, anxiety, impatience, depression, and anger. Researchers are only beginning to trace the steps by which these states of mind subject the body to stress. But whatever the mechanisms, it seems clear that the physical symptoms of stress will not vanish until we learn to control the states of mind that bring them on.

At present, researchers in these areas have naturally tended to concentrate on particular emotional states. To what kind of stress does anger subject the body? What, if any, are the physical effects of chronic anxiety or low self-esteem? These are fascinating questions, but one unsuspected connection that I would like to see explored has more to do with the underlying dynamics of the mind, regardless of the specific emotions involved: what stress is imposed by a mind that is excitable, prone to race off at the slightest provocation when events or people do not behave the way they "should"?

By now, researchers generally acknowledge that it is not so much events that subject us to stress as the way we perceive and interpret those events. Richard Lazarus of the University of California at Berkeley, for example, defines stress as a "relationship between the person and the environment that is appraised by the person as taxing or exceeding his or her resources and endangering his or her well-being." Put simply, if we interpret an event as threatening, the body responds to what the mind warns is a stressful situation. But if we see the same event as challenging, bodily responses may actually be enhanced.

My submission is that those whose minds are prone to race off in any kind of conditioned response to life's ups and downs – whatever the cause, whatever the response – are going to be subject to stress everywhere they go, simply because the mind is constantly subjecting the body to physiological arousal. By contrast, those who know how to keep their mind on an even keel will respond to life's challenges with calmness, alertness, and even eagerness. Events that others call stressful will be, for them as for Dr. Selye, "the spice of life." I want to emphasize this conclusion, because it differs significantly from current thinking. What makes the difference is not personality type but evenness of mind – which is a skill that anyone can learn.

꩜

Paradoxically, it is the mystics – supposedly babes in the woods where the affairs of the world are concerned – who give us the most practical insights into how to stay even through life's ups and downs. And one of the most surprising of these insights seems almost a paradox itself: if you want to teach your mind to stay even, the time to practice is not so much when fortune frowns as when fortune smiles.

Keeping even minded is difficult enough in unpleasant situations, when the mind strains to race off in anger or fear. But keeping calm in the face of excitement is even harder. Pleasure makes the mind race too, but because it is pleasant, our natural response is to sit back and enjoy the ride. Why not? The problem is that if you let your mind race in pleasant situations, you will not be able to keep it from speeding out of control in anger, fear, or some kind of compulsive behavior. If you want your mind to listen to you at such times, you have to keep it steady always.

Here the mystics give priceless and thoroughly misunderstood advice. When something exciting comes, they say, don't get excited. Put up with it. Soon it will be over.

This kind of advice is as welcome as a wet blanket. Everybody wants pleasure, and if it comes rarely, the least we should be able to do is enjoy it when it comes. But the mystics are not really trying to bleach the joy out of life. They are sharing the real secret of enjoyment. How can you enjoy anything, they ask, without peace of mind? It is one of life's most basic questions. Happiness requires a calm observer. When the mind gets speeded up, it is moving too fast to sit back and observe quietly, "Ah, that's good!" What the mystics are telling us is "Go ahead and enjoy; just don't get excited about it." Joy and excitement are two different things. William Blake captured the secret in well-known lines:

> He who binds to himself a joy
> Doth the winged life destroy.
> But he who kisses the joy as it flies
> Lives in Eternity's sunrise.

Actually, as your thinking slows down through the influence of meditation, excitement as such will lose its appeal. Nobody really enjoys a jangled nervous system; it is simply because of past conditioning that we confuse jangle with joy. For me today, any kind of excitement would be an unwelcome intrusion, because the still mind is so full of love and joy. Getting excited over something pleasant would be most unpleasant, because my heart is already full.

One possible connection between stress and illness is that psychological stress drains energy – energy that the body needs to stay vital, resist disease, and heal. Emotional storms – in fact, any kind of excitement – consume a tremendous amount of personal energy, which cannot help taking a toll on the nervous system – and, I suspect, on the circulatory and immune systems as well.

By nature, an untrained mind is excitement-prone, always ready to pick up some hitchhiking thought that promises to add interest to the ride. What happens is that the hitchhiker decides where to go. No wonder we find our mind out of gas toward the end of the day! It has been driving around and around, here and there, looking for joy in all the wrong places, and when we try to get started the next morning, we need some kind of psychic auto club to come out with a can of gas. We can sample all the medicines on the druggist's shelves, exercise like an Olympic champion, resort to the latest that medical technology can offer; no physical regimen can counteract the energy-wasting habits of the mind.

When I first moved to Berkeley, I was surprised to see the parade of hitchhikers that used to gather along University Avenue just where it joins the freeway. Most of them were thoughtful enough to carry signs to let you know just where they wanted to go. Compulsive thoughts carry signs too. We are going along, intent on our business, when some tempting thought standing just within our field of vision raises a sign saying "Excitement!" We think, "Great!" Who wouldn't pull off the road to give that hitchhiker a ride? Doesn't excitement mean pleasure? We get so enticed by the very thought of it that we don't think to look at what is printed on the back of the sign: "warning: this fellow may be hazardous to your security. Emotional turmoil, sleepless nights, and long-term frustration may result." He says he's going to Excitement, but the real destination is Depression.

Whatever our past conditioning, whatever our present state of mind, none of us is compelled to go on picking up excitement every time it sticks out its thumb. Every one of us has the freedom to drive by without a glance. That is the kind of training that meditation and the mantram can give your mind. If you don't put your foot on the brake, pull over, open the car door, and let excitement in, your mind is not going to be affected by it: which means that to the same degree, it will not be affected by fear, depression, anxiety, anger, jealousy, and any number of the other unpleasant states of mind that tie the stomach in knots during the day and turn our nights to nightmares.

I read recently that an estimated twenty to thirty

million Americans are subject to serious depression. One glossy drug advertisement described the symptoms in catchy language: "Depression. It can affect you in ways you would never suspect. Unexplainable jumpiness or anxiety. Unusual irritability. Sleep disturbances. Difficulty in concentrating or remembering. Physical pains that are hard to pin down. Appetite loss (or overeating). A loss of interest or pleasure in your job, family life, hobbies or sex. A downhearted period that gets worse and just won't go away. Frequent or unexplainable crying spells. A loss of self-esteem or an attitude of indifference. A combination of the above symptoms, persisting for two weeks or more, can be an indication of depressive illness and a warning to seek the advice of a doctor. . . ."

Feelings like these are all too familiar in today's world, and no one should feel guilty or inadequate if they strike home. Depression is built into our very way of life. Everywhere the media promise us happiness, pleasure, leisure, fulfillment, luxury. We want to be happy and are taught to be excited; we want to love and be loved, to cherish and be cherished, and are told we will find what we are looking for in sex. We are promised the right to have our own way, encouraged to believe that our first responsibility is to ourselves; yet somehow our relationships don't seem to thrive. More and more frequently we may look around and wonder what we are living for; life seems such a dull, meaningless round.

These are not matters of right and wrong; this is simply the dynamics of the mind. Our way of life puts the mind on a roller coaster with no seat belt, and the faster it goes, the sooner it gets jaded. One minute it is flying toward the sky, shrieking, "I'm high!" But the next minute it is hurtling down, and life seems hopeless. That is the nature of the mind: it never stops moving, and when it goes up, it has to come down. If we could interview the mind on *Sixty Minutes* and demand, "Why do you keep causing all this trouble?" it would shrug and reply, "That's how I am. I'm fickle by nature."

Human beings do not need excitement; they need meaning, purpose, a higher goal and some way of getting there. Without these, for those who are sensitive, life may soon lose its value.

Meditation is such a powerful shield that it can make the mind depression-proof, simply by slowing it down. The slower the mind, the steadier it has to be, and the less susceptible to excitement. When your meditation is going well, nothing that happens will be able to disturb your peace of mind.

By and large, meditation is a preventive measure. The time to guard yourself against depression is before you get depressed, and nothing provides a better shield than training the mind. I want to make it very clear, however, that in extreme cases, meditation should not be initiated as treatment. For those who suffer from life-threatening depression, or who are taking antidepressive drugs under a doctor's supervision, it may even be dangerous. If you are in this category, please do not jump into meditation without the close guidance of an experienced teacher. But there is a powerful spiritual tool which offers safe, fast help for anyone in times of crisis: repetition of the mantram.

In times of distress, when you try to call up the Holy Name, you may have difficulty even remembering how it goes. Your attention will be caught in your own turmoil, and every time you try to draw it back, it will rebel and slip away again. Here is where toughness comes in. No matter how many times you have to try, just keep bringing your attention back to the Holy Name again and again until your mind is calm.

When the weight of mental anguish is especially heavy, it can keep the mind from resting even at night. Here again, the best recourse is the Holy Name. Sleep does not come gradually. It falls like a curtain, and between the last waking moment and the first sleeping moment, there is an arrow's entry into deeper consciousness. If you can keep repeating the mantram until you fall asleep in it, the mantram will slip into the depths of your consciousness and work its healing wonders even in your sleep. When you are tormented by bad dreams, the Holy Name will come like a nurse to assuage your fears.

Guarding the mind against excitement is in no way attempting to run away from life. It is telling life quietly, "I am not afraid of you. I don't ask for any favors." You will never catch me holding out my hat to life and saying, "Please, I beg you, give me a few things that I like. You can put in one or two surprises if you care to, but only if they are pleasant. Don't put in anything that I don't like." This kind of begging is beneath our dignity as human beings.

Imagine getting up in the morning not even bothering to ask, "Are people going to like me? Are people going to dislike me? Are things going to go my way? Will I get jobs that I enjoy doing?" If you ask at all, it will only be to wonder, "Will I get a chance to help others?" If you do, it will not matter if you like or dislike what you have to do, or whether those around you will like you or not. All that is important is that you can make a contribution; that is what gives life meaning and value.

Even where food is concerned, you can train your mind not to get excited when things you like or dislike come. Food is a perfect training ground for the mind. I don't go in for ascetic fare; I enjoy everything I eat. But I eat only food that is wholesome and nourishing, and I never eat just to enjoy. If my life is a trust, I want everything I eat to help me live longer and work harder for the benefit of others. Whether it is food or exercise or entertainment – all of which have an important place in spiritual living – the question I ask is not "Do I like this?" but "Will this add to my capacity to give?" When your mind has been trained like this, there can never be any question of depression.

↲

Today's mania for speed strikes right at the root of our capacity for an even mind. How often we find ourselves locked into behavior and situations that force us to hurry, hurry, hurry! By now, most of us are aware that compulsive speed – "hurry sickness" – is one component of a personality that puts us at risk for heart disease. But hurry has another alarming repercussion that is less suspected: it cripples patience, which is vital for learning to steady the mind in times of trial.

A few months ago my wife and I drove to San Francisco for a movie. We got there early – one of my favorite ways of not getting pressured by time – so after we got our tickets, we decided to take a short walk. We were about to cross a busy street when a car stalled at the intersection next to us. The light turned green, and the driver of the car behind leaned on his horn. Nothing unusual; just another noisy incident in city life.

But the first driver did not simply sit and continue to crank his engine. In an instant he had burst out of his car with a snarl and was trying to drag the other driver through the window. Before we realized what was happening, they were scuffling like animals.

Fortunately a third party in the car intervened, and after more honking the intersection was cleared without injury. But if one of those men had had a gun, I realized, I might have witnessed not just a fight but a murder – all because of hurry, and the habit of getting excited when things don't go our way.

It shows how far we have traveled from patience when a few moments' delay, a trivial disappointment, an unexpected obstacle, makes a man explode in anger. Hurry makes a calm mind impossible: and without peace of mind, how can we enjoy anything, from a movie to good health? As for having things work out just how and when we want, wisdom demands that we learn to expect the unexpected. Life thinks nothing of making changes in our plans – after all, it has a lot of people in the picture. If we take personally every disruption of our schedule, we will go about feeling insecure most of the time.

In other words, patience is not only a mental virtue; it is an asset even for physical health. I'm sure you are aware of the way your heart races when you get impatient. Perhaps you have noticed, too, that your breathing becomes faster and more shallow. Doesn't it seem reasonable that if you can strengthen your patience to such a degree that other people's behavior never upsets you, your heart, lungs, and nervous system will be on vacation? Don't take my word for it; try it. At first, I agree, you will feel some stress from going against an established habit. But that is to be expected. After all, when you have been leading a sedentary life, walking only as far as the garage or the television set, it is stressful for a while to get out and jog; your heart and lungs complain. But how quickly they feel better for it! It is the same with patience; this is one of the grandest secrets of health.

Research evidence today suggests that emotional immunity to negative states of mind may well be linked to physical immunity, even resistance to disease. A person who is even minded, who doesn't get shaken if people speak ill of him or excited when they praise her to the skies – such a person, I submit, is a poor host for disease. That kind of inner toughness creates a protective buffer of what one researcher, Suzanne Kobasa, calls "hardiness": enhanced resistance to illness and the everyday stress of daily life.

So inverted are our modern values that we associate

patience with passivity and admire those who bowl over their competitors in their rush to the top. The spiritual perspective turns this right side up. "*La paciencia todo lo alcanza,*" Saint Teresa used to repeat: "Patience attains everything." Through patience, every goal can be reached.

Teresa's language would have been appreciated by her brothers, who were conquistadors in the New World. For them, to conquer meant to impose their way on unsuspecting peoples through superior military might. But for Teresa the real battle was within, and the surest weapon against the negative forces in human consciousness is patience. Patience means self-mastery: the capacity to hold on and remain loving in a difficult situation when every atom of your being wants to turn and run.

᙮

Perversely, the more we try to run from occasions that might cause us grief, the more we add to our burden of it. Trying to avoid suffering only makes suffering more likely, because we become increasingly rigid about the way life has to perform to meet our requirements. Again, no one is more insightful than Thomas a Kempis:

> . . . As long as suffering seems so grievous that you desire to flee it, so long will you be ill at ease, and the desire to escape tribulation will follow you everywhere.

"The desire to escape tribulation" is Thomas's tactful way of referring to our enslavement to personal likes and dislikes. We are held captive by so many tiny fears of life not working out: tied fast, like Gulliver, by a thousand Lilliputian cables. It's Saturday night, and you have a dinner engagement with the date of your dreams: what if the menu turns out to be uninspired? Suppose the music isn't right? And perhaps your companion is only pretending to have a good time . . . Thoughts like these run through our heads more than most people know. But if we go on worrying like this about every little unpleasant possibility, distress can follow us through life like a shadow.

How can we reverse this very natural habit of mind? By doing our best in whatever life sends without ever asking what it is going to send next. Every day brings circumstances in which we can practice this, beginning with the thousand and one little likes and dislikes that really matter very little to anybody but ourselves. By seizing every opportunity to do cheerfully things we do not like, especially when they benefit somebody else, we can gradually dissolve every fetter of anxiety about life's challenges. Slowly we begin to sit up straight, rub our aching arms and legs with indescribable relief, and wonder how we ever thought we enjoyed being tied down.

"Tribulation" is an old-fashioned word, but it describes rather accurately the day-in, day-out endeavor that is the real substance of spiritual living. It starts at the breakfast table – staying cheerful, not hiding behind the newspaper, listening with attention as your son recounts every play in last night's soccer match. It goes on at the office, where you try for the hundredth time to reconcile two co-workers who are allergic to each other. It continues late into the afternoon, when a missing file threatens to close your promising career. And after work, commute traffic is so torturous that if there were a muscle where patience is exercised, it would be swollen and throbbing by the time you pull in the driveway.

But there you are, as relaxed as if you had spent the day on a putting green! To look at you no one would guess that inside, you are toe to toe with a relentless adversary: self-will. And you are holding your own.

What makes us impatient? The mystics give a good, scientific answer: acts of impatience, repeated over and over and over. Then how do we make ourselves more patient? By trying to be more patient every day. When we meditate on passages like the Prayer of Saint Francis, the muscles of the mind, which at present may be so flabby that they can hardly bear the weight of any sorrow, grow stronger and more resilient every day. Every provocation is an opportunity. If we do everything we can every day to stretch our patience, one day it is going to be inexhaustible.

A few days ago I was in the grocery store watching an exasperated young mother contend with her little one. Hitching a ride on the shopping cart, he seemed determined to throw in all the items advertised on television; unfortunately, his fancies did not coincide with his mother's notions of nutrition. After she had taken out half a dozen items and set them back on the shelves, she announced for half the store to hear: "Patrick, there's a limit!"

Every parent can sympathize with her situation. But I wish I had been able to tell her on the spot something the mystics have proven to us with their very lives: There really is no limit. There is no limit to the patience we can develop, no end to our capacity for bearing with the sorrow that life impartially doles out.

This is a crucial issue. No matter how hard we try, aren't there occasions when we are bound to blow up at someone – our partner, our neighbor, our children, our mother-in-law? It grieves us to realize that even with our loved ones, we cannot always control our own temper. Sometimes it breaks loose and runs amok almost with a will of its own.

It is precisely at such a moment, when your temper is about to burst all bounds, that love for the Lord can come to your rescue – and the rescue of those around you. If God is the furthest thing from your mind, that is where toughness comes in. Go for a walk and start repeating the Holy Name for all you're worth – not aloud but in your mind – and keep bringing your attention back to it over and over again until your mind is calm. Then, when you go back to the scene that brought you distress, you will be able to stay relatively calm and compassionate. You can speak kindly, even when the other person's response is far from kind. If you have a very personal relationship with the Lord, you may feel almost as if a loving arm has slipped around you and set you back on firm ground. This security – knowing that the loving arm is always ready – is what makes for joy.

Remember, though, that in repeating the Holy Name like this, you are not appealing to somebody on high. You are asking the Lord who lives in the depths of your heart, "Please give me more patience, more endurance to bear this cheerfully. Release the strength I need to stand firm, so that I can help those around me to stand firm too." The mantram invariably brings help, but help always comes from within – even when it rises from recesses beyond the reach of our small, personal self.

The key here is detachment – not from others but from ourselves, from our own self-centered insistence on getting things the way we want. With detachment, life's ups and downs need hardly affect our security at all.

Meditation and the mantram clear our eyes so we can see when purely personal motives are coming into play. The mind, remember, can present us with only a fragmentary picture, never a faithful representation of the whole. When we get deep below the surface of consciousness in meditation, the mind becomes still and clear. Then we can see for ourselves to what extent our mind has distorted the picture we have of even the people closest to us. With that insight, much of what seems to threaten and distress us dissolves.

All of us, of course, believe we are the never-ending stream of thoughts that is our mind. But just as there are hurricanes and earthquakes in the world outside us, there are emotional typhoons and tremors deep in the caverns of consciousness, and this turmoil is constantly shaping and reshaping our thoughts. As long as we believe we are these thoughts, how can we avoid being shaken and blown off course by such violent disturbances?

Gradually, in meditation, our thoughts slow down further and further, until we are able to see that these storms of the mind are not who we are. We need not be blown about by emotional hurricanes; we can watch winds like anger rising, just as a veteran meteorologist would, noting changes but not getting entangled – that is, without feeling any compulsion to act on them. No one can imagine what an era of freedom this ushers in. It is not that turmoil will vanish: causing us trouble sometimes is in the nature of people, just as it is in our nature to cause trouble sometimes to others. But when the mind quiets down and we see more clearly, we gain faith that we have the inner resources to stay calm and kind no matter what circumstances come our way. With that, a good deal of life's burden of personal sorrow is lifted.

But sorrow is more than something to be endured. It can be an invaluable teacher. You must have seen those highway signs warning, "Go Back. Wrong Way!" Where roads are concerned, we all understand this warning and know we should turn around. If only we could understand life's signs so easily! Sorrow is often a warning with the same message:

"Go back. Change your direction. You are going the wrong way."

Every creature is conditioned to avoid pain; this is a built-in safety mechanism to protect our bodies from harm. When you eat more than you should, for example, you should feel reassured if your stomach aches. Your body is telling you in the only language it knows, "Please don't do this again; it's not good for me."

Similarly, mental and emotional suffering often comes as the consequence of our own thoughts and actions. Trying to hide from suffering, closing our eyes to it, means we will go on repeating the same mistakes, making the suffering worse.

When you find your mind in turmoil, when you begin to feel that you are not worth much and your life is a waste, it is time to make a U-turn. Otherwise, sorrow will only increase. So when pain comes, don't shrink away from it; that will only hurt you more. When you feel threatened, don't hide or put up hostile defenses; that will only wound you more. Try to keep your mind steady, drawing on the mantram and meditation: if there is a lesson to be learned, it will sink in. All of us have this choice. And once you have learned how to keep your mind still, you will act only from love and live only in love, which means that personal sorrow will be erased from your life. That is the purpose of pain: to urge us toward the discovery that love, joy, meaning, and peace of mind can be found only in living for all.

Most of us, as my grandmother once told me

bluntly, confuse self-pity and grief. Granny was as tough as she was loving. When I would come to her crying because my feelings were hurt, she could be terribly unsympathetic. "That's not grief," she would say. "You're just feeling sorry for yourself." Self-pity weakens us; grief, which means sorrow for others, ennobles us and releases inner resources to help.

It requires detachment and a measure of self-understanding to know when the mind is just reciting its favorite litany of "Poor me, nobody cares for me, nobody loves me." Part of the strategy is never to ask who loves you; instead, ask how you can love more.

I used to teach classes in Shakespeare in my university days, and I always remember King Lear's tragic question to his daughters: "How much do you love me? How much do you love me? How much do you love me?" Cordelia, who loved him truly, could not adorn her answer with flowery phrases, and her father flew into a rage that turned to hatred. Such acute self-will and self-pity cannot help leading to tragedy, and toward the end of the play we see Lear standing on a desolate moor, abandoned by all but those he has himself abandoned, raising his arms to the stars in despair and crying, "Look upon a man as full of grief as he is of age!"

If I were to write a play on the same subject, I would have King Lear tell his daughters, "I don't care whether you love me; I will never ask. Love is not a contract. Love me or hate me, my life will be devoted to you always." The end of the play would be magnificent: Lear standing as majestic as a real king should and saying to the heavens, "Look upon a man as full of joy as he is of love."

Sorrow is an essential part of living: not good, not something to be courted or embraced, just unavoidable. But in facing sorrow we have a choice, and wherever there is choice there is freedom. "Pain is an enemy," goes an Indian proverb, "only when we do not welcome it as a friend." Sorrow is a teacher whose lesson is to go beyond sorrow. No one likes heartburn, but we can learn from the experience that there is a limit to how much ice cream can satisfy. In the same way, we can learn from heartbreak not to clutch for happiness at any thing or person outside us.

Yet the tragicomedy of sorrow is that most of us go into the same situation again and again and still do not learn. This is the illusion that Indian mysticism calls maya. It always reminds me of the old shell game, which I used to see in my village in South India. No matter how many times we fail to guess which coconut shell covers the rupee, we are always ready to try just one more time.

In the end, sorrow comes simply from asking of life what it cannot give. As long as we believe ourselves to be physical creatures, there has to be suffering when we pursue our desires. Asking material things and outward activities to satisfy the spirit, to borrow an old Persian saying, is like asking an elephant to satisfy its hunger with a sesame seed.

Initiation into universal consciousness, it has been said, is initiation into universal empathy . . . and therefore into universal sorrow. As love deepens, unseen walls that isolate us from others begin to melt away. No longer can we pick up a newspaper and read about the hungry and homeless without feeling ourselves intimately involved. No longer can we watch passively as violence rages in Central America. That suffering will be our suffering, and it will change our lives: we will take time and resources from other activities and find ways to help. Spiritual growth means a heightened sense of sorrow, but it also brings the inner resources we need to help assuage that sorrow: strength, insight, compassion, creative action.

Opportunities for becoming more aware of the needs of others lie all around us. Helping is the true vocation of every human being, and we don't have to wait for some terrible event to come and reveal it to us. A neighbor's wife is ill – why not offer to take her children for the day? Your daughter has come home from school in tears again: you can let her go her own way, or you can rearrange your schedule and make time to listen and help. Little things, all of them, but they add up to works of love.

Most of us, at least at the beginning, can shoulder only a little burden of such sorrow at a time. Yet by the end of a day, when everything is tallied, we may find we have lifted a hefty load. Miraculously enough, we will not feel the fatigue we used to feel when our sorrows were strictly personal. In this way, even in our own rather pedestrian lives, we discover the truth of what Jesus promised: "My yoke is easy, and my burden light."

Which lover of God has not had to face mighty storms? Name anyone you like; you will find that suffering seemed to seek that person out. Can we expect divine love to come any more easily to us? Which of us would learn to be selfless if life were one long pleasure cruise? For the aspiring lover of God, stressful situations become fuel to "the fire of the soul" which consumes our ugliest, most selfish tendencies and fans the spark of divinity in us into flame. It may sound impossible, but we can cultivate the same eagerness to face every challenge to spiritual growth.

CHAPTER 6
Love

*Blessed are they that are persecuted for righteousness'
sake, for theirs is the kingdom of heaven.*

Coming from South India, I never saw snow
until I was sixteen. Not only that, I had never even seen
people who had seen snow. When I came to this country on the Fulbright exchange program, I explained to
the authorities that I was accustomed to a mild climate. The State Department thoughtfully posted me
to the University of Minnesota.

It was there that I heard about skiing. Ski enthusi-
asts, I discovered, have to get up even earlier to go skiing than I do for meditation. "You have to drive all the
way to the mountains," friends explained, "and then
get in line for the lift." And that is only the beginning of
the discomfort. "Look at all that gear you have to carry
and put on!" I teased them. "Not the least of which are
those two long fiberglass appendages that to me are
only impediments to movement. And then standing
about for hours in the snow . . ."

"You don't know the joys of skiing," my friends retorted. "When you're shooting down a fast, powdery slope, you're not a groundling any more; you're a bird in flight. The weight of your body just falls away." "The same thing happens to me every morning in meditation," I said. "Only with one big difference: wouldn't you find it more challenging to ski up the slopes?"

That really got them interested. Imagine starting from the Rhine valley and skiing straight up the Matterhorn! That is the challenge of the spiritual life, the greatest challenge you can imagine: skiing up the slopes of life, against all the downward pull of physical and emotional conditioning. To attain any worthwhile goal, even in sports, don't we have to overcome certain obstacles? Isn't a measure of pain part of the effort? It is the same with living in heaven here on earth, winning that "pearl of great price." There, too, we have to endure what it costs to overcome the obstacles in our way; but just as in skiing, if our desire is deep enough, what seems like pain to the rest of the world is dwarfed in comparison with the glory of our goal.

What sounds like a negative note in this beatitude is really proof of the depth and breadth of Jesus' universal vision. If suffering is part of entering the kingdom of heaven within, it is not because life is perverse but because living in heaven means mastering a whole new way of thinking. Remember Eckhart's words: "He who would be what he ought to be must stop being what he is." When life sends us treatment that seems unfair, sometimes at the hands of those dear to us, it is not just "trial and tribulation." These are the opportunities every human being needs for cultivating the divine love that shines alike on all, without question of right or reason or favor, "that we may be the children of our Father which is in heaven: for he maketh his sun to rise on the evil as on the good, and sendeth rain on the just as on the unjust."

Every normal human being throws up his hands at this and says, "I simply am not capable of behaving like that!" Jesus assures us emphatically: You are capable of behaving like that. Everyone is, simply by virtue of being human; for whatever our failings, whatever our limitations, the Lord lives in every heart. I am not idealizing here. I know how difficult this can be. But when someone offends you, instead of thinking over and over again, "She hurt me! She hurt me!" you can actually use the Holy Name as an eraser. All the power behind your anger then goes into the erasing, and resentment goes no deeper than writing on water. The secret of the mind is that it is a sponge: we slowly become what we soak our consciousness in. When your mind dwells on jealousy, you cannot help becoming more jealous. When it dwells on wrongs you have suffered, you are soaking yourself in anger. The only alternative is to teach the mind to soak itself in love, through the practice of meditation and repetition of the Holy Name.

Friends often lament, "But there just doesn't seem to be any end to the negative thoughts that come up! No matter how I try to be positive and forgiving, there's always something just around the corner to upset me again. I'm not sure you realize how much negativity the ordinary person has to deal with." I assure them that indeed I do understand. That is why I know that love requires a center within oneself which nothing can shake — a *sanctum sanctorum* into which we can always retire to renew our strength and security. That is the purpose of meditation.

↷

Again, because there is so much misunderstanding about suffering and spirituality, I find it helpful to look at the actual dynamics of the mind.

Mystics of all religions remind us that this life on earth is woven of opposites that are inseparable twins: pain and pleasure, sickness and health, praise and censure, defeat and success, birth and death. One minute people are handing us bouquets of roses; the next minute they are lobbing rotten eggs. If we function well only when people are kind to us, we are living only part-time. Love is a full-time occupation, a continuous state of mind.

We may not feel the need for approval as acutely as a movie star I read about who, in order to fall asleep at night, had to switch on a tape of her audience applauding. Yet almost all of us suffer when we are criticized, or when friends suddenly turn on us or let us down. By using blows such as these as opportunities to keep our mind steady, we can erase negative responses like depression and resentment from our hearts completely. And when all resentment, all ill will, all depression is gone, we live in heaven here on earth. Instead of looking at difficulties as deprivations, we can learn to recognize them as opportunities for deepening and widening our love. You don't run away from opportunities; you keep on the lookout for them. Lashing out at others, trying to "get even" when people are harsh, only wastes these precious chances for growth, which can come in no other way.

Wise spiritual directors have always recognized that for the vast majority of us, the widest opportunities for this kind of growth lie hidden in the give-and-take of everyday relationships. It is here that we can find the unity between ourselves and others by removing everything that keeps us separate, which is precisely what the practice of loving means.

One profound but simple secret is that when you love someone deeply, you want to share everything with that person. If she likes the novels of Somerset Maugham, you want to read them too. If he likes baseball, you want to feel the same attraction. When you find satisfaction even in enduring the same hardships, because you would rather be together in hardship than comfortably apart, you begin to escape from the narrow prison of separateness that is the human condition. That is why, whether we know it or not, each of us longs to discover in at least one relationship the unity which underlies all life, for even a fleeting taste of this unity brings enormous joy.

"He who knoweth not love, knoweth not God," says John the Apostle, "for God is love." The words sound so ethereal that most of us cannot connect them with daily life. What, we ask, do personal relationships have to do with the divine? I would reply, it is by discovering the unity between ourselves and others – all others – that we find our unity with God. That is why training the mind is the nuts and bolts of religion. We don't first get to know God and then, by some miracle of grace, come to love our fellow human beings. Loving comes first: learning to love others is how we move closer to the Lord. In this sense, learning to love is practicing religion. Those who can put the welfare of others before their own small personal interests are religious, even if they would deny it. And, of course, anyone who can quote scripture chapter and verse but will not put herself out for others has yet to learn what religion means.

In one of my favorite sonnets, William Shakespeare calls love "the marriage of true minds." We are so used to thinking of love as involving bodies that hearing "marriage" together with "minds" can startle us. But this is no mere turn of phrase; it holds a kernel of subtle psychology. In any relationship in which two people can hold their minds true – to each other, to compassion, to a willingness to share in sorrow as well as joy – love cannot help blossoming. What we need in order to nurture love, then, is mental disciplines that we can use to train our minds to be true.

Mystics like Thomas a Kempis tell us that the would-be lover must be a martyr. That is not particularly effective salesmanship today, but learning to stay kind when people turn against us is the essence of training the mind to love. If we do not develop this sort of inner toughness, our love will never be strong enough to support the weight of close relationships, let alone the weight of the all-embracing love to which Jesus calls us again and again: "Be ye therefore perfect, even as your Father which is in heaven is perfect."

Tradition has it that love is blind, but just the opposite is true. Love looks only to the shining goal of union; it is lack of love that is blind. The more you love, the more clearly you see the needs of others, for you are dwelling less on your own needs and desires. You know how you feel when unkind words are directed at you; when you feel one with others, you find it impossible to strike back with unkind words when someone is rude to you. No abstruse psychology is required for understanding this, simply "Do unto others as you would have them do unto you." And, Jesus would add, do it no matter what they do unto you, even when it hurts. If we want to be in love, Thomas a Kempis tells us plainly, we have to "embrace willingly all that is hard and distasteful": not in a spirit of grim self-denial, but simply in the course of trying to put others' needs before our own. Bearing sorrow cheerfully for the sake of another is the very heart of love.

This is far from the idea of romance held by the modern world, which seems to have taken lessons from commerce in all things. Today, one unkind word can be enough to make a person bristle with hostility. One well-aimed dig and we say, "I don't want to hear any more from you for the rest of the weekend!" Set aside divine love, the mystics would say, we should not even claim to have mundane love if that is how we are going to act.

Love means that regardless of what a person does to

us, we will not turn our back or move away; we will stand close and go on loving. This ubiquitous question of "Why have you done this to me?" doesn't even enter in. If you slip and hurt me, what has that to do with my love for you?

None of us, I believe, really wants to strike back at those we love. We do not really get satisfaction out of hurting people who hurt us. We have simply fallen into the habit of brooding on wrongs done to us, blowing them up to the proportions of enormous antipathies, until we finally explode.

A natural antidote to this tendency of mind is to repeat the mantram as often as we can, with as much depth of feeling as we can muster. There is no mystery about driving the Holy Name deep into the mind; it is just a matter of sincere, systematic practice. By dint of sheer persistence, making use of every odd piece of time in the midst of a very busy life, I have managed to carry the Holy Name like a lifeline down into the depths of the unconscious. If I hear even one negative phrase, the Holy Name starts up, and all the power that might have flared in animosity is harnessed to love's purposes. As Mahatma Gandhi showed, we can use this power to build bridges of understanding between those who are estranged, to light lamps of sympathy between warring communities and even nations.

In the end, personal suffering always comes from self-will. Remember that pungent phrase from the *Theologica Germanica:* "Nothing burns in hell except self-will." That leaves little room for argument. No matter how justified we may feel in getting angry, the only thing that makes us flare up is that our self-will has been violated. In the end, the whole of loving consists in removing self-will; and if we are going to choose that, we have to choose suffering, for that is what removing self-will entails.

There is anguish in taming selfish passions that are accustomed to riding roughshod over us. When you have been striking back at others for twenty years, it hurts to sit and listen to rude words without doing or saying anything harsh, trying to keep your mind from even thinking a mean thought, just "for righteousness' sake." The capacity to bear this pain cheerfully, knowing it will lead to greater love, is the very core of spiritual disciplines. After a while, the mystics say, you will find the fierce thrill of mastery right in that pain – just as you would in the pain of a cold ski slope or of "hitting the wall" on a marathon – as you get the taste of freedom. Goodness, says the Bhagavad Gita, "may taste bitter at first, but it is found at last to be immortal wine."

Going against the grain of self-will – the insistent, overriding drive to have our own way, whatever it may cost others – can be excruciating. Yet as Meister Eckhart says bluntly, we cannot know God until we are "stripped, cleansed, and purified." As long as there is self-will, we have no choice in whether to suffer. But we can choose whether our suffering is to be meaningful or meaningless. We can actually use suffering to reduce suffering, to gain a state of consciousness so grand that even a step toward it is worth the cost. We can choose to bear suffering rather than add to our burden of anger, resentment, and hostility. We can choose to suffer ourselves instead of adding to the suffering of others. This pain of purification has a purpose: to remove every obstacle between ourselves and the kingdom of heaven within.

Thomas a Kempis, then, explains this beatitude precisely. Suffering becomes sweet when we see that it removes self-will and uncovers love:

> When you come to such a degree of patience that tribulation is sweet to you, and for the love of God is savory and pleasant in your sight, then you may trust that it is well with you; . . . for you have found heaven on earth.

For everyone, there comes a turning point in spiritual striving when suffering does become sweet: not out of perversity, but because it is a necessary spur to this process of perfection. It helps to remember that nothing in personality suffers but the thick covering of selfish drives and desires that stands between us and perfect love. Having this thick covering brings suffering; getting rid of it brings suffering: but the first only ensures more suffering, whereas every step toward removing self-will means a little of our burden of sorrow has fallen away.

But at the risk of repetition, let me be clear: this is no assurance that your life will be free from grief. It is only personal sorrow that falls away. The greater your sensitivity to others, the more you will be aware of the suffering borne by those around you.

Years ago I read about a little girl whose pup was run

over and who sat on the curb sobbing and sobbing. When a neighbor tried to console her she replied, "It's just like being run over myself!" That is the price of love. For those who love God, when anyone dies, a part of them dies too. In the highest sense, this is the meaning of the Passion, the reason why the Messiah was called "a man of sorrows, and acquainted with grief." Living in all, you suffer whatever they suffer. But this awareness of unity is also the source of the greatest joy, because it brings the love, compassion, and creativity to relieve suffering wherever you go.

There is meaning in sorrow, and when that meaning is grasped, nothing in the world is more useful for us. The key lies in recognizing that we do always have a choice: not whether we are going to suffer, but when and for what. The astonishing claim of the mystic, exemplified so beautifully in the life of Jesus, is that once we begin exerting this power to choose, our suffering can be turned into joy. Eckhart says:

> Would you know for certain whether your sufferings are your own or God's? You can tell by these signs. When you suffer for yourself, in whatever way, the suffering hurts and is hard to bear. But when you suffer for God and God alone, your suffering hurts you not; nor will it burden you, for it is God who bears the load. Believe me, if a person were willing to suffer on account of God and of God alone, then even if he should fall prey to the collective sufferings of all the world it would not trouble him nor bow him down, for God would be the bearer of his burden.

If we want to draw closer to the spark of divine love deep within, our desire will be to suffer, as Christ did, whenever it helps to relieve the suffering of others.

Before Francis of Assisi fell in love with Christ he was a troubadour, composing and singing passionate love songs. This same depth of feeling he brought to his relationship with the Lord. So great was Francis's thirst to be united with Christ that one day toward the end of his life he knelt in prayer on the secluded heights of Mount La Verna and from the depths of his heart asked his Lord for two favors: first, that he should experience, as far as possible, the suffering Christ had endured on the cross; second, that he should feel the love for all God's creatures that had moved Christ to endure that suffering. These two, suffering and love, are the two intertwining poles of Jesus' life on earth.

After long hours of intense prayer, Francis rejoined his companions. He said nothing about his experiences; yet despite his efforts to hide himself, they saw on his palms, on the soles of his feet, and in his side the stigmata, the wounds of Christ's Passion. These he would carry, concealed from all but his closest followers, for the rest of his life.

Saint Teresa of Avila is probably best remembered for her celebration of the "mystical marriage" that takes place between the soul and Christ. "It is like rain falling from the heavens into a river or a spring," she says, ". . . or it is as if a tiny streamlet enters the sea, from which it will find no way of separating itself." But the joyous union with Christ that she experienced, as she herself explains over and over again, was possible only because she had first united herself with his suffering.

⌁

One simple proof of love's unbelievable power is that it is still the most longed-for commodity on earth. In an age rich in technological toys, aren't we still troubled if we have a losing record in love? Even if broken relationships and divided homes become the norm, won't we always try to have and hold something more? How much solace will we find in a fat portfolio of stocks or a warehouse of possessions? The awful truth is that no one on earth is more severely handi-capped than those who are unable to love. Without love we are desperately deprived – and that may prove to be our saving grace.

Love is so exquisitely elusive. It cannot be bought, cannot be badgered, cannot be hijacked. It is available only in one rare form: as the natural response of a healthy mind and healthy heart. The only way to se-cure it is to heal our own mind and heart. From time to time, everyone needs to be reminded that love is not something that is up to chance or fate. It is a skill, a world-class skill of mind, which anyone can gain and everyone must work to maintain, all the more so in a world that holds so little sacred.

The mystics may know of no magic to exorcise self-ish urges, but they give us powerful disciplines like meditation and the mantram with which we can learn to turn around the raw energy of negative emotions like anger, jealousy, and hate. This reversal is the whole purpose of training the mind. Harnessed for unity, that same energy is love.

The other day my wife and I were driving along a narrow coastal road when we encountered a man with a flag warning of crews busy repairing the road. Heavy rains had washed out the bank from under the asphalt, so one lane was a yawning pit with no shoulder but thin air – and, hundreds of feet below, the sea.

We sat there waiting for several minutes, unable to see what was going on. For a while it seemed that there was no one in that desolate stretch except us, the flagman, and a few cows beyond the fence at the side of the road.

Then, as if the earth itself had produced them, a stream of cars erupted from nowhere and rolled by in the other direction.

No one else in the car, I feel sure, thought anything of such an ordinary occurrence. But I immediately exclaimed, "That's just how it is in the mind!" Negative thoughts can surprise us just like that. They bunch up in the mind where we can't see them; then, without the gracious warning of a flagman, they burst in and rush through consciousness before we even realize they are coming. Whenever thinking is fast and furious, whether because of anger, fear, or some fierce desire, we have no control over what thoughts come bursting through, and very little freedom in how we respond to them either. For the time being, we are trapped in that stream of thought – which means that however we respond, the consequences of our actions are likely to be disastrous.

Once you get beneath the surface of consciousness, you begin to see and to control this kind of traffic. Eventually you can become a kind of flagman in your own subconscious, stopping thoughts with the mantram until you can let them pass by in an orderly fashion. In practical terms, this means that although your mind may still think angry thoughts, you will not get caught in them or act on them; you will have latitude for choice. It is the same with most other negative emotions: resentment, jealousy, anxiety, fear. When you enter the personal unconscious, you begin to take yourself out of the orbit of compulsive thinking – the first exhilarating step toward acting in real freedom.

Compulsive thought patterns exist only so long as we support them with our belief in their power to propel us into action. Choice is hard to exercise beneath the surface of consciousness, but choice is there. If we are bothered by certain thoughts, we should remind ourselves that it is we who rent out the precious space within the mind. We don't have to be afraid of compulsive thoughts if we don't welcome them. If we shut the door of the mind right in their face, they will soon tire of knocking.

The deeper realms of the unconscious, which are shared by all, can be compared to a mental atmosphere that every human being breathes. Just as the atmosphere outside us contains oxygen, hydrogen, and many other elements and compounds, the atmosphere of the unconscious contains primordial forces – desires, impulses, urges, instincts – that are part of the collective record of our evolutionary past. And just as chemicals in the air around us can bring on ailments like cancer, there are thoughts in the unconscious which can pollute our inner atmosphere and bring on illness in mind and even body. If for no other reason than our own health, we need to develop our own stringent standards and monitor for negative thought pollution. We will not only be doing ourselves a great service; we will be doing others a service as well.

But this inner atmosphere is not itself negative. Like the air we breathe, it nourishes life. The positive forces of consciousness – love, compassion, forgiveness, the yearning to be reunited with the divine ground of existence – spring from those depths as well, as do the laws that express the unity of life.

In this view, the mind is as much a part of the world as matter is, and moral laws describe forces as real as those defined by laws of the physical world. Sir Isaac Newton did not invent the law of gravity; it had been floating around since creation, we might say, waiting for someone to get onto the right wavelength to pick it up. It was always there, fully operative, yet thousands of innocent souls must have been hit on the head by overripe apples over the course of history before the connection was made. It took Newton's genius and the confluence of the currents of history to allow him to delve deep into the structure of life, discern this law, and see how to apply it.

Similarly, Einstein delved into those same depths.

With the wider view that Newton had opened, he was able to see gravitation as part of a larger whole and glimpse a unity in which all physical laws cohere. The relationships he found – the unity – had always been there; yet it took intense concentration, imagination, and insight to see form there, express it in laws, and work out the applications. As modern physics tells us, this is a participatory universe, whose laws are expressed in forms shaped in part by the human mind.

Spiritual laws and forces, the mystics remind us, are just as verifiable as those the physicists find. When Mahatma Gandhi said that nonviolence is the law of our being, and that it is no new discovery but "as old as the hills," he was speaking as precisely as Newton might have about gravitation. The law of life's unity is written into the very essence of creation. It comes into play whenever a person draws on the power of love and self-sacrifice to heal a relationship or stanch the spread of violence.

Yet evolution takes a great step forward when people like Gandhi, Newton, and Einstein discover such laws and articulate them in a new way, applying them scientifically to the solution of old problems. Einstein once said that even as a child, he used to imagine what the universe would look like if one could ride on a ray of light. Imagine! Most children dream of nothing more fantastical than riding on a Harley-Davidson, and here is young Albert, traveling with his imagination along sunbeams. Similarly, I like to think of Gandhi catching a ride on the force of divine love, riding it from its source deep in consciousness up to the surface of life, to show the world the way out of violence and war.

From the law of gravitation, is it too long a jump to talk about the law of love floating around in the atmosphere of our common consciousness? All we have to do is tune in and pick it up. Hate, too, is there, blowing through like a Texas tornado – don't pick it up! There is no need to bring in God or an afterlife; we all know how hatred destroys relationships between persons and races and nations. Whatever our intentions, hate gradually pollutes the atmosphere until violence erupts.

There is no use in saying to ourselves, "It can't happen here in good old Sioux Falls!" In our own century, hatred has hijacked some of the most cultured of societies. In parts of our own country, it is happening today. Unless we make a relentless, continuous effort not to open the door to hatred, we can find ourselves dwelling inside a mind that views the world with eyes of suspicion and hostility. Then we will swear that suspicion is only realistic and sympathy an attitude for fools.

"Judge not," Jesus warns, "that ye be not judged." When we keep pointing a finger of judgment at others, we are teaching our mind a lasting habit of condemnation. Sooner or later, that finger of judgment will be aimed point-blank at ourselves. It is not that people do not sometimes warrant judgment; fault is very easy to find. But judgmental attitudes and a suspicious eye only poison a situation. To right wrongs and help others correct their faults, we have to focus on what is positive and never give in to negative thinking. Love, sympathy, and forbearance require steady strength of mind.

Love means that whenever negative thoughts enter the mind, we can turn our attention to positive thoughts instead. This is all that is required to guard ourselves against lapses from love.

The key to this is giving – our time, our talents, our resources, our skills, our lives – to selfless work, some cause greater than our small personal interests. By working hard to give what we can, and by cultivating kindness and compassion under every provocation, we can escape destructive ways of thinking. Even those facing a critical illness will find that this simple pre-scription can lift the burdens of resentment, guilt, and depression from their lives.

When this skill of love becomes second nature, even when someone is cruel to us, our eyes will not be di-verted from the divine core of his personality.

This does not mean playing Pollyanna or closing our eyes to wrong behavior. It means simply that we will never lose faith in any person's capacity to change. Without that faith, people lose faith in themselves, and without faith in yourself it is not possible to improve. Everyone deserves our respect, for all are children of an all-compassionate God. This is the most effective way to help others remember their true character.

When negative thinking ceases completely, what re-mains is our real nature: love itself, universal; "love without an object," as Saint Bernard says, which sheds light wherever it turns without ever asking who "deserves" it. What a question for love to ask! "I need no reason to love," Bernard says: "I love because I love; I love in order that I may love." When we attain this state we will bask in love continuously, whatever storms may rage outside. Can you imagine any greater joy? No achievement can surpass this; no aspiration can reach higher. This exalted state is our real human legacy, and until we claim it, we have not done what we are here on earth to do.

Early in this century, Werner Heisenberg changed our thinking about the world outside us by asserting that the act of observing subatomic events cannot help affecting what is observed. Mystics are no less revolutionary than quantum physicists, and what they have to tell us can lead to a transformation in our lives. "We behold that which we are, and we are that which we behold." Those who have not learned to love see a world where love is weak, ineffectual, sentimental, hopelessly out of date. Those who live in love see a world of hope: a world of men and women who, despite their failings, are always capable of love in the core of goodness in their hearts.

"He that loveth," says Thomas a Kempis, "flyeth, runneth, and rejoiceth. He is free, and will not be held in." When your love does not depend on others, you soar like an eagle, high above the selfishness of the world and its law of "an eye for an eye," which, as Mahatma Gandhi would say, ends only when all are blind.

To see life from this lofty vantage, however, we cannot let our sight be clouded by rumors or slander or innuendo. As long as our loyalty is dependent on other people's responses, we are living in slavery; the hallmark of love is freedom. Love "manuals" are coming out now almost like pulp novels, and their popularity reminds us how urgent is the need to rediscover what love really means. The mystics give us an uncompromisingly reliable standard: love should not waver, whatever those we love may do or say.

To lay claim to love, the mystics warn, we have to develop a fortitude that no battle in history has demanded. We have to train our mind to be secure in the teeth of deprecation, calumny, injustice, and betrayal. Only in this kind of trial by fire can the human being rise above praise and censure to that unshakable compassion which, as Jesus himself showed, is the most heroic feature of the spiritual life.

In my own lifetime, I recall how often slander was spread against Gandhi, painting him in the most lurid colors imaginable. I don't think he ever wasted a word defending himself, although it must have hurt deeply when those who should have known him better believed what they read in the more sensational papers. Even when once-loyal supporters turned against him, Gandhi's compassion for them never faltered.

Saint Francis of Assisi, who endured many similar experiences, left us his secret: "He who has not learned to forgive has lost the greatest joy in life." Every one of us has opportunities to taste this joy on a smaller scale when friends or loved ones turn against us or let us down. That is when we can transform our human love into love divine.

On the Blue Mountain in South India, where I lived for many years, sandalwood trees grow in profusion. Beautiful images of the Lord are carved from the wood of these trees, which has a lustrous texture and such a haunting fragrance that sandalwood paste is used in temple worship. If you take an axe and cut into the sandalwood tree, rich perfume comes forth; the deeper you cut, the more intoxicating the fragrance will be.

All of us, Jesus would say, can learn the lesson of forgiveness the sandalwood teaches. The deeper we are wounded, the sweeter should be our response; that is the only way to heal our wound and also to change that person's heart.

If we cannot cultivate this kind of patience, we need not bother to say we love; time will prove otherwise. We should simply use the word "like." The law of liking is: Like me and I will like you; dislike me and I will dislike you. Love is not a business contract or a trade agreement; love is a given.

Those whose responses always spring from love, in Meister Eckhart's phrase, "carry God with them in all things." That kind of love is divine. The true lover knows it is the nature of most people to change their loyalties, to modify their affections in rhythm with the ebb and flow of personal desires — and still the true lover will love.

These are marvelous challenges. It is when you begin thinking "How much will I get out of this person?" that relationships become a burden. When you are concerned only with how to give more, you feel no burden at all. Which one of us is free of self-centered thinking, even in our most intimate relationships? It may take the form of "Is she always going to be faithful?" or "Is he always going to cater to me?" Whenever we start making demands like these, at that moment the relationship turns from love.

According to the mystics, love "attempts what is above its strength." But it is just as true that love brings a surge of strength for overreaching its own limitations. When you free yourself from the conditioning of stimulus and response, so that not a ray of energy is wasted on the broken record that repeats, "What is he going to think of me," immense personal resources are released for giving. Nothing is too much for a lover to attempt, because the resources for loving have no limit. Where once we found it impossible to work with certain people, now it becomes not only possible but desirable. Those people are so hard to work with that they need somebody with patience. Seen through the eyes of love, the most difficult conditions become opportunities for helping those whom others shun. That is how the miracle of love works.

We can learn to extend our love wider and wider; without exaggeration, there is no limit to its extent. Even if for the present we can love only one person – and then only when the circumstances are just right – by daring to face difficult situations with understanding and good will, we can learn to love even people who dislike us. To me, nothing is more miraculous.

When I first came to this country in the late fifties, I was puzzled to see huge beams of light sweeping the horizon at night. I thought it must be some strange meteorological phenomenon like the aurora borealis. A friend corrected me: it was searchlights, advertising an after-hours sale on used cars. Similarly, when meditation and the Holy Name have erased selfish desire from your mind, a kind of searchlight sweeps consciousness continuously, bathing it in light. This quiet inner light marks the presence of the man or woman who has achieved life's highest goal: not only to love Jane and Chuck and little Betsy, but to love everyone on earth, without exception.

As our desire to draw closer to the Lord within us deepens, it draws self-centered desires into it like tributaries into a great river. The power of that love swells until it becomes cataclysmic; we begin to inspire other people through the transformation we have wrought in ourselves. They say to themselves, "I knew him when he was nothing but trouble, and now look at him! There is hope even for me." In this way, we quietly begin to be a force for good.

The Lord is love itself. Christ asks us to endure persecution "on my account," and his account has no limits. We can write checks on it anytime we need to, anywhere we happen to be, and there will always be resources to cover the draft. The more we get ourselves out of the way, the easier will be our access to this limitless treasury of love in the depths of the heart.

When our relationships become strained, we can ask ourselves what Jesus would have done – or, when that seems too lofty, what Saint Teresa or Saint Francis would have done. The example of such figures shows with what thoroughness divine love can transform ordinary men and women, who began with all the human frailties we recognize in ourselves. They show us that if we want to learn to love, we have to rise above low and demeaning responses – little by little, day by day, situation by situation. It is not at all easy; it has never been easy for anybody. Yet nothing is more rewarding.

The Lord is in everyone; therefore we must practice love and trust and selfless service with everyone everywhere. Whenever you look into another person's eyes, remember that you are looking into a city where the Lord dwells – and remember always that our arms and hands were given to us for others' rescue, not for their ruin.

We come from God and dwell in God, the mystics say, and to God we shall return. This supreme Being, whom galaxies cannot contain, lives in the small confines of every human heart. Whenever I hear what a miracle the artificial heart is, I remind myself that the greatest miracle is that the Lord is enshrined in the heart of the soul. Whatever we may do, he never gives up and moves away; he is always there. We should learn to give every person the same kind of respect, and never give up on anybody. When we can do this, we will live in joy always. Even tragedy cannot drive this joy away, because it comes not from what life gives us but from our boundless capacity to give.

Love of this power and sweep has very practical consequences. Tensions are released, conflicts resolved; vitality, enthusiasm, creativity, and resourcefulness are renewed for us every day. Every human faculty, in fact, comes to function beautifully. The reason is simple: we are no longer squandering and fractioning our energy on ourselves. All our vitality is merged in one mighty force which we offer to life as a great gift, and life itself repays us abundantly. This is the wonderful reward that divine love brings.

⟴

Finally, we are getting to the bottom of love's mysteries. We are no longer confusing love with the urge to be intimate with two or three people who satisfy our emotional needs; we are talking about catching a ride on a force powerful enough to make our trouble-plagued world a paradise. It takes years of practice, but the same mental power we expend every day in keeping private desires burning can slowly be harnessed in bringing people together, in healing relationships, in resolving some of the long-standing difficulties that stand between us and a world at peace.

The regular practice of meditation and repetition of the mantram can be compared to building a road deep into the unconscious, where the forces of love and hatred play. Ask your grandparents how much engineering effort went into building some of the highways in this country. Rivers had to be spanned, slopes graded, mountains tunneled through. The road into deeper consciousness requires every bit as much skill and painstaking attention. The challenges — and the dangers, I might as well say — are practically unending. But the reward is access to a realm where personalities and events can be seen as fluid energy, waiting to be shaped by the power of love.

It is only when we live on the surface of life, driven about by personal urges, that little things can satisfy us or upset us. As we sink below the surface, we begin to feel the draw of a current of irresistible love, carrying us toward the very depths of consciousness. There is no "I" or "you" in these deep realms; there is only all. The self-naughting which is such a recurring theme in the literature of mysticism is simply preparation for being admitted to this divine condition. The camel trying to squeeze through the eye of a needle is a lively illustration of how little selfhood we must have in order to get in.

Yet paradoxically, it is only here, where the sense of a separate personality is zero, that all our human needs are met. As the very nature of God implies, our needs are infinite. The Lord is our very Self, and nothing less than his infinitude can satisfy us. "How could I find rest anywhere else," asks Augustine, "when I was made to find my rest in thee?" This is not metaphysics; it is the plain dynamics of love. Our need is for a state of unity that will never leave us; nothing less will do. Only in the depths of the soul, beyond time, place, change, and circumstance, can we find the fulfillment of our deep need to love.

Even in the midst of turmoil and trouble, those who have learned to turn their back on personal grievances and return kindness for unkindness live in heaven on earth. No external event can shake the security this love brings. Those who possess it may live in the midst of Manhattan or in the suburbs of Sacramento; they still live every day in the kingdom of heaven. That is their permanent state. They don't have to try to love; they cannot help it, and everyone who comes within their orbit will be touched by their lives.

Laboring under conditions we would find too primitive to believe, with the handicap of superiors who put up obstacles to her work, Saint Teresa of Avila carried her love throughout Spain; ultimately it spread around the world. The king of Spain at that time was an inordinately powerful and wealthy man; yet was he able to have that kind of influence over history? All the crowned heads of Europe together had not one percent of Teresa's impact. Burning love enabled her to do the impossible: to reach deep into the hearts of people everywhere and stir them to change their lives.

Teresa was not a bit shy about giving away her secret: *Amor saca amor,* "Love begets love." Even if you try to resist love of this magnitude, she says, it reaches out like a sword and opens up your heart to draw love out of you.

When Gandhi came back to India from South Africa in 1915, a stranger in his own country, who would have dreamed that he would bring the British Empire to its knees? Yet it was not Gandhi who brought it down, as he would have been the first to admit. It was the power of love, working through the hearts of millions of responsive people in India, in Great Britain, and elsewhere around the world.

Whatever their differences in language and lifestyle, great lovers like Teresa and Gandhi saw the Lord in the heart of every person around them. This is the vision that enabled them to treat others with love and respect even in the heat of opposition. It may take time, but no one is immune to this kind of love; it draws a response from everyone.

For men and women with this kind of vision, love becomes a passion that will not let them rest. No matter what comes in the way, they are going to carry forward that work. Physically, of course, there comes a time when they disappear from this earth, just as Teresa and Gandhi have. But their work continues. Their lives continue, working through those they inspire.

Mystics would say that the spirit of someone like Teresa of Avila is abroad, looking for ordinary human beings like us to pick up. We read her life and words and they stir something deep inside us, moving us to take up spiritual disciplines and make changes that seemed impossible before. In this way, with our whole-hearted consent, divine love can take possession of our life and gradually make it an instrument of peace on earth.

More than one lover of God has called him the hunter of souls. Here is Teresa:

> When that tender hunter from paradise
> Released his piercing arrow at me,
> My wounded soul fell in his loving arms,
> And my life is so completely transformed
> That my Beloved One has become mine
> And without a doubt I am his at last.

Teresa of Avila wrote a number of exquisite love poems like this about the one she called "His Majesty," who hunted her down with inescapable grace and shot her separate self out from under her. After that shot she could well have said, like Paul, "I died, and yet I live: yet not I, but Christ liveth in me."

Every human being finds this painful. Yet if the day comes that it happens to us, we too will sing our joy; for after this wound we can no longer behave selfishly. We are bonded by compassion to all who suffer. We can forgive them their lapses because we recall only too clearly what the affliction of self-centeredness is like; and we can help them because our hearts are free to give.

Only then, when we have given up once and for all the frantic effort to shape the world around ourselves, do other people trust us completely. Until that time we cannot guess what being loved and cherished really is. We have a saying in India: "When the lotus blooms, it doesn't have to go looking for bees." Bees are always bumbling around in search of flowers; that is their job. Similarly, we human beings are all searching for love. Those who have learned to give compassion freely, asking nothing as collateral, have no need to take out an ad in the classified section saying "Love Available." We seek out such people and are drawn to them; we just can't help ourselves.

Lest we doubt the joy of it, here is the testimony of the English mystic Richard Rolle, as true and as eccentric a troubador of God as Saint Francis was, and one of the earliest poets of the English language. Read it aloud and listen to the way it sings of joy:

Song I call, when in a plenteous soul the sweetness of eternal love with burning is taken, and thought into song is turned, and the mind into full sweet sound is changed. . . . O singular joy of love everlasting, that ravishes all His to heavens above all worlds, them binding with bands of virtue! O dear charity, in earth that has thee not is nought wrought, whatever it hath! He truly that in thee is busy, to joy above earthly is soon lifted! Thou makest men contemplative, heaven-gate thou openest, mouths of accusers thou dost shut, God thou makest to be seen and multitude of sins thou hidest. We praise thee, we preach thee, by thee the world we quickly overcome, by whom we joy and the heavenly ladder we ascend.

And again Rolle tells what transformations this love works in the souls of those it seizes:

But this grace generally and to all is not given, but to the holy soul imbued with the holiest is taught; in whom the excellence of love shines, and songs of lovely loving, Christ inspiring, commonly burst up, and being made as it were a pipe of love, joying sounds. The which [soul] mystery of love knowing, with great cry to its Love ascends, in wit sharpest, and in knowledge and in feeling subtle; not spread in things of this world but into God all gathered and set, that in cleanness of conscience and shining of soul to Him it may serve whom it has purposed to love, and itself to Him to give. Surely the clearer the love of the lover is, the nearer to him and the more present God is. And thereby more clearly in God he joys, and of the sweet Goodness the more he feels, that to lovers is wont Itself to inshed, and to mirth without comparison the hearts of the meek to turn.

The triumphant, joyful note of freedom in those lines is the sure mark of the mystic. Above all else, the lover of God is free, because freedom is the breath and soul of love. "As long as you stand hat in hand begging life for favors," my spiritual teacher used to tell me, "life will have only contempt for you." When people get anxious and insecure, allowing themselves to become upset over every little thing, it is essentially because of this attitude: they are forever asking life for favors. And Granny would add: "Don't make demands on life that life cannot fulfill."

It took decades of frustration for me to understand those words, but today I don't make any demands on life at all. All I need is opportunities for giving, which life has no power to withhold.

Not long ago I was leaving San Francisco with some friends at the end of a gorgeous day. Commuters were streaming into the main arteries of the city, and as we turned onto Van Ness Avenue and headed north I thought to myself that it would take half an hour just to reach the Golden Gate Bridge. Ahead of us a long row of forbidding red lights warned me to settle back and repeat my mantram. But as we drove, miraculously enough, light after light turned green. The friend who was driving me timed it perfectly; we never so much as slowed down until we saw the red towers of the bridge poking overhead into the mist.

That is how our lives can be. With this one commitment to live for all, your personal life becomes smooth sailing. Minor problems which used to mean gridlock will break up and get out of your way.

Then a new joy enters your life. Most of us, I imagine, truly believe that just doing our thing, doing what we want, is the height of a good day. But the joy of loving and serving others is a million times greater. Once we get even a taste of this joy, we will not be able to restrain ourselves from giving and loving more.

Isn't being in love the highest joy we know? Romance must sell more books, more movie tickets, more concert seats, than all other subjects combined. Now imagine for a moment how much joy there must be in love that can never fail, that never ends or wavers or runs dry. Imagine the joy of never losing faith in someone we love, in loving him just as intensely no matter what he does. We would get to keep the joy of our love and never lose it. Then try to imagine feeling that kind of continuous, unconditional love not just for one person but for all. That is the joy these mystics have found.

If we live selfishly, not all the angels in the celestial spheres will be able to drag us into heaven. But if we love all life, all people, all creatures, we have found heaven already; we live in heaven here on earth. The choice is ours, and it is within our reach, as Fra Giovanni testifies in haunting words:

There is nothing I can give you which you do not have, but there is much that while I cannot give it, you can take. No heaven can come to us unless our hearts find rest in today. Take heaven. No peace lies in the future which is not hidden in this present instant. Take peace. The gloom of the world is but a shadow behind it, yet within reach is joy. There is radiance and glory in the darkness could we but see, and to see we have only to look. I beseech you to look. Life is so generous a giver, but we, judging its gifts by their covering, cast them away as ugly or hard; remove the covering and you will find beneath it a living splendor, woven of love, by wisdom, with power. Welcome it, grasp it, and you touch the angel's hand that brings it to you. Everything we call a trial, a sorrow or a duty, the angel's hand is there, the gift is there and the wonder of an overshadowing presence. Our joys too, be not content with them as joys. They too conceal diviner gifts. And so at this time I greet you, not quite as the world sends greetings but with profound esteem and the prayer that for you, now and forever, the day breaks and the shadows flee away.

CHAPTER 7

Mercy

Blessed are the merciful, for they shall obtain mercy.

"The possession of God," says Ruysbroeck, "demands and supposes active love. He who thinks or feels otherwise is deceived." To be full of love, full to overflowing, so full that we give love freely to everyone around us – in the end, the mystics ask, isn't this what we all want in life, more than anything else? This full measure of love has a healing effect not only on those around us, but also on ourselves.

The whole message of original goodness is that we do not have to work to draw this kind of love from some external source. A full reservoir of love is lying right inside us. In meditation we are digging deep into our own consciousness, tunneling toward this infinite reservoir that lies waiting to be discovered and manifested in our daily life.

"Come unto me," Jesus promises, "all ye that labor and are heavy laden, and I will give you rest. Take my yoke upon you, and learn of me, for I am meek and

lowly in heart: and ye shall find rest unto your souls."
When we are kind, tender, compassionate, and forgiving, we get a glimpse of the healing power of this reservoir of mercy within.

But I do not want to soften this statement from the
Beatitudes: "Blessed are the merciful, for they shall obtain mercy." If we listen to it with our hearts, we will
hear a thunderclap. Who will obtain the mercy we all
long for from life? Only the loving, only those who
show mercy to others. Only those who forgive others
will enjoy the healing power of forgiveness in themselves, because in showing mercy to others we are being
merciful with ourselves as well.

The reason is simple: only then are we abiding by
life's most fundamental law, that all of us are one. If I
give love to others, it means, I stand to benefit from
that love as much as they. Not necessarily immediately,
not necessarily directly, but that love has to come back
to me; for I have added to the measure of love in the
world, the mystics say, and I am part of that whole.
Similarly, if I add meanness, stinginess, resentment,
hostility, then sooner or later that sort of treatment
will be shown to me.

This is not so occult as it may sound. After all, when
someone treats us unkindly, isn't it natural that we begin to avoid that person, speak curtly, even be unkind
ourselves? When a person is regularly unkind, it conditions our expectations; then, when that person surprises us with something thoughtful – it does happen!
– we may shun him anyway, simply out of habit. It is
the same with kindness: when we can count on a per-

son to be loving, we give our love freely in return, and allow a wide margin for those rare times when he or she might act otherwise. "She's never like that," we tell ourselves. "Something terrible must be preying on her mind." That is how our responses to life come back to us.

In Hindu and Buddhist mysticism, this common-sense principle is called the law of karma. The word karma has been much misunderstood, but its literal meaning is simply action, something done. So instead of using exotic language, we might as well refer to the "law of action," which states that everything we do – even everything we think, since our thoughts condition our behavior – has consequences: not "equal and opposite" as in physics, but equal and alike. The comparison with physics is deliberate, for this is not a doctrine of any particular religion. It is a law of life, which no one has stated more clearly than Jesus: "Judge not, that ye be not judged. For with what judgment ye judge, ye shall be judged: and with what measure ye mete, it shall be meted unto you." Paul puts it more tersely: "As we sow, so shall we reap." The working of this law is not necessarily negative, as this Beatitude shows: if we sow mercy, we shall receive it in ample harvest.

Even if we follow these arguments intellectually, however, how many of us act as if this law really applied to us? We let mercy wait while we pursue goals we understand. A luxurious home overlooking the sea through a forest of pines; prestige in our job, success for our children: don't all of us dream that such things can make us happy? We slave for them. "That is not enough," Jesus would say quietly. Our need is for love, and we can get it only in the measure that we give.

Instead of pursuing external satisfactions, Jesus tells us, we need to let mercy rule our decisions from day to day, and our long-range goals as well. Then the forces of life will rise up from within to protect us. They will protect our health by keeping us clear of physical addictions and emotional obsessions. They will protect our mind by keeping it calm and detached. People will surround us with affection and support when they see we care about them more than we do about ourselves. And as death approaches, it will hold no fear for us. We will know for certain that the forces of mercy from which we draw our life flow through creation from an endless source, and will never cease flowing.

Just as our currency was once guaranteed by gold reserves, every word Jesus delivers in the Beatitudes is guaranteed by his life. How many times Jesus forgave in the face of cruelty! It is the example of his life that gives his words on forgiveness the power to penetrate our hearts even after two thousand years.

Even on the scale of international politics, when some minister of state proclaims, "We have been provoked and our only course is retaliation," Jesus' reminder of mercy should echo in our ears. What a challenge he is issuing us! But if forgiveness is truly a law of life, then retaliating only makes others more angry, less open to discussion, and more vengeful than before. If we will only put forward a helping hand, Jesus is urging us – even before we are asked – the laws that govern human nature above and beyond political persuasion or race or religion will eventually stir a deeply human response, which can defuse the most desperate of situations. Later I will let Mahatma Gandhi tell us of his experiences putting mercy to work on large-scale social problems. His experience is an abiding affirmation that practicing this Beatitude can bring about no less than the end of war and the beginning of real peace, which this world has scarcely known.

"Be kind, be kind, be kind." That is the prescription for holiness issued by a wise medieval mystic. Half its wisdom lies in its insistence on being kind over and over; for to make kindness the mind's natural response even in the unconscious requires years of practice. Until we descend into the depths of the mind, we simply have no idea what resentments have accumulated there. "In these regions," says the theologian Paul Tillich,

> we can find hidden hostilities against those with whom we are in love. We can find envy and torturing doubt about whether we are really accepted by them. And this hostility and anxiety about being rejected by those who are nearest us can hide itself under the various forms of love: friendship, sensual love, conjugal and family love.

Even today, in this age of practical psychology, people are so insecure that without realizing it, they often try to raise themselves up by tearing somebody else down. When we get even a glimpse of the unity of life, we realize that in tearing others down we are tearing ourselves down too. Sitting in judgment on other people and countries and races is training your mind to sit in judgment on yourself. "Forgive us our trespasses, as we forgive those who trespass against us." As we forgive others, we are teaching the mind to respond with forgiveness everywhere, even to the misdeeds and mistakes of our own past.

Yet true forgiveness is no simple matter of shaking hands and murmuring, "Forget it, old boy." Careful files are being kept inside. Little grievances, injuries that don't deserve a second thought, are being recorded deep in consciousness, marked "Store Indefinitely. Top Secret." These are the episodes that come up in dreams, cause us conflicts, and often push us to erupt in unexpected bouts of temper. In very deep meditation you will actually catch sight of some of these hang-ups. And you gasp: that grudge you have been feeding all these years has been responsible for emotional sore spots and health problems you never suspected.

Indulging in anger is pointing a poison-tipped arrow inward, aimed straight at ourselves. It taints our thinking, poisons our feelings, turns our relationships adversarial. If we continue to think resentful thoughts, mistrust spreads in consciousness like some toxic underground chemical until we have a permanent disposition for suspicion. When anger pollutes our internal environment to this extent, we don't need particular events to trigger suspicion; it has become an automatic response, draining us of energy like an insidious hidden leak. Our nervous system and vital organs react angrily on their own, without any connivance from the mind. The long-term effects, as I said earlier, can be disastrous: heart disease, stroke, extreme emotional stress, perhaps even lower resistance to disease and impaired capacity to heal.

⌖

To counter this tendency of the mind, we need some way to gain access to the deep reservoir of mercy within. But how? This is a question that will touch every choice we make, because part of the answer is that we must learn to harness and use wisely the energies of our lives.

Energy conservation is the basis of spiritual engineering, for vital energy provides the power we need to tap the infinite source of goodness and mercy that lies at the core of consciousness.

In Sanskrit, vital energy is called *prana,* which literally means "the energy of life." Prana is the energy that drives the whole organism we call ourself: not only the physical body, but the mind as well. All creatures consume vital energy. In the ancient Hindu tradition, it is said that we come into life with a given supply of this energy, enough to power a certain number of breathing cycles. Our natural human life span, according to this view, is allotted not in calendar years but in the number of breaths we take. The word expire means literally to reach the end of this span of breaths — interestingly enough, at about one hundred and twenty years of age. Anything less is considered a premature death, "death by unnatural causes."

If this theory is true, it may help to explain why these ancient sages claim a close connection between mental states and longevity. Our breathing rhythm, the measure of how fast our reserves of vital energy are being consumed, is regulated in part by our state of mind. Security, compassion, patience, forgiveness – all these are accompanied, if you observe closely, by a relatively slow breathing rhythm and heart rate. Positive states of mind like these conserve energy and lengthen the life span, leaving a reserve of resilience and resistance for facing challenges. Every time we are able to remain calm under pressure, or merciful while under attack, we are making a big deposit into the vault of vital energy within.

Learning to control attention is the key to gaining access to this energy and using it wisely. No skill in living is more useful. It is William James again who writes that the ability to direct attention "is the very root of judgment, character and will." Human attention is the equivalent of a turbocharged sports car with space-age aerodynamics: we can use its power to take us wherever we want. We can turn corners with a flick of the wrist, brake fast if necessary to avoid an accident; we can even turn the ignition off when the engine needs a rest. "An education which should include this faculty," James continues, "would be the education *par excellence*." Sadly, I know of no curriculum in any educational system in the world for learning this most basic of skills.

When you can keep your attention where you want it, vital wealth accumulates, like savings earning compound interest. You become so loaded with cash reserves that it becomes very difficult to upset you. When J. Paul Getty lost five dollars, do you think he called in the police? Even five hundred would scarcely have been noticed. Mastering attention can make you that kind of tycoon with your vitality; you can take great losses without ever losing your balance.

Yet most of us live from hand to mouth, writing energy checks every time we think life has let us down. What a way to go through life, squandering our vital wealth just to keep ourselves in emotional poverty! Our piggy bank never gets full enough to make a deposit, so if somebody grabs a nickel from us, naturally we cannot sleep.

All of us need ways to conserve and replenish our emotional reserves. What meditation can do over a period of many years is open up access to a limitless supply of vital wealth. After all these decades I still meditate for hours every day, just as an oil tycoon drills for oil and natural gas, to tap greater and greater resources for carrying on this work. The miracle is that once you reach this stage, maintaining complete and uninterrupted attention no longer requires effort. Full attention, and therefore full vitality, becomes your natural state.

When somebody is talking to me, for example – even one of the children in the midst of a conversation among adults – I never fail to give my complete attention, no matter what else is going on around us.

"Quality attention," some psychologists call it. The natural tendency of the mind is to wander, but I have taught it to focus and stay still. After years of practice it cannot behave in any other way. The bonus is priceless: intimate, unbreakable relationships.

One benefit of this kind of control over attention is the capacity for unshakable loyalty. I never give up on anybody, and I am not exaggerating in the least when I tell you that no joy in life is more exhilarating. When Saint Francis insists that it is in loving that we are loved, this is what he means. When your love for others cannot be shaken by anything they do, you never ask whether they love you; it is irrelevant. That is what unconditional love means, and naturally it draws a loving response.

Young people, to me, are the real wealth of any country. That is no mere cliché; it is a living truth. And the best way to help our young people discover and harness their inner resources is by teaching them to master their attention, beginning with our own example. Giving children our full attention is the best way to make them secure; and with the steadiness that comes from a trained mind, we will not lose faith when they run into the problems that young people run into everywhere. Our support will give them a safety net while they are learning to deal with life, which today is an unparalleled challenge for anyone. With that net, even if they fall, they are much less likely to get hurt.

Attention is trained not only during meditation but throughout the day, by keeping your attention off yourself and focused on the job at hand. Going through the day with a one-pointed mind is itself quite an achievement. But after many years of effort, imperceptibly, a tiny hole opens in consciousness. You will have to work for a long time, like a woodpecker, to open that hole further. Years of peck-peck-pecking away lie ahead. But when the opening is wide enough, you can shine your attention like a powerful flashlight into deeper realms of consciousness.

This is an extraordinary experience, for which nothing in the external world can prepare us. Everywhere you look you see the forces of consciousness at play, surging through the shadow-world of the mind. There is anger, barreling through like a freight train; don't get in its way! And there is desire, rising nebulous from the deep. The marvelous thing about watching these forces is that without even realizing it, you begin to understand that they have no intrinsic power to compel your actions. You are not linked inextricably to the thoughts these forces conjure up: in fact, you are not your mind at all.

As your concentration deepens, the beam of its searchlight penetrates farther and farther into the gloom. It is the power of harnessed passions which gives that light such enormous penetrating power. Slowly, unconscious forces are coming under the control of your conscious mind.

Meditation is the drill we use day by day to widen that opening. Ultimately it enables us to reach deep into the unconscious, almost to the seabed of consciousness, and draw these clamoring forces into one irresistible surge of love. "This abyss of wisdom," says

Saint John of the Cross, "now lifts up and enlarges the soul, giving it to drink at the very sources of the science of love."

ↇ

This reservoir of energy in the depths of consciousness is available to all human beings, but access is far from easy. Like an exclusive country club surrounded by unscalable walls, the vaults of the unconscious are jealously guarded. There is only one way to get hold of the Gold Card that allows uninhibited admission: we have to live entirely for the benefit of all. Only then will the Lord allow us past the gate.

For this, mastery of attention alone is not enough. With concentration must flow what in traditional religious language is called devotion: love of God. We already have the capacity for devotion, the mystics say, even if we don't know it. The problem is that it is locked up in any number of personal attachments: to our home, our job, our clothes; even in compulsive attachments to family and friends. Let me emphasize again, this is quite different from loving God in all; here the emphasis is on our needs and wants.

Most of us carry strong personal attachments and sincerely believe that we love deeply. But when we are emotionally entangled with someone, we cannot really be aware of that person's needs or how we affect his life. Our preoccupation is with ourselves: that our feelings not be violated and that our wants be fulfilled. One frank Christian mystic goes so far as to describe attachment as "mercenary love." We say, "I will love Clothilde so long as she does A, B, and C and never dreams of doing X, Y, and Z." This is more akin to a business contract than to love. Love means always taking into consideration how our words and actions might affect those around us. This is how we make our love more pure.

A compulsive attachment is trapped energy, and its pressure builds up tremendously over time. We have difficulty pulling our attention away from the other person and devoting this energy to the kind of lofty goal that alone can give life meaning. Conversely, real love opens up the very wellsprings of vitality for selfless service. When we learn to love truly, selflessly, all the power that had been trapped in private, personal attachments comes gushing up into our lives.

All this ties in closely with self-indulgence. Every time we yield to a personal desire, there is some satisfaction, of course, but we have also written a check on our vital energy account. After we have been dashing off checks right and left for some time, depression often sets in. We feel so drained that we just can't cope with the rigors of the day. This low-energy ebb is the manager of the bank inside reminding us, "Don't write so many checks. They're starting to bounce!"

This happens whenever the mind gets excited, and the more agitation there is in the mind, the more energy is lost. My submission is that the exhilaration from certain potent drugs and from sexual stimulation makes a particularly large draw on our energy reserves. Since not only the heart and lungs but all physiological systems – including the immune system – draw on this energy for proper functioning, anything that depletes energy reserves regularly is likely to take a toll on health. Compulsive self-indulgence is always debilitating, and over time it may well lower our resistance to disease.

I took some young friends to a frozen yogurt shop the other day, and while they were deciding between White Chocolate Macadamia and Very Raspberry, a hand-printed sign on the counter caught my eye: "Now is not the time for self-restraint." It gave me pause. How little we understand the vital connection between self-restraint and love! Excessive indulgence actually drains our power to love, blocks our vision of others' needs. Our senses and passions are always on their feet, waving their arms in our face and exclaiming, "Hey, you, I want this! Look over there, how can you resist that!" With all this hullabaloo, it takes effort even to notice that other people are around.

It always surprises listeners when I say that people who have a strong sex drive should congratulate themselves. They have a lot of gas in their tank, a lot of vital energy in reserve. But gas is to be used, not drained; if you let your car sit with a hole in the tank, you are likely to be out of fuel when you need it most. The stronger a person's sexual desires, the more vital it is that the power behind these desires be harnessed. What I never hesitate to deprecate is adults continuing to maintain teenage attitudes about sex long after they have passed the age of discretion. And it is not only behavior that drains vitality. Reading about it, seeing stimulating movies, fantasizing – all these consume large amounts of prana.

Behind sexual desire is a very natural longing that is not really physical: the longing to escape the loneliness of separate existence. The closer we learn to feel to other people, the less we will be driven by the physical urge for sex, for the urge will be fulfilled much closer to its source. As we deepen our relationships far below the physical level, the sexual drive will be transformed naturally into a dynamo of creative power: the power to help, the power to love.

✧

Several years ago my wife and I visited a retreat in the Southwest, where I was to speak on meditation. It was my first visit to that part of the country, and I found the scenery spectacular in its beauty.

One day our hosts took us to see a stunning chapel built up against the red sandstone of the desert hills. As we entered, I felt as if I had received a blow. Right in front of us rose a lifelike sculpture of Christ in agony on the cross. The eyes were hollow with pain and the mouth seemed to be crying out, "Haven't I suffered long enough? Can't you all join hands now and lift me down from this cross?"

Whenever we utter an angry word or raise a hand against our neighbor, we are driving in another nail to keep Jesus up on that cross. The principle underlying the Passion is that out of his infinite mercy, the Lord has taken our suffering upon himself. As long as any living creature is in pain, so is Jesus, for he lives at the heart of all. Wherever violence breaks out, no matter how cleverly we try to justify it, we are crucifying the spirit of Christ.

"Patience" and "passion" both come from a Latin word meaning to suffer or endure. When we speak of the Passion of Christ, we are recalling the suffering he endured on the cross. But it is good to realize that whenever we practice patience – cheerfully bearing with somebody who is irascible, or enduring discomfort rather than imposing it on others – in a small way we are embracing the principle of the Passion. Each of us can bear a little of such self-denial, and with practice, our shoulders can grow broad enough to carry some of the burden of those we love. In this way, the mystics tell us, by practicing mercy throughout our lives, we take upon ourselves some of Jesus' burden of pain.

This does not mean becoming blind to what others are doing. That is not what mercy and forgiveness mean. I know when somebody is being rude or unkind, but it does not impair my faith in that person or lower him in my eyes. I keep my eyes on the core of goodness I see in him, and act toward him as I would have him act toward me. There is only one way to make others more loving, and that is by loving more ourselves.

What we are looking for in others is generally what we find. "Such as we are inwardly," Thomas a Kempis says, "so we judge outwardly." Psychology can go no deeper. If we want to follow Jesus' dictum to "judge not," we must change who we are; then others will change in our own eyes. When we ourselves are trust-worthy, for example, we see others the same and trust them accordingly – and when we do, interestingly enough, our trust is often rewarded. Trust is a two-way street. It is the same with our other judgments about life: it's amazing how quickly the world we live in conforms itself to our ideas about it.

You can test this intriguing law in the laboratory of your own life. If someone at work absolutely seems to enjoy making things rougher for you, try treating that person with extra respect – and go on showing him respect no matter how he acts. In a surprisingly short time, I predict, his behavior will begin to verify your faith in his better side.

Yet I need hardly remind you how hard it is to start letting down old, ingrained hostile defenses. Experience, we believe, does not teach us that others are trustworthy; it teaches us that we had better watch our flanks. The memory of past letdowns can weigh down any sensitive human being, making trust an elusive commodity to acquire. Worst of all, when negative memories cast a shadow of mistrust over our relationships, we lack the vitality we need to withdraw our attention and act with kindness, as if those shadows were not there. That is why any effective reformation of character has to start with reforming the thought process itself.

Here the power of the Holy Name makes itself felt. Each time your thoughts start to wander down dark alleyways of the past, by drawing on the Holy Name you can call them back and point their feet in the direction you really want them to go. Gradually, with practice, your thoughts will wander much less frequently; in time, they may even forget the address of those alleyways they once haunted.

Repeating the Holy Name is a powerful way to harness a very natural tendency of the human mind: to brood. Every compulsion gets its grip from this tendency. The mind takes a trifling remark or incident, no bigger than a limp balloon, and starts to inflate it by thinking about it over and over and over, blowing it up with its attention until it fills our consciousness and we cannot think about anything else.

When the mind starts this blow-up routine, the Holy Name restores your perspective by letting out the air. Every time the mind pumps, the Holy Name pricks open a little hole and lets some of your attention get free. The balloon may not collapse immediately – after all, an emotion like anger or resentment has powerful lungs. But right from the first, it will not get so obsessively large, which means you have introduced a measure of free choice. Next time you will find your freedom even greater.

When, after years of sincere repetition, you make the Holy Name an integral part of your consciousness, it can take even a grievous injury and reduce it to such a minuscule size that forgiveness comes easily. Afterward, when you recall the incident, there will be no emotional charge. Then personal relationships become effortlessly comfortable. You will be able to work easily even with people who have done you a bad turn, because past memories will have no more power to compel you than would the memory of some old film.

Once at a swimming pool I saw a fascinating device that moves around the pool keeping the water clean. The Holy Name is a pool sweep for the mind, sweeping away resentment and frustration before they get a chance to build up during the day. A burden of resentment, carried around for years, translates into constant mental turmoil, which expresses itself in physical and psychosomatic ailments. A mind kept clean of resentment, whatever the provocation, not only is resourceful and secure but also makes the body less prone to physical problems.

It is not quite accurate, however, to say that anger is swept away. Another way of describing the process is that emotions like anger are transformed. Anger is power. When I see instances of injustice – which I do every day now in the newspapers and magazines – I get enormously angry. For example, coming from India, I still identify with the plight of the Third World. I grieve every time I am reminded that half a billion people, most of them children, go to bed hungry each night. I don't have to see them face to face to feel their suffering; they are right there in my consciousness. But as that anger rises, it is transformed into creative energy for selfless action. That is why you will never hear me waste a word on judging, haranguing, and complaining. My time and energy go into teaching others how to live by the unity of life, so that these wrongs can be set right. Anger is now a kind of backyard oil well, to draw on when I need power. Mahatma Gandhi was instrumental in showing us how crude anger can be transformed into refined energy to drive the engine of mercy.

The machinery for this transformation is very simple in design: we have only to cease making selfish demands on life. I don't try to clutch at people any longer, or to cling to pleasures. I don't rely on applause and appreciation for security, because I depend entirely upon the Lord within. That is why anxiety has gone out of my life; frustration has fled; every negative emotion is but a distant memory.

I have come to have an all-consuming passion for every creature on earth: for all countries, all races, all animals. My appeals to help save the elephants in Africa, in danger of extinction from poaching because of consumer demand for ivory, is a natural part of the unitive vision. It is said of Margery Kempe, an English mystic of the fourteenth century, that "if she saw a man with a wound, or a beast, or if a man beat a child before her, or smote a horse with a whip, she saw our Lord being beaten or wounded." Sri Ramakrishna, one of the greatest of India's mystics, used to feel such wounds on his own body.

Such a tremendous backlog of energy can be locked up in anger and resentment that we can visualize it as a Hoover Dam right inside, blocking our energy flow on every level from the physical to the spiritual. The most effective way I know to channel the enormous power of anger is to turn it around, turn it into mercy, by pouring it into the peaceful resolution of problems that threaten to erupt in violence between individuals and communities and nations. Working for the sake of all releases a virtual flood of creative energy into our lives.

꘎

In practice, mercy is just what Mahatma Gandhi meant by nonviolence. Nonviolence is much more than a technique for righting social wrongs; it is the mercy which Jesus beseeches us to practice in every arena of our life. "In my opinion nonviolence is not passive in any shape or form," Gandhi wrote. "Nonviolence, as I understand it, is the most active force in the world." He is talking about the mercy that flows from our heart when we have smashed through the dam of hatred.

I like to think of Gandhi as an energy tycoon, constantly drilling for the oil of mercy and pumping it up to allay violence, harnessing anger's fierce power in constructive action. But he is extremely practical about how we must go about this process of drilling. "If one does not practice nonviolence in one's personal relations with others and hopes to use it in bigger affairs, one is vastly mistaken. Nonviolence, like charity, must begin at home."

One man who took Gandhi at his word was Martin Luther King Jr. When I was at the University of Minnesota as a Fulbright scholar in 1959, some of the students in my dorm came to my room one evening and said, "You're interested in Gandhi. Someone you should hear is speaking tonight. Come on." Still new to the country, I hadn't even heard about Martin Luther King, but I went and sat with them, right in front.

The auditorium filled until it was packed. Then a quiet black man stood up, walked to the podium, and began to speak. I couldn't believe my ears: he was speaking the very language of Gandhi, not quoting him but speaking with the unmistakable conviction of living, personal experience. Later I found that he had been to India to learn about Gandhi's experiments in nonviolence.

In one shining passage from a recent biography, King recalls a night in 1956 when his work, his family, his very life were threatened by the roused forces of oppression. While his wife and child slept, he sat in despair at the kitchen table with his head in his hands, about to give up the struggle. From the depths of his consciousness he prayed aloud: "Lord, I'm down here trying to do what's right. . . . But Lord, I must confess that I'm weak now. I'm faltering. I'm losing my courage."

And a voice from within uttered clearly: "Stand up for righteousness. Stand up for justice. Stand up for truth. And lo I will be with you, even until the end of the world."

In that moment, King tells us, he lost his fears of failure; he lost the very fear of death. And from that night on, his work began to bear miraculous fruit.

We may not be called to face such challenges, but wherever we have difficulty getting along with somebody, that is a precious opportunity to start drilling for mercy. "It is only when you meet with resistance," Gandhi wrote, "that your nonviolence is put on trial."

I confess to having been baffled for decades by that phrase "getting even." If you really want to get even with someone, be more forgiving; kindness exchanged for unkindness comes out even. What people call getting even is only getting odd. That wise old fellow Ben Franklin understood: "Next to knowing when to seize an opportunity," he said, "the most important thing to know in life is when to forgo an advantage."

"Mutual forbearance," wrote Gandhi, "is nonviolence. Immediately, therefore, you get the conviction that nonviolence is the law of life, you have to practice it towards those who act violently towards you, and the law must apply to nations as [to] individuals." Then he adds, "Training no doubt is necessary. And beginnings are always small."

I must tell you that even though I grew up in Gandhi's India, my own beginnings in this art were small indeed. My village in South India had no high school until I entered my teens, so of course there were quite a few older fellows in my class who had finished the lower grades years before. Some were twice my age and seemed twice my size too. Having been out of school for so long, most of them didn't know how to answer questions or even do sums, and they resented a little fellow like me being good at most kinds of schoolwork. When we did an assignment in class, the boys in back of me naturally wanted to see my work. They didn't even have to ask; they had only to give me a certain look and I got the message.

These fellows knew I was gentle at heart, and when I passed down their street on my way home from school they would be out on the veranda waiting for me, making disparaging remarks about my appearance. They would start with my hair and work their way gradually down to my feet, and I used to get upset.

My mother was duly sympathetic. "You are a nice-looking boy," she reassured me. "What do they know? Don't listen to them."

That was gratifying but not very helpful, so I went to my grandmother. "Granny, what shall I do?"

"Well," she said, "there are two ways to deal with this kind of situation. One is to remember that what they are saying is untrue, and just repeat your mantram and ignore them. After a while, when they see that you're not bothered, they'll stop."

This too was not what I was looking for. "What's the other way, Granny?"

"The other way," she said, "is for me to take care of it for you."

I said, "Let's try your way."

So we did. Granny never lost her temper, but she had a way of speaking that made even brave men prefer to face a sword. To this day I don't know what she told those boys, but ever after there was an awed respect in their manner and they never bothered me again.

I tell such stories on myself whenever people say, "Oh, it's easy for you to say 'forgive and forbear'; that's your nature." Not at all. I was not born like my granny, utterly impervious to deprecation. Harsh, taunting words used to hurt me deeply. But gradually I absorbed her unshakable security, based on the sure awareness that the Lord is ever present in our heart of hearts. "The Lord is with me; I shall not fear."

Interestingly enough, I had a cousin who solved this problem an utterly different way. He actually enjoyed courting trouble, because he knew he was good at dealing with it. So where I went out of my way to avoid the bigger boys, my cousin made a point of swaggering down their street, daring them to do so much as raise an eyebrow. They never bothered him either.

"To practice nonviolence in mundane matters is to know its true value. It is to bring heaven upon earth." Gandhi is claiming in all humility that he doesn't live on earth; he lives in heaven. And it is a heaven in which all of us can dwell when we lose the capacity to feel ill will no matter what the provocation.

When we meet someone with this capacity for mercy, something changes in the depths of our unconscious. Those who merely touched the hem of Jesus' garment, the apostles tell us, received a gift of peace. I believe it was William James who observed that when we meet a saint, a little of our "native meanness" dies. To be hostile is more difficult after that; to be forgiving is more natural. The more we love such a person, the more possibilities open up in our own mind to become merciful, like a window opening inch by inch into deeper awareness.

The scriptures of all religions say that those who tap the reservoir of mercy within eventually become a river of love, which no adversary or adversity can stop. What is the reason for that power? The explanation is simple: whenever you give love to somebody who doesn't know how to love, you educate that person. Even the most insecure and most embittered among us cannot resist for long a person who gives out pure, unconditional love. "Behold the Lamb of God," exclaims John the Baptist, "which taketh away the sin of the world!"

An ancient Sanskrit saying, "*Ahimsa paramo dharma,*" states categorically that nonviolence is the highest law of life. All other laws arise out of it. That is the meaning and significance of mercy in the loftiest sense of the word. If we refer all our decisions, large and small, to this one supreme law, we will get the answers to every raging question of our day.

Gandhi came to this same conclusion. "During my half a century of experience, I have not yet come across one situation when I had to say that I was helpless, that I had no remedy in terms of nonviolence." That is why he is much, much more than just the father of the Indian nation; he is a beacon light to the modern world and to generations yet unborn.

"I am an irrepressible optimist," Gandhi continues. "My optimism rests on my belief in the infinite possibilities of the individual to develop nonviolence. The more you develop it in your own being, the more infectious it becomes, till it overwhelms your surroundings and by and by might oversweep the world." Whenever we forgive unkindness, we are passing on this infection of mercy of which Gandhi speaks. In the heart of every human being lies a noble response to anyone who will neither retaliate nor retreat: a deep, intuitive recognition that here is someone who sees in us all the inalienable good in human nature. That is the source of our unfathomable response to Jesus, to the Buddha, to Teresa of Avila and Francis of Assisi, and of course to Gandhi himself.

"I have known from early youth," Gandhi says, giving away his native genius for love,

> that nonviolence is not a cloistered virtue to be practiced by the individual for his peace and final salvation, but it is a rule of conduct for the whole of society, if it is to live consistently with human dignity and make progress towards the attainment of peace, for which it has been yearning for ages past. One cannot be nonviolent in one's own circle and violent outside.

This knocks the bottom out of claims by governments that they are waging righteous wars, wars to make the world safe for peace. When we are violent in one sphere of life, we kindle violence everywhere we reach.

Statistics remind us how far we have traveled from this law of mercy. "Today," Michael Renner writes in *State of the World 1995,* "military budgets are still as high as they were in the late seventies, when U.S.-Soviet détente came to an end. . . . Global military spending since World War II has added up to a cumulative $30-35 trillion . . . resources that could help reduce the potential for violent conflict if instead they were invested in human security. . . . For example, the price paid for two warships ordered by Malaysia in 1992 would have been sufficient to provide safe drinking water for the next quarter-century to the 5 million Malaysians now lacking it." If Jesus were here today, he would ask us bluntly: When millions of children are going hungry and people don't even have safe water to drink, how can we go on wasting more than a million dollars a minute on the machinery of war?

A total of six countries – the United States, the former Soviet Union, France, Great Britain, China, and Germany – accounted for almost 90 percent of world arms exports over the last twenty years. Most of these exports, of course, went to underdeveloped nations whose resources are desperately needed by their own people. If even two or three of these arms-exporting powers would join hands and work together to relieve some global problems instead of fueling war, every technological obstacle to a safer, healthier planet could be removed. No one would lose by this kind of joint effort. In fact, everyone would gain: not only from a safer globe, but from relief from the crippling economic burden of a war economy.

If we want to see mercy on a global scale, ordinary people like you and me have only to make it a top priority of our lives. The *Theologica Germanica* tells each of us to "be to the Eternal Goodness what his own hand is to a man." It might begin with examining our means of livelihood, refusing any job that threatens life.

There are plenty of challenges to mercy right around us, here in the wealthiest country on earth, and every one can find some way to help. I learned this from Gandhi. People often do not realize that most of Gandhi's efforts to free India were spent not on marches and demonstrations but on improving the lot of the poor. He traveled all over the subcontinent asking each of us, even children, to make some contribution. He was so successful that today all over India there are modern hospitals for women and children named after his wife, Kasturbai. Those who can afford to pay give what they can; for those who cannot, treatment is free.

᪥

Blessed are the merciful, for they shall receive mercy. It is at the time of death that we receive the final gift of a life of mercy, a life we have lived for all.

Below the surface of consciousness, we can speak roughly of two grand domains. What I call the personal unconscious is the region in which our personal problems arise, shaped by the conditioning of what we have thought, done, and experienced in the past. During the first half of meditation, by digging deeper and deeper into consciousness, we learn to traverse this region, which brings the resolution of most of our personal problems.

This formidable achievement can seem like the end of the spiritual journey, and many have taken it as such. But beyond the personal unconscious stretch the limitless reaches of the collective unconscious, which lies below everything that is personal and separate. Here in these unfathomable depths lies the answer to the mystery of death.

In these dark realms, which have never before been penetrated by the light of our conscious mind, our image of ourself begins to change as the infinite resources of the unconscious come into our hands. Slowly, without even meaning to, we begin to lose our fear of death. This is an amazing realization; for as Jung says, at these depths the fear of death is written in the hearts of all. Yet it is in these depths that we discover experientially what we may have hoped or believed, but never known: that death is not the end for anyone. It is only a gateway, a passage to another state of being. More important, we see that at the very core of ourselves we are neither body nor mind but that small spark in the soul, "uncreated and uncreatable," which can never die.

In the Sanskrit scriptures death is called our friend, because it is awareness of death that gives meaning to life and prompts us to search for what is deathless. Without this awareness, we let life slip by as if it could last forever. Every day time is robbing us of our vitality and of our cherished ideals; we have not a minute to waste in selfish, separate pursuits. When we take this fact of life to heart, we know death to be our loyal friend, always prodding us on toward self-realization.

Against the backdrop of reincarnation, the Tibetan mystics have a picturesque way of describing what happens to personality after the body is shed. I always emphasize that if we live rightly today, there is no need to worry about the next life at all, let alone the influences of the past. But even if we do not believe in reincarnation, these Tibetan theories give a helpful perspective on doing our best here and now. At death, they say, the soul enters a kind of cosmic waiting room called Bardo, where we get a certain time for "R and R" – rest and recuperation – before going on to our next life. These two Rs are our first priority. After being knocked about on the freeway of human existence, we need a chance to recover from the wounds we have both suffered and inflicted. Otherwise we will not be in good shape to learn from our next life, which is the point of being reborn.

But two other Rs are equally important. After rest and recuperation, our next priority in Bardo is reflection. We live in a compassionate universe, and everybody is expected to learn something from life each time around. Bardo gives us a chance for "emotion recollected in tranquility": to review our past and ask ourselves in detachment, "Why did I do such foolish things? Why didn't I do more for other people? What so possessed my attention that I forgot to seek to realize God?" Such questions can be painful, but their purpose is not to punish or torture us. We need to learn from past mistakes what to do and what not to do in order to make our life better the next time around.

Then comes the last R: resolution. "Next time," we say, "I am not going to make these same mistakes, whatever the temptation. I am going to remember what life is for." With this high resolve we are ready to come into life again, where we will be born into just the right context for facing the same trials with new wisdom and courage. That new life, for almost everybody, will be a little better than the last. In particular, if we have been meditating sincerely and following spiritual disciplines, all the momentum of our search will be carried over to our next life. The very fact that you are reading a book like this, these mystics would say, is part of that momentum: you are picking up where you left off last.

Death is a kind of major surgery which every creature has to undergo. Body and mind are severed, and awareness of all that makes up our separate, individual personality is cut away. Without preparation or understanding, this experience can be as painful as crashing headlong into an immovable wall. The only thing that can get us through this wall is the unshakable faith that our deepest Self does not ever die.

Every time we meditate, we can be said to be rehearsing for this moment of surgery, learning that we are not the body but the deathless Self. More than that, we are uniting our passions into a force powerful enough to penetrate the wall of death. At life's last ebb, the immense power of this unified desire can pour into repetition of the Holy Name, which becomes a lifeline we can hold on to while the body is shed.

I have sat by the deathbed of more than one devoted friend and seen this lifeline stretch deep below the conscious level, where it enables us to hold on to the Lord long after awareness of the outside world is gone. Physical trauma is still there, of course. But panic is gone, the panic of loss and self-dissolution, and the fear of the unknown which so fills the human heart with anguish. We know that our story is not ended, and if we have lived in mercy we know for certain that the next chapter will be richer and more fulfilling than the last. David showed this depth of faith in lines that teach us what this Beatitude means: "Surely goodness and mercy shall follow me all the days of my life, and I shall dwell in the house of the Lord forever."

CHAPTER 8
Peacemaking

Blessed are the peacemakers, for they shall be called the children of God.

"Peace," according to Spinoza, "is not an absence of war. It is a virtue, a state of mind, a disposition for benevolence, trust, and justice."

From this one quotation, you can see how far beyond politics the mystics' definition of peace goes. If peace would only be approached as "a virtue, a disposition," the balance of terror in which most nations on earth hang would soon vanish. Arms limitation treaties are a necessary first step; but even if all weapons were to disappear from the earth, Spinoza might tell us today, that would not guarantee peace. We must actively cultivate peace as a virtue, trying to make it a permanent state of mind.

Good people around the globe today are concerned about taking the external steps necessary to promote peace, but if we want a lasting solution we must search deeper, into this largely ignored dimension within ourselves. If we acknowledge the relevance of this dimension, we can hope to do away with war; if we continue to ignore it, no external measure can be of lasting help.

There is a vital connection, the mystics assure us, between the peace or violence in our minds and the conditions that exist outside. When our mind is hostile, it sees hostility everywhere, and we act on what we see. If we could somehow attach a monitor to the mind, we would see the indicator swing into a red danger zone whenever consciousness is agitated by forces like anger and self-will. Acting in anger is not just the result of an agitated mind; it is also a cause, provoking retaliation from others and further agitation in our own mind. If negative behavior becomes habitual, we find ourselves chronically in a negative frame of mind and continually entangled in pointless conflicts – just the opposite of peaceful and pacifying.

"A disposition for benevolence." What a remarkable psychologist is this Spinoza! Millions of people get angry every day over trifles; when this goes on and on, the mind develops a disposition for anger. It doesn't really need a reason to lose its temper; anger is its chronic state. But we should never look on angry people as inherently angry. They are simply people whose minds have been conditioned to get angry, usually because they cannot get their own way. Instead of benevolence, they have developed a habit of hostility. For peace, Spinoza tells us, we need only turn that habit around.

In order to do effective peace work, to reconcile individuals, communities, or countries, we have to have peace in our minds. If we pursue peace with anger and animosity, nothing can be stirred up but conflict. In the end, the tide of violence we see rising day by day can be traced not to missiles or tanks but to what builds and uses those missiles and tanks: the minds of individual men and women. There is where the battle for peace has to be won. As the UNESCO constitution puts it, "Since war is born in the minds of men, it is in the minds of men that we have to erect the ramparts of peace." A familiar truth, but one we still have not learned.

How can peace ever emerge from actions prompted by suspicion, anger, and fear? By their very nature, such actions provoke retaliation in kind. If Mahatma Gandhi were here to look behind the scenes at our international summit meetings and accords, he would say compassionately, "Yes, these are a good beginning, but you need to follow them up. You're sitting at a peace table, but there is no peace in your hearts."

I knew hundreds of students in India during Gandhi's long struggle for independence from the British Empire. I met hundreds more in Berkeley during the turbulent sixties, when students all over the country were honestly trying to work for peace. I watched their relationships with one another, especially with those who differed with them, and I saw that these relationships often were not harmonious. If your mind is not trained to make peace at home, Gandhi would ask, how can you hope to promote peace on a larger scale? Until we develop enough mastery over our thinking process to maintain a peaceful attitude in all circumstances — a "disposition for benevolence" — we are likely to vacillate when the going gets tough, without even realizing what has happened.

After some of those demonstrations that were capturing headlines, I used to remind my friends that agitating for peace and actually bringing it about are not necessarily the same. Stirring up passions, provoking animosity, and polarizing opposition may sometimes produce short-term gains, but it cannot produce long-term beneficial results because it only clouds minds on both sides. Progress comes only from opening others' eyes and hearts, and that can happen only when people's minds are calmed and their fears allayed. It is not enough if your political will is peaceful; your entire will should be peaceful. It is not enough if one part of your personality says "No more war"; the whole of your personality should be nonviolent.

One of these students told me with chagrin that he once found himself using his fists to promote peace. Things just got out of control. "How did that happen?" he asked incredulously. "I never would have dreamed of doing such a thing!"

I told him not to judge himself too harshly: after all, the will to strike back is part of our biological heritage. When push comes to shove, unless we have trained ourselves to harness our anger — to put it to work to heal the situation instead of aggravating it — it is monumentally difficult for most of us to resist the impulse to retaliate.

In situations like these, one first aid measure is to leave the scene and take a mantram walk. The force of your anger will drive the mantram deeper, bringing you closer to the day when you can rise above those fierce negative forces. Each repetition of the mantram, especially in trying moments, is like money put into a trust account in the Bank of Saint Francis. One day that account will mature, and you will become an instrument of peace. You may have no idea of what capacity you will serve in: after all, Francis himself hadn't a clue to the direction his life would take when he began placing stone upon stone to restore the chapel at San Damiano. But you can be sure that the banker within will provide you with enough compassion, security, and wisdom to make a creative contribution to solving the problems of our times.

The mystics are tremendous psychologists. It has taken more than two thousand years for secular civilization to begin to accept that penetrating aphorism of Ruysbroeck, which expresses a central tenet of spiritual psychology: "We behold that which we are, and we are that which we behold." If we have an angry mind, we will see life as full of anger; if we have a suspicious mind, we will see causes for suspicion all around: precisely because we and the world are not separate.

When suspicion lurks in our hearts, we can never quite trust others. Most of us go about like medieval knights, carrying a shield wherever we go in case we have to ward off a blow. After a day of carrying a shield around at the office, who wouldn't be exhausted? We take the shield to bed with us for seven or eight hours and wake up wondering why we still feel worn out. And of course, with a big piece of iron on one arm, we find it hard to embrace a friend or offer a hand in help. What began as a simple defense mechanism becomes a permanent, crippling appendage.

Statesmen are no different: they too are human beings, albeit with a most important job. When they go to the conference table, they too carry their shields. Worse, their suspicions may prompt them to carry a sword in the other hand, or to sit down with a clenched fist — which, as Indira Gandhi once said, makes it impossible to shake hands. Yet that is just how most nations today come to the peace table, desiring a meeting of minds but prepared to fight to get their own way. They don't expect peace, they expect trouble: and expecting trouble, I sometimes think, is the best way of inviting it.

When we change our way of seeing, we begin to live in a different world. If we approach others with respect and trust, with a great deal of patience and internal toughness, we will slowly begin to find ourselves in a compassionate universe where change for the better is always possible, because of the core of goodness we see in the hearts of others. That is how I see the world today. It is not that I fail to see suffering and sorrow. But I understand the laws of life and see its unity everywhere, so I feel at home wherever I go.

Wernher von Braun, the pioneer of astronautics, once said that for those who know its laws, outer space is not the hostile environment it seems but very friendly. Traveling in space is as safe as sitting in our living rooms — so long as we understand the rules of space and abide by them. Similarly, those who know the laws of the mind live in peace and security even in the midst of storms. They choose not to hate because they know that hatred only breeds hatred, and they work for peace because they know that preparation for war can only lead to war. When people wonder if programs like "Star Wars" will work, I reply, "That is the last question we should ask. The first question is, Can wrong means ever lead to right ends?" Can we ever prepare for war and get peace?

"One day," said Martin Luther King Jr., "we must come to see that peace is not merely a distant good but a means by which we arrive at that good. We must pursue peaceful ends through peaceful means." In his speech accepting the Nobel Peace Prize in 1964, King said:

> Nonviolence is the answer to the crucial political and moral questions of our time; the need for man to overcome oppression and violence without resorting to oppression and violence. Man must evolve for all human conflict a method which rejects revenge, aggression and retaliation. The foundation of such a method is love.

It is a living law, a law governing all of life, that ends and means are indivisible. Right means cannot help but lead to right ends; and wrong means – waging war, for example, to ensure peace – cannot help but result in wrong ends. Gandhi went to the extent of telling us to use right means and not worry about the outcome at all; the very laws of our existence will ensure that the outcome of our efforts will be beneficial in the long run. The only question we have to ask ourselves is, Am I doing everything I can to bring about peace ? at home, on the streets, in my own country, around the world? If enough of us start acting on this question, peace is very near.

What we do with our hands, the mystics say, is a direct expression of the forces in our minds. Even our technology is an expression of our deepest desires. The crisis of industrial civilization, which could create the conditions of paradise on this earth and yet threatens to destroy it, only reflects the deeper division in our hearts. Instead of blaming our problems on some intrinsic flaw in human nature, we must squarely take responsibility for our actions as human beings capable of rational thought – and then change our ways of thinking. It is not so difficult, after all; it has happened many, many times in the past as humanity has evolved.

In other words, this responsibility has a heartening side: if it is we who got ourselves into these habits of hostility, fear, and suspicion, we have the capacity to get ourselves out too. Simply to understand this is a great step in the right direction, where we do not sit back and bemoan our irrational "animal" behavior but accept that our violence-torn world is an expression of our way of thinking and feeling. The terrible dilemma which we face is the ultimate result of our mode of life, our motivation, the kind of relationships we have cultivated with other people, other races, and other countries, our whole philosophy of life. Here again is Martin Luther King Jr.:

I refuse to accept the idea that the "isness" of man's present nature makes him morally incapable of reaching up for the "oughtness" that forever confronts him. . . . I refuse to accept the cynical notion that nation after nation must spiral down a militaristic stairway into the hell of nuclear destruction. I believe that unarmed truth and unconditional love will have the final word in reality.

In this presumably sophisticated world, it is considered naive to be trusting. In that case I am proud to say that I must be one of the naivest people on earth. If someone has let me down a dozen times, I will still trust that person for the thirteenth time. Trust is a measure of your depth of faith in the nobility of human nature, of your depth of love for all. If you expect the worst from someone, the worst is what you will usually get. Expect the best and people will respond: sometimes swiftly, sometimes not so swiftly, but there is no other way.

When statesmen and politicians view other nations through the distorting lens of hatred and suspicion, the policies they come up with only keep the fires of hostility smoldering. "If you want peace, prepare for war." "My enemy's enemy is my friend." "Hate those who hate us – and, if possible, threaten them as well." Maxims like these scarcely constitute a path to peace; this is only the path of stimulus and response. Jesus gave us a path that matches means to ends: "Do good to them that hate you." This should be the basis even of foreign policy. There is no surer route to building trust and dispelling fear, the prime mover behind all arms races.

Because we see as we are, not only are our policies backward but our priorities are upside down. We long for peace but work for war, often under the label of "defense." That is where the time, talent, and resources of some of our "best and brightest" go. Being a scientist is a tremendous responsibility. If just half a dozen top scientists from the research laboratories of great universities like Stanford, Harvard, MIT, and the University of California should withdraw their support from work that serves military purposes, it would be a tremendous contribution to peace. Instead, some of our best scientific thinking and technological talent continues to contribute, directly or indirectly, knowingly or unknowingly, to war. No one has appraised the result better than General Omar Bradley back in 1948, whom I quoted at the beginning of this book:

> We have grasped the mystery of the atom and rejected the Sermon on the Mount. . . . The world has achieved brilliance without conscience. Ours is a world of nuclear giants and ethical infants. We know more about war than we do about peace, more about killing than we know about living.

These are strong words, but we need a strong reminder of how ridiculous our values have become. General Bradley's language reminds me of an episode I once saw in a run-of-the-mill Indian movie, in which a simple villager goes to Bombay for the first time. When he comes back, his friends ask him what he thought of the big city. "Such tall buildings," he says, "and such small people." That is our world, "nuclear giants and ethical infants."

When I first arrived in this country, at the Port of New York, friends took me to Times Square to ooh and aah at the architecture. I went, but I didn't ooh and aah. That puzzled them. "Oh, you're just acting blasé," they said. "You know you've never seen a skyscraper before. Aren't you impressed?"

"Buildings don't impress me," I confessed. "People do. I may not have seen a skyscraper, but I have met and walked with a man to match the Himalayas, Mahatma Gandhi. Show me someone big like that and you'll see how impressed I can be."

Do you remember the movie in which Charlie Chaplin goes on looking for the top of a skyscraper until finally he topples over backward? That is not going to happen to me, and it should not happen to you. We should never be impressed by something just because it is big, whether it is a big building or a big bomb. These are not the signs of an advanced civilization, and they have nothing to do with progress and growth. One real "ethical giant" is of much more significance in history.

I believe it was Prince Edward, the Duke of Windsor, who went on a shooting expedition when visiting India many years ago and managed to get separated from the rest of his party. Finally the others started firing into the air to make their position known. "Ah!" Edward exclaimed when he heard the shots. "The sound of civilization!"

Today, instruments of destruction have become so deadly that however sophisticated the technology, nations that concentrate on developing, selling, and stockpiling weapons might be said to be losing their claim to civilization. We can make a rough map of the truly civilized world: the bigger the arsenal of nuclear weapons, the weaker the claim to being a civilized power. To be truly civilized, a government must subscribe to the highest law: respect for life, to the point of being unwilling to kill or to cause others to kill.

I am a very hard-nosed person. I do not get impressed by speeches and rallies and media coverage about arms control. How much are we willing to give, and give up, to make peace a reality? That is the question. It is not just what we say and write but how we order our lives — how we apportion our time, distribute our resources, and behave in everyday relationships — that counts for peace.

George Kennan, a veteran statesman who has lived through thaws and freezes in the Cold War since 1945, wrote daringly after forty years of nuclear stalemate between the United States and the Soviet Union:

> I see no way out of this dilemma other than by a bold and sweeping departure, a departure that would cut surgically through the exaggerated anxieties, the self-indentured nightmares, and the sophisticated mathematics of destruction in which we have all been entangled over these recent years, and would permit us to move with courage and decision to the heart of the problem.

Soon afterwards, of course, the Soviet Union began to collapse, impoverished by pouring its resources into preparation for war. But I would still apply Mr. Kennan's words to many other conflicts around the world today. As I write this, more than thirty "major" wars are raging. Many of the fiercest are not wars of one army against another, but fratricidal attempts by members of one religion, one sect, one race, one ethnic group, to destroy another completely. Mr. Kennan is talking about nothing less than a complete reversal of the ways of thinking that drive this kind of conflict. In all such cases, both sides peer at each other through a curtain of suspicion, mistrust, and fear which distorts vision and allows no other way of seeing. How can peace ever come in such a climate? To have peace we must learn to see where we stand on common ground, beginning with certain basic truths: that people in all countries are essentially the same, whatever governments happen to be in power, and that neither side threatens the other as much as this kind of conflict threatens them both.

To change course like this, we human beings have to learn to talk to each other even when our opinions differ. And that requires respect. Nothing closes communication more swiftly and effectively than this business of painting the other side with an all-black brush. If it were not so tragic, it would be amusing to compare how often the same comments are hurled like missiles by both sides. Each claims to be innocent of all wrong and views the other as the epitome of evil.

Citizen exchanges can do wonders to dissolve such barriers on the personal level before tensions flare into all-out war. It pleases me very much to see high school and university exchange programs include teachers and students from countries whose governments disagree with ours. We can send more students, more scholars, more artists and dancers and musicians and athletes, to countries with whom we differ politically; they do more for peace than most politicians. It is due to such a program – the Fulbright exchange – that I first came to this country, and I still work to fulfill the spirit of Senator Fulbright's vision. I still work for international peace – not by giving lectures on literature, but by showing how to banish mistrust and suspicion from the mind and discover that all people everywhere are one.

Rich or poor, powerful or not so powerful, ally or antagonist or nonaligned, the peoples of every nation need help and understanding if the world is to escape from the complex web of violence and environmental destruction that threatens us all. This is not rhetoric. We are already seeing how problems on the other side of the globe a few years ago have thrown up unexpected ramifications in our own backyard.

This is an opportunity for every one of us. Our children face right now the dreadful realities of terrorism, senseless violence, and poisoned water and air. If we remember this always, it will bring the motivation to work hard for our children, for their lives, for their world.

Our children deserve to grow up in a peaceful

world, and it is our responsibility to do everything we can to see that they get the chance. This is why our schools are so important – and let me repeat, the home is the most important school of all. Teachers should not have to declare themselves "educators for social responsibility"; that is their role. I want to see that hundreds of millions of children understand this basic choice and have the opportunity to make it. When they reach voting age they should be able to tell anyone running for office, "If you support war, you are not going to get my vote. You must stand squarely and unequivocally for peace; then I'll see that you get in." If enough of us say that and mean it, the struggle is as good as won.

One very serious obstacle to children growing up with this point of view was pointed out a few years ago on the front page of the *Christian Science Monitor* during the Christmas shopping season. The headline read, "Toy Companies Ride Military Wave and Watch Kids Catch It." How early the seeds of violence are sown! Toys are not neutral; they influence children's thinking and emotions, for better or worse. When my young friend Christina was two, she used to bring her dolls with her to the dinner table. When I asked her, "How is your little one today?" she would say, "She has a cold." "Does she wake you up by crying at night?" "No, she just sleeps." Those dolls were real to her. Children need toys that are fun, but they also need toys that inspire them, toys that make them more sensitive to other people and creatures. So many toys today do just the opposite.

The *Monitor* article went on to supply illustrations: "Tricycles with bazookas attached; guns that shoot beams of infrared light at the opponent. Dolls with bad breath, or those with controversial messages, like Grace the pro-life doll and Nomad the Arab terrorist. These and other toys are on more wish-lists than ever before." Children cannot be held responsible for putting violent, tawdry stuff on their Christmas lists. It is we adults who are responsible: well-intentioned parents, grandparents, relatives, and friends; television programmers and media manipulators; and especially those who make and sell whatever promises to bring in a profit, regardless of the values it may represent.

Every parent can play a useful role in reversing this trend – particularly every mother. When you give toys to children, or allow them to buy them for themselves, you have to consider that you are not just giving them something to entertain them; you are giving them an instrument that may influence their thinking and living for decades.

Of course, big money is involved in toys today. Isn't it involved in most of our big problems? "Controversy" over such toys, the *Monitor* continued, "has not hurt sales. Laser Tag, which is number five on *Toy and Hobby World* magazine's most-popular lists, is expected to bring in a hundred million in sales this year." (Laser Tag involves shooting at opponents with a light-gun; when a person is hit, his target gives off an electronic death rattle.) That is a hundred million from the pockets of parents. The president of the company that makes Laser Tag says that the toy merely "puts a high-tech spin on a time-honored game." Laser Tag, he says, "is a vehicle to bring children together." It brings them together in insensitivity to violence, and it fosters the thinking that perpetuates war.

Developments like these will bear bitter fruit in the lives of , and that is why every parent has a responsibility to think about this issue, write about it, and speak about it to others. I admit, this is undramatic work. Nobody is likely to give you recognition or put you on the front page of the newspaper. But this is the kind of work that expresses real commitment to peace. If a thousand or so mothers and fathers speak up on this issue, within ten years we will see a completely different kind of toy market in this country. Toys that help, inspire, and strengthen while they entertain are quite within human reach.

But the surest way to educate children for peace is through our personal example. This is the responsibility of every one of us – not just parents, but everyone who has contact with young people. Children quietly absorb what we teach through our actions and attitudes, so there is no more powerful way to show them what the silent power of a peaceful mind and a loving heart can do.

One of the things that impressed me deeply about Gandhi, for example, was his ability to calm a violent crowd. I don't think anywhere in this country are you likely to see crowds like those in India. You got an idea of them in the film *Gandhi*: tens of thousands of people gathered in one place; and in those days they were sometimes in no mood to be nonviolent. Often Gandhi stood before an angry crowd clamoring for retaliation, "an eye for an eye." I have seen him quiet them just by raising his hand, and with one reminder make them stop to think: "An eye for an eye only makes the whole world blind." After a few minutes we would all go away calmer and braver, having tasted a little of the peace that was in the heart of this spiritual giant. The eyes, the voice, and the gestures of such a person communicate with people even from a distance and bring them peace.

We may not be called on to face multitudes or to calm the storms of nations, but we can all begin by calming storms in the teacup of our homes. This is the only way we can help our children to grow up in peace and security. We may not have found a world at peace ourselves, but it is quite within our power to create one for the next generation – if we will only make peace, rather than personal profit or pleasure, the first priority in our lives.

Family relationships are so important that we cannot afford to relegate them to secondary status, putting children or partner after our job and income and status. Nothing is more important than the children of our nation, our only essential resource; and each of us, remember, is their teacher by our example. Every morning after meditation I ask myself what I would be without my grandmother, my spiritual teacher. I might have acquired a well-trained intellect, but I would never have learned how to train my mind, the most precious skill on earth.

✧

No one can be blamed for thinking, "This is out of my reach! Human nature is, after all, only human. Isn't survival of the fittest a biological imperative? Isn't violence part of our very nature?" Most scientists would agree. "What I think I know of the history of our species," says a distinguished professor of animal behavior and Nobel laureate from Oxford, Niko Tinbergen, "makes me afraid that in the struggle between rational, long-term insight and nonrational, short-term motivation, it will be the latter that will win."

No one would argue that this fear is groundless. At the same time, biologists sometimes need to be reminded that human beings are not the same as animals. My body is that of an animal, but I am not my body. The spark that burns in me, in you, is lit from the fire of heaven.

I respect research that draws on animal physiology to help us learn more about physical health, but when it comes to drawing conclusions about human character on the basis of animal studies, I draw the line. The human personality, though it has fascinating correlates in the brain and throughout the rest of the body, is not physical and cannot be biologically explained; and the core of personality, the Self, is not even mental but wholly spiritual. Nothing the physical sciences can discover, therefore, can limit what you or I can become. An animal may have little choice in pursuing its food, comfort, and survival; but you and I have the capacity to choose to go against profit and pleasure and every other conditioned motivation for the sake of others, or simply for the sake of an ideal.

This is a supremely human trait, yet we can see it burgeoning even in animals that are highly advanced in evolution. The elephant, for example, is an extremely powerful creature that will not knowingly harm any other animal. The female elephant considers all calves her own and will protect all the young of the herd from harm at the risk of her life. I have seen a huge elephant step out of the way to avoid crushing a tiny frog that you and I would probably never notice. And not long ago I read of a dog that escaped from a burning building and then ran back inside to rescue the little girl it loved. Even when it comes to animal behavior, then, I do not always agree that creatures are biologically determined to behave selfishly, motivated solely by short-term gratification.

When I was a professor in India, I used to see learned papers reporting on experiments on how rats behave when put under pressure. I used to tell my students, "You're not rats!" Don't ever put yourselves in the category of rodents. Theirs is a different world, and I wonder sometimes how deep our understanding of that world goes when we observe an animal doing certain things and draw conclusions about what it means.

So much in the field of human psychology is based on animal experiments that we should not be surprised when research reports give a pessimistic picture of human motivation. It has been said that it is scholarly to be pessimistic: if you are optimistic, you must not have done your homework very well. If that is true, I am no scholar. I am incorrigibly, though realistically, optimistic, because I know that beneath even the most selfish, violent behavior there lies in every human personality a spring of goodness, flowing from the sea of love that is the Self.

In fact, this "disposition for benevolence, trust, and justice" which Spinoza defines as peacemaking flows from that very aspect of our nature which is not part of an animal heritage, but distinctly human. It is a skill, a skill in thinking, and like any physical skill — swimming, skiing, gymnastics, tennis — it can be learned by anyone who is willing to practice.

This approach should have immense appeal today. We know how to teach computer programming and coronary care nursing. The mystics tell us simply to do the same with peace: to approach it as a skill which can be systematically learned if we apply ourselves to the task. If there is no peace in the world, in our communities, or in our homes, it is not because war is built into our genes; it is because we have no idea of the requisite mental skills of peacemaking. With no way to learn these skills, we move farther from peace every day.

When we first set out to learn this "disposition for benevolence," of course, the going will be rough. The conditioning of stimulus and response, "an eye for an eye," is strong. But as meditation deepens, you find there is a fierce satisfaction in letting go of your own way so that things can go someone else's way instead. Gradually you develop a habit of goodness, a hang-up for kindness, a positive passion for the welfare of others. In terms of emotional engineering, you are using the mind's enormous capacity for passion to develop the power to put other people first: and not just verbally, but in your thoughts and actions as well. Eventually kindness becomes spontaneous, second nature; it no longer requires effort. There is nothing sentimental about this quality, either; kindness can be as tough as nails.

We can see in the life of Gandhi how he developed this disposition for kindness. Even as a young man in South Africa, he wrote that he was unable to understand how a person could get satisfaction out of treating others with cruelty. Yet this attitude was not enough in itself to prevent him from reacting with anger when provoked. It took years of practice to drive this conviction so deep that it became an integral part of his character, consciousness, and conduct.

Why do we feel we have to lash out against others? The mystics give a very compassionate explanation: because we have uneducated minds. If the mind acts unruly, that is simply because we have not put it through school.

This kind of education is scarcely available anywhere in the world today. I have had the privilege of being associated with great universities both in this country and in India, and I deeply wish that in addition to educating the heads of their students, they could teach the skills that enable us to educate our minds and hearts. It is what we know in the heart, not in the head, that matters most; for what we believe, we become. "As a man thinketh in his heart," the Bible says, "so is he."

For most of us, intellectual knowledge has very little say in the choices that shape our lives. You may know in painful detail about the harmful consequences of smoking, but if you have ever smoked, you know how shallow that knowledge is when measured against the power of habit and desire. I have seen a physician pondering X-ray films of a diseased lung with a lighted cigarette between his lips.

Similarly, you may know from bitter experience how destructive anger can be, but that makes it no easier to keep your temper the next time something provokes you. The reason is simple: there is very little connection between the intellect and the will. Intellectual knowledge is on the surface of consciousness; addictions, urges, and conditioned cravings arise deep in the unconscious mind. And the vast majority of us cannot bring our will to bear in the unconscious; even in waking life, the will may have little to do.

When you reach a certain depth in meditation, however, all this changes. You gain access to the will even below the surface of awareness, which means you can actually get underneath a craving or negative emotion and pull it out. This is the most challenging adventure life offers: to tunnel slowly under a craving for tobacco or alcohol, overeating or drugs, and remove it like a weed. After decades of sustained effort, you finally get to the roots of the primordial drives that take their toll on the lives of every one of us: self-will, anger, fear, and greed.

Let me change metaphors to make a practical illustration. All these forces – anger, for example – can be thought of as powerful physical forces like electricity. Electricity can destroy us, but when harnessed, it can also bring us light and warmth. In the same way, we can learn to use anger as a positive force, devoid of any ill feeling, to heal divisions between persons and nations and to find creative solutions to conflicts. When we have gained mastery over our responses, when deepening meditation brings insight and creativity, when will and desire have fused into a passionate determination to act only for the good of all, we have simply to flip a switch to redirect the current into its new channel.

To do this takes a great deal of preparation, of course. The mind has to be trained to listen to you when all it wants to do is turn tail and run, or lash out in retaliation. The muscles of the will have to be made strong enough to reach for that switch when everything in you is screaming, "You're wrong!" This takes a lot of work, but the day will come when, in the heat of a conflict, you will be able to say quietly, "Let's look at this problem together and see what we can do to solve it."

In presenting the connection between meditation and peace, then, I am not advancing moral or ethical arguments. I am presenting the dynamics of acquiring a new disposition of mind. Through the practice of meditation and its allied disciplines, every one of us can become a peacemaker by making "a disposition for benevolence" our natural state: that is, by teaching the mind to be calm and kind.

The purpose of meditation is to bring lasting peace to the mind. This is not a superficial suppression of hostility, but a profound, joyful, enduring peace of mind. It can pervade our consciousness to such an extent, Gandhi says, that even in our dreams we will not feel animosity toward anyone. Imagine! Most of us find it difficult in our waking moments to have love in our hearts always, but such is the power of these tremendous spiritual disciplines that once they are mastered, even in the unconscious no wave of anger will be able to rise.

In fact, this is how your meditation will be tested. You will have been meditating regularly for years, perhaps decades, when someone dear to you bursts out against you in cruel words. It would be only natural for your mind to be so agitated that anger, anguish, vengeful feelings, perhaps nightmares, follow you into your sleep. But Jesus says no. Natural it may be, but not necessary. Hatred does not have to be the human response to hatred. We have the capacity to love and forgive; and if your meditation is really good, these are the forces that will sweep up from the depths of your consciousness in your sleep, healing your heart and releasing new resources for reaching out to the person who has wronged you.

To do this, as Spinoza says, requires a deep trust – trust in the native goodness within others and in ourselves. I was not born with this kind of trust – neither, in fact, was Gandhi – but today, after many years of training my mind, if somebody says something unkind to me it doesn't bother me very much. What does bother me is the other person's state of mind, because I know what sorrow the habit of unkindness brings. It's a wonderful reversal of sensitiveness.

No philosophical conviction can confer this depth of security. It requires some glimpse of the Self, the Lord within, who is one and the same in all. Spinoza uses a medieval phrase for this that appeals to me very much: *sub specie aeternitatis.* Seen from the aspect of eternity, each of us is but a mode of one infinite reality that dwells in the heart of every finite creature. When you are always aware of this deep, underlying unity, how can you be upset by apparent differences? Who can make you feel threatened or insecure? The message of all great religions is the same: Regard everybody as yourself, because everybody is you. Whatever others may say or do, you will know that the Lord lives in them, and you will always treat them accordingly.

Yet it is not enough that this core of love is always present. We have to learn to express it, which requires gaining the capacity to say no to the conditioned demands of physical nature. That is why I teach meditation, to bring about this gradual but fundamental change in consciousness. I wait for those moments when somebody tells me, "I don't know how to be kind." I say, "I can teach you – or rather you can teach yourself, through the practice of meditation." Memorize a passage on kindness, on goodness, and then drive it inward every day, deeper and deeper into consciousness. If you persist, you will become that kind, good person on which you meditate; it cannot fail.

The other day I went with a friend to take his car in for minor repairs. The mechanic lay down on his back on his little moving dolly and vanished under the engine, where he could look around and see just what needed to be done: a screw that needed tightening, I suppose, or maybe loosening. This is what we do in meditation. It takes a long, long time to get under the engine that is the mind – and hard work, daring, and a great reservoir of devotion to the task. But no skill is more worth learning. When you get deep in consciousness, you can actually look up at the workings of the mind with wrench in hand. Then transforming anger becomes a mechanical problem; overcoming fears becomes a matter of tightening or loosening a screw.

The only reason we are not able to do this kind of fix-it work is that we have not learned how. There is no school where this skill is taught. Powerful disciplines for training the mind do exist, handed down to us from the great traditions of every religion. Yet they are largely ignored in today's world; in West and East alike, we are in danger of losing this precious legacy.

Augustine, who had a very modern perspective on the workings of the mind, asks pointedly, "I can tell my hand what to do and it will obey me. Why can I not do the same with my mind?" If the mind gets angry and you tell it to calm down, it is likely to retort, "Who do you think you are to talk to me like that? Why should I listen to you?" It's like a gawky teenager protesting, "Dad, you never sent me to school! How can you complain because I can't read?"

I have real sympathy for the untrained mind, so

uneducated and illiterate. It is big and powerful but all thumbs, all turmoil and tempestuousness, bumbling through life like a Saint Bernard puppy and knocking everything over. Yet this clumsy creature can be taught anything we care to teach it, if we only have patience and persevere – and once it has learned how to behave, this embarrassing and unpredictable liability becomes our greatest ally. "Neither your father nor your mother," the Buddha says, "neither husband nor wife nor child, can be such a loyal friend as your mind when it has been trained." It will stand by you in all circumstances. When you go among unkind people, your peaceable mind will enable you to be kind to them and quiet their hearts, which is the only peacemaking approach that really works.

All the mind's habits of unkindness can be unlearned. If the mind is coaxed further and further into positive words and actions, the unkind person will gradually think, feel, and act kindly; the unloving person will think, feel, and act out of love. To all who are agitated, insecure, unhappy, there quickly follows peace of mind.

When the mind is trained over a long, long period, you will not need effort to meet hatred with goodness. Goodness will be your mind's spontaneous response. An educated mind has a very casual style. It has its diploma, so it knows it can stay cool under provocation – which means we lose all fear of anger; we know we will not lose control.

Patanjali, one of the finest teachers of meditation in ancient India, implies that when you live in the presence of someone who will trust you over and over again, you cannot help rising to be worthy of that trust. Gradually you become so tired of letting him down that you become trustworthy.

This does not mean that we should look the other way when someone does something unworthy of him. It means that we must have the inner toughness to hold fast to our faith that there is in that person a core of goodness that does respond to trust and love. Whether between individuals or between nations, without this faith, peace is not possible.

If we want to be real peace workers, then, we have to work on removing anger from our personality: not suppressing it, but harnessing it into love poured into concerted action. If we can do this, opportunities for peace work will open up everywhere in our lives. I appreciate the yearning for peace that is expressed in truly nonviolent demonstrations and vigils, but as the Buddha said, those who help the world most are those who help to banish anger, greed, and fear. No one is more active on the path of peace than those who try every day to reduce their own selfish passions and self-will. They may not be participating in demonstrations, but they deserve to be called children of God, for they are true peacemakers, spreading peace everywhere through their daily lives.

Conversely, when someone is being selfish, he or she is actually contributing in a small measure to war. You may refuse to be in the fighting forces, you may be a peace advocate of the most vocal kind, but these things are not enough to make you a peacemaker. I never lay the blame for war at the door of the military. Wherever there is anger, selfishness, greed, or self-will, a foundation for war is being laid, and all of us must accept a share of the blame.

It is this gradual raising of popular consciousness that will bring about peace. We should demand of our politicians that they stand for peace, but we should never look to them to guarantee it; they have vested interests. The military cannot ensure peace because it is conditioned for war. It is ordinary citizens, you and I, who make the final difference. Lisa Peattie, professor of urban anthropology at MIT, puts it persuasively: "The power to move the system must come, I think, from a sort of great popular uprising, a refusal, a mass defense of human life." The former prime minister of Sweden, Olaf Palme, agreed:

> It is very unlikely that disarmament will ever take place if it must wait for the initiatives of governments and experts. It will only come about as the expression of the political will of people, in many parts of the world.

I am respectful of governments, but I have no illusion that peace will come through their efforts. It is governments that have got us into this dilemma, with our support; now it is we, the people, who must take the lead in insisting on a wholly different approach. It is not first-strike capacity but first-trust capacity that we should be pursuing with all our might. It would cost a good deal less, and it would release economic and human resources into the bargain. Isn't this the message that Jesus' life conveys? Each one of us, by establishing peace in our minds and practicing it in all our relationships, can hasten the day when peace will reign on earth.

"Some day," said Dwight D. Eisenhower, who was president when I first came to this country,

the demand for disarmament by hundreds of millions will, I hope, become so universal and so insistent that no man, no men, can withstand it. We have to mobilize the hundreds of millions; we have to make them understand the choice is theirs. We have to make the young people see to it that they need not be the victims of the Third World War.

Again, these are the words not of a peacenik but of a great general. Eisenhower knew, as every insightful general knows, that if we want peace we cannot count on whoever is sitting in the White House or Number 10 Downing Street. If each of us, through the example of our own lives, can inspire two more people every year to meditate and to live at peace with those around them, it will have an incalculably great effect in creating a climate of peace. That is my ambition, and that is why I say I am a terribly ambitious man. You and I make peace. You and I make war. It all depends on us.

In other words, if we want to change the world, we have to change ourselves. Unfortunately, that is not where most people begin. Most of the leaders I have met, both here and in India, strike a more familiar tone: "Let me reform you, Diane, and you, George, and of course you, Bob." That is often the reason why well-intentioned efforts to change conditions in other countries fail to get the effects at which they aim. The great spiritual teachers of all religions – Jesus, Saint Francis, Saint Teresa, the Buddha, Mahatma Gandhi – say in re-freshing contrast, "Let's start with ourselves."

It is an astonishing truth: there is only one person in the world I can hope to control, and that is myself. I may learn to govern the way I think, but I can never govern the way you think. How much of our behavior reveals that we have not grasped this truth at all! Viewed from this perspective, daily life takes on the qualities of a comedy of errors. I want you to stop being angry, so I get angry with you. I want your mind to be patient when I say something offensive, to be under-standing when I say something incomprehensible. I'm always worried about what you are doing and feeling when I should be worrying about my own feelings and behavior. I can only change myself: but in doing that, I do influence how you act too. There is no other way to help a person change.

Yesterday my wife and I had an encounter with a flock of quails. These curious creatures know how to fly, but they prefer not to. When we drive up, they just go on walking right down the middle of the road. It is only when they get desperate, when the fender is a foot or two away, that they bother to use their wings and clatter up together out of the way.

We human beings are much like that. We know how

to fly, but we have forgotten. We have come to think of ourselves as plump, pedestrian quails, bipeds without wings. Often it is only after one quail takes off that the others even consider the possibility. One bird suddenly says, "Look! I may be a quail, but I'm in the sky!" Then the others look around and think, "Fancy that! Maybe I can fly too." Two or three others try, and abruptly there is a great flapping of wings and everybody is in the air.

The solution to rampant violence, to international suspicion and the specter of a nuclear nightmare, begins with a challenge to each of us: Change yourself. If you can change yourself, you can reach anybody. We should always remember that there is great hope for the world, because one person changing himself has effects that reach much farther than we see. As Gandhi said, if one man gains spiritually, the whole world gains with him. Wherever there have been beneficial changes in history, that is how they have come about. And we don't have to wait until the other person, the other nation, decides to change. Why don't we change first? Through the practice of meditation, it all lies within our reach.

CHAPTER 9
Desire

> *Blessed are they which do hunger and thirst after*
> *righteousness, for they shall be filled.*

I don't think I have ever come across a more penetrating summary of the human condition than one given thousands of years ago in the Upanishads, the earliest source of the Perennial Philosophy yet found:

> You are what your deep, driving desire is.
> As your deep, driving desire is, so is your will.
> As your will is, so is your deed.
> As your deed is, so is your destiny.

Spinoza once said penetratingly that most of us mistake our desires for decisions. When we think we decide to buy something, go somewhere, see someone, all too often the choice is being made not by us, but by unconscious desires. Unless we develop some capacity to direct our desires, living in freedom is only an attractive idea.

The intellect, so useful in making decisions on shallower levels, simply cannot operate at the deep level of desires. All it can do is rationalize actions we have already been forced to take. That is why even little desires like smoking a cigarette or polishing off two servings of dessert, even when we want to say no to them, can sometimes get the better of us. It is not fair to criticize people for such peccadillos, as if getting addicted were something they chose to do.

In Hindu and Buddhist spiritual psychology, this control of the unconscious is considered almost a kind of magic. That is one connotation of the word *maya*: a kind of cosmic sleight of hand in which the senses cast a spell over us with their promise that if only we indulge them, they will make us happy. Regrettably, they have no power to do anything of the kind. But if we fail to see through their game of illusion and go on giving them what they clamor for, we go through life more and more frustrated, longing to get from sensory experience what it can never give.

I met many young people caught in this game in the sixties, when I was teaching meditation in Berkeley just off Telegraph Avenue – "where the action was." I knew that many of the people coming to hear me were sampling a smorgasbord of drugs. I used to say: "This is a come-as-you-are party. Come with whatever difficulties and addictions you have, learn to meditate, and listen to what the great mystics say about fusing desires and directing them to a supreme goal. Then let us see what happens." Hundreds of them, I am happy to say, gave up smoking and drugs without any direct appeal on my part. When they learned to take the energy that fueled those desires and direct it to goals which have the power to fulfill desires, addictions simply fell away.

I went so far as to tell my meditation class on the Berkeley campus – which numbered a thousand in those days – that Berkeley students had what it takes to understand the spiritual psychology of desire: a good intellect, some measure of sophistication, and just a dash of wickedness. That went down very well, because this is just how most of us like to imagine ourselves.

"A dash of wickedness" here means the daring which prompts us to experiment with experiences we suspect are likely to burn our fingers. In our younger days we all have a built-in margin for this kind of experimentation: to eat this, smoke that, sniff this, experience that. Gradually, however, we need to learn that indulging such desires only leaves us hungrier than before.

In those days I had a young friend in Berkeley with an inordinate fondness for pastry. Delicacies of any kind had a hold on him, but Danish was his undoing. Unfortunately, on his way to work every morning he passed an excellent bakery – and every time he got on the bus, he confessed, he found himself polishing off a morning snack.

This kind of thing has never been a problem with me, so I began with what seemed obvious. "Are you hungry in the morning?" I asked. "Be sure you have a good, hearty breakfast before you set out."

"I tried that," he said. "I'm not hungry at all."

I must have looked puzzled. "It's not something I

decide to do," he explained. "It just happens. I'm walking along the sidewalk with absolutely no intention of putting anything in my mouth, and as I pass by, not even glancing at the cherry strudel in the window, this invisible hand reaches out and drags me in. The next thing I know I'm back on the sidewalk with a white bag in my hand."

In my simplicity I suggested: "Why don't you just leave your wallet home?"

He looked aghast. "You mean you want me to steal?"

Most of us feel the same way about strong desires: we think we have no choice but to yield to them. But believe me, there is no joy in yielding to a compulsive desire. All yielding can do is give us a little respite from desire's demands – and make them stronger the next time. Joy comes not from yielding, but from gaining the freedom to choose.

When you have been meditating seriously for some time, for example, if you have a craving for alcohol or drugs, you can find a fierce thrill in just fighting it out. There is combativeness in our makeup not so we can fight others, but so we can take on these urges and see how much satisfaction we get in beating them.

Compulsive desires are part of the human condition, but today we have an additional problem: for almost all of us, our desires are exceptionally well trained. We send them to clinics where big-name trainers from the University of Madison Avenue coach them in what to crave. We buy them velour warm-up outfits with racy stripes, and shoes with aerodynamic design features that cost a hundred dollars. Just a hint of Pavlov's bell and they take off – and like runners in peak condition, they easily outstrip our will.

Recently I went to get some shoes that would be comfortable for walking. One pair fit well enough, so I asked the man the price. He replied, "Ninety-nine ninety-five."

"Dollars?"

He looked irritated.

"In India," I explained, "I could get comfortable shoes for just a fraction of that."

"Mister," he retorted, "there are shoes and shoes. With most shoes, after you put them on, you still have to move your feet. Put these on and they do the running for you."

That is the kind of shoes our desires sport these days. They take off running and we watch. We don't have to do a thing. The job of the will is to keep pace with desires and outrun them when necessary, but for most of us our will has been sleeping like Rip van Winkle. We drag him out in his pajamas and say, "Come on, Will, I need you to beat these desires!" But sometimes we can't even find the track.

When people want to give something up but say they just don't have the willpower, this is their situation: they do have a will; it just has to be trained. Meditation, as it turns out, is a perfect clinic. It has no self-interest; it operates solely on our own donations of enthusiasm.

I am not going to hide from you the fact that this training is going to be painful. Don't they say "No pain, no gain"? At the outset, every muscle in Will's flabby body is going to ache. But if you are resolute, he will begin to shed those excess pounds and approach the lean, sleek profile of a panther.

Training the will is such a serious topic that I might as well lighten it for a moment. Shaw once remarked that his method was to take pains to find the right thing to say and then to say it with the greatest levity. So in that vein, here is a cartoon I saw recently, probably in the *New Yorker*. A tortoise and a hare are dining in a Chinese restaurant, and both have just opened their fortune cookies. The tortoise reads aloud: "Slow and steady wins the race." He looks at the hare, and the hare says grumpily, "I refuse to disclose." You can guess.

In other words, don't start out by enrolling Will in the Boston Marathon. Train him steadily, every day. Eventually you will discover one of the most exhilarating secrets of life: there is no limit to the extent to which the human will can be trained.

In fact, the will has so much potential that eventually you can safely say, "It's true, I've given those desires a big head start. But I'm not worried. We're going to catch up." All desires know is to run flat out, so they don't even notice when Will begins to jog around the track. But gradually he gains speed, like a panther kept for a long time on a leash. He shoots around one final time, and when the tape comes into view no desires are in sight.

I hope I have made it clear that I am not anti-desires. It is just that I am so solidly pro-will. When your will is running smoothly in front, no desire can ever lead you around by the nose.

⊹

Training the will begins with making wise choices about where desires lead us – and practically speaking, that begins with food. Through choices about food, we begin to make choices about the mind.

This body of ours is made of food; that is the first reason why we have to be so careful about what we put into it. I do not go in for fads or fancies. I follow the advice of good nutritionists, who tell us in detail what is best for us to eat. Similarly, I like to think of myself as a sort of nutritionist for the mind. Selfishness, resentment, anger, lust – all these are junk food for the mind, and just as our body suffers setbacks on a steady diet of junk, the mind loses its balance and resiliency on a steady diet of junk thoughts.

When you go to a grocery store, don't you have a choice in what to place in your cart? We haven't yet reached a state in which the manager follows us around saying, "You have to buy two boxes of Crunchy Nuggets today." And if we do buy Crunchy Nuggets because they were right there by the cash register, no law says we have to put them in our mouth. With the body, then, making choices is relatively easy. But with the mind it is different. To paraphrase Augustine's poignant question: "When I tell my hand what to put in my mouth, it obeys. Why can't I tell my mind what to think?"

Now, the mind too is a kind of store. Consciousness,

in fact, is the biggest chain store in the cosmos: an out-let in every individual mind. The Buddha calls this common or collective consciousness *alaya-vijnana,* "the store where thoughts are kept." By comparison, Safeway is just a mom-and-pop operation. The problem is that we don't mind our store. A double-trailer truck full of jealousy chips comes and we say, "Drop off as many cartons as you like. Can't stock too many of those!" Efficient grocery store managers simply would not work that way. They would say, "I didn't order that stuff, so get it out of here!"

Twenty-five years ago, when the ways of this coun-try were still dawning on me, we used to pull into a gas station and see a little sign on top of the tank: "Free Tumbler with Fill-up." I used to ask my wife, "What is the tumbler for, to drink the gas?" I didn't see any con-nection.

That is the way junk thoughts appeal too. "Hey," jealousy says, "buy a few cartons of these, send in the tops, and we'll give your ego a rebate: fifty cents' worth of self-will." And we buy it. But fifty cents doesn't last long. Soon we find our mind full of junk anxieties, and the relationship we were agitated about is going down-hill rapidly. Who was minding the store? When jealous thoughts appear at the loading dock of the mind, med-itation enables you to say, "I never asked for you guys. Drop yourselves off at the nearest dump."

Scientists tell us that the body is constantly chang-ing. New amino acids, minerals, and so on from the food we eat are always replacing what the body loses through wear and tear. Perhaps a sixth of the body gets turned over like this each year. At that rate, we get a completely new body every six years! By changing our eating habits, we could get just the body we want.

This may not be quite accurate where the body is concerned, but with the mind it is literally true. The mind can be replaced completely, just as you can replace the engine of your car. It takes much longer than six years to replace the store of consciousness with healthful, loving, healing thoughts, but it can be done. The key is knowing how to change your desires at will.

Desires that are good for our health, for our happiness, for our relationships, don't usually come attractively packaged. That is why we push them to the back of the shelf and put our energy into desires that promise fun. Here we need to develop some hardheaded business discrimination. We have to learn to evaluate everything — eating habits, work, entertainment, exercise — not for the immediate pleasure it promises, but for its long-term benefit or loss.

In other words, every desire has consequences that will affect our lives. One of the reasons I like to refer to Augustine is that as a young man, he was full of very human desires that we can readily understand. He was passionate about poetry, passionate about truth, passionate in his love affairs, and passionate to find God. These are desires with serious consequences, and until he was thirty or so, Augustine burnt his fingers badly. That is why his voice carries conviction when he tells us later that none of his experimentation with life's desires "brought fulfillment or peace of mind."

Everyone discovers this, the mystics say. Everyone

suffers the consequences of desires that do not fulfill. But not everyone learns. That is the purpose of pain.

I have friends who would never have taken to meditation but for the load of suffering they bore for earlier escapades. Sometimes the burden is physical infirmity; more often it is emotional anguish. Worst of all is a sense of total alienation.

Most of these people found their burdens immensely eased by taking to meditation. Eventually they gained enough self-knowledge to say what every spiritual figure tries to pass on to us: "Blessed be the day I suffered so much, because it forced me to search for God."

❧

Not all powerful desires, of course, are harmful in where they lead. One deep desire which plays a vital role in spiritual evolution is what Sir Peter Medawar, the distinguished British biologist, called the "rage to know." This is not an insatiable curiosity about facts and circumstances, but a driving need to understand the secrets of life. It can produce great scientists, but it also produces great philosophers and mystics; for it is this same desire that makes us yearn to know for certain what life is and whether it has a purpose, and what, if anything, awaits us after death.

Pursuing this deep desire is a little like breaking codes. When I was a Boy Scout, I once astonished my grandmother by talking to a cousin just by waving two flags. "My scoutmaster taught me a secret code," I explained. I don't think she knew what I was talking about; she wasn't terribly interested in codes. But she knew how to read all the codes of life, which the vast majority of us never suspect.

I remember vividly the morning our scoutmaster took a small patrol of us tramping into the tropical forest a few miles from our village. A man from a forest tribe came with us as our guide, and although he evidently felt ill at ease in our village, he was as much at home in the forest as I felt in my own room. We would be crashing along behind him and suddenly he would stop and say, "Shhh, listen! There's a tiger." We couldn't make out a thing. But to him every sound was a message, in a language we couldn't even hear.

For most of us, a moment comes at least once – perhaps a loved one dies, or life deals a blow that dashes our hopes to pieces – when we pause to reflect, and questions float up into our minds: "What has happened to my friend? I was with him only last week; where is he now?" "My lover is gone; is this the end of our love?" And perhaps the lines from Omar Khayyám spring to mind:

> There was the door to which I found no key:
> There was the veil through which I could not see:
> Some little talk awhile of me and thee
> There was – and then no more of thee and me.

When questions like these arise, we often plunge into distractions in order to forget again, pretending that life on earth is not a profound riddle whose solution matters. But some people pursue the questions. They go on to ask themselves: Why am I here? Why is there so much sorrow and violence in the world? Why do children die? And they cannot rest until their questions get answered. These are people who, more than anything else in life, want to understand.

For this kind of deep understanding, we have to break the code of desires; for it is only when desire is understood and mastered that life's meaning can be seen. This is the purpose of meditation, which plumbs the depths of consciousness where our deep desires arise. In its climax we grasp at last the secret that Augustine hinted at in such deceptively simple words: "How can I find rest anywhere else, Lord, when I am made to rest in thee?"

All desire, the ancient codebooks of the scriptures suggest, arises ultimately from the sense of being a finite individual, separated and estranged from the whole. There is a kind of primal loneliness about this state, a hunger for reunion, that is expressed in the myth of Eden I referred to in the first pages of this book. In the mysticism of Christianity, Judaism, and Islam, the apple of the Fall is the temptation to think of ourselves as separate creatures, whose first concern is personal satisfaction. From the loneliness that gripped Adam and Eve in the wake of this first isolation in themselves — and which grips the rest of us who follow them — arose the haunting conclusion that prompts all human desires: "I am alone, separate from the universe, and I feel hungry and incomplete. Therefore, what can complete me, what can fill my hunger, must be waiting for me somewhere outside."

In evolutionary terms, this root loneliness is a force

four and a half billion years old – as old as life itself. Ultimately, it is behind all our attempts to fulfill ourselves in the world outside us. Yet it is an extremely positive power, for it also drives the struggle for reintegration which motivates spiritual and cultural growth.

How is it that this deep desire for reintegration, essentially the same in all of us, expresses itself so differently in different individuals? The answer is that this root desire arrives at the threshold of our everyday awareness only after being filtered through various layers of personality. These are the strata of personal and biological conditioning – drives, habits, aversions, and so on – that give each of us our own particular personality profile.

Like strata of the earth's surface, the mystics would say, this profile is the record not just of one lifetime, but of thousands of years of biological conditioning over the course of evolution. Such layers acknowledge the heritage of our jungle ancestry; but it is equally accurate, in spiritual terms, to say that they trace the path we have wandered for eons from the Garden of original fulfillment.

In Sanskrit, these layers of conditioning are called *koshas:* sheaths or jackets that cover our real Self. They are five. Innermost is what might be called the ego-sheath, for it imposes the sense of separateness, the sense of "I." But in Sanskrit it is also called the "sheath of joy," because at this level, consciousness is so rarefied that only a little sense of a limited personality separates us from our real Self.

Outside this level of awareness lies what is some-

times called the "higher mind," the seat of clear understanding, judgment, and will. This layer, in turn, is
covered by the "lower mind," the turbulent region of
our emotional life. Enveloping this is the layer of sensory awareness. And outermost of all is the only component of personality that we can see: the physical body.
All these levels have habits and conditioning of their
own, which affects the way life's basic desires find individual expression.

When I was a boy, I was delighted the first time I saw
a prism take clear sunlight and spread it in a rainbow of
colors across our school wall. These sheaths of consciousness, too, act as planes in a prism, scattering a
unitary spiritual yearning into a million different emotional and physical desires.

In each of us, then, what starts out as a simple longing for unity becomes particularized. We see it through
the fantasies and emotions of the mind, then try to satisfy those emotional needs with sensory satisfactions in
this particular physical frame which we believe is what
we are. We try to fill ourselves by eating, to forget ourselves in drinking, to find our home in the universe by
traveling, to complete ourselves through physical
union with another human being who is searching for
the same thing. Through these filters, what begins as a
simple appreciation of the beauty in another person
may end as a compulsion to possess – and the more we
clutch, the less we find; for no one can rob beauty and
have it for his own.

I confess that in my university days, even though I
had read about these forces, I too did not suspect that

they might be as real as the force of gravity. Still less would I have understood that they are resources of infinite power from which any human being can learn to draw. Today I know these things from personal experience. It is my spiritual teacher, my grandmother, who showed me what a vast world of love and creativity the human being can command when the immense power of our original goodness is tapped and directed toward a lofty spiritual goal.

⌇

To undo the conditioning imposed by these planes of personality, we begin by redirecting where our desires go. More easily said than done! Even a strong will is not always enough to accomplish this kind of mental engineering. What meditation allows us to do, one step at a time, is to climb down into consciousness as we would into a deep swimming pool, so that over years of practice we manage to enter the levels where particular desires arise. Only from these depths can we resist a misdirected desire and direct its power wisely.

Sensory attractions may seem compelling, but compared with deeper desires they really have little power. Even when they seem overwhelming, as with my friend's attraction to Danish pastry, their power over us really comes from a deeper stratum of personality — often, for example, from our emotional needs. It is in the filter of emotional attachments that most of our personal difficulties arise. And most strong emotional attachments get their strength largely from our thinking about ourselves.

Thoughts, that is, gain power from the attention we give them. Every time we start turning over in our minds sixteen ways to fulfill a cherished desire, that desire puts on weight; that is, it gets that much more power to force us to do what it demands. If we think about it all the time, it becomes huge like a Japanese sumo wrestler. That is a compulsion.

Most of the energy we spend on daydreaming, rehashing the past, planning a future tailor-made for ourselves, is at best a waste of energy. At worst it locks us further into habits we want to change.

Letting the mind idle with its desires running is like letting your car sit out all night with the engine running: when you want to get going in the morning, you are out of gas. Worse, when the mind is left unattended like this, any passing desire can just climb in and take off. Then you find yourself walking out of the bar or the pizza parlor wondering, "Why did I go and do that?"

One of the reasons why repeating the Holy Name can be so effective is simply that it saves so much wasted mental energy. When the mind wants to run on about something that is neither useful nor beneficial, we can learn to start up the Holy Name and turn the key of this enormous mental engine to Off.

Once you taste this blissful stillness, you know you are not your thoughts. That is a tremendous achievement, for it brings access to the limitless resources of the unconscious.

The University of California at Berkeley, as you may know, has one of the finest research libraries in the world, but undergraduate students can benefit from it only partially. They are not allowed into the library stacks, so they have to stand in line to petition the clerks to get a book for them, and then pray the book is in. But graduate students are not subjected to these indignities. All they have to do is flash their card and the clerk at the gate will wave them through. Then they can wander through the books at will, nine tiers of shelves, marveling at what they find and picking out whatever they need.

That is how it is when you know you are not your thoughts: you get a security clearance into the deepest resources of consciousness. You don't have to petition for more patience and then wait and pray it will come. You can go straight in, deep in meditation, and when you reach the tollgate of the unconscious, you just establish your identity and your mind will wave you through.

We may not know it, we may not believe it, but in our hearts every one of us longs to get at the immense wealth of the world within. Even the lady who goes to play blackjack every weekend is looking to break the bank inside, the infinite treasury of love which is our legacy as human beings. In other words, all of us want to love and be loved. When we have removed all the jealousy and greed and resentment in our hearts, what remains is pure love.

As we descend into the depths of the mind in meditation, we gradually strip away layer on layer of selfish conditioning. Why should anybody love us when the only thing we are concerned about is ourselves? Care for others, share with others, even if it means ignoring your own comforts and pursuits and urges; then people will naturally love and cherish you. When you make yourself zero, Gandhi would say, the Lord adds an infinity of digits beyond.

"Be ye therefore perfect," Jesus challenges us, "even as your Father which is in heaven is perfect." It means: Let's see you really exercise your courage, stretch your patience, deepen your love beyond limit. Life will supply opportunities in plenty. If you want spiritual growth, there is no need to retire to a wilderness hermitage or even to a tree house in your backyard. We can reach for perfection right in the middle of life, while holding down a responsible job.

But who has the energy for this kind of effort? Even if we do want to reach beyond ourselves, which of us has the vitality, endurance, and dedication? The mystics are so full of vitality that we may think we have to be born like them in order to follow in their footsteps. Fortunately, it isn't so. Every one of us has access to deep reserves of vital energy of which we are largely unaware.

Gandhi, in his seventies, used to work hard for fifteen hours a day seven days a week. Often he and his staff would not get to bed until midnight, but he would rouse everyone at three in the morning to get going again; there was work to do. That is your capacity too, he used to tell us. We have learned to use only a small fraction of what we have.

Where did Gandhi get those tremendous reserves of energy? Not from being frugal about using it, obviously, since he poured his heart into energetic effort right and left for decades. Rather, he got his vitality from spending it.

I know this sounds like a plain contradiction, but that is precisely how vitality works. Just as athletes train their bodies, we can train the mind until it becomes marvelously fuel-efficient. Few effects of meditation are more dramatic.

I have always been a hard worker, like my mother and especially my grandmother. Yet I am the first person to be amazed to see that today, at an age when most men have retired, I have immeasurably more vitality than I did in my twenties. I work longer and much more effectively, but without fatigue or burnout, and I need only a few hours of sleep a night. After decades of training in meditation, there is no agitation in my mind; so very little energy leaks out.

The secret is simple: I seldom think about myself. This is what drains vitality, because it is dwelling on ourselves that churns the mind with excitement, craving, anxiety, competition, and disappointment. If you want a life full of vitality, the mystics say, don't waste your energy in thinking about yourself. Think about others. You will find it not only conserves personal energy, it actually brings you to life.

The thrust of our contemporary civilization is just the opposite. "Don't ever forget your personal needs," popular magazines warn, "or you'll become a zombie." Saint Francis would say this is picking up the stick by the wrong end. If we want our personality to shine, to be aflame with beauty, we must learn to love. "O divine Master, grant that I may not so much seek to be consoled as to console, to be understood as to understand, to be loved as to love." This is the formula for a personality that draws all hearts, and its secret lies in forgetting ourselves in working for the welfare of all.

Saint Francis, Gandhi, Saint Teresa – far from being zombies, great lovers of God like these are among the most original figures in history. They burst on the world with the vitality of a dozen ordinary souls. Every one of us, they testify, has this kind of vitality in abundance; we simply do not know how to get at it. That is the purpose of meditation.

Ultimately, all the energy that drives the functions of life comes from a single source, a vast kind of reserve of undifferentiated power. We can think of this energy as an immense trust fund of "evolutionary energy," kept in a cosmic bank. At birth a checking account is opened in our name, credited with a certain measure of vital energy – not a large amount, but enough to see us through the ordinary energy expenses of our life. To this minimum, the bank in its mercy credits a little extra to cover the mistakes most of us make in learning to invest.

From birth to death, this modest checking account is all the vitality we have to draw on. We never suspect there is any more. Yet this is only the interest on a vast cosmic trust, which the bank is just waiting for us to come of age and claim. As with a financial legacy, we need to establish our credentials before we can make withdrawals. And the main credential is that we be living for all. For this vast account is held in trust for all of life. It becomes available to us only when we have a deep need to give to others and have reached the limits of what we can draw on in ourselves.

Gandhi drew on this cosmic account every day, and it allowed him to accomplish almost superhuman things. Another way of putting it is to say that Gandhi had learned to tap the power that lies in the very depths of the unconscious. Or, following Saint Teresa of Avila, we might speak of a perpetual wellspring of grace, from which the soul can always go to be filled from within. "He leadeth me beside the still waters," says David. "He restoreth my soul." This endless pool of vitality is there for every one of us to tap, if we can only find and uncover it.

This is what is meant by making ourselves "pure in heart." When we practice meditation, repeat the mantram, and put the welfare of others before our personal interests, we are digging for this spring of living waters, removing all the strata of self-will and selfishness that cover it. In the end, the mystics of all religions say, it is not we who actually open up this spring. That is up to the Lord, who is within. But we have to make all the effort. Our job is to purify the mind, to get every obstruction out of the way.

✧

For the vast majority of human beings, the strongest urge is sex. Very few today understand that when the mystics harp on the need to master sexual desire, it is not because sex is "wrong" but because this deepest of urges is an immense source of power. Such is the pull of sexual desire that it lays down a direct track into the unconscious. This is the secret of its strength: it draws straight from the treasury of power in the unconscious, the longing for fulfillment that reaches back into Eden in the depths of the heart.

The difficulty with handling this secret channel of power is that until sexual desire is mastered, it moves down a one-way street. We have no say in where it takes us; it just grabs us, throws us in the trunk, and takes off with the accelerator pedal on the floor. Before we know it, we are dumped back where we started, often with some souvenirs of the Land of Physical Desire – jealousy and insecurity – slipped into our luggage.

In meditation we slowly gain the capacity to buck the flow of this fierce traffic. Meditation is a kind of mental engineering project, laying down a lane by which we can, when we choose, travel back against the flow of conditioning into the realms of the unconscious, where our deepest resources lie. This does not mean sex is stifled; it simply means we have a choice. We can use it for a few moments of personal pleasure, or we can draw on its power to make a lasting contribution to the rest of life.

Given the conditioning of our times, I think it is only natural to think of sex in terms of private satisfaction, particularly in youth. In his compassion the Lord gives us leeway for experimentation, so that we can learn for ourselves how little the senses can really gratify. But as we grow older, we are expected to learn from our experiences and set our aspirations on a higher goal. When this happens, we begin to look everywhere for more gas, more drive, more love with which to solve the problems that living poses. And no source is greater than sexual desire.

In the Indian scriptures, sex is evolutionary energy. Its physical expression is only the tip of the immense iceberg in consciousness which is pure desire. Locked within it is the creative drive behind evolution, so intensely compressed that when this drive is released and harnessed, it can shoot us straight to heaven. This power is our rocket to the stars. But its evolutionary purpose is wasted on the pursuit of pleasure. If we really want to grow spiritually, we have to learn to master this immense source of power; otherwise toward the end of our lives we may find ourselves without enough gas to reach our goal. As you can see, this is not a moral issue; it is essentially a matter of spiritual engineering.

Mahatma Gandhi had a grand insight which I didn't even begin to understand until I went deep in meditation. When sexual desire comes under complete control, he said, it turns into longing for God. That one observation explains why those who offer their whole life, all their desires, to the Lord are not suppressing their faculties or stunting their humanity. On the contrary, by drawing on this endless tank of energy that is sexual desire they bring all their faculties into glorious play.

In Hindu mythology the god of physical passion, called Kama, has five flower-tipped arrows in his quiver. They look pretty, but as all of us know, they go in deep. These arrows correspond to the five senses, but they can also be described as five aftereffects of overindulgence in sex: jealousy, insecurity, loss of freedom, enervation, and loneliness. Similarly, what we get when we transform this energy are five incomparable boons: vitality, security, creative freedom, emotional endurance, and compassion for all.

In every religion, the mystics assure us that through many years of hard work – of intense meditation and continuous striving – all desires can be brought together, to flow like the Amazon River from an endless spring of love within. When you can give your devotion completely to the Lord in the depths of your heart, you will have an eternal source of inspiration, creativity, and joy, "a well of water springing up into everlasting life."

⊷

I have a number of teenage friends, and in some ways I think teenagers see through the allure of sex better than those who are older and more experienced. Young people can be sensitive and sharp-eyed. They look around and see where the pursuit of pleasure has taken the previous generation, and I believe they are ready to understand that to love deeply, the sexual faculty has to come gradually under control. To love, you have to banish jealousy; you have to rise above possessiveness. In other words, you need to see the other person as more than just a physical creature.

Love takes a lot of effort. A self-centered Romeo cannot love. All he can promise is: "I love you, Juliet . . . as long as I am the center of your universe and you keep orbiting around me."

Yet love is what everyone wants, and young people in particular need to be shown that it is worth working for. This is the responsibility of those of us who have lived longer, who have burnt our fingers enough to know what physical passion can and cannot give. No matter what we preach at young people, it is our example that they watch, in our lives and in the mirror of the media. If we want a world with a goal higher than pleasure, we have to strive for it in our own lives. It is my fervent hope that thousands of young people in this country who have not yet become entangled in sex as a compulsion can learn to transform this force and become powers for love.

I want to repeat some lines from Mechthild of Magdeburg, a lay sister in a Cistercian abbey in Thuringia, central Germany, and a contemporary of Eckhart's, who gives us the reason for our soul's need for love:

> I was created in love; therefore nothing can console or liberate me save love alone. The soul is formed of love and must ever strive to return to love. Therefore it can never find rest nor happiness in other things. It must lose itself in love.

God is home, Augustine says brilliantly; all of us are abroad. We are perpetual tourists in this world, gazing wonderingly at all the strange sights. Only when we get tired of sightseeing do we begin to look for a way to get home.

Nothing more transfigures the human spirit than when all personal desires fuse in the desire to return to our native state of unitive consciousness. Far from being self-indulgent, this is the highest ambition imaginable. It enables us to hope and work and live for making our world a little better for others to live in, particularly the children who will follow us. And it leads, in the end, to the highest summit of awareness that a human being can reach for, the Mount Everest of the spirit.

Not long ago a friend of mine was going to India and asked if he could take a message for me. I said, "Give my love to the Himalayas." How can one convey the splendor of mountain ranges that spread over fifteen hundred miles across the roof of the world, with peak after peak above twenty thousand feet? The first time I saw them, it was not only their height that stunned me but their unutterable purity – so pure that it seemed to enter my heart. Himalaya literally means "the home of snow." It is the purity of this perpetual snow that makes the Himalayas the perfect symbol of the eternal home in our hearts which we call God.

George Mallory, who made the first recorded ascent of Mount Everest in 1924, was asked by journalists why he felt he had to risk his life on an impossible challenge. Mallory gave an epic reply: "Because it is there." Millions of people hear reports of the Himalayas but nothing stirs inside them. Most of us are so engrossed with playing pigeon on the plains, picking up whatever crumbs of satisfaction we can find, that we never think of the words of the Psalms: "I will lift up mine eyes unto the hills, from whence cometh my help" – the towering mountains of the spirit, wrapped in perpetual purity. Mallory was one of those rare individuals who lifted up his eyes and felt a deep inner stirring which would not let him live in peace. He died making his ascent, but his courage lit a path for others to follow to the top.

To me, this is the real glory of human nature. "Let there be dangers; bring them on! I don't ask for a guided tour with a guarantee of success; all I ask is the strength and courage to go on trying. I want more than anything else to live to the full height of my being." Self-realization can be attained only by facing difficulties which appear to be almost impossible. That's why I often poke fun at the words "fun" and "pleasure." Once you raise your eyes, what satisfaction can you get from pecking about on the plains? It is challenge that makes a human being glow, effort that hardens our muscles, danger that fuses our dedication and desire.

Many more attempts to climb Everest followed Mallory's, until in 1953, Sir Edmund Hillary and Tenzing Norgay reached the summit for the first time in history. I still remember the enthusiasm with which my students in India responded to the news. One day, I thought to myself, I hope to have the privilege of teaching young people the exploits of great mountaineers of the spirit: climbers like Mechthild, Eckhart, Gandhi, Saint Teresa, Saint Francis. I think it was a young woman from Berkeley who, after she reached the crest of Everest herself, coined a slogan I still see on T-shirts: A Woman's Place Is at the Top. I say, "Right on! And a man's place is right there beside her." Nobody should ever be content to crawl on the ground looking for the crumbs of pleasure that life offers. The place of every one of us is at the summit of living.

In meditation we learn to reach into consciousness, get hold of our biggest desires, and fuse them into an irresistible force that can lift us like an eagle, as Saint Teresa says, and carry us to the peak of spiritual awareness. It is not a luxury for our civilization to hold out this goal; it has become a necessity. When human beings reach a state where physical wants are more than satisfied, if they do not have a lofty, snow-clad peak to gaze on, to plan for, and to climb, they cannot help indulging in destructive behavior. Human daring is meant for this purpose, and if we do not engage it, all that power will turn against us. The social problems which challenge our future – drugs, violence, AIDS, alienation, war, the despoliation of the environment – all, in the end, are fed by desires turned desperate because they can be fulfilled only on higher ground.

Something in the human spirit demands to challenge impossible odds. One of the sages in the Upanishads tells us what the climb to the summit of consciousness is like. "Don't expect a path of convenient rocks," he says. "You'll have to climb up the edge of a razor." This is the path of glory that all of us are born for, our path to a beauty and a joy which cannot be imagined.

Mahatma Gandhi stirred me like this; that is why I talk about him so much. Here was a man barely five and a half feet tall, but when I set eyes on him he seemed to tower above the rest of us like the Himalayas. Something stirred deep within me, as if to say: That is my destiny too: to stand where I can see all people as my people, all countries as my own. That is my home.

Two or three years ago, along with thousands of others in the San Francisco area, I awoke one morning to read in the paper that in the course of its long swim home, a humpback whale had somehow got in through the Golden Gate and was trapped in the shallows of the Sacramento River Delta. These majestic, sensitive creatures, who come to us from fathomless depths like visiting rulers from a kingdom we can never see, stir the unconscious. Humphrey the humpback caught the city's heart, for without deep waters no whale can thrive.

For almost a week, while the papers had a field day, Humphrey could not be coaxed from his new bathtub back to the sea. Finally somebody got the bright idea of enticing him with the recorded underwater songs of whale Loreleis. They must have picked the right tunes for awakening nostalgia, because Humphrey leaped and turned and began to make his way to freedom, distracted only momentarily by the inexplicable lure of the Richmond Bridge. As he churned triumphantly out the mouth of the bay, traffic backed up in both directions while whale-lovers stopped in the middle of the Golden Gate Bridge and stood at the railing to cheer.

We are like that, the mystics would tell us: great creatures made to roam in the deep waters of the spirit, caught in the shallows of a narrow vision of who we are. Yet in the voices of the mystics and scriptures, the echoes from poetry and myth, we hear "deep calling unto deep." Wordsworth records it in his suggestively titled "Intimations of Immortality":

> Hence in a season of calm weather
> Though inland far we be,
> Our Souls have sight of that immortal sea
> Which brought us hither,
> Can in a moment travel thither,
> And see the Children sport upon the shore,
> And hear the mighty waters rolling evermore.

Midnight or early morning, while the world sleeps, when awareness of the outside world falls away in profound meditation, these words may come to life. Then you will see the "immortal sea which brought us hither," will hear it calling; and you will see too the way back to your real home.

When we regain our native state of unity, we ask nothing more of life. It is not that the spirit of searching is dead: spiritual fulfillment is not the end of growth, only a new beginning. But we no longer ask who we are and why we are here; we know. And in place of the world that once baffled and frustrated us, we dwell in a compassionate universe whose forces are friendly once they are understood.

"Having this," the Bhagavad Gita says, "what more is there to ask for?" All we need is opportunities to give, to serve, to love – which is, without exaggeration, to live in Eden here on earth.

Reading the Mystics

One of my hopes in writing this book was that the quotations I chose might stir some readers to explore for themselves the poetry, power, and contemporary relevance of the world's great mystics.

To me, reading the mystics is not merely a pleasure; it plays a vital role in spiritual growth. Until we turn inward in meditation, most of us cannot guess how thoroughly the mass media have saturated our minds with a low, purely physical image of human nature. To undo this conditioning, these images must be erased from consciousness and replaced by the loftiest ideals to which we can aspire. This is the job of meditation and the Holy Name. But their work becomes infinitely easier if we start saying no to some of the tawdry stuff that goes into the mind through our eyes and ears, and replace it with the inspiring words and personal example of men and women whose love of God can set fire to our lives.

That is why, whenever I teach meditation, I always make spiritual reading one of my eight essential points. After your evening meditation, instead of stirring your mind up again with the violence and vulgarity on TV, go to bed with a book of pure spiritual inspiration – not philosophy or psychology, however helpful these may be at other times, but the direct words or life of someone who has realized God.

I rarely recommend books *on* mysticism, preferring to go straight to the sources. Nevertheless, there are books which let the mystics speak for themselves in a readable and reliable setting. I often use *The Perennial Philosophy,* by Aldous Huxley (Harper, 1945) and *Treasury of Traditional Wisdom,* edited by Whitall N. Perry (Harper, 1971).

Of the individual mystics I quote in this book, almost all can be found in the Paulist Press "Classics of Western Spirituality" series, now the best source for Christian (and some Jewish and Islamic) mystics otherwise out of print: Ruysbroeck, Juliana of Norwich, Origen, and many others, including the anonymous works *Cloud of Unknowing* and *Theologia Germanica.* Some, true classics, are available in many other editions as well: Augustine's *Confessions,* Brother Lawrence's, *Practice of the Presence of God,* Thomas a Kempis's *Imitation of Christ,* and the works of the great Spanish mystics Teresa of Avila and John of the Cross. The mysticism of the early church is well represented in *The Desert Fathers,* translated with an excellent introduction by Helen Waddell (University of Michigan Press, Ann Arbor Paperbacks, 1957).

Meister Eckhart in particular has benefited from new translations. My quotations are based on that of Raymond Blakney *(Meister Eckhart: A Modern Translation,* Harper, 1941), which I have used for decades. But devoted scholarship has since produced a solid critical edition of Eckhart's works, and readers today can take advantage of two new English translations: *Meister Eckhart,* translated with an introduction by Edmund Colledge and Bernard McGinn (Paulist Press, Classics of Western Spirituality series, 1981), and the three-volume edition by Maurice O'Connell Walshe *(Meister Eckhart: Sermons & Treatises,* Shaftesbury, England, Element Books, 1987).

Quotations from the Indian scriptures are from my own translations, *Bhagavad Gita* (Nilgiri Press, 1985) and *Upanishads* (Nilgiri Press, 1987), both of which have introductions and notes presenting the key ideas of Indian mysticism to the Western reader. The quotations from Mahatma Gandhi are from my *Gandhi the Man* (Nilgiri Press, 1977), which is neither biography nor anthology but seeks to understand how Gandhi transformed his personality. Many other selections from Gandhi are in print. Of the many biographies, Louis Fischer's *Gandhi: His Life and Message for the World* (Mentor, 1945) still gives one of the most sensitive introductions to Gandhi's life.

The Jesus Prayer, probably used in the times of the Desert Fathers, is enjoying new popularity today, partly because of the underground classic *The Way of a Pilgrim* (translated by R. M. French, many editions). A good historical account is *The Jesus Prayer,* by "A Monk of the Eastern Church" (Crestwood, N.Y., St. Vladimir's Seminary Press, 1987). But for practical use of the Prayer, or for repetition of the Holy Name in any other form, I recommend my own *The Unstruck Bell* (Nilgiri Press, 1993), which is written not for monastics but for ordinary lay people in the modern world. It is accessible to anyone and full of examples from personal experience.

Index